Politics and Opinion
in the Nineteenth Century

JOHN BOWLE

Politics and Opinion
in the Nineteenth Century

An Historical Introduction

A GALAXY BOOK

New York   OXFORD UNIVERSITY PRESS   1964

First Published 1954
First Published as a Galaxy Book, with corrections, 1964
Printed in the United States of America

CONTENTS

Book I

THE POLITICAL THOUGHT OF THE ROMANTIC AGE

Book II

THE POLITICAL THOUGHT OF THE AGE OF DARWIN

CONTENTS

PREFACE

IN the volume to which the present study is a sequel the main development of Western political thought from the origins to Rousseau was examined. It was then pointed out that by the close of the eighteenth century constructive principles of self-government had been partially realized in important areas of Western Europe and North America. They were summed up in terms of rationality, justice, compassion and freedom.

It was also predicted that this kind of government, as further developed, would probably in time control the surge of modern industrial society and gradually supersede the national and class conflicts which are its bane. 'A mere century and a half,' it was suggested, 'though fraught with fateful and tremendous change, has not diverted the fundamental lines of political thought, though it has developed and extended them.' Constitutional government was already embodied in successful institutions over powerful areas. In a broader context, it might well form a basis of the world order to which we are summoned by modern science.

Since these words were written, six years ago, the situation has greatly deteriorated. Yet, in spite of ideological conflicts, supra-national institutions exist and governments are heavily committed to their promotion. They seem bound to fail unless supported by beliefs adapted to modern conditions. A new inspiration for con-stitutional government is therefore necessary. It will be cautious and empirical — contemporary political thinkers dislike abstractions — but it must also reflect the elementary moral and biological prin-ciples which have been proved to promote survival. If civilization is preferable to barbarism, wealth to poverty, life to death, such political methods must now be accepted. Political philosophy to-day, on both sides of the ideological frontier, is faced with facts which render many pre-atomic ideas obsolete. It now seems clear that nothing short of world peace through world commonwealth can ensure survival in the radically changed environment created by the hydrogen bomb. Modern political philosophers are a luxury or a menace unless they recognize this need.

One of their principal tasks is to elucidate the constructive and destructive elements in nineteenth-century political thought. The present volume is an introduction to this analysis. It attempts to indicate, in broad outline, how the present situation has come about. The book is addressed not simply to specialists, but to a wider public; in particular to those engaged in politics and administration, and to those beginning to study political thought in Universities. It is of direct personal concern to all who read these pages that the misuse of science should be arrested and political thought swiftly directed to that end.

The survey is therefore planned to set present problems in an historical perspective. It should lead to a fuller study of the writers concerned; to illuminating comparisons between them; even to a new approach. Following the design of the earlier work, a full, if simplified, account will be given of representative writers who were to shape the future, though often immediately disregarded. With the increasing complexity and range of political thought, the net has been cast more widely, though important writers have had to be omitted. Those examined express influential and contrasting points of view. In the first book, for example, the romantic Herder and Hegel are compared with Bentham and both with the conservative de Maistre. Saint-Simon's collectivist attack on traditional society is compared with that of Godwin and Owen, and both related to the revolutionary ideals of Mazzini and the liberal compromise of de Tocqueville and J. S. Mill. These thinkers have been fully described at the expense of minor figures of rather similar outlook. The French writers Chateaubriand and Constant, for example, have been omitted; de Bonald gives way to de Maistre; Cobbett to Proudhon; Guizot to de Tocqueville. These limitations have been deliberately accepted. Considerable space has also been devoted to Utopian and anarchist ideas. If often embodied in fantasy, they contain flashes of original and now useful insight.

In the second book, British liberal writers at first preponderate. They were then at the peak of their influence. Militant nationalism has been represented solely by Treitschke, the most influential of its exponents, though there was much similar propaganda in other countries. Acton, rather than the pluralist lawyer, Gierke, represents the later nineteenth-century idea of liberal commonwealth. Two sociologists, Durkheim and Graham Wallas, have been included, not as the climax of the book, but as portents of the future, for sociology now increasingly absorbs political thought. Essential historical background has been roughly indicated, particularly in the opening and concluding chapters. The main theme is the development of liberal constitutional commonwealth into social democracy to meet

PREFACE

the needs of mass civilization. The attack on this central tradition ‧ made by nationalist aggression, class war and nihilism is then examined. Finally the prospects of reinforcing commonwealth by modern sociology are briefly indicated, for constructive political thought seems likely to develop along these lines.

Such reinforcement is urgent. Under modern conditions nineteenth-century myths of class war, nationalist aggression and political nihilism are fatal. Unless these pre-atomic conflicts can be transcended by a more moral, responsible and impartial view of politics, the prospect is catastrophic. Political ideas must be basically revised before the biological challenge to the whole species, irrespective of political allegiance, created by the discovery of nuclear power. If this adjustment cannot be made, mankind will fail in its most elementary biological response, adaptation to environment. It may well be cast upon the scrapheap of evolution.

Today, within a few decades, scientific invention has superseded many traditional political institutions. Nuclear weapons now threaten the destruction of the main centres of culture, with consequent paralysis and spreading collapse. Before this fact the most ruthless politicians, hardened in the abuse of power, stand dwarfed and irrelevant. The catastrophe they may provoke would destroy the organized society in which they move. A new assessment of political ideas is therefore imperative. It is the most immediately important study that exists. In this context the following pages have been written, in the hope of contributing to clarify and mobilize opinion upon questions which will determine the life or death of modern society.

The author has many obligations to acknowledge. First to the Leverhulme Trustees, whose award of a Research Fellowship gave him the leisure to write the book, and in particular to Lord Haden Guest. Sir Isaiah Berlin has kindly given his help and advice. Mr F. M. H. Markham, Fellow of Hertford College, Oxford, and Mr David Pears, student of Christ Church, Oxford, have also both made valuable comments and suggestions. The author is under a particular obligation to Professor L. H. Butler for his help and criticism in reading most of the original draft. The author's thanks are also due to Mr F. W. D. Deakin, Warden of St. Antony's College, Oxford, and to the late Mr A. B. Rodger, Fellow of Balliol, who have advised him on certain political and economic aspects of the book.

Oxford, October 1962.   JOHN BOWLE

INTRODUCTION

THE EXPANSION OF EUROPE

THE rich variety of nineteenth-century political thought reflects the evolution of a swiftly changing society. The ideas of Plato and Aristotle were determined by the city state, the scholastic arguments of St. Thomas by Catholic Christendom, and the outlook of Locke by a mercantile commonwealth. Nineteenth-century political philosophers were also conditioned by their surroundings. Their bias was historical and environmental. Today, abstract political ideas are increasingly discarded. Political philosophy, no longer a branch of metaphysics or an aspect of revelation, seems part of the age it mirrors and whose course it partially determines. This outlook is largely due to the historical trend of nineteenth-century opinion. The development was salutary. Certain political problems are perennial, but the idiom employed and the pace and scale of events are necessarily different. Before surveying representative Western political thought in the nineteenth century and relating it to the problems of our own time, one must recall the social, economic and geographical background.

From the neolithic age to the gradual beginnings of industrial society, Europe had developed along a chequered but successful course. From sparse peasant cultivation, originally looking to Mediterranean centres of culture and subject to the incursions of Steppe warrior invaders, the European peoples had achieved, by the later eighteenth century, a slow but cumulative mastery of environment, an elaborate minority culture, and a world-wide expansion. They had already penetrated the Americas and Siberia, conquered India and the East Indies, planted outposts in Africa and the Far East, opened up the Pacific and Australasia.

This astonishing expansion was achieved through a growing population and unprecedented technological skill. With the rise of great industry, both these tendencies were to be intensified. Population dramatically increased, and the technological superiority of Europeans was confirmed. The nineteenth century was to be the greatest age of European expansion. If by the mid-twentieth Europe was in retreat, great new Continents had been populated, and predominant world power had passed to North America, the

13

heir of Europe. In the West a vast Atlantic civilization was beginning to emerge. In the East, centred on the Soviet Union, the massive, still relatively primitive, foundations of a Eurasian supra-national society.

During this tentative and gradual evolution civilization had necessarily been confined to minorities. They had lived off the land; off small-scale mining and commerce. The rule of the warrior and the priest had been slowly modified by commercial oligarchies; after the liberal revolution of 1789, the middle class were to translate economic into political power. But it was not until the rise of great industry that one could even imagine the extension of a minority civilization to the masses. Under pre-industrial methods of production wealth was narrowly limited. The price of the culture and initiative of elites was paid by lives of toil and monotony for the vast majority. Naturally, in so varied an environment, the social pattern had differed widely. The early farmers of Attica, Latium or Wessex, attained the rudiments of self-government. In more elaborate and far flung societies, exploitation became more pronounced. The peasants of the Forest cantons about Lucerne, or the fishermen of Friesland or Scandinavia might assert an independence which reflected their isolation from the centres of European power; the great cities of Flanders and North Italy a parochial civic vitality. But in pre-industrial times the masses were generally submerged. On its higher levels, this society was more dynamic and varied than the only other contemporary civilization which could compare with it — the vast agricultural empire of China whose rulers in the nineteenth century still regarded interlopers from the West with contempt. But the horizon of the great peasant majority was strictly bounded by the confines of their village and their market town.

In this preponderantly static picture there is one element of contrast. The status of the rural masses of Eastern and Western Europe was becoming different. Already by the twelfth century, in the West, the rise of cities had altered the primitive social pattern which survived the decline of civilization of Antiquity. The emancipation of the serfs was slowly but inevitably to proceed. With the expansion of commerce and administration, medieval society needed new blood. Not only the Church, but the secular world, called for talent and enterprise. The bourgeoisie of England, France and the Netherlands, the military and commercial adventurers of Italy and Portugal and Spain, came predominantly from the land. The interaction of a maritime and continental environment — the key to Western European variety and enterprise — had provoked widespread emancipation along the Mediterranean and Western seaboards.

In Eastern Europe the picture was different. Here the lack of effective government, the conflict between Teuton and Slav, the threat of Tatar and Turkish invasion, the monotony of great plains and continental climate, the constriction of maritime enterprise, had retarded the rise of an urban middle class, and stereotyped the ancient order of noble and serf. By the eighteenth century, in the nation-states of the West, the ruling minorities were commercial and urban, as well as aristocratic and clerical. But the polyglot Hapsburg Empire still sprawled over Central and Eastern Europe; Polish and Lithuanian barons ruled over vast estates where the livestock included a backward peasantry, and the emancipation of the serfs in Russia was to wait until 1861. Though the basis of all European society was still agricultural, slow moving, conservative, East and West saw a growing difference of social pattern and methods of government.

Such was the broad picture presented by pre-industrial Europe at the close of the eighteenth century. This society had now come to the threshold of world domination. It was a civilization of dynamic enterprise, of brilliant intellectual and artistic culture, of great variety and initiative. By modern standards, it was one of profound social injustice and glaring privilege. The peasant masses on which it depended, and to which it gave leadership and sometimes even opportunity, were still illiterate, and still rural. Towns which were the focus of government and learning, of commerce and communications, were still the natural complement to their surroundings, of field and vineyard, meadow and mountain. They were linked by roads which would appear in modern eyes execrable. Much of their traffic went by river or canal, the slow barges moving on the Scheldt or the Loire, or through the intricate waterways of Lombardy. The mountain barriers were still immensely formidable. The bulk of merchandise from Italy came over the relatively easy Brenner into Bavaria, or along the winding coast road — the ancient Via Julia Augusta — which skirts the Ligurian Alps along the Mediterranean. The oceanic routes were slow and dangerous, though already there was a great volume of trade about the world. Eastward round the Cape to Malacca or Calicut, across the mid-Atlantic to the sugar islands of the West Indies, or to the sandy harbours of Boston and Connecticut, the creeks and islands of the Potomac; northwards to the forests and fisheries of Labrador. But all this vigorous world of agriculture and

15

commerce was not radically different from the civilization of Antiquity, save that it was on a wider, Atlantic, scale. It presented the same problems that had baffled the rulers of the Roman Empire, and ultimately brought their society to collapse. How to extend civilization to the masses? How to increase their purchasing power, to open markets which could continue to expand? How to create wealth which would counterbalance the dissipation of treasure and energy in war? Despite the abundance enjoyed by minorities, it was a civilization, like that of the traditional East, still basically agricultural, technologically primitive and generally poor.

With the application of science to production through new technology, the old problems became more urgent, though nearer possible solution. The nineteenth century was to see not only the emancipation of the middle classes, but in the West the appearance of a new urban proletariat. In England, already, the masses were no longer rural. And the twentieth century was to see an internal proletariat throughout Europe, and an external proletariat in Asia and Africa, both heavily dependent on great industry and on a cosmopolitan network of investment and exchange.

Three great events thus determined the social framework and political problems of the nineteenth century. First, the development of a world economy, centred on Western Europe and North America. Secondly, the Western liberal revolution which emancipated a professional and managerial class and gave free rein to capitalist enterprise. Thirdly, the rise of a politically conscious proletariat, urbanized and industrial. Meanwhile the peasant countries of Eastern Europe and Asia began to stir beneath the impact of Western economy and Western ideas. The tempo of industrial and technical change was destined to accelerate; the possibilities of progress and catastrophe to be stepped up. Environment was to alter at a pace which bewildered and demoralized men whose ancestors for millennia had been accustomed to the slow responses of an agricultural society; a society poor and limited, provincial and slow, but one which had been secure from utter disruption.

II

In face of the formidable problems already apparent, what were the predominant political ideas which had reflected and determined the evolution of pre-industrial Europe? In the changing and uneven development of so large and diverse an area, no single political theory could obviously predominate. In Periclean Athens or Republican Rome some degree of self-government might be realized, but the Rome of Marcus Aurelius or the Byzantium of Constantine had been autocratic. While English local government might flourish under Elizabethan Conciliar administration, the reception of Roman law in the Germanies and the development of France under Richelieu or Prussia under Frederick II promoted despotic power. The picture is contradictory and complex. Yet when all the contrasts are admitted, certain tendencies in Europe are original compared with other civilizations. They were realized, as might be expected, where the characteristically European environment is most marked: along the Mediterranean and Atlantic seaboard or in mountainous areas where despotism was difficult. In the sum of these intermittent, scattered, but cumulative and ultimately predominant tendencies, there emerged the rudiments of a Western political tradition.

Its hard-won development has been sketched in a previous work, and its nature and originality defined. Its pedigree is familiar, with its roots in Greece, in Israel and in Rome. Like all movements of thought, it has been fluctuating and sometimes obscure, but its accumulated or interacting effects have determined institutions and conduct. Imperfectly attained, standards had been set. They had encouraged clarity of thought, diminished the abuse of power, mitigated the worst horrors of the struggle for existence within society, and allowed a measure of personal freedom for creative minorities.

If one reflects on these tendencies and considers what Western civilization would have been without them, these elements in the diverse European inheritance appear the most distinctive. They have brought with them instability and conflict, but also unprecedented knowledge; in particular, command of environment, the most original Western achievement. The habit of self-government, which embodies this tradition, was to go far to tame power. Now rooted as well in North America, it has inspired the structure and objectives of the United Nations. In wide areas the callousness and conflict, normal in history, have often given place to negotiation and compromise.

By the end of the eighteenth century this tradition of constitutional commonwealth was already in being. How far was it to be enriched or diminished? How far was it able to dominate the critical transformation from an agricultural to an industrial society? How far can it be restated in terms of modern scientific knowledge so as to carry through unbroken the initiative of the political elites of pre-industrial Europe? These questions are the theme of this volume.

If the idea of constitutional commonwealth was the most valuable element in Western political thought at the close of the eighteenth century, already, since the sixteenth, it had possessed serious limitations. It was no longer cosmopolitan, being caught up in the development of the national sovereignty of the successor states of Medieval Christendom. It had also, in most of Europe, been swamped by the rise of centralized royal power. It had always been bounded by the limitations of its setting. It had emerged gradually and tentatively only in favourable areas; it had often fought a losing battle with arbitrary power; and it was still predominantly oligarchic. Originally, its setting was cosmopolitan, coming down from Antiquity — a civilization of cities, held together by a far flung bureaucratic and military rule which reflected the order of the *orbis terrarum*. Backed by religious sanctions, it had carried over into medieval times in terms of a world Christian commonwealth, subject, in theory, to Pope and Emperor, in which the realms of Christian kings had their ordered place. But this sense of Christian unity had been steadily diminished since the fourteenth century, and for all the resurgence of the Counter-Reformation, the Papacy had become no longer the spiritual guardian of all the West, but another power in the kaleidoscope of European politics.

By the time this study begins, the medieval idea of commonwealth had been largely swamped in the most powerful states of Europe by dynastic power. First Spain, then France, then Prussia, had seen the establishment of centralized government on a great scale. The 'enlightened' despotism of Joseph II identified the remnant of the Empire with absolutism. Only in England and the Netherlands, in parts of Switzerland and Scandinavia, had the idea of commonwealth effectively been maintained. And if, across the Atlantic, in the Puritan communities of Massachusetts and Connecticut, and in the easier world of Virginia, Georgia and the Carolinas, the ideas of Locke had taken root, the colonies were not yet powerful, and in the broad panorama of dynastic Europe, constitutionalism was at a discount. Such, after all, was the picture to be expected in a Europe which had witnessed through the seventeenth and eighteenth centuries the rise of great nation states, of government bureaucracy and commercial capitalism.

Yet imposing as institutions may be, ideas harmonious with the drift of social and economic change are more decisive. With the rise of the Western bourgeoisie in the seventeenth century, the English and Dutch commonwealths had become the centre of a new outlook. For all their limited area, the political as well as commercial initiative was with these Northern maritime peoples. The prevalent political fashions of the nineteenth century were largely to be determined by their institutions and ideas. This tide of political opinion was to spread to France; it was to look to Locke and the English and American institutions he had contributed to inspire. Although, therefore, in the late eighteenth century, the structure of absolutism still looked formidable, it was widely destined to crumble.

But the old regime was to leave its legacy. Internally the bureaucratic structure of monarchy remained; the prestige of centralized power, the unmedieval assumption that all initiative must come from government. While the medieval city was grouped round its cathedral, and the eighteenth-century town round its palace, the nineteenth-century industrial dynamo centred on its government offices. And when the old monarchies were supplanted by Napoleon, or even by the rule of middle class parliamentary majorities, the power of bureaucracy was by no means diminished. The sovereignty described by the Utilitarian writer Austin superseded the diffused authority of a medieval commonwealth, and the affinities of Rousseau are as much totalitarian as they are liberal.*

In the external field the legacy of dynastic sovereignty was more obvious. Indeed, it became exacerbated. The nation in arms proved more belligerent than the old governments. The conscription imposed by Napoleon, let alone that of 1870, was far more comprehensive and efficient than the levies of the old order. When the Industrial Revolution began to transform society, the triumph of liberal ideas in the West was to assure that constitutionalism would dominate the nineteenth century. But it was to be set in a framework incompatible with its medieval origins, of the internal and external sovereignty of the nation state. And national sovereignty was to be based not upon the sanction of a cosmopolitan Natural Law which reflected the divine order of the universe, but upon the new and dangerous doctrine of national popular Will.

III

Against this background, the rise of liberal constitutionalism and a *laissez-faire* economy will be examined. Reflecting the ideas of the

* See in particular, Sir E. Barker, *Social Contract*. Oxford University Press, 1947.

Western bourgeoisie, with their expanding economic and political interests, the former achieved far-flung extra-European success. It remains the accepted framework of Atlantic civilization and its dependencies. It has been widely adopted by non-Europeans, and it has determined the nature of attempts towards world government. It allows the adaptation of society to profound change by negotiation within a framework of law. It may therefore solve the two over-riding problems of the twentieth century — the building of a great popular civilization without the disruption of society by class conflict, and the control of competing national sovereignties through their assimilation into a world order.

The greatest constitutional success in the mid-nineteenth century was probably to answer the threat of revolution by legalizing trade unions. When, following the democratic revolution, the masses came to the threshold of power, they found in constitutional states, two institutions awaiting them, the ballot box and the national sovereign state. In consequence, in areas suited to constitutional democracy, internal disruption was avoided. External disruption was ensured. Liberal constitutional commonwealth, unlike its medieval predecessor, was no longer cosmopolitan. Whether it can again become so is one of the most important questions of the mid-twentieth-century.

During the period to be surveyed, it greatly enlarged its area, in particular over vast colonial territories in the British Commonwealth. By the twentieth century its centre of gravity was to shift to North America. The politics of the United States might be dominated by big business; unstable, raucous and corrupt, but in America liberalism achieved what it had never achieved in Europe. It spanned a Continent. Democratic principles and constitutional tradition remained the backbone of this immense civilization. That they did so was decisive.

In this wide extra-European setting, three major attacks developed. First, the socialist revolution, on the one hand Utopian or anarchical; on the other, Marxist. Next, the humanitarian nationalism of Mazzini degenerated into the ferocious nationalism of which Treitschke is the most extreme exponent. Finally, following the widespread loss of religious faith during the mid-century, there developed a nihilist attack on the basic assumptions of Christian and Humanist commonwealth. All these movements, like the constitutionalism they attacked, radiated from Europe. But, in their primitive forms, they tended to emanate not from the West, but from Central and Eastern Europe where arbitrary power was habitual.

The conflict of ideas was made steadily more dangerous by increasing power of governments. In Germany, in particular, the power of bureaucracy increased. This internal threat, even in the Welfare State, will be a major theme of this study. Its external consequences were worsened by closer economic interdependence and by scientific invention.

This continuing scientific progress was also marked by the appearance of a new sociology. Its development is the next outstanding feature of the political thought of the age, parallel with the rise of liberal constitutionalism and social democracy, with the revolutionary, nationalist and nihilist attack. It was a valuable new departure, and it will later be more fully considered. As political thought becomes, as it must, more deeply influenced by environmental and psychological knowledge, this contribution will be better appreciated. If modern conditions demand social democratic world commonwealth by consent, it seems best achievable through an alliance of sociology with constitutional government. And it may be that, as the mists of metaphysical dogma dissolve, the social landscape may become more precise and the world more habitable. This nineteenth-century application of scientific method to the study of society was of deep significance.

I V

Meanwhile the rush of scientific invention conditioned the whole background of the time, transforming Europe from a slow-moving agricultural society into a mechanized and changing civilization. The period with which this study begins marked the first great transformation in pace and scale. The slow-moving Europe of the mid-eighteenth century had been primarily agricultural, qualitatively unchanged since the Neolithic Revolution. There had been commerce and small capitalism; cities and maritime expansion; elaborate minority cultures, great art and literature and music, the flower of a complex civilization. But there had never been anything similar in kind to modern industrial society, even in the massive and far flung structure of the Roman, Byzantine and Chinese Empires. The transformation was naturally gradual and irregular. When Great Britain, Belgium, France and the Rhineland were already heavily industrialized, the peasant countries of Eastern Europe remained predominantly conservative. But the pace was set by the West. Here, increasingly, the population became urban. Not in the sense of the old bourgeoisie, living off the commerce of an agricultural society, but radically dependent on the factories and mentally conditioned by new surroundings. The typical Western man became a town dweller, free from the old routines; literate and articulate for the first time in history.* Unless it could dominate and come to terms with him, the old minority culture was ultimately doomed, breeding its own barbarians. It had to aim consciously at a mass civilization or peter out. That challenge, vividly perceived by de Tocqueville and J. S. Mill, liberal social democracy was belatedly to accept, in the West with considerable success. The penalty of failure was to revert to more primitive tribal patterns of dictatorship, as in Hitlerite Germany. In Russia the old method of autocracy in new guise rose heavily to the occasion. Here there was probably no alternative. Such was the first aspect of the transformation, still gradually going on, and still not much advanced over great areas of the world.

But these areas could not escape the tentacles of the new industries and technology. The world economy became more and more closely interdependent. Though the eighteenth century merchants of London and Amsterdam made their fortunes from trade in Chinese and Indian markets, the English were not then dependent on foreign imports and world trade, nor were the Dutch yet deeply involved with an East Indian Empire. While Governor Pitt and his kind were pouring wealth into England, factory operatives in Lancashire were not dependent on the chances of Japanese competition; and while decisions taken in Lombard Street might affect speculators in Paris, the basic conditions of peasant life were not subverted, as the livelihood of industrial millions in Great Britain and Germany was to be determined, by the decisions of Wall Street.

These facts were coincident with a revolution in transport. As the slow shift of economic power dwarfed Europe, the facts of geo-politics became global.† By the twentieth century the centre of Atlantic power settled in the breadth of the United States, its main potential competitor the vast but still relatively backward and ill co-ordinated area of the Soviet Union.

As the Atlantic liner moves up the estuary of the Hudson, these

---

* See ORTEGA y GASSET, *The Revolt of the Masses*, Allen & Unwin (1951 ed.).
† See H. J. MACKINDER, *Democratic Ideals and Reality*. London, 1919. Pelican edition, 1944. A pioneer work which still retains its force.

facts are dramatically apparent. First the fantastic silhouette of New York appears gradually in the distance. Then, behind the first cluster of sky-scrapers, appears another range which seems even more formidable. Here is the capital of an Atlantic world. But once in the dark canyon of Wall Street or beneath the cliffs of glass and steel around the Rockefeller Plaza, one senses that this power is not merely Atlantic. It is based upon the huge cities of the Middle West, Chicago and St. Louis, on the vast plains of Iowa and Illinois, and away, over the Rockies round the curve of the world for three thousand miles, upon the wealth of California. Here is power, broad-based on a Continent; power that looks out also over the Pacific to the Far East. It radiates over Central America and the West Indies, the mountain states of the Andes, the steaming forests of Brazil. It represents, in its glittering and unprecedented reality, the harnessed force of the twentieth century. And as the giant planes roar out of the great airports across the continents and oceans, the banal and sordid aspects of this civilization are dwarfed by the dignity of world authority. Power which can move mountains and divert rivers, which, if controlled by cosmopolitan institutions in which America must inevitably give the lead, can transform the future of mankind by the subjugation of the earth, the conquest of disease, the creation of plenty, the banishment of fear. Meanwhile, in the central massif of Eurasia, a vast and brutal industrial and political revolution is creating an opposite centre of supra-national power. It can either destroy itself and cripple the outer world in conflict, or collaborate, following ideas suited to the twentieth century, in the creation of plenty and peace.

All this can be done if practical methods of world government can be achieved. If the old and fundamental Western political tradition is not abandoned, and the principles of rationality, of justice, compassion and freedom are reinforced by science. There is then no obstacle to the building of a civilization of unprecedented range and well being. Such a project need not imply materialism. It would be the foundation of a future mass civilization, broad-based on the peoples of the whole world, on those external and internal proletariats whose standards of living and awareness must now be transformed if a world society is to be realized.

To this point has the rush of industrial and technical change carried the leading peoples of the planet in the mid-twentieth century. They are haunted by the penalties of their power. By the memories of Coventry and Rotterdam and Warsaw; of Cologne, Dresden and

Berlin; by the ruins of Hiroshima and Nagasaki; by the sinister nuclear experiments which punctuate the current armament race. All is jeopardized by the continuance of arbitrary power made more terrible by science. And still the change from the old slow-moving world of agriculture and commerce is only beginning over vast areas of the world. The traditional society which created the forms of self-government in small but favoured areas of Western Europe, implied, over most of the world, the rule of tyranny and force. The inhabitants of these countries still statistically outnumber the peoples over whom the various forms of constitutional government prevail. As the Asian peasant, or the Sahara tribesman, looks up to see the echeloned bombers of civilization gleaming in the sun, and hears the howl of jet engines as the swift formation vanishes in the haze, the contrast seems so fantastic as to seem irrelevant. Yet it symbolizes the problem of the modern world. For the mentality of peasant and tribesman still lurks in the minds of the rulers and the masses of mankind. How can the outlook and institutions of the agricultural past, and the ancient destructive impulses of the subconscious mind, be adapted to the precarious, changing, yet immensely powerful machinery of industrial and atomic civilization?

The swift change is extraordinary. But it has already begun to affect political thought. All mentality is conditioned by its setting, and already modern political ideas reflect the increasing command of environment, internal and psychological, as well as external and material, which has marked the slow turning of civilization into its second great age. The age of heavy industry and vast potential wealth; of atomic power and radio; of television and supersonic speed; of urban living and professional science, which has emerged out of the slow centuries of peasant agriculture, of illiteracy and leisured privilege, of resignation and routine. The political theory of such an age is naturally Humanist and practical. To the traditional religious view it is arrogant. But the field of knowledge has expanded in the last two centuries to reveal the hard realities of nature and the limitations as well as the glory of life. Man, it seems, must now make himself. By political wisdom, scientific knowledge, and organized mutual aid. And, in the making, realize the power and compassion of Mind.

BOOK I

THE POLITICAL THOUGHT OF THE ROMANTIC AGE

CHAPTER I

THE ORIGINALITY OF THE ROMANTICS: HERDER: HEGEL

T H E political thought of the later eighteenth century had seen the decline of the concept of Natural Law. Both Thomism and the enlightenment had assumed a transcendental sanction; one the revelation of Christianity, the other the rational benevolence of a Supreme Being. But Hume's analysis had not only been hostile to revealed religion; it had undermined the 'enlightened' confidence in reason itself.

It was the ambition of Rousseau, Kant and Hegel to find a way out. That road seemed to lie in a deeper, more systematic introspection. The nineteenth century was to be original in the exploration of intuition. The cult of will displaced the apprehension of a clear cut transcendental order. Reality was immanent, diffused, creative. Here is the first original aspect of the time. And with it, reflected in political thought, an emotional response to total experience, a deepened humanism. While political theory was thus enriched, the effects of this outlook could also be disastrous. As the classical theory had its limitations, romanticism had its dangers. In the loss of political realism and of the old sense of European order.

The second original aspect of the nineteenth century was the expansion of professional knowledge; the systematic mastering of environment. This achievement was also humanist. Its tentative beginnings are early interwoven with the thought of seventeenth- and eighteenth-century political philosophers. But it was not until the mid-nineteenth century that it became formidable. It is expressed by the English Utilitarians and later reinforced by the immense expansion of scientific knowledge in the age of Darwin. Starting with mainly legal reform, it developed towards the wide ramifications of modern welfare legislation and sociology.

Against this background, a novel aspect of nineteenth-century political philosophy is the preponderant influence of the Germans. Here French and English influence met a new challenge. The Germanies had long been regarded as backward and provincial. The miniature courts of their princes were a by-word for dullness, and German pedantry and beer-swilling were proverbial. When the chances of dynastic succession saddled the English with George I, a Bolingbroke or a Marlborough regarded his entourage and his mistresses with contempt. Apart from the respect inspired by the European genius of Leibnitz or by the military virtuosity of Frederick II, the prestige of Germans in the West was negligible. They made good mercenaries to put down rebels in the Highlands or in America.

By the 'thirties of the nineteenth century there is a different and juster picture. In England, Coleridge and Carlyle, J. S. Mill, Jowett, Matthew Arnold, the world of classical scholarship and advanced theology, looked to Tübingen, to Heidelberg and Bonn. Apart from the cosmopolitan prestige of Goethe and Kant, the transformation had owed much to two Swiss publicists. Rousseau gave the first broad momentum to the cult of romantic introspection, and Madame de Staël's *De l'Allemagne* had presented Germany to intellectual Europe. In English political thought this admiration was to persist into the late nineteenth century with the neo-Hegelianism of Bradley and Bosanquet. What was the magnetism, the originality, which had so transformed the reputation of the German people?

The qualities of the German mind seemed to meet the situation created by the decline of eighteenth-century rationalism. The great figures of Goethe and Kant came to dominate the early nineteenth century. The destruction of a united clerical front in Germany by the Reformation, and the diversion of German liberalism into speculation rather than action, both contributed to this result. Among the diverse states of the Germanies there was no movement so massive as the French Revolution. The champions of French enlightenment had been passionately anti-clerical. They had to be: it was not only the lofty eloquence and range of a Bossuet they had to challenge. They were harassed by a church entrenched in a centralized and powerful state. Apart from their Gallic tradition of sharp realism, it was natural for these writers to be exasperated and necessary for them to attack. In the mild atmosphere of a Lutheran Court the position was very different, and it was notable how many German thinkers were pastors, like Herder, or pastors *manqués*, like Hegel. But a distinctive and original feature of the age was the rise of the middle-class secular intellectual. He was not a brilliant creature who frequented court and salon — a Leibnitz or a Voltaire — but a dim or vaguely prophetic figure who held his audience from the professorial rostrum. His books were conned by bourgeois amateurs, savants and students, alone and intimately, in untidy libraries in a haze of tobacco smoke. The consensus of these professional and amateur middle-class minds was increasingly to influence the trend of political opinion.

It was a serious body of thought. These people were not frivolous or cynical, with the hardness of the great world. They were often introspective, preoccupied with problems of conduct. If they were aristocrats, like Chateaubriand or Lamennais, they were Bohemian aristocrats. Kant and Hegel, with their regular middle-class lives, were also typical. They were writers, living by a wide public, their reputation won by originality and eloquence. They were the secular prophets who had stolen the mantle of the priests.

In this setting the exponents of political theory were naturally different from the staid and generally official characters whose works had held the field since Antiquity. The solid statesmen, the eminent divines, the responsible lawyers and administrators, are joined by writers more in the tradition of Rousseau, or by cranks of genius like Saint-Simon, Comte and Proudhon, living in poverty by their pens. There were rebels, also, who made a better living by castigating their Age.

The majority of political writers in the Middle Ages had belonged to a formidable and European Church. John of Salisbury was a civil servant, who died Bishop of Chartres; St. Thomas himself was eminent in his order; Bracton a clerical administrator. With the learned doctors of the sixteenth and seventeenth centuries it was the same tale. If they were not clergy, they were lawyers and adminis-trators, as were Fortescue, Bodin and Grotius. Hobbes had been one of the first to stand entirely on his own fame, with no public position, execrated by official circles, if sustained by patronage. Voltaire and Hume had played a lone hand, but they were men of the world, not critical of organized society. But with Rousseau the role of the Bohemian, the rebel, the middle-class publicist, more akin to the musicians and the playwrights, had begun. The role was to be continued by Carlyle; later by Schopenhauer and Nietzsche. These people belonged to no great disciplined order; they are backed by no European authority and their outlook tended to be coloured by national tradition. When they rebel, they become outcasts and refugees, as were Marx and Lenin, appealing away from the bour-geoisie to which they belong to the masses without. They are no longer a clerisy: they are an intelligentsia.

Nearly all these writers are secular but earnest. They are trying to restore to society the meaning and justice taken for granted in the orthodoxy of the Middle Ages, and they differ from the philosophers and law-givers of Antiquity, since in general they represent and contribute to a vast middle-class public and command a far wider audience. It was this seriousness and this introspection, and sometimes this irresponsibility, which was the political hall-mark of the Romantic Age.

The cosmopolitan origins of this movement cannot here be investigated. It was predominantly a phenomenon of the North — not Mediterranean. It drew much of its vitality from the investigation of a national past, going back into the Middle Ages and beyond. It was bound up with the new philology, with the study of ancient languages; embodied in *Percy's Reliques*, in Macpherson's *Ossian* and in weird Scandinavian mythology. In France it led to a new feeling for history, expressed in Chateaubriand's *Les Martyrs*, and Thierry's Anglo-Saxon and Merovingian studies.

For political theory it was decisive.* It emphatically and permanently increased the sense of history, of environment, of tradition. Its weakness, particularly apparent in Germany, was emotional instability. Where Burke, in England, already a unified national state, could combine his mystique with constitutionalism and a new sense of imperial trusteeship, his German counterparts, a Müller or a Fichte, living in the political crisis and backwash of the Napoleonic wars, were naturally lost to the cosmopolitan tradition of the old Europe, and devoid of Burke's pervading sense of the possible. The German writers, in particular, were liable to a State idolatry reflecting the amorphous political situation of their country.† It was thus in Germany that the movement was most typical and powerful, in its originality and its weakness, and it will be worth examining two representative German political philosophers, out of many, in greater detail.

II

Herder is highly original, Hegel the more influential and better known. Herder stands at the beginning of a new school of German political thought, and will here be taken as the most representative figure of its first cosmopolitan phase.‡ His origins were Baltic,

* For a study of this background see EMERY NEFF, *The Poetry of History*. Columbia University Press, 1948; also R. B. MOWAT, *The Romantic Age*. Harrap, 1937.

† It has been said, with truth, that a German without a state was like a Frenchman without a mistress.

‡ See R. D'O. BUTLER, *The Roots of National Socialism*. Faber & Faber, 1941, for a powerful analysis of the Romantic and subsequent aspects of German nationalism.

something new in the history of European political philosophers.*
He had fought his way out of a bleak environment, intending to become a Lutheran pastor. At the ancient University of Königsberg
Kant was then predominant. He saw the possibilities of the brilliant
youth; allowed him to attend lectures without a fee, put the latest
books in his way, encouraged him to master Hebrew and Greek.
The influence of Johann Georg Hamann, with his cult of Northern
folk poetry, also enriched Herder's mind. The 'fifties and 'sixties of
the eighteenth century saw a growing appreciation of Scandinavian,
Celtic and Early English poetry, and a new approach to Homeric,
Biblical and Medieval studies.† Herder's range was to be encyclo-
paedic. If his expression was sometimes confused, his political
outlook was always historical. For Herder, indeed, history was time-
travel, a feeling oneself (*einfühlen*) into the past. He related contemporary life to wilder times. 'On the way through the narrow
Skagerrak', writes Professor Neff, of the voyage in 1769 which marked
a turning point in his development, 'to the broad North sea, glimpses
of the bleak, mist-shrouded mountains of Norway, their green bases

* Johann Gottfried Herder, 1744-1803. Born at a remote village in East Prussia, son of
a village schoolmaster. In 1762 he attended the University of Königsberg, where he came
under the influence of Kant and Hamann. From 1765 to 1769 he was a Lutheran pastor
at Riga in the Grand Duchy of Latvia, where he followed up his studies of northern folk
poetry. In 1767 he published *Fragments on Recent German Literature*, which coincided with
the publication of Lessing's brilliant literary criticism, vindicating Shakespeare. Three
years later, appeared his *Journal of my Voyage in 1769*, which states the purpose of his life
work. After travelling in France and Holland, he became pastor at Buckeburg, the provincial capital of the small Duchy of Schaumberg-Lippe. In 1772 he published his
Considerations on the Origins of Speech, and in the following year, after a fortunate meeting
with the young Goethe at Strasbourg, he published, jointly with Goethe, *German Character
and Art*, a landmark in the comparative study of early literatures. In 1774 appeared his
Still Another Philosophy of History, a preliminary sketch for his later masterpiece. Through
the influence of Goethe, Herder was summoned to fill the post of Court preacher at
Weimar, where he lived for the rest of his life. In these congenial surroundings, he produced his *Folk Songs*, 1778-79, which contained remarkable translations of early poetry,
and in 1782-83 his *Spirit of Hebrew Poetry*, which applied the new standards of literary
criticism to Biblical literature. In his Biblical studies Herder had been influenced by the
rationalistic methods of Spinoza. His greatest work, *Thoughts on the Philosophy of the
History of Mankind*, appeared between 1784 and 1791. Herder maintained that a pattern of
history exists which can be ascertained by observation and sympathetic understanding,
and he relates history to biology and environmental studies. The influence of this original,
sometimes disordered and often brilliant work has been considerable on historical studies,
and Hegel's *Philosophy of History* owes much to it. Herder was a dynamic, extravert
personality; although his egoism and sensibility made him quarrelsome, he had great
personal magnetism. His writings were collected and edited by B. Suphan in thirty-two
volumes, 1877, who also published a *Selection*, 1884-87. See NEFF, op. cit. and R. R.
ERGANS, *Herder and the Foundations of German Nationalism*. New York, 1931.

† For an account of the English contribution to these studies see Professor D. C.
DOUGLAS, *English Scholars*. Cape, 1939. In particular his chapters on 'The Saxon Past'
and his account of Hickes and Wanley. Professor Neff points out that Hamann had been
influenced by that curious character Edward Young, author of *Night Thoughts*, whose
Conjectures on Original Composition he had read with approval.

bathed in deep fjords, told him why the Eddas and Ossian exhaled wildness of a different quality from that of the Odyssey. In vivid retrospect Herder wrote of his voyage. "Suddenly out of business, tumult, and the foolish rivalries of the bourgeois world, out of the easy chair of the scholar . . . upon a deck on an open boundless sea amid a little state of men who have severer laws than the republic of Lycurgus . . . believe me, there skalds and bards get read far differently than from a professor's desk." The stuff of history, Herder now believed, was action, instinct, atmosphere; the spirit of people in its geographical setting.'[1] He loved the weird, the romantic, the remote. Like Horace Walpole, a very different character, he made a cult of the Gothic. 'My life,' he wrote rather self-consciously, 'is a procession through Gothic arches.' He glorified the German language and German national spirit. He approached politics through literature. For he sought by the study of language to understand the atmosphere of other times.

Herder was also convinced of the importance of the new botany and biology, first systematized by Linnaeus and Buffon. He understood, like Montesquieu, the effect of geography on civilization, contrasting the maritime and mountainous environment of the Greeks with the riparian background of near Eastern cultures. But unlike the aloof and universal Kant, who could write *Zum Ewigen Frieden* with a world-vision, and unlike Goethe, the cosmopolitan aristocrat, with his Olympian view, Herder's approach to politics, his deep sense of the Germanic past, made him profoundly nationalistic. 'Herder', writes Mr. Butler, 'replaced the traditional conception of the politico-juridical state by that of the folk nation . . .'[2] He stressed the word, 'Folk . . . an imprecisely suggestive word; it surpasses *people* in the very German quality of *Innigkeit*, a blend of inwardness and fervour.'[3] He sensed the collective personality of a people in Time. Like Burke, he brought to the angular and calculating rationalism of the eighteenth century a revived sense of community; unlike Burke, he had little feeling for political liberty and for institutions which could ensure it. He was hostile also to the Catholic view of European order coming down from Rome. His cult of the North, of the barbaric enterprise of a Teutonic 'Volk', whose tradition, he believed, dominated Scandinavia, England and the Frankish conquerors of Gaul, was concentrated on the cult of Germany. Like most German romantics, he expressed a certain neglect and inferiority before the brilliance and commanding authority of eighteenth-century France. He meant to vindicate the German national spirit;

the spirit of the Rhine and the Harz, of the rolling uplands and mountains of Bavaria and the broad Baltic plains. 'Let someone therefore defend the national spirit . . . and show by examples that Germany has since the earliest times had the fixed national spirit in all classes, still has it at the present time, and according to its organization will have it everlastingly. The writer of such a history deserves more than a civic crown; a wreath of oak, beech, spruce and linden boughs.'⁴ Herder insisted on national self expression: 'Only through the consciousness of nationality can the folk retain its deep roots.' Yet he had breadth and generosity. Like Mazzini after him, he had a romantic vision of a world where nations, working out their proper qualities, could live harmoniously and learn from one another. 'No nationality,' he wrote, 'has been solely designated by God as the chosen people of the earth; above all we must seek the truth and cultivate the garden of the common good.' Hence no nationality in Europe may separate itself sharply, and foolishly say, 'With us *alone*, with us dwells *all* wisdom.'⁵ Herder thus encouraged a powerful and often valuable stream of political thought. Unlike many of his followers, he was a humanist and a Christian. In spite of his hostility to Catholicism and the Latin tradition, he tried to reinterpret Christianity; to reconcile passion and reason; to find a way out of the scepticism of the Enlightenment; away from the hard brilliance, wit and pride of the men of the world, of Hume and Gibbon and Voltaire. If, like Luther, he thought with the blood, his violence was theoretical and his sense of the past poetic. He is among the followers of Rousseau, with his cult of the people. He glorified the freedom and nobility of primitive races, the tribal and bardic past. And often he goes deeper than Rousseau in his understanding of the human spirit. For, like Vico, he had singular intuition. He sought to understand man's place in nature, the decisive influence of environment, of historical explanation. He is one of the fathers of nineteenth-century historicism. This Baltic genius contributed much to European thought. He is profoundly German; in this Germanity is both his weakness and his strength.

For he had profound defects. His political outlook was vague and unstable. Like so many of his kind, civilians leading their relatively sheltered lives, he had little understanding of the hard realities of politics, through which the seventeenth and eighteenth century noblesse of the sword and the robe had cut their way; little apprehension of the appalling consequences of political miscalculation, none of the political experience of a Washington or a Jefferson.

The ideas of Herder and his kind were thus original and creative, but dangerous. They led to the cult of the Volk, but not to the idea of self-government; and they took for granted the disruption of the old cosmopolitan Europe into nation states, with the vaguest realization of the obvious political consequences, of which Rousseau had been well aware.* Yet, in his introspective insight, his struggle for truth, his attempted reconciliation of sense and reason, his insight into early cultures, his insistence on the totality of experience and the reality of will, Herder is forerunner of the most original developments of nineteenth-century political thought. Where Hegel has probably won excessive respect, it is likely that the influence of Herder, as historian and political thinker, deserves more recognition. For he symbolizes the romantic cult of history, the appeal away from contract and self-interest and a mechanized society to an organic national tradition. He is attempting to put a new myth in place of the old rationalism or the Utilitarian sanctions now becoming influential in England. There is no more representative exponent of early romantic nationalism, with its sanguine political hopes and literary appeal.

III

The rise of the Western middle classes to political, economic and intellectual predominance had been expressed in France by the Revolution and by Napoleon's Code Civil. In England it was

* See ROUSSEAU's *Extrait du Projet de la Paix Perpétuelle de M. L'Abbé de Saint Pierre et jugement sur la Paix Perpétuelle. Political writings of Rousseau.* Edited C. E. Vaughan, vol. I, pp. 365-88. It shows that Rousseau was vividly conscious of the problem. In principle he agrees with St. Pierre. He stresses the natural bonds of culture, history and interest which make for the unity of European civilization, and agrees that the 'public Law' of Europe has no authority. The remedy should be a force 'coactive et coercitive', ensured by a perpetual alliance and a perpetual Congress, or European Diet. Aggressors should be 'mis au ban de l'Europe' and proscribed as public enemies. The advantages of ending 'l'impolice européenne', he writes, are too obvious for argument. 'C'est une insulte que je ne veux pas faire au lecteur de lui prouver qu'en générale l'état de paix est préférable à l'état de guerre.' The plan, he insists, as have many after him, does not even demand a high level of morality; it is a matter of interest. Moreover, it could easily be brought about by rulers — 'for all we have to assume is enough sense to see their interest and enough courage to arrange their own welfare'. 'If,' he concludes, 'in spite of all this, the project remains unexecuted, that is not because it is chimerical, it is because human beings are insane and that it is a kind of lunacy to be wise in the midst of madmen.' Here Rousseau expressed a conclusion still arguable.

Among other causes of the failure of such a project, he also cites the pride of princes, who think it beneath their dignity to submit to law, and the self-interest of ministers who gain in importance in war-time. Summing up, he thinks the project can probably only be brought about by a revolution which would entail worse evils than the international disorder it attempts to remedy, a conclusion probably no longer valid in an age of misapplied science.

marked by the doctrines of Bentham and by the Reform Bill of 1832, with its far-reaching administrative sequel. The German contribution was expressed at once in dynamic metaphysical theory, and in the development of an all too efficient bureaucracy.

After Herder, German romantic political thought is broad and complex. Its vague liberal idealism was sometimes cosmopolitan, more often nationalistic. Herder and Hegel, figures of European significance, must be set against this background. The dominant influences were originally Kant and Goethe; the one insisting on moral self development and austerely denying the significance of the phenomenal world; the other stressing aesthetic and intellectual liberation. Between Herder and Hegel the most important figure is Fichte, who reached the height of his influence in Berlin after Jena, and who turned to economic as well as to metaphysical and political theory. In reaction against the cosmopolitan outlook of Adam Smith, he devised a theory of state-controlled economic autarchy as well as a metaphysical state theory with Hegelian affinities. His influence on German thought in the nineteenth century was fundamental.*
The change in Fichte's opinions from cosmopolitan individualism to a romantic cult of the state is highly significant. An 'idealist' philosopher in the Kantian tradition, concerned to realize the liberty of the free will, he was early influenced by Rousseau and an ardent champion of the Revolution. His cult of personality then implied a critical attitude to the state. After the Napoleonic invasions, his outlook radically changed. Only a strong government, he believed, could guarantee individual freedom; the freedom of the small peasantry and lower bourgeoisie which he had most at heart. His originally cosmopolitan outlook became narrowed into a violent democratic nationalism, and his cult of personal free-will became merged in the assertion of political and economic independence through the state. He became the great interpreter of romanticism into collectivist terms.

Like the early Fichte, most of the older writers in this age had been cosmopolitan and liberal. Schiller, like so many of them, was fundamentally a religious genius, and projected his personality into an idealist dramatization of history. Wilhelm Schlegel, Professor of Literature at Bonn, wrote translations of Shakespeare which contributed to a German romantic cult; the Bavarian novelist, Jean

---

* J. G. Fichte, 1762-1814. Rector of Berlin University, 1810-12. See in particular *Reden an die Deutsche Nation* (1808), trans. R. F. Jones and G. F. Turnbull. Chicago, 1922. The collected works in eight volumes were edited by I. H. Fichte. Berlin, 1845-46.

Paul Richter, and the brilliant and short-lived von Hardenberg (Novalis), were predominantly liberal mystics. Following the reaction against the Napoleonic invasions, there can also be heard a primitive and bloody minded note in this serious Romanticism. The poets Arnim, Kleist, and Arndt, the last from Rügen on the Baltic, composed ferocious battle songs on consecrated daggers, 'cohort — stormers', and rivers of blood. The paradox of German idealism and violence pervades this literature.

In Hegel the paradox is still there, the noisy manifestations of 'Sturm und Drang'. With it went a forceful and original genius of European range. The introspective Humanism of the German Romantic Age had been expressed by Herder in a cult of organic community, of the Volk, and in a new historicism. Overshadowing Herder, yet developing his essential idea, Hegel was to exercise a more powerful influence on the nineteenth century. Although his great reputation in Germany was comparatively short lived, his ideas later deeply affected foreign political philosophers. From the least valuable part of Hegel's philosophy, Marx was to take the dialectical aspect of his materialism. The Marxist interpretation of this mystical concept was still to determine the politics of otherwise hard-boiled realists in the Kremlin in the middle-twentieth century. And today it is extraordinary to observe how this originally Hegelian idea, inverted by Marx, forms the basis of a powerful dogma. In its name purges are conducted, heresy hunts unleashed, the party line laid down, and foreign policy apparently determined. Such is the power of political theory; so docile men of action in believing, or cynical manipulators of myth in exploiting, the distorted ideas of dead philosophers who have spent their lives lecturing to small audiences in academic surroundings. Painfully elaborated, often sinister with power, this nineteenth-century dogma still commands belief.

Hegel would doubtless have been horrified. His objectives were never revolutionary. But this son of a small customs official, educated for the pastorate, achieved astonishing influence.* 'Political genius,'

* Georg Wilhelm Friedrich Hegel, 1770-1831, was educated at Stuttgart and Tübingen, where he read theology and obtained the degree of Doctor of Philosophy in that subject, with the report that although he possessed sound mediocre ability, he was deficient in philosophy. The bias of his early studies was classical and this appreciation of Antiquity coloured his later thought. After leaving Tübingen in 1793, he earned a meagre livelihood as a tutor at Berne and Frankfurt, but in 1799 inherited a small legacy from his father. He put this opportunity to good use. In 1801-2 he was studying at Jena and in the latter year published his *Constitution of Germany*. But he obtained little academic recognition, and in 1807, the year of the publication of his *Phänomenologie des Geistes*, he

he was to write, 'consists in identifying yourself with a principle.' That principle was the national state. For doubting yet religious minds he provided an imposing and comprehensive philosophy. Today his most valuable contribution seems his sense of time, his relation of the observer, in his shifting context, to the observed in history, his assertion of the relativity of much historical thought.

Hegel faced the deepest problems of his age. But like many men of genius he was reckless in eloquence and involved in expression. He endowed the state with a dangerous glamour and lacked the salutary suspicion of power which has inspired more realist thinkers. He is in the tradition of Luther, who also thought with the blood, regardless of political consequences. There is more wisdom in a few pages of Aristotle's *Politics*, or in the unpretentious views of Locke, than in all the heady eloquence of this successor of Rousseau.

In cutting a way through the jungle of Hegelian metaphysics, one may remember that Hegel's thought was early defined. This merciful dispensation allows the student of political theory to disregard many later assertions of metaphysical dogma with which this curious genius impressed his contemporaries. Like Herder, he lacked the sense of form, and the German language, not the most lucid of media, reaches, in the view of good judges, some of its most occult, if numinous, convolutions in the later writings of this philosopher. 'Commentary on Hegel,' writes Dr. Sabine, 'has on the whole tended to take too seriously the parade of legal precision and the formidable terminology in which he finally cast his philosophy. There is now no doubt that his main ideas were first suggested to him by his

took to editing the *Bamberger Zeitung*. He then turned schoolmaster, and as Rector of the Aegidien Gymnasium at Nuremberg he proved a success. This post he held until 1816. In 1811 he had married: from 1812 to 1816 appeared his *System of Philosophy*. In 1816 he succeeded Fichte in Berlin. In 1821 appeared his *Fundamentals of the Philosophy of Right*. The next ten years saw the climax of his career; his lectures became the object of a cult. In 1830 he was Rector of the University, and in the following year decorated by the Prussian king. He died, working to the end, in the cholera epidemic of 1831. As a personality he was unprepossessing and of meagre appearance; his delivery was painful and his voice weak. He was a good family man and addicted only to snuff: he spoke, apparently, with a broad Swabian accent. The best German edition of his writings was made by G. LASSON, *Hegels Werke*. Leipzig, 1907-28. *The Philosophy of History*, based on his lectures in Berlin, was translated by J. Sibree. London, 1857.

There is a large Hegelian literature. For the best British Neo-Hegelian exposition see E. CAIRD, *Hegel*. London, 1880: see also B. BOSANQUET, *The Philosophical Theory of the State*. London, 1899. For a hostile criticism, see L. T. HOBHOUSE, *The Metaphysical Theory of the State*. London, 1918. See also A. D. LINDSAY, 'Hegel, the German Idealist', in *Social and Political Ideas of the Age of Reaction and Reconstruction*, edited F. J. C. Hearnshaw, New York edition, 1949; H. A. REYBURN, *Hegel's Ethical Theory*. Oxford, 1921, and M. B. FOSTER, *The Political Philosophies of Plato and Hegel*. Oxford, 1935. E. CASSIRER, *The Myth of the State*, pp. 248ff. Newhaven, 1946, has some interesting comments.

early studies of European culture, especially the history of Christianity.'*

Hegel's *The Philosophy of Right* contains the most elaborate explanation of his political ideas: his *The Philosophy of History* is a more popular work. Both will here be examined. For Hegel created a new philosophy of world history. Where Burke had expressed the continuity of the English past, and Herder of the development of the German Volk, Hegel took the plunge into total world-historical philosophy. It combined a belief in the emerging consciousness of the 'Absolute' with the social realization of individual will. Here is not merely the assertion of particular nationalism, but a whole metaphysical philosophy to justify, or to explain, the mission of the nation state.

The Philosophy of Right first appeared in 1821. It is available in English in a good critical edition.† The argument is presented in 360 numbered paragraphs, to which are subjoined Hegel's remarks, or explanatory notes. It is further complicated by additions taken from notes at Hegel's lectures by his earlier German editor, Gans, here separately collected. Finally, Professor Knox has added eighty pages of his own exposition. *The Philosophy of History*, which will later be examined, is based on lectures delivered between 1822 and 1831. It contains a long introduction and four parts; the Oriental World, the Greek World, the Roman World, and — the culmination — the German World. It ranges over the whole field of History, as it was known at the time. 'The subject of this course of

* G. H. SABINE, *A History of Political Theory*, pp. 624ff, q.v. for a good short account of Hegel's political ideas. On the other hand, Hegel's obscurity greatly contributed to his prestige. As Georges Sorel points out (*Matériaux d'une Théorie du Prolétariat*, p. 21), he was in his day the outstanding creator of myth, if, by the 'seventies on the continent, he was out of fashion. Take, for example, how 'Boris d'Yxkull, baron estonien, tout récemment encore officier dans l'armée russe, a raconté avec une curieuse sincérité comment il s'attacha à Hegel; il *ne comprenait à peu près rien à son cours*, mais il était attiré par cette obscurité même, et *surtout par le sérieux profond de Hegel*.' P. ROQUES, *Hegel, sa Vie et ses Œuvres*, p. 170.

† *Hegel's Philosophy of Right*, translated with notes by T. M. KNOX. Oxford, 1942. Reprinted 1945. Text 223 pp. Additions from notes at Hegel's lectures (interpolated by Gans in his edition, 1833), pp. 224-97. Translator's notes, pp. 298-376. The German edition needed a double title: *Naturrecht und Staatswissenschaft im Grundrisse* (Natural Law and Political Science In Outline), and *Grundlinien der Philosophie des Rechts* (Elements of the Philosophy of Right or Law). 'The difficulties of translating *The Philosophy of Right*,' Professor Knox remarks, 'begin with the title.' After a preface and introduction, the book is divided into three parts; Abstract Right; Morality and Ethical Life. Under the first come Property, Contract and Wrong. The second part includes 'Purpose and Responsibility, Intention and Welfare, God and Conscience.' The third deals with the family (marriage, capital and education), and with Civil Society (the system of Needs, the administration of Justice, and the State). The last section is divided into a discussion of Constitutional Law, International Law and World History. Under the former the 'internal' constitution is examined — Crown, Executive Legislature — and 'sovereignty vis-à-vis foreign states.'

lectures,' Hegel begins boldly, 'is the Philosophical History of the
World.'*

The Philosophy of Right was described by Lord Lindsay as a 'profoundly inspiring and illuminating work';[6] Lord Russell, on the
other hand, regards Hegel's influence as disastrous; 'he seems to
think that everything important takes the form of war'.[7] The
political philosophy of both books is 'a doctrine which, if accepted,
justifies every internal tyranny and every external aggression'.

What was it in Hegel's philosophy that appealed to academic
liberal thought and also provokes such scathing denunciation? It
was new since it introduced a new relativity in political thought. It
regarded all ideas and institutions as changing, and all ideas as
coloured by their immediate setting, an aspect of development of
consciousness in Time. It also defined society as something alive and
'becoming' rather than a utilitarian harmony of interests. Hegel, it
was believed, provided sanctions for a dynamic constitutionalism,
a living harmony of individual and society. He foresaw, it is argued,
the possibilities of the nineteenth-century constitutional nation
state, then a new phenomenon. He based this community on a
harmony of self-correcting wills. 'No political philosophy,' wrote
Lindsay, 'has given such an adequate account of the constitutional
state.' Here is a new political theory, no longer desiccated into
pragmatic utilitarianism after the destruction of the old concept of
Natural Law, or hide-bound with the eighteenth-century conventionality of Burke or the Catholic reaction of de Maistre. Here, once
more, is an alternative; a standard by which government can be
judged. Expelled, Natural Law returns in a new guise. It has hitherto been too rigidly defined: now from the depth of Hegel's intuition,
it emerges as historically creative will. He has carried on Rousseau's
mission to provide an alternative — the living will, ascertainable by
negotiation from the broad life of the state. Individuals are thus fulfilled in the life of whole peoples; family interest, economic organizations, corporate bodies within the state, are reconciled in the wider
harmony of the whole society. The state lives by its components; in
them a mystical sanction is restored against the Benthamite attempt
to justify society by mere 'cunning of reason'. Here is a creative
society inspired by Rousseau's General Will, without the misleading
convention of contract, elaborated by a new philosophy. In this
perpetual becoming are realized the emergent values of life, though

* *The Philosophy of History* by GEORG WILHELM FRIEDRICH HEGEL, with prefaces by
Charles Hegel and the translator, J. Sibree. Revised edition. New York, 1944, 457 pp.

it is hard, even for philosophers, to catch up with it. 'When philosophy paints its grey on grey, one form of life has become old, and by means of grey it cannot be rejuvenated but only known. The owl of Minerva takes her flight only when the shadows of evening are falling.'

This outlook is at once dynamic and conservative. According to Hegel, only what is 'real' is 'rational'. In one aspect it implies release: in another, acceptance of fate, its own justification. Here is none of Marx's determination to improve; rather a consecration of the *fait accompli* — profoundly reactionary. God is history: the state is the bland, inexorable fact. The achieved living thing is reality and nothing else.*

This philosophy is rooted in universal history. Hence the claim that Hegel 'really brought historical method into political philosophy', though it seems an odd method to most historians. Since, it is claimed, the state is rooted in particular wills, 'The principle of the modern State has this enormous strength and depth, that it lets the principle of subjectivity fulfil itself to the most independent extreme of personal particularity, and yet, at the same time, brings it back into its substantive unity, and thus preserves particularity in the principle of the State. The idea of the modern State has this peculiarity; the State is the embodiment of freedom not according to subjective liking, but according to the concept of Will, that is, in its universal and divine character.'[8]

Here is the old Kantian assertion of liberty through Will. This Will can be realized through the family, in economic enterprise, and through the state. In this sense Hegel was not totalitarian. Liberty, he declared, 'is only deep when it is differentiated.' The State supplies the adjustable constitutional framework within which voluntary activities of individuals and groups can find harmony and fulfilment. Thus mankind can make its own Natural Law, and a way out has been found for the perennial problem, whether the world reflects a cosmic order which is favourable, indifferent, or hostile. The knot is cut by the exercise of creative Will.†

Here, briefly sketched, is the attractive side of Hegel's political philosophy. It reflects the fundamental concern of the political thought of the Romantic age, already described. How, by introspection, by the contemplation of history, by the study of man and his works, to find a basis of value outside the dogmas of orthodox

* Vide *infra* for F. H. Bradley's development of this idea.
† See my *Western Political Thought*, p. 81, Cape, 1947.

Christianity — or one which can perhaps be reconciled with some form of Christian belief? The nineteenth century, it has already been remarked, was original in the exploration of intuition. Of all the German thinkers who devoted themselves to this task, Hegel was the most extraordinary and the most impressive. It was natural that he should become one of the major prophets of the nineteenth century.

Yet for all their range, these German romantics were provincial. Theirs was a romanticism of the North — devoid of the political realism of the Mediterranean or of the universality of Rome. They made the romantic error of reading into political institutions qualities which in the eyes of realists who conduct them they do not possess. Hegel thus perceived the internal possibilities of the early nineteenth-century nation state. His limitations were in the international field. They were to prove singularly pernicious. *The Philosophy of Right* and *The Philosophy of History* contain most of the nonsense which has subsequently bedevilled political thought. The merits of the writer who prided himself 'on teaching philosophy to speak German', are outbalanced by his wild ideas of the relations of states and peoples. Hegel had no conception of European order, or of cosmopolitan Law. Though deeply influenced by Kant, he scorned Kant's vision of world-citizenship and perpetual peace; he accepted and glorified conflict. How did this romantic philosopher, admired by English idealists, come to so bellicose a mind? To understand this paradox one must examine Hegel's idea of history.

It is the medium in which the 'Absolute', which is Thought thinking about Itself, achieves self-realization in space and time. 'In History its act is to gain consciousness of itself as mind'⁹ . . . 'it is its nature to have γνῶθι σεαυτόν as the law of its Being.' 'This apprehension is its Being and its principle, and the completion of apprehension at one stage is at the same time a rejection of that stage and its transition to a higher.' Thus, in the 'bourgeois' state, the first 'thesis' is the growth of utilitarian laws. But, morally, they are not enough: they clash with the 'antithesis' of conscience. This conflict is then resolved in the 'synthesis' created by the morally superior and total life of the state.

For, according to the peculiar Hegelian logic, the Absolute realizes itself through the Dialectic, a triadic movement of thought. It moves by opposites. This process — the key to Hegelian Idealism — achieves some curious results. It reflected, he believed, the 'inner go' of events. This confounded the plans of statesmen, and was only occasionally understood by philosophers. This claim to apprehend the secret of the Universe was developed by Hegel's followers. It reached its most dogmatic statement in the Hegelian aspect of Marxism. Within the triadic structure 'History is mind clothing itself with the form of events'. Here is a transcendental and complex pantheism. It displays a new violence, and it is entirely abstract. There is naturally no evidence for the working of this 'dialectic' in history. All Hegel's historical affirmations were as much an act of faith as the most elaborate assertions of St. Augustine.

For Hegel the pattern was clear and compelling. This extraordinary poetry of ideas, like one of the symphonies of his contemporary, Beethoven, presents a total panorama of experience. 'In the course of the work of this world mind,' he writes, 'states, nations and individuals arise, animated by their particular deterministic principle which has its interpretation and actuality in their constitutions and in the whole range of their life and condition.' These entities become 'the unconscious tools . . . of the world mind'. Then 'the shapes which they take pass away', while 'the Absolute mind prepares and works out its transition to its next stage'. It is a dramatic, world embracing picture. Like the World-Spirit in Thomas Hardy's *Dynasts*, Hegel's Absolute recks little of humanity. In the life-panorama good and evil have their actuality, but 'World-history is above the point of view from which these things matter'.[10]

Politically such ideas could be extremely dangerous. Hegel had the conviction of a seer. In the majestic self-realization of the World-Spirit, each of the arbitrary chosen 'stages' of history is a 'necessary moment in the idea of the world mind . . . the nation whose life embodies this moment secures its good fortune and fame'. It does not need deep reflection to unmask this assertion. The very concept of a nation in this sense is a romantic idea. Apparent already in Burke and Herder, it was recent in history. In fact all the European peoples derive their technology, language and ideas from common sources in Antiquity; moreover Hegel's knowledge of world history was inevitably limited. Here, in fact, is a manifestation of romantic early nineteenth-century nationalism; the cult of the Volk; the cult, of course, of Germany. And Hegel gives the nation a charter which would have made Bodin shudder.* 'The Nation State', he writes, 'is mind in its substantive rationality and immediate actuality, and is . . . absolute power on earth.'[11] This hideous remark is followed by a joyful acceptance of war. Since fully developed nations are sovereign, they are in a state of Nature in relation to one another. The

* See *Western Political Thought*, pp. 289-93.

clash of their 'Wills' can only be settled by war. In the noisy self-realization of the World Spirit these wars are likely to be frequent, for nations, according to the dialectic, successively dominate each other. 'The nation,' he wrote, 'to which is ascribed a moment of the Idea . . . is entrusted with giving complete effect to it . . . this nation is dominant in world history during this one epoch, and it is only once that it can make its hour strike.'[12] Here is something different from the liberal reconciliation of individual and society, from the merging realization of self-critical wills. Here is the desire to dominate; to assert that national sovereign power which the Germans had always lacked, and which in the nineteenth and twentieth centuries they were to wield with such terrible effect. Hegel was of course obsessed with the political weakness of Germany; living in the Napoleonic period of collapse, of negation, he hoped, following the dialectic, for the reaction, for the re-affirmation of German might. He aspired, Dr. Sabine believes, to be the Machiavelli of a new Germany. Both thinkers had the same admiration for 'virtu'. As Cassirer remarks, 'Hegel's sinister assertion that "men are foolish to forget the *Truth* that lives in power" contains the clearest and most ruthless program of Fascism that has ever been propounded by any political philosopher.'[13]

Naturally Hegel denies the existence of Law in international affairs. 'When its hour has struck,' this parochial European society, the nineteenth-century nation state, becomes for its glorious moment a law unto itself. 'In contrast with this, its absolute right of being the vehicle of this present stage in the world-mind's development, the minds of other nations are without rights, and they, along with those whose hour has struck already, count no longer in world history.' It is a curious conception. The Absolute must needs express itself in terms of the Philistine and clumsy manifestations of state power — often one of the least interesting aspects of human activity.* Meanwhile, the dominating nation is scheduled to get as good as it gives. Following the dialectic, the affirmation of power provokes its negation. 'It presses in on world history,' but its initiative is followed by decline, and the emergence of a higher principle as the pure negation of its own. Mind 'passes over' to a new favourite. 'After this period', the declining nation has 'lost the interest of the Absolute'.

This must be very embarrassing. Hegel finds it difficult to account

* Hegel had not the realism of Halifax, when he remarked 'The Government of the world is a great thing, but it is a very coarse one too, compared with the Fineness of Speculative Knowledge.' *Political Thoughts and Reflections*. See *Complete Works*. Edited Sir W. Raleigh. Oxford, 1912.

for the numerous and forceful peoples who have co-existed without dominating one another. So he asserts that after its culminating peak, a nation may 'drag out its existence without rhyme or reason in manifold enterprises at home and abroad'. In this discouraging atmosphere most history is passed by all peoples. Not content with these heady assertions, Hegel appears to sanction the personal tyranny of outstanding individuals. Seldom have the dreams of an intellectual who admires violence been more elaborately expressed. 'All action,' he asserts, 'including world historical actions, culminate in individuals.'[14] They are 'the living instruments of what is in substance the deed of the world mind'. Owing to limitations which they do not share with Hegel, these heroes are often unaware of their own significance. After Hegel, Mussolini and Hitler had the advantage of knowing it. For when a nation state, beginning as an unselfconscious 'horde', develops institutions and sovereign power, 'It is the absolute right of the Idea to step into existence in clear cut laws and objective institutions . . . This right is the right of heroes to found States.'

Having denied equality of rights among states, Hegel denies equality of rights between civilized peoples and barbarians. 'The same consideration justifies civilized nations in regarding and treating as barbarians those who lag behind them in institutions . . . the civilized nation is conscious that the rights of barbarians are unequal to its own, and treats their autonomy as only a formality.'[15] This outlook was not very fortunate in the nineteenth century. It was to be reflected by Hegel's nationalist disciples. On Hegel's principles, also, no treaties are binding. 'Since states,' he had written, 'in their relation of self subsistence are opposed to one another as particular wills, and the validity of treaties depends on this, and since the content of the particular will of the state is its welfare, this particular welfare is the highest law in the relation of one state to another.'*

Such, in brief, in their internal and external aspects, are the outstanding political ideas expressed in Hegel's *The Philosophy of Right*. Where the former had their attractive side in providing a philosophy for the new constitutional state, the latter, while all too obviously seductive to those who demand a political religion, were extremely dangerous. In the Introduction to *The Philosophy of History* these ideas are more fully elaborated. Here, in little more than a hundred

---

* Grotius's opinion that 'the moment we recede from right we can depend on nothing', was a wiser contribution to international affairs. This Hegelian attitude was to find more violent expression in the political theory of Treitschke.

pages, are again most of the theories which have since most seriously perverted political thought. *The Philosophy of History* turns on the Hegelian concept of Reason. This is 'proved by speculative cognition', to be 'substance as well as infinite power'.[16] From this curious assertion, it follows that history is fate; 'the rational necessary course of the world spirit'.[17] But it is not realized through mere individuals. 'In the history of the world, the individuals we have to do with are Peoples.'[18]

This idea goes along with a dualism unintelligible to modern physics. For Hegel insists upon the antithesis between 'spirit' (*geist*) and 'matter'. 'The nature of spirit may be understood by a glance at its direct opposite — matter. As the essence of matter is gravity, so, on the other hand, we may affirm that the substance, the essence of spirit, is Freedom'. One might have expected it to be hot air. This 'Spirit is self-contained existence': it 'knows itself'. And history is the result of its realization. 'Two elements therefore enter into the object of an investigation; the first the idea, the other the complex of human passions — the one the warp, the other the woof of the vast arras-web of human history.' Spirit, originally unconscious, can thus realize itself. Again he insists, as in *The Philosophy of Right*, the process has little to do with human values. 'The history of the world is not a theatre of happiness. Periods of happiness are blank pages in it, for they are periods of harmony; periods when the antithesis is in abeyance.'* The tides of spirit, he again declares, are embodied in *World Historical Individuals*. When Caesar obtained the 'autocracy of Rome . . . It was not, then, his private gain merely, but an unconscious impulse that occasioned the accomplishment of that for which the time was ripe. Such are all great historical men. . . .'[19] The intoxicating idea was to be fully employed.

Those 'heroes of an epoch' must be 'recognized as its clear-sighted ones; their deeds, their words are the best of that time'. Hegel regards the man of action, the conqueror, as supreme. Alexander, a name not hitherto very popular among philosophers,† is cited as one of these fated 'world historical' men. 'When their object is attained, they fall off like empty husks from the kernel. They die early, like Alexander; they are murdered, like Caesar; transported to St. Helena, like Napoleon.' Here is the tragic, romantic touch.[20]

Yet, in general, before the sweeping manifestations of world

---

* pp. 26-7. Compare Bentham's good sense; vide *infra*, pp. 63ff.
† Diogenes had told him to 'get out of his sunlight'.

history, mere individual achievement is ignoble and insignificant. 'The so-called well or ill-faring of those isolated individuals cannot be regarded as an essential element in the rational order of the Universe.'[21] It is not the individual who reflects the world spirits' self-realization, but the state. Here, again, is the most familiar notion which Hegel bequeathed to the political mythology of the nineteenth and twentieth centuries. First the claim to understand the 'necessary' process of history and the universe; next the cult of the 'World historic' hero; now the cult of the state. This cult is unpractical and romantic. For Hegel Near Eastern inventors or Neolithic farmers do not 'count'. 'Only those people can come under our notice who form a state.' 'It must further be understood,' he continues, 'that all the worth that a human being possesses — all spiritual reality, he possesses only through the state ... The state is the divine idea as it exists on earth.'[22] Here is the most blasphemous definition of modern nationalism. He proceeds to introduce the term 'totality', and to trample down the distinction between government and society. For him the state is everything. The 'substance' which inspires it is the 'volksgeist' — 'the spirit of the People itself'.[23] It does not reflect the right of individuals: it creates them. 'The State, its laws, its arrangements, constitutes the rights of its members; its natural features, its mountains, air, and waters, are *their* ... fatherland ... the history of this state their deeds ... it is this matured *totality* which thus constitutes *one* being, the spirit of *one* people.'[24]

Having created his nationalist mythology, Hegel eloquently elaborated it. Nations are the equivalent of individuals. 'Each particular national genius is to be treated as only one individual in the process of Universal History.' Armed with this clue, the Hegelian can comprehend the course of events. 'Having, therefore, learned the abstract characteristics of the nature of spirit ... in its complete realization in phenomenal existence — namely, the state — nothing further remains for this introductory section to contemplate, but the course of the world's history.'[25] Since world history is concerned not with individuals or their morality, but 'the activity of the Spirit of Peoples',[26] its perspective is simplified. The 'essence of spirit is activity', and 'a nation is moral — virtuous — vigorous, when it is engaged in realizing its grand objects ... it has attained full reality'. Once this object is achieved, 'it has its desire'.[27] After that the essential supreme interest has vanished from its life, for interest is present only where there is opposition. Here again is the Hegelian obsession with conflict, doubtless psychologically explicable. 'The nation,' he continues, with a singularly false comparison, 'lives the same kind of life as the individual when passing from maturity to old age. . . .'[28]

After this welter of assertion and analogy, Hegel turns to a vivid account of the geographical basis of history. He surveys the geography of the Americas. 'America is, therefore, the land of the future, where, in the ages that lie before us, the burden of the world's history shall reveal itself — perhaps,' he concludes hopefully, 'in a contest between North and South America.'[29] He examines the geography of the old world, dividing it into the region of 'arid elevated land with its extensive steppes and plains', the great river valleys, and the coastal regions. Here his classification is sound, and his treatment of the effect of environment on mentality and institutions suggestive. To those familiar only with eighteenth-century historians, this broad and imaginative picture must have seemed a revelation. It contributed to the spread of the ideas with which it was enmeshed. Africa is the 'land of childhood', which 'lies beyond the day of self conscious history': Hegel makes great play with the atrocities committed in African kingdoms, and allows himself a joke about the 'case of a negro in London, who lamented that he was now quite a poor man because he had already sold all his relations'.[30] 'From those various traits,' he remarks, 'it is manifest that want of self control distinguishes the character of the Negroes . . . At this point we leave Africa not to mention it again.'[31]

We now find ourselves in the 'real theatre of history', and consider the various regions of Asia and Europe, with a fine imaginative grasp. There follows a short and wild reversion to abstractions in a 'classification of historic data'. 'The history of the world,' Hegel asserts, 'travels from east to west, for Europe is absolutely the end of History . . .'[32] World History is divided into four phases, corresponding to advancing stages of self-consciousness. The first is realized in the East. Here is a patriarchal order, most fully developed in China, where the state is based on the family — 'a prosaic Empire because the antithesis of form, viz. Infinity, Ideality, has not yet asserted itself' — a merciful dispensation, one might think. This phase of limited consciousness may be compared, he says, like Vico, with the childhood of the race — a strange remark about the highly sophisticated Chinese.

The second phase was realized in the Greek world. This may be compared to the 'boyhood of History'. 'Here we have individualities forming themselves.' A beautiful, unconscious, brief harmony was then realized of 'form and idea'. The third phase is 'the Roman state, the severe labours of the Manhood of History'.[33] It is marked by universal Law and the individual's reaction (antithesis) against it. The Spirit 'leaves the Godless world' and 'begins a new inner life'. The fourth phase of world history is Germanic. 'This would answer in the comparison with the period of human life to old age.' The contrast between the Ecclesiastical state (the reaction from the Roman Empire) and the Barbarian world, produces a synthesis, the reconciliation of Church and State, so that the 'spiritual is no longer an element foreign to the State'. The present climax of world history is thus the Kingdom of Prussia.

The rest of this extraordinary, violent and imaginative work ranges, within the limits of early nineteenth-century knowledge, once more over the history of the whole earth. Leaving aside the metaphysical notions which serve as the framework of Hegel's vision, and recalling the limited historical outlook of the time, it will be seen that these reckless and suggestive generalizations immediately enriched the outlook of the romantic age. China, India, Assyria, Persia, Judaea, all are swept into the net: Hegel's immense and often uncritical reading* brought together a body of facts and opinions which were to colour the outlook of historians for decades. His treatment of the Greek world, the relation of the Greek spirit to Nature and in his sketch of Greek political institutions, are all remarkable. There follows a fuller description of Rome and the rise of Christianity, and the climax, naturally, is reached in the fourth part, which deals elaborately with the German world.

It is a romantic vision. Of noble barbarians 'deluging the world, and overpowering in their course the inwardly rotten, hollow political fabrics of the civilized nations'.† The period is sub-divided into three phases, the first extending from the fall of the Roman Empire to Charlemagne; the second witnessing the 'thesis and antithesis' of Church and State; the third extending from the time of the Emperor Charles V to the present. 'In the German aeon, as the realm of totality, we see the distinct repetition of earlier epochs,'[34]

---

* Ninus, king of the Assyrians – a familiar figure in medieval legend (see Isidore of Seville's remarks on him, quoted *W.P.T.*, pp. 151-3), gives occasion for a peculiarly wild statement that the troops who accompanied him numbered '1,700,000 and a proportionate number of cavalry'.

† It is now known that the numbers of the barbarian war bands who dominated large areas of the Continent and gave their names to extensive kingdoms — Visigoths, Burgundians, Lombards and the like, were quite small. 'Their largest armies seem to have numbered no more than a few thousand fighting men, the whole army of the Visigoths which destroyed the Roman army at Adrianople in 378 A.D., could be contained in an enclosure formed by its chariots.' See SEIGNOBOS, *A History of the French People*, p. 51.

and the climax is reached in an 'hegemony of self cognizant thought', when the 'Peoples will the right in and for itself.' For the 'knotty heart of oak' underlying the national temperament of the Germans was broken down and mellowed by the terrible discipline of the Middle Ages. 'The two iron rods which were the instruments of this discipline were the Church and serfdom.'[35] Now, with modern self-consciousness, the 'human spirit has come to stand on its own basis' and 'Humanity beholds its spiritual firmament restored to security.' For with the Reformation 'the time-honoured and cherished sincerity of the German people' had been 'destined to effect this revolution out of the honest truth and simplicity of its heart'.[36] The rest of the world was engaged in predatory enterprises to the Far East or America: among the Germans 'we find a simple Monk' looking for God. The Reformation is the greatest landmark in human freedom. It naturally occurred in Germany; 'the pure inwardness of the German nation was the proper soil for the emancipation of the spirit'.

The greatest defender of this Protestant liberty was the 'world historical' figure of Frederick the Great. 'Frederick II may be mentioned as the ruler who inaugurated the new epoch in the sphere of practical life — that epoch in which practical political interest attains Universality and receives an absolute sanction ... Frederick II merits especial notice as having comprehended the general object of the State.'[37] In conclusion, Hegel writes, 'In the Protestant world there is no sacred, no religious conscience in a state of separation from, or perhaps even hostility to, Secular Right.'[38] He concludes with a panegyric of the vision evoked of the 'glory of the Idea mirroring itself in the History of the World'. 'This is the true ... justification of God in History ... What has happened, and is happening every day, is not only not "without God", but is essentially His work.'[39]

Hegel had thus developed four major ideas. First, the conception of the dynamic constitutional state, reconciling individual wills in a self-transcending freedom, an idea later adapted in more sober context by British neo-Hegelians. Next, he had defined the Dialectic, the process of the Absolute's self-realization, through thesis and anti-thesis, to synthesis in Time, whereby whole epochs of changing civilization, with their own, to them all pervasive, intellectual climates succeed one another. This idea was to be appropriated and transformed by Marx. Thirdly, Hegel depicted world history as the clash of successive world-historical nation states and glorified the perennial conflict in terms of world-historical individuals. In contrast to Mazzini, the other most influential political philosopher in the international affairs of the nineteenth century, Hegel accepts and glorifies war as the natural relation between peoples. This view was to find a strident expression in late nineteenth-century Germany in the writings of Treitschke, and to blend with subsequent misinterpretations of Darwinism. Finally, Hegel enveloped all these metaphysical ideas in an imaginative sense of the spiritual significance of changing experience, and a far-ranging romantic vision of world history and geography, a poetic view of the mission of successive world-historical peoples in contrasting environments. For he believed that history is the accomplished visible manifestation of the Absolute on earth. The Rational was the Real. His philosophy was the most elaborate and abstract result of that exploration of intuition which was the first original manifestation of the political thought of his age.

CHAPTER II

STEAM-INTELLECT 'IMPROVEMENT':
BENTHAM: AUSTIN

T HE early nineteenth century made two vital and original contributions to political thought: first a deeper introspection leading to the idea of emergent Will, historically ascertainable, and, secondly, an expansion of professionalized knowledge and administrative skill. Herder and Hegel, both romantic thinkers, were pioneers of the first aspect; the English Utilitarians of the second.

They were anything but romantic. As Lord Russell has wittily observed, 'the intellectual conviction that pleasure is the sole good, together with a temperamental incapacity for experiencing it, was characteristic of the Utilitarians'.* If the engaging Bentham might have been absolved from this judgment, a quasi-Evangelical sense of mission made this generally irreligious doctrine widely acceptable. The Utilitarians descended from an old and tough tradition; from Hobbes, Helvétius and Hume. They had much in common with the rather complacent Deism of Paley, whose theology long dominated the Cambridge curriculum. They contributed to a new constructive idea of government which aimed at improvement through legislation. Though their outlook was often provincial, their influence was world wide. The course of English politics, in particular, was consciously and unconsciously determined by their influence during most of the nineteenth century. They stand to the reforms of the mid-nineteenth century as the Webbs stand to the Welfare State, for Peel was influenced by their outlook as well as the Whigs. 'Tory men, and Whig measures', Disraeli was to observe.

Their affinity with Hobbes is striking but limited. They agree with him that government is justified by its usefulness. In their view, as in his, the transcendental sanctions of religion and Natural Law are moonshine. But where Hobbes advocates a neutral adjustment of competing egotisms, Bentham and his followers are more benevolent and constructive. They believed in the ameliorative function of the state and showed the characteristic late eighteenth-century desire for

---

* BERTRAND RUSSELL, *Freedom and Organization.* Allen & Unwin, 1934, p. 119, q.v. for an entertaining and penetrating introduction to the Utilitarian philosophy and its setting.

'improvement'. They are concerned, in their famous phrase, 'with the greatest happiness of the greatest number'. Though Bentham did not believe in God, he believed in Progress. As Professor Ayer has well remarked, 'He tried to turn judgments of value into judgments of facts and at the same time to retain their emotive force.'*

He had the eighteenth-century belief in the rationality of mankind, and he was convinced of the importance of institutions in determining behaviour. Primarily a legal reformer, Bentham was born and bred a Tory; he later became radical but he remained a constitutionalist. More practical than Hobbes, he held that happiness is not likely under a tyrannical government, but under a system responsible to the governed, flexible and amenable to public opinion, if exercised through untrammelled sovereign power.

Bentham is by far the most original and representative of the Utilitarians. His influence on jurisprudence may be compared to that of Adam Smith on economics. 'He found the philosophy of Law a chaos,' wrote J. S. Mill, 'he left it a science.' This claim is excessive. The constitution Burke admired was not a chaos, and Bentham never created a 'science' of Law, but he asserted useful principles of action at a critical time. This development, expressed in the concept of positive Law, derived ultimately from Hobbes, 'a perverse and unwilling progenitor of Liberal thought'.† It was to find its most precise and influential expression in the writings of John Austin, whose theory of government will also be examined.

II

Two of Bentham's numerous writings will here be shortly surveyed. First, *The Fragment on Government*, which dispelled much prevalent confusion created by the myth of the 'Social Contract'. It was a brisk, well written attack on one aspect of Blackstone's portentous *Commentaries*. Secondly, *The Principles of Morals and Legislation*, which provided a new basis for 'improvement'.

Bentham's most obvious and immediate ancestor was Hume, whose analysis of the limits of reason had marked so great a turning point in political thought. Adam Smith's doctrine that a free market would promote the development of society, also deeply influenced his mind. His optimism reflected the dominant outlook of the French Enlightenment, as well as the English Deists, but un-

* See his 'The principle of Utility' in *Jeremy Bentham and the Law*, pp. 250ff.
† R. B. McCullum, Preface to the Blackwell's *Political Text of J. S. Mill*, p. xiii.

like so many of these writers, Bentham was extremely practical. His home-spun good sense was continually exercised by particular problems. It is difficult to imagine a greater contrast than that between the mind of the meticulous Englishmen, Bentham and Austin, and the sweeping romantic thoughts of the German visionary philosophers. If Bentham's philosophical background is incoherent, and the vast confusion of his writings ill co-ordinated, he has a characteristic concern with the possible.

Bentham belonged to the eighteenth century. He was born three years after the 'Forty-Five, and he lived on into the year of the Reform Bill. He had about him a touch of the reckless individualism of the richer eccentrics of that time, and he must have been a very extra-ordinary old gentleman. On his father's side he was the great-grand-son of a successful pawnbroker. His mother came of Hampshire trading stock from Andover.* Like John Stuart Mill, he was a very

* Jeremy Bentham, 1748-1832. Son of Jeremiah Bentham, a London lawyer who had made money in land speculation. Educated at Westminster School and Queen's College, Oxford. Barrister of Lincoln's Inn. In 1765 inherited a small private income. In 1776 published *A Fragment on Government* which brought him the friendship of Lord Shel-burne in whose house at Bowood he met the celebrities of the day. Shelburne, he said, 'first made him feel he was something'. In 1785 he visited Russia, where his younger brother, Samuel, was organizing a model colony in the Ukraine for Prince Potemkin: he travelled out through the Levant and back, in 1788, by the Baltic. In 1789 appeared his *Introduction to the Principles of Morals and Legislation* and in 1791 he wrote *Panopticon or the Inspection House*, outlining his extraordinary ideas for a model prison. He had now come into a considerable fortune and won some recognition abroad. In 1791 he had also written his *Essay on Political Tactics*, an excellent study of English methods of government, for the benefit of the French Revolutionaries. But the Revolutionaries did not take his advice, though they made him an honorary French citizen. In 1794 the English Government surprisingly accepted the project of the *Panopticon*, though it was not until 1799 that a site was found in Millbank. In 1802 appeared Dumont's translation, *Traités de Législation Civile et Pénale*; the book circulated in France, Russia, Spain and Latin America. Bentham corresponded with the Tsar Alexander, with Bolivar and other rulers. The Russian, Swiss, and Portuguese governments were all to ask Bentham for Codes of Law, for which he attempted to provide a model in his improved *Constitutional Code*. This formed the main occupation of his later years. Meanwhile Bentham's political views had become radical, following the repudiation of the Panopticon scheme, which disillusioned him with politicians. In 1808 he had met James Mill who influenced him in favour of democratic government. The volume of his works is vast and only the most important of them have been here mentioned. For example, he wrote an anonymous attack on the Catechism. Quantities of manuscript were left by him to University College, London, much of it still unpublished. He also left his body to the College to be dissected; his skeleton, clothed in his usual garments, is still kept there in accordance with the principles set out in his pamph-let *Auto Icon, or the Uses of the Dead to the Living*. Mummified ancestors, he suggested, might alternate with trees on an estate: 'Copal varnish would protect the face from the effects of rain.'

The most intimate and detailed account of Bentham and of the Utilitarians is LESLIE STEPHEN's *The English Utilitarians* (3 vols., 1900). The best modern essay is Wilfred Harrison's Preface to the *Fragment on Government and Principles of Morals and Legislation*. Blackwell's Political Texts, 1948. See also JOHN PLAMENATZ's study, *The English Utilita-rians*, Blackwell, 1949; HALÉVY, *The Growth of Philosophic Radicalism*, 1928, and SIR WILLIAM HOLDSWORTH, *A History of English Law*, vol. XIII (ed. A. L. Goodhart and H. G. Han-bury), 1952, a masterly exposition, pp. 43-144. In Bowring's edition of the Collected

precocious child and is said to have been found reading Rapin at the age of three. No more than the poet Cowper did he enjoy the rough and tumble of eighteenth-century Westminster School, which he described as 'hell'. And since he left to become an undergraduate at Queen's College, Oxford, at the age of twelve, it is not remarkable that, like Gibbon, he obtained little profit from the University. Here, says his biographer, Leslie Stephen, 'laziness and vice were still prevalent . . . and brutal horseplay was still practised on the younger lads'.* But he was fortunate in possessing a good private income and later a considerable fortune. He was one of those well-to-do English eccentrics through whose initiative much reform has been brought about.

Bentham provoked lively affection in those who knew him. Though he led a retired and rigidly ordered life, and was nervous in society, he was the host to many house parties at Queen's Square Place and at Forde Abbey, Dorset, which he rented from 1814 to 1818. He was musical, and popular in society. He preferred home-brewed ale to wine, and enjoyed hot ginger nuts and strong coffee. One of his contemporaries wrote: 'it is impossible to conceive a physiognomy more strongly marked with ingeniousness and philanthropy'. In his later years his dress was rather eccentric 'and consisted chiefly of a grey coat, light breeches, and white woollen stockings hanging loosely about his legs, while his venerable locks, which floated over his collar and down his back, were surmounted by a straw hat of the most grotesque and indescribable shape . . . he wended round the walks of his garden at a pace faster than a walk, but not so quick as a trot.'[1] John Stuart Mill remarked of him that he was a 'boy to the last', and at the age of 82 he describes himself as 'codifying like any dragon'. This extraordinary vitality is a mixed blessing for his commentators, for it caused him to turn from one project to another and to start similar subjects several times over.

The influences which went to form his mind are manifold. Apart from Hume, probably the most decisive was Francis Hutcheson, the philosophical Deist and critic of Hobbes, who had been Professor of Moral Philosophy at Glasgow from 1729 to 1746. Here he had

* *The English Utilitarians*, vol. I, p. 173, q.v. for a vivid description of his personality.

Works, vols. X and XI, will be found the fullest account of his life. See, as well, C. W. EVERITT, *The Education of Jeremy Bentham*, 1931, and C. K. OGDEN, *Introduction to Bentham's Theory of Legislation*, 1931, and his edition of BENTHAM'S *Theory of Fictions*, 1932. This last work makes Bentham a pioneer of the Sociology of Knowledge. Here, like Pareto, but without Pareto's withering sarcasm and schematic jargon, he foreshadowed the investigation of the meaning, or lack of it, of many current political terms.

enjoyed a great reputation and influenced Hume and Adam Smith.* Hutcheson was a follower of Shaftesbury and Bishop Butler, a Lockian sensationalist who accepted the limitations of Locke's position and made the best of them. He insisted on the reality of an instinctive moral sense, and found room for choice by arguing that the moral sense was the one instinct of which the deliberative mind consistently approved. Taking the opposite view to Hobbes, he had maintained that the desire for self-approval led not to savage competition for 'glory', but to a desire for social approbation leading to useful action. Man was egoistic, but not anti-social. This position, while not depending on revelation, deduced co-operative action from instinct. Hutcheson had, further, anticipated the Utilitarian 'calculus' of pleasure and pain, by attempting to devise, in a very Scots manner, 'a mathematical calculation of the subjects of morality'. And in his *Enquiry Concerning Moral Good and Evil* (Sec. 3, para. 8) he had coined the useful if not startling phrase, 'the greatest good of the greatest number'.

Another source of Bentham's ideas were the writings of Helvétius. An atheist who believed in the perfectibility of mankind, Helvétius regarded morals as relative. Like the more high-minded Hutcheson, he attempted to equate public with private interest.† Following Locke's sensationalist philosophy, he assumed that the mind is *tabula rasa*, reacting to external impressions. He believed in equality of natural endowment and that personality could be transformed by education. He wished to sweep away traditional government and establish a rational régime which would deliberately condition character. Since institutions determine conduct, he thought that legislation, which he regarded as a science, was a weapon of decisive power. Though man was moulded by environment, he could make himself. This idea was assimilated by Bentham, who was influenced by Helvétius's religious views. He also derived his impatience with tradition from another French influence. A faith in the intellectual

* Francis Hutcheson, 1694-1746. Born at Drumalig, County Down, son of the Presbyterian Minister at Armagh, whose forebears had come from Ayrshire. Educated at Killeleagh and Glasgow University, 1710, he started a school in Dublin, but between 1725 and 1728 he won celebrity by publishing a series of essays, *An Inquiry into the Original of our Ideas of Beauty and Virtue* (the second edition is called *Enquiry concerning Moral Good and Evil*); an attack on Mandeville; an essay on the *Nature and Conduct of the Passions and Affections*; *Thoughts on Laughter*, an attack on Hobbes; *A System of Moral Philosophy*, etc. See T. FOWLER, *Shaftesbury and Hutcheson*.

† Claude Adrien Helvétius, 1715-71. Born in Paris, son of the chief physician to Queen Marie Leczinska of France. Appointed to the lucrative office of Farmer General in 1738. Published, 1758, *De l'Esprit*, which attained wide influence, and was burnt by order of the Sorbonne.

direction of society and a contempt and misunderstanding for the past had marked most of the Encyclopedists. As Bury well observed, 'They felt a sort of resentment against history.'[2] They wished to make a fresh start. Diderot's patron, the Baron d'Holbach, for example, had attacked the idea of original sin and preached militant atheism. He had applied a determinist philosophy to ameliorate the predicament of man. These French writers took a world-wide view of the problems of humanity: like the Stoic and Epicurean philosophers of Antiquity, they had a universal range. Unlike the old philosophers, they were full of confident initiative and determined to change the conditions of society. Both their breadth, their shallowness, and their enterprise were to be apparent in Bentham's thought.

This confidence was also reflected in a more cautious form by British thinkers by whom Bentham was influenced. The Unitarian Dr. Priestley was confident that civilization would advance.* 'The plan', he wrote, 'of the Divine drama is opening more and more.' He brought to the atheistic and ruthless manifestos of the French philosophers a more pious confidence. James Dunbar, Professor of Philosophy at Aberdeen, who wrote *Essays on the History of Mankind in Rude and Cultivated Ages*, also modified the generalizations of French aristocrats with a more canny caution. On the whole, he ventured to think, when all considerations were fully taken into account, the prospects of humanity might not appear altogether discouraging. The general belief in Progress had spread from the worldly and opulent salons of Paris to the more frugal circles of academic Aberdeen.

Meanwhile, the comfortable and pedestrian Paley, always on such easy terms with his Creator, added his Argument from Design to the general equanimity. In admirable prose, the *Principles of Moral and Political Philosophy* and *Evidences of Creation* deployed his ordinary and satisfying case.

Finally, among major influences, must be counted the well-known Italian reformer, the Marchese Cesare de Beccaria.† He remarkably anticipated some of the doctrines of Adam Smith and Malthus, but his principal achievement was in penal reform. He desired not merely to punish crime but to prevent it, and essayed the daunting

* See his *Essay on the First Principles of Government*, 1768, and his *Lectures in History and General Policy* in 1788. As a respectable Unitarian, who believed in one God, no Devil, and twenty shillings in the pound, he was naturally shocked by the frivolity of the Parisian philosophers. He is admirably described by Professor Basil Willey in *The 18th Century Background*.

† 1738-94. Born at Milan, where in 1768 he became Professor of Law and Political Economy. Published in 1764 his *Dei Delitti e delle Pene*.

task of reforming the criminal law of eighteenth-century Lombardy. His book, which attained wide fame, was translated into French, and prefaced with an anonymous Essay by Voltaire. Like Hutcheson's lecture, Beccaria's contained the magic formula 'La massima felicita divisa nel maggior numero'. This interest in the reformation of law was fundamental to Bentham's mind. At home, too, a critical approach to English law had already been made by Daines Barrington, the well-known lawyer and littérateur, the friend of Horace Walpole and Dr. Johnson, whose *Observations on the More Ancient Statutes from Magna Charta to the Twenty First of James I* had appeared ten years before Bentham's first publication.

Apart from these influences, continental and British, there was the pervasive influence of Adam Smith, with his confidence in the beneficent working of the economic system. This was to be reinforced by Malthus, with his assertion of hard facts of natural competition by an increasing population for a limited food supply. In view of these economic and demographical considerations, Bentham came to believe that the function of government is not to regulate but to release; not to suppress but to adjust. Reformers must convert law and administration to this end.

Such was the background to *A Fragment on Government* which appeared in 1776.* It carries on its title page a quotation from Montesquieu: 'Rien ne recul plus le progrès des connoissances qu'un mauvais ouvrage d'un auteur célèbre; parce qu'avant d'instruire, il faut commencer par détromper.' (*Esprit des Lois*, LXXX, chap. xv).

The opening words of the Preface are full of optimism and the whole written in a brisk clear style. 'The age we live in is a busy age; in which knowledge is rapidly advancing towards perfection. In the natural world, in particular, everything teems with discovery and with improvement. The most distant and recondite regions of the earth, traversed and explored — the all vivifying and subtle elements of the air so recently ... made known to us — are striking evidences, were all others wanting, of this pleasing truth.' Here is a writer full of confidence and devoid of subtlety. The keynote is at once struck in the word 'improvement'. And Bentham immediately draws the

---

* 'Being an examination of what is delivered on the subject of Government in general in the Introduction to Sir William Blackstone's *Commentaries*, with a Preface, in which is given a Critique of the work at large'. It is a short work, running only to 112 pages, of which thirty-three are devoted to the Preface. After a brief introduction, the five chapters are entitled: 'Formation of Government', 'Forms of Government', 'British Constitution', 'Right of the Supreme Power to make Laws', and 'Duty of the Supreme Power to make Laws.' There are marginal subheadings pointing the argument.

political moral with the slogan which was to carry his movement to a widening public. In all this progress of science and knowledge, he says, the problems of human welfare have not been faced in the light of 'this fundamental axiom', for 'it is the greatest happiness of the greatest number that is the measure of right and wrong'.

If knowledge of distant countries is valuable, he continues, it is equally important 'to be made better acquainted with the chief means of living happily on our own'. With these colours nailed to the mast, the young reformer sails in to do battle with Blackstone, the most famous lawyer of his day. Bentham's principle of Utility also inspired Austin, who followed up the attack. It struck at the roots of traditional sanctions for law and Government. The British Constitution, glorified by Burke, had in fact been considerably modified in the eighteenth century. It was not destined to collapse at the sound of Utilitarian trumpets, though Bentham's improvements were to be assimilated into the fabric of the law.

But Bentham declared that its theory was 'nonsense upon stilts'. Here was injustice, inefficiency, corruption. And Austin, following Hobbes, argued that law is not law unless enforcible; strictly, it could only be the command of a superior. Both maintained, for example, that the venerable idea of Natural Law had legally no meaning.

Blackstone's view, in modern terms, has been brilliantly defined by Vinogradoff. This 'alternative view regards Law not as the command of a sovereign, but in its material content as the opinion of the country on matters of right and justice. Instead of being traced to the deliberate will of the legislator, its function was assigned to the gradual working of custom, the proper function of legislation being limited to the declaration of an existing state of legal consciousness, and not as the creation of new rules by individual minds. As regards the state, the Law was assumed to be an antecedent condition, not a consequence of its activity.'[3]

This tradition as expressed by Blackstone the Utilitarians brushed aside. They assumed that mankind was actuated by calculation. If sound reasons for improvement were demonstrated, they would follow them. It was rather a simple assumption. Blackstone's view may have been complacent, but it was subtle and more realistic. Since, as Clarendon and Halifax had already pointed out, and Bagehot was later to emphasize, mankind is not in general swayed by reason but by emotion, society is, in fact, inspired by conventions and myths, so that the utilitarian aim of survival and well being is generally promoted more by habit and loyalty than by calculation. This loyalty is commanded by institutions and ideas, varying with time and space, and it had been so commanded throughout history back to primitive times. Ideals of Natural Law, abstract Justice, and the like, had been the idiom of classical and Christian civilization from which the English constitution had emerged. Such beliefs had often restrained the worst abuses of power and asserted the interests of the commonwealth against tyranny. When Hobbes, in a rather similar manner to Bentham, had described what he felt to be the facts of power, the old appeal to Natural Law and other symbols of society had been eloquently invoked against him. Blackstone had now rewritten the history of English institutions in the light of similar assumptions.

He had written in a world which had profoundly changed. Cartesian rationalism had long been undermining the traditional outlook, originally derived from revealed religion and the cosmopolitan Catholic Church. Moreover, the old doctrines of social contract and the state of nature were ceasing to command belief. Whatever the faults of Bentham's political psychology, he was representative in asserting that the old sanctions were losing power. They had been losing it ever since the disruption of medieval Christendom.

And when Bentham declared that 'the fabric of felicity' must be reared 'by the hands of reason and Law', he expressed not only the greater sensibility of his time but accepted the challenge of a new environment. Massive industrial change was already beginning to demand a fundamental readjustment of society. In asserting that the constitution needed revision Bentham was right. He was wrong in the naive assumption that society could be conducted purely by rational calculation.

Blackstone was then in the full tide of his reputation. A master of exposition, he was the first lawyer to make the history of English institutions readable.* Bentham had attended his lectures, and

* Sir William Blackstone, 1723-80. Educated at Charterhouse and Pembroke College, Oxford. In 1741 he entered the Middle Temple, an occasion he marked with a poem, 'The Lawyer's Farewell to his Muse'. In 1744 he was elected a Fellow of All Souls College, Oxford. His interests were wide and versatile. As a youth he had dabbled in poetry, and written a treatise on architecture; he was a life-long student of Shakespeare. As Fellow and Estates Bursar he helped to complete the great Codrington Library, to rearrange the archives, and to rescue the endowment of the College from the depredations of an expanding Founder's kin. As one of the Delegates he had attempted to reform the administration of the Clarendon Press. In 1755 he began lecturing on Law in Oxford. In 1758 he was appointed Vinerian Professor of English Law, and in 1759 he published his edition of the Great Charter. In 1761 he was made Principal of New Inn Hall, Oxford, and elected Member of Parliament for Hindon, Wilts. In the same year he married Sarah Clitherow, by whom he had nine children. In 1763 he was Solicitor

early felt antipathy to the great lawyer's 'frigid pride'. In the famous *Commentaries on the Laws of England*, with their wide circulation and incomparable prestige, Bentham already discovered a 'grand and fundamental' blemish — 'the antipathy to reformation'. In Blackstone's Introduction, he says, what pass for his general principles will be found under the heading of 'Law Municipal', 'an account, such as it is, of the nature and origin of Natural Society, the mother, and of Political Society, the daughter of law *municipal*, duly begotten in the bed of Metaphor'. Here Blackstone has distinguished Statute and Common Law, and given 'a general account of Equity, that capricious and incomprehensible mistress of our fortunes, whose features neither our Author nor perhaps anyone, is well able to delineate'.[4] Here is the digression which forms the subject of the *Fragment*, in its own turn part of an unpublished *Comment on the Commentaries*.

Bentham now presses home his attack. He at once declares the 'grounds of that war which, for the interest of true science and liberal improvement, I think myself bound to wage against this work'. It is Blackstone's massive complacency which Bentham finds intolerable, so typical, he insists, of the majority of the legal profession. Of course, Blackstone does not claim to be more than an expositor: the office of 'censor' or critic, which demands the outlook of a 'Citizen of the World', is outside his admitted range. But he has exceeded his function. Like 'a bigoted or corrupt defender of the works of power', he has tried to crush criticism with scorn and insult. Yet critics are vitally important, since the majority of mankind cannot bring 'rude establishments to the test of polished reason'.[5] The eighteenth-century phrase is revealing.

There follows a spirited attack on lawyers, never a popular profession. 'A passive and enervate race,' he calls them, 'ready to swallow anything, and to acquiesce in anything: with intellects incapable of distinguishing right from wrong, and with affections alike indifferent to either: insensible, short-sighted, obstinate: lethargic . . . deaf to the voice of reason and public utility: obsequious only to the whisper of interest and to the beck of power.'[6]

General to the Queen. From 1765-69 appeared the four volumes of the famous *Commentaries*: they went into eight editions in Blackstone's lifetime, brought him over £14,000, and won great reputation in France and America. In 1766 he resigned both his academic appointments: two years later he was Member of Parliament for Westbury, and in 1770 he became a Justice of the Common Pleas. He died in 1780, and is buried at Wallingford, near Oxford. Blackstone was a fine crusted character with a taste for good living and college port. Anyone familiar with the statue of this formidable worthy in the Codrington Library at All Souls, will understand that Bentham was taking on an alarming adversary.

This fine cadence leaves no doubt of the young lawyer's opinion of most of his colleagues. The attack is pressed home by damaging footnotes on current controversies and legal fictions. Criticism is the more urgent because of Blackstone's prestige, since 'popular fame enters not into nice distinctions'. This fame is in part deserved. 'He it is, in short, who, first of all institutional writers, has taught Jurisprudence to speak the language of the Scholar and the Gentleman: put a polish upon that rugged science; cleansed her from the dust and cobwebs of the office: and ... decked her out ... from the toilette of classic erudition.'[7]

His entire strategy is, none the less, erroneous; his exposition hopelessly confused. He forgets the sovereign test, Utility. Law should promote happiness: offences are light or serious in proportion as they diminish it. Blackstone thinks only of the British Constitution, but Bentham's principle is universal. What would be suitable for one country, 'would serve, with little variation, for ... any other'.[8] Able as Blackstone's limited exposition may be, in a wider view it is wholly inadequate. In this constricting and misleading confusion, jurisprudence is 'Rather as a game of crambo for lawyers to wet their wits at, than as a science that holds in her hand the happiness of nations.'* With this phrase Bentham brings a breath of air into what he considers the fusty chambers of the law, and suggests the broad possibilities of his new approach. His object, he concludes, is to 'put the reader upon thinking for himself'. In spite of unpopularity, he is determined to 'persevere without deviation in the lines of truth and utility'; to 'prefer the still whisper of enduring approbation, to the short-lived bustle of tumultuous applause'.[9]

The Utilitarians have the reputation of being a dull crew, but this spirited attack shows Bentham an able controversialist, and defines his fresh and sensible ideas with elegance and precision. Unfortunately, this clarity is not apparent in his later writings.

After this preface, he narrows the attack. A sketch of the main argument must here suffice. Bentham first scouts Blackstone's view of the contractual origin of government, and makes short work of the doctrine of the state of nature. 'I was in hopes,' he writes, 'that this Chimera had been effectually demolished by Mr. Hume.' 'The indestructible prerogatives of mankind have no need to be supported on the sandy foundation of a fiction.'[10]

---

* p. 28. Bentham here quotes Selden's notion 'he had hit upon as a schoolboy', that classical learning was a game devised by parents to keep children quiet, and the personages of Antiquity fictitious. The law, says Bentham, often seems just such a fraud.

On the contrary, the 'foundations of all virtue are laid in utility'. Under 'Forms of Government', Bentham also attacks the supernatural sanctions, which 'divert us' from 'sounding into the shallows of his doctrine'. 'Theology,' he notes in the margin, 'on such an occasion as this impertinent.' Blackstone's classification of governments is artificial. Even his account of the British Constitution is antiquated and confused, and his attribution of superior wisdom to the aristocracy unwarranted. Bentham draws up a pseudo-geometrical theorem in which he parodies Blackstone's demonstration that 'the British Government is all-perfect'.[11] But rulers, he insists, ought to be respected for merit, not accepted for their station. 'For my part,' he concludes, 'if ever I stand forth and sing the song of Eulogy to great men, it shall be not because they *occupy* their station but because they *deserve* it.'

Bentham's exasperation with tradition, his desire for efficiency, his brisk intolerance, his faith in reason, and his rejection of historic myth, all are apparent. His attack was radical. In the light of the new doctrine of the sovereignty of the legislator, even the independence of the judiciary is questioned. Law is simply the command of a superior. Not the 'declaration of an existing state of legal consciousness'. Government exists solely for the preservation of society; its justification is pragmatic. By this standard all institutions should be judged. Bentham is concerned primarily not with a just constitution but with forceful legislation. He employs Hobbesian sovereignty as a means to improvement. In the words of Pollock, 'the formula of the greatest happiness of the greatest number is made a hook to put in the nose of Leviathan that he may be tamed and harnessed to the Chariot of Utility'.*

Such is the brisk argument of Bentham's *Fragment on Government*. It was as much an act of faith as any beliefs defended by Blackstone. In assuming a public power of rational calculation, Bentham defied the experience of most practical politicians. What a contrast are the views of this kindly reformer with the outlook, for example, of Halifax the Trimmer, who believed in 'good resolute nonsense backed by authority', or of Bagehot, with his appreciation of the 'cake of custom'.

The *Introduction to the Principles of Morals and Legislation* first drafted in 1780, and published in 1789, was a more elaborate work.†

* SIR F. POLLOCK, *History of the Science of Politics*, p. 101, quoted by HOLDSWORTH, op. cit., p. 131.
† Bentham deals first with 'pleasures and pains, their kinds'; 'circumstances influencing sensibility', and 'human dispositions in general'. In the twelfth chapter he turns from the

Where the Fragment was primarily critical, here Bentham's constructive programme is deployed. The short Preface is followed by seventeen chapters, ranging over a broad discussion of the principle of utility.

Like Austin after him, Bentham again defines his revolutionary conception of a 'science' of law. It is 'to the art of legislation, what the science of anatomy is to . . . medicine'.[12] He dwells upon the difficulties attending his enterprise. '. . . truths that form the basis of political and moral science are not to be discovered but by investigations as severe as mathematical ones, and beyond all comparison more intricate and extensive . . . There is no King's Road, no Stadtholder's Gate, to legislative, any more than to mathematic science'.[13] With this modest and laborious proviso, which contrasts characteristically with the numinous gestures with which Hegel gets to work, Bentham goes to the heart of his subject.

The first chapter further defines the basic principle of Utility. 'Nature', it begins, 'has placed mankind under the governance of two sovereign masters, pain and pleasure.' The principle of Utility 'recognizes this subjection . . . Systems which attempt to question it deal in sounds instead of sense, in caprice instead of reason, in darkness instead of light.' By this principle the actions not only of individuals but of governments must be judged, since communities are the sum of the individuals composing them. He repudiates all other sanctions. 'Ought and ought not,' he says, are meaningless terms unless related to this standard. He thus, again, sweeps aside all traditional and abstract sanctions for morality.

For what, he asks, is the alternative? All principles other than utility are unreliable. Take, for example, asceticism — 'generally inspired by fear of future punishment at the hands of a splenetic and revengeful Deity', and in any case only a principle of utility misapplied. Nor is the principle of 'antipathy' more satisfactory. It leads to burning heretics and 'quarrels between Bigendians and

---

motives to the consequences of action. How far is an act mischievous? How far deserving of punishment? When is punishment unprofitable and when necessary? He discusses how punishment should fit the crime, and the division of offences – this fourteenth chapter being the longest in the book. He concludes with a discussion of the limits of Penal jurisprudence. Nine years later, in the year of publication, he added a section which sketches the way in which his conclusions could be worked out. The treatise occupies 323 pages of Harrison's edition. It was first printed in 1780, but Bentham postponed publication for nine years until he satisfied himself of the validity of his approach. 'I had got into a mizmaze,' he says, 'I could not see my way clearly; it was a dark forest – for the vast field of the law was around me with all its labyrinths.' When the first edition did appear it was very small, 'and half of that devoured by rats'. The definitive edition appeared in 1823. See C. K. OGDEN, op. cit., Introduction, p. xxi.

Littlendians'.[14] With ironic wit Bentham baits the orthodox, adding barbed examples to his generalities. As for 'a revealed will, contained in the sacred writings . . . that is a system which nobody ever thinks of recurring to at this time of day, for the details of political administrations'; indeed it is 'universally allowed, by the most eminent divines of all persuasions to stand in need of pretty ample interpretation'. It is impossible to know the will of God. Neither 'asceticism', antipathy, nor the invocation of Divine will are satisfactory bases for legislation. But 'the principle of utility neither requires nor admits any regulator than itself.'

Having dealt in this devastating manner with the alternative, Bentham proceeds to justify his principle in more detail, analysing the sanctions or sources of pain or pleasure — physical, political and moral, and attempting to estimate 'The value of a lot of pleasure and Pain, how to be Measured',* and dealing with 'Pleasures and Pain, their kinds'.

The result is often clumsy, laborious and quaint. The attempt to calculate the amounts of pleasure and pain, multiplied by the number of individuals concerned, and related to the effect of the action upon the whole, is often like a complicated cookery recipe. But in enumerating pleasures, Bentham is singularly entertaining. He classifies the pleasures of sense, of wealth, of skill; of amity, of a good name; of power, of piety and benevolence. The pleasures of malevolence are also included†. And those of memory, imagination, expectation, association and relief. Correspondingly, pains are also listed; with insight, elaborated in footnotes. When attempting to analyse 'complex' pleasures, Bentham gets into deep waters; in particular, when he tries to separate the pleasures of sense and of association derived from the contemplation of a rural scene.[15] He proceeds to a laborious account of the 'Circumstances influencing sensibility'; of 'Health, strength, hardiness etc. habitual occupation and pecuniary circumstances, education and climate.' Frame of body, he says, often indicates the tone of mind, but appearances are apt to be deceptive. 'Oliver Cromwell, whose conduct indicated a heart more than ordinarily callous, was as remarkably profuse in

---

* Memorized as:

        Intense, long, certain, speedy, fruitful, pure,
        Such marks in pleasures and in pain endure.

                                        p. 151n.

† They are derived 'from pain suffered by (1) Human Beings; (2) other animals'. 'Those may also be styled the pleasures of ill-will, the pleasures of the irascible appetite, the pleasures of antipathy, or the pleasures of the malevolent or dissocial affections,' pp. 157-8.

tears.'[16] This rudimentary psychological inquiry proceeds to 'Human actions in general', always on the assumption that the 'business of government is to promote the happiness of society, by punishing and rewarding'. There follows a wearisome and complex attempt to assess the motives and circumstances of actions, and Bentham gives an elaborate description of their repercussions and relativity, taking as an example the assassination of the Duke of Buckingham.[17] He proceeds, in a chapter on 'Intentionality' to an even more conjectural description of the possible intentions of Sir Walter Tyrrel, when, by mistake or design, he shot William Rufus in the New Forest. The inconsistency of popular opinion is again remarked. Today if 'a man assassinates his lawful sovereign ... the motive is ... universally looked upon as abominable, and is termed fanaticism; formerly it was by great numbers accounted laudable, and was by them called pious zeal'.[18] 'Good will', on the other hand is a consistent motive. It coincides with Utility. For 'the dictates of utility are ... the dictates of the most extensive and enlightened benevolence'. They are, in fact, in modern terms, the rationalization of a profound instinct for mutual aid. All laws should aim at increasing happiness. Since punishment is in itself evil, it is only justified if it prevents greater mischief. It is not expiation; it must be fitted to the crime. He describes cases where punishment is groundless, unprofitable, or unnecessary.[19] Large fields of conduct are debarred from interference by the Law. Offences are either private, self-regarding, semi-public, public, or 'heterogenious'. It is not, he maintains, the business of government to prevent private sexual irregularities. 'With what chance of success', he asks, 'would a legislator go about to extirpate drunkenness and fornication? ... such a mass of evil would be produced as would exceed a thousandfold the utmost mischief of the offence. The great difficulty would be in procuring evidence.'[20] Such 'self-regarding' offences should remain outside the cognizance of the law. In particular, since they are 'many of them apt to be more obnoxious to the censure of the world than public offences, owing to the influence of the two false principles, the principle of asceticism and the principle of antipathy'.[21]

Bentham's argument had been incisive, revolutionary and consistent. Discarding abstract sanctions, he attacks the evils of existing law, and armed with weapon of 'Utility', proceeds to his objective, beating through psychological thickets and morasses to constructive conclusions. His aims are security and well being. In a society so improved, the economic forces defined by Adam Smith would have free play. Throughout, his concern is for ordinary human happiness. He has no use for the kind of speculations made by Grotius, Pufendorf, and Burlemarqui, whom he criticizes on the ground that they 'take for their subject the pretended *law of nature*; an obscure phantom, which in the imaginations of those who go in chase of it, points sometimes to *manners*, sometimes to laws; sometimes to what law *is*, and sometimes to what it ought to be'.[22]

Bentham's positivism was, of course, very limited. It achieved great results. He subordinates institutions to life. To the expiatory side of punishment, so much stressed by de Maistre, he is indifferent. That the collective guilt of society should be redeemed by sacrifice, would have appeared to Bentham a gross superstition. Yet, to this day, such motives are still apparent in the laws of civilized societies.

Government is here regarded not as a mystery, but as an instrument for the betterment of immediate conditions. And if Bentham grossly over-estimates the rationality and benevolence of mankind, and assumes their loyalty to institutions through calculating self-interest, rather than emotion symbolized and created by suitable myths, often no less suited to the public good than the planning of intellectuals, he gave a vast impetus to the reform of inefficient institutions all over the civilized world at the close of the eighteenth century. In England, where law and administration have always been flexible, his ideas were gradually worked into the texture of Law and the life of institutions, so that they at once promoted and reflected the transformation of society during the nineteenth century and framed a way of life now taken for granted. It remained for this reformist conception of government, which in Bentham's theory is starkly deprived of theoretical sanction and entirely pragmatic, to be reinforced by the liberal cult of the general will, as interpreted by T. H. Green. Meanwhile, in the field of jurisprudence, Austin continued the attack.

III

John Austin was another individualist and original writer, with a more conservative outlook than Bentham, who cleared the ground for a new analytical jurisprudence and penetrated more deeply than Bentham to the real basis of sovereign power. Taking an Hobbesian approach, he discarded Hobbes's philosophical arguments, and empirically examined the facts of law and government in early nineteenth-century England.* Largely ignored in his own day, he is famous for his theory of sovereignty, aptly described as 'all or nothing', and for his clear analysis of its ultimate sanction, not in calculation but in habit and way of life.† This outlook had roots in the sixteenth century with the rise of the nation state; it had first found expression in Bodin's definition of 'majestas', and an elaborate

* John Austin, born 1790, the eldest son of Jonathan Austin of Creeting Mill, Suffolk, who made a fortune in the Napoleonic Wars; he entered the army at sixteen and served in Sicily: in 1816 he sold his commission and in 1818 he was called to the Bar. Two years later he married Sarah Taylor of Norwich and they settled at Queen's Square, Westminster, as close neighbours of Bentham and James Mill. Temperamentally unfitted for success at the bar, Austin gave up his practice in 1826 and retired to Bonn, where he studied German Jurisprudence and found German academic society congenial. In 1828 he was appointed to the Chair of Jurisprudence at the newly founded University College of London through the influence of Bentham and Mill. Since he regarded 'clear notions on the foundations of Law and Morals' as 'essential to the welfare of the human race', he took elaborate care over his lectures, but the new science of Jurisprudence he had in mind was beyond the range of his audience. He took his students very seriously, but they were only concerned to pass their examinations, and 'flocked to the lecture room of his colleague Mr. Amos'. In 1832 Austin resigned his chair. 'It was a blow', writes his wife, 'from which he never recovered.' In the same year he published his *Province of Jurisprudence Determined*, destined to become the most famous treatise in Jurisprudence in the later nineteenth century. It was designed as preliminary to a larger work, *The Principles and Relation of Jurisprudence and Ethics*, which was never written. Though urged to publish a revised edition of the introductory book, Austin never republished. In 1833 he was appointed to the Criminal Law Commission, but resigned, and in 1836 to the Commission on the Administration of Malta. Here his work was appreciated by the Maltese, but he got little credit from the British Government, and owing to political changes in London found himself abruptly dismissed. Disgusted with this further rebuff and disappointed of the 'quiet humble nook in the rich domains of learning' which he desired, Austin threw in his hand. He was comparatively poor, but a small private income went further abroad, and he was, happily, endowed with a 'disinterested hatred of expense'. The Austins retired to the continent, to Karlsbad, Dresden and Bonn; from 1844 to 1848 they lived in Paris. The Revolution of 1848 drove them back to England and they settled in a cottage at Weybridge, where Austin cultivated his garden and spent probably the happiest period of his life. 'He wanted no excitement and no audience.' In 1859 he published a conservative pamphlet, a *Plea for the Constitution*, and in the same year he died.

Austin was an inhibited, scornful and fastidious character. His memory was phenomenal and he could be forcefully eloquent, but he was dogged by illness. Brougham is said to have remarked 'if John Austin had had health, neither Lyndhurst nor I would have been Chancellors'. Austin was, in fact, a self-tormenting perfectionist, dissatisfied with all he wrote, with an uncontrollable intellectual conscience. But, like Hobbes, he was 'rare at definitions'; a founder of English nineteenth-century analytical jurisprudence.

The second edition of the *Province* appeared in 1861, and *Lectures on Jurisprudence* (two volumes), with a biographical notice by his wife, in 1863. (Third edition, revised R. Campbell, 1869.) There is an extensive literature of criticism and explanation. See W. J. BROWN, *The Austinian Theory of Law*; ANSON, *Law and Custom of the Constitution*, and DICEY, *Law of the Constitution*, pp. 69-72. HEARNSHAW's *Essay in Social and Political Ideas of the Age of Reaction and Reconstruction* is tiresome and misleading on Austin's idea of sovereignty, but there is a good essay by C. A. W. MANNING in *Modern Theories of Law*, 1933, and see in particular, W. W. BUCKLAND, *Some Reflections in Jurisprudence*, Cambridge, 1949, for an extremely able analysis.

† See LORD LINDSAY, *The Modern Democratic State*, pp. 217ff, q.v. for a criticism of Austin's position.

philosophical defence in Hobbes's *Leviathan*. Austin believed that societies were only truly 'political' when they were subject to centralized sovereign power. Strictly speaking, for example, the pluralist and abstract concepts of law current in the Middle Ages would prevent these societies from being termed 'political'. International 'Law' is not law in the true sense of the term, since there is, as yet, no world sovereignty to enforce it, and sovereign states, though bound by ties of custom and convenience, cannot be said to form a political society. This realistic conception of law and sovereignty reinforced the new Benthamite idea of government as a constructive force. It won widespread approval by the mid-nineteenth century, although, with the rise of a more historical jurisprudence, there has since been a reaction against it, expressed by Gierke, Maitland and Duguit.

Whatever the limits of Austin's view of political sovereignty — and it long dominated men's minds — his lucid analysis of legal terms was salutary. And this was the task which he set himself primarily to perform. Through the fog of legal controversy, which the layman approaches with trepidation, this fact is clear.

Lord Melbourne is said to have remarked of the *Province of Jurisprudence Determined* that it was the dullest book he had ever read. In fact the style is generally clear, if dry, and sometimes achieves a severe eloquence. Austin's quasi-scholastic method, which deals first with the objections to his case before stating his own, sometimes, indeed, makes the perusal of his book an obstacle race. But his argument raises fundamental problems of political and legal thought. His greatness lies in his sharp 'positivist' distinction between law and political myth. A utilitarian, and confining the term law to enforceable commands, he admits that habit and custom are the main foundations of public authority. Yet his utilitarian hatred of myth tended to blind him to its sometimes salutary power in determining this way of life. Hence the excessive rationalism of the political tradition to which he contributed. 'Calculation', he hoped, would be 'the guide to sentiment'.

The analysis is empirical, pragmatic and clear. His subject was the 'Province of Jurisprudence Determined' — and although, as Mr. Buckland points out, he describes it as a 'Philosophy of Positive Law', he uses the term in the early-nineteenth-century sense of a 'science'. The book is a prolegomena, an attempt to clear the ground. The great work on jurisprudence and ethics it was designed to introduce was never written. Austin's field is confined to the description of legal concepts as they then existed in England. Its relevance is, therefore, limited, valuable and exact.*

This East Anglian lawyer, compared by Hearnshaw to a mole, and termed, rather unkindly, by Dr. C. K. Allen 'this all too earnest seeker after truth', makes a striking contrast to Hegel on Man, Society and the Cosmos. The comparison is highly instructive. While Austin was reduced to abandoning his Chair of Jurisprudence for lack of an audience, Hegel was engaged in his apotheosis in Berlin. But it was the dowdy, limited Englishman who had the greater good sense. Both certainly lived up to the legend of their national characteristics. With his empirical bias, Austin naturally admired Locke, whom he describes as 'the greatest and best of philosophers'. He understood Locke's limited objectives. And as Locke was the exponent of the interests of the commercial oligarchy of 1688, so Austin, like Bentham and Mill, was the spokesman of the early-nineteenth-century bourgeoisie. He believed in utility and free trade; in education and conservative improvement. He was scornful of metaphysical abstractions, and believed that slogans do harm. Although his estimate of human nature was low, and he regarded the prospect of universal suffrage as a return to barbarism, he was anxious to clear up the mysteries of the law and create a 'science' out of it, in order to improve mankind. 'It really *is* important', he wrote, with a touch of exasperation '(though I feel the audacity of the paradox), that we should think distinctly, and speak with a meaning.' Like Bentham, he believed in the power of reason, and hoped that the masses would become reconciled to their condition if they studied the new science of political economy as expounded by Malthus and the elder Mill. He would have disliked the views of Bagehot or Sorel on the power of myth. Austin had little historical sense and his view of society now seems static, for he wrote before the idea of evolution had captured men's minds. Hence the criticism of his views by Maine, the pioneer historian of Law in the 'sixties. He was, in fact, typical of his angular age — a conservative, but a conservative utilitarian.

Much has been made of Austin's short career in the army and how it gave him the mentality of a drill sergeant. But he was not a great success in the army, spent most of his time reading books, and early sold his commission. Anyone can perceive that here is the work not of a martinet, but of a most sensitive and disinterested mind,

* He does not mean by philosophy, writes Buckland, 'at all what Mr. Oakeshott means by it'.

anxious merely to detect the truth, whatever the consequences. Austin is always practical, within his definition, 'scientific'; he merely points out what he believes to be the facts and the objective in view. On that objective he had no doubts. '. . . The final cause . . . for which government ought to exist', he wrote, 'is the furtherance of the common weal to the greatest possible extent'. This is 'the only ultimate object of good or beneficent sovereignty'.[23]

The term 'beneficent' implies a moral judgment. For Austin positive morality reflects the 'laws' set by 'God to the human creature'. These 'laws', which are distinct from human positive law, he declares, following Bentham and Paley, reflect the principle of utility. This principle is the 'proximate test'. In this light Austin examines the best form of government in a given setting, and the distinction between free and despotic states. There is no need for moral denunciation: it is a question of relative success. Utility naturally condemns the 'loading' of subjects with onerous duties. Thus, if 'political or civil liberty has been erected into an idol, and extolled with extravagant praises by doting and fanatical worshippers', it is 'not as being liberty, but as conducing to the general good', that it is 'an object deserving applause'.[24] For always and only utility is the 'index' to God's commands.[25] Within this frame Austin distinguishes 'true positive Laws of purely human original', which are enforcible commands, from general rules of Nature and morality and from metaphorical laws of fashion and honour, or the 'laws' of gravity. The last, for example, are not human laws at all, yet 'through these misapplications of a *name*', the field of jurisprudence has been 'deluged with muddy speculation'.[26] Hence his famous definition. 'If a *determinate* human superior, *not* in a habit of obedience to a like superior, receive *habitual* obedience from the *bulk* of a given society, that determinate superior is sovereign in that society, and the society (including the superior) is a society political and independent.'[27] Its writ runs only so far as it can impose its will.

On what does this sovereign depend? It actually depends not, as Bentham held, and as it should, upon a rational calculation of interests, but upon a habit of obedience. Even in absolute monarchies, the ruler depends upon his bodyguard and upon the apathy of his subjects. 'The monarch is the superior of the governed . . . but the governed, collectively or in the mass, are also superior to the monarch, who is checked in the abuse of his might by his fear of exciting their anger; and of rousing to active resistance, the might which slumbers in the multitude.'[28]

Habit, not contract or calculated consent, is the basis of sovereign power.* It is thus conditioned by certain 'principles', habitually observed and embodied in a constitution, representing collective tradition and habitual political procedure. Ultimately the legal sovereign depends on it, since all depends on an 'embodied habit of life'. Here, the 'all or nothing' Austinian concept of sovereignty is modified.† The basis of sovereignty is thus latent and negative: it 'slumbers in the multitude . . . a reflex of habitual obedience'. Such sovereignty, says Manning in a good simile, is 'like a lighting system which is backed by a power plant which is mass habit', and by its control the light is distributed.²⁹ Within its decisive sphere, this control is absolute. Supreme power is therefore not bound by legal limitation: it is the law. And such real law must be sharply distinguished from the myths which condition public opinion and masquerade under the terms Natural Law and natural rights.

This position descends from Hobbes, who regarded sovereignty as what existing power could exact in the light of the psychological facts. It is, therefore, to be expected that Austin should cite him. 'It is affirmed by Hobbes', he writes, 'in his masterly treatises on government, that "no law can be unjust", which proposition has been deemed by many an immoral and pernicious paradox.'‡ But Hobbes merely says 'in unguarded terms' that no positive law is legally unjust. For supreme power, Austin affirms, bound by positive law, is 'a flat contradiction in terms'. It may be unconstitutional, but so long as it can command habitual obedience, it is not illegal.

Like Hobbes and Bentham, Austin scorned the abstractions whereby medieval and Stoic thought had attempted to control power: unlike Hobbes, he had a flexible standard — utility. Popular habits could be modified by education; there is not the pessimism, the determinist psychology, which petrifies Hobbes's thought and grounds his state upon fear. But Austin agrees with Hobbes in his denial of personal innate natural rights. Government is not subordinate to them in a political society. It can 'confer what rights'

---

* See MANNING, op. cit., p. 194. 'The flock', he writes, 'owes its continued existence as such not merely to the sheep dog, but to the fact that the average sheep is content to trot along in the middle and rarely, if ever, becomes a marginal case.'

† 'If this point were pressed' (the distinction between constitutional and positive law, the former being positive morality), 'it would mean that the basis of sovereignty is the feelings in the minds of the people in regard to the constitution as a result of which they absolutely obey a determinate person or persons.' A. D. LINDSAY, *The Modern Democratic State*, p. 228. Manning drily remarks, 'It is a wise community that knows its own sovereign.'

‡ *Province*, p. 276n. The cadence of this sentence is worth attention by those who think Austin unreadable.

... utility commends 'and what duties'.[30]. Here, reinforcing Bentham, is a charter for improvement by legislation.

But no vindication of the Rights of Man. Austin turns savagely on their champions and cuts to pieces the 'jargon' they employ. 'In most of the communities the result has been determined', he writes contemptuously, 'by the ... prevalent *talk*.'[31] Demagogues incite the masses with meaningless terms, so that 'having bandied their fustian phrases and "bawled till their lungs be spent", they must even take to their weapons and fight their difference out'.

Consider, for example, the loss of the American colonies. Had the British government proceeded as Burke advised them, on plain grounds of interest and 'utility', they would not have endeavoured to enforce a pedantic 'right' where their commands could not run. Hence the hatred and lasting bitterness. It always follows the pursuit of abstractions. 'For, it is only in the ignorance of the people, and in their consequent mental imbecility, that governments or demagogues can find the means to mischief.'[32] Hence the 'bestial antipathy begotten by the original quarrel'. These are strong words. They reflect Austin's fastidious distaste for impulsiveness and unreason. Of course, he concludes bitterly, they ignored Burke's good sense. His advice was not to 'the dull taste of the stupid and infuriate majority'. They went on blindly, mouthing their fatuous abstractions. ' "They'd a *right* to tax the colonists, and tax 'em they would: Ay, *that* they would" — just as if a *right* were worth a rush of itself.' 'Mr. Burke,' he concludes, 'would have taught them better. He would have "laid the fever in their souls" with the healing principle of utility.' They would not, he might have added, have taken much notice. It is extremely dangerous, he insists, for 'ignorant and bawling fanatics' who 'make such a pother about liberty' to appeal either to natural rights or Divine Law and Natural Law, against actual legal government. They are merely criticizing the law: they cannot legally defy it. 'All Blackstone means when he says that if law conflicts with God's law it is not binding, is that it ought not to have been imposed.' The confusion of what ought to be with what is, can only be tendentious. 'To say that a human law which conflicts with the law of God ... is not *binding* or not *valid*, is to talk stark nonsense.'[33] There are no rules laid up in heaven. God's purpose is revealed only through the dictates of utility. There are, indeed, certain rules and customs which have grown up in all places and times and whose value is obvious. They may be termed natural 'laws', but the term is misleading. They are neither the reflection of a divine original or of true positive law: they reflect, in modern terms, the pressure of environment. They are so 'strikingly obvious' that anyone can understand them.* But there is no need, he declares, to call them the 'laws' of God. And they have 'gotten the specious name of "natural" because they are suggested by necessities pressing in on all mankind'.

Besides disposing to his satisfaction of these quasi-legal myths, Austin reiterates his scepticism about international 'law'. As already indicated, it depends only on moral sanctions, since there is no habit of general obedience to a supra-national law and it is the nature of sovereign power to brook no superior. It 'inevitably follows that the law obtaining between nations is not positive law'. Yet he holds no brief for the Hegelian national state. The good of mankind, he argues, is 'the aggregate' of the pleasures which are respectively enjoyed by the individuals who constitute the human race. He objects even to the collectivist tone of the city-states of Antiquity, and speaks of individuals being 'sacrificed for an empty phrase'. 'Mankind', 'Country', 'public' — they are nothing but concise expressions for a number of individual persons considered collectively or as a whole. If this good is immolated for a collective person, 'the general good would be destroyed by the sacrifice'. Such were the views of this realist contemporary of Hegel. They were to be heavily criticized by the neo-Platonists and neo-Hegelians in the later part of the century, by T. H. Green and Bradley. But it was self-interest, not self-sacrifice, which in Austin's opinion rendered society efficient. No sound utilitarian, he said, with an unwonted flash of humour, ever contended that 'the lover should kiss his mistress with an eye to the common weal'. In love biological duty and interest coincide. In spite of his definition of sovereignty, and his hostility to Natural Rights and Natural Law, the open society need not count Austin among its enemies. His sovereign is not judge of all men, judged of none. If government becomes the enemy of its own people, if the light in the power house is wasted, or short-circuiting through corruption, then at last the power-plant of mass habit and opinion will cut out.

Since it is the basis of all power, he concludes, the habit of life which government reflects must be improved and enlightened. As the multitude become 'more and more acquainted with the leading

* For example one might describe it as a 'natural law' that men wish to preserve themselves (vide Spinoza). In fact, that it is better to be alive than to be dead is a natural 'law' which badly needs translation into positive law by the human race in the century of the atomic bomb. Vide *infra*, p. 481.

principle of utility', and recognizes law and government for what it is, they will not be deluded by the false glamour of Natural Rights and revolutionary slogans. Like all his generation, Austin had grown up under the shadow of the French Revolution, and in the 'twenties had seen the mob violence which was the sequel to the Napoleonic wars. If only the people would become clear-headed, they would respect the rights of property and the necessity of positive law. Hence the new and lucid science of jurisprudence he has begun to define must be diffused among them. If they read Mill and Malthus, they will comprehend the economic system: if they read Austin, they will comprehend the science of government. All depends on knowledge. 'A small fraction of the sums which are squandered in needless war, would provide instruction for the working people: would give this important class that portion in the knowledge of their age which consists with the nature of their callings and with the necessities of toiling for a livelihood.' They will then no longer 'blindly persist in hereditary opinion', but become, according to their station, the rational and orderly citizens of a modern state. They will accord the legislator his initiative in reform without appealing to the destructive myth of Natural Rights. Austin thus hopes, like Bentham, that the power of reason will overcome the power of myth, and underestimates, in his zeal for clarity, the mainly emotional basis of the habit of life he admits to be the basis of power. This rationalistic assumption was to colour predominant English political thought until modern sociologists, of whom Graham Wallas was the pioneer, were to restore a juster view.

With such an aim, with such power, and with such limitations, Austin had none of Saint-Simon's vision of the possibilities of great industry or Coleridge's sense of the hierarchical and emotional needs of society. Yet this conservative Utilitarian philosopher had done great service to legal and political thought. He had made a cool and accurate analysis, following the principles of Hobbes and Bentham, of the facts of contemporary law. He had distinguished what actually happens from what ought to happen, and he had helped to temper an instrument of sovereign government which would be sharp and handy for the reforming legislation of the mid-nineteenth century. He had provided Benthamite legislators with a criticism of prescriptive right and entrenched custom which was to be extremely formidable.

CHAPTER III

THE COUNTER-REVOLUTIONARIES
DE MAISTRE: COLERIDGE: CARLYLE

THE political ideas of the German Romantics and the English Utilitarians both represent a new middle-class outlook and initiative. Herder and Hegel and their followers desired to find a sanction for society in creative Will, rooted in History and expressed in terms of the Nation state. They are introspective, delving to find values compatible with Christianity, or even a substitute for it. Their thought is serious, poetic, with a deep Germanic sense of the totality of life. It lacks humour, it is liable to be unpractical, and often it achieved political results shocking to its originators.

Bentham and his followers, on the other hand, aim always at immediate and practical objectives. Careless of metaphysical consistency, the Utilitarian political philosophers were determined to master environment in the old Baconian tradition. They believed in knowledge; in the power of cool calculation and self-interest; in the ultimate reasonableness of mankind. They were highly successful reformers of Law and Administration. They were also provincial and doctrinaire enthusiasts, blind even to the realism of the main stream of English political thought, with its keen sense of politics and human nature. Although their influence was to predominate in England through the mid-nineteenth century, and modernize the administrative framework which was to stand the strain of the twentieth, their theoretical assumptions were meagre and inconsistent, if seldom pernicious.

The Hegelians and the Utilitarians had a common belief in the new freedoms of bourgeois civilization. Neither were sympathetic to the French Revolution; both were its beneficiaries. In reaction to previous orthodoxy, Hegel endeavoured to define a new ideal transcending the brittle eighteenth-century rationalism, with its cult of an abstract secularized Natural Law, and its mechanical view of society based on contract. For Bentham life was a crusade against the ancient and organic abuses of established convention; against the pervading and stifling aura of tradition; against the 'Juggism' of the law and organized religion. Hegel believed in the poetic and prophetic power of emergent Mind 'dreaming on things to come';

Bentham in the efficiency of what Peacock was to call 'the Steam Intellect Society'. Behind the banners of Hegelian romantic mysticism and utilitarian 'improvement', the bourgeoisie of the early nineteenth century was to advance.

To many minds it was not an advance. It was a disastrous, Gadarene stampede. To those bred in the old cosmopolitan Catholic outlook, in the ways of eighteenth-century aristocracy, or in the Tory tradition of Church and State, the parochial vulgarity of the new Nationalism and 'Reform' seemed intolerable. And these intransigent conservatives were reinforced by the alarm of writers of sensibility and discernment, disillusioned by the consequences of the French Revolution and disquieted by the first and distant intimations of the age of the common man.

There have always been minds to whom civilization has seemed precarious. In the early nineteenth century they were profoundly alarmed. The Catholics at the loss of faith and of the sense of European Christendom; the aristocrats by the destruction of hereditary privilege and of the qualities in life it made possible; the humanists by the threat to personality from a raw materialism. In view of the long-term sequel to the bourgeois paradise of the nineteenth century, it is by no means certain that they were wrong.

Catholic disgust with liberalism had the most impressive pedigree. The belief in Original Sin went back to the roots of Pauline Christianity. In the early fifth century St. Augustine had described with formidable eloquence and arresting metaphor the dangers of organizing society 'apart from God'. 'Remota justitia', he had written, 'quid sunt regna nisi magna latrocinia?' — 'without justice what are Kingdoms but brigandage writ large?' And by justice he meant the transformation of society into a Christian Commonwealth. To this eagle vision the confidence of the Utilitarians would seem a dusty heresy. Indeed the belief of Atheists or mild Deists in calculated self-interest and rational benevolence appeared curiously simple to minds long settled in the European Catholic outlook. Did these people imagine, they asked themselves, as Dostoevsky was later to demand, that the masses of mankind could face freedom?

The irresponsibility of Liberal nationalism naturally distressed all those brought up in a Latin tradition of European order. Even Hegel, after painting so broad and colourful a picture of world history, could imagine its present culmination in the Prussian State. For all his range, this German was a provincial. He had no more part than Wagner or Treitschke were to have in the lucid amenities of

Latin civilization; in a world order deriving from Antiquity and the Middle Ages. Michelet and Macaulay, too, were hypnotized by the limited and recent phenomenon of the nation state.

For the bureaucrats of the old regime the new ideas seemed totally disruptive. For the Rhinelander Metternich, in Vienna, who was to be the centre of a long rearguard action, there could be no compromise.* Civilization, they believed, demanded discipline. The cult of the Nation State was bound to destroy the principle of dynastic legitimacy on which European order must depend. By undermining privilege, Liberal reformers must themselves be swamped by the forces they released. The assertion of unbridled popular nationalism could only produce a welter of conflict. Hope of reform was a delusive rebellion against the conditions of life; treason against the traditional leadership which could save the people from exploitation by the demagogues and adventurers of whom Napoleon had been the terrible example. Only an organic and agrarian conservatism could preserve the welfare of the masses and the values of civilized society. This outlook also reflected the minds of the landowning aristocracy. And it detested and feared the new industrialism.

For conservative poets and philosophers, too, the dogmas of reform and revolution had always seemed repellently naive and politically disastrous. The disgust of the exponents of Catholic and aristocratic tradition, of European agrarian and bureaucratic order, was reinforced by writers driven to doubt the capacity of mankind for political improvement and to appeal to authority. Their protests are numerous and forceful, ranging from the neo-Catholicism of de Maistre and de Bonald to the Conservatism of the Lake poets; from the genial satire of Peacock, to the radical but reactionary denunciations of Carlyle. During the 'thirties, the young Disraeli also began to make his exotic reinterpretation of Burke.

Three of these writers, de Maistre, Coleridge and Carlyle, will here be taken as representative. De Maistre made the most sensational contribution which will be fully examined. He writes as a European brought up in a cosmopolitan tradition; as a Catholic administrator who had seen the consequences of the Revolution. Coleridge was more insular, but he had a more kindly and equally penetrating insight. Like Wordsworth, he had welcomed the Revolution, but the Terror and Napoleon had brought disillusion. It was a natural development, and it is unlikely that even the

---

* See SIR LLEWELLYN WOODWARD's admirable *Three Studies in European Conservatism* in this context.

republicanism of Shelley or the liberalism of Byron would have survived the full consequences of the bourgeois triumph, had they lived to see the umbrella of Louis Philippe succeed the sword of Missolonghi.

Carlyle, who belonged to a younger generation, and whose influence on the Victorian age was to be so powerful, was inspired with a neo-Calvinist indignation and made a cult of Heroic individuals. At once a radical and a prophet, he proclaimed general woe to a materialist epoch and denounced the consequences of political 'reform' and industrial 'progress'. All these three writers were passionately concerned to redeem a serious situation.

There were others whose influence was to be destructive. The Byronic legend had an extraordinary European influence, not merely in terms of the championship of submerged nationalities. Its hatred of government encouraged the demand for liberty, but, as Mazzini was to point out, the liberty was anti-social. From the cult of egoist despair was to derive the pessimism of Schopenhauer and, in part, the nihilism of Nietzsche. Romantic introspection could display an ugly as well as a humanitarian face. But it was only following the long-term misinterpretation of the conclusions of Darwin — the Newton of the nineteenth century — that this stream of thought came to full influence in the more elaborate manifestation of nihilism and despair. We are here concerned, not with these later aberrations, but with three representative exponents of Catholic, Anglican and radical conservatism in the early nineteenth century.

II

The most vivid and the most extraordinary of these writers was the Count Joseph de Maistre.* In the wide range of his works the

---

* Joseph de Maistre, 1754-1821. Born at Chambéry, Savoy. His father had been an important official, and he studied at Turin and entered the Savoyard Civil Service. On the annexation of Savoy by the French Revolutionary armies, he was driven into exile at Lausanne, and here he wrote *Considérations sur la France*. He joined the Court of King Charles Emmanuel in Sardinia, and in 1802 he was appointed Minister to St. Petersburg where he remained till 1815. In 1810 he wrote *Essai sur les Principes Généraux des Constitutions Politiques*, and in 1817 the *Du Pape*. The *Soirées de St. Pétersbourg* was his last and unfinished work. See also the posthumous *Mémoires et Correspondances*. He died at Turin. His brother, Xavier de Maistre, wrote introspective fantasies, notably the *Voyage autour de ma Chambre*, 1794. De Maistre's complete works were published at Lyons in fourteen volumes, 1884-87. See also GRASSET, *Joseph de Maistre*, and CAGOURDAN, *Vie de Joseph de Maistre*. E. FAGUET, *Politiques et Moralistes du 19e Siècle* also contains the best introduction to the ponderous neo-Thomist theories of De Bonald. Also C. BESSE, *Le Paradoxe Célèbre de Maistre sur la guerre*, 1916, and I. BERLIN's brilliant *The Hedgehog and the Fox*, London, 1953, which relates de Maistre to Stendhal and Tolstoy.

Considérations sur la France, the *Du Pape*, and the *Soirées de St. Pétersbourg* are the most striking. De Maistre combines an Augustinian conviction of original sin with a Hobbesian political pessimism. He was a writer of brilliant, imaginative and incisive prose. He is the most profound and eloquent of those who despaired of the new secularism and the new democracy. He has even been described as an arch-forerunner of Fascism, but his affinities are more patristic. In asserting that government is a mystery backed by force and faith, in his despair of Constitutionalism, and in his detestation of the mob — (do you want, he asks, 'to unmuzzle the tiger'?) — he has, indeed, affinities with the twentieth century. But his outlook is fundamentally religious; he has far more in common with St. Augustine than with Sorel or Pareto. 'I have never denied the inconveniences of absolute power,' he writes, 'I want to diminish them; but one finds oneself between two abysses.'

Temperamentally at odds with the dominant tendencies of his time, he regarded the rise of science as a monstrous perversion, a falling off from a superior and older wisdom. He denounced fundamental developments of modern culture, and savagely attacked its most characteristic qualities. They could lead, he thought, only to perdition. 'Sous l'habit étriqué du nord, la tête perdue dans les volutes d'une chevelure menteuse, les bras chargés de livres et d'instruments de toute espèce, pâle de veilles et de travaux, elle se traine, souillée d'encre et toute pantelante, sur la route de la vérité. . . . Rien de semblable dans la haute antiquité.'[1]

It was a curious vision of science. He not only dismissed liberal ideas; he was also blind to the development of professional knowledge, the other hopeful aspect of the nineteenth century. For all his eloquence, his learning is amateurish, and his brilliant verve leads to folly. He implicitly believes, for example, in the reality of the Flood — what gigantic sins, he remarks, must have been committed to justify so stupendous a catastrophe! He thought the wisdom of the ancient Egyptians superior to all subsequent knowledge, and from their architecture that the Etruscans had been supermen. All this nonsense emphasizes the gulf between the early nineteenth-century view of science and the professionalized knowledge of the 'sixties and 'seventies.* Yet the poetic force of his despair make his writings singularly arresting.

In the immediate field of politics his outlook is responsible but

---

* 'Count de Maistre,' writes the pioneer anthropologist Tylor, in 1871, 'with his usual facility of taking an argument up at the wrong end.' *Primitive Culture*, I, p. 128.

exclusive. He insists that men are led not by calculation but by myth. Of voting, he remarks, 'une addition n'est pas un organisme':[2] contract is an abstraction, and the revolutionaries were planning for '30 million men without ancestors'. Society is, in fact, based, as Burke and Coleridge also maintained, on emotion: 'un sentiment obscur, puissant parce qu'obscur, irréfléchi, spontané, tenant de la foi, tenant de l'instinct héréditaire et mystique, irrational sous toutes ses formes . . .' It is a view typical of the romantic reaction against the eighteenth century, and foreshadowing the psychological outlook of the twentieth.

A professional administrator, de Maistre wished to conserve not the rule of aristocracy, but the rule of kings. He held that the privileges of the old nobility interfered with government; but he wished to hedge about the kingly power with a *noblesse de robe*. His conception of rule is flexible and humane, if absolute. He thought that the monolithic sovereignty of the popular state, with rule by demagogues in the name of the people, would be the inevitable result of 'freedom', for the general will was a fraud. Hence, given the nature of men, the need for monarchy administered by a patriciate.

His most closely argued work is the *Du Pape** with its onslaught on the French Revolution, though the *Soirées de St. Pétersbourg* is the more striking.

The Revolution is something without precedent. It is 'Satanic'.[3] In de Maistre's neo-patristic view, it is the result of cumulative intellectual arrogance, the logical outcome of the teaching of Locke and Voltaire. 'Humanity is struggling against the torrent of errors to which it has abandoned itself . . .' In this crisis, with the foundations of civilization collapsing, de Maistre declares the one remedy — the absolute authority of Rome. For the Pope is the 'grand demiurge de la civilisation universelle'.[4] De Maistre is a good European; his book reflects the ancient unity of the Christian world.

In exercising this authority, the Pope is no mere personal tyrant. He rules as head of a great institution, the symbol of supreme world sovereignty. Such an authority there must be, because, de Maistre declares, like Austin, sovereignty is of its nature absolute. The need for government is primordial. It derives from original sin. 'L'homme, en sa qualité d'être à la fois moral et corrompu, juste dans son intelli-

* It runs to 396 pages and is divided into a Preliminary Discourse, four Books and a Conclusion. The first book deals with the Pope in relation to the Catholic Church; the second to temporal sovereigns, the third to civilization in general, the fourth to the schismatic Anglican and Russian Churches.

gence, et pervers dans sa volonté, doit necessairement être gouverné.'
Without judgment ('sentence'), there will be 'combat'. There is no
choice; no question of contract; 'sovereignty results directly from
human nature'.* With Burke, he believes that mankind and their
rulers are mutually interdependent — 'born into society'. 'Sovereigns do not exist by the grace of their peoples, sovereignty being
no more the result of their will than the existence of society itself.'
The people gain more from this symbiosis than the prince, who is
sacrificed to his obligations.

In this organic interdependence most societies have their being. In
Europe, alone, the 'audacious tribe of Japhet' has always followed
an unusual course. They have attempted to restrain sovereign
power. The rest of the world — 'the immense posterities of Sem and
Cham' — have generally acquiesced in despotism tempered by
assassination. 'Do what you like,' they have told their rulers, 'and
when we are tired of it we will cut your throats.' Europeans have
been more subtle. They have set themselves the great problem —
'how to restrain power without destroying it'.⁵

De Maistre considers and rejects Constitutionalism. 'Only England, favoured by the sea . . . and a national character that lends
itself to these experiments, has been able to do something in this
line.' And already the famous edifice of 1688 seems rocking on its
foundations. France, of course, was in worse case. Here the most
dangerous remedy has been applied — 'la révolte, remède terrible,
pire que tous les maux'. Consider the consequences: they have
merely, amid the shame of foreign occupation, placed on the throne a
'b italique instead of a B majuscule'. It was only to be expected.
'Revolutions started by the wisest men are always finished by madmen.' And they founded their doctrines on sand. For the rights of
man give no basis for sovereignty, no basis for the control of power.
From Protestantism has come the vain idea of the sovereignty of the
people, 'a dogma which has been transferred from religion into
politics'. It is worthless, for Sovereignty is a high mystery, 'a sacred
thing, an emanation of divine power — of its nature unlimited'. Even
in England, where it is said to be limited, they have only diminished
the power of the king, which by itself is not supreme. But when the
three powers which in England make up the sovereignty are in
accord, what can they do? 'Il faut répondre avec Blackston — tout.'

Then what is the answer? Must it be that 'the oath of fidelity

---

* *Du Pape*, p. 133. In the first three chapters of the second book will be found the most
essential of de Maistre's political ideas.

exposes men to tyrants; resistance without rules to anarchy?' There can only be one solution. If temporal sovereignty is mysterious, it can be controlled only by another and superior mystery — the supreme authority of the Pope. Thus alone can the problem of freedom and order be solved; not by an assertion of popular rights, not by an appeal to a fictitious contract, but by recognition of one supreme and august authority, the embodiment of civilization itself.

Against these profound considerations, de Maistre continues, Rousseau's facile optimism looks absurd. 'Man was never born free.' Anyone who has studied his 'dismal nature' knows that man in general is far too wicked for freedom.[6] 'La maxime retentissante "l'homme est né libre et partout il est dans les fers", que veut-elle dire? . . .' The opposite to this mad assertion is the truth. In pre-Christian times slavery was the normal condition of the vast majority of mankind. Aristotle's view that some men are slaves by nature was right, and Lucan made the sinister observation, 'humanum paucis vivit genus'. This grim outlook, normal in Antiquity, was only gradually altered by the Christians, who alone could have achieved the change. The profound mistake of modern 'progressive' thinkers is to believe that freedom without Christianity is possible. For such is human wickedness, unredeemed, that it can only be controlled by slavery. This alone diminishes the egotism of an unregenerate world. The alternative can only be Christianity. By a kind of 'spiritual grafting', it diminishes 'natural bitterness of will' and enables men to live peaceably, but in a world of liberal utilitarianism there are too many 'wills loose in the world'. The Supreme Authority must be the Church.

Such, for de Maistre, is the predicament; and such the remedy. He concludes with a panegyric on the Church, an appeal to Anglicans to return to the fold, an attack on the 'vulgar innovations' of Luther and Calvin, and a fine evocation of the splendour of Rome.

Eager to restore Christian unity, de Maistre actually cites Hume and Gibbon on the Antiquity of the Catholic Church. Even these sceptics admit that the Church was prior to 'nearly all political establishments in Europe'; that by the fourth century, doctrine was already defined and that the 'seeds of the Papacy were sown even in the apostles' time'. Is it likely, he demands, that Christianity would have become perverted, as the Protestants maintain, so soon after the Redemption? That would deny the wisdom of God. Here is the supreme Protestant error; we must 'efface this word Protestantism from the European Dictionary'.[7] For only a united

European Church can control the innovating and ungovernable quality of the European mind. Only the Church, which has alone endured for eighteen centuries. 'What hidden force has done this — against all rules of probability?' Only a superhuman institution could have so survived.*

De Maistre concludes with a prose-poem on Holy Church. 'Je te salue, mère immortelle de la science et de la sainteté, *salve magna parens.*' The Papacy has been the supreme force of civilization. The citadel of the pagan world was the Pantheon: it was transformed to the stronghold of the Saints. As in Milton's ode *On The Morning of Christ's Nativity*, the theme of the conquest of the Pagan Gods is sung. St. Peter eclipses Janus; St. Francis, Pluto; the miraculous St. Xavier drives before him Bacchus, the fabulous conqueror of India. 'La Divine Marie monte sur l'autel de Vénus Pandémique. Tous les Dieux hommes disparaissent devant L'homme Dieu.'

Here, already, are all de Maistre's outstanding themes. A similar outlook is apparent in the curious *Soirées de St. Pétersbourg.*† Here the treatment is different: where the *Du Pape* is forcefully systematic, the *Soirées* are cast in the form of casual conversation. They form a strange and often extraordinary sequence of ideas, profound and eccentric. While the motives implicit in the *Du Pape* are further illuminated, the illumination reveals some dark corners. And the queer supplement, the '*Traité sur les Sacrifices*', shows an odd pre-occupation with blood.

The opening of the *Soirées de St. Pétersbourg* is singularly attractive. De Maistre and two companions, a Russian Privy Councillor and a spirited young Frenchman, the 'Chevalier de B.', are being rowed on the Neva in the long twilight of a Northern summer. There is a superb sunset, reflected on the clouds and in the flaming windows of the Imperial palace. In the soft air the Tsar's standard hangs drooping from its mast, and across the full flowing river float the songs of the Russian boatmen. The inner harbour is alive with

---

* In attacking the Church the philosophers of the Enlightenment had seized the opportunity created by the Protestants. The supreme architects of ruin were Luther and Calvin, 'ces deux hommes de néant avec l'orgueil des sectaires, l'acrimonie plébienne et la fanatisme des cabarets'.

† *Les Soirées de St. Pétersbourg*, ou Entretiens sur le gouvernement temporel de la Providence, suivis d'un Traité sur les Sacrifices, par le Comte Joseph de Maistre, deux tomes. Bruxelles 1838. The books are divided into eleven discussions. Six take place in the first volume, the first two are the most interesting and will here be examined. The third attempts a moral justification for the hereditary transmission of physical defects: the fourth deals mainly with crime and its remedy, prayer. The fifth and sixth books are also mainly concerned with prayer and its efficacy. The second volume opens with an extraordinary and notorious chapter on war.

pleasure craft; further out are the big foreign ships, crammed with the exotic merchandise the opulence of Russia can command. The evening deepens into golden twilight, unpaintable and strange. As they drift in the silence, the Chevalier observes that they should have on board one of those political 'monsters who weary the earth'. 'And what would you say to him?' 'I would ask whether he found this sight as lovely as I do.' 'My dear Chevalier,' replies de Maistre, 'lost souls never have good nights or beautiful days.' 'So you really think the wicked unhappy?' 'I wish I could believe it, but I see them flourishing . . . A little account for them in this world would not have spoilt anything.'

So the main theme of the *Soirées*, the question of divine justice and original sin, is introduced. De Maistre proceeds to depict the first tea party in the annals of political thought. They hold a symposium on justice, this time not in the grove of the Academy or on Cicero's estate at Arpinum, but round a tea table on the terrace of the Sardinian Minister's residence in Petersburg. Here they discuss the joys of the wicked and the misfortunes of the just — 'C'est le grand scandale de la raison humaine.' The ways of Providence in the world are examined. What is the explanation of human suffering? It reflects evil which comes not from God but from original sin. Here, again, is an Augustinian view. And what is the explanation? Menu, 'grand législateur des Indes', declared that Brahma created the genius of pain: he is a demon of black aspect and fiery eyes. His task is to save mankind from sin.

De Maistre proceeds to his well-known *tour de force* — the evocation of the executioner.[8] Who is it that sustains the fabric of society? he asks. Not the king, not the first Minister, not the highest dignitaries of the Church. It is a more humble, a more sinister figure — the *bourreau*. In the human family here is the ultimate authority. A strange being, set apart, he lives in queer solitude, alone with his mate and brood. When the day for duty arrives, the executioner appears before the seething crowd. Some criminal — a poisoner, perhaps — awaits him. He proceeds to break him on the wheel. First he extends the victim; then ties him down. Soon the horrible silence is broken by the crack of bones. As they splinter beneath the iron, come screams of agony. Then the criminal is detached. He is deposited upon the wheel, broken limbs entangled with the spokes. With drooping head, with parched and gaping mouth, with matted hair, the victim can mutter only the bloody words that pray for death.

Before this ghastly spectacle, what are the feelings of the executioner? If he is a good professional, they are exultant. His heart beats high; not with pity, but with pride. No one, he says, can break a man so well as I do — 'nul ne roue mieux que moi'. I am the best executioner in the world. And so, passing through the ranks of his shrinking fellows, the *bourreau* collects his pay. Back at home, he sits down to a good meal.*

Upon the shoulders of this sinister creature society inevitably rests. He is at once 'L'horreur et le lien de l'association humaine' — the horrible mystery, the inescapable bond. Take him away, at once order gives place to chaos, thrones collapse, society dissolves. For God, the author of sovereignty, is the author of punishment. Sovereign power, with its ultimate and terrible sanction, is the only answer to original sin. Its decisions are in general just; if sometimes the innocent perish, such is the law of life: 'c'est un malheur comme un autre'. After this harrowing description, the discussion turns to illness. Physical disorders, de Maistre maintains, are in general the 'suites funestes de la volupté'; ill temper, gormandizing and incontinence — all have their penalties. Most suffering is deserved. Such is the pessimistic outlook behind de Maistre's political opinions.

The Chevalier begins the next conversation by refusing a second cup of tea, a drink which, as a southern Frenchman, he distrusts. 'Élevé, comme vous savez, dans une province méridionale de la France, où le thé n'était regardé que comme un remède contre le rhume', he has long lived in circles addicted to its consumption. Good Frenchman that he is, he has never brought himself to like it. Tea may even increase illness. Nonsense, says de Maistre, all illness is really unnecessary. It could be abolished by prayer and the abandonment of sin. The reign of physical evil could be indefinitely restrained by this supernatural means. For illness is caused simply by wickedness, 'le péché original, qui explique tout', and which, one must remember, is still always going on. A sobering consideration. It is the tragedy of mankind that alone of the animals they are aware of sin. Rousseau — 'l'un des plus dangereux sophistes de son siècle . . . avec une profondeur apparente qui est toute dans les mots' — was wrong to speak of noble savages. All savagery results from degeneration. Mankind is not progressing, it is groping back towards lost realms of light. Hence the desire for learning. 'No

* Emile Faguet (op. cit., p. 3) thinks that the tour de force ought not to be taken too seriously; . . . 'encore que cette page du bourreau qui, à la bien entendre, n'est qu'une saillie d'humeur un peu patibulaire, à la Swift, ait eu un peu trop aux yeux de nos pères le caractère d'une leçon en Sorbonne, à prendre au pied de la lettre'. It remains the key of the political argument.

beaver, no swallow, no bee wants to know more than its forebears.'
Hence man's greatness and his sorrow. For his will is broken and
divided. Ovid and St. Paul echo one another: . . . *video meliora,
proboque, Deteriora sequor*; 'For the good that I would I do not: but
the evil that I would not, that I do . . . Oh wretched man that I am
who shall deliver me from the body of this death?'[9] Everywhere and
at all times there is a dark inclination to wickedness. This dualist
horror of life, expressed by many previous writers, had not before
found a romantic expression in political theory.

The second evening is also distinguished by the deployment of de
Maistre's curious and often fruitful ideas on the nature of speech. He regards it as an expression of the creative capacity of the human spirit,
something which moulds the environment of the race. He comes to
examine the genius of language in describing the origins of civilization, and touches on subjects raised by Vico.[10] As in the *Du Pape*, he
insists, 'where you see an altar, there you will find civilization'.
And like religion, speech is mysterious. It is as 'old as eternity', and
'toute langue particulière naît comme animal'.[11] It is a creative
process. Why can primitive peoples create a language while modern
philologists fail? Once the process becomes self-conscious, it becomes
sterile. Surely, the Chevalier suggests, the origin of speech throws
light on the origin of ideas? Here if anywhere, is evidence for creative mind. In an interesting attack on Hobbesian materialist sensa-
tionalism, de Maistre appears from an unexpected angle as a defender
of Cudworth, of all people.[12] To materialize the origins of ideas is
profoundly degrading; 'reason loses its wings and crawls like a rep-
tile'. On the contrary, intellect is not merely passive but creative;
since intelligence reasons upon impressions, it has the power to
generalize, expressed in words. De Maistre shocks the rationalist
Chevalier by vindicating St. Thomas, who, for clarity and precision,
he declares, is one of the greatest minds.[13] 'Truth', said St. Thomas,
'is the equation between the affirmation and its object.' Its apprehension is a natural and creative act. Man, de Maistre insists, thus
lives by the spirit, and the spirit is thought. This creative power
cannot be explained. One cannot analyse the human spirit; one
can only observe its operations. A clue to this creative activity may
be found in the study of language. Citing Plato and using an Hegelian phrase, de Maistre remarks, 'La pensée est le discours que l'esprit
se tient à lui-même.' Now 'la pensée et la parole ne sont que deux
magnifiques synonymes', and 'être' is the soul of all verbs. You can
affirm anything without its pre-existence.

These are suggestive and original ideas. They are embedded in discursive conversations which extend into a curious analysis of war.[14] The Chevalier has no difficulty in defining war. It is to obey the king's orders, he says with soldierly precision. But why are all the best soldiers so extremely polite? Because, even in the heat of action, they are trained to behave with poise, as virtuous wives, de Maistre points out, are chaste even in the transports of wedded love.

Violent death, he insists, is the law of all life; war is the reflection in human society of an inscrutable decree. It 'is divine in itself, because it is one of the laws of the world'. Like the executioner, it is a 'mystery'. Hence its strange glamour. Though there is nothing apparently so much against nature, there is nothing so attractive. After all, were public opinion sufficiently against it, war would be impossible. Yet it was far more difficult, says the Russian Senator, for Peter the Great to abolish beards than to get cannon fodder, even when he was constantly defeated. And why has war never been suppressed? Why was the scheme of the Abbé de Saint-Pierre received with mockery? Because on this subject the human race is mad. This madness can only be explained through some 'occult and terrible law which demands human blood'.[15] De Maistre quotes La Bruyère with effect. 'If anyone told you that all the cats of a large country assembled on open ground, and after having caterwauled (miaulé) their fill, had flung themselves on one another, tooth and claw, with the utmost ferocity; that after this mêlée the corpses of nine or ten thousand animals had been left on the field to infect the air for ten leagues with their decay, wouldn't you say this was the most atrocious sabbath you had ever heard of? And if the wolves did the same — what howls and butchery! And if both cats and wolves told you that they loved glory, wouldn't you laugh at the ingenuousness of the poor creatures?'

Of course, he again asserts, only original sin can explain human behaviour. 'Observe,' he says, 'that this terrible law of war is only a chapter of the general law that weighs on the Universe.' 'Dans le vaste domaine de la nature vivante, il règne une violence manifeste.' 'The decree of violent death is written on the very frontiers of life.' Species prey on species and man is the worst killer of all. King of the animal creation, he 'stuffs the crocodile, tears the guts from the lamb to make music for his harp . . . and uses whalebone to stiffen the girl's corsage'. His tables are 'covered with corpses'. But what animal exterminates man? Only man himself. Yet, insists the Senator, man is a moral being. To fulfil this law of destruction he must, therefore, periodically become insane. 'Don't you hear the earth crying for blood?' he says. The blood of the animals, of criminals, is not enough to assuage so vast a collective guilt. Wars there must be; so periodically, 'la guerre s'allume'. Nations are seized by a frenzy, something different from anger or hate, and drawn to destruction without knowing whither they are bound. Young men who enlist with alacrity are 'innocent murderers' . . . the 'passive instruments of an irresistible hand'. Thus is accomplished the 'great universal law of the violent destruction of living beings'. It will continue until all evil is redeemed, 'until the death of death'. Meanwhile, 'l'ange exterminateur tourne comme le soleil autour de ce malheureux globe'.

In a strange panegyric on war, de Maistre seems to parody himself. It is a divine enigma, surrounded by mysterious glamour. The protection of Providence is accorded to great generals, who seldom get killed themselves — or only when their 'glory' is at its height and their mission accomplished — for they are the instruments of God's vengeance for accumulated crime. War, too, is incalculable. It is not always the most powerful who win. Indeed, the remark attributed to Turenne, that 'God is on the side of the big battalions' can be misleading. The most mysterious and unexpected results occur,* and often the victors are worse off than the vanquished. Sometimes, too, those who win wars suffer greater moral degradation than the defeated. Moreover, war gives rise to remarkable poetry. After this peroration, de Maistre loses himself in another panegyric on the Psalms.

Such is the nightmare envisaged by this sensitive observer. Crazy as much of the argument may be, it is worth pondering in the twentieth century. Like lemmings to the sea, it seems, the human race rushes periodically to perdition. The worst misinterpretations of the Darwinian struggle for existence pale before the visions of this original and tormented mind.†

* Under the Emperor Arnoulf, says Liutprand of Cremona, for example, Rome was taken through the action of a hare, which got up in front of the besieging army. The soldiers pursued it, shouting, and the defenders, thinking an assault was in train, lost their nerve and took to flight. De Maistre admits that this is a tall story, but thinks it as credible as the tale of the Capitoline geese.

† Penetrating as de Maistre's insight may be, it is curiously unhealthy: this morbid strain is strongly apparent in a queer last work on the history of sacrifice. Primitive peoples, de Maistre begins, have always held God in awe. They may call Him Father, but they believe themselves to be in the hands of powers which demand propitiation. Even the idea of a beneficent God is accompanied by the conviction of guilt, to be assuaged only

For, here indeed is a Manichaean hatred of the 'flesh'; a psychological repulsion, a projected guilt. What sub-conscious furies drove de Maistre to this cult? The very tension increased his imaginative power, infused his nervous and brilliant style. Here is no Hobbesian materialism, but something far more sensitive. For de Maistre is at heart a romantic, shuddering at the collapse of the aristocratic order to which he belonged, horrified at the blasphemy of philosophers who believed that man could make himself. Discounting the possibilities of technical progress and the promise of the new science and industry, he despairs of mankind. Though at one with his contemporary, Saint-Simon, in the conviction that society needed religion, his outlook is diametrically opposed to Saint-Simon's acceptance of life. Only by the assertion of a mysterious authority, of the world embracing sovereign power of the Pope, could the natural wickedness of society be controlled. It is a strange kind of Christianity, in which there is little compassion. It belongs rather to the old world of Patristic Theologians and medieval heresy, than to the materialist outlook of the future, when totalitarian Dictators were to regard all truth as relative and ideas as instruments of political warfare. For de Maistre declares human motives wicked and the remedies brutal, but he desires government by an administrative patriciate, loyal to an hereditary king. His affinities are not so much with the parvenu bureaucracy and purblind manœuvres of the dictators of modern mass society, but rather with a more hoary medieval tradition. Of all the figures who have contributed to the colourful tapestry of political ideas he is one of the most singular.

by blood. This is because flesh is the enemy of spirit, he says, in the old Manichaean way, and blood is the 'vital fluid' of the flesh. Modern doctors agree on this question; he quotes the 'celebrated Hunter' (*Treatise on the Blood*), 'wee [sic] grow out of it'. A similar propitiatory idea is apparent in the widespread custom of ritual prostitution. If thus appeased, the seductions of 'Vénus toute entière à sa proie attachée' will not disrupt legitimate love. There is also a passage on bull fighting, with elaborate notes. The almost universal practice of sacrifice among primitive peoples reflects this sense of guilt and appeasement. So the Druids propitiated the dead, and the Aztecs systematically cut their prisoners' throats. Consider, he says, the cannibals of Peru and the Indian practice of Suttee, which not only provides presents for the Gods, but discourages wives from killing their husbands. Lurking beneath the surface even of civilized society there is always savagery. The French Revolution was the supreme example; in the twinkling of an eye occurred behaviour worthy of the Iroquois and Algonquins: 'voilà l'homme naturel'. Of course, the mystery reflects a profound human need. Pagan ideas of redemption by blood sacrifice anticipated Christianity, 'Sine sanguine non fit remissio'. The supreme blood sacrifice was made on Calvary. Our own age has naturally produced similar notions. Mussolini's conception of war and Professor Toynbee's view of history as a process of redemption through suffering are crude and highly sophisticated versions of these ideas.

While de Maistre had stated with piercing insight his neo-patristic view of life and flung his counsel of despair in the face of the early nineteenth century, the English poet Coleridge was to develop the ideas of Burke with a new mystical content, while Carlyle was to bring a general indictment against the 'improving' materialism of the time. Carlyle was the more widely influential; like Ruskin, he coloured the outlook of most of the leaders of the Victorian age. But Coleridge made a more immediate contribution to conservative thought, standing between Burke and Disraeli in that rather curious pedigree.

It was curious, since English conservatives were singularly indifferent to ideas. Their approach had always been empirical: it goes far back to the level-headed outlook of Anglo-Saxon and Scandinavian law and custom, to the solid building of medieval administrators, to the manœuvres of Elizabethan statesmen and the common sense of the men of 1688. It reflects the northern knowledge of 'what one is about' noted by W. P. Ker in the Sagas, the capacity to look at political problems without excessive excitement.[16] Given this practical bent, it had always been easy for English politicians to get along with a rather inconclusive political theory. This distrust for neat abstractions and rigid dogma is still apparent in the dislike of English Trade-Unionists for dialectical materialism. Burke had clothed this empirical approach with a matchless eloquence — perhaps it took an Irishman to do it — and the exotic figure of Disraeli further embellished the English conservative tradition. 'Man was made', he was to say, with Oriental emphasis, 'to adore and to obey'.

Coleridge was to contribute many penetrating and some foolish observations.* As Professor Willey points out, he became the 'leading

* Many of Samuel Taylor Coleridge's opinions are to be found in his *Table Talk*. His principal political works are *The Courier*, 1810; *The Friend*, *The Statesman's Manual*, 1816; *Lay Sermons*, 1817; *On the Constitution of Church and State*, 1830; *Essays on his own Time*. See the *Complete Works of Coleridge*, 7 vols., 1884. For an excellent study of Coleridge see BASIL WILLEY, *Nineteenth Century Studies*. Professor Feiling has a suggestive article in HEARNSHAW, *Social and Political Ideas of the Age of Reaction and Reconstruction*. R. J. WHITE, *The Conservative Tradition* (British Political Tradition Series, edited Alan Bullock and F. W. Deakin. Kaye, 1950), has many quotations from Coleridge and a stimulating introduction on Conservatism in general, though his account of Conservative Foreign Policy is hardly representative. There is an admirable short treatment of Coleridge in SIR WILLIAM HOLDSWORTH's *History of English Law*, XIII, p. 148. For Wordsworth's political ideas, see particularly *On the Convention of Cintra*, 1809. Also A. V. DICEY, *The Statesmanship of Wordsworth*. For a general survey, see CRANE BRINTON, *The Political Ideas of the English Romanticists*.

English representative of the European reaction against the eighteenth century'. For his early revolutionary enthusiasm and his notions of 'Pantisocracy', there can be no place in a study of this scope: his more influential opinions are expressed in his maturer writings. They are engulfed in a spate of generalities. Professor Feiling ruefully remarks that they form 'scanty islets in the delta of an intraversable river system' . . . 'It is however possible', he continues, 'to construct out of the ceaseless digressions something like a theory of the state.'

The core of that theory is an Anglican ideal of commonwealth and a scepticism of political reform. Utopia can never come about by Act of Parliament, still less by the decree of arbitrary power, whether despotic or popular. The art of government is so uncertain, the dangers of the abuse of power so menacing, that it is barbarous to make politics the dominant fact in life. Society is more important than government, and private life than public affairs. Persons, said Coleridge, must never be sacrificed to things. This view is fundamentally religious, whether stated in terms of Christianity or Humanism. It drew its inspiration mainly from Burke. 'His political teaching', writes Holdsworth, 'was in fact an application of Burke's principles to the needs and intellectual conditions of his day',[17] but Coleridge added the Kantian ideal of morality, and a kind of Platonic cult of the 'Idea' of Church and State. Development of character, the fulfilment of personality, was the objective. The stress on character is found also in Carlyle, though he regarded Coleridge's attempt to revive the contemporary Anglican Church as impracticable.* Although, therefore, Coleridge was influenced by German metaphysics, he never advocated the German totalitarian state and idea of Law as might. He also defended the Constitution against the radical belief in popular will which might lead to over-riding it in the name of a 'mandate'; and he formulated an ideal of Church and Clerisy which would stand over against the materialism of a knowing, cocksure, pursuit of Progress. The Church, he believed, was 'the appointed opposite of them all collectively — the sustaining, correcting, befriending opposite of the world'. Hence his influence on Thomas Arnold of Rugby, that tidal force in early Victorian England, who partially realized the Coleridgean conception of Clerisy when he reformed the casual freedoms

* It was absurd, he said, 'to bring these dead Churches, this English Church especially, to life again'. See BASIL WILLEY, op. cit., p. 108. Carlyle thought Coleridge 'flabby and irresolute' and he explained his great influence because 'he could still, after Hume and Voltaire had done their best and worst with him, profess himself on orthodox lines'.

of the old public schools and created a new spirit of earnest purpose
in the new ones. This influence is also reflected in the Christian
Socialism of F. D. Maurice and Kingsley. Like Wordsworth,
Coleridge greatly admired the better aspect of the seventeenth-
century Commonwealth; where Carlyle idolized Cromwell, they
admired Milton and Vane. There was also a strain from the
romantic revival, with its interest in monks and medieval theology.
Coleridge, as Feiling well remarks, comes to political theory like
the benefactor in a medieval painting, bearing his miniature church.
These mixed elements contributed to the Tractarian Oxford Movement and to much clerical excitement at the time. This conservative
interest in religion was later encouraged by Disraeli, who regarded
the Anglican Church as a safety valve for religious enthusiasm.

Coleridge's hopes for the Anglican Church were combined with
the romantic patriotism, so powerful during the Napoleonic wars
and their aftermath, to which Wordsworth gave superb expression.
This patriotism, with its faith in character and distrust of innovation,
reinforced belief in a Constitution inherited from 'time out of mind'.
Like Burke, he objected to the theory of individual natural rights.
He detested the Jacobins because they were ready to commit murder
for an idea. No political myth was worth that wickedness. And no
new-fangled utilitarian doctrine, Malthusian or Ricardian, was worth
the sacrifice of personality of high or low. Education should be a
training of the whole man, not as Austin conceived it, an instruction
of technicians in economic 'Laws' to explain that they must keep
their station since utility demanded it. They should be kept contented in a commonwealth wherein every man has his place, his
obligations and his rights. 'In every patent of Office,' Burke had
said, 'the duty is included.' Man is born to society, and born to
religion. There must be balance, order, hierarchy. The utilitarian
world of calculating individuals was a nightmare. To Coleridge it
was the more deplorable that the Deist clergy should have adopted
and sanctioned the morals of the market place, and abandoned the
speculative and lofty theology of the ancient church.

In the economic sphere Coleridge was also a conservative. Property was an extension of personality; it should be widely distributed,
but it was not for the state to create social justice. Hierarchy must
be preserved, and all fulfil themselves in their proper station. Thus
alone, he believed, could happiness be brought about. No rigging of
the political structure can alter the fact that character is the basis
of the good life; character which reflects a right relation to God and

the commonwealth into which we are born. All must be framed by
an organic time-honoured constitution, by rights which ensure fundamental liberties safeguarded by the Common Law. Such a frame
will prevent the degeneration which is as likely as progress, and
protect society from subversion by arbitrary power. For if that frame
is broken, the name of just and unjust can no longer exist; all is
tyranny, however it may be tricked out in the guise of popular will.
The *vox populi* was as likely to be *vox diaboli* as *vox Dei*. The power of
the mob can be as arbitrary as that of a monarch,* and once the
frame of society is broken, the idea of a majority becomes meaningless. For it is an artificial creation only applicable to organized
society. There must always be a standard to which government is
answerable. What better than a Constitution — 'a work of art and
a work of time' — which embodies the way of life of a nation down
the centuries? A commonwealth is not 'a mere problem of arith-
metic', it is 'a solemn fraternity'.

In this setting policy should be empirical, evoked by events rather
than imposed upon them; an adjustment rather than a plan. Intuition, the feel for a situation, is a surer guide than dogma. All must
be in terms of human values and rooted in local patriotism: 'we must
learn to love the little platoon'. Coleridge detested centralized
power and planning, a mechanical view of society — 'the general
conceit that states and governments ought to be constructed as
machines . . . the consequent multitude of plans and constitutions,
of planners and constitution makers, and the remorseless arrogance
with which the authors and proselytizers of every new proposal [are]
ready to realize it, be the cost what it might in established rights, or
even the lives of men'.†

These are wise words, poignantly relevant after more than a
century. They contain the essence of Coleridge's political creed.
Family, friendship, private life, property, the relation of man to
God and his fellow beings, these are the values to be conserved. In
every scheme for improvement the human cost must be counted,
in view of complex and incalculable chance. The state, above all,
can never be a law unto itself. It must be judged by the same
morality as individuals.

This was the doctrine which Coleridge opposed to the Utilitarianism he thought so dangerous and shallow. It was the view of

* In that sort of game, Burke had remarked shrewdly, 'the people are apt to be the
losers'. See *W.P.T.*, p. 435.
† Quoted by White from the *Statesman's Manual*, p. 66. See also Coleridge's remarks
there quoted on the 'Disease of Excessive Organization'.

an Anglican humanist and a poet.* It derived from Burke, the Romantic movement, and Kantian philosophy, with its stress on character and moral intuition. In one sense it was unpractical, in another realist. Before the tide of democracy which de Tocqueville saw as inevitable, the hierarchy of the eighteenth century could not be conserved. The grand old constitution Coleridge admired sheltered abuses and inefficiencies which an age of expanding techniques could not tolerate; the frightful consequences of the early Industrial Revolution demanded legislation which only a new and more positive conception of state power could bring about. This aspect of Utilitarianism, the Conservatives were to assimilate under Peel. But Coleridge, like Burke and Johnson, had little part in the raw industrial civilization which was transforming the face of England and shifting the whole balance of economic power. How could there be character and contentment in the world depicted by Dickens and by Engels and denounced in *Sybil*? 'The two nations' needed new methods of government to grapple with the massive problems of great industry. Yet by his scepticism of politics, his assertion of human values and personal responsibility, by his cautious and empirical view of policy, Coleridge gave a salutary warning to his compatriots not to hope too much of improvement. He advised them, like de Tocqueville, of the dangers of centralized democratic power, and warned them to regard political fanatics of both sides with the suspicion always characteristic of the predominant strain in English political thought. Here, in contrast to the cosmopolitan and Manichaean outlook of de Maistre, is an insular and more sanguine convervatism. It reflects the humanity of the best traditions of Anglican Churchmanship, deriving from Hooker and Jeremy Taylor and Cudworth, and comes perhaps nearer the Christianity of the gospels than the desperate visions of de Maistre.

IV

'Laissez-faire — leave them to do? The thing they will *do*, if so left, is too frightful to think of!'[18] Such was Carlyle's opinion of the people. His view of Utilitarian philosophy was no better: 'fantastic tricks enough man has played in his time . . . but to fancy himself a dead Iron Balance for weighing Pains and Pleasures on, was reserved

---

* A similar outlook is well expressed by another admirable humanist of the time, Thomas Love Peacock, though without Coleridgean Metaphysics. See, in particular, his views on Malthus (Mr. Fax) in *Melincourt*, quoted by LORD RUSSELL in *Freedom and Organization*, pp. 97ff, and of Dr. Folliott on the 'March of Mind' in *Crochet Castle*.

for his latter era. There stands he, his Universe one huge Manger, filled with hay and thistles to be weighed against each other; and looks long eared enough'.[19]

Brought up in a Calvinist tradition, Carlyle never abandoned its gloom or escaped its atmosphere. A reactionary, in the sense of one revolted by his age, he was also a radical — the Scots stone-mason's son, always conscious of the people. For this most vehement of Victorian prophets the world was still divided between reprobate and elect, and life a cosmic drama of fated reward and punishment.* An artist and a moralist, Carlyle detested the common and the dull. He believed in an aristocracy of talent: 'the wise . . . a race apt not to be found in the high roads at present or only to be transiently passing there, with closed lips, swift step and possibly a grimmish aspect of countenance'. A sense of the glare of cosmic fires behind the ordinary scene inspires the mood Carlyle so skilfully communicates. This mood had pervasive influence on his age, and from the early *Sartor Resartus* to the bitter *Shooting Niagara*, he faced the deepest question of his time. 'Is there no God, then; but at best an absentee God, sitting idle, ever since the first Sabbath at the outside of His universe and seeing it go?'[20] Brought up on the Old Testament, he hankers for spiritual calm. In the famous *Past and Present*, he remarks of Abbot Sampson's monks: 'Our Religion is not yet a horrible restless Doubt, still less a far horribler composed Cant; but a great heaven high Unquestionability, encompassing, interpenetrating the whole of Life.'[21]

He was, further, influenced by Goethe, Schiller and Fichte, and like Coleridge, he was one of the first writers to exploit the richness of German thought, then little known in England. Technically inaccurate and one-sided, he remains, as Professor Gooch remarks, the great portrait painter among English historians. A sense of the living past, of personality in history, of high drama and local colour, inspires his extraordinary but effective style. He makes a singular contrast to Gibbon, another great master of panoramic history. With Ruskin, who greatly admired him, Carlyle became part of the

---

* Thomas Carlyle. Born Ecclefechan, 1795, died Chelsea, 1881. His principal works are *Sartor Resartus*, 1833-34 (book form, 1838); *The French Revolution*, 1837; *Heroes and Hero-worship* and *Chartism*, 1839; *Past and Present*, 1843; *Life and letters of Oliver Cromwell*, 1845; *Latter-day pamphlets*, 1850; *Life of Stirling*, 1851; *Frederick the Great*, 1858-65; *Shooting Niagara*, 1867. For critical accounts of his political ideas see R. S. DOWER, chap. II of HEARNSHAW, *Social and Political Ideas of the Victorian Age*; CASSIRER, *The Myth of the State*, pp. 189ff; NEFF, op. cit., chap. v; G. P. GOOCH, *History and Historians in the Nineteenth Century*. For his life see R. GARNETT, *Life of Carlyle*; JULIAN SYMONS, *Thomas Carlyle*. Gollancz, 1952.

conscience of the age; like a recurrent thunder-storm, he rumbles round the mid-Victorian horizon.

The political views of this Calvinist without a creed reflect the sensibility of a poet and the moral indignation of a Covenanter. Early influenced by Scott and Herder, he always saw politics and history in human and immediate terms. He felt the personal force of Cromwell and Frederick; the sense of place: the 'wild cattle roam in those ancient solitudes; the scanty sulky Norse-bred population all coerced into silence'.[22] Like Kierkegaard and Nietzsche and modern existentialists, he saw everything subjectively, through the bars of his rampant egotism; hence his frequent misjudgment of politics, in contrast with the objectiveness of his contemporary, de Tocqueville. He had won his reputation as a prophet, striking representative attitudes of denunciation and defiance in an uncertain world. His political doctrines are thus incidental to his morality. As Cassirer points out, 'he never tried to give more than a life-philosophy and he never meant to separate this philosophy from his personal experience'.[23] Here is no historical system as attempted by Hegel, rather a series of flashing intuitions.

This moral insight and fervour explains the cult of secular heroes, a modern elect. 'Great Men are the inspired (speaking and acting) Texts of the Divine Book of Revelations, whereof a Chapter is completed from epoch to epoch, and by some named History.'[24] Such a gospel was moral and romantic. History and politics are determined by genius, the most vivid manifestation of life. Carlyle loathed the ordinary and the mean; Bentham's simple objectives are made to shrivel, as the mellow interests of pagan Antiquity had shrivelled before the blaze of St. Augustine's moral indignation: are 'mammon and machinery the means of converting human souls, as of spinning cotton?'[25] Hence his detestation of the Industrial Revolution. Like Marx, he believed it was destroying all human values. In one of his best-known passages, he writes, 'Is it a green flowery world, with azure everlasting sky stretched over it, the work and government of a God; or a murky, simmering Tophet, of copperas fumes, cotton-fuzz, gin riot . . . created by a Demon, governed by a Demon . . .' with no escape save into 'liquid Madness sold at ten-pence a quartern?'[26] The passage was to be quoted by Engels in his first book.[27] To such a pass he believed great industry and laissez-faire had come. 'Specific mutual division of the spoil in a world left well alone . . . what a black, Godless, waste-struggling world in this once merry England of ours.'[28] This state of affairs obsessed him; for decades he reiterated the problem — 'how to deal with the Actual Labouring Millions of England'.[29]

Malthus roused his particular detestation; the blind cruelty of unemployment his fury. A good Scot, he quotes Burns on a poor man seeking work, 'that he might but be put on a level with the four-footed workers of the Planet'.[30] Yet in spite of this radicalism, Carlyle had no sympathy with liberal reform. He reserves his most splenetic phrases for liberal democracy; 'Divine commandment *to vote* ("Manhood Suffrage" — Horsehood, Doghood ditto, not yet treated of)!'[31] He had no doubts about the tide of democracy, which de Tocqueville and J. S. Mill accepted as inevitable and endeavoured to canalize. It was heading for disaster: '*Democracy* to complete itself;' he wrote, 'to go the full length of its course, towards the Bottomless or into it, no power now extant to prevent it or even considerably retard it . . . Complete "liberty" to all persons; Count of Heads to be the Divine Court of Appeal on every question and interest of mankind.'[32] His views on Rousseau were ferocious: '. . . and now has not Jean-Jacques promulgated the new evangel of a Contrat Social; explaining the whole mystery of government . . . to universal satisfaction? Theories of Government! Such have been, and will be; in ages of decadence'.[33] All such theory fades before the actual and mysterious course of events, for men are not automata nor is soul 'synonymous with stomach'. Personality determines history. Carlyle's native individualism had been enriched by the aristocratic humanity of the admired Goethe. This European genius, with his many-sided sensibility and range, had thought politics of secondary importance to the adventures of the spirit. Carlyle's sense of Election had been reinforced by this Olympian attitude; the Scots desire for theocracy merged with the German belief in the superior man. '"The equality of man"', he exclaims, 'any man equal to any other; Quashee Nigger to Socrates or Shakspeare; Judas Iscariot to Jesus Christ; and Bedlam-Gehenna equal to the New Jerusalem . . . poor mankind!'[34]

Society, he believed, like de Maistre and Coleridge, must be inspired not by calculation but by common beliefs. Aristocracy and priesthood should be in genuine and effective relation to the mass. Yet there could be no salvation in outworn dogmas or a sentimental return to the past: still less in liberal 'reform'. Like Comte, he was groping for a new myth. What he termed 'the calling in of new supplies of blockheadom, gullibility, bribeability, amenability to beer and balderdash', was merely the expedient of 'traitorous politicians grasping at votes'. The task was something far higher: 'to embody the Divine Spirit of that Religion in a new Mythus'.[35] 'Thought Heroes' must revive religion, reinterpreted for their age; and 'Industrial Heroes' must recivilize the material world. 'One way or other,' he insists, like de Maistre, 'the world will absolutely need to be governed.'[36] Such Heroes, an aristocracy of talent who 'draw their patent of nobility direct from God', will command loyalty by something far stronger than cash nexus, and govern through the only natural bonds of society. Of course they will meet hatred and misunderstanding; all superior talent is hated by the mob, and when, he asks 'was a God found agreeable to everybody?' 'The regular way is to hang, kill, crucify your gods and execrate and trample them under your stupid hoofs for a century or two till you discover that they are gods and then take to braying over them, still in a very long-eared manner!'[37]

In this predicament, Carlyle, like Luther, sought salvation in works — another secret of his influence on his age. Following Kant, he grounded everything on Duty. So, whatever his doubts, a man will discover his 'America is here or nowhere'. 'Be no longer a chaos but a world,' he writes, 'whatever thy hand findeth to do, do it with thy whole might. Work while it is called Today, for the Night cometh; wherein no man can work.'[38]

History is thus a Miltonic conflict between creative genius and the idiocy of the mob. Carlyle's haunting sense of the depths that lurk beneath the veneer of civility and his flair for moral indignation makes his message vibrant.* Through the cloudy or clotted rhetoric even of his more unreadable pages, this feeling for mystery flashes through. His ironic pity for the world is comparable to de Maistre's dark sense of tragedy and sin, but, unlike de Maistre, he is a provincial with no refuge. He was convinced that the Creeds must be restated by new prophets. The nature of this restatement he never defined.

A hatred of materialism which followed from his poetic insight and cult of personality, thus drove him to denounce the two major impulses of his time — the French and Industrial revolutions. He felt, as Ruskin was to feel, 'that the career of cheap and nasty' was morally pernicious. He poured out his wrath and scorn on what he held to be the destruction of standards by the new democracy and upon the horrors of the new industrial cities. In reaction to this dis-

* It has been observed that the descendant of Lowland peasantry has affinities with another proletarian genius, D. H. Lawrence.

belief in the people, he was driven to assert some very curious opinions. Already in *Past and Present* he can speak of 'noble loyalty in return for noble guidance — not as a bewildered bewildering mob; but as a firm regimented mass, with real captains over them . . .'[39] In the later *Shooting Niagara*, he comes near to a rough blue print of Fascism. In spite of Professor Willey's and Cassirer's arguments, one cannot deny that his admiration for drill sergeants and desire to put the whole population at their disposal, under discipline and conscription, are clearly and violently expressed. Nor is his attitude to colonial enterprise favourable to coloured populations. It is upon the colour question that he voices his most virulent opinions. He declared that the negroes for whose emancipation the American Civil War was ostensibly fought — in fact it was fought to preserve the Union — were not worth the bloodshed: 'they were three million absurd Blacks'.

For all these proto-Fascist leanings, Carlyle's ideal was too individualist, too much of his century, too romantic, to be closely relevant to the mob ideologies of our own time. Like Nietzsche, he would never have admired the average man magnified, or as Willey remarks, 'mistaken Hitler for a Cromwell, any more than Plato would have mistaken him for a Philosopher-king'.[40] Carlyle could rate Shakespeare — 'clear, all-piercing like sunlight, lovingly melodious' — as more important than the Indian Empire. 'He is the grandest thing we have yet done . . . Indian Empire will go, at any rate some day: but this Shakspeare will not go.' Here is hardly the voice of rampant imperialism. For the heart of his creed was the cult of genius. With Nietzsche, he desired a new Myth and a new élite. So he blasted the ordinary routine of life into triviality in the Old Testament Scots-Hebraic style. The natural leaders and benefactors of mankind were easy to recognize. And, indeed, there is truth in such a view. Who cares now for Metternich compared with Beethoven, Palmerston compared with Darwin? It is not the politicians and planners who fundamentally enrich life. And for the rest, for the men of talent and good will, there was always work to be done. It was a gospel well suited to an age so rich in talent — a congenial doctrine to the struggling young agnostics of the time. Hence Carlyle's influence. His political limitations are obvious: he had little sense of the politically possible. Further, as in Nietzsche, there is an element of the pathological in this acrid self-centred indignation — in the incessant girding at the limitations of mankind. Yet this prophetic impulse was pervasive. Agonizingly aware of the

finer shades of personality and the cosmic background to life, he had
the sense of mystery of a great artist. All was grounded on the old
Calvinist tradition combined with the new Germanic doubt and
violence of the Romantic age. Carlyle lived on until 1881, so that
he seems to belong to the mid-nineteenth century. But, like Mazzini,
his gospel was formed in his youth and he never altered it. He
remains the radical but reactionary prophet of Scots Old Testament
morality and German introspection.

CHAPTER IV

SAINT-SIMON: TOTALITARIAN AND TECHNOCRAT

THE two most original aspects of early-nineteenth-century political thought have been surveyed and the conservative reaction indicated. The romantic cult of historically developing will, originally derived from Rousseau, had been dramatically enriched by German philosophers. This idea of will was elaborated, and often paganized, in the later nineteenth century.

The second original aspect of the time, the new professional competence, was to come to fuller achievement in the 'sixties and 'seventies. Disregarding speculations which he held to be meaningless, Bentham had been inspired with a new passion for improvement; his influence on the reform of institutions was to be world wide.

Against this background of metaphysical and Utilitarian thought and of the conservative reaction against it, a much more revolutionary approach was now being made. If the dominant political fact of the time had been the French Revolution and its consequences, the over-riding economic fact was the development of new industrial techniques. Hitherto no political theory had fully taken account of them. Adam Smith and his followers had attempted to explain the working of economic laws, and Bentham to adjust political institutions to them, but no one had advocated a way to bring the process under fuller control and even enhance the new possibilities of production. Smith and Bentham had demanded the release of economic forces, but they had insisted that the economic process should take care of itself. It remained for a French aristocrat to make a new approach and to advocate a total economic transformation of society. His ideas were further elaborated by Comte. Both were authoritarian revolutionaries. The other aspect of revolution was communitarian and anarchist. It was expressed in the writings of Godwin, Fourier and Owen. None of these thinkers won immediate power. Often their ideas were so wild as to be ludicrous. But they were original: their influence was cumulative and insidious; and it still persists. They raised questions often now more topical than in their own day. It will be worth according their eccentric writings more attention than at first sight may seem justified.

Saint-Simon was original in combining the two characteristic strains in early-nineteenth-century thought. On the one hand, like Kant and Hegel, he faced the problem of contemporary religion, and evolved a cult of Humanity which was further elaborated by Comte. On the other, like the Utilitarians, he faced, and faced far more radically, the crisis of the Industrial Revolution. An eccentric character in his day, Saint-Simon is in retrospect a central figure of the early nineteenth century. In his confused and voluminous writings many streams of thought combine, and from them many derive. Here is a European humanism, a new historical sense, a new conception of the social function of technology, and a crusade against poverty and war. If Saint-Simon often shot wide of the mark, he was shooting at the right targets. His influence on subsequent political thought was eventually to be profound. He cannot be regarded, like Godwin, Babeuf, Fourier, and the other revolutionaries, as merely Utopian. His ideas must be set in a wider context. These ideas and those of Comte are worth careful examination. In a subsequent chapter the pedigree of the more left-wing socialism will also be examined, as a background to the federal anarchy of Proudhon and the state socialism of Marx and Engels, later to be considered.

Claude Henri de Rouvroy, Comte de Saint-Simon, is one of the pioneers of the early nineteenth century. The large body of his works, and the confused and turgid manifestoes of his followers, present a deterrent aspect to the historian, but his originality and his influence are incontestable. Born of an historic family that claimed descent from Charlemagne through the Counts of Vermandois, Saint-Simon was an aristocrat with an overmastering idea.* In the

* Claude Henri de Rouvroy, Comte de Saint-Simon, 1760-1825, was the great-nephew of Louis de Rouvroi, Duc de Saint-Simon, 1675-1755, author of the famous *Memoirs of the Regency*, whose honours and fortune he would have inherited but for his father's quarrel with the Duc. He early displayed an independent temper; at thirteen he refused to attend his first communion, so that his father took the drastic step of having him put in prison. But the spirited boy overpowered his gaoler and escaped. Later, when bitten by a mad dog, he immediately procured a pistol with which to commit suicide at the first onset of hydrophobia. He was early influenced by D'Alembert and the Encyclopedists, whose effect was lasting. In the American war, he reached the rank of Colonel. He was stunned by a cannon ball when Rodney captured the *Ville de Paris*, and narrowly escaped being thrown overboard for dead. He tried to persuade the Mexican government to cut a canal between the Carribean and the Pacific, and the Spanish government to construct one from Madrid to the sea via the Guadalquivir. After these adventures, and a dissipated youth, he was able to cope with the French Revolution. He at once renounced his titles, but, says his Victorian biographer, A. J. BOOTH, *Saint-Simon and Saint-Simonism*. London, 1871 (q.v. for a lucid and entertaining account), 'If in public he affected to despise the advantages of birth, he was careful to secure those of wealth.' In collaboration with Baron von Redern, a Prussian Ambassador to England, he purchased the whole of the Church lands in the Department of Orne and big properties in Paris. When Robespierre had Saint-

course of his often tragic life, he sacrificed everything for this over-mastering aim. He was always confident of his own genius, and spent the last francs of the pittance allowed him by his family upon printing his works. Starting life with brilliant prospects, he fought with distinction in the war of American independence, made and lost a fortune, and then devoted himself to the exposition of his confused and eloquent ideas. But throughout the wide range of his writings, from the first anonymous *Lettres d'un Habitant de Genève* to the repetitive pages of the *Nouveau Christianisme*, written in the year of his death, there run two dominant themes. They are the overwhelming social importance of applied science, and the need to create a civilization of the masses. When devising the fantastic organization of the Council of Newton, or advocating, in 1814, a Parliamentary union between England and France, or in conducting his own life, Saint-Simon may appear insane: in analysing current politics and stressing the need for appropriate beliefs in society according to its changing historical development, for expert leader-

Simon imprisoned for eleven months, the Baron escaped and later bought out Saint-Simon's interest for an inadequate sum. Saint-Simon then turned to the study of mathematical physics and the common man. His first book, *Lettres d'un Habitant de Genève*, was published in 1803, when Saint-Simon was well over forty. He was now impoverished and forced to accept an appointment at the Municipal pawnshop. From this slavery he was rescued by Diard, a former valet. In 1807-8 he wrote his first major work, *Introduction aux Travaux Scientifiques du 19e siècle* (2 vols.). On the death of Diard, Saint-Simon secured a small allowance from his family and a sub-librarianship at the Bibliothèque de l'Arsenal which he held till 1813. In that year he wrote his *Mémoire sur la Science de l'Homme* of which he made sixty manuscript copies; these he distributed to eminent persons with an appeal for their support. In 1814 appeared his next published work, *De la Réorganisation de la Société Européenne*, which had some success. His subsequent writings were published by subscription, in which two industrialists took the lead. In 1816-18 appeared his *L'Industrie* in the periodical the *Producteur*; in 1819, *La Politique* and *l'Organisateur*, the last involving him in a prosecution. In 1821-22 he published his *Du Système Industriel* but again found himself in penury. He therefore attempted suicide, but without success. 'Is it possible,' he remarked to Comte, 'that a man can live with seven slugs in his brain?' In 1823-24 appeared the *Catéchisme des Industriels*, written in collaboration with Comte. In 1825, the year of his death, he wrote the *Nouveau Christianisme*.

Saint-Simon was a man of great personal charm and a brilliant conversationalist. His portrait shows a dandified figure with a handsome face, a sensitive mouth and fine eyes. The bibliography of Saint-Simon and the Saint-Simonians is baffling. The Paris edition in forty-seven volumes (1865-76) *Œuvres de Saint-Simon et d'Enfantin*, includes ten volumes of his works (vols. 15, 18-23, 37-40), but omits the *Introduction aux Travaux Scientifiques*. The *Œuvres Choisies de Saint-Simon* is more convenient. Brussels, 1859. There is a modern selection, edited by C. Bouglé. Paris, 1925. See also C. BOUGLÉ et E. HALÉVY, *Doctrine de Saint-Simon Exposition première année 1829*. Paris, 1924, which contains an admirable preface. There is also M. G. HUBBARD's *Saint-Simon, Sa vie et ses travaux*. Paris, 1857. A. J. BOOTH, op. cit., gives a detailed if rather unsympathetic account, and M. LEROY, *La Vie de Saint-Simon*, is worth consultation. See also E. DURKHEIM, *Le Socialisme*, ed. M. Mauss. Sir Alexander Gray, too, has an entertaining chapter on him in his *Socialist Tradition*. The best English selection and translation is by F. M. H. MARKHAM, with its admirable and comprehensive introduction, and its full account of Saint-Simon's followers, their doctrine and their subsequent influence. (Blackwell's Political Texts, 1952.)

ship and for the abolition, by modern techniques, of poverty and war, he appears a genius. From Saint-Simon, Comte took his most important ideas — a 'positive' sociology, an anthropocentric religion with a vast historical background, and the direction of an industrial society to a planned end. Saint-Simon was a founder of socialism, but he was too much of an eighteenth-century authoritarian to accept 'levelling' Natural Rights. Rather he is the pioneer technocrat. A forerunner of the cult of efficiency and control that was to colour the outlook of the bureaucracies of the nineteenth and twentieth centuries, and which was insidiously to turn many socialist champions of liberty to collectivism. Where Adam Smith and Bentham shared Saint-Simon's passion for 'improvement', they deny his collectivist and organic view of society. Laissez-faire was to Saint-Simon a doctrine both morally and psychologically pernicious. With Burke, de Maistre and Coleridge, he insists on social beliefs, loyalties and ceremonials. But he demands that they should be suited to their age. This gospel of historically necessary regeneration was to attract Mazzini, who owed much to him. He also differed profoundly from de Maistre in his deep and obsessive admiration for the promise of modern science. Where de Maistre looks back to St. Augustine and the Middle Ages, Coleridge to a traditional hierarchy and Carlyle to a new one, Saint-Simon looks forward to the technocratic enthusiasms of the Welfare State and in some sense to the historically conditional outlook of Marx. The admiration for material progress, characteristic both of Social Democracy and of Marxism — the dominant philosophies of the modern world — was eloquently and naively expressed by Saint-Simon's indefatigable pen.

Like most of his contemporaries, he was dominated by the aftermath of the French Revolution and Napoleonic Wars. All about him he saw symptoms of social collapse. Yet he was convinced that 'L'humanité n'est pas faite pour habiter des ruines'. Meanwhile the scientists, to whom he believed in the course of historical development the initiative should now pass, seemed unable to formulate a coherent world view. Descartes, he said, 'avait monarchisé la science, Newton l'a républicanisé, vous n'êtes pas . . . que des anarchistes'. Specialization, the bane of leadership, was already setting in. But Saint-Simon was convinced there could be no healthy civilization unless the scientific élites, from whom, with the expansion of knowledge, leadership must derive, could formulate and diffuse a commanding ethic which would reflect the new cosmology. Here is the first and most uncompromising affirmation of Saint-Simon's doctrine. Its importance and its originality is obvious in the context of its time.

The second is the demand that industry, the result of applied science, shall by-pass conventional politics and use its untrammelled and unprecedented power for the betterment of mankind. Above all, for the betterment of the masses — for the 'amelioration of the moral and physical existence of the most numerous and poorest class'. Saint-Simon had grasped and formulated the aspect of modern civilization which makes it profoundly different from any of its predecessors. His simple and vigorous mind understood a situation beyond the range of his more politically minded contemporaries. For within his limits he saw all things with the clarity of the obsessed. His outlook was not subtle: on the broad possibilities of betterment he had no misgivings. Brought up, like Bentham, in the rationalism of the eighteenth century, he was convinced of the reality of progress. Though he frequently claims divine inspiration, his outlook was irreligious and worldly. Quite feckless in his personal life, he was convinced that without solid material foundations there can be no spiritual and moral improvement. Hence his insistence on raising the standard of life of the whole people by science and administration. With a common sense which was to appeal to the deepest currents of nineteenth-century materialism, the ideas of this eighteenth-century aristocrat were to reach out beyond the Romantic Age and appeal to the confident administrators both of the Welfare State and modern totalitarian government. Such are the two overmastering ideas, coloured always by romantic historical relativism, which run through his works, though the development of his thought is superficially incoherent and contradictory. Within this framework his doctrine may be roughly divided into four phases. There is the first phase of wild romantic ideas and philosophical speculation, which ranges over the widest field and forms the most extraordinary aspect of his thought. This was followed, after the fall of Napoleon, by a brief concern with international affairs, represented by the project for the unification of Europe in 1814 and coinciding with the collaboration of the young Auguste Thierry, later the interpreter of Merovingian and Anglo-Saxon history. The third phase is marked by attention to industry and the possibilities of technocratic government; the last by concern with a new religion, expressed in the final *Nouveau Christianisme*. These divisions are, of course, arbitrary, they overlap, and the two main themes already mentioned run through them all; but in the confusion of Saint-Simon's works, and those of his followers, they provide the clue to his significance.

No study of Saint-Simon's ideas can be complete without attention to their sequel. On the one hand, the antics of Enfantin and the Saint-Simonian Church belong often to the realm of farce; on the other, the influence on Auguste Comte and his followers contributed to serious speculation.

The first of Saint-Simon's writings, *Lettres d'un Habitant de Genève*, has been given rather too much attention.[1] It was anonymous and absurd. Even the author had misgivings. He never referred to its existence and allowed his close friend, Olinde Rodrigues, to suppose his *Introduction à la Philosophie du XIXme Siècle* to be his first work. Yet the pamphlet is worth attention for its startling slogans and because it strikes a note that echoes in all the other complexities of Saint-Simon's thought, right through to the *Nouveau Christianisme*.

'Plus d'honneur pour les Alexandres, vive les Archimèdes!' he wrote. The phrase, with the slightly crazy atmosphere of the early Revolution, at once briskly states a dominant and original theme. Under the direction of the 'Archimèdes', 'tous les hommes travailleront'. The other popular side of technocracy is here also foreshadowed. It was a significant departure. Most political theorists before Saint-Simon had regarded leisure as a supreme good: the ideal had been the warrior, the landowner, the contemplative philosopher. Aristotle regards the lion as the king of beasts. For Saint-Simon it was the beaver. An eccentric aristocrat first held up this industrious animal for imitation. The ideal was later to be imposed upon the proletariat by middle-class intellectuals and administrators, though the natural affinities of the people are probably with more inconsequent creatures.*

The Letters centre on a crazy scheme for a world elite. It will be composed of twenty-one men of genius, paid for by opening a sub-

---

* To support his materialist psychology Saint-Simon was anxious to prove that the intelligence of animals is in proportion to the complexity of their physique. Now the physiologists had placed the monkey immediately after man, but Saint-Simon held the beaver to be above the monkey in the scale of mind. Fortunately he discovered a zoologist who assured him that the beaver was physiologically more complicated than the monkey. Scientists, he declared, had been misled into overestimating the latter by assuming that, since God made man in His image, the monkey came next nearest to the Divine Likeness. But 'l'organisation du Castor est supérieur aux singes'. The monkey has indeed means of prehension, but the beaver has 'the abduction muscle of the thumb ... which increases its sense of touch'. Moreover, it has more 'tubes' in its physiology. The monkey, indeed, 'shows vivacity in its conceptions', but, as Kipling was to observe of the *Bandar Log*, it is incapable of carrying them through. The Beaver was thus vindicated, to Saint-Simon's relief, for it is a social animal and eagerly engages in communal works. See *Mémoire sur la Science de l'Homme. Œuvres*, vol. 40, pp. 49-50.

scription before the tomb of Newton. The plan would increase the prestige and freedom of creative spirits upon whom progress depends. They would be free of Universities, who attempt, says Saint-Simon, first to suppress original thought and later to sterilize it. 'Quand on en a fait des academiciens, ils se sont presque toujours endormis dans leurs fauteuils': Richelieu, that despot, knew this and founded the French Academy. Italy is full of Universities but produces few men of genius. That is why England, which is free, boasts so many great thinkers. Men of genius of all countries are at present deprived of travel and tied to routine tasks. What a privilege for humanity to arrange that these natural leaders get their reward! Among civilized people one plants trees for the future. Among the Turks, on the other hand, one cuts them down. Men of genius should also be cultivated. And they should have contact with the masses. After all, they are worth looking after — they are rare enough! Contemplating the prospect of his Council of twenty-one, he thinks there will be vacancies.

After this spirited vindication of the claims of genius, Saint-Simon appeals to the men of learning, to the men of property, and to the masses. To the first, he remarks, they must provide leadership to conquer the inertia of mankind. 'Allons,' he says, to the mathematicians (of all people!) 'puisque vous êtes en tête, commencez'[2]— 'the sceptre of public opinion is in your hands'. Turning to the landowners, he adopts a more realistic tone. The intellectuals, he declares, have started the revolution. Since it is inevitable, the men of property had better control it. Make yourselves 'regulators', he says, yours is the real power. Turning to the masses, and speaking with careful simplicity, he points out that in England, where men of learning are numerous and free, the people live well; they can read and write and 'in that country the town and even the country workers eat meat every day'. In Russia, on the other hand, when a savant annoys the Emperor, he cuts off his nose and ears and sends him to Siberia. And there the peasants are as ignorant as horses: they are underfed, too, ill-clothed and beaten. Such are the consequences of neglecting men of genius.

As for the rich, hitherto, he admits, they have exploited the people. 'Force them', he says, 'to enlighten and instruct you, make them use their heads for you as you use your arms for them: do them the service of relieving their boredom.' Like Marxists after him, Saint-Simon endows experts with great prestige. They can foresee the future: 'le savant, mes amis, est un homme qui prévoit'. Those who understand the workings of society, who have the correct explanation, should be obeyed. And of course social questions can be explained — by physiology. This evocation of the prestige of science foreshadowed a dominant current of modern thought. There follows a naive appeal to the masses, who on Sundays, of course, enjoy the work of writers, sculptors and musicians. It is only fair that the artists should be suitably rewarded. Creative work, he explains, is exacting. Parks of 'Culture and Rest', and the cult of approved writers, in part reflect the idea.

This threefold appeal is followed by the voice of God Himself. The Deity appears to Saint-Simon in a vision, and gives detailed instructions for the new cult of Newton, with its temples and encircling laboratories, and declares that He intends to 'make the earth a paradise'.[3] Naturally, war will be abolished, but since Africans are bloody-minded and Asiatics idle, there must be European world domination. The Founder of the Religion (presumably Saint-Simon) will command the Armies of the Faithful and make a good beginning by driving the Turks from the continent. The vision ends with a picture of an industrious and peaceful world. A copy of the document was sent, with a covering letter, to the First Consul, who ignored it.

Such was the anonymous manifesto in which Saint-Simon launched his campaign. It is ridiculous but original; impracticable, but important. It presents already that mixture of genius and farce which was to mark all the work of this extraordinary being and of his disciples.

As Saint-Simon's writings develop they elaborate this outlook and provide evidence for its origin. The *Introduction aux Travaux Scientifiques* (1808), and the *Essai sur la Science de l'Homme* (1813) are particularly revealing. In the first the greatness of Descartes is affirmed, who 'in my view, replaced belief by reasoning and observation'. But Bacon was the greatest pioneer of practical humanism, for he applied scientific method to the betterment of the condition of man. Between them, these two great thinkers 'demolished the whole structure of the ancient temple of wisdom. They took the human intellect and fashioned it in a crucible'. This benificent work was carried on by Newton and by Locke. Saint-Simon's line of descent from the Encyclopedists is here plainly apparent.[4] But there remains vital work to be done; the formulation of a new religion compatible with Baconian science. 'The scientific opinions formulated by these philosophers should then be clothed in forms which will make them sacred, in order that they can be taught to the children of all classes and the illiterate, whatever their age.'[5]

This conviction is reiterated in the *Essai*.[6] 'Religion', he insists, 'for a man of the intelligence of Bacon is not anything but a general scientific theory. The purpose of a theory is to organize facts. . .' And Bacon, 'who was as great a man as he could be in thought, speech and action, considering the age in which he lived', would today be horrified at the little progress achieved in organizing politics and society. In the name of the famous philosopher, Saint-Simon appeals to the intellectual leaders of France to unite. At present even the *Institut de France* heads a 'precarious and mongrel' exis- tence: the abilities of the most eminent savants are at the mercy of courtiers and politicians. A revolt of the competent is necessary. The more so, since the power of governments must inevitably dimin- ish before the vast development of modern industry, a world wide revolution. This contrast is driven home by Saint-Simon's best- known utterance. Suppose, he writes, that France suddenly lost three thousand of her leading intellectuals, scientists, engineers, poets, painters, bankers and technicians, 'it would require at least a generation . . . to repair this misfortune'.[7] Let her lose in the same day 'Monsieur the king's brother, Monseigneur le Duc d'Angoulême', all the great courtiers and bishops, ten thousand of the greatest land- owners: the situation would be harrowing, but not desperate. Society would carry on. There would be no difficulty in filling the gaps. By this vivid example, Saint-Simon 'underlines the most important fact of modern politics' that the human race is still 'politically barbarous'. For, 'in every sphere, men of greater ability are subject to the control of those who are incapable'. The two major themes of Saint-Simon's gospel are thus steadily developed in his more general argument. He continually insists on the need for a popular religion based on science, on the sweeping aside of the old political order, and upon the control of modern society by experts and managers, in whom he had singular faith.

The second phase of Saint-Simon's thought was devoted to inter- national affairs. It is contained in his broad project for a European government. In the tradition of Sully, Saint-Pierre and Kant, he attempts a radical solution of this ancient problem. The work of the last century, he says, has been revolutionary; that of the nine- teenth ought to be one of organization. The fall of Napoleon pro- vides that opportunity.[8] The recent chaos had been due to the destruction of the framework of European society. But we need not

choose between barbarism and stupidity, for public opinion rules
the world. In the first book he therefore appeals through a survey
of history to the Parliaments of France and England. Before the
fifteenth century, he says, all Europe was part of a single political
organization. This order was wrecked by Luther, who destroyed
the prestige of the United Church, 'Depuis la Traité de Westphalie
la guerre a été l'état de l'Europe.' From that time dates the world of
power politics and standing armies. From this disorder England has
benefited and now aims at world domination; 'free and happy within,
she is hard and tyrannous without'. Yet without England, Europe
will never be united. This cannot be done suddenly, but together
France and England could dominate Europe.[9] The Congress now
assembled at Vienna will be useless, for it is composed of representatives of sovereign states, concerned only to further their national
interests. Multiply these Congresses, they can only lead to war.
The statesmen, he says, are caught in a system they cannot change:
'There is a routine in politics from which no one dares to break away,
although experience has long warned us that the method must be
changed . . . So the massacres continue and no one knows when they
will end.'[10] Like Sir Thomas More in a different context,[11] Saint-Simon
draws a vivid and salutary picture of the manœuvres of sovereign
governments. Austria, he says, will insist on the domination of
Italy, on keeping Galicia and the Illyrian provinces, on the control
of Germany. Sweden, 'map in hand', will say it is 'natural' she
should rule Norway; France will claim the Rhine and the Alps;
England will declare that she is charged by nature to rule the seas.
There can be no such thing as a balance of power. 'L'équilibre des
puissances est la combinaison la plus fausse qui puisse être faite.'

The evil has been evident before. Henri IV and Sully and the
Abbé de Saint-Pierre attempted to face it. Saint-Simon examines
the Abbé's scheme. It is inadequate, since it is inorganic, being simply
an alliance of princes, which perpetuates the abuse of power. A
real European government should be organic and homogeneous,
independent of national authorities, occupied with general European interests and based on a European public opinion. Such a
project, he maintains, is not visionary, since the medieval church
reflected these conditions. A similar system is needed, adapted to
modern circumstances. There must be a European government.
National Parliaments must 'recognize the supremacy of a general
parliament, superior to all national Governments and armed with
power to judge their differences'.[12] Such an administration can only

be effective if it expresses a common will, but as Montesquieu pointed out, 'c'est l'institution qui forme les hommes'. First create a European parliament, and a new outlook will emerge. Saint-Simon has no doubt in this now topical question.

European order must be based on constitutional government. It already exists successfully in England. A Lower House of Parliament should be chosen, not from politicians, but from men eminent in the Arts and Sciences, in Law and business. Each million of the sixty million literate persons in Europe are to elect a scholar, a business man, an administrator and a magistrate. They are to possess a high property qualification and hold office for ten years. For a few brilliant professional men without property a large salary will be provided. There will also be a House of Peers, nominated by the King and hereditary, supplemented by twenty ennobled intellectuals and disposing of large annual revenues. The Head, or King, of Europe — Roi du Parlement Européen — will initiate the whole scheme. So nice is the choice that Saint-Simon, with becoming modesty, reserves his recommendation.

This European parliament will have sovereignty over a town and its surrounding territory, and will impose necessary taxation. It will occupy the minds of the European peoples in constant projects of great international works: for example, it will join the Danube to the Rhine by canal and the Rhine to the Baltic. It will have complete control of European education and it will draw up a basic moral code to which all must subscribe. Beyond this, it will allow complete toleration. Here, at last, will be the basis of an organic European Society.

It can be brought about only by an Anglo-French union, the focus of a peaceful and expanding Federation. Both countries are menaced by revolution, both have common interests. England need then no longer practice a Machiavellian egotism, which by cold calculation foments new wars in Europe; she will no longer need to commit crimes or face bankruptcy. She can be saved by union with France.

Saint-Simon was equally hopeful about Germany. The Germans have hitherto been regarded as 'les vulgaires des nations de l'Europe'; in fact they are full of good will. And they, too, are heading for revolution. Here is half the population of the continent — a people of 'noble and genuine character'. Organized under a Liberal government, what a part they might play! It is essential, he concludes, to unite the Germans into a single state. Finally, Saint-Simon admits that his plan may have immediate weaknesses, but insists that, in principle, it is the only way to secure peace. He rightly emphasises the need to break the old political routine, which hypnotizes both peoples and statesmen, that the problem must be treated from a European aspect. He declares that in time the European peoples will insist in the regulation of 'points of general interest'. 'The imagination of poets has placed the Golden Age in the cradle of the human race, in the ignorance and grossness of primitive times': on the contrary, 'the Golden Age of the human race is not behind but before us'. Then, at last, the social order will be perfected. Our ancestors have not seen it, but one day our children will achieve the goal. It is for us to point out the road.

Such was Saint-Simon's contribution to the problem of European and world peace. Wild as it may seem, today it is extraordinarily topical. Here are the usual elements of penetrating vision and fantasy. Saint-Simon had grasped and driven home the need for a supra-national order, for a European constitutional government concerned with practical projects transcending national interests, and for the creation of a European public opinion. He was a pioneer of the modern idea of European union. His disciple, Comte, was to carry this programme on.

Having defined those fruitful and fundamental ideas on international affairs, Saint-Simon turned to problems of economics and known. Of the resulting works, his *Nouveau Christianisme* is the best religion. This short dialogue often displays the repetitive arguments of a failing mind. Its theme is the brotherhood of man; the need to adapt religion to new conditions, above all, to ameliorate the lives of the masses. Saint-Simon criticizes both Catholics and Protestants in turn, and insists that only on a basis of material betterment can moral and spiritual progress be achieved. A modern form of Christianity must abolish poverty and war.

The Catholics, he believes, have been the greatest heretics. They oppress the laity and are ignorant of technical progress. They only study theology. Consider the condition of the Papal states, at one time a flourishing territory, now a pestilential marsh. The clergy are blind to the possibilities of mass production and paralyse industrial enterprise. Turning to the shortcomings of the Protestants, he again concentrates his attack on Luther. It is true that Luther rendered a great service by exposing the abuses of the Catholic Church; but he also is a heretic; he missed his chance. He should have seen that true Christianity ought to make men happy not only in heaven but on earth.[13] By the sixteenth century material progress had far ad-

vanced beyond the conditions of Antiquity. It was no longer enough
to acquiesce in poverty. Today a new Christianity should organize
the whole world to conquer it. The Protestants missed their opportunity when they prosecuted religious wars. What an impious
spectacle to see the clergy of both belligerents singing Te Deums in
victory and invoking God in disaster! War, like poverty, must be
swept aside in a new crusade for a 'positive good', an intelligible
project for physical well being. We now know the dimensions of the
planet; we must make it the flourishing possession of the entire
human race. Thus the rich will remain secure and the poor will
improve their condition. Saint-Simon is no levelling Socialist, no
democrat, though he passionately desires to improve the condition
of the people. He insists on the leadership of technically competent
elites backed with an emotional appeal suited to the popular mind.
Luther, he wrote, had made religion prosaic; a vital religion should
harness poets, orators and artists into a commanding and attractive
cult. Further, it is absurd to set so much store by the Bible. The
main argument summed up in the formula reiterated throughout
with monotonous but effective insistence — 'Toute la société doit
travailler à l'amélioration de l'existence morale et physique de la
classe la plus pauvre; la société doit s'organiser de la manière la plus
convenable pour lui faire atteindre ce grand but.' This programme
must be propagated immediately, and since 'les forces intellectuelles
de l'homme sont très petites', it must be put over to the masses by
simple propaganda. Far from inciting the poor to violence, the project will unite the interests of elites and people and avoid revolution.
The interest of elites 'sont essentiellement lés mêmes que ceux de la
masse du peuple'. Intellectuals are workers; the natural leaders of
the people. But none of this progress will be possible unless the
synoptic vision of medieval Christendom can be restored and
transformed by scientific knowledge. The whole scheme is based on
the belief in progress which Saint-Simon had assimilated from the
philosophers of the eighteenth century, in particular from Condorcet.
A new scientific religion is 'the only social doctrine which is suitable
to Europeans in the present state of enlightenment and civilization'.[14]
Here is the revolutionary historicism of the Romantic age, which
asserts a new ideology and leadership in a new phase of history.
The outstandingly important science is now 'the science that constitutes society'. The dialogue concludes with an appeal to the
Princes of the Holy Alliance. 'You', he says, 'are the successors of
Caesar', of ruthless temporal power. 'You keep two million men

under arms, you tax to capacity. What are you doing for the poor?' 'Listen to the voice of God speaking through my mouth; turn to true Christianity again, leave your power politics and devote yourselves to the swiftest possible amelioration to the lot of the poor.' The dialogue ends with the formula which gives it unity and impact.

Here is the final manifesto of Saint-Simon's life. It has the usual combination of vision and impracticability and it defines the greatest questions of the day. How to provide leadership for the masses based on science, now inevitably the dominant ideology; how to restore creative leadership and abolish poverty and war; how to transform the environment of mankind by a drive for clear-cut practical objectives. The statement of such a programme was a great contribution to political thought. The fanaticism, the touch of madness in Saint-Simon's gospel, the repetition of a few dominant ideas, in time increased its influence. It was to be systematized, dehumanized and elaborated by Comte. At the end of his life the old prophet remarked 'Rappelez-vous que pour faire de grandes choses, il faut être passionné.' This simple and selfless devotion gives Saint-Simon his greatness.

II

The immediate sequel was less reputable. The attempt by his followers to found a Saint-Simonian Church forms an odd episode. They evolved a kind of Pantheism, a cult of Life. 'Dieu, c'est la vie conçue dans son universalité absolue, dans sa unité et sa multiplicité, sous toutes ses manifestations', wrote Eugène Rodrigues, brother of Olinde Rodrigues who subsidized Saint-Simon. The spirit of the universe was expressed in the phrase 'I am that I am, I am all that has ever been, and all that is to be.' The Saint-Simonians hoped to commune with it through love. Eugène, who died young, after 'une touchante histoire d'amour contrarié', was the most intelligent of the disciples — a student of St. Augustine and St. Thomas. He had found the neo-Catholicism of de Maistre and de Bonald retrograde, disfigured by a dualist distrust of life.

On a different level was the conduct of the able and forceful Enfantin, who constituted himself the supreme Father of the Saint-Simonian Church, attempted to discover a 'femme Messie', and became involved in a prosecution at the Cour d'Assises de la Seine in 1832. The account of this trial makes interesting reading, in the best tradition of French farce.* Enfantin and his companions were accused of offences against public morals. The jury consisted of small bourgeois, among them an oculist, a chemist, a goldsmith, a paper maker, and a 'marchand de nouveautés'. The Supreme Father's tactics at once embarrassed the President. 'Who are your Counsel?' he was asked. 'They are these two ladies.' 'Vous ne pouvez avoir pour conseils des personnes du sexe féminin . . . (étonnement chez tous les assistants).'[15] Was Enfantin, asked the President, the author of an article entitled 'De la Femme', published in the *Globe* of January 1832? Had he not described himself as 'La loi vivante'? Both the accusations were admitted. It was pointed out, however, that Enfantin was of respectable family and an old pupil of the École Polytechnique. His gospel was to reconcile the flesh to the spirit in a cult of Love: the Manichaean conflict must be transcended. Appetite and intellect 'must be reconciled, and the function of the new religion was to educate both'.

At this point the prosecuting council played a trump card, but suffered a tactical reverse. There was a sensitive woman, he said, among Enfantin's followers. She had been revolted by the practices of the Sect. Gentle and timid though she was, she had denounced them. Her name was Cécile Fournel, and 'here the tone of voice of the advocate took on an increasingly pathetic note'. The move failed, for the witness jumped up in Court and disowned not Enfantin but the lawyer. 'Mieux éclairé', she confessed, 'j'ai reconnu la réalité de ces doctrines.' Whereupon the President said tartly, 'if you interrupt again I'll have you put out of Court'. Subsequent revelations were very shocking to the jury. As the case progressed, some curious goings on came to light. The Saint-Simonian Church contained priests and priestesses, who 'far from mortifying the flesh, will educate it; they will know all the charms of decency and modesty, but above all the grace of abandon and delight'. In vain their Counsel protested that the doctrine exercised a restraining influence on the more radical liberals and socialists; that they had no desire to undermine bourgeois society; that they had contacts all over the world. Indeed, among the 'thoughtful population of Germany many enlightened men have approached us'. 'Nous sommes religieux,' they declared: 'nous aimons le juste milieu'

* See *Religion Saint-Simonien, Procès en la Cour d'Assises de la Seine, le 27 et 28 Août 1832.* Paris, 1832. 398 pages. It is prefaced by a revealing illustration of three romantic and Christlike figures, with noble foreheads, beards and commanding eyes, dressed in low-necked blouses and draped in what appear to be tunics. For details of the Saint-Simonian costume, see F. M. H. MARKHAM, op. cit., p. xxxvii.

(laughter in court). They were not, they insisted, a political party, but a movement for the moral betterment of society and the development of industry on a grand scale. They aimed at the peaceful and progressive emancipation of the workers. They even hoped gradually to transform the army, 'so that every regiment shall be a school of Arts and Technology and that every soldier shall come out of it a good workman'. And they advocated the immediate development of the railway from Paris to Marseilles.[16]

Neither these arguments, nor a further scene by Enfantin, convinced President or Jury. The former 'several times shook his head as a sign of impatience'; the latter pronounced the defendants guilty. Enfantin and his companions were sentenced to a year's imprisonment and a substantial fine. The Society was dissolved. After doing his time, the supreme Father left for Egypt with a few followers. These youthful aberrations did not prevent Enfantin later playing a notable role in the development of the French railways and of Algeria, to the contempt of Mazzini. As Markham points out, many Saint-Simonians played notable parts in the economic enterprises of the Second Empire. But the original movement, with its fantastic costumes and emotional extravagance, belongs to the world of the romantic 'thirties, to the Paris of Victor Hugo and Berlioz. The main line of descent became more austere. For political thought Comte's development of the ideas of Saint-Simon is more important. The ideas of this unattractive philosopher will now be examined.

CHAPTER V

COMTE'S SECULAR RELIGION

THE ideas so eloquently put about by Saint-Simon received a systematic, more powerful, but not less eccentric development at the hands of Auguste Comte.* Like Saint-Simon, he regarded himself as a Messiah, and faced poverty and persecution for his beliefs. He is often regarded as a founder of systematic sociology, but John Stuart Mill's verdict is more exact; he helped to make systematic sociology possible. His synthetic religion is a remarkable manifestation of the nineteenth-century cult of man. As a sociologist Comte belongs to the mid-century. Many of his ideas were rooted in the period of the Revolution and its immediate reaction. His precise religious notions were a humourless elaboration of the cult of the Supreme Being and of Public Festivals, bizarre aspects of the French Revolution. Further his early atheism and romantic cult of Man — and Woman — derived from that time. But Comte's historicism, his belief in sociological laws, his attempt to assimilate all knowledge into one scientific world-view, are more characteristic of the age of Marx and Spencer.

* Isidore Auguste Marie François Xavier Comte, 1798-1857, was born at Montpellier, fourth child of Louis Comte, an official in the local taxation office, who lost his appointment since he refused to condone the corruption of local politicians. Comte attended the École Polytechnique from 1814 to 1816, when he was expelled for indiscipline. In 1817 he became secretary to Saint-Simon, with whom he later quarrelled. For most of his life he earned a poor living as a tutor of mathematics, an occupation which may have encouraged his low estimate of the average intelligence of the human race. His *Cours de Philosophie Positive*, in six volumes, was published 1830-42. It was based on lectures delivered from 1826 to 1829. The lectures nearly cost Comte his life, for after the third one he broke down and jumped into the Seine. The *Système de Politique Positive* appeared 1851-54; the *Catéchisme Positiviste* was published in 1852. Following the break-up of his marriage in 1842 (Madame Comte, he complained, 'espéra toujours le transformer en machine académique') he met Clothilde de Vaux, 'a circumstance of a personal nature which it is impossible', says J. S. Mill 'not to notice'. She died in 1846 and the *Système* is dedicated to her memory. Comte quarrelled with his publisher and his disciples and in his later years partly depended on the support of English admirers.

There is an extensive Comtian literature. Contemporary studies include E. LITTRÉ, *Auguste Comte et la Philosophie Positive*. Paris, 1863; J. F. E. ROBINET, *Notice sur la Vie et L'Œuvre d'Auguste Comte*. Paris, 1860; J. S. MILL, *Auguste Comte and Positivism*. London, 1865; G. H. LEWES, *History of Philosophy from Thales to Comte*, vol. II. See also E. CAIRD, *The Social Philosophy of Comte*, 1885, a masterly exposition, and BASIL WILLEY, *Nineteenth-Century Studies*. London, 1948. Also H. GOUHIER, *La Vie d'Auguste Comte*. Paris, 1931, and his indispensable *La Jeunesse d'Auguste Comte et la Formation du Positivisme*, two volumes. Paris, 1933-36; E. SELLIÈRE, *Auguste Comte*. Paris, 1920; L. J. GUILMAIN, *La Sociologie d'Auguste Comte, ce qu'elle doit à la Biologie du début du XIXe siècle*. Alger, 1922; E. FAGUET, *Politiques et Moralistes du dix-neuvième Siècle*, vol. II. Paris, 1903, one of Faguet's most brilliant studies; G. DUMAS, *La Psychologie de deux Messies positivistes*, 1905, and LÉVY-BRUHL, *La Philosophie d'Auguste Comte*.

Like Saint-Simon and Proudhon, Comte was a voluminous writer, and his extensive works are unredeemed by distinction of style. His earliest writings can be crisp and clear, but his larger works are more repetitive. The reader who desires to investigate them will be wise to concentrate on the early and originally unsigned *Plan of the Scientific Operations necessary for the Regeneration of Society*, written in 1822, while he was still collaborating with Saint-Simon;* upon the second volume of Harriet Martineau's condensed translation of the *Course of Positive Philosophy*, and upon the 'General View of Positivism,' contained in the first volume of the *System of Positive Polity*.[1] Most of Comte's doctrines are succinctly expressed in the first work. Apart from the convincing internal evidence of the debt of the disciple to the master, and in spite of Comte's characteristic repudiation of it, there can be little doubt that the Comtian gospel is a systematized extension of Saint-Simonian ideas.† But Comte far surpassed his predecessor in organizing ability. This genius from the Midi had a powerful intellect and no sense of humour. During his maturity he practised what he termed 'cerebral hygiene', and refused to read the writings of his contemporaries, an expedient for which something may be said. He concentrated instead on Homer and Dante. His work, therefore, reflects a rather crazy lucidity and an uncompromising dogmatism. This intellectual arrogance and isolation is at once his weakness and his strength: while it sometimes led him into ludicrous eccentricity and rendered him singularly unaware of the realities of current political power, it enabled him to face the starkest problems of the nineteenth century without a qualm, and to answer them with a staggering confidence. The anthropocentric bias of Comte's mind, his systematizing power and imaginative relation of history to biology, gave his ideas an apparently scientific and formidable content. To intelligent contemporaries the gospel of the *Plan* and of the *Cours de Philosophie Positive* must have appeared something to be reckoned with.

For all his eccentricities, his influence has been profound. He was one of the first writers fully to apply a crude sociological method to the study of society; to relate politics to total environment in time and space; to mathematics, physics and biology. He attempted a complete picture of the evolution of social life through the three great

* See *System of Positive Polity*, vol. IV, appendix III, pp. 527–89. See also the *Producteur*, 1825, on 'Les Sciences et les Savants', and on 'La Pouvoir Spirituelle'.

† See J. B. BURY, *The Idea of Progress*, p. 291. 'The fundamental idea of *positive* philosophy had been apprehended by Saint-Simon long before he was acquainted with his youthful associate.'

stages he elaborately and arbitrarily distinguished.* He summed up, as Mill and Caird point out, an old empirical tradition, which he related to the broad new vista of environmental studies. Later sociologists had far more data than were ever at Comte's disposal, and the ambitious total explanation he devised was to be discarded by a more practical and scientific discipline. But he marks a turning point. Spinoza, Vico, and Montesquieu in their respective spheres, had approached a sociological outlook; Vico, in particular, swept the whole field of history with his curious vision, attempting to trace the evolution of the human spirit from within. More directly, de Brosses, Turgot and Condorcet had foreshadowed Comte's approach. The first's *Du Culte des Dieux Fétiches* had appeared in 1760; the second's *Discours sur le Progrès Successif de l'Esprit Humain* (1764) had sketched the major divisions of history in a manner rather similar to Comte's, and anticipated his theory of the accumulation of knowledge; the third had published *Esquisse d'un Tableau des Progrès de l'Esprit Humain* in the same year. Hegel had also approached political theory with a world-ranging view and seen the past in clearly defined stages of development, but his metaphysical assumptions were not remotely scientific. In Comte, for all the limitations of his technique, there is something new. The beginning of an alliance between political thought and a range of sociology impossible before the nineteenth century. The systematic emphasis on environment, and the interpretation of the eighteenth-century idea of progress as based on command of it, characterized an age of expanding technical efficiency. Comte's interpretation tends to be angular and arbitrary. The exclusion of aesthetic and religious experience; the assumption that the accumulation of 'facts' in the light of scientific laws is somehow more 'real' than direct intuition, the impoverishment of total experience, all are marks of mid-nineteenth-century science. There is a confusion, too, of individual and social psychology. But the division of history into theological, metaphysical and positive phases has proved singularly fruitful. Comte's sociology remains a landmark of nineteenth-century thought. Hence the surprising influence this eccentric could command, the respect his earlier work inspired in writers so fastidious as Lecky and J. S. Mill, the influence on

---

* These divisions have no scientific basis. As T. H. Huxley remarked in a letter to Charles Kingsley, 'You are perfectly right in saying that Comte knew nothing about physical science . . . the law of the three states is mainly evolved from his own consciousness.' Comte's Grand Être he thought 'as big a fetish as ever nigger first made and afterwards worshipped'. T. H. HUXLEY, *Life and Letters*, edited Leonard Huxley, vol. I, pp. 434-5. (Eversley edition.)

English writers of his time — George Eliot and John Morley; the interest his often repellent writings possess today.[2] While his works are vast and generally arid, they are not confused. His writings may often seem a desert, but they are not, like Proudhon's, a welter. All is systematized, all madly coherent. If in doubt, the reader can always turn to the extraordinary charts which explain the text.

The doctrine may be examined under four aspects. First, there is the Positivist cult of man. Comte boldly asserts an anthropocentric outlook. 'The moral grandeur of man', he wrote, 'when freed from the chimeras that oppress him, was foreseen by Goethe and still more clearly by Byron.'[3] Since, following the conclusions of Hume and Kant, there can be no direct knowledge of reality, only of phenomena, real understanding can be attained only by a cult of the human spirit. Since life manifests itself most intensely in man's own mind and in the accumulated knowledge of the race, it is time to brush aside all theological and metaphysical explanations of the universe, and to concentrate on the study of facts. The old ideas of natural law, revelation, and the rest, are no longer meaningful. They are irrelevant assertions.

This attitude reflects the ultimate defeat of romanticism. It is the logical end of the Wordsworthian cult of nature, or the Byronic cult of sardonic hedonism. Comte, a philistine of genius, a dry mathematical analyst, was devoid of all but the crudest sensibility, and devoid of tact. He rushed in; he computed; he spoke. 'At the age of fourteen', he writes, 'I had naturally ceased to believe in God.'[4] 'Petit montpelliéran au sang vif', he had been expelled from the École Polytechnique for insubordination. He quarrelled bitterly with Saint-Simon, to whom he owed so much; he was at odds with his wife whom he treated abominably; at odds with his disciples. There was no one, he declared, fit to succeed him as High Priest of Humanity. 'I am not yet able to find a successor, nor even a colleague.'[5] But with monomaniac self-confidence he worked on. He died in the full spate of production, his vast projected works unfinished — his dying words, 'quelle perte irréparable!'

Yet, as Professor Willey remarks, Comte was a figure central to the nineteenth century. With his cold, precise reason, he faced the situation of his age. This 'positivist' outlook was not one of despair. If man cannot fathom the mysteries of the universe, he can master his environment and perfect himself. Let us face, says this ruthless prophet, the bleakness of the modern world: admit that religion and philosophy are projections of the mind, and set about the betterment of man's condition. If Comte's tactics were crazy, his strategy may have been correct. 'Compassion,' it has been well remarked, 'armed with scientific knowledge, may yet inaugurate the new Utopia.'⁶

He was, he believed, in command of the situation. 'The destination of society now come to maturity is neither to inhabit for ever the old and miserable hut which its infancy erected, as kings suppose, nor to live eternally without shelter after having left it, as the people imagined.' Its destiny is rather this, that aided by acquired experience, it should with all the accumulated materials, construct an edifice fitted for its needs . . .'⁸ And again, 'The primary object, then, of positivism is two-fold, to generalize our scientific conceptions and to systematize the art of life.' This art will be based on the unification of all knowledge. 'The science of society, besides being more important than any other, supplies the only logical and scientific link by which all our observations of phenomena can be brought into one consistent whole . . . the establishing of this great principle is the most important result of my system of Positivist Philosophy.' Comte desired to be the Aquinas of the nineteenth century. Such is the second, 'scientific' aspect of Comte's doctrine. Man and society are to be regulated according to sociological law.

The third aspect of Comte is political, technocratic and authoritarian. Following the precise and systematizing quality of his mind, he was no revolutionary; and being devoid of much sense of political reality, of human motives and the shifting preponderance of interest over opinion, his view of society was static. There was to be little freedom, which man, in any case, cannot endure.* 'Following M. Comte's frenzy for regulation,' writes J. S. Mill, 'liberty and spontaneity on the part of individuals form no part of his scheme.'⁹ He was not very interested in political power: he believed that moral feeling and public conscience were the ultimate sanctions. 'Political power will fall into the hands of the great leaders of industry . . . Unworthy as they seem at present, they will gradually become less so as spiritual regeneration proceeds.' Meanwhile, he desired a popular dictatorship, combined with freedom of discussion, and 'the diffusion of positivism' by an 'occidental committee'. For Comte was a good European, and projected and caricatured the programme of European Union of the mid-twentieth century. His goal was nothing less than a positivist world order. The abuse of political and industrial power would be controlled by the combined moral force

* For an admirable treatment of this theme see ERICH FROMM, *The Fear of Freedom*. Routledge & Kegan Paul, 1942.

of a priesthood of humanity, who would renounce political and economic authority; by the pervasive influence of women, to whom all education up to fourteen was to be confided, and by the public opinion of the working classes, of whom Comte had a high opinion. The whole structure depends on a quasi-religious foundation. For Comte devised a synthetic religion, worked out in grotesque and elaborate detail. It is the sanction of the entire plan. Here, again, is courage and insensibility. No one who understood the nature of religious experience would have the audacity to devise such a plan. Such manifestations must be traditional and spontaneous. While a Guy Fawkes's day can quite naturally be added to the year as the sequel to a memorable event, the design to impose an artificial and elaborate calendar is bound to meet with little success. This typically intellectualist construction, while it provides material for entertainment, has little relevance to the mysterious tides of popular belief. Here Marx and Sorel, to say nothing of the Catholic Church, make Comte's scheme puerile.

Yet, in one principle he was right. A vigorous society demands its myth; if the old religion is to be abandoned, a new one must take its place. If theology and metaphysics give way to positivism, the sheep cannot be permanently abandoned. If they are, blind guides will lead them to perdition, as the twentieth century was to witness. In the event, Comte's cult of humanity, of brotherhood and compassion, could not stand for a moment before the dark appeal of Marxist determinism and hatred, the attractions of militant nationalism, or even the temptations of commercial greed. Comte, a Christian might observe, had forgotten original sin.

Such are the four main features of the positivist creed: the cult of man, the belief in science, in authoritarian government and in a new religion. A survey of the more important aspects of his writings will reinforce this view. As Caird points out, the whole doctrine is consistent in principle and must be taken together. J. S. Mill, for example, shocked at emotional extravagance, could accept the earlier but reject the later writings.* He was certainly misguided. Given the original repudiation of religion, the cult of humanity was the inevitable sequel. That Comte's conception of it was grotesque does not make a more sophisticated version unthinkable. To reconcile intellect and emotion; to relate philosophy to history and politics,

* 'Others may laugh, but we could far rather weep at the melancholy decadence of a great intellect.' J. S. MILL, op. cit., p. 199. This new emotion was due to the crisis suffered by Comte following his meeting with Clothilde de Vaux. Compare Mill's attachment to Mrs. Taylor.

to design a pattern for social life based upon the latest psychology —
on the manipulation, perhaps, of the chemistry of the body — it is
a theme as old as the *Laws* of Plato and as new as the nightmare of
Brave New World. His doctrine centred on the idea of Humanity,
a 'Great Being', whose existence contains the past and future of the
race and its accumulated achievements. 'The very conception of
Humanity', he writes, 'is a condensation of the whole mental and
social history of man . . . It implies the irrevocable extinction of
theology and war.'[10] 'Get rid of Providence', he says, like Saint-Simon,
'take hold of things'. Influenced by Lamarck, who maintained that
acquired characteristics are inherited, Comte believed that biology,
in particular the study of the brain, could be the basis of this confident control. 'The grand object of human existence is the constant
improvement of the natural order that surrounds us; of our material
condition.' This will be the foundation for spiritual experience.
Control of environment will be based not only on biology and
psychological studies, but on a new understanding of history, on the
accumulated knowledge which distinguishes mankind from the
animals. For humanity alone can capitalize its efforts. As the illusion
of God fades, the Great Being takes its place. No abstraction, but a
human achievement. The Great Being has duration in time; all manifestations of human life are part of it. Behind that Being is inscrutable
will. As his mind matured, Comte became an agnostic rather than an
atheist; for atheism, he argues, is merely the reverse of the theological assertions of the primitive phase of history, equally without
meaning.

Within these limits, sociology can now proceed according to
known laws. 'Now that history has been, for the first time, systematically considered as a whole, and has been found, like other phenomena, subject to invariable laws,' Comte writes, with sublime
confidence, 'the preparatory labours of modern science are ended.'*
These 'invariable laws' are described in the *Course of Positive
Philosophy*, which interprets the whole of history in these terms.†

* Compare Marx's similar nineteenth-century confidence in total 'scientific' explanation.
† *Cours de Philosophie Positive* (second edition), 6 vols. Paris, 1864. Vol. I, *Les Préliminaires Généraux et la Philosophie Mathématique* (18 lectures), contains (chaps. 1 and 2) the
general objective and plan of the course and a chart (pp. 7-88). The remaining lectures
are on mathematical subjects. Vol. II (lectures 19-34), *Philosophie astronomique et la Philosophie de la Physique*, deals with astronomy, optics and electricity. Vol. III (lectures 35-45),
Philosophie Chimique et Philosophie Biologique, contains an interesting lecture on animal life
(p. 483ff) and a 'Final consideration on the positive study of the moral and intellectual or
cerebral functions.' Vol. IV, *Partie Dogmatique de la Philosophie Sociale* (lectures 46-51),
are more relevant to political theory, and contain important passages. Notably 46 —

The first, Theological, stage is subdivided into periods of Fetishism, Polytheism and Monotheism, the corresponding political organizations of the first two being theocratic and military. Slavery and serfdom are their respective social characteristics. The great contribution of the third period is the disruption of the totalitarian front of state power dominant in pre-Christian civilization, and the assertion of a spiritual power apart from the state. That, he says, following de Maistre, was the great achievement of Medieval Catholicism.

With the decline of Christendom in the early fifteenth century, the next great age of European history began — the confused yet powerful 'Metaphysical' era, articulate by the late sixteenth century and reaching its most negative and destructive phase by the seventeenth. It emerged through the weakening of religious emotion, from the transition from Fetishism and Polytheism to Monotheism. Far from intensifying religious feeling, it diminished it, ending in a feeble Deism which marks the decline of religious belief into metaphysical abstraction. This negative tendency further developed into the anarchic assertion of liberty and equality, crystallized in the absurd dogma of the sovereignty of the people, which makes wise government impossible and destroys the influence of elites. In this stage private property and economic individualism predominate.

With the coming of Positivism, this negative period is ended. A new orthodoxy will develop, corresponding to the rise of great industry which will supersede military power. This outlook has abandoned 'all inaccessible researches on the ground of their utter inutility'. It recognizes the 'inanity' of the attempt to explain final causes, and is directed to the spiritual regeneration of the civilized world.[11] The basis of this society is the fact of Progress, in the sense of continuous, ascertainable, development according to laws first

'Considérations politiques préliminaires sur la nécessité et l'opportunité de la physique sociale'– and 51 – 'Fundamental Laws of Social dynamics or general theory of the natural progress of Humanity.' Vol. V (lectures 52-55), *La Partie Historique de la Philosophie Sociale*, contains the main contribution to historical philosophy, analyses the Theological Age of Fetishism, Theocracy and Militarism, the Age of Polytheism and Monotheism. It concludes with a general appreciation of the metaphysical state of modern societies and 'the growing disorganization of theocratic and military society'. Vol. VI (lectures 56-60), *Complément de la Philosophie Sociale et les Conclusions Générales* (774 pp.), describes the general characteristics of the positive stage, and the convergence of the spontaneous principle of evolution in modern society towards a final organization of a rational and pacific regime. The work ends with a retrospect and conclusion for future policy.

Since the book is composed of lectures given over a long period, it is repetitive and diffuse. There is an abridgement by HARRIET MARTINEAU, *The Positive Philosophy of Auguste Comte*. Freely translated and condensed, in two volumes, 1853. 'The great extent of the work has been and will always be', remark her publishers, of the full text, 'a serious obstacle to its general acceptance.'

apprehended by the nineteenth century. The Metaphysical phase is over, the Positivist age begins.

Following the systematization of mathematics, physics and biology, all of which have passed through the three stages defined, the time has now arrived to formulate the master science of Sociology. It is divided into social statics and social dynamics. All social phenomena must be studied in these terms; given such an approach, a science of politics becomes possible. Political thought is no longer confined merely to the state, but concerned with the whole broad panorama of society in time and space. And the core of the whole doctrine is Comte's religion of humanity.

The *System of Positive Polity* is based on the conclusions of the former book.* It contains a detailed prospectus of the application of the new principles to the service of mankind, stresses the third, or political aspect, of Comte's teaching, and defines the precise nature of the new religion. All is still conditioned by his over-riding theme, the cult of Humanity and the division of history into the three great stages. It is also conditioned by the disillusionment of Comte's generation with the consequences of the Revolution. The influence of de Maistre on Comte has already been indicated; he wished to combine authoritarian governments with the moral rule of a priest-

---

* *The System of Positive Polity, or Treatise on Sociology*, Instituting the Religion of Humanity, by AUGUSTE COMTE. The Principle, Love; the Basis, order; the end, Progress. Republic of the west. Order and Progress. Live for others. London, 1851. Sixty-third year after the great revolution. Four volumes. Vol. I (618 pp.), trans. H. J. Bridges, contains the *General View of Positivism* (pp. 1-317), next, the *System of Positive Polity* (pp. 325-593) and an appendix containing the writings of Clothilde de Vaux. The whole is prefaced by a long and fervent dedicatory epistle. 'To the sacred memory of my eternal Friend . . . gratitude, regret, resignation.' The *General View* contains six chapters. The Intellectual Character of Positivism, its Social aspect, its Action on the People, its Influence on Women and relation to Art, and the Religion of Humanity. The *System* opens with the Nature and Plan of Scientific Synthesis, and an Indirect Introduction, concerned with Cosmology, Mathematics, Physics and Chemistry. There follows a 'Direct synthetic Introduction', dealing with Biology, Animal and Social Life, and the Theory of Cerebral Function. Vol. II, *Social Statics*, or the abstract theory of Human order (trans. F. Harrison, 387 pp., 1852), contains seven chapters, devoted to the general theory of Religion, to Property, to the Family, to Language and the Social organism. The sixth deals with the Priesthood, the last with the general limits and varieties of Human society. Vol. III, *Social Dynamics* or the General Theory of Human Progress (trans. J. H. Bridges, 1853, 536 pp.), in seven chapters, treats of Human Evolution, of the Age of Fetishism, the Theocratic state, 'the Positivist Theory of the Greek elaboration', and of 'the Roman incorporation'. The sixth chapter describes the Positivist theory of Catholic Feudalism, and the final chapter the Political Theory of the Western Revolution. Vol. IV, *The Synthetic Presentation of the future of Man* (trans. R. Congreve, 1854, 653 pp.), contains five chapters and an appendix, which includes the original 'Plan' or 'Prospectus', 1822. Topics covered are the fundamental theory of the Great Being, a general view of the Affective Life or Systematic definitions of the Positivist System of Worship; a general view of the Intellectual Existence of Man, of his Active existence, and a Philosophical Estimate of the Present by the co-ordination of the Future with the Past. After a Final invocation, the Appendix of Comte's earlier essays concludes, suitably enough, with an examination of Broussais's *Treatise on Irritation*.

hood, devoid of political and economic power, but commanding the support of mass opinion. But Comte was not a Royalist. 'Man,' he said, 'in spite of himself, belongs to his epoch . . .'[11] and Kings are at variance with facts. Yet the doctrine of popular sovereignty, a typical abstraction, is equally outdated. It is an ideological weapon in the old struggle against monarchy, and 'weapons of war cannot be metamorphosed into instruments of construction'. It leads to the people regarding government as 'a natural enemy encamped in the midst of our social system'. Freedom of conscience prevents the establishment of a new orthodoxy and 'tends to hinder the unique establishment of any system of general ideas, without which, nevertheless, society cannot exist'. No society, he maintained, could function without the psychological relief of organized religion, of common beliefs. Only thus could anti-social instincts be fully reconciled to the necessary demands of society. Ideas of individualist contract were worthless; civilization must be organic. Hence Comte's admiration for the Catholic Church, 'that noble but premature achievement'. Positivist society, untrammelled by the Christian obsession with original sin, will 'accomplish what in the Middle Ages could only be attempted . . . Affections which Catholicism had asserted to be altogether alien to our nature and to be entirely dependent on superhuman grace', can now be harnessed to the service of humanity. Grace is no longer necessary. The bold assumption has increasingly dominated the modern world.

This optimism is reflected in Comte's curious political programme. The basis of society is the family, so that the political superstructure is relatively unimportant. The real function of government should be limited to the creation of ordinary security and well being. As one assigns the care of roads and drainage to experts, so government should be the concern of specialists. Democratic doctrines are futile and dismember the body politic by placing power in the least capable hands.[13]

This Platonic assumption that government is the affair of experts, which follows so closely Saint-Simon's technocratic ideas, is taken to notable extremes.[14] Since modern power is ultimately industrial and financial, bankers form the apex of the pyramid. There will be a committee of three of them, dealing respectively with industry, commerce and agriculture. Below will be an administrative and industrial patriciate, whose wealth will be inherited, since this method of transmitting it seems 'the most natural'. In the Comtian religious calendar there will be a special month devoted to the expression of feelings of veneration for this class. 'The higher dignity of the banking element' will be 'asserted.'[15] In return, these plutocrats will feel themselves to be 'knights of industrial chivalry'. If they fail to live up to this ideal, they will be brought to book by moral strictures, finally by social ostracism. The masses, meanwhile, will enjoy basic security and accept the limitations of their lot. In the thirteenth month of the Positivist Calendar there will be a festival of the Proletariat, in which great Inventors — Watt and Montgolfier, who invented the balloon — will be commemorated, and in which the masses will be honoured for their 'dutiful acceptance of their existence as plebeians'. They will draw a basic wage, also payable during periods of unemployment, and a supplementary wage proportionate to work performed. Housing, wages, and the like, will be public utilities and capitalists regarded as custodians of the public interest. There will be no effective system of political representation, but government will ultimately be controlled by public opinion, mobilized by priests and women and powerfully expressed among the common people. Like Saint-Simon, Comte believed strongly in the integrity of the masses, who were, nonetheless, to be kept in contented subjection. While the nobility are anti-social, and the bourgeois engrossed in the pursuit of political and economic power, the workmen, from the nature of their occupations, which are not so absorbing as to prevent continuous thought, even during the hours of labour, 'are more often of a philosophic turn of mind'.[16] The subjects of these meditations were not, in Comte's opinion, the lottery, the prize fight or the *Variété*. Moreover, any intellectual deficiency could easily be remedied by philosophers. He foresees a solidarity of all classes who stand apart from the political and economic administration: ultimately, it seems, a disappearance of class distinctions following intensive and universal education. This will be entirely in the hands of women until the little scions of Humanity attain the age of fourteen; after that, they would proceed to an elaborate and exacting discipline until the age of twenty-one. Although women will be entirely dependent on their relations, and if necessary on the state, their influence will be all-pervasive, incalculable and decisive. The structure of Comtian society depends on them. 'Unless the new philosophy can obtain the support of women, the attempt to substitute it for theology in the regulation of social life had better be abandoned.'[17] 'Now of all the elements of which society is constituted,' he remarks, in an incongruously Aristotelian manner, 'women are the most aesthetic.' On this topic, as on nearly everything else, Napoleon was wrong. 'According to the lower views of the subject, such as those coarsely expressed by the great hero of reaction, Napoleon, procreation and maternity are the only function of women.' On the contrary, owing to her ethereal nature, her primary function is elevated companionship. Exclusive, indissoluble, eternal, 'the theory of marriage as put forward by the positivist becomes totally independent of any physical motives'. It follows, naturally, that widowhood will last for life. Upon these idealistic assumptions Comte depends for the inspiration of his regenerated society. Its religious aspect will later be more fully discussed.*

Given this stratified and harmonious order, international affairs will soon be put to rights. Great modern states will gradually dissolve into a more manageable area — the size of Belgium, for example, or less — and a new spirit of Occidental patriotism will arise. Working men, in particular, will soon attain a cosmopolitan outlook. 'During the five centuries of revolutionary transition, which have elapsed since the Middle Ages, we have lost sight of the fact that in all fundamental questions we form one political system . . . it rests now upon the basis, inadequate though it be, of community in industrial development, in aesthetic culture, and in scientific discovery.'[18] This European body, centred on France, he regarded as the 'nucleus of Humanity', and in it he included the United States. Here he hoped for a great future for his philosophy, which would give the Americans new 'coherence' and spiritual power. On this basis, positivism would spread about the world, particularly after the establishment of the positivist Occidental Committee, with headquarters in Paris. It will contain eight Frenchmen, seven Englishmen, six Germans, five Italians and four Spaniards, regionally

---

* The core of this religion was Comte's passionate devotion to the memory of Clothilde de Vaux, expressed in the extraordinary dedication of the *Système*, and in his inclusion in an appendix of 'the only work ever published by my sainted colleague'. Her story, entitled *Lucie*, reflects the melancholy circumstances of Mme de Vaux's marriage, and the poem, 'Thoughts of a Flower', her poetic sensibility. The former is a remarkable little melodrama. It concerns the deserted wife of a young man of distinguished family, afflicted with a 'funeste passion de jeu', who had disappeared under a terrible charge: he had been accused of assassinating a banker. The angry creditors promptly pursued the widow, who was unable to obtain a divorce. The story continues in the letters of 'Maurice' and 'Roger', who describe successive disasters. 'Nouvelle douleur, le monstre qui l'enchaîne à lui a été arrêté sur la frontière et conduit au bagne de Toulon, où il va subir sa peine' (in the galleys). 'O Roger,' writes Maurice, with epigrammatic insight, 'la vie a de rudes épreuves!' Finally the young woman dies and her lover blows his brains out. The following verses are representative of the poem:

Je nais pour être aimée, o merci, bon destin,
Quand le rossignol s'inspire
Sur ma tige en se jouant
Pour laisser résonner son chant
La Nature entière expire.

recruited. This harmonious body will be reinforced by four women, of whom two will be French, with the special task of disseminating positivism among the Mediterranean nations, who are evidently expected to prove difficult.* This Council as 'pioneers of the final order of society', will carry on a 'European Movement'.

There will be a common Western Navy and a common coinage, termed a 'carolus', after that founder of European unity, Charlemagne. There will also be an Occidental College, whose students will enter the positivist priesthood. They would, in general, come from the working class, but talent from any quarter would be welcome.[19] Those interested in cosmopolitan education will find Comte's detailed report on this project entertaining.† There would also be a banner and a flag, predominantly green, suitable for the Western Republic. The former 'should be painted on canvas; on one side the ground would be white; on it would be the emblem of Humanity, pictured as a woman of thirty bearing her son in her arms. The other side would bear the religious formula of the Positivists: "Love . . . Order . . . Progress", on a ground of green, the colour of Hope and therefore most suitable for emblems of the future'. The political flag, on the other hand, was intended to float freely, so 'it does not admit of painting . . .'. It will have a green centre bordered by the relevant national colours. 'Order and Progress' will be inscribed on one side; 'Live for others' on the reverse.

From this European nucleus the positivist committee will expand. Russia will be initiated into the Union by Poland, of all countries; later, Indian and Chinese delegates will attend. There will be two Negro representatives, one from Haiti, and one from Africa — a bold idea, in view of the customs of many inhabitants of the dark continent at the time.

The fourth, religious, aspect of the Positivist programme, already stressed, is fully elaborated. Humanity will be worshipped — 'an organism in time and space . . . the Great Being who manifests to the fullest extent all the highest attributes of life'. This scientific-humanist ideal was dynamic. The Great Being is not immutable and apart. By its nature it is relative, intimate; changing as the experience of mankind becomes enriched. Here the loneliness of individuals will be resolved; throughout their lives they will be sustained by the elaborate and continuing ritual of the Positivist

* The order in which states would join the organization preoccupied Comte; at first he thought England would be the last; on second thoughts the discreditable place was assigned to Germany.

† Published by the Positivist Society, 1849.

Church. Comte's religion has been well described as Catholicism minus Christianity. Great servants of mankind will attain the only possible immortality by being commemorated in the calendar of the Positivist year. The artist, now frustrated and dependent, will find opportunities for his genius in the service of the Positivist Church. Such a religion was impossible 'until the science of sociology had been founded; and this was done by my discovery of the Laws of historical development'. Within this framework, 'henceforth the true men of science will rise to the higher dignity of philosophers, and by so doing will necessarily assume something of the sacerdotal character'.[20] Far from being specialist technicians, the scientists, as in Saint-Simon's programme, will become a priesthood. And the new religion will become universal since science transcends frontiers, race and creed.*

Private devotion will be systematic; it will be practised three times a day, in all for two hours. Public sacraments and festivals will mark the phases of the individual's life and the cycle of the year. The daily meditation of Positivists will be a work of art, since each worshipper will compose his own prayer. Private adoration will be directed to beloved individuals, and will be carried to the point of 'hallucination'. 'Effusion' follows — in rhapsodical prayer. Naturally it will be a religion, not of petition, but of contemplation.

The 'Child of Humanity' will pass through nine stages in its career, each marked by a sacrament. Initiation takes place at·fourteen — 'refusal . . . being given only in the extremely rare cases of radical incompetence for scientific culture'.[21] One's career is decided at Destination: Marriage takes place for men between the ages of twenty-eight and thirty-five, for women between twenty-one and twenty-eight, following a period of chastity lasting three months. At forty-two the status of Servant of Humanity is attained; retirement comes

* The Comtian religion found disciples in academic circles in England. For example, Richard Congreve, Fellow of Wadham College, Oxford, wrote a large three-volume collection of essays and sermons on Comtian themes. He called the new religion 'Human Catholicism', and advocated a Western Republic. Annual sermons were delivered at the Positivist school (19 Chapel Street, Lamb's Conduit) on the Festival of Humanity. The movement cast its net wide. 'There is a slight increase in numbers in India' writes Congreve, 'so far as I know, in the U.S. we are in a stationary condition. In South America the two centres of Brazil and Chili are in active correspondence with me.' Nearer home, 'there has been steady persistence in Liverpool', but in Birmingham progress was slower, and there was 'less readiness outside to see what the new religion offers'. Subscriptions to the sacerdotal fund for the year 97 (1885), amounted to £305 15s. 10d., with a balance of £21 18s. 11d. (II, p. 570). Congreve denounced the 'absolute international anarchy that characterizes our time', doctrines of competitive individualism and of the survival of the fittest. He also strongly disapproved of the partition of Africa (II, p. 616).

at sixty-three, after which one becomes an auxiliary to the Priesthood. Finally, comes Transformation, when one becomes a memory. Seven years after, when opinion has had time to settle, one is incorporated into the Great Being and commemorated by an inscription, a bust or statue, according to merit. Those adversely criticized are ignored. But really wicked characters are exhumed; the body of the condemned is 'borne in a fitting manner to the waste ground allotted to the rejected'.* Major criminals, like Napoleon, will be held up to perpetual execration in the Positivist calendar. Caesar, St. Paul and Dante are honourably celebrated, but their commemoration would be followed by the 'repudiation' of Julian the Apostate and, naturally, of Bonaparte, 'the latter being the more criminal of the two, the former the more insensate'. Joan of Arc, of course, will be commemorated. She will have a solemn festival, not only for France, but for all Western Europe; but in case this celebration should make women reckless, the 'anomalous' nature of her career will naturally be pointed out.[22] The judgment of society will thus extend beyond the grave. Comte's social system is, indeed, a prig's paradise. As Bagehot remarks, 'who can doubt that Comte would have been hanged by his own hierarchy?'[23]

The Calendar of the Positivist year is not perhaps so grotesque. It will be constructed independently of the vagaries of the moon; it contains thirteen months and a day, and will open with a Festival of the Year.† The first six months will be devoted to celebrating the major virtues of humanity; to parental and fraternal love, to marriage, to the relation of masters and servants. The next four will commemorate the development of the race, the age of Fetichism and the stages of nomad, sedentary and sacerdotal life, with a special commemoration of the use of Iron. Under Polytheism, Greek sages will be venerated, and the ninth month will be devoted to the 'Adolescence of Humanity'. In this epoch Abraham and Moses, Charlemagne, King Alfred and St. Benedict are remembered: Mohammed, too, is venerated, but there is also to be 'an extraordinary festival on the Monday commemorating the Battle of Lepanto'.[24] The tenth month will witness the glorification of women; the eleventh will celebrate the virtues of the Priesthood, with festivals

---

* Compare, again, Plato who directs that the bodies of the incorrigible are to be 'buried in silence beyond the borders'.

† Comte thought of everything and the animals were not forgotten. 'Care will be taken to pay fitting honour to the animal races which are man's auxiliaries' (IV, p. 121), and there will be a special day devoted to '. . . Man's alliance with the sociable animals – special honour being paid to the Associates in succession, to the Dog, the Horse and the Ox' (I, p. 126).

of Art and Science. The twelfth will mark the glorification of the Patriciate. Finally, it is the turn of the proletariat, whose good sense and docility are celebrated, and the whole year ends in a kind of All Souls Day, in which the memories, if not the souls, of the faithful departed are glorified.

It was a strange fantasy this 'self-intoxicated doctrinaire' had elaborated.[25] Yet, one reflects, is it really more improbable than the Calendar of the Christian year, with its martyrs, its days of mourning and its festivals, would have appeared to Cicero? It seems ineffective because it is not organic, some slow expression of the folk mind: but in its bloodless artificial way, it reflects fundamental concerns of human life. It is not altogether removed from the themes of primitive ritual. Behind the austere gaze of this nineteenth-century academic bourgeois can be seen the lineaments of the Corn King and the Spring Queen.

The absurdity of this religion naturally distressed Comte's followers, who thought him a great sociologist. Comte himself had few misgivings; 'Auguste Comte croit la déchristianization de ses contemporains assez complète pour qu'il soit permis de renverser leurs habitudes.'[26] He could remark, 'I am sure that I shall preach Positivism in Notre Dame.'

This detailed and elaborate new religion was to reinforce the political, scientific and philosophic principles which emerged from his study of sociology. There, in spite of obvious later absurdities, Comte's contribution was massive, formidable and apposite — the fruit of a fierce individualism, intellectual arrogance and deliberate isolation. The whole system is rooted, like Hegel's, in an attempt to unify all experience, and in an elaborate view of history. It asserted that mind and environment interact, and it arbitrarily divided thought and history into its three stages, with elaborate sub-divisions. Where Marx asserted that environment was predominant, Comte attributed more initiative to mind. In applying the law of the three stages of knowledge to all history and all sociology, Comte went far beyond the evidence. Nor was his knowledge of history particularly profound within the range of his time. But in making such an approach at all, so massive and systematic; in asserting the reality of progress in terms of control of environment and accumulation of knowledge, in facing the greatest problem of his time — the loss of Christian belief — and in accepting the limitations of mind and yet asserting the value of life, Comte made a contribution to the thought of his age which fundamentally altered its development. Like Saint-

Simon, he combines genius with the obsessions of a crank; like Saint-Simon, he changed the course of nineteenth-century opinion. But by foreshadowing the full range of modern sociology, he made a contribution of his own. In a crude and angular hypothesis, riddled in detail by modern expertise, he charted new ground. And in this work he continued a great tradition. The pedigree of his attempt at a philosophy of scientific humanism has its roots far back in the writings of Bacon, Descartes and Spinoza. In its acceptance of the limitations of mind, it recalls the philosophy of Hume. Its positivism recalls, also, the resolution of Bentham to master environment, regardless of metaphyscial speculation. It is based upon obsolete science, and its political programme takes little account of the heavy realities of power, or the wickedness and folly of statesmen and of the peoples they represent. But Comte asserts that the highest values of life are human, that the Life Force, as far as man can apprehend its mystery, reaches its peak in human experience, that the achievements of mankind should be commemorated and that humanity forms one great brotherhood. He reaffirms in a different and richer idiom, an ancient Stoic ideal of universal citizenship, on a wider scale and with a new, agnostic, contemporary sanction. This vision was combined with authoritarian politics, reminiscent of Plato at his worst, and inadequately symbolized by a religion and a Calendar which, because not spontaneous, appears absurd. This fact does not diminish the major contribution made by this uncompromising intellectual to the study of politics and sociology. It aimed, in his own Saint-Simonian words, at 'an object far higher than satisfying our scientific curiosity; the object of reorganizing human life'.

CHAPTER VI

ANARCHISTS AND UTOPIANS
GODWIN:FOURIER:OWEN

THE term anarchist has baleful associations. But if the theory of anarchism led to sanguinary excesses, the majority of its exponents cannot be tarred with the brush of crime. Moreover, the belief that all government is iniquity has a very ancient pedigree. Apart from its classical and medieval manifestations, the religious upheavals of the sixteenth and seventeenth centuries had produced many experiments in communitarian anarchy and secession, particularly in central Europe and North America. Their inspiration had been religious. With growing scepticism, the tradition turned secular in the hands of Godwin and Fourier; and with Proudhon, atheist. The pedigree went on to the Russian revolutionary Bakunin, to Sorel whose sardonic anarcho-syndicalism was influenced by Marx, and to Kropotkin, the most remarkable modern exponent of this form of revolution.

Only religious conviction could have induced Anabaptists, Mennonites and Moravians to brave the seventeenth-century Atlantic and found their settlements in New Jersey, Connecticut and the Hudson valley.* The impulse came mainly from central Europe. Socinian communities were long widespread in Lithuania and Poland, and Bohemian heresy traced its origins to Huss and beyond, while the Thirty Years' War had naturally encouraged emigration from the Germanies. The English Interregnum also gave rise to the multiplication of sects. Extremist political thought found expression in the conduct and opinions of Levellers, Diggers and Quakers, for Quakers were then very different from their modern representatives. The early tradition of communitarian anarchy was rooted in nonconformist religion. The aim of all these movements was simple. To change men's politics by changing their hearts. All depended on personality, on the worth of individuals; on the spiritual priesthood of all believers. Once these principles were asserted, the need for

---

* See A. E. BESTOR, *Backwoods Utopias, the Sectarian and Owenite Phases of Communitarian Socialism in America, 1663-1829.* Pennsylvania Press, 1950. Dr. Bestor points out that only in America did the transition take place gradually between religious and secularized communitarianism.

government would dissolve. And along with the cult of individuals, went the cult of the small beloved community.

The main scene of these movements in the seventeenth century had become American. Following the successful revolt of the Colonies, the new Republic became the greatest stronghold of communitarian enterprise. The movement had thus attained an Atlantic background. Fourier, for example, had little influence in France; he inspired considerable experiments in the United States. Owen attempted to repeat at New Harmony the success he had achieved at New Lanark.

All these experiments are generally regarded by men of affairs as impracticable. Nor have they obtained better treatment at the hands of most revolutionaries. Marx and Engels, for example, pour scorn on communitarian theory, just as the practical politicians, from Guizot to Bismarck, would have dismissed them. The radical, but not anarchist, political tradition, later expressed by John Bright and Henry George, was to have a powerful political future. But the anarchist communitarian theory of politics, which had little immediate influence, and is notorious through its lunatic fringe, produced more original and perhaps, ultimately, more constructive ideas.

For they went further than the political radicals. They objected to politics altogether. All government, in their opinion, was evil. The aim was a network of self-governing, self-sufficient communities within the loosest federation. While the contribution of Tom Paine (1737-1809), the apologist of the American and French Revolutions, and of Cobbett (1762-1835), that pioneer popular journalist, made a great stir in the history of political radicalism, the present study will concentrate upon four representative figures in the anarchist and communitarian pedigree.

Godwin and Fourier, Owen and Proudhon, all made their contribution. Where Proudhon had the greatest range, Owen was a principal ideological founder of British socialism, a stream of thought to be reinforced by William Morris. While Fourier and Owen wished to expand modern production, they also desired to restore the balance between industry and agriculture, escape the evils of megalopolitan civilization, and subordinate industry to human requirements. The whole movement is still the long-term secularized version of perennial religious motives. It asserts old values realized in an agricultural setting into a world of urban industry and bureaucracy. Since that time the evils of centralization have vastly increased. In view of modern techniques of diffusing electric and nuclear power, projects for decentralized self-sufficiency are worth attention.

Proudhon is the most interesting and relevant of all these writers. His outlook is European, and with his contribution the next chapter will be concerned. Here the political theory of William Godwin will first be considered, then the queer Utopian visions of Fourier. Finally Owen's plan for a peaceful educational and economic revolution will be examined.

II

William Godwin's reputation was won early by a single book, the *Enquiry concerning Political Justice and its Influence on Morals and Happiness.** The rest of his rather unhappy career was an anti-climax, and his main notoriety through his relationship to Shelley.

The *Enquiry* was a very remarkable work. Like Paine's *Rights of Man* and Cobbett's political pamphlets, it had phenomenal success, in part a succès de scandale owing to Godwin's odd views upon marriage. Its impact was due to vigour and candour of style and the deceptive lucidity of a well-planned, if slightly crazy, argument. 'No work in our time', says Hazlitt, 'gave such a blow to the philosophical mind of the country . . . Tom Paine was considered for the time a Tom Fool to him, Paley an old woman, Edmund Burke a flashy sophist. Truth, moral Truth, it was supposed, had here taken up its abode.'[1] Like Herbert Spencer, Godwin was an individualist and a prig. Brought up in the atmosphere of East Anglian Dissent, his sublime confidence in Reason reflects the Deist assumption that Reason is Virtue and Error Vice. All is suffused by a Platonic cult of abstract ideas and a conviction of progress. Along with this abstract belief, which he shared with the Encyclopedists, whose authoritarian views he disliked, went the English nonconformist distrust of government. 'Even in its best state', he declared,

* William Godwin, 1756-1836, like Paine, an East Anglian, born at Wisbech, Cambridgeshire, son of a dissenting Minister, whose calling he at first followed at Ware, Stowmarket, and Diss. In 1783 he took to journalism in London and in 1793 his *Political Justice* appeared. In 1794 his novel *Caleb Williams* was published. In 1797 he married Mary Wollstonecraft who died the same year. Their daughter subsequently eloped with Shelley and wrote the romance *Frankenstein*. Godwin had now turned playwright, publisher and antiquary. In 1803 he produced a life of Chaucer, in 1822 he went bankrupt, in 1828 appeared his *History of the Commonwealth*, and in 1831 he obtained the small office of Yeoman Usher of the Exchequer. The best edition of the *Enquiry* is edited by F. E. L. Priestley with an admirable introduction and notes. (Three volumes, Toronto, 1946.)

Government is 'but a necessary evil'. Decentralized democracy is the answer: in time, even that will become unnecessary.

This emancipation will come about through the gradual conversion of opinion. Godwin was a pacific, if extreme, anarchist. Since public opinion rules all things, 'the chains fall off themselves when the magic of opinion is dissolved'.[2] Before the spreading initiative of individuals everywhere, the evils of government will fade away. War will be abolished, since it is unreasonable; moral restraint will solve the problem of population, renunciation that of poverty. Unlike Adam Smith, Saint-Simon, Owen and Marx, Godwin is not interested in releasing the new industrial productivity. Like Proudhon, he detests organization and wants to stabilize on a balanced, predominantly agrarian, economy. If he denounces existing government, he detests even more the Collectivist solution.

Godwin was, indeed, concerned with fundamental problems. Hence his influence on Coleridge and J. S. Mill. He desired to moralize politics. Active, indefatigable, disinterested, the missionaries of Godwinian rationalism would transform society by discussion. Political truth, he insisted, was ascertainable through argument. Can we suppress discussion? he demands, like Milton: 'Can we arrest the progress of the enquiring mind?' 'Intellect has a perpetual tendency to proceed.'[3]

In the light of this morality, Godwin surveys the deficiencies of government. He sets his 'System of Equality' against war, poverty and general wickedness. Man, he declares, 'is not a vegetable'. He is a reasonable creature. Truth, when adequately communicated, is irresistible. Society, moreover, is constantly changing; an 'everlasting innovation' is in the true interest of mankind. For progress is a fact: 'let us carry back our minds to man in his original state'.[4] Men must be regarded not only for what they are, but for what they have it in them to become. With this spontaneous development government must never interfere. Its function, as Herbert Spencer was to maintain, should always be diminished.

For consider, says Godwin, the evils brought about by Government. Most of his book is concerned with them. 'May it not happen', he asks, 'that the grand moral evils that exist in the world, the calamities by which we are so grievously oppressed, are to be traced to political institutions as their source and that their removal is only to be expected by their correction?'[5] Externally, government means war: 'Satiated with petty mischiefs and the retail of insulated crimes, he [man] rises . . . to a project that lays nations waste and thins the population of the world . . .' He proceeds 'in the midst of gaiety and pomp, to execute his horrid purposes'. Internally, even in civilized society, 'hundreds of victims are annually sacrificed at the shrine of positive Law and political institutions', while, over most of the world, governments are despotic. 'Dungeons, chains and racks are the most approved and established methods of persuading men to obedience, and impressing upon their minds the lessons of reason.'[6] Meanwhile the wretchedness of the poor is increased by the luxury of the rich, 'the bitter aggravation of their own calamity'. In consequence the poor are induced 'to regard the state of society a state of war'. Tyranny, exploitation and violence make human society worse than that of beasts.

This frightful situation is unnecessary. With Owen, he held that environment determines character. Change the institutions and society would be transformed. Since monarchy and aristocracy are hopelessly discredited, the least bad form of government is demo-cratic. For all its shortcomings, which Godwin freely admits, 'it is a system of government, according to which every member of society is considered as a man and nothing more'.[7] All men are equal and democracy implies self-respect. All have the right and duty to par-ticipate; all are reasonable and responsible. Godwin echoes the Leveller's assertion that the 'poorest he in England, hath a right to live as the richest he'.[8]

In an educated democracy political imposture will be unnecessary. Sound public opinion is more reliable than fraud, which 'takes for granted that a true observation of things is inadequate to teach us our duty'.[9] And, besides, the bubble of political imposture is always liable to burst. Democracy should also be decentralized. With the French Revolution in mind, Godwin dislikes National Assemblies. They should be confined to adjusting the differences between dis-tricts and 'consulting respecting the best way of repelling invasion'. Their authority should be employed 'as sparingly as the nature of the case will admit'.[10] If the power of central government is closely cir-cumscribed, there will be little chance for 'the tyranny of a multitude drunk with unlimited power . . . here the demagogue will discover no suitable occasion'. There must be local self government and differences should be settled by 'juries'. At first the threat of force must be kept in reserve, but in time it should be sufficient for juries no longer to compel but to 'invite'.[11]

If Godwin detested government, he was no immediate revolu-tionary. With his belief in the power and reason over conduct and faith in perfectibility, he held that the evils of society were destined to disappear before rational enlightenment. 'We are not concerned', he wrote, 'to vindicate any stain of violence, we do not assume that levelling principles are to be acted upon through the medium of force.' Human nature is constantly changing, and even national characteristics are not constant.* Public affairs have only to be left alone. Before the influence of education they will 'find their level and work out for good'. Revolutionary political parties are no remedy against oppression, but themselves equally tyrannical.

There is only one remedy — anarchism. It can be achieved through the capture of majority opinion. 'Give the people guides and instructors,' he wrote, with his doctrinaire confidence, 'and the business is done. This, however, is not to be accomplished but in a gradual manner.' Once its scope is understood, the atmosphere of education will be transformed. 'It will then scarcely be thought more necessary to make boys slaves than to make men so.'[12] With the beating and barbarism of the old public schools in mind, he declares that instruction will proceed, as it should, 'with a firm step and genuine lustre, when those who conduct it shall know what a vast field it embraces'.

Like other anarchists, Godwin reinforced his beliefs by preaching an austere morality.[13] His most resounding utterances reflect this puritanism. He wished to abolish the marriage laws, not to encourage promiscuous depravity, but to convert people from regarding sex as important. Intellectual affinity is what counts. And the present system is a legalized monopoly. 'So long as I seek by despotic and artificial means to retain my possession of a woman, I am guilty of the most odious selfishness.' Love marriages contracted by the young generally prove a mere 'making the best of an irretrievable mistake'. So he advocates temporary unions which 'leave room for repentance'. 'No ties,' he insists, 'ought to be forced upon either party preventing them from quitting the attachment, whenever judgment directs them to quit it.'[14] Such startling propaganda can always command an audience, and odd morality is often combined with advanced political opinions. The alliance of free love with anarchy rendered Godwin's doctrines notorious.

These views reflect his assertion of individual liberty. Once individuals are free, the natural virtues of mankind will

---

* For example, 'Diodorus Siculus describes the Gauls as particularly given to taciturnity, and Aristotle affirms that they are the only warlike nation who are negligent of women.' A singular contrast, Godwin remarks, with the modern French.

predominate. Tyranny, war, poverty and immorality are not the result of original sin. They result from the bewilderment of men and women of potential good will. 'The true reason', he insists, 'why the mass of mankind have so often been the dupes of knaves,' has been the mysterious and complicated nature of the social system. Once annihilate the quackery of government, and 'the most home-bred understanding might be strong enough to detect the artifices of the state juggler who would mislead them'. This faith in 'home-bred' intelligence and in the capacity to act upon it, is fundamental. Shall we not ultimately find, he had already asked, that juries themselves, and every other form of public institutions, will be 'laid aside' as unnecessary?

William Godwin was plainly a doctrinaire. Yet his criticism of government has justice. Whatever the psychological miscalculations on which his remedies are based, and however fatuous his belief in the rationality of mankind, who can deny the vast iniquities which he so briskly pointed out?* His anarchism is valuable not in its constructive proposals, but for its assertion of humane ideals and its expression of a perennial mood of resentment against government. Its weakness was in Godwin's dislike of Christianity and failure to realize the need of an alternative belief, which alone could sustain anarchy.

III

Where Godwin had based his views on rampant individualism, Fourier was of more communitarian mind. He insisted first that the possibilities of modern production were unlimited, secondly that work should be enjoyable. He influenced Engels, William Morris and the French socialist Jean Jaurès.

Fourier believed that existing society thwarted the profoundest instincts of mankind.† Far from repressing the passions, one should

---

* This horror of power, however exercised, was to be carried further, into revolutionary violence, by the Russian anarchists of the later nineteenth century, of whom Bakunin is the most notorious: see MICHAEL BAKUNIN, Œuvres. Edited J. Guillaume. His most important works are Fédéralisme, 6 volumes. Paris, 1907-13; Socialisme Antithéologisme, 1867-68, and L'Empire Knouto-Germanique et la Révolution Sociale, 1870.

† Fourier, François Charles Marie, 1772-1837. Born at Besançon, he spent most of his life as a small clerk, mainly at Lyons. He wrote Théorie des Quatre Mouvements et des Destinées Générales. Leipzig, 1808; Théorie de l'Unité Universelle (1822); Le Nouveau Monde Industriel et Sociétaire (1829). See Œuvres Complètes (actually incomplete), 6 volumes. Paris, 1846-48. Also Victor CONSIDÉRANT (Fourier's principal disciple), Destinée Sociale (1834-38) and Exposition Abrégée du Système de Charles Fourier. See also PELLARIN, Fourier, Sa Vie et sa Théorie and H. BOURGIN, Fourier. Also ALEXANDER GRAY, op. cit. and GIDE and RIST,

encourage them. They will then develop their natural and productive harmony. His earliest work he describes as 'Prospectus et Annonce de la Découverte'. For this supreme discovery, he believed, heralded a new age of unprecedented well-being. Hitherto all history had been a record of misery and crime. Like Godwin, he believed that war and poverty are the direct result of institutions: 'les modernes tombent de plus en plus dans la démence politique'.[15] Economic competition leads to poverty and war. 'Il attaque l'humanité en masse, en suscitant des guerres stipendiées qui forcent les peuples à se déchirer tour à tour.'[16] All this frustrates the grand process of the Universe, the 'immensity of well being which God reserves to us'.

Fourier combined the wildest cosmic speculations with an exact materialism. He believed that the Creation was destined to rise in a crescendo of well-being to its climax, and after a vast period of felicity, to decline into the confusion of its origins. The fantastic time-chart which explains his system, belongs not to the realm of serious speculation but to the more amiable kind of asylum.* So do his visions of 'Anti-Lions' and 'Anti-bears', docile animals who take the place of their present ferocious prototypes in the coming period of harmony. Fourier's fantasies of good living probably reflect the straitened circumstances of his own life. He sets particular store by the kitchen; by the gigantic French meals which everyone will enjoy; 'les mets de troisième classe, qui seront le pis-aller du peuple, surpasseront en délicatesse ceux qui font à present les délices de nos "gastronomes" '.[17] These succulent fantasies combine with speculations about free will to make up a large part of his writings. Like Godwin, Fourier is more convincing when he criticized society than in sketching his alternative. But his description of social 'parasites' is worth attention and has something in common with the views of Saint-Simon, from whom, however, he dissociated himself.

Consider, for example, he says, the armies which distract the most enterprising youths from work, the customs-officers, the bureaucrats, 'les légions de Régie'. Nine-tenths of the merchants and half the manufacturers are redundant, a handicap to society, quite apart

* This extraordinary document, to be found at the end of Œuvres, vol. I, is well worth unfolding.

History of Economic Doctrines (1915). Gray (pp. 169ff), is particularly entertaining on this author, who he says is 'scarcely to be read without loud guffaws of uproarious and irreverent laughter . . . Let no one approaching Fourier,' he warns us, 'imagine that he is taking up a volume marked by the decorum, the austerity and the conventionality of John Stuart Mill.'

from 'agents of positive destruction', such as strikes.[18] His grotesque 'Anatomy of Supreme Pleasures'* and the nicety of his directions for exploiting the less desirable impulses of children, also diversify his visions.

In brief, Fourier proposed to eliminate wasteful competition, and oppressive government, by organizing self-sufficient and mainly agricultural units of production. They would be based on an adequate estate and provide for about sixteen hundred persons, who would be organized in 'series' and groups. Inspired by mutual and organized emulation, and with a basic standard of life guaranteed, these 'Phalanstères' would in time proliferate by example and supersede the present monstrous economy of the world. Inspired by their harmonious passions and the disappearance of the distinction between producer and consumer, the 'Harmonians' will in time produce fantastic wealth. It is bound to become prodigious. 'Le luxe d'Harmonie se porte sur le travail utile, sur les sciences, les arts, et notamment sur la cuisine.'[19]

Along with this expanding production, will go an educational revolution. The majority of mankind are now miserable and repressed — 'marmots civilisés'. Fourier's 'Education Unitaire' will release the whole man. It will start from infancy by organizing good children into corps of industrious Bambins, Chérubins, Séraphins, and bad ones into 'little Hordes' who will enjoy the scavenging. It will raise mankind to perfection in body and mind. As Owen was to maintain, environment and education can transform personality. Our present teachers — slaves to abstractions — know how to produce Neros; we know how to turn potential Neros into men like Gods.[20]

In contrast to Godwin, Owen and Proudhon, Fourier believed in a benevolent Creator, who had designed mankind for life in the better circumstances of the future. Hence all human impulses were good, even inconsequence and idleness — both suitable for better times. The society of the future would not run against the grain of human nature, but prove an age of tremendous achievement through impulses properly adjusted and energies properly employed. Like Godwin, and in contrast to Proudhon, Fourier detested the family, which he regarded as anti-social. The inhabitants of his Phalansteries were to practice various degrees of free love. There was to be no levelling down of incomes; merely the guarantee of basic affluence

* DORVAL's *Parcours du Plaisir* . . . 'On peut, par exemple, dans le cours d'une heure', etc. — an apotheosis of Lifemanship, IV, p. 188.

for all. Everyone was to go their own way, with freedom to change their occupation and cultivate individual tastes. Fourier was an amicable and tolerant anarchist, not a communist of austere moral views. The mixture of Harmonians of different social levels was to transcend the class war. Competition between groups and the vivid intensity of personal intercourse, amorous, gastronomic and intellectual, would put politics out of their heads. Capitalists who supported the movement would be rewarded by fantastic titles, and much time would be spent by Harmonians in visiting colleagues in their different vocations about the world.

This economic and educational revolution, by housing the population in self-supporting, autonomous and self-conducted luxury hotels, in which all the occupants would work and play in industrious harmony, would solve the problems of poverty, war and wickedness.

Like Saint-Simon, Fourier relied on the help of the rich. To the day of his death he believed a benefactor would arrive who would give his scheme its start. He waited for him daily and pathetically at an appointed hour for years. His prophecies are combined with fantastic physical and biological speculations and worked out in bizarre detail, but his attack on the frustrations and perils of society cannot be dismissed. Nor in principle, his hope for a better future — his conviction, curious in the time of Malthus — that 'economists forget to take into consideration the neglected but ameliorative possibilities of civilization'.[21] His dreams of the potential wealth of modern industry, released from maldistribution, state tyranny, nationalism and war, have been partially realized by the range and power of modern inventions. Given the power of modern technology, economic nationalism and class war may yet be transcended. Fourier struck a gallant, if eccentric, blow against the dreary fatalism of Malthusian economics. 'Moi seul,' he proclaimed, 'j'aurai confondu vingt siècles d'imbécillité politique.' His boast was not entirely unjustified.

IV

In contrast to the immediately neglected visions of Fourier, Robert Owen's scheme for the regeneration of society was relatively sober. This pioneer of British Socialism had an original, candid and one-track mind. Like Bentham, he came to maturity in the eighteenth century, implicitly believed in the rationality of mankind, and held to a few simple ideas with invincible tenacity. This single-mindedness made him successful. Like other wise publicists, 'he never argued; he merely reiterated his views'. 'Mr. Owen the Philan-thropist' was described by a contemporary as 'always a gentle bore'.

This powerful, pervasive influence was exerted to attain two main objects: the reform of education and the abolition of unemployment. They were to lead to a third — a world co-operative Commonwealth. It will be worth examining Owen's ideas under two heads; first his theory of education; secondly, his co-operative plan.

He came to this visionary purpose with a record of practical suc-cess. A self-made cotton-spinner, the son of a small saddler in Wales, he had been confronted at New Lanark with singularly intractable material.* His original workmen combined hard drinking and dis-honesty with sectarian fanaticism. He had to deal with 'dispossessed Highland crofters who hated factory life and found solace in the bottle, and pauper children drafted there by the Public authority'.²² While earning substantial profits, Owen converted this tough com-munity into a famous show place. This success gave him a prestige which few political theorists can immediately command, and a sanguine view of economic difficulties for which he later paid the penalty.

Owen's *A New View of Society* is coloured by one overmastering idea. Men, he declares, are not responsible for their characters. All is determined by heredity and environment. And the last is under human control. If the full power of society were exerted on the

---

* Robert Owen, 1771-1858, was born at Newtown, Montgomeryshire, the son of a small saddler and ironmonger of Methodist persuasion. At nine he became a draper's assistant, and was next apprenticed to a prosperous linen draper at Stamford. Although his employer offered him the succession to the business, Owen migrated to Manchester in 1789 and set up as an independent cotton spinner on a capital of £100. He had arrived at the peak of the cotton boom, and at twenty was offered a partnership. By 1795 he was one of the leading manufacturers of the city. His company was soon able to buy New Lanark, the best equipped spinning mills in Scotland, of which he became managing director in 1800. Having married the daughter of the former owner, he settled down to transform New Lanark Mills. In 1813 he first published his *New View of Society*, and in 1815 started an agitation for factory reform. In 1817 he wrote his *Report on the Poor Law* and in 1821 his *Report to the County of Lanark*. Though at first widely supported by in-fluential opinion, Owen's religious views made him unpopular and he resolved to found a new community in the United States. He therefore bought 30,000 acres in Indiana. Four years later the experiment was wound up at the loss of £40,000. But Owen's writ-ings had won him a growing working-class following, and he became the leader of the new trade union movement which culminated in the Grand National Consolidated Trade Union (1833-34). Following the government's attack, marked by the episode of the Tolpuddle Martyrs, the immediate movement collapsed, but since 1825 the Co-operatives had been widely developed, and led to the foundation of the Rochdale Pioneers Co-operative Society in 1844. Owen's later years were devoted to educational reform and spiritualism. For his Biography, see, in particular, the *Life of Robert Owen, Written by Himself* (1857) and G. D. H. COLE's *The Life of Robert Owen*. London, 1930. Also, J. MACABE, *Robert Owen* (1920); L. DOLLÉANS, *Robert Owen*. Paris, 1905 and his son, ROBERT DALE OWEN's *Threading my Way* (1874). The best selection is in the Everyman Edition, edited G. D. H. COLE.

individual from early childhood, character could be transformed. A peaceful social revolution could thus solve all the miseries of poverty, ignorance, unemployment and war. Owen was primarily an educational reformer. His objective was a transformation of personality, starting before the age of two. The core of his doctrine is in the nursery school. Children, he insists, can be trained to acquire 'any language, sentiment, belief or other bodily habits and manners, not contrary to human nature'. Human beings, for example, even the best, are now all 'localized animals, peculiar to some of the innumerable districts into which irrationality has divided the world'.* And the outlook of each generation is entirely determined by that of adult society. This situation has been constant since earliest times. Parochialism and intolerance have been ineffaceably stamped upon mankind. Now, at last, has come Owen's supreme discovery. It follows that 'the governing powers of all countries should establish rational plans for the education and general foundation of character of their subjects. These plans must be devised to train children from their earliest infancy in good habits of every description . . . They must afterwards be rationally educated, and their labour be usefully directed. Such habits and education will impress them with an active and ardent desire to promote the happiness of every individual, and without the shadow of exceptions, for sect or party or country or climate'.[23] They must be inculcated by an inexorable, untiring benevolence. Here is a Quakerish calm and persistence. Nothing short of madness, Owen insists, will 'long resist a firm, determined, will, directing persevering kindness'.

He is never in doubt of the goal. It is enhancement of life — a sober, practical, humanism. The basis will be physical well-being; sobriety, order, recreation, good sense. The ideal is thoroughly civilian.† Like most socialist thought in England, it is constitutional, not politically revolutionary. 'The rich and the poor, the governors and the governed, have really but one interest.'[24] It is an appeal, in the Benthamite manner, to the rationality of all mankind. For in

* A New View of Society or Essays on the Principle of the Formation of the Human Character, and the Application of the Principle to Practice. 'Any character, from the best to the worst, from the most ignorant to the most enlightened, may be given to any community, even to the world at large, by applying certain means; which are to a great extent at the command and under the control, or easily made so, of those who possess the government of nations.' By one of His Majesties Justices of the Peace for the County of New Lanark (1813), 76 pp. (Everyman Edition, op. cit.).

† He loathes militarism. The Napoleonic Wars are 'these transactions in which millions have been immolated. The direful effects of Napoleon's government have created the most deep-rooted disgust in notions which could produce a belief that such conduct was glorious . . .'

the light of Owen's discovery, 'a correct knowledge of human nature will destroy all animosity and anger among men, and will prepare the way for new arrangements which will be introduced without violence'. Like many other reformers, including Marx, Owen repudiates the past. He lays down that 'the past ages of the world present the history of human irrationality only, and that we are now but advancing towards the dawn of reason, and to the period when the mind of man will be born again'.[25] This regeneration is perfectly possible. 'Whence,' he then asks, 'have wickedness and misery proceeded? I reply, solely from the ignorance of our forefathers!'* No longer nurtured on 'illusions in direct opposition to existing facts', humanity can at last become adult, responsible, prosperous and secure.

The problem of poverty will be solved. 'All men, by judicious and proper laws and training', may 'readily acquire knowledge and habits which will enable them, if they are permitted, to produce far more than they need for their support and enjoyment; and thus any population, in the fertile part of the earth may be taught to live in plenty and in happiness without the checks of vice and misery.' Malthus's nightmare will dissolve. 'For man knows not the limit of his power for creating food.' Moreover, properly exploited, the sea affords inexhaustible abundance. Unemployment, too, can be abolished, if governments, foreseeing the fluctuations in the demand for labour, 'provide perpetual employment of real utility'.

Religious hatred and nationalism will also fade away. Once admit that no one is responsible for his opinions, but reflects the tradition in which he has been bred, and all the rancour of nationalism and bigotry will give place to charity and understanding. The teaching of innumerable sects and religions now divides the human race. Each arrogates to itself the truth. Through this insanity the rest of mankind are regarded as heretics and enemies. Yet no one is to blame for believing the ideas implanted by his predecessors and surroundings. Let these illusions die, Owen demands, 'for in consequence of them, man has been always instructed from infancy to believe impossibilities — he is still taught to pursue this same insane course, and the result still is misery'.[26] Mankind is now further embittered by being forced to accept impossible moral standards. Hence hypocrisy, hatred, and war. Yet the truth is plain. 'Man . . . never did, nor is it possible he can, form his own character.' Let this,

* Address delivered at New Lanark on opening the Institution for the Formation of Character, on January 1st, 1816.

once and for all, be admitted. Then, at last will come the emancipation of the human mind.

Here is a kind of rudimentary positivism. This indefatigable philanthropist, who brushed aside all illusions, inculcated one remedy from which all the rest would follow. Each child is to be told, on his entrance to the new playground, '. . . in language which he can understand, that "he is never to injure his play-fellows; but that, on the contrary, he is to contribute all in his power to make them happy" '.[27] This 'simple precept, if no counteracting principle be forced upon the young mind, will effectively supersede all the errors which have hitherto kept the world in ignorance and misery'. Owen wrote before Freud.

This clear, ardent, and reiterated propaganda at first won widespread attention. The deceptive simplicity of his argument was in tune with the age of the March of Mind. The simple rationality he assumed remained unquestioned by advanced opinion. And his revolution was to be gradual. 'Beneficial change can alone take place by well-digested and well-arrayed plans, temperately introduced and perseveringly pursued.'[28] Of course, the 'bandages' which obscure human sight were only gradually to be removed. In his address at New Lanark, Owen adopts a Saint-Simonian tone of paternal explanation.

His fierce onslaught on the iniquities of sweated child labour in the mills also won support. His immediate programme of education, with its then unusual stress on recreation, fresh air and exercise, commanded wide sympathy. Whatever his political and economic Utopianism, Owen was a great pioneer of education. His ideal was simple and hygienic. 'What ideas individuals may attach to the Millenium I know not; but I know that society may be formed so as to exist without crime, without poverty, with health greatly improved, with little, if any, misery, and with intelligence and happiness increased a hundredfold.'[29]

It is a characteristic ideal; far reaching and humane. Circumstances, he believed, made it urgent that it should be immediately pursued. Like Saint-Simon, Owen believed that the Industrial Revolution had confronted governments with an inescapable choice. Either they might deliberately keep the 'lower orders' in ignorance and brutality, retaining their own precarious position under the threat of unemployment and revolution; or they might endeavour to solve the problem by education and by creating mass purchasing power.

Both these objects Owen was convinced he could achieve. The theory behind the first has already been examined. Education could make the masses 'Truly benevolent and kind to the whole of the species, and, with the certainty of a mathematical demonstration, render all men charitable.'[30] Strange doctrine in the days of Malthus, laissez-faire, and the post-Napoleonic depression. The second objective, he believed, could also be attained. This time by the other aspect of his communitarian plan. The argument is most fully developed in the *Report to the County of Lanark*, which must have made curious reading for its recipients.

It was essential, he argued, to create wider purchasing power. 'The markets of the world,' he wrote, 'are created solely by the remuneration allowed for the industry of the working classes.'[31] He is concerned to 'recreate and extend demand in proportion to the scientific improvement'. Like Fourier, if with a more sober judgment, he believed that scientific production could create unprecedented wealth. This long term objective coincided with the immediate purpose of his Plan.

Owen proposed to establish 'villages of Co-operation'. They would at once give employment, and serve, on the principles of New Lanark, as model communities. They were to be predominantly agrarian and self supporting. In time, he believed, their profits would allow the extension of a movement which would peacefully transform society. Although, immediately, the plan was never successfully attempted in England, and met with disastrous failure at New Harmony, its legacy as a stimulant to the Co-operative movement was to persist.

The ideas behind Owenite Socialism are often very odd indeed. In spite of their practical purpose, Owen's villages have affinity with the Phalanstères. Starting from the basic assumption, afterwards adopted by Marx, that labour, properly directed, is the source of all wealth, he declares that 'the whole population might participate in the benefits from the increase of scientific productive power'.[32] If the labour standard of value were adopted, the working class would no longer be 'slaves of an artificial system of wages'.

The basis of labour must be the land. But it must be individually cultivated. The first objective of the Plan is 'to cultivate the soil with the spade instead of the plough'. 'The spade' Owen continues, with a theoretical dogmatism worthy of Saint-Simon, 'wherever there is sufficient soil, opens it to a depth that allows the water to pass freely below the bed of the seed or plant . . .'[33] But, 'the action of the plough upon the soil is the reverse of that of the spade...' That is, indeed, a 'mere surface implement, and extremely defective in principle'. Owen, of all people in this context, then coolly turns to attack 'closet theorists', and to cast aspersions on the ignorance of farmers.[34] By this reversion to prehistoric methods of cultivation, society was to be redeemed. It is not remarkable that the landowners of Lanark failed to appreciate the Plan.

Given this return to the spade, Owen maintains at least sixty million labourers could be healthily employed. The total population of the island could be raised to a hundred million. The greatly increased wealth resulting would be distributed by a fair exchange, according to the labour expended — by papers, for example, 'representative of the value of labour'.

The agrarian communities would include from eight hundred to twelve hundred persons, and a village would require between six hundred to eighteen hundred acres. The workman will thus no longer be 'separated from his food', and the whole population would in time be engaged in agriculture, with 'manufactures as an appendage'. This community would reside in 'a large square, or rather parallelogram'.[35] Food, clothing and education would be provided. They would eat together 'as one family'. And 'if to partake of viands so prepared, served up with every comfort, in clean, spacious, well-lighted, and pleasantly ventilated apartments, and in the society of well-dressed, well-trained, well-educated, and well-informed associates possessing the most benevolent disposition and desirable habits, can give zest and proper enjoyment to meals, then will the inhabitants of the proposed villages experience all this in an eminent degree'.[36] The ideal takes its place in the pedigree of the Welfare State.

Ventilation will also be scientifically arranged. 'The parties will have no further trouble than to open and shut two slides . . .' And their clothes will also be well ventilated. Like the Saint-Simonians, they will wear the tunic or kilt. 'The Romans and the Highlanders of Scotland appear to be the only two nations who adopted a national dress on account of its utility, without, however, neglecting to render it highly becoming . . .'[37] Such robust exposure, it is well known, promotes good morals; 'sexual delicacy and virtue will be found much higher in nations when the person, from infancy, is most exposed.' The really immoral people are those who go about muffled to the eyes.

If these hygienic, rational, and self-sufficient communities can be established, a new mentality will emerge. Human nature now distorted and maligned, will be transformed not only by education but by a new economy. The poisonous division of labour will be abolished. Men will become once more versatile, healthy and intelligent. Thus employed, the lower classes will abandon thoughts of revolution. They will have 'every motive not to interfere with the honours and privileges of the existing higher orders'.[38]

Owen concludes with an elaborate simile. 'The conduct of mankind,' he declares, 'may not unaptly, be compared to ... an individual who, possessing an excellent soil for the purpose, desired to raise grapes but was ignorant of the plant.'[39] In the mistaken impression that 'the thorn was the vine', he cultivated it with immense pains. But irrigation, manure, incessant care, all proved ineffective. He, therefore, concluded that no human agency could raise grapes from such a soil, and sought refuge in supernatural assistance. With revived hopes, he again cultivated the thorn: with equally discouraging results. It only produced tougher and more varied prickles. So the misguided cultivator concluded that 'the power which had created the soil had ordained that it should produce only prickles, and that the grape would one day or other, in some way or other, be an after-product of the seed of the thorn'. He then abandoned all expectation of present success, and consoled himself with the hope of a distant and better future. 'This', concludes Owen, 'is an accurate picture of what human life had hitherto been.' Yet, all the time, human nature, properly understood, could yield immense harvests of benevolence. All is a matter of changing education and economic environment. And 'unlike ... all former great changes, this may be effected without a single evil or inconvenience'.[40]

Such was the dream which inspired Owen's disinterested propagandist career. It was to lurk, rather incongruously, behind the early development of the Trade Union and Co-operative movements. As the Fabians concentrated on the practical, the immediate and the ordinary, so Owen's objectives are thoroughly bourgeois. And as in the 'nineties, William Morris expressed the sentiment and the ideals which were the complement to the administrative programme of the Webbs, so Owen appealed to the hearts of the people. This strain of ordinary good sense inspired by sentiment, already anticipates the background of the British Welfare State. Here is no doctrine of class war and violent revolution; rather, in secular terms, an ideal deriving from the kindly but determined exponents of the communitarian Utopias of the seventeenth century. This tradition, before the challenge of the Industrial Revolution, found a new secular spokesman in Robert Owen. If his immediate economic plans were unpractical, he was a great educational reformer. He voiced, in plain terms, the conviction of generations of benevolent, individualist, and obstinate humanitarians, that 'something must be done'.

v

By the 'thirties of the nineteenth century, anarchist and communitarian thought had found an eloquent expression. First through the individualist ideas of Godwin, who with telling phrase and burning indignation, had contributed to the development of English political radicalism. He represents the priggish intellectual's form of anarchism. Fourier and Owen are less concerned with politics. Their objectives are educational and economic. Both are convinced that human nature has been maligned and mishandled. Both are determined to abolish laissez-faire, restore a healthy relation with the soil, and further release the immense forces of modern scientific production. They are convinced, as were Marx and Engels, that the development of these forces were still rudimentary. Unemployment, boom and slump, imperialist wars, are all, they write, a sign of maladjustment; not endemic in the nature of things. Fourier was wildly unpractical: Owen more effective, but immediately Utopian. And both were to be surpassed in range, ingenuity and eloquence by Proudhon.

CHAPTER VII

PROUDHON'S ATTACK ON THE STATE

SELDOM are the circumstances of a writer's early life more closely reflected than in the confused but ultimately consistent development of Proudhon's mind.* His outlook, like Cobbett's, is rooted in the land. The son of tough peasantry from Franche-Comté — his father was a wine cooper, his mother had been a cook — he spent his youth in the fields and woods around Besançon. Here, on the western slopes of the Jura, he developed a pagan pantheism. 'Till twelve my life was passed almost entirely in the country, in small rural tasks or herding cows.' Though without illusions about rural life, Proudhon always remained a countryman. He well knew the hard routine of peasant labour and the peasant lust for the soil. 'The industrial worker', he would insist, 'has nothing in common with the peasant; quite apart from his dialect, he doesn't speak the same language.'

* Pierre Joseph Proudhon, 1809-65. Born at Battant, a rural suburb of Besançon, the eldest of five children, he was brought up in severe poverty. Awarded a free place at the College of Besançon, he was punished for 'forgetting' the books he could not afford. When at the local prize-giving he was crowned for 'excellence', no one of Proudhon's family appeared, and he returned home to find them threatened with arrest. 'That evening,' he writes, 'we supped off bread and water.' To help his family he early took work as a printer and proof reader. Here he acquired an enthusiasm for philology and learnt Hebrew through the encouragement of his friend Gustav Fallot, the editor of a Latin *Lives of the Saints*, who told him that he was 'inevitably a writer'. In 1830 he took to itinerant work: 'cinquante francs dans ma poche, un sac sur le dos, et ma cahier de philosophie pour provision, je me dirigeai vers le midi de France'. His first publication was entitled *Essai de Grammaire Générale*, but the failure of the enterprise, says his biographer, was rendered irremediable by the suicide of the publisher. He now applied for the Pension Suard, a subvention awarded to young Doubsois of promise. After intense academic intrigues – Proudhon's opponents objected that being a printer he had a livelihood already; that he was the wrong age; that the *Essai* was not his own work, etc. – he obtained the award. Congratulated by the local bourgeoisie on his chance to gain 'une belle position', Proudhon replied that he was 'enfant du peuple, Filius Fabri'. 'Quelle fureur,' he commented, 'de bien-être matériel.' He would devote his career, he said, to the betterment of his own kind. Following his *Lettre de Candidature de la Pension Suard* (1938), appeared the *De la Célébration du Dimanche*, in which he inserted many subversive ideas, and which already gives the clue to his programme. But the real shock to his supporters at Besançon came with the notorious *Qu'est-ce que la Propriété?* (1840). Proudhon next took employment with Gautier Frères, at Lyons, in a coal business which specialized in water transport. In 1843 appeared his *De la Création de l'ordre dans l'Humanité* and, in 1844-46, his *Système des Contradictions Économiques, ou Philosophie de la Misère*. From this time dates his intimacy with Marx and Bakunin. The Revolution of 1848 proved an opportunity and a disappointment. He edited a paper *L'Avenir* and was elected Deputy of the Department of the Seine. But he was unsuccessful as a politician and his 'People's Bank' failed. In 1849 he was imprisoned for attacks on Louis Napoleon, but his imprisonment did not prevent his marriage to a proletarian girl, or the spate of his publications,

This passion for the land was bound up with deep memories of boyhood. With tenacious satisfaction he recalled long summer days by the Doubs. 'What pleasure,' he writes, 'to roll in the long grass that I would have liked to crop (brouter) like my own cows . . . to run barefoot under the hedges . . . often on the hot June mornings I would pull off my clothes and bathe in the meadow dew.' 'He could hardly distinguish,' he writes, 'between me and not me' — 'moi c'était tout ce que je pouvais toucher de la main'. To this sunlit world of boyhood the harassed writer would return. 'Without knowing it,' he says, 'and in spite of being baptised, I was a sort of practising pantheist — it is the philosophy of all those brought to sensibility by age, education and literature, who have not arrived at the abstract and the ideal — two things which in my view it is best to postpone as long as possible.'

This outlook was fundamental.* To his death Proudhon felt his deepest roots in peasant life. This writer of confused genius was a child of nature — far more genuine than Rousseau, with his self-dramatized introspection. Along with this love for the soil, went a deep-rooted anti-clericalism; the hatred of the emancipated peasant for the curé. Proudhon's detestation of the Church came from his conviction that the Christians blasphemed life — by what he regarded as their obsession with sin, their denial of instinct, their

* These views are most fully expressed in the De la Justice (vide infra).

l'Idée Générale de la Révolution au XIXe siècle (1851); Confessions d'un Révolutionnaire; La Révolution Sociale, etc. Released in 1852, he wrote his most voluminous and anti-clerical work, De la Justice dans la Révolution et dans l'Église addressed to the Cardinal Archbishop of Besançon. When again threatened with imprisonment, he fled to Brussels; a good Frenchman, he disliked the Belgian climate and the enforced consumption of Belgian beer through the high price of wine. In 1861 appeared his la Guerre et la Paix, which is coloured by illness and exile. Following an amnesty, he returned to France, and in 1863 appeared his important Du Principe Fédératif. He died at Poissy in 1865. The la Capacité Politique des Classes Ouvrières appeared posthumously. Proudhon's writings and correspondence are voluminous, and only his outstanding publications are here given. He was personally an upright, straightforward, character, whose literary powers could have won him a comfortable living: instead he chose poverty and the championship of his class. His portraits show a stocky, square, man with a fine forehead and level eyes concealed behind the curiously small spectacles of the period.

The best though incomplete edition of his works is the Œuvres Complètes de P-J Proudhon, vols. I-XI. Edited C. C. A. Bouglé et H. Moysset. Paris, 1923, which all contain admirable introductions. There is an earlier complete edition in 33 volumes. Paris, 1865-76. There is also a short selection, with a brilliant introduction by C. Bouglé, Proudhon. Paris, 1928. The most vivid portrait of the man is SAINTE-BEUVE's P-J Proudhon, Sa vie et sa Corréspondence, 1838-48 (first edition 1872, reprinted Paris, 1947). See also EMILE FAGUET, op. cit., 3e serie (1900); P. BOURGEAU, P-J Proudhon et La critique de la Démocratie. C. BOUGLÉ, La Sociologie de Proudhon; A. AMOUDRUZ's excellent Proudhon et L'Europe. Paris, 1945, q.v. for a good bibliography; N. BOURGEOIS, Les Théories du Droit Internationales chez Proudhon. Paris, 1927. See also Professor D. W. BROGAN, Proudhon. Hamish Hamilton, 1934, and SIR A. GRAY, op. cit., chap. x.

parasitic regard for work as a curse, when in fact it is a blessing, and by their crawling preoccupation of self. He was more hopeful about the nature of mankind. 'I have lost faith in God,' he wrote, 'I have found it in humanity.' He was thus, like his contemporary, Comte, an early representative of a powerful current of nineteenth-century opinion. This self-confidence was reflected in his own early life. He never hankered for middle class employment and enjoyed his wanderings as an independent compositor. He recounts with gusto his devastating interview with the Mayor of Toulon, 'a complacent little man in gold spectacles', who had denied him employment or even advice. It is a classic scene of scarification, the official being immortalized like a fly in amber. Unlike many of his class who have climbed by their talents into the upper ranks of society, Proudhon never despised his own kind; he realized their limitations, but he knew their strength.

This basic peasant outlook combined with a passion for scholarship, expressed in the Latin and Greek quotations which reinforce and sometimes divert his argument. His original ambition was to be a philologist, and he was a man of deep, if scattered, erudition. This learning is brought to the service of his anti-clericalism, which reaches a level of vitriolic hatred anticipating the idiom of Georges Sorel. Christianity, 'imported from the East in a revolutionary epoch . . . saturated with Jewish and Egyptian ideas, is an expression of the poverty of the masses, of the despair of the people, of the degradation of slaves'. It was indeed the reaction to Pagan pride, but 'the epoch of Christianity is the real era of the fall of Man'. Now will come another, Hegelian, reaction into a third epoch of justice and humanism. For Christianity represents a violation of conscience. What a horrible doctrine is the idea of original sin — a declaration of universal indignity! It is incompatible with Proudhon's over-riding conception of social justice — the key to his thought. For justice, say the Christians, is a stranger to this lost world; only by redemption can there come salvation from sin. Such pessimism is revolting to the peasant genius, with his kinship with nature, his cult of life. Proudhon's mind was profoundly irreligious; it was powerful, not subtle. His analysis of the Lord's Prayer — singularly shocking to Christians — shows a total blindness to the finer shades of religious experience. The human race, he says, bound under its original sin to beg its bread — what degradation!

Proudhon's cult of humanity, of marriage and the family, did not imply equality of the sexes. He combined the usual romantic phrases of his time and nation with a strict view of women's place in society. 'Le farouche philosophe de Besançon avait de la femme l'opinion le plus défavorable' says Perrin, the biographer of Sorel. This view is exaggerated. Firmly relegated to the role of helpmeet, and her economic capacity assessed at eight to a man's twenty-seven, woman is also a personified conscience. She is man's hope and consolation. She is 'turris eburnea, Domus aurea, janua coeli, stella matutina, Rosa mystica — quelle puissance dans ses regards!' She is even 'refugium peccatorum'. But nature, he insists, has not made her the equal of man.* Here, again, is a peasant outlook. Woman is essentially the helper, the complement of man. The nineteenth-century romantic phrases are superimposed, an exercise in rhetoric and paradox, on the ideal of family co-operative enterprise. A more ethereal ideal was not for Proudhon's rather Philistine mind.

This idea of comradeship, or 'mutualism', is further developed in his economic thought, technically so incompetent, morally not unattractive. And his political views were subordinated to economic 'mutualism'. Like Godwin and Kropotkin, Proudhon was a Puritan moralist, who detested the state as the enemy of justice. Yet although a revolutionary, he was implacably hostile to authoritarian communism. Hence the profound divergence from Marx, and the bitterness of Marx's attack on a man he had once admired. Proudhon wished for a moral, classless, society, stabilized on an austere economic level. He looked for 'a system of equilibrium between free forces, of which each is assured of exercising the same right on condition of fulfilling the same duties . . . a system in consequence essentially egalitarian and liberal, which excludes all acceptance of rank and class'. In this sense Proudhon was an anarchist. Along with this idea, went an onslaught on 'la grande propriété'. Proudhon also firmly asserts natural rights. 'Man as a citizen draws his rights directly from the dignity of his nature': 'Service for service — such is the Law.' It is the old Levelling idea of commonwealth in a different setting. 'Here the worker is no longer a slave of the state, drowned in a communitarian ocean; he is a free man, really sovereign, acting under his own initiative and personal responsibility.' Proudhon thus attempts to evade the antithesis of individual and state. His anarchy did not imply violence and terror, but a world of spontaneous self-governing producers. As his thought matured, this anarchism was translated into terms of Federation. Internally the centralized state

* See *De la Justice*, vol. IV, pp. 179-201 for the alleged 'Infériorité physique, intellectuelle et morale de la femme'.

was to be weakened by contracts between groups of producers, agrarian and industrial, for specific ends; externally, the power of sovereignty was to be simultaneously diminished.

The debt to Saint-Simon is clear in the stress on production, on the discarding of political power, but here is none of the authoritarianism of Saint-Simon or of Comte, which Proudhon strongly repudiates. His self-governing producers were to transcend class conflict. This view was to find rather similar expression half a century later in the views of Kropotkin, and with the Marxist class antagonism bitterly emphasized, in the writings of the anarcho-syndicalist, Georges Sorel.[1] Proudhon's debt to Rousseau is also apparent, in his passionate belief in the moral stature of the common man.

This self-governing federal society was, of course, incompatible with industrial capitalism. Like Godwin and Cobbett, Proudhon's agrarian mind never fully understood the problems of great industry. He hated urban capitalist civilization. 'La grande propriété,' he writes, 'envahie tout.' False values are created; mere singers and artists earn more than industrious peasants; women are judged 'only by their beauty'. All this springs from a fundamental injustice, the maldistribution of property.

Such are the landmarks in Proudhon's thought. The reader faced with the welter of his works may be wise to bear them in mind. The peasant origin and self sufficiency, the cult of work, the anti-clericalism, the belief in the family and woman's place in it, the ideal of 'mutualism', of economic co-operation with its hatred of large property, the programme of political anarchy and Federation — all are related to social justice based on the dignity of man.

This view Proudhon proclaimed with violent reiteration. Already in the Preface to the second edition of the trenchant *De la Célébration du Dimanche*, he inserted his attack on property. We live, he says, in an age of fundamental revolution, comparable to the Christian revolution of Antiquity. Just as the Christians denied Caesar, the republic, the pagan gods, so we now question everything. 'What is Royalty we ask — a myth? What is religion — a dream of the Spirit? What is God — the eternal X? What is property — theft?' The notorious phrase is already coined. It was to be used with fullest effect in Proudhon's first large and ambitious work — *Qu'est-ce que la Propriété?* 'La propriété,' he declared, 'c'est le vol.'* To this slogan

---

* *Qu'est-ce que la Propriété?* ou Recherche sur le Principe du Droit et du Gouvernement. Premier Mémoire, 1840, p. 131. The book is divided into five chapters, (1) A scheme of the

he constantly recurred. It made him seem a more desperate revolutionary than he was, and it won for him a haunting notoriety. He was extremely proud of the phrase. 'Il ne se dit pas en mille ans deux mots comme celui-là. Je n'ai d'autre bien sur la terre que cette définition de la propriété, mais je la tiens pour plus précieuse que les millions de M. de Rothschild.'*

Why not, he asks, admit the truth? If, asked to define slavery, I replied 'assassination', no one would object. 'I am only anticipating history by a few days . . . I write the preamble of a future constitution — La propriété c'est le vol. What a transformation of ideas!'² The large book, written in six months, contained Proudhon's most passionate convictions.

He also developed views on sociology. Like most of his generation — Comte, Marx and Spencer — he believed in a science of politics. 'The work of our species', he wrote, 'is to build the temple of Science, and that science includes man and nature.' Man's task is to transform environment by knowledge. 'I said to myself, one day, why in society is there so much pain and poverty — must man always be miserable?' Here is the Saint-Simonian belief in control and betterment. This conviction blends curiously with his anarchism. Where Saint-Simon and Comte believed in an alliance between science and authority, Proudhon believed that his free Federalist producers would understand scientific method.

Proudhon's attack on property brought him the notoriety he desired: 'Il n'existe rien de semblable à mon livre.' In this assertion Proudhon was right. The Academicians in Besançon had indeed got their money's worth. He had struck at the most sensitive point of middle class opinion. Henceforward he was a marked man. Though in fact he desired a diffusion and equalizing of property rather than its abolition, from that time he became an ogre.

During his employment at Lyons, Proudhon wrote his next large work, the *Système des Contradictions Économiques, ou Philosophie de la Misère*. Its title at least is well known, since it was the object of

---

* Actually the phrase seems to have been coined by WARVILLE DE BRISSOT, *Recherches Philosophiques sur le droit de Propriété dans la nature*, see LECKY, *Democracy and Liberty*, vol. II, on the history of Socialism *passim*, and JANET, *Histoire de la Science Politique*, vol. II, pp. 662-5.

Work and the Idea of Revolution. (2) Property considered as a Natural Right. (3) Of Labour as the efficient cause of the Domination of Property. (4) Why Property is impossible: because it exacts something from nothing: because it is homicidal; by it society devours itself. The negation of Equality. (5) Psychological explanation of Justice and Injustice, and definition of the Principles of Government; moral sense in men and animals. Definition of the form of society.

Marx's ferocious attack in his *Poverty of Philosophy*. As Filmer won dubious fame as the victim of Locke, so Proudhon, in this context, has been known as the victim of Marx. Like Filmer, today Proudhon has also won recognition. Meanwhile, the book, a mixture of Hegelian philosophy and economic speculation, is not his masterpiece. The later *De la Justice* is more comprehensive, and the posthumous *De la Capacité Politique des Classes Ouvrières* shows better judgment.

Proudhon himself set much store by the *Contradictions*. He wanted it to make a stir. 'If I could set all the world by the ears, I should achieve just the result I want — universal reconciliation through universal contradiction.'* The book is primarily concerned with economic theory. It was written at white heat, and confused by second-hand Hegelian ideas. 'Le style', wrote Proudhon, 'en sera rude et âpre: l'ironie et la colère s'y feront trop sentir; c'est un mal irrémédiable. Quand le lion a faim, il rugit.'† Here is an onslaught, confused but powerful, on the long prevalent orthodoxy of laissez-faire; an attack on the economic individualism deriving from Adam Smith, Malthus and Ricardo. It also applied Proudhon's conception of Hegel's Dialectic to political economy — 'a pretentious speculative muddle', said Marx.‡ 'You open a book of political economy,' complains Sainte-Beuve, 'and you find a chapter about God.' Yet

* Quoted by R. PICARD in his Introduction; '*Hegelianisme féroce et naïve*', he remarks. See his edition, *Rivière*. Paris, 1924. Two vols. The first volume of this large work contains a prologue in eight chapters. The first deals with the Insufficiency of Economic Science; the second with Value, the third with Division of Labour, and its antagonistic Social effects. The fourth (of particular interest) describes the impact of the machine on Liberty and what means should be taken to counteract it. The fifth and sixth chapters describe the effects of competition and monopoly, and the seventh the power of the Police and Taxation. The eighth abandons these economic subjects to examine the 'Responsibility of Man and God in view of the Law of Contradiction'. The first volume concludes with An exposition of the 'Myth of the Fall and of the Myth of Providence' and with a final account of the 'Retrogradation of God'. The second volume (chapters XI-XIII) returns to more limited topics: the balance of Trade, the power of Credit (as orthodoxly conceived) to create Poverty; and the influence of Property towards Depravity (diminution of the hypothesis of God by Property). Chapter xv examines the paradox of the bourgeois state, which is impossible without organization, yet dies of it. The bourgeois state is the creation of poverty. And poverty results from the ideas of orthodox political economy. The whole work ends with a résumé and conclusion. Marx had something to get his teeth into.
† SAINTE-BEUVE, op. cit., p. 59.
‡ Picard's admirable edition contains an Appendix giving Proudhon's own marginal comments on MARX's *Misère de la Philosophie*. 'Quelle bêtise . . . En vérité, Marx est jaloux', writes Proudhon. 'Bavardage . . . allons, cher Marx, vous êtes de mauvaise foi et tout à la fois vous ne savez rien,' etc. etc. etc. A proper mare's nest. The Hegelian preoccupation occasioned a characteristic anecdote. Herzen relates how, in the rooms of a mutual friend, Proudhon and Bakunin were discussing Hegel far into the night. When the visitor came back next morning to take their host to visit the Zoo, he found that the two philosophers had forgotten to go to bed. In the best tradition of intellectual Bohemianism and in precisely the same positions, they were absorbed in the same theme.

in this rambling and portentous work, will be found most of Proudhon's master ideas. The attack on the existing economy; the remedy by 'mutualist' credit and a People's Bank; the hostility to the state, the vindication of the family and the demand for social justice.

The appearance of the book in 1846 increased Proudhon's prestige. He attempted during the Revolution of 1848 to assert himself as a practical politician and economist. But he never reconciled his hatred of the centralized state with the need to use it to impose revolutionary policies, and soon fell out with the politicians. During his consequent imprisonment, he returned to his métier as a writer. The vast range of his *De la Justice* (1861) marks the climax of his anti-clericalism and provides the fullest materials for his biography. The reader is recommended to study the full text, which forms one of the most interesting documents of its time.* The argument is extremely well constructed. Though overweighted with digressions and examples, it forms the fullest statement of the themes already enumerated. All societies must have their inspiration. Hitherto it has been transcendent, revealed religion and abstract metaphysics. Today these sanctions are dead and a decision must be taken. Either the Church or the Revolution is right. There can be no compromise. The inspiration of modern society must be found in the conscience of man, and in this new Puritan Humanism alone can social justice be found.

In primitive societies mankind projected the ideas of God and justice into abstractions. This is an 'optical illusion': man now makes himself. The principle of modern society is 'la dignité humaine ...' 'C'est un loi de la nature que l'être intelligent et libre fasse lui-même ses mœurs'.[3] This optimistic belief, a matter of feeling rather than logic, repudiates original sin: it assumes high qualities in ordinary individuals which Hobbes or de Maistre would deny. Since all depends on the intrinsic worth of personality, Communism is no remedy. 'Moins que jamais, nous ne pouvons reprendre le joug communiste.' There are roughly equal numbers of each sex; nature has not therefore exacted the 'murderous subordination' of the

---

* *De la Justice dans la Révolution et dans L'Église.* 4 vols. (op. cit.). It contains twelve studies. The first treats of the problem of Justice, the second of Personality, the third of Goods. The fourth analyses the State, and the fifth Education. The sixth deals with Work and the seventh with Ideas. The eighth is concerned with Conscience and Liberty, the ninth with Progress and Decadence, the tenth and eleventh with Love and Marriage, and the concluding study with the sanctions for Morality. It will be seen that there are few aspects of life omitted from this survey. It is subtitled 'Studies in practical philosophy addressed to his Eminence Cardinal Mathieu, Archbishop of Besançon.' With vitriolic politeness, the argument is addressed to the Archbishop in person throughout.

specialized termites from mankind. Social justice can come only from spontaneous individual initiative. We must feel it passionately, 'Comme un amour, une volupté, une joie, une colère.'* This atheist Humanism sets a gulf between traditional and modern society. It informs all social relations with a new morality. Justice is the product of mutual regard; spontaneously felt, and with increasing civilization, reciprocally guaranteed. This dignity is innate, not assertive: 'la gloire est cet instinct d'enflure ridiculisé dans la fable de la grenouille et du bœuf'.⁴ It is equally detestable in nations and in men. Dignity is a private virtue and private life must remain outside public affairs. But character is the mainspring of commonwealth. Doctrines which derive the inspiration of government from imposed power or contract are pernicious. 'La liberté, suivant Hegel . . . est zéro.'⁵ Hobbes and Bentham, who equate right with interest, reduce all to licence and calculation.⁶

The essential problem is moral. Hence Proudhon's bitter attack on orthodox laissez-faire economists: 'ils font bon marché', he wrote, 'de la vie, de la liberté, de l'intelligence des masses.'⁷ Here, before history, is their crime. The economic problem can be solved only through 'a system of reciprocal service'. Mutualism must supersede hierarchy. Proudhon's sense of human dignity is particularly outraged by Malthus and his followers. They sacrifice life to economic laws of their own devising, and abdicate humane initiative. They are reduced to 'moral restraint' as the sole palliation for poverty. What, in human terms does this mean? It amounts to the degradation of marriage: 'morale des Malthusiens, *morale de cochons*'.⁸

In politics, as in economics, it is the same. Anarchy is not the business of mankind, yet government is perennially unpopular and unstable. Police, education, propaganda, all are needed to maintain political authority; yet the basic human institutions, marriage and the family, spontaneously persist. This spontaneity should be transferred to government. Universal suffrage is not enough; it must be inspired by mutual service. If asked what would you do the day after the revolution? Proudhon would reply: 'assert a new way of life'.

This would transcend all frontiers. It is therefore the answer to the question of European order. Federation would 'guarantee all liberty and law, without soldiers or priests'.⁹ 'La fédération est la forme politique d'humanité.' How to attain this ideal? By converting public opinion. Then one day, before the criminal manœuvres

---

* Proudhon rejects Enfantin's interpretation of Saint-Simon as a spiritual tyranny. If it emancipates the flesh, it degrades the mind (I, p. 386).

of governments, the masses will say 'No'. The objective is to bring this 'No' into being. Put government in the predicament of the King who was asked 'Que ferais tu, Sire, si quand tu dis Oui, tout le monde disait Non?' These remedies assert human values against the poison of abstract ideas. They that live by the ideal perish by the ideal. The 'elimination of the Absolute' is the first task of 'cerebral hygiene'. Proudhon devotes a whole chapter to the 'corrupting influence' of the Absolute.[10]

Raison d'État and Raison d'Église are both equally pernicious. The Roman Imperial ideal was imposing, but its decadence was inevitable and ended in the total destruction of liberty. The puritanical Proudhon makes a long and zealous digression into the morals of Antiquity. Elagabalus, for example, was a perverted idealist. This embodiment of eroticism, 'omnisexuel, omnianimal, omnimode . . . dans son hermaphrodisme épuise tous les inventions de la volupté'. His queer habits are described in some detail. As for Septimius Severus, he was incompetent, and Maximin beastly. All are examples of the decadence of imposed power. Indeed, this decadence of Antiquity proves the rottenness of a civilization inspired by abstractions. The Catholic Church is no better, and Communism would come to the same end. By its negation of personality, property and family; by its denial of human dignity and its 'Esprit d'Église'. It also makes for sexual aberration: 'comme ses contraires, il est du point de vue des relations amoureuses, fatalement pédérastique'.[11] After this unexpected allegation against the Marxists, Greek erotic fashions are elaborately attacked. They are flagrant consequences of sophisticated idealism. And indeed the ideals of the Greek Anthology contrast strongly with peasant married comradeship. Proudhon does not mince words. Gross depravity, he declares, was celebrated by the Greek poets. What idealist hallucination! It is the same now. Honest workers do not pursue these aberrations, but the intellectuals — the artists, the writers, and, he reminds the Archbishop, the priests. Boys and girls who dream of love should remember where Platonic ideals are apt to lead.*
And if the Greeks were bad enough, Roman debauchery was 'titanic'. All this perversion results from satiety and boredom, from over-sophistication and social injustice. In matters of sex, Proudhon was a militant moralist. Marriage and the family, he reiterates, rooted in practical life, are the foundation of society. Catholic asceticism and misguided abstract ideals have deprived women of

* De la Justice, IV, pp. 69ff passim, Corruption du Mariage, etc.

their mission, but the 'conjugal pair' are now to be vindicated. Revolution will deliver marriage from the taint of idealism and the contempt of intellectuals. As the long Christian eclipse of the human spirit wanes, the glorious day of progress and emancipation is coming in: — 'the self justification of humanity by itself'. At long last the dignity of man is to be vindicated.

In his exile Proudhon devoted himself mainly to international affairs. The *La Guerre et la Paix* is a curious document.* It begins with a description of war which owes much to de Maistre, and ends by asserting that war in its natural purity has been spoilt by nineteenth-century capitalists and bureaucrats. Modern war is a *reductio ad absurdum*, and likely to die out. It has been well remarked that Proudhon liked war, but not armies. Historically he declares, war has always been 'the most splendid, at the same time the most horrible, manifestation of our species'.† 'So speaks de Maistre . . . a thousand times more profound in his theosophy than the self-styled rationalists whom his writings scandalize.' Man preys upon his own species. He thus shows his creative originality. 'Wolves and lions, no more than beavers, go to war among themselves . . .' Man's warlike habits show his greatness, for without them 'he would have lost his revolutionary faculty'. When philanthropists wish to abolish war, they risk degrading the race. In modern conditions one must find a substitute. War's primary cause is always economic: it is 'fille de famine'.[11] Its objective has always been plunder; in primitive times 'heroic pillage'. With the advance of civilization, this impulse becomes sophisticated and more horrible. It becomes perverted into a government industry, into exploitation. What promotion it brings, what bureaucracy — and for the business men, what speculations! This is war in its most advanced phase.[12] Armies are now supported no longer by pillage, but, a huge vested interest, by the taxes of their own people. In the mid-twentieth century this thought seems apposite. War, he declares, will end when mass opinion decides it shall do so. Peace, he concludes hopefully, will be the work of the nineteenth century.

Proudhon shows an hostility to nationalism rare at the time. He cared nothing for Mazzini and Garibaldi, whose exploits dazzled his contemporaries; nothing for the wrongs of Poland or Hungary. For nationalism meant the glorification of the centralized state. The

* *La Guerre et la Paix, Recherches sur le Principe et la Constitution du Droit des Gens*, edited H. Moysset. Paris, 1927.

† For the best treatment of this theme, see J. U. NEF's masterly *War and Human Progress*. Chicago, 1950.

break-up of the loose-knit Austrian empire would multiply such concentrations of power. How right had been the diplomats of the Treaty of Vienna! Proudhon is one of the earliest defenders of that settlement. As for liberating the people of the Austrian Empire, 'one might as well talk of reasserting the Saxony of Witukind, the realm of Austrasia and the Visigoths'. Such enterprises are 'wars of fantasy'. This kind of thing, in any case, is outmoded: 'the end of the period of wars will coincide with the end of Christianity'.[14] There is no 'natural cause' for the campaigns of the Crimea and Lombardy: 'la politique de guerre est épuisée'. France today holds the keys of war and peace. She has the mission to inaugurate the abolition of war. 'L'humanité ne veut pas la guerre.'

Federalism will end it. 'Le Fédéralisme,' he wrote, 'alpha et omega de ma politique'. The *Du Principe Fédératif* contains some most valuable ideas. They reflect, in particular, a detestation of the centralized state. 'Les grands états modernes', says Bouglé, 'sont aux yeux de Proudhon autant de monstres tentaculaires.' He thus set himself against one of the major tendencies of the nineteenth century, centralized democratic nationalism. The sovereign nation state, inherited and developed from the eighteenth century, had constricted the new forces of industrialism and democracy: Proudhon, though a French patriot, defied this powerful tendency. He observed, too, the growing inequality of states, its consequences for minor powers; and his deep-seated sense of the paramount importance of economic life convinced him that peace was imperative. A society of producers implied international federation. The characteristic nineteenth century identification of nationality with government, of national cultures with sovereign power, never appealed to him. Hating the centralized state, he favoured polyglot minorities. 'It was not at all bad for the fraternity of nations,' he writes, 'that there should be Flemings, and Germans and Italians and Basques in France . . . minorities make people understand that justice is more than language.'[15] The power of the bourgeois state must be diminished from within. If its internal authority is undermined by federation, external, supra-national federation will become easier. Since the power of modern great states means war, says Proudhon, we must weaken them all. A 'fraternal equilibrium' is the goal — outside the state as well as within. In this field, he complains, the Revolution lacked initiative. The people accept the unitary framework inherited from the old regime. But the evils of national sovereignty are the same, whether royal or democratic.

Here, indeed, is an agonized protest against the course of power politics. Proudhon's pacific, mutualist society implied the defeat of the state. 'If', he declared, 'the progress of mankind is to be accomplished in the sense of individual liberty, corporative, local communal, provincial, national, . . . it is inevitable that, after some oscillations, the great states lose their centralizing character.'[16] To this confederation of federations he also wished parliamentary democracy to be subordinate, since it implied centralized power, and indeed had made a poor enough showing in the France of Proudhon's experience. So bitterly did he dislike French liberal constitutionalism that he wrote 'the best way of making the people lie is to establish universal suffrage',[17] a comment on the 'Caesarism' of Napoleon III. This false democracy must be abolished, as the monarchy was destroyed before it. Under such régimes, parliamentary or dictatorial, the people are crushed by the authority whose power is wielded in their name.

Proudhon's proposals for European Union also deserve study. 'A man is a man,' he says, 'both in the state and in Europe.' Here contract becomes cosmopolitan. He does not desire a European superstate, but specific contracts for defined purposes within a confederation. As one of his commentators remarks, 'To multiply juridical ties between the peoples, at once supple and strong, is to advance towards a logical constitution for mankind.'[18] Unhappily Proudhon's advice could hardly then be taken by politicians involved in the going concern of the nation state, even had they desired to do so. The momentum of administration, the development of international politics, the realities of nineteenth-century power, brushed aside the protest of this eloquent, indefatigable and politically powerless writer.

On the other great problem of the nineteenth century, the development of the class struggle, Proudhon had also much to say. The posthumous *De la Capacité Politique des Classes Ouvrières** displays a more temperate judgment and a greater clarity than his other works. It also shows less hostility to the methods of democratic suffrage, and is often regarded as his masterpiece. It opens with a vivid evocation of the Paris of June 1st, 1863, under the hated government of Louis Napoleon. The Parisian workers had rejected the

---

* *De la Capacité Politique des Classes Ouvrières.* Edited M. Leroy, Paris, 1924. 420 pp. It treats of working-class democracy; the development of the working-class Idea; the creation of Economic Rights, etc. The fourth chapter is of particular interest on municipal liberty and for federalist criticism of the unified bureaucratic state. The book concludes with an affirmation of the solidarity of middle-class workers with the masses.

official opposition candidates. They favoured independent supporters of the *Manifeste du Soixante*. Paris, wrote Proudhon, was seething with excitement. No longer 'the new, monotonous, tiring town of M. Haussmann, with its rectilineal boulevards, gigantic hotels . . .' it was again the Paris of the old revolutionary days, 'whose ghosts appeared in the starlight'.[19] For now the people were asserting their own will. Here was no mere rising of clients and serfs, and no stampede into Caesarism. In 1789, 1804, and 1815, 'the people had voted for its Emperor, never for itself'. And after regaining the suffrage in 1830, they had merely elected bourgeois politicians. Now, at last, comes real proletarian initiative. 'That is the most significant event of our nineteenth century, and should not be any more astonishing than polygamy and slavery in the time of the patriarchs, or feudalism or Papal supremacy in the middle ages.'[20] At last the masses have become Something. And like the middle classes in 1789, they now aspire to become Everything. The people are on the march. All over the French countryside the peasants are moving with a fixed idea — to get the land. In spite of industrial development, the old agricultural interest still predominates. In the cities, too, the people are on the move. And since the renewal of the suffrage, rural and urban masses are at one. 'The thought inspiring both is fundamentally the same: it is the complete emancipation of the worker, the abolition of the salariat — the expulsion of the alien.'[21] The whole working class is inspired with the same impetuous aim. The days of Caesarism will soon be past. In a characteristic simile Proudhon remarks, 'the people have behaved like a hungry bull. Wanting to wake the keeper, it shoves a horn in his side'. But this massive instinctive, movement must have an Idea. 'Yes,' he says, '. . . you've got the numbers and the power, but you must have an Idea too. You won't get anywhere without that.'

So he tells them some home truths. Why, for example, not support their own natural leaders? 'Educated minds exist in the working class, and plenty of them capable of leadership . . . twenty times more able, and, above all, more worthy to represent the people, than the lawyers, journalists, writers, pedants, intriguers and charlatans, on which it lavishes its votes.' Yet the masses reject them. They dislike really democratic candidates. With an old, instinctive, deference before the arrogant stare of the salaried class, 'the proletariat lowers its eyes like a girl'.[22] They are sluggish, too, in exercising their power. Even in 1863, twenty-five per cent failed to vote. Now at last is the time to affirm a proletarian 'consciousness of self as members of the commonwealth'.[23] In 1848 class consciousness emerged. The rudiments of an idea exist; the next step is to realize it. It has not yet been taken. That is what we now look for — independent action, not 'manifestations moutonnières'.[24]

But Proudhon most emphatically repudiates class war. Although class division has created solidarity, it is evil. It must be surmounted. 'The division of modern society into two classes — one of paid workers, the other of capitalist exploiters being flagrant . . . Can this dangerous division be overcome?' His ideal was egalitarian, but harmonious. Proudhon was a moralist and leveller, not a prophet of class conflict. Sooner or later, he says, the democratic idea is bound to transform society, but it must not be yet another mere affirmation of caste.[25] Popular responsibility must follow popular power. This is the moral of the greatest fact of the nineteenth century, the result of the pioneering effort of French democracy. 'The social fact of incalculable significance . . . the arrival of the most numerous and poorest class in political life'.

And what a task confronts the people! Since their great effort in 1789, the middle class have morally collapsed. They have failed in thought and will: they can think only of power and profit, they are rotten with corruption. They despise the people as the nobility never despised the peasants. They are 'no longer a class powerful in numbers, work and genius, which wills and thinks, which produces and contrives, which governs and commands — it is a minority that exploits and speculates — a rabble'.

Here, still, is the voice of the peasant moralist. It is also the voice of Proudhon's generation — of the disillusioned romantics. Down the river near Rouen, the son of a provincial surgeon was also composing his indictment of the bourgeoisie. Hatred of 'Bovarysme' was to contribute to the literature of revolution. The meanness, the egotism, the boredom, of petit-bourgeois life, combined with the corruption of politics, to contribute to the legend that the bourgeoisie was finished. Proudhon, like Sorel after him, vied with Marx in creating the profoundly misleading myth.

Yet he reiterates that the people's revolution should not be just another turnover of power and privilege, a new domination of one class for another. Class distinction, he insists, is 'not in the nature of things'. The workers ought not to be led by bourgeois doctrinaires; too often they then become cruel and inept imitators of the middle class. They ought rather to gain by the absorption of professional intelligence and skill. Both should be reciprocally absorbed in a new society. 'The day when the people constituting the majority will have seized power . . . and proclaimed the reform of the economic and political system, according to the aspiration of a new kind of law and the formulae of science, will be the hour of their final fusion.'[26]

In spite of his former revolutionary bitterness, this is Proudhon's final answer to the class war. It is one of vision, humanity and sanguine hope. It reflected the moral purpose of all his thought. The supreme fact of the nineteenth century, he believed, had been the collapse of the old religious sanctions. But Society must have its beliefs. The new principles of social justice must emanate from man himself. All politics must be subordinated to life, to the essential dignity of man. Among revolutionary Utopian thinkers, he is perhaps the most sensible.

Proudhon's influence on the development of French syndicalist thought was decisive. Individualist, confused, voluminous in exposition, politically a failure, he left few immediate disciples. In the economic context of the time, Marx's ideas were more appropriate; with modern developments of diffused power Proudhon's theories are of increasing interest. They were always moral. Like Godwin, but with greater realism, this Jura peasant genius was convinced that personality must come before government. From the moral reform of personal and family life, the mutual humane exchange of services, and the transcending of national frontiers in a common interest, will follow the moralization of political and economic life before which the monstrous problems of the modern world would dissolve.

CHAPTER VIII

HUMANITARIAN NATIONALISM: MAZZINI

T HE contribution of Italian writers to political thought has alternated between lofty ideals and cynical realism. On the one hand Dante, Vico, Mazzini; on the other, Machiavelli and Pareto. It is the contrast between the worlds of Perugino and Petronius, of Dante and Norman Douglas. This Mediterranean paradox is already familiar in Greek theory and practice in the time of Plato and Thucydides.

The effect of the Romantic Movement upon the Italians was naturally sensational. Mazzini was its greatest political prophet.*

---

* Giuseppe Mazzini. Born 1805 at Genoa of a substantial professional family, his father being Professor of Anatomy at the University. At fifteen he was much affected by a 'tall black bearded man of severe aspect', who demanded aid for refugees from the failed revolution in Turin. He expressed his adolescent melancholy for the Italian cause by dressing from that time onwards in black. In 1827 he joined the Carbonari, with whom he was later disillusioned, and following the revolution of 1830, he was imprisoned at Savona. Released, he established himself at Marseille, where he lived for a year hiding in one room, editing *La Giovine Italia*. This he greatly enjoyed, 'writing articles and letters, seeing travellers, affiliating the Italian sailors . . . tying up bundles'. The paper was 'smuggled out in barrels of pumice stone and cans of pitch'. Following the suicide of his best friend, Jacopo Ruffini, in prison, Mazzini and his mistress, Giuditta Sidole, settled in Geneva, where he inspired an expedition for the liberation of Savoy, conducted by a Polish general who embezzled the funds. In 1835 he began to publish *La Jeune Suisse*. In 1837 he fled to London where at first he endured great poverty. Though forced at one stage, like Marx, to pawn his overcoat, he was sustained by remittances from his parents. In 1840 he became acquainted with the Carlyles and began to make a name as a journalist. The revolutions of 1848 proved his opportunity, and he was acclaimed on a balcony in Milan by the revolutionary populace. 'Bodies of citizens paraded the city armed with fowling pieces, rifles, swords, pitchforks and old halberds carrying Tricolour flags' and shouting 'Viva Pio nono, Viva L'Italia, Viva la Reppublica'. Following the defeat of Carlo Alberto's armies at Novara, Mazzini moved to Rome, where from March to July he acted as Triumvir during the famous siege. He later took refuge in Switzerland and organized various republican risings from Lugano. Returning to London, he continued his propaganda for united Italy. But he detested the policy of Napoleon III and Cavour which created the Italian Kingdom under Piedmont. In 1866 he was elected to the Italian Parliament and offered an amnesty; both these offers he refused. He continued his propaganda and conspiratorial intrigues, even after Rome had become the capital of united Italy in 1870. He died at Pisa in 1872. Mazzini was a man of striking appearance. 'One knew at once', wrote an observer, 'that slight figure in a dark closely fitting dress with the marvellous face of pale olive, in shape a long oval, the features fine and bold rather than massive, the forehead full and high under the dark hair, the whole expression impassioned and sad, the eyes large, black and preternaturally burning' (quoted in BARR, op. cit., p. 144). He cared little for health, lived wholly for ideas, and would remain for days in one room. He was violently temperamental. 'There are moments,' he writes, 'when I could roll on the floor biting myself like a snake', op. cit., p. 75. Like Marx, he found his main indulgence in cigars.

During a lifetime of conspiracy and exile, with a brief phase of action and glory during the siege of Rome, this eloquent idealist created a liberal pan-European movement. He also formulated a theory of liberal nationalism destined largely to determine the outlook of powerful peoples and statesmen far into the twentieth century, reaching its climax after the First World War with the establishment of the new nation states of Eastern Europe; its decline with the failure of the League of Nations. Mazzini was not only an Italian patriot: he was the cosmopolitan prophet of liberal democratic Europe and America. Further, he attempted to transcend the class conflicts that Marx regarded as inevitable. He thus faced the two major problems of the modern world — international and class conflict. That he did so is the secret of his remarkable and lasting influence.

Like Saint-Simon, to whom he was much indebted, Mazzini, who was a liberal humanist, also endeavoured to meet the central challenge of the nineteenth century, the decline of religious belief. He formulated a cult of Humanity and progress derived from an interpretation of Dante, from Vico and from Condorcet. As a boy he would read the latter's views on progress at Mass, the book disguised between the covers of a Missal. He had a great belief, too, like so many middle class romantics, in the nobility and grandeur of the people. Reacting against the materialism of Bentham, which he said was concerned with the kitchen, he sought, like other idealists of the day, to regenerate mankind through the new sense of historic nationality which was an original aspect of the time. Like Burke, Herder and Hegel; like Michelet, and Macaulay, he was passionately conscious of his country's past: this faith was made more poignant by the contemporary condition of Italy. His beliefs he summed up in the formula, 'one sole master, God; one sole Law, Progress; one sole interpreter of that Law on earth, the people, with genius and virtue as its guides'.*

It will be apparent that Mazzini was an optimist. He was also a persistent conspirator. But his enterprises tended to collapse. Like

* 'The Holy Alliance of the Peoples', 1849. *Life and Writings*, VI, p. 277.

The basic English authority for his writings is the six-volume selection *The Life and Writings of Joseph Mazzini*. Smith, Elder, London, 1890 (2nd edition). This is indispensable, though the translation is seldom felicitous. For the full works see *Scritti editi ed inediti di Giuseppe Mazzini*, 40 vols., Imola, 1905-31. For his life see G. O. GRIFFITH, *Mazzini, Prophet of Modern Europe*. London, 1932; also STRINGFELLOW BARR, *Mazzini, Portrait of an Exile*, for a vivid account with a good bibliography. New York, 1935. *The Duties of Man and other Essays* are published in the Everyman Edition. See also G. GENTILE, *Mazzini*. Caserta, 1919. The biography by Bolton King is not now to be recommended.

most of the writers with whom this study is concerned, he was also unpractical in his own affairs.* This simplicity, the incomprehension of sheer laziness and cynicism, the apparent failure of the sense of the facts, was occasionally to make his long-term influence dangerous. He glorified the lineaments of established state authority with new trappings, created unreasonable expectations of the nation state and sometimes gave it false glamour.

Mazzini was a secular saint; a propagandist of the first order. He was a brilliant writer, the selfless indefatigable creator of a myth. And the masses believed in him. All over Europe German minorities, Poles, Hungarians, Serbs, Croats and Bulgars, were emerging into nationality. Their history was written for them, as in Bulgaria, Serbia and Greece, by a new class of intellectuals who looked to Mazzini. Already in South America Bolivar, whatever his motives, had emancipated whole nations from the old imperialism of Spain, and all about the world during the nineteenth century, and still today, inarticulate peoples have been stirred to national consciousness by the romantic words of this Italian exile. These generous ideas were turned too often to serve the perennial game of power. The peoples and their leaders were seldom what Mazzini thought them; the humanitarianism which cloaked the facts of competitive sovereign power and racing armaments, may have masked the need for cosmopolitan institutions backed by effective force. They certainly led to delusive hopes of free collaboration among interested politicians and economically hostile systems. Yet a great and moral influence was exercised by this dedicated and indomitable figure.

Much sentiment has been poured out over the memory of Mazzini, who was one of the first exiles to be regarded by the British ruling

* During the 'forties in London his business ventures were singularly unsuccessful. He invested, for example, a considerable sum in five or six hundred pounds of Italian sausage, a large quantity of spaghetti and some olive oil of an unsaleable kind. After tortuous negotiations, these commodities were sold at a loss. Nor was he, apparently, more practical as a revolutionary. His directions for the conduct of guerrillas are amateurish, if high minded. See his *Rules for the conduct of Guerrilla Bands*, with their touch of Verdi (vol. I, appendix). Guerrillas are to show respect for individual rights and property; they must spare the crops. Nor must they execute 'justice' on their own account. (Mussolini's end would have been discountenanced.) They should subsist on booty taken from the enemy, and 'the blanks caused among officers by war will be filled up on the principle of universal suffrage'. Besides rifle and bayonet, their weapons should include a dagger, bread and spirits, a thin strong cord, a few nails, and 'if possible a large axe'. They will signal to one another by horn or trumpet. The great point is to keep communications open and make friends with the peasants. Mazzini's cult of the 'Noble Dagger' was violently expressed in 1856 (*On the Theory of the Dagger*). 'From the Dagger of the Vespers to the stones of Balilla and the knife of Palafax, blessed be in your hands every weapon that can destroy the enemy and set you free.' He concludes, appealing to liberal sympathizers, 'if you do not like our daggers, why not give us guns?'

classes as a pet, and, indeed, on the romantic view of the Risorgimento in general. A reassessment is, perhaps, overdue. But if Mazzini be set in a new light, against his own intellectual pedigree, and against the consequences of the gross perversion of the romantic nationalism in which he believed, he remains an important and inspiring figure. As Treitschke is the prophet of later post-Darwinian militarist nationalism, so Mazzini belongs to the first half of the century — the humanitarian apostle of the nationalism of a more generous age.

The background to his ideas is characteristic. The son of a well-to-do professor in Genoa, and brought up by a formidable Jansenist mother who long continued to influence his mind, Mazzini was early familiar with Livy and Tacitus, and he early absorbed the ideas of the French Revolution through his study of an old Girondist publication, the *Chronique du Mois*. He also assimilated from Dante, in particular from the *Monarchia*, the conviction of the world mission of Rome and of the need for government to further the fulfilment of life.* This influence is reflected in the most valuable and cosmopolitan elements in Mazzini's thought. There was also the usual background of Voltaire and Goethe and Byron. Mazzini was a brilliant critic who deliberately renounced literature for politics.

Two turning points stand out in his life. At twenty-four he was shut up in the fort of Savona. In a cell looking on the open sky and the Mediterranean, with only the voices of fishermen audible below, he was confined with a Bible, a Tacitus, a Byron and a green-finch. Debarred from action, he devised an attractive programme, La Giovine Italia — the Gospel of Young Italy. Eighteen years later, came the second great moment of his life. As dominant Triumvir of the short-lived Republic, he ruled Rome.† All the long years of cloak and dagger conspiracy, of penury in London (though he developed in retrospect an affection for the fog) led to this brief realization of the republican ideal formulated at Savona. But where Lenin and Hitler achieved power, Mazzini's rule was ephemeral; he later passed long years in exile or in unsuccessful conspiracy against Cavour and the Italian monarchy, with which he refused to be reconciled.

The political thought of Mazzini, as may be expected, is eloquent, repetitive and diffuse. The best known documents are *Thoughts on*

* See *W.P.T.*, for this aspect of *Monarchia*, pp. 233-6.
† Anyone who examines the relics of this romantic time in the Castle of St. Angelo will sense the desperate tension of the siege. See G. M. TREVELYAN's *Garibaldi's Defence of the Roman Republic*, for a fine evocation. London, 1907.

Democracy in Europe (1847), *The Holy Alliance of the Peoples* (1849), *Europe, its Condition and Prospects* (1852), and *The Duties of Man*, of which the first four chapters were written in 1844 and the rest by 1858. There is much, also, to be found in the earlier writings and in the brilliant literary essays. If one takes a cross-section of the entire writings, rather than examines them seriatim, two main themes dominate Mazzini's thought. They are clear and strong through all the vicissitudes of exile and political change. First is the attempt at mass moral and religious regeneration through a new cult of progress and nationality; second, the desire to create a new popular economic and social brotherhood, thus attaining within the state the harmony achieved in Europe. The two themes are complementary and inseparable.

The first is always European, though based on a passionate belief in potential, if not actual, Italian leadership. Like the other Romantics, like Rousseau and Hegel, Mazzini detested the hard cosmopolitan realism of the eighteenth century: he believed that the future was with the peoples and that the 'law' of progress was realized in the collective life of the human race affirmed by Dante.[1] Bentham and the Enlightenment must be transcended; they can only be transcended by the nation, the intermediate term between humanity and the individual. 'Without the nation there can be no humanity . . . nations are the citizens of humanity, as individuals are the citizens of the nation.'[2] Within this 'family' each nation should perform its special mission and Europe must be reconstructed according to 'national vocations' into a 'certain number of states, as nearly as possible equal in population and extent'. 'The nations', wrote Mazzini, 'will be sisters.'[3] They will become more intimately associated through democracy so that the Europe of the peoples will be spiritually one. All will be united in the belief that 'Progress is the Providential Law'. On the private side of this regenerated world, the family will be a sanctuary, property the reward of labour, and religion, a little vaguely, 'the supreme synthetic educational formula'. In the name of God and the people we are one.

Like Saint-Simon, Mazzini believed in the leadership of intellectuals, a belief reflected in the long line of political professors who have contributed to nationalist movements since his time, particularly in countries where a new intelligentsia has suddenly come to power. He even translates his idea into a cosmopolitan spiritual order with Saint-Simonian and Comtian affinities. 'A few men,' he writes, 'rendered venerable by knowledge and virtue, intellect and love, and by sacrifices nobly endured for the sake of the common faith of Europe and America, would form a supreme council of the association.'[4] They will 'transmit . . . the European idea'. This revolution is hostile both to eighteenth-century materialism and the Catholic Church. It is romantic; at once Nationalist and Pan-European; anti-clerical, looking to liberal intellectuals for leadership and peoples for support. Writing in 1847, on the verge of the great upheavals of the following year, Mazzini was ready for his opportunity. But most of these ideas had already been formulated in 1832, when he was appealing for Young Italy to remake herself and Europe, when the Papacy, he declared, was infested by senile Cardinals and intriguing Vatican politicians,* and 'when in the entire Catholic world de Maistre alone remained to the Pope'. The King and the executioner were indeed real enough for Mazzini.

Hence the passionate renunciation of all the old order. Humanity, he constantly insists, needs new symbols; the old ones are rotten. Church and Monarch are a façade and the new foundation of government must be the general will. He sets himself to find a moral law whereby the general will can be disciplined.† There must be new inspiration, a new religion. 'Religion and politics are inseparable. Without religion political science can only create despotism or anarchy.'[5]

Where can this faith be found? In the "progressive authority of the People, the collective and lasting interpretation of the Law of God', for 'the spirit of God descends now upon multitudes'. It is the old theme of the nineteenth century; the exploration of intuition — this time collective. To clinch the argument, Mazzini makes a final and, to modern ears, rather ironic statement. 'National sovereignty', he says, 'is the remedy universally accepted for preserving society.' God is God, and humanity, through the nation, His prophet.

For Nationalism, he wrote in 1849, was the great redeeming force of the age. It was everywhere — 'in Italy, in France, among the Slavonians, at Pesth, at Vienna, from the extremity of Sicily to St. Petersburg'. Everywhere there are 'holy prophetic sounds of the new order'; its slogans are Fatherland, Liberty; Nationality, Equality, Fraternal Association. As a young man he had written of the poetry of the modern era in the tramp of republican armies, in the Guer-

* See R. B. MOWAT, *The Romantic Age*, chap. x. London, 1937, for a good description of the atmosphere of Rome between 1815 and 1848.
† Compare T. H. Green — another liberal philosopher of greater academic speculative power, *infra*, pp. 274ff.

rilleros in Spain.* It had 'overflowed in Germany in students who marched to battle to the songs of Korner and Arndt'. It was incarnate in the Polish exiles. 'Poets,' he had written, 'brothers of the eagle, why look behind?'† After 1848, the great dilemma posed by Napoleon on St. Helena must be decided. 'Europe,' he had said, with his wicked insight, 'will be either republican or Cossack in forty years.' A republican harmony, in Mazzini's view, was the answer. This vision was pervaded by a world embracing humanism. The collective life of the race achieved by the Romans, 'populus ille sanctus pius et gloriosus', had been recognized by Christ. Mazzini invokes Dante's vision of Humanity.

> Onde si muovono a diversi porti
> Per lo gran mar dell' Essere, e ciascuna
> Con istinto a lei dato, che la porti.‡

It was an ideal of civilized harmony. In 1847, he wrote, 'I abhor the usurping and monopolizing nation, conceiving its own grandeur and force only in the inferiority and the poverty of others; but who would not welcome with enthusiasm and love, that people which, understanding its mission in the world, should find its security in the progress of all surrounding it?'§ Such was Mazzini's ideal of harmony and progress. It was a noble ideal. And it contributed to many liberal illusions.

The second aspect of Mazzini's political thought is concerned with the condition of the people, with manhood suffrage and the education of the masses, the emancipation of women, the destruction of clerical and feudal privilege. He had a Saint-Simonian concern with the problem. 'A large portion of . . . care and attention', he wrote, 'will be directed to the amelioration of the condition of the most numerous and most suffering classes.'‖ Since 'the epoch of individuality is concluded', the epoch of association must begin — the modern era, after the final apotheosis and bankruptcy of individualism in Byron and Napoleon, will be a social world.¶ Privilege will be the reward of capacity, and there will be a 'gradual diminution of the class compelled to sell their labour'.• There will, indeed, be a fusion of classes in an inspired nation-state. Fraternity is the

* Goya took a more realistic view.
† *Thoughts Addressed to the Poets of the Nineteenth Century*, I, p. 131.
‡ *On the Minor Works of Dante*, 1844. IV, p. 177n.
§ *Thoughts upon Democracy in Europe*, VI, p. 98.
‖ *The writers of Young Italy to their Fellow Countrymen*, vol. I, p. 171.
¶ *Thoughts addressed to the Poets of the Nineteenth Century*, I, p. 131.

answer to economic conflict. This concern with the working people was reflected in Mazzini's life. They were not for him merely an abstraction; there is no patronizing tone. In his London exile he early set himself to help Italian peasant boys, lured into the slums from their own land, and set to beg by evil taskmasters in London.* Mazzini denounced this odious traffic. He founded a night school; he expanded it into classes for working men. The organization spread to Boston and New York. He taught in the school himself; for it was 'holy work', he said. Here is one of the most attractive aspects of Mazzini. This humanity, one may think, explains his detestation of actual politics, of the Machiavellian calculations of Cavour. It is thus that one of his most elaborate and well-known works *The Duties of Man*, is prefaced by an address to the Italian working classes. He hoped to get rid of Machiavellianism by an appeal to the good hearts of the people. The impersonal and inhuman attitude of the bourgeoisie to the masses has had its reward; they have come to regard each other with the same cruel impersonality.[7] In the war of gold and graft, all human relations are dissolved.

Against this anarchy the workers must set not another materialism, but a new brotherhood. The doctrine of individual rights, originally middle class, is not enough. It may 'suffice to arouse men to overthrow the obstacles placed in the path by tyranny, but it is impotent where the object . . . is to create a noble and powerful harmony between the various elements of which the nation is composed'.[8] This new morality implies elevation, improvement, education; liberty and new horizons. 'God exists, because we exist, God lives in our conscience, in the conscience of humanity.' The people have before them a 'material world magnificent in beauty and pregnant with life . . . increasing in power and vigour in proportion to new increased activity'.[9]

Set against this cult of life, the Pope is merely a Manichee.[10] Doctrines of original sin and the Fall of Man are blasphemous. As Galileo is said to have muttered 'Eppur si muove', so Humanity, undaunted, must raise its eyes to the sun. If we can rid ourselves of the old eighteenth-century individualism, and launch out into the world of true fraternity and association, there opens a splendid future before the precursors, the vanguards of the human race.[11] They will go forward with the cry which marks all 'great and noble revolutions — the "God Wills It", of the crusaders'. For the law of

* 'By day the elder lads are given an organ, the younger a squirrel or white mouse, and each is bound to bring in a certain sum of money every evening.'

life is self-expression: 'act and live according to your law'. It is 'your first, or rather your sole, duty'. And to make this freedom possible there must be a constitution, for 'in countries despotically governed there is no society'. So the creative self-fulfilment of humanity will come about, the 'Ascent of Humanity' will be consolidated; and through time and space, mankind will 'realize the successive incarnations of God'. It was a bold belief, typical of the brave days of the nineteenth century. It was guaranteed to Mazzini, the 'Apostle of the Fraternity of Nations' — by his faith, absorbed from Condorcet, in the Law of Progress.[12] In this light, Humanity is a vast army, advancing for the conquest of lands unknown. The conception is linear, pre-Darwinian, and eighteenth century.

It could be, none the less, exhilarating in the stuffy world of Metternich and the Reaction. As Byron had written:

> Yet, Freedom! yet, thy banner torn but flying,
> Streams like the thundercloud *against* the wind!

In this light, Mazzini, in his most serious essay in political theory *Thoughts upon Democracy in Europe*, subjects the doctrines of Bentham, Saint-Simon, Fourier and the Communists, to an often penetrating analysis.[13] Their doctrines are always related to the central problem — the emancipation of the people.

Some pessimists may declare that civilization is going down, that the barbarians are at the gates. On the contrary, writes Mazzini, we are on the threshold of a new creative age. The utilitarian materialists, with their individualism, have destroyed the sense of duty and human solidarity which the new age demands. 'Nourished from the tenderest youth with the doctrines of Helvétius, evidently devoid of all religious sentiment, and disinherited of the common inspiration of humanity by his contempt of the past — how should [Bentham] have dwelt upon anything but the sensations, or the instinctive sympathies and antipathies of the individual?'

Bentham was, indeed, extremely influential. But he had the mind of an anaemic clerk. And his ideas were not new. 'Panem et Circenses' are as old as the Roman Empire. He helped cleanse the world of great abuses, but his philosophy was pernicious — the 'barren Godless formula of interest'. With Saint-Simon, came the first serious attack on individualism. '. . . The most important, I will venture to say, the most advanced manifestation of the spirit of new things that breathes through the era.' Bold it was, and sincere. But Saint-Simon, the collectivist, sinned against liberty. His motto was not 'all through the People, but all for the People'. 'All these materialist Utopias must die of spiritual inanition.' The subsequent careers of his disciples are revealing; 'at the present time they are almost all zealous servants of Louis Philippe. Enfantin directs I know not what railway works'.[14] Such is the end of collectivist technocracy.

The Utopian anarchist, Fourier, on the other hand, went too far on the opposite road. His individualism is equally repellent. His objective is the 'beggar's broth' enjoyed by the apes in the witches' coven in Goethe's *Faust*. 'This is Malthus crowned with roses.' It leads to senseless luxury and the morals of the 'Otaheitans', those voluptuous South Seas Islanders. Fourier would merely create an 'anarchy of animal propensities'. Far from having destroyed 'twenty ages of political imbecility', he could depict, with total lack of poetic insight, only a world of gross indulgence. Like Carlyle, Mazzini saw in materialist Utopias not the basis of the good life but the pig trough.

As for the Communists, the fate they desire for the world is just as squalid. Where Saint-Simon would destroy freedom and Fourier create simian anarchy, the Communists would combine the worst of both. They would organize society 'after the manner of bees and beavers, upon a fixed immutable model'. And they claim that 'on such a day, and year, one or other of [their] chiefs found beneath his pillow the secret of the world'. Mazzini attacks them particularly (it was the year before the *Communist Manifesto*) for lack of intellectual leadership.* He declares that their system is tyranny. It is at the root and the end of Communism and pervades it throughout. 'What is the point of great buildings and public works, if they house barbarians?' Sorrow and death, the destruction of personality, can be the only end. The Communist tyrants will be masters of mind as well as body; they will 'strive by corruption to reassume the hereditary dictatorship of the ancient castes'.

Proudhon's ideal of self governing producers is equally materialist — preoccupied with the stomach. His Federalism and Contract are artificial. There is only one sound idea in all this Utopian literature, the need for greater production to alleviate the condition of the people. But increased production will come with fuller life, not as its own end. All these materialist ideals end in spiritual death. Mazzini had thus traversed with trenchant criticism all the main

* In 1852 he was to qualify this statement; 'with the exception of Marx, who is desirous of being the chief of a school at any price' (VI, p. 244).

trends of revolutionary thought here already examined. His ideas
are still well worth attention.

So the second main theme of Mazzini's thought is worked out —
the redemption of the masses. It runs parallel with the redemption
of Europe through romantic nationalism. Both themes unite in the
cult of Italy and of Rome, the centre of the world, from which the
unity of Europe and mankind has already been twice affirmed, first
by the Empire, then by the Church. Now the time is ripe for a third
Rome — of the European peoples. In 1852 Mazzini again evokes
this ideal. It is a broad vision. Of united Germans, of Poles and
Southern Slavs; of liberated Rumanians; of Greece with Constantinople redeemed; of the Iberian Peninsula united and a northern
'Union of Odin' under the Swedes. To crown all will be a united
and regenerate Italy, 'planting upon the Capitol and the Vatican
the inviolability of the human soul for the whole world'.[15]

To this European order the French and English must contribute.
Conceit and insularity must be abandoned — by the French, with
their 'aplomb de maître', their cultural arrogance, their materialist
egotism; by the English, with their commercial minds. For the
French are 'supple, pliant, full of self-confidence'; instinctively they
monopolize, with their lucid, facile, language. Today they are sunk
in myopic self-interest, and are so complicated that they have lost
the power of intuition. 'Analysis', he writes, with some insight, 'has
almost destroyed in France the conception of life.' After these critical
remarks about the then most powerful nation in Europe, Mazzini
turns to the English. They are, as usual, insular, selfish and cold.
Already in the 'thirties, he had remarked in these phlegmatic
islanders 'a certain exclusively analytic tendency inborne in the
Anglo-Saxons and strengthened by Protestantism'. This has led
them to be cautious in experiment, though with them an advance
once achieved is 'achieved forever'. Now, after 1848, the caution
seemed maddening. Mazzini states a theme familiar, a century later,
in another context. 'If England persists in maintaining this neutral,
passive, selfish part, she will have to expiate it, a European transformation is inevitable . . . the Peoples will remember . . .' The new
Europe will turn on the supine English and tell them 'live your own
life, and this life will be more and more restricted by the gradual
inevitable emancipation of [the] colonies'. Blind to the possibilities
of United Europe, England will end as a third rate power. Mazzini
concludes by attempting to bring American moral pressure to bear
on the unimaginative English. There is an appeal to Anglo-American

solidarity: 'let England accept American ideas and baptise again her alliance by a policy worthy of both'. Mazzini, the Italian exile, will bring the two great Anglo-Saxon nations together. Already President Wilson is in the offing. Mazzini had, indeed, created a new, pan-European theory of romantic liberal nationalism. The two great problems of the age had been challenged by this inspiring, if not always realistic, outlook. Europe would be restored to a new spirit by regenerate nationalism and united in the resulting harmony of free peoples. Class-conflict would be transcended in a new brotherhood. And the question behind it all, the most searching of all questions, would be answered by a new religion of humanity.

This gospel drew strength from deep roots. It has been already pointed out how Europe had been influenced by romantic historians who had emotionally reinforced the national traditions inherited from the eighteenth century, and how they had provided the dominant middle classes with a new past and a new tradition. Where Proudhon was a voice crying in the wilderness, Mazzini appealed to all that public who had absorbed the ideas of progressive liberalism in a national setting. The legends of Joan of Arc, of Magna Carta, of Charlemagne, of Republican Rome, were combined in the cult of progress and liberty. The old conception of dynastic sovereignty and European order defended by Metternich, had given way to the revolutionary ideal of the self determination of peoples, of the manifest destiny of the nation state.

CHAPTER IX

THE LIBERAL COMPROMISE
DE TOCQUEVILLE: JOHN STUART MILL

THE early-nineteenth-century cult of historically developing Will and the Utilitarianism of Bentham and Austin, had run parallel both with a strong conservative reaction and with revolutionary undercurrents of thought. These had been expressed in the technocracy of Saint-Simon and Comte, in the Marxist dialectical materialism here later to be examined, in communitarian doctrine, Proudhon's federalism and the humanitarian nationalism of Mazzini. None of these currents of thought, except the Utilitarian, had produced much effect on policy, though the mysticism of Hegel and Mazzini had already coloured much advanced opinion. Saint-Simonians, Comtists and Marxists were then little regarded by politicians or peoples, though in influential circles the practical ideas of Owen had provoked interest.

This neglect was natural. The framework of society was still based on a solid, if largely inarticulate tradition, with its roots in a pre-industrial past. This structure of government, inherited from the eighteenth century, was highly centralized in France, well established in England, and closely interwoven with the fabric of society. Far from diminishing the power of governments, the Revolution had increased it, while in England the wars and class conflicts of the turn of the century had strengthened the solidarity of the ruling class. The effects of the two dominant events of the time, the Democratic and Industrial Revolutions, were therefore contained and worked out within a strong institutional frame which was in time adapted to the new conditions. Administrative improvement in France and in Napoleon's conquered territories, the English reforms after 1832, the achievements of Stein in Prussia, met the immediate demands of the age which followed middle-class capture of political power. They made the incitements of the more extreme political thinkers still peripheral. For the tide of prosperity in the West, with its increasing Colonial interests, was with the rising bourgeoisie. In spite of the protests of reactionaries and revolutionaries, the age was their century.

The widespread habit of reading history backwards, and the

temptations of political bias, tend to depict a time seething with discontent. In fact the revolutionaries whose ideas were later to be powerful were an obscure and generally squalid minority in an age singularly rich in all kinds of achievement. An age confident and pugnacious; preoccupied with money-making, society, travel and sport; engaged in a great variety of industrial, learned, literary, musical and artistic enterprise. The wealth and social display of the upper classes was overwhelming; the prosperity of the middle class substantial and widespread; professional men and creative artists reaped their harvest from broad fields. The career open to talent emancipated thousands. Injustice and iniquity there might be, peasant poverty and industrial friction, but the surge of nineteenth-century expansion, admired even by Marx in the *Communist Manifesto*, sustained one of the richest, most creative, and most powerful societies in history.

To most responsible Western administrators the situation did not appear revolutionary, though it was evidently set for change. There was no question of the subversion of government; no break in administrative continuity. In England the panic over the Reform Bill and the Chartists had proved evanescent, and in France the Revolution of 1830 had left the basic centralized structure intact. What were the opinions of practical, moderate, reformers, determined to contain the new forces and adapt the existing structure of society to them? It is time to turn to their then predominant contribution to nineteenth-century political thought.

Two such writers are outstanding and representative: Alexis de Tocqueville and John Stuart Mill. Both were constitutionalists; both were convinced that the democratic revolution must be accepted; both were alive to the dangers and promise of the new order. The first examined American society as the only current example of democracy in action, and applied the lessons to France; he also made the first thorough and objective analysis of the nature and causes of the Revolution. The second, brought up in Utilitarian individualism, realized the limitations of that philosophy and sought both to inspire it with greater humanity and to maintain the tradition of liberty, resilience and leadership in the approaching democratic world. At the height of his influence during the mid-century, Mill combines traditional English individualism with a more humanitarian conception of government. These writers are both statesmen of distinguished calibre. They endeavoured to adapt constitutionalism to democracy and pointed out the dangers of national sovereign power when combined with democratic rule. Liberal reform thus found expression in a more sophisticated humanism, and enriched a constitutional tradition inherited from the eighteenth century and from origins deep in the medieval, barbarian and classical past. The success of this form of government was decisive in the Atlantic-Oceanic world, and considerable on the European Continent: in some vital European areas, although lip service was almost everywhere paid to it, its success was only superficial. In others negligible. And in the sphere of international relations constitutionalism failed.

It is clearly worth dwelling with some attention on the ideas of these two remarkable liberal writers. For we are here concerned with the central stream of political development in the nineteenth century, destined to be a sheet-anchor of sanity in the welter of violence loosed on a later generation by the exponents of national and class war.

II

De Tocqueville's *Democracy in America* is dominated by one overmastering idea.* 'The whole book,' he writes, 'which is here offered

---

* Alexis Charles Henri de Tocqueville was born in 1805, of a family of Norman nobility. His father was Prefect of Metz, where de Tocqueville was educated, completing his studies by qualifying in law in Paris. He was appointed to the minor post of juge auditeur in the Court of Versailles. He had already formed a life friendship with Gustave de Beaumont, another young official, who survived him and edited the complete edition of his works. A liberal aristocrat, de Tocqueville lacked enthusiasm for the new regime of Louis Philippe, and in 1831 obtained leave of absence for eighteen months to study the prison system of the United States at his own expense. Accompanied by de Beaumont, he made a thorough study of American conditions. He produced *De la Démocratie en Amérique*. Paris. Vol. I, 1835; vol. II, 1840, and de Beaumont produced a novel concerned with slavery (*Marie, ou L'esclavage aux États Unis, Tableau des mœurs américaines*. Paris, 1835, 2 vols. See GEORGE W. PIERSON, *Tocqueville and Beaumont in America*. New York, 1938). The success of de Tocqueville's book was immediate and overwhelming, and came as a surprise to him. 'I ask myself', he said, 'whether they are really talking about me?' 'It seems', replied his publisher, 'that you have created a masterpiece.' His reputation was at once assured. From 1839 to 1848 he was deputy for la Manche in Normandy, and with the revolution of 1848 he obtained a short term of high office, being appointed Foreign Minister in the Government of Odilon Barrot. After the coup d'état of Louis Napoleon in 1851, he retired from politics and devoted himself to his other great work, *L'Ancien Régime*, of which the first volume was published in 1856. In 1850 he also began his devastating and brilliant *Souvenirs*, which were continued during the winter of 1850-51 at Sorrento and completed the next year at Versailles. They remained unpublished until 1893, and give an arresting and subtle picture of the French political scene during the crisis of 1848. There are numerous editions of the *Democracy*, of which the best in English is *Democracy in America*, by ALEXIS DE TOCQUEVILLE, the Henry Reeve Text as revised by Francis Bowen and now further corrected and edited with introduction, editorial notes and bibliography by Phillips Bradley. Knopf, New York, 1945. 2 vols. *L'Ancien Régime* is edited by G. W. Headlam. Oxford, 1904, and the *Souvenirs* by Luc Monnier. Paris, Gallimard, 1942. There is a brilliant essay on de Tocqueville in E. FAGUET, *Politicians and Moralists of the 19th Century* (Trans. Galton), and an abridged translation of the *Democracy*, edited H. S. Commager, in the World's Classics. O.U.P., 1946.

to the public, has been written under the influence of a kind of religious awe, produced in the author's mind by his view of that irresistible revolution which has advanced for centuries in spite of every obstacle, and is still advancing.' This democratic revolution has transformed the 'body of society', and a 'new science of politics is needed for a new world'. De Tocqueville was an administrator and politician, versed in the ways of government; a man of the world as well as a political theorist of the first quality. He takes a detached and impartial view. And although his diagnosis is grave, it is not, in the *Democracy in America*, pessimistic.

If the stream of events may sometimes appear uncontrollable, our fate, he insists, is in our own hands. The great task of the nineteenth century is to accept and educate democracy; to prevent the abuse of power to which it is liable. Under the old order, central power was limited by an aristocracy: 'Custom and usage had established certain limits to oppression.' There was recognized inequality, but not 'degradation of soul . . . and the social state thus organized might boast of its stability, its power, and above all, its glory'. The new society is profoundly different; in some aspects more ignoble, in others more humane. But in France the ruling classes have made no attempt to come to terms with it. Yet can one imagine that 'a social movement, the causes of which lie so far back, can be checked by . . . one generation? Can it be believed that the democracy which has overthrown the feudal system and vanquished kings will retreat before tradesmen and capitalists?'[1] It follows that 'the first of the duties that are at this time imposed upon those who direct our affairs is to educate democracy, to reawaken, if possible, its religious beliefs; to purify its morals; to mold its actions; to substitute a knowledge of state craft for its inexperience, and an awareness of its true interest for its blind instincts, to adapt its government to time and place, and to modify it according to men and to conditions'.

In the first place, a democracy is liable to obliterate standards, to destroy individual liberty. And it will never achieve 'the wild virtues' of aristocratic and traditional societies. Properly organized, on the other hand, it will have its own merits. Agreed obedience to utilitarian Laws 'through quiet and rational persuasion'; voluntary associations with their own dignity; a sober sense of political and social responsibility. Properly handled, this widespread self respect may even counteract the forces tending to materialize life.

De Tocqueville, as a young man, displayed a certain optimism.

Like Saint-Simon, he did not believe that the human race was created 'to live among ruins'. 'I cannot believe', he writes, 'that the Creator made man to leave him . . . in the intellectual wretchedness that surrounds us. God destines a calmer and a more certain future for the communities of Europe.' With this hope in mind, in particular for France, de Tocqueville set himself to study democracy in America.

In the resulting study he undoubtedly composed one of the great books of political thought; a nineteenth-century document which can compare with the old masterpieces. A first-hand knowledge of the text shows wisdom and insight on every page. Here only an introductory sketch can be given, which may suggest a thorough examination of the original. It is even more rewarding then the better known *L'Ancien Régime*. The author combines penetrating worldly judgment with admirable style, an eye for detail and atmosphere. The reader gains contact with an intellect of extraordinary distinction, concerned with fundamental social problems and rich in political understanding. It is significant that one of the few masterpieces of nineteenth-century political thought was written by a Frenchman about America. It puts most Utopians and revolutionaries in their place.

The first part of the book examines environment and institutions; the second, their effect on the outlook of American society. It is concerned also with more general speculations. As de Tocqueville emphasizes, his work reflects a thorough study of documents and a wide consultation of informed opinion. Some will consider it a defect, he says, to advocate no particular political cause and to write without any startling originality. 'I have not', he declares, 'undertaken to see differently from others, but to look further.'* The open-

---

* The *Democracy in America* is designed in 2 volumes. The first contains eighteen chapters of which the following are representative headings. After a Preface and Introduction, the first four are concerned with 'The Exterior Form of North America', 'The Origin of the Anglo-Americans', 'The Social Condition of the Anglo-Americans', and 'The Principle of the Sovereignty of the People of America'. The fifth chapter deals with the 'Townships and Local Government of New England', and is of particular importance and value. The sixth, seventh and eighth chapters deal with the 'Judicial Power', 'Political Jurisdiction' and the 'Federal Constitution'. Chapters IX, X and XI with 'Popular Government', 'Political Parties and the Liberty of the Press'. There follow chapters on 'Political Association', 'Suffrage' and the 'Advantages of Democratic Government'. Chapter XV, which is particularly well known, treats of the 'Unlimited Power of the Majority in the United States and its Consequences'. Chapter XVI analyses the 'Causes which Mitigate the Tyranny of the Majority'. Chapter XVII deals with the 'Causes which tend to maintain Democracy in America', in particular with American religion. The final chapter faces the problem of 'The Present and Probable Future Condition of the Three Races that inhabit the Territory of the United States'.

The second volume is divided into four books, entitled respectively, 'The Influence of Democracy on the Action of Intellect in the United States' (twenty chapters); 'The Influ-

ing chapter, with its vivid geographical survey, at once displays de Tocqueville's imaginative grasp. He compares the exotic world of the 'translucent Caribbean . . . where death lurks beneath a brilliant exterior', with the relatively austere environment of New England. Here everything is 'grave, serious, and solemn' — a land of 'granite, rocks, dark trees and primaeval forests'. It is the cradle of North American civilization.

The America of de Tocqueville's day was still comparatively untouched by the development of big business, by the vast immigrations from Central Europe and by the expansion into the far West. It was still predominantly a country of small townships. White wooden houses on village greens overlooked the sprawling estuaries of the New England coast or commanded the hills of Connecticut and the expanses of Massachusetts. Here place names reflected settlement from southern England and East Anglia — Wareham, Taunton and Plymouth; Yarmouth, Boston and Norwich. Porches and window frames recalled their prototypes in Bridport and King's Lynn.

Here the Puritan settlers had brought an ancient tradition of self-government. They were not disreputable adventurers, but solid families emigrating not through poverty but through principle. Set upon the 'triumph of an idea', the Founding Fathers had acclima-

ence of Democracy on the Feelings of the Americans' (seventeen chapters); 'The influence of Democracy on Manners properly so called' (twenty-six chapters) and 'The Influence of Democratic Ideas and Feeling on Political Society' (eight chapters). The first two chapters of Book I discuss why Americans show a greater flair for general ideas than their forefathers, the English. The third and fourth chapters discuss religion and American democracy; and the eighth chapter points out that American ideas of equality imply the indefinite perfectibility of man. The tenth chapter points out the practical bias of the American mind, and chapters XI-XIII how the Americans have modified the English language. The first chapter of the second book suggests that Americans set more store by equality even than liberty, and the eighth chapter discusses how Americans control individualism by enlightened self interest. Chapters X and XI deal with the taste for physical well being in America and 'the peculiar effects of the love of physical gratifications'. Chapter XII asks 'Why some Americans manifest a sort of fanatical spiritualism' and Chapter XIII 'Why the Americans are so restless in the midst of their prosperity'. The third book discusses (chapter II) how democracy renders 'the habitual intercourse of Americans simple and easy', and inquires why Americans show so little sensitiveness in their own country but are so much more sensitive in Europe. Servants, wages and family life are then discussed, and chapter XV deals with 'The Gravity of the Americans and why it does not prevent them from often doing inconsiderate things'. 'And why, it is asked [chapter XVI], is the National vanity of the Americans more restless than that of the English?' And why is the aspect of society in the United States 'at once excited and monotonous'. The third book concludes with a discussion of War and Democracy. The fourth book is of particular value. Why, it is asked (chapter II) are Democratic Governments naturally favourable to the concentration of power? The sentiments that lead to it are analysed, and its advantages and disadvantages discussed (chapters III and IV). Chapter V points out that Sovereign Power is increasing in Europe, although thrones are unstable, and chapter VI asks 'What sort of Despotism Democratic nations have to fear?' The book ends with an admirable retrospective survey and conclusion. It will be apparent that it is still highly topical.

tized political procedures which were to dominate the United States. 'The general principles which are the groundwork of modern constitutionalism', wrote de Tocqueville, 'were all recognized and established . . .' The civilization of New England had been 'like a beacon set upon a hill'. And if, south and west of the Hudson, there had been a different society, the great Southern landowners had collaborated with the revolution. From Virginia had come its greatest leaders. Yet the revolution had been democratic; 'the doctrine of the sovereignty of the people came out of the townships and took possession of the state'. This habit of self government was in time to dominate the whole area. For all its subsequent expansion, the civilization of North America developed within the same constitutional frame. Lincoln's genius was to express it.

It is an old story. From Greek civic assemblies, out of the parochial concerns of primitive Rome, from the Moots and Things of Anglo-Saxon and Scandinavian farmers, from the civic vitality of medieval communes, the habit of self government had come down. Now, in the New World, this ancient tradition, acclimatized to new surroundings and strengthened by a disciplined religion, was destined to its greatest expansion. In this development the habit of local government was fundamental. De Tocqueville describes the annually chosen 'select Men', the 'rotation of banal offices' willingly assumed; the titheing men, hog-reeves, and fence-wardens, all in direct Anglo-Saxon descent.[2] Here the conduct of local business is easy, since the people feel their part in it. They collect their own taxes, build their own schools. There is initiative and responsibility; 'the French government lends its agents to the *commune*; in America . . . the township lends its agents to the government'.[3] County administration through Justices of the Peace is neither centralized nor oligarchic. This institution has been borrowed from England and democratized: it is unknown on the Continent of Europe — 'a sort of middle term between the magistrate and the man of the world',[4] subject, like anyone else, to the Law.

In its widest aspect American government is decentralized, if State administration is concentrated. Normally casual, in emergency it can be tightened up, for all is based on consent. Hence its vitality. 'Despotism', he remarks in a memorable phrase, 'by itself . . . can maintain nothing durable.'[5] 'Do what you may, there is no true power among men save in the free union of their will.' If this principle be observed (and how often and disastrously it is disregarded), there will be no lack of vitality. For nations, de Tocqueville rightly remarks, scotching an old, false and still widespread analogy, 'do not grow old as men do'.[6] American energy springs from the whole people and compares well with the atmosphere of most European states. It reflects vigorous provincial liberties which can counteract both the tyranny of democratic majorities and of traditional despotism. 'Those who dread the licence of the mob, and those who fear absolute power, ought alike to desire the gradual development of provincial liberties.' Here de Tocqueville touches on one of his main themes, also dominant in *L'Ancien Régime*; the danger of democratic tyranny. 'I am convinced', he wrote, 'that democratic nations are the most likely to fall under the yoke of centralized administration.' It had been a mistake, for example, to abolish the ancient and varied provincial institutions of France.

De Tocqueville also examines the powers of the President, its extent and limitations, and remarks quaintly that the President's functions as Commander-in-Chief are insignificant because the United States' armed forces are extremely small. Equally incongruous today are his remarks on American political parties. They are not, he says, highly organized. But in spite of democratic politics, there is a gulf between the propertied classes and the rest. The rich pretend to be egalitarian, but are in fact extremely exclusive. 'Next to hating their enemies, men are most inclined to flatter them.' Hence a characteristically American parade of pretended equality.

In considering the influence of the press on American life, de Tocqueville breaks new ground. Here is the first elaborate treatment of a new problem. The 'sovereignty of the people', he remarks, 'and the liberty of the press . . . may be regarded as co-relative.'[7] But the press is no mere adjunct to popular opinion. It creates it. And the press appears sometimes to have 'passions and instincts of its own'.[8] It is extremely powerful, a new factor in political and social life, something without precedent on such a scale. 'In America, as in France, it constitutes a singular power, so strangely composed of mingled good and evil that liberty could not live without it, and public order can hardly be maintained against it.' Yet its rule is manipulative rather than creative, for it must work with the material to hand. 'The press cannot create human passions, however skilfully it may handle them where they exist'[9] — a remark worth pondering by ambitious propagandists.

Yet the power of the press in America, though considerable, is less effective than in France. He remarks on the already preponderant role of advertising. 'Three-quarters of the enormous sheet is filled with advertisements', a practice which has since continued. In France, on the other hand, politics take up nearly all the space. Moreover, the prestige of journalists in America is low. There are too many newspapers for the press to develop much power. The day of the syndicated columnist has not yet arrived. Indeed, the journalists of the United States, he remarks, are generally in a humble position, with scanty education and a vulgar turn of mind. Far worse than their French colleagues . . . whose spirit 'consists in a violent but frequently an eloquent and lofty manner of discussing the great interests of the state. The characteristics of the American journalists consist in . . . a coarse appeal to the passions of his reader; he abandons principles to assail the character of individuals, to track them into private life and disclose all their weaknesses and vices. . .' Nothing can be more deplorable.

De Tocqueville concludes by a warning of the growing and immense power of the press in democratic states. It is second only to the political power of the people itself. Its influence is further extended by the peculiar American susceptibility to abstract ideas. Once they have taken up an opinion, 'be it well or ill founded, nothing is more difficult than to eradicate it from their minds'. This tenacity is also apparent in England. The explanation is simple. When one is free to choose one's opinions one clings to them.

While concerned primarily with the immediate American scene, de Tocqueville was shrewd enough to foresee that the obvious destiny of the United States was world power. Given the geographical advantages of the huge area, no political conflicts were likely to prevent expansion over the entire continent. 'Thus,' he concludes, 'in the midst of the uncertain future, one event at least is sure . . . the Anglo-Americans will alone cover the immense space contained between the Polar regions and the Tropics, extending from the coast of the Atlantic to the shores of the Pacific Ocean.'[10] He foresaw the existence of a hundred and fifty million Americans, with a common outlook, language and way of life. 'The rest is uncertain, but this is certain: and it is a fact new to the world — a fact fraught with such portentous consequences as to baffle the efforts even of the imagination.' When most of his contemporaries had their eyes firmly fixed on the power politics of Europe, and when Americans were held by European conservatives in little regard, de Tocqueville foresaw the dominant strategic and economic outcome of the twentieth century. With singular foresight, he also sensed the prospect of the other focus of world power. With his strong feeling for geography, which distinguishes him from most political philosophers of his time, he realized the possibilities of Russia. As the Americans had been coming to economic and political power, 'while the attention of mankind was divided elsewhere', so the Russians, also, were 'proceeding with ease and with celerity along a path to which the human eye can assign no term'.[11] De Tocqueville stressed the deep significance of the contrast between these two expanding societies. The one pacific and relying on private initiative, giving 'free scope to the unguided exertions and common sense of its citizens'; the other, military, centralized, bureaucratic; its conquests 'won by the sword', and all the authority of society 'carried on a single arm'. With his shrewd foresight, he concluded of these two peoples: 'their starting point is different, and their courses are not the same; yet each of them seems to be marked out by the will of Heaven to sway the destinies of half the world'.

When he turns from the political scene and describes the American way of life, de Tocqueville's observations are equally acute. He relates American democracy to religion, science and the arts; to language and literature, and he observes the effect of the universal cult of prosperity. He describes, too, with sympathetic insight, the domestic habits of Americans and relates them to public life. Here is not only sharp political insight, but one of the first of innumerable attempts to interpret America in terms of field sociology. It compares well with most of them.

The inhabitants of the United States, he observes, are individualists who desire quick results. They are not, indeed, interested in abstract philosophy, but if Americans do not read Descartes, they instinctively act on his advice. Their society is mobile and their tradition weak; each man makes his own judgment for practical ends. There is not much capacity for abstract thought but a great capacity for swift improvisation. The American tendency to treat language as an implement and the vogue of pragmatism in their philosophy are here foreshadowed. Yet though Americans are individualists, they tend to be alike, and singularly subject to ready-made opinions. This condition is likely to prevail in all modern democracies. It results not merely from political institutions, but from widely held beliefs: 'it may be foreseen that faith in public opinion will become a species of religion . . .' This danger was also to be stressed by J. S. Mill. Here, concludes de Tocqueville, is 'matter for profound reflection for those who look on freedom as a holy thing.'[12]

This is the more dangerous since, to a Catholic, the religious life of

Americans is generally transient and distracted. In spite of their original Puritan beliefs, individualism and the pursuit of material welfare tends to diminish religion. To maintain its influence in democracies, religion should concentrate upon essentials and simplify its rites; otherwise it may be isolated in 'the midst of an infidel people'. Theocracy and asceticism, in particular, are unlikely to succeed in democratic societies which believe in progress. Only by 'respecting all democratic tendencies not absolutely contrary to itself' can religion maintain its influence. Thus the clergy in America are not aloof from their people: they accept current standards of well-being. If they 'endeavour to amend their contemporaries . . . they do not quit fellowship with them'. Here he foresaw the technique of many rich and successful religious movements.

American democracy is optimistic. Where institutions are fluid, mankind is thought perfectible. Conservative societies may conceive 'amelioration', but not fundamental and constant change; for them 'everything is in its fit place', and the social order, like ships or furniture, must be durable.* How different is the view of progressive, technologically competent democrats! De Tocqueville cites the observation of an American sailor from whom he inquired why American ships were not built to last. He had replied that the ships would soon be obsolete anyway.

De Tocqueville also inquires into the comparative poverty of American art and poetry. How far is this a democratic or merely an American phenomenon? He decides that it is predominantly American; due in part to Puritanism, in part to the preoccupation with money and business of almost the entire society. Moreover, it was always possible to import from Europe the culture there was no time to create at home. Had the Americans been isolated, they would probably have created their own ideas. The lack of indigenous culture is nɔt therefore likely in all democracies. But their outlook will have certain peculiarities. When 'the chief cause of disparity between the fortunes of men is the mind', democracies, while naturally Philistine, will respect education as a ladder for success. The number of graduates will therefore increase; but their achievement will be mediocre, if their output is immense. There will be heavy specialization; vast accumulations of facts, mistrust for the broad view. Democratic intellectuals are also apt to be 'unremitting in their efforts to point out the weaker points in their neighbours'

---

* This economically conservative outlook is still apparent in the relatively liberal Encyclicals of Leo XIII, vide *infra*, pp. 383ff.

opinions'. Here, in a nutshell, are some major tendencies of modern academic life. This deficiency in pure speculative power may accompany competent technology. It is likely to spread to all democratic societies, and measures should be taken to counteract it. 'In the present age the human mind must be coerced into theoretical studies.' Governments ought deliberately to encourage and maintain the highest faculties of learning and invention.

There is another dangerous aspect of democracy. It is the contrast between the insignificance of individuals and the immensity of society. Men compensate for petty personal lives in glorification of the state, in immense public projects and grandiose buildings. This dwarfing of personality is reflected in political thought. In aristocratic states, where policy is decided by the few, historians record the personal control of affairs. To 'master . . . his lot, and to govern his fellow creatures,' they believe, 'man requires only to be master of himself.' It is also understood how large a part mood, chance and sheer casualness play in decisions. In democratic societies, on the other hand, historians tend to interpret events by impersonal laws and tendencies. Contemplating the massive course of policy, men lose the confidence of those nurtured in public affairs and tend towards fatalism. This attitude is congenial to the general public. Here is an extremely shrewd observation on middle class thought: it throws an interesting light both on Hegel and Marx. It is a pioneer contribution to the sociology of knowledge. Such 'doctrines of necessity', de Tocqueville insists, are extremely dangerous. If this outlook 'infects the whole mass of the community and gets possession of the public mind, it will soon paralyse the activity of modern society, and reduce Christians to the level of the Turks'. Another and repellent aspect of democracy is the need for mediocre demagogues to obtain publicity, without which they will cease to command the votes of their constituents. But the Americans are singularly patient of this infliction. They show 'their long experience of Parliamentary life not by abstaining from making bad speeches, but by courageously submitting to hear them made'.

Democratic peoples are also vulnerable in a crisis, for while aristocrats take luxury for granted, but if necessary can do without it, and while the poor are inured to privation, the middle class, having struggled to obtain security and comfort, dread to lose it and are perpetually afraid of doing so. Their policy is therefore liable to be wavering and opportunist: on occasion timid. A symptom to be familiar in the politics of the twentieth century. This preoccupation with security also renders its victims restless. Further, the lack of a recognized hierarchy makes snobbery more acute, while preoccupation with wealth and social advancement diverts men from public life. When the old leisured aristocracy has ceased to exist, 'the place of government is as it were, unfilled'. Here is the opportunity for unscrupulous and ignorant politicians.

All these tendencies, which have since been amply fulfilled in America and elsewhere, must be foreseen and counteracted. Democracies can be trusted to create material prosperity, but they are liable to spiritual degradation. It is therefore vital for governments to maintain standards and ideals. It is also demoralizing if, as well as being preoccupied with material welfare, the people cease to believe in an after life. De Tocqueville suggests that the best way for governments to avoid this danger is to act as if they believed in one themselves. Where, unfortunately, 'irreligion and democracy coexist, the most important duty of philosophers and those in power is to be always striving to place the objects of human actions far beyond man's immediate range'. 'Circumscribed by the character of his country and his age, the moralist must learn to vindicate his principles'.[13] Next to religious beliefs, an encouragement to morale is to inculcate a sense of responsibility to future generations. This idea has since often blended with a democratic outlook, and reached wide influence; it is, statistically, unusual in history.

This concern for morale is the more necessary in laissez faire democracies where the economic system disrupts the relationships both of rich and poor. The new industrial rich have little solidarity; they are a fluctuating class and each for himself. Unlike the landed aristocracy, their object is not 'to govern the population but to use it'. They recognize few obligations: 'I am of the opinion on the whole,' writes de Tocqueville, 'that the manufacturing aristocracy which is growing up under our eyes is one of the harshest which ever existed in the world.'* Since it is disunited, it is, indeed, not yet really dangerous. But if inequality again invades the world, 'this is the channel by which [it] will enter'.

The effect of democracy on family life is striking. It diminishes tradition and emancipates the young. The impact of young America on this French aristocrat was evidently considerable. And the independence of American women was even alarming. 'In America', he remarks, 'there is, strictly speaking, no adolescence.'[14] He contrasts

* For a striking account of the American climax of this phenomenon see BERTRAND RUSSELL, *Freedom and Organization*.

the formal and frigid tone of correspondence in aristocratic circles
with the idiom of democratic domestic life, and 'nowhere are young
women surrendered so early and so completely to their own guidance'.
Yet Americans are extremely respectable. It seems that the emancipation of women has had salutary effects, for 'morals are the work
of women'. It is true, de Tocqueville remarks, rather unkindly, that
an American girl 'scarcely ever displays that virginal bloom in the
midst of young desires ... which usually attend the European woman
in the transition from girlhood to youth', but she is neither timid nor
ignorant. She knows where she is and what she wants. Indeed, he
confesses, 'I have been frequently surprised and almost frightened
at the singular address and happy boldness with which young women
in America contrive to manage their thoughts and their language.'
In a society with fluctuating standards, where 'paternal authority
weak and marital authority contested', the Americans have successfully relied upon the competence and resolution of their women.
Moreover, wives support their frequent vicissitudes of fortune with
unquenchable energy.

The conclusions de Tocqueville drew from the American scene
were mixed and sometimes paradoxical. In the first place, he felt
it to be unique. 'I find no parallel to what is occurring before my
eyes.'[15] In general, he notices a universal levelling — in fortune, talent
and achievement. And he finds few outstanding individuals. But
'customs are mild and laws humane'. If less brilliant and less extreme than in Europe, life in democratic America is more easy and
tranquil. Social intercourse, he remarks, rather surprisingly, is softer.
'When I survey this countless multitude of human beings, shaped in
each others likeness ... the sight of such universal uniformity saddens
and chills me, and I am tempted to regret that state of society which
has ceased to be.' But this democratic mediocrity has its consolations. 'A state of equality is perhaps less elevated, but it is more
just: and its justice constitutes its greatness and its beauty.' It may
or may not be better than more traditional societies. It is certainly
different and it must certainly be accepted. For it is the destiny of
all democratic societies in the nineteenth century to work out 'that
species of greatness and happiness which is our own'.[16] A democratic
order is inevitable; within it there is a wide freedom of manœuvre.
De Tocqueville repudiates the idea of inexorable fate; of 'some insur-
mountable and unintelligent power, arising from anterior events,
from their race, or from the soil and climate of their country. Such
principles are false and cowardly'.

For America is the pattern of the future. 'We cannot prevent the conditions of men from becoming equal, but it depends upon ourselves whether the principle of equality is to lead them to servitude or freedom, to knowledge or barbarism, to prosperity or wretchedness.' How that responsibility has been discharged the mid-twentieth century bears witness. De Tocqueville had certainly posed the major question of his time. This famous book, written with a most anxious and responsible foresight and a sharp observation, shows shrewd judgment of political realities and of how to deal with them. Here, says de Tocqueville, are the facts. Pleasant or unpleasant, they must be accepted. Intelligent minorities who wish to maintain standards in what is obviously to be the society of the future will know how to act. He distinguishes between features peculiar to America and those likely to be common to all democratic states. And he interprets democracy according to the egalitarian political ideas of the French Revolution and the current belief in laissez-faire. It is not an exhaustive definition, but in the context the most practical. Here is the shrewdest and most comprehensive analysis made in the early nineteenth century of the new liberal democracy. De Tocqueville, in many respects, shows an Aristotelian realism and certainty of standards. Apart from his other writings, all of them valuable, this early masterpiece greatly contributed to the sophistication of liberalism, and the promotion of constitutional self-government.

III

De Tocqueville had faced the implications of the democratic revolution, made a penetrating examination of the only existing democratic state, and defined the problem of preserving standards and leadership in mass society. His friend John Stuart Mill tackled the same question with a different background and with remarkable foresight.*

* John Stuart Mill, 1806-73, eldest son of James Mill, the radical Utilitarian disciple of Bentham, who came of small farming stock in Angus, Scotland. James Mill and Bentham between them devised an education for the boy so extraordinary that it is a tribute to the force of his mind that he survived it. (See MILL's *Autobiography*, LESLIE STEPHEN and BERTRAND RUSSELL, op. cit.). He began Greek at the age of three, and was subjected to unrelenting pressure until the age of fourteen, when he was allowed to visit Bentham's brother in the south of France for a year. He is said to have remarked 'I never was a boy, never played cricket', but it is unlikely that the young prodigy would have enjoyed the game. At sixteen he was already writing for the periodical press, and the next year, in 1823, he followed his father into the employment of the East India Company. Here he remained, in considerable prosperity, rising in 1856 to become Chief of the Office, at a salary of £2000 a year, then a position of affluence. Two years later he retired on a substantial pension, since he disapproved of the direct rule of India by the English government. His duties as an administrator, in which he was highly successful, did not

THE LIBERAL COMPROMISE

Three aspects of Mill's thought demand attention. First, his contribution to nineteenth-century sociology, closely bound up with his attempt to construct a new philosophy of knowledge. Influenced by Comte, Mill brought a broader view to Benthamite improvement. This part of his *Logic* is a landmark in the new professional competence; it anticipates, in purpose if not in method, the development of modern sociology. The second and most famous aspect of his thought was expressed in the *Essay on Liberty* and the *Considerations on Representative Government*. Following de Tocqueville, he here asserts that only liberty can secure the resilience and initiative needful for success. Mill also asserts the power of reason in politics through knowledge and good will. He carried on and enriched a most valuable strain of English thought, at once lucid, practical and humane. A third aspect of his political writings is his championship of women's rights. His views on this burning question will also be examined.

interfere with his writing. He was a regular contributor to the *Westminster Review*, the paper of the so-called Philosophical Radicals, whose influence was to be reflected in the reforms after 1832. In 1831 began his long and sometimes difficult friendship with Carlyle, which survived the burning of the manuscript of the first volume of the *French Revolution* by one of Mill's housemaids. MILL's *System of Logic* was published in 1843, and in 1848 appeared his *Principles of Political Economy*. Both books won him celebrity. In 1851, after the death of her first husband, he married Mrs. Taylor, with whom he had been on terms of romantic friendship for twenty years. This well-known Victorian relationship throws an unexpected light on the political philosopher. 'Having got rather into the sphere of scandal,' writes Jane Welsh Carlyle, in 1837, 'I may mention before leaving that John Mill and Mrs. Taylor get on as charmingly as ever. I saw them together very lately looking most ecstatically "moony" at one another and sublimely superior to the rest of the World.' (Letter to John Stirling, quoted in *Jane Welsh Carlyle*, by TRUDY BLISS, p. 60. London, 1950.) In 1859, the year after her death and his retirement from the India House, he published his masterpiece, the *Essay on Liberty*, with its affectionate dedication. The *Considerations on Representative Government* appeared in 1861, and the *Utilitarians* in the same year. His *Autobiography*, published in the year of his death, was also written about this time. Mill was of frail physique and nervous temperament, and possessed considerable personal charm. Thomas Hardy, with characteristic precision, describes Mill's appearance as a candidate at the Westminster Election in 1865. 'He stood bareheaded and his vast pale brow, so thin skinned as to show the blue veins, sloped back like a stretching upland, and conveyed to the observer a curious sense of perilous exposure. The picture of him as personified earnestness surrounded for the most part by careless curiosity, derived an added piquancy . . . from the fact that the cameo clearness of his face chanced to be in relief against the blue shadow of the Church, which, on its transcendental side, his doctrines antagonized, but it would not be right to say that the throng was absolutely unimpressed by his words; it felt that they were weighty, though they did not know quite why.' *The Later Years of Thomas Hardy*, by F. E. HARDY, p. 119. Macmillan, 1930.

See SIR LESLIE STEPHEN, op. cit., and H. ELLIOTT, *The Letters of John Stuart Mill*. The best edition of the *Liberty* and *Representative Government* is by R. B. McCallum, already quoted. The introduction admirably relates Mill's views to his setting and to the problems of the modern world. The article by R. S. Dower in HEARNSHAW, *Social and Political Ideas of the Age of Reaction and Reconstruction*, is inadequate, and misleading in its belittlement of Mill; but there is a penetrating essay by JOHN PLAMENATZ, *The English Utilitarians*. See also Professor BASIL WILLEY, op. cit., for a broader treatment. For a disconcerting insight into Mill's neurotic personality, see F. A. HAYEK, *John Stuart Mill and Mrs. Taylor*. London, 1952.

The influence of Mill on the Victorian age was extraordinary. Though an unstable personality and hardly a great original mind, he is a master of empirical political thought. And if the calibre of writers is to be judged by their effect on policy, Mill must rank high. As logician, economist and political philosopher he was regarded as a prophet in his own age. This study must mainly be concerned with his political contribution. His outlook is wary but confident, logical but humane. As a seasoned administrator in the East India Company, he better understood the difficulties of policy than had Bentham or his own father. Nor had he their dogmatic force of mind. He was an intellectual with unbending moral standards, regarded by his more worldly contemporaries as Quixotic and by Disraeli as a 'governess'. But he had a shrewd sense of the possible and an extraordinary power of intellectual synthesis. Like the great majority of his generation, he believed in progress and in the security of the culture he represents. This confidence was justified by Victorian economic and naval preponderance. Within a century the nice problems of conduct and free discussion, even the basic freedoms Mill asserted, were to be threatened by régimes which deny even the existence of the problems which he defined. Such a future would have seemed to him a disaster both terrible and unlikely. Yet his principles have, in fact, remained extremely powerful in the West. Mill is no priggish and parochial writer, dwarfed by the Marxist revelation, elaborating moral questions since swamped by the convulsions of our own age. His view of society, expressed in limpid and forceful prose, is more realistic and ultimately more effective, than the visions of Hegelian and Marxist determinism. He is concerned, in his context, to maintain social variety and vitality. He states, often with unsurpassed precision, the truth that, without intellectual and moral freedom and responsibility, societies ossify and decline. Mill's *A System of Logic* attempted, under the influence of Comte, to provide a new basis for philosophy.* His treatment

---

* *A System of Logic.* Ratiocinative and Inductive. Being a connected view of the Principles of Evidence and the Methods of Scientific investigation. Two vols. London, 1843. The work is significantly prefaced by a quotation from the first 'lesson' of the *Cours de Philosophie Positive.* Translated, it asserts that Positivism alone 'can be considered the only solid basis for the social reorganization which ought to end the state of crisis in which the most civilized peoples have so long existed. So long as individual minds do not adhere, by unanimous opinion, to a certain number of general ideas capable of forming a common social doctrine, one cannot deny that the state of nations will necessarily remain revolutionary, in spite of all the political palliatives which can be adopted, and which can, in fact, only lead to merely provisional institutions. It is equally certain that after this meeting of minds in the same community of principles has been brought about, the appropriate institutions will necessarily flow from it, without any severe dislocation, the greatest confusion having already been dissipated by the mere fact of agreement'.

of the moral sciences, in which he includes sociology, is a facet of this broader undertaking to provide a common outlook.*

In the wide range of knowledge, he says, the study of society presents the most conspicuous gap. This is natural, for it is the most complex and the most difficult subject of study in which the human mind can be engaged. Here, if anywhere, new principles will be useful, 'if "the proper study of mankind", is not destined to remain the only subject which Philosophy cannot succeed in rescuing from Empiricism', and 'a blot upon the face of science'.[17] He will first indicate what sociology is not, then make a new approach. He evades the pleasure-pain reflex philosophy by declaring that character, the effect of habitual will, transcends it. 'A Character', says Novalis, 'is completely fashioned will.' There must be a science of character, or Ethnology, based on the study of successive 'states of mind'. 'The Laws of the formation of character exist.' It cannot, naturally, be an exact science, but it can be as much a science as meteorology and 'Tidology'. The most important aspects of society, which are most in need of control, can thus be approximately ascertained. 'For purposes of political and social science,' he concludes, 'this is sufficient. An empirical sociology is possible.'

This 'science of character' studies the effect of total environment on mind, and mind itself. Both circumstances and psychology must be fully analysed. Here is a comprehensive programme, surveying the wide range of behaviour in varying conditions, and the equally various ideologies these environments have provoked.

In his 'General Considerations on the Social Science', Mill sketches a 'science of man in society, of the actions of collective masses of mankind, and the various phenomena which constitute social life'.[18] Here is foreseen a new, professionalized knowledge. It is 'but of yesterday that the conception of a political or social science has existed, anywhere but in the mind of here and there an insulated thinker. Yet we must realize that there are laws that govern society independently of human will'. Philosophers and statesmen have hitherto imagined that the world could be 'whatever they chose to make it'. They did not understand that 'there were limits to the power of the human will over the phenomena of society'. Social science, like medicine, has too long proceeded on narrowly empirical lines; trying to 'cure disease, without knowing the laws of health'. Now there is hope 'that general laws . . . do really admit of being ascertained'.

* Op. cit., vol. II, Book VI. On the Logic of the Moral Sciences, pp. 475-624.

The old ways of speculation are now obsolete, examples of 'what sociology is not'. He calls them the 'chemical' and 'geometrical' methods. The traditional and tedious citation of historical examples, culled at random from varying places and times — always the saws and instances of conventional opinion — are hopelessly irrelevant. Historical examples cannot be isolated from their setting. Here is the 'chemical' error. The 'geometrical' fallacy is equally widespread. A single aspect of politics is isolated to explain a complex society; the 'unbending practical maxims', the universal precepts of the dogmatist, 'such . . . are those who make the assumption of a social contract or any other kind of original obligation and apply it to particular cases . . .' Take, for example, the argument of Hobbes. His apparently devastating thought is profoundly unsophisticated. Hobbes assumed one motive — fear: ' — not by implication, but avowedly'. In his view 'dread of each other is the one motive by which human beings were originally brought into a state of society and are still held in it'.[19] And this view is eked out 'by the double sophism' of original contract. Mill even criticizes the Benthamite 'interest philosophy' in which he was himself bred. The Benthamites argue that since all men are actuated by self interest, the best form of government is representative, where the aims of rulers and peoples will coincide. But such rare enlightenment is peculiar only to certain nations at certain times — all is modified by setting and intellectual climate. Queen Elizabeth, for example, was not responsible to the people, yet 'everything that the people had most at heart the monarch had at heart too'. And in primitive societies (and most others) the Benthamite rule cannot apply, since the people have no idea what is good for them. 'Had Peter the Great, or the rugged savages whom he began to civilize, the truest inclination towards the things which were for the real interest of those savages?'[20]

There is also no universal panacea in politics. The Benthamite creed was a fine weapon of political warfare in the struggle for reform: it does not and cannot give a total explanation of the art of politics. The Chemical and Geometrical methods are both misplaced and obsolete. There is only one constructive way of studying society — 'The Physical or Concrete Deductive method', which verifies its generalizations by the facts. This technique has been defined by Comte, 'the greatest living authority on scientific method in general, and the only philosopher who, with a competent knowledge of those methods, has attempted to characterize the Method of Sociology'.[21] So the ideas of the six volumes of Comte's recently published *Cours de Philosophie Positive* were filtered through the austere and practical mind of Mill, to find a wide publicity in the popular success of the English writer's attempt to construct a new philosophy of knowledge.

Since all science of government is conditioned by environment and its effect on character, Mill admits that English political economy, a science which he defends against Comte's accusation of artificial abstraction, is certainly too parochial. 'Empirical laws of human nature are tacitly assumed by English thinkers which are calculated only for Great Britain and the United States.' The steady concentration on self interest, the incessant urge to work, is far from characteristic, for example, of the inhabitants of the more genial parts of Europe, where laziness and pride often predominate over the desire for wealth. What is applicable to the inhabitants of Dumfriesshire is not applicable to the inhabitants of Catania. This discovery, long ago apparent to Montesquieu and Burke, here modifies the provincialism of Utilitarian thought. It was now made by a representative of a skilled class of administrators, avid for facts, avid for system, determined and destined to change the world.

With a complimentary reference to Vico as a pioneer philosopher of history, Mill declares that progress comes not from environment but through mind. Ideas ultimately determine progress. The expanding, shared, knowledge of elites is the key to advance. The new study of sociology can now close the last gap in the foundations of his *System of Logic*.

Mill thus makes his limited but lucid contribution to the most characteristic nineteenth-century social preoccupation — the study of man. And where Herder and Hegel sought metaphysical sanctions, the English philosopher, following Comte — without Comte's eccentricity or range — looks to the new field of professional competence, to that unprecedented power of analysis, which was to make its overwhelming and disconcerting contribution in the long researches of Darwin. The mild sociological chapters of the *System of Logic*, coming as early as 1843, are a notable example of English assimilation and bowdlerizing of extreme, original and far ranging foreign ideas. And where, in the English-speaking world, one read Comte, a hundred read Mill.

The *Essay on Liberty* and *Considerations on Representative Government* in which Mill's vindication of elites is further developed, are no parochial plea for the amenities of bourgeois life. They are a statement of obvious facts which no rulers can afford to ignore.

The main theme is expressed by the quotation from von Humboldt which precedes the dedication of the *Essay*. 'The grand leading principle, towards which every argument unfolded in the pages tends, is the absolute and essential importance of human development in its richest diversity.' Mill's vindication of liberty derives from a fine pedigree of English humanism. From More's *Utopia*, and Milton's *Areopagitica* and Locke's *Essay on Toleration*. It also has a broad European pedigree in classical and medieval tradition. It deserves the renown it was accorded by Victorian opinion. The *Considerations on Representative Government* contain detailed suggestions for reform, ranging both over domestic politics and problems of federal and colonial government. Here is the new administrative technique of the mid-century.

The masterpiece, the *Essay on Liberty*, had been written when Victorian individualism had reached its height. To the emancipated English professional classes, governments still seemed identified with eighteenth-century corruption and inefficiency, a constant theme of radical attack. Yet, in spite of the political liberty his class enjoyed, Mill was deeply apprehensive of the tyranny of opinion, in part doubtless owing to the high-minded unconventionality of his private life. It was then, as apparent from the novels of the time, more formidable than the power of government. Like de Tocqueville, he foresaw the dangers of universal mediocrity, of the coincidence of popular intolerance and state power. Nowhere is the case more cogently stated for the maintenance of quality than in the writings of this originally Utilitarian philosopher.

The *Essay* is widely familiar. Only its main arguments will here be recapitulated.* After defining his theme, Mill criticizes the curious belief in an infallible popular will among early-nineteenth-century liberals, and points out the dangers of democratic government. The power of mass opinion, he warns his readers, may well be politically expressed: 'the majority has not yet learnt to feel the power of government as their power, or its opinions as their opinions: when they do so, individual liberty will probably be as much exposed to invasion from the government as it already is from public opinion'.[22]

Naturally Mill's idea of Utility goes far beyond Bentham's. 'I

---

* It is divided into five chapters; the first introductory, the second on Liberty of Thought. The third treats of Individuality, as one of the Elements of Well being; the fourth of the Limits of the Authority of Society over the Individual. The fifth deals with 'Applications' and contain a devastating attack on the evils of bureaucracy, which still makes topical reading. The whole work occupies 104 pages of the edition quoted.

regard utility as the ultimate appeal ... but it must be utility in the largest sense, grounded on the permanent interests of a man as a progressive being.' Push-pin is no longer as good as poetry. Mill also assumes that progress is likely, and that it can be furthered by discussion. These originally eighteenth-century assumptions still colour the liberal democratic outlook. It is fashionable to disparage them, but they still largely dominate the most powerful countries in the world.

This liberty, Mill thought, was threatened, not, as Marx was to insist, by economic forces which made it illusory, but by mass opinion and bureaucracy. Though he admired Comte as a socio-logist, he disliked him as a politician. 'M. Comte ... aims at estab-lishing a despotism of society ... surpassing anything contemplated in the political ideal of the most rigid disciplinarian among the ancient philosophers.' And, apart from Comte, Mill feared pro-foundly the stifling power of average opinion. To avert these dangers he made his classic vindication of intellectual liberty. 'If all mankind minus one were of one opinion', he declares, 'mankind would be no more justified in silencing that one person than he, if he had the power, would be justified in silencing mankind.' Repres-sion of opinion 'robs the human race'. In a well-known passage on the dangers of conventional opinion, Mill remarks that mankind 'can hardly be too often reminded that there was once a man named Socrates, between whom and the legal authorities ... there took place a memorable collision'. He refers also, rather primly, to 'the event which took place on Calvary ... eighteen hundred years ago'. Both these 'lamentable transactions' were brought about by res-ponsible and respected men. Marcus Aurelius, one of the most lofty spirits of Antiquity, persecuted the Christians, for 'this strange history of the crucified God was not credible to him'. Nor is persecution salutary: history teems with examples of truth put down by perse-cution. Intolerance means intellectual stagnation: 'the price paid for this sort of intellectual pacification is the entire moral courage of the human mind': truth may be 'thrown back for centuries'. Success also ossifies and diminishes the power of doctrine. For example, the early Christians must have been very different from modern ones; in those days their enemies could say ' "See how these Christians love one another" (a remark not likely to be made by anybody now).'[23] Diversity of outlook is the mark of a living society, and 'a contemporary author has spoken of the "deep slumber of decided opinion" '. Take, for example, the 'paradoxes of Rousseau' that 'explode like bombshells'. He was even more wrong headed than his opponents, yet his contribution was valuable.[24] It is not the controversialists who gain by the clash of opinions, but the 'disinterested bystander . . . and there is always hope when people are forced to listen to both sides'.

Character, too, cannot be formed without free choice. 'Individual spontaneity' is the key to progress. And-character is the objective. Von Humboldt remarks that the end of man is 'the highest and most harmonious development of his powers . . . it really is of importance not only what men do, but also what manner of men they are that do it'. Like Godwin, Mill insists that 'mankind at present are but starved specimens of what nature will produce'. All progress is due to a small minority of creative and original minds. 'These few are the salt of the earth; without them human life would become a stagnant pool.' They not only create new institutions, but sustain those which exist. Society depends on genius: and 'genius can only create freely in an atmosphere of freedom. The initiation of wise or noble thought comes, and must come from individuals'.

Yet, all around him, Mill sees only increasing mediocrity. 'Already energetic characters on any large scale are becoming merely traditional' and 'the greatness of England is now all collective'. It seems a strange picture of the mid-Victorian age, with so many intellectual and material triumphs before it; so rich in literary genius, administrative enterprise and scientific invention. But Mill is determinedly pessimistic. He quotes de Tocqueville's remark that Frenchmen now tend all to look alike, declares that it applies even more to the English, and closes the chapter on a note of urgent warning. Once standards are gone, he says, it is impossible to recover them. Mankind no longer realize what they have lost.

The simple Utilitarianism of his upbringing was thus abandoned and a broader ideal of conduct and personality defined. It sometimes appears rather anaemic. Public opinion, if it agrees with Mill's principles, is even evoked against the failings of the average sensual man, 'who pursue[s] animal pleasures at the expense of . . . feeling and intellect'. He must expect to be 'lowered in the opinion of others and to have less share in their favourable sentiments' — an amenity he may well be ready to forego. Like the ideal of More and Milton, Mill's good life is rarefied, with 'human beings . . . for ever stimulating each other to increased exercise of their higher faculties'. But, unlike his predecessors, he dislikes state interference in personal affairs; when it does interfere, it interferes in the wrong way. He attacks the Puritan tyrannies of the Commonwealth and early New England, and points out the dangers to property of democratic feeling, and the 'notion that the public has a right to a veto on the manner in which individuals shall spend their income'.

Mill was no socialist. He warned his generation of the consequences of the doctrine. 'We have only further to suppose a considerable diffusion of Socialist opinions, and it may become infamous in the eyes of the majority to possess more property than some very small amount, or any income not earned by manual labour.' Production, too, may be diminished by restrictive practices in industry and technical advance delayed.

Constantly aware of the tides of puritanical jealousy and egalitarianism beneath the surface of society, he attacks American attempts at Prohibition and English Sabbatarian intolerance. 'Though the feeling which breaks out in the repeated attempts to stop railway travelling on Sunday, and in the resistance to the opening of Museums, and the like, has not the cruelty of the old persecutors, the state of mind indicated by it is fundamentally the same.' He even reprobates persecution of the Mormons, with their shocking practice of polygamy — after all, only a result of teaching women that marriage is the sole object of life, so that many of them 'prefer being one of several wives, to not being a wife at all'.[25] He deprecates a crusade against these people.

Education is vitally important. He even suggests that it should be compulsory 'up to a certain standard', though he wisely remarks 'that State education should be strictly limited', and 'one among many competing experiments'. He further advocates extensive public examinations, at that time a new instrument of selection. If civilization cannot intellectually vanquish barbarism, the sooner it 'receives notice to quit' the better. Ideas, not bayonets, are ultimately victorious.

Summing up, he remarks that there are three objections to government interference. First, if the thing can be better done privately; second, if it is good for private individuals to do it; third and most cogently, if it implies an unnecessary increase in the powers of government. There follows a valuable passage on the dangers of benevolent power. Every extension of the public administration 'converts more and more of the active and ambitious part of the public into hangers on of the government . . . If the roads, the railways, the banks, the insurance offices, the great joint stock companies, the universities and the public charities, were all of them branches of the government; if, in addition, the municipal corporations and local boards, with all that now devolves on them, became departments of the central administration; if the employés of all these different enterprises were appointed and paid by the government and look to the government for every rise in life, not all the freedom of the press and popular constitution of the legislature would make this or any other country free otherwise than in name'. Mill's warning seems singularly apt.

Moreover, the more effective a bureaucracy, the greater the evil. The best minds are absorbed by it. Thus recruited, the system lumbers on under its own momentum; the bureaucrats themselves are its slaves and liable to sink into 'indolent routine', If they now and then 'desert that mill-horse round, rushing into some half examined crudity which has struck the fancy of some leading member of the corps', they may become a 'pedantocracy'.

In view of these possible evils, one must be vigilant to observe where the disadvantages of state power predominate over the benefits derived from the 'collective application of the force of society, . . . for the removal of the obstacles which stand in the way of its well being'. Too zealous a hindering of the hindrances of the good life may lead to worse evils than those originally removed. 'The worth of the State in the long run, is the worth of the individuals composing it.' This admirable and obvious conclusion, fundamental to liberal thought, and so far removed from all forms of collectivism, is followed by a classic and closing admonition. 'A State which dwarfs its men in order that they may be more docile instruments in its hands, even for beneficial purposes — will find that with small men no great thing can really be accomplished; and that the perfection of machinery to which it has sacrificed everything will in the end avail it nothing, for want of the vital power which, in order that the machine might work more smoothly, it has preferred to banish.' Such was the telling and realistic conclusion of Mill's vindication of liberty. The *Considerations on Representative Government*, with their detailed suggestions for reform, are inspired with the same idea of a creative society.

There was a livelier side to Mill's contribution. Hitherto few influential political philosophers had championed the cause of women. Their legal disabilities had persisted into mid-Victorian times. Mill was a formidable champion of women's rights. His essay *On the Subjection of Women* is uncompromising.[26] As he well knew, he was attacking a 'deeply rooted prejudice'. 'The principle', he writes, 'which regulates the existing social relations between the sexes — the legal subordination of one sex to the other — is wrong in itself and now one of the chief hindrances to human improvement.' This situation is an anachronism; like slavery, it reflects 'the taint of brutal origins . . .' from the 'very earliest twilight of human society'. The progress of mankind has moved from status to contract: today 'no male human being' in civilized society is held to status. Women, alone, as such are disabled. They are educated for slavery, for meekness, for resignation. 'In the case of women, each individual of the subject class is in a chronic state of bribery and intimidation combined.'

These are strong words. They stirred strong passions in Victorian England. Behind Mill's trenchant phrases can be discerned the wave of feminine emancipation. Within a century of Mill's challenge, able women had invaded Parliament and the professions, transformed the prospects of feminine education and broken the legal sanction of domestic tyranny.

'Their social subordination,' Mill insisted, was an anachronism. It '. . . stands out an isolated fact in modern social institutions' . . . 'as if a gigantic dolmen, or a vast temple of Jupiter Olympius, occupied the site of St. Paul's'.[27] To those who retort that the nature of women demands and even enjoys subordination, he replies that the ideal of meek womanhood is false. 'What is now called the nature of women is an eminently artificial thing — the result of forced repression in some directions, unnatural stimulation in others.' One side of woman's personality is subjected to 'hot-house and stove cultivation' — the other is left 'in the snow'. But the Macassar oil and the ringlets, the bare shoulders and the crinolines, concealed a more masterful future. How little, he argues, are the possibilities of women understood! They have never been allowed the chance to develop them. And if they are given freedom, they will not act against their own instinct. 'The anxiety of mankind to interfere on behalf of nature, for fear lest nature should not succeed in effecting its purpose, is an altogether unnecessary solicitude.'[28] But so long as the legal bondage of women persists, there can be no freedom — no opportunities. The interdiction on the ownership of property, modified only by settlements which do not imply control, made their position worse than that of a Roman slave, who was allowed personal chattels. And even a slave often had the right 'to refuse to her master the last familiarity'. Not so the Victorian wife.[29] The children, moreover, are entirely in their father's power, whatever his character. Only proved adultery can obtain divorce, and that with great difficulty. All these consequences follow from the legal despotism of the male. Yet 'not a word can be said for despotism in the family which cannot be said for political despotism'. And even if the full letter of the law is not often enforced, the situation is intolerable. 'The despotism of Louis XVI was not the despotism of Philippe le Bel, or of Nadir Shah or of Caligula', but it provoked the French Revolution. Law should not assume the good-will of the well meaning majority, but cater for the worst. Today 'the vilest malefactor has some wretched woman tied to him, against whom he can commit any atrocity except killing her, and if tolerably cautious can do that without much danger of the legal penalty'. Here are vistas of Dickensian domestic horror. 'The breadth and depth of human misery caused in this shape alone by the abuse of the institution, swells to something appalling.'[30]

The unfitness of man for unbridled political power is a 'commonplace', but the power granted to husbands is tyrannical. The family becomes a 'school of despotism' when it ought to be a school of freedom; 'the true virtue of human beings is fitness to live together as equals'. This ideal seems obvious. It was beyond the average morality of Mill's contemporaries. Yet he assumes, in his liberal way, that it will be realized. The sensibility which makes the present situation intolerable is the price paid by those rare spirits who can see into a better future. 'To see the futurity of the species has always been the privilege of the intellectual élite or of those who have learnt from them; to have the feelings of that futurity has been the distinction and usually the martyrdom of a still rarer élite.' The thought is familiar in the novels of Thomas Hardy, so representative of thoughtful Victorian opinion.

Until the family becomes the scene of a real moral training, the whole body politic must remain rotten.[31] The first step in this emancipation must be the right of women to keep their own property and their own earnings. At present 'what is mine is yours, and what is yours is not mine'. Turning to the wider sphere of public life, Mill makes an even more startling claim in the context of his time. He demands the suffrage for women.[32] He cites the political ability of Queen Elizabeth I. Women have intuitive perception which 'means a rapid and correct insight into present fact'.[33] Further, hysterics and fainting fits are already going out of fashion, and women who take exercise 'very rarely have any excessive susceptibility to nerves'. Men, it may be objected, have larger brains; 'I reply that in the first place the fact is doubtful.' He knows a scientist who has weighed many brains and the heaviest belonged to a woman. In any case, the mere argument of size is irrelevant: an elephant is not more intelligent than a man. After this lapse from his usual cool rationality, Mill points out that there are, obviously, very conflicting views on the nature of women. 'An oriental thinks that women are by nature peculiarly voluptuous . . . an Englishman usually thinks that they are by nature cold.' After this reflection on his compatriots, Mill remarks that the French regard women as fickle, but that the English regard them as models of fidelity, thus striking the balance even. In any case, 'both in a good and bad sense the English are farther from the state of nature than any other modern people . . .' they 'not only act but feel according to rule'. So far had the muffled processes of English convention already advanced. All this disqualifies them from understanding women, whose possibilities are far greater than is generally recognized. Consider, he says, the famous women of Antiquity — Sappho, greatest of lyric poets; Corinna who surpassed Pindar; Aspasia, from whom even Socrates took advice. If only they were not obliged by their dependent position to spend so much time making themselves attractive, there is no telling what they might not do. Think of 'the great and continued exercise of thought which all women who attach importance to dressing well (I do not mean expensively, but with taste . . .) must bestow upon their dress . . .' It would 'go a long way towards achieving respectable results in art or science or literature'.[34] As for the usual charge that women are incapable of detachment, Mill observes that 'It has still to be proved that women are oftener misled by their personal feelings than men by their personal interests.' And would mankind be the better off if women were free? Unhesitatingly he affirms that they would. 'The law of servitude in marriage', he insists, 'is a monstrous contradiction to all the principles of the modern world.'[35] Public life would be enriched by their participation; men would cease to be demoralized by their dependence, and the reserve of talent, always inadequate, would be greatly increased. Why, already, he observes quaintly, the influence of women counts for a great deal 'in two of the most marked features of European life, its aversion to war and its addiction to philanthropy'. Moreover, this influence is increasing since males have become more domesticated; and the cult of 'rough amusements' and 'convivial excesses' diminish. With greater refinement, men desire a relation of intelligent equality. This 'unspeakable gain' in private happiness would sweeten the whole atmosphere of society; it would diminish the love of power. It would diminish boredom.

This admirable ideal has greatly enhanced the amelioration of society since Mill's day. His conclusion is moving enough. Why add, he asks, to the evils nature inflicts by 'jealous and prejudiced restrictions'? Why promote the impoverishment and not the enrichment of life? Why, indeed? Mill's arguments, amid the imbecilities of national and class conflict, should not be forgotten, either on this or on wider themes.

IV

Such were the contributions of de Tocqueville and John Stuart Mill to the advancement of sociology, the adjustment of institutions and the development of the liberal compromise. Both saw clearly the major problems of their age; both reinforced constitutional government. The outlook to which they contributed dominated their century. The attempt to assimilate democracy and maintain standards had considerable success in its native setting. Both these writers took the situation as they found it. They endeavoured, by close observation and foresight, to adjust existing institutions by insight and knowledge. They were convinced that professional competence inspired by wise purpose can guide and adapt a constitutional society without recourse to revolution or dictatorship. They were shrewd, practical and humane — the fine flower of the privileged mid-nineteenth century civilization they represent.

BOOK II

THE POLITICAL THOUGHT OF THE
AGE OF DARWIN

CHAPTER I

MID-CENTURY PROSPECT: THE IMPACT OF DARWINISM

THE high European culture which found political expression in the ideas of de Tocqueville and J. S. Mill, was largely secured by a *Pax Britannica* based on resources which were extra-European. Constitutional government was predominant, and a confident assumption of progress became widespread. The most influential and representative liberal thought was thus formulated in England, then the main focus of world power. It is upon English writers, representative of this sanguine outlook, that attention will now be directed, and upon the knowledge of the life of institutions which grew up within their culture. The Marxist, nationalist and nihilist attack upon this prosperous society will then be examined. The weakness of liberal middle-class civilization, of which these English writers were representative, was economic and international. Beneath the imposing achievement, two problems remained implacable — the threat of national and class war. Behind the façade of ornamental royalty, the colossal wealth, the cultural and technological achievement, the military and naval might, was an undercurrent of political barbarism.

The earlier nineteenth century had been full of confidence. The dashing French romantics, the 'improving' Utilitarians, the admirers of Macaulay and Mazzini, all believed that once reaction had been defeated, wars and oppression would disappear. The Utopian prophets of socialism also depicted prosperity and brotherhood. All were good Europeans. Spirited patriots, like Mazzini, dreamt of a European Commonwealth. The critics of the new democracy were numerous, but a minority. The prevalent tide of opinion before 1848 was hopeful. Western Europe was to be the political arena of the liberal heirs of the Revolution. It was the age of the political professors, the apex of liberal romanticism. After 1848 the scene darkens. While intellectual discovery is increasingly original, more fundamentally important, the political signs become increasingly ominous. The conflict between the new industrial working class and the bourgeoisie in France was sealed in blood on the June barricades in Paris. The failure of the Frankfurt parliament transformed the project of a liberal greater Germany into a smaller, Prussian dominated, confederation. The Hapsburg power, challenged by the Vienna revolution, and shaken by the rebellions of subject peoples, was forced to appeal for Russian intervention. In the 'fifties and 'sixties, while new ideas crowded upon one another, the bloody fiasco of the Crimea, the first taste of Prussian blood and iron at Sadowa, and the long hard fought campaigns and devastation of the American Civil War, were followed by the mechanized horrors of the Franco-Prussian conflict. The age of post-Napoleonic progress was becoming an age of battle. The new railways and factories could serve other purposes than to create plenty for a free market. After 1848, when the tattered fabric of Metternich's dynastic order had been swept aside, Europe was confronted not with benevolent liberalism, but with that forerunner of twentieth-century dictatorship, Louis Napoleon, and by Bismarck's Machiavellian mind.

Along with the growth of power-politics, backed by popular nationalism and great industry, there also grew up an increasing menace of class war. If Marx and Engels were disappointed by the failure of 1848, the hatred that it left gave the doctrine of the *Communist Manifesto* a new, if delayed, impetus. And by the 'sixties, when the more massive reserves of *Das Kapital* were deployed, Marx reinforced the flaming dogmas of 1848 by a new, apparently realistic, sanction. He claimed to have discovered a science of politics. A total explanation, far surpassing Comte's, comparable only to Darwin's explanation of the whole biological field. By now the historicism of the early Romantic age, the cloudy intuitions of Hegel, and the imaginative power of Scott, Chateaubriand, Thierry and Carlyle, had become 'scientific'. New political doctrines were reinforced by the idea of inevitable progressive evolution, even if achieved through the massive and cruel conflicts of perennial class antagonism. But there were more sceptical prophets than Marx and Engels, both still typical of their age in their belief in progress. There was Treitschke, for example, who preached a cult of war for its own sake, a gospel tricked out with specious liberalism and brilliant historical narrative. In more sophisticated minds there was nihilism. The despair of Schopenhauer, with its Byronic early nineteenth-century origins, was deepened by a new cult of the political negations of the East. This despair of politics was carried further by Nietzsche's post-Darwinian philosophy. This tormented genius, maddened by the apparent implications of the new knowledge, was to launch a brilliant attack on all traditional values. His elaborate and unrepresentative ideas were later vulgarized into a popular myth. Preposterous theories of racial superiority, for which no scientific foundation could exist, further bedevilled the minds of the lower bourgeoisie, now, in the most powerful states of Europe, for the first time on the threshold of political and economic influence.

The demographical background was without precedent. The industrial and technical revolutions were now working themselves out, not only in England, but in North-Western and much of Central Europe. A massive increase in population is evident by the early years of the century. It was now producing its cumulative effects. Not only was the population of Europe enlarged, but great new migrations crossed the Atlantic and the outer oceans to transform the economy of the United States and to colonize Canada and Australasia. This increase of population went along with the growth of great industrial cities. They were centred on the new industries, now linked by rail and steamship with their customers and competitors across national frontiers, and with the agricultural and mining areas which formed their sources of supply. All this mechanical expansion was determined by a network of cosmopolitan finance, centred increasingly on London. The early railway speculations, the later ventures of the Saint-Simonians, French colonial expansion in North Africa, the rise of the industries of the Low Countries and the enormous expansion of British manufactures in the first half of the century, were now surpassed by the enterprise of mid-Victorian England and of American big business after the Civil War. By the ventures, too, of the speculators of the Second Empire, by the rise of the great heavy industries of Westphalia and the Ruhr, by the exploitation of Africa and South America, and by intensified European enterprise in the Far East. In this increasingly world-wide megalopolitan setting — urban is too traditional a word — the masses in the leading nations came to political consciousness and power. So great was the scale of transformation that in a society with the intellectual solidarity of medieval Christendom, or of traditional China, the threat of disruption would have been formidable. But this demographic change coincided with an intellectual revolution which seemed to threaten to cut traditional values and culture from their roots. The dangers earlier foreseen by de Tocqueville and J. S. Mill became more imminent; the challenge to the ruling classes more searching. With the waning of traditional beliefs, there was a danger of a collapse of leadership, similar, on its wider scale and more dynamic context, to the loss of grip by the ruling minorities

of Antiquity on the predominantly rural proletariat of the Mediterranean world. There was a danger, still menacing, of the industrial
masses turning hostile to the civilization which had brought them
into being. As spiritual *malaise* had contributed to sap the life of
pagan Antiquity, so the political fanatics of the later nineteenth
century threatened to dislocate the far more vigorous society which
had developed from the era of the Revolution.

In political thought there was a marked degeneration. In particular in continental Europe, where the new scepticism had been
taken more seriously than across the Channel, where political dogmas
are never popular. Here, absorbed in money-making, society and
sport, secure from foreign attack, an amiably Philistine ruling class
remained largely aloof. The masses were uninterested. In England,
as in the United States, where a more emotional and intense preoccupation with business obtained, existing political institutions held
firm. Energy which might have inspired revolution or nationalist
aggression, was canalized into more rewarding expansion across
new continents and oceans. The paranoiac nationalism of Treitschke
and the esoteric blasphemies of Nietzsche were irrelevant in the
mining camps and railroads of the New World. They had their own
argot. But where ancient national grievances and festering class
antagonism poisoned the minds of continental Europeans, the
nihilism of politically irresponsible intellectuals filtered through.
And where clerical reaction had been evicted, the devils of class
hatred and nationalism entered in.

The predominant trend of later-nineteenth-century political
thought on the European continent, if not in England and North
America, thus fomented a danger always implicit in the national
political structure of Europe since the Revolution. This trend was,
indeed, encouraged by intellectuals disorientated by the impact of
Darwinian ideas. But defective institutions, proceeding, as Saint-
Simon had pointed out, of their own momentum, were probably
more decisive for the collapse. The ineffectual criticisms of Sully,
Saint-Pierre and Kant had been carried on by Saint-Simon and
Comte, but they no more influenced policy than had their predecessors. J. S. Mill might write that the American Supreme Court
was a model for the world, 'the first great example of one of
the most prominent wants of civilized society, a real international
tribunal',[1] but the political structure of Europe was still wholly
determined by national sovereignty. As the new peoples, the
Italians in the nineteenth century, the Poles and Czechs, Magyars,

Serbs and Bulgars, in the twentieth, won their independence, all were determined to identify their national culture with sovereign power.

Apart from nationalist political theory, the masses were dragooned by a concentration of government which de Tocqueville had foreseen, the paradoxical legacy of 1789. And when the guns opened on the Franco-German frontier in 1870, they heralded the age of huge conscript armies, of the head-on collision of the bureaucratic powers denounced by Proudhon, which had often escaped control of those who imagined they were in command. The legacy of the seventeenth and eighteenth centuries, the sovereign state, had developed into the Juggernaut of modern nationalism, its course unrestrained by dynastic interest and eighteenth-century inefficiency. Against this background, the political thought of the later nineteenth century is set. It was to be dominated by the intellectual revolution created by the reception of Darwinism.

II

While Comte, Proudhon and Mazzini, de Tocqueville and J. S. Mill, were making their varying contributions to political speculation, a broad change of intellectual climate had long been building up. This gradual transformation, brought to decisive dimensions by Darwin, is comparable only to that wrought by Copernicus and Newton. In some respects the Darwinian contribution was more intimate and pervasive. Where the astronomers had revolutionized the earth's place in the cosmos, Darwin revolutionized man's place in nature. Theologically the implications seemed equally disconcerting. That it is still under a century since the publication of the *Origin of Species* in 1859 is often forgotten, so completely has the new knowledge been assimilated. While the political controversies of the nineteenth century are still vehemently alive, the battles of T. H. Huxley and Bishop Wilberforce are now remote. Only a few mopping-up operations have still to be conducted. It is a significant discrepancy between accepted science and the doubts and controversies of political opinion. The nature of the new knowledge and its implications for political thought, still not adequately realized, are worth examination.

So great a change of outlook did not occur suddenly. Evolutionary ideas of a kind had long been in the air in the eighteenth and early nineteenth centuries. By the 'fifties concepts of evolution were

widely familiar. But Darwin's contribution was decisive.* Two outstanding conclusions emerged from his laborious experiments. First,
man was no longer in a special category of creation. Like the other
animals, he was part of Nature; no longer the product of a
sudden fiat, but of evolution, the spontaneous interaction of environment and life. It was a change shattering to orthodox opinion.
To minds conditioned by the dogma of special creation, by Baby-
lonian and Hebraic folktales of the early Iron Age, it appeared
deeply disturbing. The orthodox theology of Fall and Redemption
seemed, at most, symbolical.

The first conclusion implied the second. The alteration of
the sense of time. Now the whole prehistoric past was opened up,
human history dwarfed in the total panorama. With Darwin and
Huxley, the piled-up evidence seemed to descend like an avalanche
upon the defenders of orthodoxy. And in the silence that followed
the long rumbling of the discharge, nineteenth-century thinkers
looked about them to observe a landscape radically transformed.†
For the first time in history, the conclusions of scientists dominated
public opinion. Hitherto the clergy and the metaphysical philosophers, the lawyers and the rhetoricians, had determined the course
of political thought. Now a new and inescapable influence had to be
taken into account.

The scientists had received little official encouragement. In the
early nineteenth century scientific posts were few, ill-paid, and
carrying little prestige. But in a society so wealthy and enterprising,
with political liberty taken for granted, scientists could put up with
being ignored since they were not persecuted. While the penalties
of heresy encompassed medieval speculation, nineteenth-century
pioneers had to face nothing more formidable than public obloquy.
The tolerance and the creativeness of laissez-faire society indirectly
contributed to startling results.

The background they depicted is today assumed. In the 'fifties,

* The publication of *The Origin of Species by Natural Selection* in 1859 had been preceded
by joint papers by Darwin and Wallace in the previous year; HUXLEY's *Man's Place in
Nature* appeared in 1863; DARWIN's *Variation of Animals and Plants under Domestication* in
·868, *The Descent of Man* and *The Expression of Emotions in Men and Animals* in 1871 and
1872.

† Huxley wrote of his scientific contemporaries, 'the publication of the Darwin and
Wallace paper of 1858, and still more of the "Origin" in 1859, had the effect upon them
of a flash of light which, to a man who has lost himself on a dark night, suddenly reveals a
road, which, whether it takes him straight home or not, certainly goes his way . . . The
"Origin" provided us with the working hypothesis we sought . . . My reflection, when I
first made myself master of the central idea of the "Origin" was, "How extremely stupid
not to have thought of that".' LEONARD HUXLEY, *Life and Letters of T. H. Huxley.* 1908
Edition, vol. I, pp. 245-6.

ordinary opinion still widely accepted the grotesque conjectures
of a Restoration archbishop, for Ussher's Chronology declared,
with convincing precision, that in four thousand and four, exactly,
the creation had come about.

Thus two overwhelming ideas gradually combined to produce the
broadest transformation of thought for centuries, with profound
effects on political theory. Such an alteration in the whole status of
man caused a profound difference between modern political thought
and the ideas even of the eighteenth and seventeenth centuries, let
alone of the Middle Ages and of Christian and Pagan Antiquity.
And the hypotheses were not the hazards of individual intuition, the
brilliant but unsubstantiated conjectures of eighteenth-century
generalization, but the convergent result of a new kind of systematic
knowledge.

The most decisive discoveries were made by a naturalist of
Aristotelian breadth of mind. Since the political implications of his
outlook were to be much distorted, they are worth a closer view. In
popular belief, the doctrine of Darwin was sombre and, indeed,
ferocious. This version is still widely entertained. It was to darken
political thought for decades. In fact, as Mr. Penniman well points
out, the tentative and sympathetic approach of Darwin was more
akin to that of an intelligent farmer than to the urban and mechanical outlook of most Victorian intellectuals. It was severely misinterpreted by current opinion: '. . . while the work of Darwin had
a far richer content, and far deeper meanings, it was this superficial
interpretation in terms of a mechanized civilization that caught the
popular imagination, and proved to be the rock on which many
eminent social philosophers stumbled for years to come'.[2] The competitive and ruthless aspect of Darwin's picture commanded most
attention.

According to the actual hypothesis, survival and success were
determined solely by the power of an organism to adapt itself to
environment, and by the natural competitive selection of those
varieties of species best able to multiply in the widest context.
Since population always presses on food supply, there is, indeed, a
'struggle for existence', but the 'fittest' are not necessarily the
toughest. They are those best suited to survive in given surroundings. Not the comparatively rare beasts of prey, but the gregarious
animals, have in practice achieved the most lasting and widespread
adaptation and the greatest biological success. Further, the 'law'
of natural selection is neutral; not imposed, but deduced from the

facts. This lesson of biology was later to be reinforced by the field-work of Kropotkin, who applied his conclusions to political thought. Meanwhile, Darwinian terminology unduly stressed the predatory aspects of the struggle for existence, at the expense of the organic interdependence the overall picture more emphatically displays. This bias was natural in a mechanized and individualistic society, nurtured in laissez-faire economics. In spite of the protests of Carlyle, Ruskin and Matthew Arnold, the outlook long dominated average opinion. Pseudo-Darwinian influence was to reinforce Malthusian and Spencerian doctrines of competition and callousness, which were already established in the field, and so encourage nationalist power politics and class war. Properly appreciated, Darwin's comprehensive and verifiable picture of man and society was to point through understanding to control. In the picture so presented the ideas of Herbert Spencer and Marx, with their respective conflicts of individuals and classes, reflected biological evidence less accurately than the temperate views later set out, for example, in Kropotkin's *Mutual Aid*.* A proper study of the Darwinian hypothesis will scotch the delusions which demoralized much later nineteenth-century political thought; and a study of biology has salutary and generally neglected lessons for political theorists.

Before examining the political effects of the new ideas, it is worth recalling the stages which led up to their full impact. It was the culmination of a long development. With the pioneering work of Linnaeus and Buffon in the mid-eighteenth century, modern biological and anthropological studies had first been mapped. The classification of the earth's strata according to time was the basis of the new approach. This had first been authoritatively achieved by Lyell in 1830.

The evidence unearthed by geologists and anthropologists was disconcerting and inescapable. Ingenious attempts were made to misinterpret it. Notably by Dr. Buckland, later Dean of Westminster, who had written that misleading work *Reliquiae Diluvianae* (1823), and in the same year discovered the 'Red Lady of Paviland', who subsequently proved to be the remains of an Aurignacian male.†
In 1833, Dr. Schmerling of Liège had discovered part of a human

---

* 1902. See also his *Paroles d'un Révolté*, 1885, and *La Conquête du Pain*, 1888. The best biography is by G. WOODCOCK and I. AVAKUMOVIC, *Kropotkin the Anarchist Prince*, q.v., also H. READ, *Kropotkin, Selections from his Writings*.

† An irreverent contemporary wrote:
> Some doubts were once expressed about the Flood,
> Buckland arose, and all was clear as mud.

Quoted by SIR GEOFFREY FABER, *Oxford Apostles*, 2nd edn., 1936.

skull — the Engis Cranium — in the compromising vicinity of bones of animals long extinct. It has subsequently been classified as upper Palaeolithic. Five years afterwards, Boucher de Perthes found flint implements in deposits of great antiquity at Abbeville, though the significance of such discoveries was immediately denied.* In 1843 Cowles Pritchard, a Bristol doctor, published a pioneer work of Ethnology, the *Natural History of Man*. In an attempt to retain traditional views, he made the daring suggestion that Adam and Eve had been black, an idea received with widespread consternation. During the 'fifties fresh evidence accumulated. The most sensational discovery was made by Dr. Schaaffhausen and Dr. Fuhlrott of Bonn. In a cave near Düsseldorf, in the homely woods of the Neanderthal, were found the remains of a creature whose receding jaw and beetling brows proclaimed what seemed at once a human and a simian affinity. Controversy raged as to whether the Neanderthaler, with his sinister sounding name, was human, an idiot, or an ape.† And the obviously bestial characteristics of this branch of the human stock contributed to the horror with which the new knowledge was regarded. Indeed, it gave an unfortunate twist to the whole problem. 'The human bones and cranium from the Neanderthal', wrote Dr. Schaaffhausen eagerly, 'exceed all the rest . . . in those peculiarities of conformation which lead to the conclusion of their belonging to a barbarous and savage race . . . They may still be regarded as the most ancient memorial of the early inhabitants of Europe.'‡

Such was some of the sparse but accumulating evidence of a prehistoric background already available when Darwin published his first epoch-making work. The 'sixties and 'seventies were to see far richer finds. The Aurignacian discoveries in the Dordogne, the sensational cave at Altamira (1879), the Grimaldi finds near Menton, more extensive evidence of Neanderthalers in Belgium and the Balkans — a whole family of them trapped and calcined in a cave in Croatia. But the discoverers even of this later evidence were met with obstinate scepticism. In 1859 the relatively rare finds available had not much shaken orthodox opinion, and were little known outside a small and specialized circle. It required intensive efforts of propaganda for the new facts to get a hearing. And by the mid-

---

* As when fossil mastodon bones, found in the Alps, were at once attributed to Hannibal's elephants.

† The statue since erected on the spot throws little light on this problem.

‡ Quoted by PENNIMAN, op. cit., p. 68. Though contemporary with more advanced human types, the Neanderthaler was proved to be unrepresentative, and, if related at all, only very remotely ancestral to Palaeolithic man. See CARLTON S. COON, *The Races of Europe*, q.v. for the best account of this subject.

century the means of such diffusion had increased. Sir Humphry Davy and Faraday were now famous: the growth of the Royal Institution and the establishment of the British Association, with its annual meetings, in 1831, had all contributed to enhance the prestige of science, while the overwhelming development of factories and railways and the Great Exhibition of 1851, had greatly increased popular interest in technology of all kinds. Nor had the feverish doctrinal controversies which had recently disturbed the calm of the Anglican Church increased its hold on public opinion.* The time was ripe for new prophets. The Oxford Movement had roused passionate public interest. During the 'thirties, in the words of Sir Llewellyn Woodward, 'the domination of ecclesiastical subjects and religious beliefs was a real domination; everything else was seen at second hand'.³ Now these doctrines seemed dwarfed by the great issues the scientists were to raise. But the clergy, says Woodward, never met the liberals on their own ground. 'For all their intellectual ability, the Oxford reformers knew little or nothing of the physical and biological sciences.'⁴ But the controversy had created an atmosphere inimical even to moderate Biblical criticism. Hence the hostility even to *Essays and Reviews* (1860), the work of liberal theologians.

Bishop Wilberforce proved more representative of Anglican opinion. He occasioned Huxley's resounding dialectical victory at the British Association's meeting in Oxford in 1860.† The contest and its repercussions roused passionate public interest. The works of Darwin, Lyell and Huxley were 'torn from the hands of Mudie's shopmen as if they were novels'.⁵

By the 'sixties a new disconcerting outlook had thus been defined and consolidated. It was controversial and revolutionary. When in fact the Darwinian hypothesis pointed to a new anthropology and a new social science far more convincing than anything spun by Comte or Spencer out of their own minds, the proven and liberating

---

* See also SIR GEOFFREY FABER, op. cit., for some interesting light on them.

† This notable scene is one of the highlights of the Victorian age. About 700 people were packed into the small south room of the New Museum at Oxford, where the Bishop of Oxford rallied Huxley by inquiring whether it was through his maternal or paternal ancestry that he claimed descent from a monkey. There followed a memorable reply. 'Mr. Huxley slowly and deliberately arose. A slight tall figure, stern and pale, very quiet and very grave, he stood before us and spoke those tremendous words . . . He was not ashamed to have a monkey for his ancestor; but he would be ashamed to be connected with a man who used great gifts to obscure the truth. No one doubted his meaning and the effect was tremendous. One lady fainted and had to be carried out; I for one (says the narrator) jumped from my seat . . .' Admiral FitzRoy was present and said he had often expostulated with his old comrade of the *Beagle* [Darwin] for entertaining views which were contradictory to the first chapter of Genesis. HUXLEY, op. cit., pp. 267-71.

knowledge was received with general hostility. The scientists were represented as blasphemers who declared that men were descended from gorillas. All that they had generally maintained was a remote common ancestry for man and his simian relatives. It followed, naturally, that destructive and revolutionary political theorists seized upon these agnostic arguments and invoked scientific sanction for national and class war. Meanwhile, as before emphasized, the growing prestige of science wrought an unprecedented change in the idiom of political thought. Political theorists had hitherto appealed to the examples of classical Antiquity, to transcendent Stoic or Christian Natural Law. They had cited the dogmas or the heresies of religion, or the laws of geometry, as had Hobbes, or the feelings of romantic emotion, as had Rousseau, or philosophical intuition, as had Hegel. Now a new fashion increasingly held the field. Appeal was made to the grim facts of a struggle for existence. They were held to justify ruthless individualism and 'jungle' law. Nations were incited to battle, not by the rival dogmas of Calvin or the Jesuits, but by appeals to pseudo-scientific doctrines of race. Already, in 1853, Count de Gobineau had launched his foolish notions of racial superiority. Defined on a supra-national level, they were not yet politically pernicious. But they were soon followed by doctrines which more closely identified race with state. Hegelian ideas of national conflict were thus given a new and bogus scientific sanction, to come to their culmination in the twentieth century. This misuse of pseudo-scientific terminology reached its most familiar and powerful nineteenth-century manifestation in the claims of Karl Marx to have discovered a science of politics. Characteristically Victorian claims, still doggedly believed. The influence of mid-nineteenth century popularized science is constantly apparent in the pages of *Das Kapital*.[6] And Hitler's views on the mission of the Aryan 'race' are familiar.

Apart from these powerful aberrations, Darwin's influence greatly enriched the world. The historical bias of nineteenth-century humanism was now to be deepened and emphasized by a new grasp of fact. It was also to be widened and enriched by the development of anthropology and the comparative study of law and institutions. The study of man was no longer intuitional, in the romantic vein, but systematic, methodical, sometimes too objective and mechanical. Of this approach Comte has been the forceful if unscientific forerunner, and Mill the more cautious advocate. After Darwin, the sociology they publicized was to be vastly expanded and developed. Properly handled, it began to promise a reinforcement of constitutional methods of government; misinterpreted, pseudo-science was to lead to the grossest abuse of power. And by the end of the century there was to come a second great scientific contribution, only fully developed in our own time. As the prehistoric past had been revealed, so the psychologists were to explore the depths of the sub-conscious mind. The combined political influence of Darwinian environmental studies and Freudian psychology was to be profound. It has still to be constructively exploited.

The new environmental influence pervades later-nineteenth-century political thought. Saint-Simon, Comte, Fourier had all over-simplified human motives. The new approach was more cautious, comprehensive and realistic. By modern standards it was over-ambitious. If Maine and Bagehot were conservative, the belief in progress was predominant. The immense sales of Winwood Reade's *Martyrdom of Man*, with its undercurrent of crude optimism, are significant. Meanwhile, the great gift of Darwinian science to political thought was an all-pervading sense of biological environment and of the need to study political questions in terms of it.

Against this intellectual background the development of English thought will now be examined. First, the individualism of Herbert Spencer, and the confident sweep of Buckle and Lecky; next, the contribution of Maine and Bagehot and of the pioneer anthropologist Tylor. This outline will lead to a full analysis of the ideas of T. H. Green, the greatest liberal political philosopher of his age. The lines of counter-attack will then be traced: the doctrine of Marx and Engels, with its roots in the revolutionary 'forties; the ferocious nationalism which found expression in the political writings of Treitschke. Next, the more insidious internal attack. It was inspired by the belated influence of Schopenhauer and by the brilliant eloquence of Nietzsche. The Papal attitude defined in the Encyclicals of Leo XIII and Acton's liberal Catholicism will then be described, a criticism of all the main tendencies of the time. In conclusion, a short view will be taken of the political and social ideas destined most immediately to influence the twentieth century. They were the proto-Fascist political philosophy of Sorel; the theory of social democracy as expressed in England by the Fabians and William Morris, in Germany by Bernstein, and in France by Jaurès. Finally, the new environmental sociology of Durkheim and the pioneer social psychology of Graham Wallas will be examined and its constructive possibilities suggested.

CHAPTER II

THE IDEA OF PROGRESS
HERBERT SPENCER: BUCKLE: LECKY

I T is often stated that the arid Utilitarian ideas which prevailed in liberal England during the early and middle nineteenth century produced a poverty of thought only redeemed by later neo-Hegelian metaphysical philosophy. Actually, during the domination of the Utilitarians, an astonishing variety and vigour of political and sociological speculation was achieved. As the following chapters will show, the post-Darwinian writers on the life of institutions in the 'sixties and 'seventies — Maine, Bagehot and Tylor — all mark in their fields a pioneering technical skill and a new maturity. They were all empirical and realistic, with a tough acceptance of agnostic conclusions; determined to improve human conditions by organized knowledge. Their outlook was cautious, and their creed the integrity of truth based on tested, if limited, evidence. They assumed constitutional government; the continuance and extension of rule by consent within the law; a decline of militarism. This form of government they accepted as the most useful and the best calculated to further the pursuit of the free inquiry and economic enterprise which made for prosperity and peace. All were, in fact, sheltered by the economic and naval predominance of England. Their optimism was none the less qualified. For they were wise men, with a long historical sense.

More representative of current opinion were the popular philosophers and historians, of whom Herbert Spencer, Buckle and Lecky may be taken as representative. The former exercised very great influence in his time, and although the quality of his political thought today seems dubious, his leading ideas must be examined. Among the liberal historians more pleasant reading will be found in the pages of Buckle and Lecky, whose writings, with their large circulation, at once formed and reflected the outlook of the dominant classes of Victorian England.

It has been fashionable to disparage the work and deride the judgment of the able and eloquent exponents of Victorian learning. Within the idiom of their time, their books display a range, a judgment, and a vitality which makes them masterpieces of style and erudition. As the reader is caught up in the long rhythm of their carefully wrought periods, held by the striking and curious facts with which their argument is driven home, and entertained by the learned and elaborate footnotes which point but never swamp their argument, he surrenders to the attack of a culture at the height of its confidence and pride, and feels the impact of one of the great self-sufficient periods of thought.

Today their optimism must seem alien: judged in the context of its time it was realistic. To dismiss their work as a monument of high bourgeois complacency seems a provincial judgment. In the work of Lecky and Bagehot, in particular, may be found the expression of a culture which puts the neurotic defeatism of much contemporary writing in the shadow it deserves.

Two predominant streams of thought have hitherto been apparent in early-nineteenth-century England. On the one hand, the rather inarticulate conservative tradition derived from Burke, carried on by Coleridge and adapted by Peel and the young Disraeli. On the other, Utilitarianism. Although based on laissez-faire, it had already inspired much useful legislation. To the Left of it had been the anarchism of Godwin and the republicanism of Paine; to the Right, the more mature liberalism of John Stuart Mill, later to blend into the liberal outlook of T. H. Green, with its more organic conception of the state. But before this mellowing of the old radical tradition, there was to intervene a prophet from the dissenting middle class who combined nonconformist hostility to government with an attack on even rudimentary welfare legislation, and a new, apparently scientific, justification for the most savage aspects of Malthusian economics. If Mill helped to civilize the Utilitarian creed, Herbert Spencer helped to barbarize it.

II

The annals of English eccentricity, and indeed of political thought, can show few more curious figures than Herbert Spencer, who attained an extraordinary and cosmopolitan celebrity in his own time, although his reputation has since much fallen off. As Sir Ernest Barker observes, he probably had 'A greater vogue than any other [thinker] in the last sixty years . . . Spencer's philosophy seems to set the stamp of authority on the prima facie philosophy of the ordinary man.' He was the representative political philosopher of the mid-Victorian progressive radicals. His fame was certainly not due to any command of style. For all his range and force, he expressed himself with banal repetition. And seldom can any author have created so enormous an 'œuvre', to whom composition was agony — he dictated most of his books in short bouts — and for whom the circumstances of early life and education were so unpropitious.* Achieved fame meant little to him. 'As contrasted with the aggregate of preceding pains,' he wrote in the Benthamite jargon which seldom left him, though he was never Bentham's disciple, 'the achieved pleasure is insignificant.' Yet he was driven irresistibly to self expression. 'This architectonic instinct,' he says, 'tyrannizes over me.' He was convinced he had found a total explanation of nature and society.† 'Once having become possessed of the

* Herbert Spencer, 1820-1903, was born of obscure Wesleyan origin. After a scrappy education, he became a railway engineer, and displayed throughout life an ingenuity for inventing unworkable gadgets. (See the illustration of his design for a 'new invalid bed' of grotesque inconvenience in *Autobiography* – or 'natural history of myself' – vol. II, p. 496.) From 1848 to 1853 he was Assistant Editor on the *Economist*, when he met many leading men and came under the influence of the Godwinite radical, Thomas Hodgskin. In 1842 he had written some articles on the 'Proper Sphere of Government' for the *Nonconformist*, and in 1851 appeared his first important work, *Social Statics*, which won him considerable reputation. In 1853 he courageously abandoned journalism, and a small bequest from an uncle enabled him to complete his *Principles of Psychology*, 1855. It was written at le Tréport, at Brighton, and in Wales, and cost its author a nervous breakdown from which he never fully recovered. There followed a series of essays in the *Westminster Review*, and in 1860, in spite of financial anxiety, he projected the vast scheme of his *Synthetic Philosophy*. It appeared in instalments: *First Principles*, 1862; *Principles of Biology*, 1864-67; *Principles of Psychology*, 1872; and *Principles of Sociology and Ethics*, 1876-96. His best known other writings are *The Study of Sociology*, 1873; *The Man versus the State*, 1884; and his *Autobiography*, 1875-93, posthumously published. After a severe struggle, Spencer attained prosperity through the large sales of his books, particularly in America.

Most of this extraordinary amount of work was achieved by a hypochondriac. His persistence in overcoming this disability was astonishing. Though he lived to be eighty-four, he was so excitable after his breakdown in 1855, that he could not read consecutively for more than three-quarters of an hour. Lecky writes: 'What is amazing about him is that . . . for many years past there has been something the matter with his brain, which only works three hours a day . . . he has written all his books in this state. They have all been dictated; his reading is chiefly done by secretaries, and he spends much of the afternoon playing billiards at the Athenaeum.' (*A Memoir of the Rt. Hon. W. E. H. Lecky*, by his wife, vol. II, p. 113.) When travelling by train, Spencer arranged a kind of hammock suspended from the rack; and when bored by conversation, he made 'use of ear-stoppers which, when I cannot conveniently leave the room, enable me to shut out the voices of those around sufficiently to prevent me from understanding what is said'. He found the microscope too exciting for more than three minutes' contemplation; cards were out of the question, 'and I have not tried backgammon since 1887, when being at the time in a low condition, the game caused a serious relapse'. Spencer was unmarried. He remarks, in his characteristic idiom, 'frequently when prospects are promising, dissatisfaction follows marriage, rather than satisfaction . . . after all, a celibate life has probably been the best for me as well as for *some unknown other*'. See his *Autobiography*. Williams & Norgate, 1904, 2 vols., 546 and 542 pp.; D. DUNCAN, *The Life and Letters of Herbert Spencer*, 1908; and LLOYD MORGAN, *Spencer's Philosophy of Science*, 1913. SIR E. BARKER's *Political Thought in England, 1848-1914*. Oxford University Press, 2nd edn., 1947, has a good chapter on Spencer, and regards him as of great importance. See also HEARNSHAW's *Social and Political Ideas of the Victorian Age*, chap. III. Sabine, on the other hand, dismisses him in a couple of pages. (*History of Political Theory*, pp. 671-3.)

† Lecky remarks drily, 'He has nearly finished the first volume of the *Sociology*, and seems very confident that it will be a complete explanation of human life' (op. cit., p. 113).

concept of Evolution in its comprehensive form,' he writes, 'the desire to elaborate and set it forth was so strong that to have passed life doing something else would, I think, have been almost intolerable.'[1]

Spencer became celebrated because he expressed two major aspects of nineteenth-century popular thought; nonconformist radical individualism and the primitive science of the pre-Darwinian decades, carried forward into the later years of the century. Although Spencer was a great systematizer, he never had a very coherent philosophy. His interest today lies not in his 'science' of evolution, certainly not in his dismal style, but in his remarkable range of information and his often just criticism of government. That aspect of his writings is well worth attention.

Before one examines it, the radical and 'scientific' backgrounds are worth a glance. The first derives from his family and from the influence of Godwin and Hodgskin; the second from German ideas assimilated through Coleridge, and from Lamarck's pre-Darwinian concept of evolution, with its stress on the inheritance of acquired characteristics. The key books in Spencer's development, the *Social Statics* and the *Principles of Psychology*, appeared well before the *Origin of Species*. Spencer never got beyond the science of the 'fifties, though he claimed the sanction of Darwin for some aspects of his idea of evolution.

The Wesleyan background is of greater interest. It was dreary to a degree. There are vistas of small tradesmen, 'pin manufacturers', and petty schoolmasters. His Taylor grandmother, he declares in his 'Statement of Extraction', was 'of the Glasgow lower middle classes and was resident in Derby'. His Spencer grandfather, who had taught the 'Commercial Division' of the local school for decades, was, not unnaturally, 'a melancholy old man . . . rarely showing any signs of pleasure'. His father seems to have been more human, though he refused to answer his wife's remarks if he thought them silly. The mother was equally uninspiring: 'My own proceedings and plans she always criticized discouragingly, and urged the adoption of some commonplace career.' It says much for the boy's tenacity and spirit that he ever got out of this environment. There were also various contentious uncles who 'disagreed' incessantly and gloomily with one another. But they were all enthusiasts for temperance movements, with a habit of what Spencer calls 'forecasting', described by one of them as 'a tendency to dwell too much upon possible forthcoming evils'. Indeed, the most unprepossessing uncle 'had none of those higher traits without which the display of individuality becomes repellent'. 'No Spencer ever dances,' remarked one of them, when pressed to take part in some local festivity. But they later proved helpful. They died at critical moments of Spencer's career, leaving small legacies which tided over the worst phases of his literary struggle. The most successful of them, the Reverend Thomas Spencer, had been to St. John's College, Cambridge. He was the extremely unpopular Rector of Hinton Charterhouse, near Frome in Somerset. To his household Spencer was relegated at the age of thirteen, and here he received all the education he ever got. In the angular if homely world of early Victorian railways Spencer began his career. At Bromsgrove, Worcester and Birmingham he worked during the boom of the 'forties in the old Great Western and other lines. The small savings thus accumulated paid for printing *Social Statics*, the keystone of his reputation.

The radical individualism, the serious dim tenacity of this background, are writ large in Spencer's opinions and hostility to government. It had its historical roots in the world of Lilburne and Bunyan and eighteenth-century nonconformity. Reinforced by the influence of Hodgskin and the London intellectuals on the *Economist*, it dominates Spencer's mind.

The other and previous aspect, the claim to have discovered a science of politics, is common to most nineteenth-century political thought. Spencer based it on inadequate data and confused analogies, and he carried it to inordinate lengths. Hence a basic contradiction in his argument. For his social organism was never organic. It 'evolved', he maintained, according to laws current throughout the animate and the inanimate Universe, yet it was combined with an extreme particularism. The development of individuality was the goal of life. Puritan independence is emancipated from theology and translated into scientific terms, while laissez-faire is biologically reinforced. As, in all creation, evolution eliminates the inferior and unadaptable in human society and subjects the survivors to salutary competition. The process works through the Lamarckian inheritance of acquired characteristics. Spencer thus claimed to give radical individualism a new philosophy. Hence his popular fame. In face of the onslaughts of Carlyle and Ruskin, here was a new, and apparently scientific, argument. Yet, out of all this welter of systemization, which seems at first sight akin to the ideas of Comte, but which differed profoundly from Comte's doctrine in its hatred of authority, there emerges a realist distrust of government. This is already expressed in the youthful Essays for the *Nonconformist* and elaborately worked out in *Social Statics*, a remarkable book which Spencer's later ideas mainly reflect.* Government, he insists, like Godwin, is a transient evil. 'As civilization advances, governments decay.' The less government the more progress. It merely marks a certain stage in civilization. Today, with our societies, companies and associations, the legislature is 'dwarfed'. 'The time was when the history of the people was the history of its government. It is otherwise now.' Further, like Buckle and Bagehot, he believed that society was moving away from militarism to commerce and peace. Spencer 'forecast' pretty exactly what was not to happen.

By disparaging government he rejected Benthamite improvement. That should come from individual enterprise. And morality cannot depend on government. This descendant of radical non-conformists detested the successors of Hobbes. Happiness, too, can never be calculated. Consider its relativity. 'Progress is necessary to the well-being of the Anglo-Saxons; on the other hand the Esquimaux are content in their squalid poverty . . . An Irishman delights in a row; a Chinese in pageantry . . . the Heaven of the Hebrews is a "city of gold and precious stones, with a supernatural abundance of corn and wine"; that of the Turk — a harem peopled by houris; that of the American-Indian, a "Happy Hunting Ground".'[2] To calculate 'the greatest happiness is a task beyond the ability of any finite mind'. No one — least of all the clumsy agency of government — has a right to impose a planned pattern of behaviour. Nor is there need. For social morality is a matter of intuition, 'a true fundamental intuition which can be logically unfolded into a scientific morality'.[3] It is based on the conduct of individuals, determined by the 'Law of Equal Freedom'. State interference is therefore intolerable and the claims of the state conditional. 'If every man has freedom to do all that he wills, provided he infringes not the equal freedom of any other man, he is free to drop connection with the state — to relinquish its protection and to refuse paying toward its support.'[4] This right of withdrawal (asserted by Puritan Radicals in the mid-seventeenth century), exists because the people are the source of power. The state is, after all, nothing but a 'joint stock protection company'. If additional tasks are assigned to it, friction is bound to follow. The

* *Social Statics* or The Conditions Essential to Human Happiness Specified, and the First of them Devoloped, 1851. (Revised Edition, 1868, 504 pp.) See particularly 'The Rights of Life and Personal Liberty'; 'The Right to Ignore the State' and the 'Limit of State Duty'. The coincidence of Spencer's and Comte's titles *Social Statics* was fortuitous. He owed little to Comte. See his *Reasons for Dissenting from the Philosophy of M. Comte*, 1864.

vanity of politicians discredits the state by expending its functions far beyond its proper sphere. Spencer rejects Burke's notion that man is born into a society existing in time as well as space: he is unaware of tradition and myth; his state is inorganic, the antithesis of the Hegelian totality. He gave mechanical doctrines of laissez-faire a new lease of life.

Since society is in continuous evolution, legislation for the 'benefit of the mass' is uncertain. It is best to leave matters to the force of nature. 'As we turn over the leaves of the earth's primaeval history . . . we find . . . never ceasing change.' The fact of progress proves the beneficence of evolution. Ethical Laws are as clear as the Laws of Physics, and 'those terrible truths which glare out at us from the gloom of the past' depict by contrast the progress of our time. Progress has come about, not through government interference, but by obeying the 'Creation's silent command, do this'; by the instinctive adaptation of individuals to environment whereby the best have survived and perpetuated their kind. The doctrine of Natural Rights had received a new and incongruous sanction. So time and personality colour political thought. The idiom of the seventeenth century is religious; in the nineteenth it is 'scientific'.

If man has a natural right to make his own blunders, it is no business of government to save men from themselves. Political reformers, with their clumsy mechanism; their blind bureaucracy, try to supersede the 'laws of existence'. 'Irresistible as they are subtle', the Laws of Life should be let alone. Competition must inevitably result in progress. The misinterpretation of Darwinism, so widespread in the late nineteenth century, owed much to the delusion that Spencer spoke for the new biology. In his *The Man Versus the State*, published to recall the liberals of the 'eighties to the old principles of laissez-faire, Spencer dilates upon the beneficent results of natural competition.* 'The process of "natural selection" as Mr. Darwin called it, co-operating with a tendency to variation and to inheritance of variations, he has shown to be a chief cause (though not, I believe, the sole cause) of that evolution through which all living things . . . have reached their present degree of organization and adaptation to their modes of life. . . . And yet, strange to say, now that this truth is recognized by most cultivated people — now that the beneficent working of the survival of the fittest has been so impressed on them

---

* *The Man Versus the State*, 1884, contains the following chapters. The New Toryism; The Coming Slavery; The Sins of Legislators, The Great Political Superstition and a Postscript, pp. 267-412. It is bound up with the abridged edition of *Social Statics* in Spencer's collected works.

that, much more than people in past times, they might be expected to hesitate before neutralizing its action — now more than ever before in the history of the world, are they doing all they can to further the survival of the unfittest!'⁵ Here, in a work which had sold 12,000 copies by 1884, is the specific invocation of Darwin to sanction Spencer's special conception of the 'fittest' — a competitive citizen in a laissez-faire industrial state.

With this rather limited ideal in mind, Spencer transfers the worst aspects of nature to human society. Writing thirty-three years after the publication of *Social Statics*, he reverts to a passage, which he declares to have been reinforced by experience. 'Note further, that their carnivorous enemies not only remove from herbivorous herds individuals past their prime, but also weed out the sickly, the mal-formed, and the least fleet or powerful. By the aid of which purifying process, as well as by the fighting so universal in the pairing season, all vitiation of the race through the multiplication of its inferior samples is prevented; and the maintenance of a constitution com-pletely adapted to surrounding conditions, and . . . most productive of happiness, is ensured.' The progress of mankind is similarly guaranteed 'By that same beneficent, though severe discipline to which the animate creation at large is subject: a discipline, which is pitiless in the working out of good: a felicity producing law which never swerves for the avoidance of partial and temporary suffering. The poverty of the incapable, the distresses that come upon the impru-dent, the starvation of the idle, and those shoulderings aside of the weakly by the strong . . . are the decrees of a large, far-seeing benevolence.'

Such was the considered social philosophy of Herbert Spencer. In distorted form it served for a rule of conduct for many lower-bourgeois businessmen of Victorian England, in the milieu depicted and scarified by the young H. G. Wells.

'Humanity', Spencer continues, 'is being pressed against the inexorable necessities of its new position — is being moulded into harmony with them, and has to bear the resulting unhappiness as best it can. The process *must* be undergone, and the sufferings *must* be endured. No power on earth, no cunningly devised laws of statesmen, no world-rectifying schemes of the humane, no communist panaceas, no reforms that men ever did broach or ever will broach, can diminish them one jot.'⁶ In the light of this curious fatalism, the ferocity of nineteenth-century revolutionaries becomes intelligible.

Reinforcing this philosophy is the characteristic mid-nineteenth-century belief, shared by Comte and Marx, that history can be explained by an all pervading law, by which all political life is determined and to which governments must conform. That this law was unpleasant evidently gave subconscious pleasure to Spencer's nonconformist, if agnostic, conscience. Hence the serious and prophetic tone: the rather sadistic emphasis.

With this apparently scientific sanction behind it, the old radical distrust of government was pungently and sometimes usefully expressed. 'It is a gross delusion to believe in the sovereign power of political machinery,' Guizot had remarked. To encourage the people to count on great improvements through government action can lead only to disillusion and discontent, even to revolution. Spencer objects to state intervention in education or in medicine or in town planning. The idea of 'doing everything for everybody' can lead only to the citizen being turned into a 'grown-up baby'.[7] The menace is particularly severe in education. 'Moreover it is proposed by many that the state, regarded as an undoubtedly competent judge of what constitutes good education for the poor, shall undertake also to prescribe good education for the middle classes — shall stamp the children of these, too, after a state pattern, concerning the goodness of which they have no more doubt than the Chinese had when they fixed theirs.'[8] Compulsory insurance will be the next step, 'by which men during their early lives shall be forced to provide for their old age'. All this benevolent interference is dangerous and unnatural. 'The liberty which a citizen enjoys is to be measured, not by the nature of the governmental machinery he lives under, whether representative or other, but by the relative paucity of the restraints it imposes on him.'[9] 'The despot is still a despot whether his motives for arbitrary rule are good or bad.' Once state interference is admitted, there can be no end to it. Why not, he asks, citing an example then ridiculous, if now familiar, control the distribution of food and clothes? Why not reconsider the Tudor sumptuary laws and 'take a hint from the old Norman practice and fix the time at which people should put out their fires and go to bed'? Nor is state power any the less dangerous if exercised by a democratically elected majority. 'The rule of the many by the few we call tyranny; the rule of the few by the many is tyranny also, only of a less intensive kind.' By no sophistry can coercion be made equitable. All government interference is immoral. The goal to which all society is moving is its abolition. Spencer repudiates the most fundamental doctrines of the

Welfare State. 'Misery results from misconduct'; economic failure is the same as moral iniquity. 'There is a notion', he writes, . . . 'that all social suffering is removable, and it is the duty of somebody or other to remove it. Both these beliefs are false. To separate pain from ill-doing is to fight against the constitution of things.'[10] Quoting the Biblical saying 'if any would not work neither should he eat', Spencer reiterates, with Malthus, that a 'creature not energetic enough to maintain itself must die'. Suffering is the beneficent law of life: it is due to the 'ill working of . . . human nature',[11] and to this evil will be added the tyranny of organization. The machinery of communism — Spencer uses the term indiscriminately for socialism — has to be 'framed out of existing human nature', and 'that those who rose to power in a socialistic organization would not scruple to carry out their aims at all cost, we have good reason for concluding'. If to the normal centralization of the socialist state, there were added the demands of defence, the state tyranny would be intolerable. 'It would need but a war . . . to at once transform a socialistic adminis- tration into a grinding tyranny like that of ancient Peru; under which the mass of the people, controlled by grades of officials and leading lives which were inspected out of doors and in-doors, laboured for the support of the organization which regulated them, and were left but with a bare subsistence for themselves.' Spencer foresaw pretty clearly the dangers of the combination of garrison and Welfare State. Such development he regarded as retrogression. He believed that evolution was pressing mankind towards a civilian, industrial civilization. It was a petit-bourgeois ideal, a combination of radical individualism and nineteenth-century science, intolerant of the idle or the picturesque; undistinguished, uncharitable, with a vicious intolerance of 'good for nothings'. Like Saint-Simon, Spencer admired the beaver rather than the lion. But he detested the state.

He was, nonetheless a safe enough thinker — no revolutionary. Though he shared Proudhon's hatred for the tentacular nation state, attacks on property would have revolted him. For the individualism of Spencer led to a distant and Utopian goal. In fact, he was very distrustful of popular rule. He foresaw, often with insight, the evils of centralized social democracy. Like de Tocqueville and J. S. Mill, he was afraid of the tyranny of the mob. 'While old kinds of coercive government are dissolving,' he warned his readers, in his cacophonous way, 'new kinds of coercive government are evolving.' Spencer was the prophet of the triumphant liberalism of the Repeal of the Corn

Laws: by the 'fifties he was afraid of a reaction. 'The old coercive shell having been cast off, a new coercive shell is in course of development.' He was to have little sympathy or understanding with the neo-Hegelian liberalism of the 'seventies, or with the state socialism of the Fabians. He remained, to the last, a mid-Victorian radical individualist.

His distrust of the state inspires a formidable attack on the theory of positive sovereignty defined by Hobbes and developed by Austin. In the transition from a military to an industrial society, from status to contract, the mystical pretensions of authority had been abandoned. It has now been revived: 'the great political superstition of the past was the divine right of kings. The great political superstition of the present is the divine right of parliaments'.[12] Hobbes and Austin, in particular, made a retrograde 'assimilation of civil authority to military authority' — and the latter has added the nineteenth-century superstition of the 'divine right' of majorities.

In face of this monstrous claim one must demand — What is the basis of this positive sovereignty? It does not exist. 'Neither single-headed ruler, nor many-headed ruler, can produce such credentials.' Quoting an earlier article in the *Edinburgh Review* on 'Railway Morals and Railway Policy' (1854), Spencer cuts at the root of unlimited parliamentary sovereignty in a manner not without interest today. Austin's contention that government creates rights is a shallow sophistry. Natural rights exist long before government, which does not create rights but recognizes custom. All primitive societies are ruled by custom; witness the habits of the Dyaks, the Kirghiz and the Bechuana. Blood-feud is private justice, and property exists before positive law.* Again, Spencer brings a biological sanction to the defence of natural rights. Granted that life is worth living, the individual has the right to self-preservation. This implies the right to carry on life sustaining activities, so long as they do not interfere with the 'law of equal freedom'. If a man is bound to status, freedom is impossible, and the 'militant' state which tyrannizes over him perverts the main object of life — the preservation of individuals. 'Those who, denying natural rights, commit themselves to the assertion that rights are artificially created by law, are not only flatly contradicted by the facts, but their assertion is self destructive.'[13] In consequence there is no divine right of majorities, even if constitutionally expressed in democratic forms. For the functions of government are strictly limited. It is a 'committee of management'; public life

* Compare MAINE, *Early Institutions*, infra, p. 250.

becomes impracticable when over-regulated, and all these errors come from 'the superstition that government is subject to no restraints'. 'The function of Liberalism in the past was that of putting a limit to the powers of kings. The function of true Liberalism in the future will be that of putting a limit to the powers of Parliament.'[14] The argument seems worth pondering.

Spencer's outlook, like that of Buckle and Lecky, was always conditioned by his view of history as progress from 'militancy' to an industrial civilization. The garrison state was the greatest enemy of liberty, and the condition of contemporary power politics prevented the realization of his civilian ideal. 'So long as the religion of enmity predominates over the religion of amity, the current political superstition must hold its ground.'[15]

The argument is driven home with greater force in the *Principles of Sociology*. The 'ultimate political regime' will be a 'developed industrial type', where citizens harmoniously collaborate within a frame of contract rather than status. It can only come about in peace. 'The conclusion of profoundest moment to which all lines of argument converge, is that the possibility of a high social state, political as well as general, fundamentally depends on the cessation of war.' War is obsolete in an industrial society. 'From war has been gained all that it had to give ... Peaceful federation is the only further consolidation to be looked for.'* Economic and social competition might be salutary, but militarist power politics were not sanctioned by the laws of life. Here the civilian radical in Spencer overcame the early Victorian biologist.

Though his *Principles of Psychology*, which brought on his breakdown, is well suited to produce a similar state of mind in most readers, Spencer endeavoured, like Hobbes, to build a solid foundation for his political philosophy.† Today it seems rather primitive: in the mid-nineteenth century it seemed formidable. Philosophically minded readers, practised in the severe discipline of Mill, regarded

---

* *Principles of Sociology*, vol. II, pp. 663-4. (1893 edition.)

† *The Principles of Psychology* (1855. Two vols., 2nd edition, 1870) 'was an inquiry concerning the basis of our intelligence ... and of the gradual differentiation of the psychical from the physical life which accompanies the evolution of life in general'. It is divided into eight parts. The Data of Psychology (seven chapters), on the nervous system and scope of the science; The Inductions of Psychology (nine chapters), Substance of Mind and Analysis of Feelings; General Synthesis (eleven chapters), Life and Mind as Correspondence; Special Synthesis (nine chapters), Nature of Intelligence, Memory, Feelings, Will; Physical Synthesis (ten chapters), Nervous System, Psychical Laws, Results, with an appendix on anaesthetics and narcotics. Vol. II, Special Analysis (twenty-seven chapters), Reason, Perception, Space, Time, Motion; General Analysis (nineteen chapters), Assumptions of Metaphysics; Positivist Justification of Realism, Corollaries, Language, Aesthetic Judgments.

it with respect. For more amateurish minds, the *Principles of Sociology* provided greater human interest. Spencer had a remarkable appetite for facts, and took full advantage of the harvest of new information about primitive and outlandish people which the travellers of the mid-century had produced. These massive three volumes are relieved by many instances of curious customs and primitive parallels to modern usage. In dealing with social privilege, for example, Spencer produces many remarkable examples. 'We learn from Bastian that among the Toloffs the use of the mosquito curtain is a royal prerogative;' while among the Tasmanians, 'the old men get the best food', and 'Sturt says, "only the old men of the natives of Australia have the privilege of eating the Emu".'[16] While 'in Fiji, Seeman says, cannibalism was restricted to the chiefs and gentry'. In matters of prestige, he points out that 'In China great fatness is a source of pride in a mandarin,' while Speke says that in Karague 'fattening is the first duty of fashionable female life'. At Darfur 'if the Sultan being on horseback, happens to fall off, all his followers must fall off likewise'.[17] Spencer proceeds to cite many entertaining examples of competitive hospitality, elaborate trophies and military ceremonial, relating them to customs current in his own country. Moreover, in the vast and ill co-ordinated data elsewhere assembled, Spencer accumulated gold amid the dross. All this immense labour, inspired by a characteristic mid-nineteenth-century belief in progressive evolution, which colours all his extensive work in sociology, can be here only briefly touched upon.

The basis of this outlook was agnostic. Since there could be no 'positive answer' to the riddle of existence, values must reflect 'states of mind'. A rather similar belief, in more sophisticated form, was to inspire much early-twentieth-century Humanism — the Cambridge followers, for example, of G. E. Moore — Lytton Strachey and Maynard Keynes. 'Modes of consciousness,' wrote Spencer, 'standing in place of positive answers, must ever remain.'[18] These 'states of mind' are intermittent, and confined to a minority, since men are feeble, inconstant, and in the mass, grossly dull. But 'in both cultured and uncultured there appear lucid intervals'.

There were thus elements of a fairly satisfying philosophy for intelligent minds in the midst of Spencer's 'scientific' dogma. In expressing the quiet and stoical agnosticism he shared with Huxley and their circle, and which was the sober English counterpart of the violence of Schopenhauer, Feuerbach and Nietzsche, Spencer rises far beyond his usual pedestrian style. He could even regret the consolations of religion. Dilating on the mystery of life, he wrote 'when we think of the myriads of years of the Earth's past, during which have arisen and passed away low forms of creatures, small and great, which, murdering and being murdered, have gradually evolved — how shall we answer the question — To what end? . . . and along with this rises the paralysing thought — what if, of all that is incomprehensible to us, there exists no comprehension anywhere?' The universal mystery of death evokes this reflection. Since 'the relation of mind and nervous system are such that the cessation of one accompanies dissolution of the other, while, simultaneously, comes the thought, so difficult to realize, that with death there lapses both the consciousness of existence and the consciousness of having existed', he came to regard religion with sympathy. It was based on a 'community of needs'. He felt only dim regret at his inability to 'accept the solutions offered, joined with the wish that solutions could be found'.[19]

Spencer also combined strict morality with agnostic conclusions. Here is at once a new sceptical outlook and a new assertion of non-conformist individualism in scientific terms. Radical 'natural rights' are given fresh sanction through biology, and distrust of government combined with revived laissez-faire. All this is supported by a parade of scientific knowledge expressed in Malthusian terms. Honest, provincial and dogmatic, facing the facts as they appeared to many 'advanced' mid-nineteenth-century minds, Spencer brought the prestige of a primitive sociology to revive old doctrines of savage and mechanical competition. While he contributed some salutary criticism of the state, he presented society as the scene of bitter and inevitable competition. His grim views of the social 'laws' which governed men and other animals were extensively popularized, and his world-wide influence helped to darken the horizons of political thought in the later nineteenth century.

It was natural that this appeal to scientific sanctions and rein-forcement of laissez-faire should provoke violent attack. In particu-lar, Marx and Engels endeavoured to outbid such appeals to 'scienti-fic' sociology by a more massive 'scientific' hypothesis. But before turning to Marx's attack on laissez-faire and 'Utopian' socialism which had been going on since the 'forties, it will be well to restore the balance by considering more attractive mid-Victorian thought, of which Spencer was by no means representative.

The influence of Henry Thomas Buckle* on contemporary opinion was extensive and remarkable. Though criticized by academic historians — Stubbs remarked 'I don't believe in the philosophy of history, so I don't believe in Buckle' — his book achieved widespread popularity and immediate success. It expressed in popular form the dominant belief in progress, the most characteristic myth of the age. Written with the ample and flowing phraseology of the high Victorian style, it still makes good reading, if its optimism provokes a wry smile. Buckle insists on the importance of environment and upon a broad view of history. He is hostile to the 'metaphysical' approach, but determined to 'grasp the subject in the whole of its natural relations'.[20] He believed that human affairs are determined by ascertainable laws, and that historians, by confining themselves to the mere relation of events, were limiting the importance of their calling. 'In all other great fields of inquiry, the necessity of generalization is universally admitted, the noble efforts are being made to rise from particular facts in order to discover the laws by which these facts are governed.' Comte, he maintained, had 'done more than any other to raise the standard of history'.[21] We have, he says, a 'right' to expect that if history is subjected to scientific method, its 'laws' will be discovered, since 'the marked tendency of advancing civilization is to strengthen our belief in the universality of order, of method and of law'. Yet at present, he says, there is no leadership in this field, and 'the most celebrated historians are manifestly inferior to the most successful cultivators of physical science'. These historical laws, he maintains, result from the interplay of mind and environment. While he held that the action of mind was decisive, he also believed that 'large and general causes ... working upon the aggregate of society, must produce certain consequences, without regard to the volition of those particular men of which the society is composed'.[22] In principle this outlook has much in common with the views of Marx and Engels, though Buckle's 'Laws' were very different from those which they claimed to have discovered. Its prevalence, following the popular success of Buckle's writings in the 'sixties, is significant. Like Marx, Buckle set great store by the new science

---

* Henry Thomas Buckle, 1821-62. The son of a city shipowner, he early inherited £1700 a year. He was privately educated and travelled extensively, becoming a notable linguist. He took fourteen years to complete his *The History of Civilization in England*, which appeared in 1857 and 1861. He died in Damascus in 1862. 'For two things he never grudged money, books and cigars.' See H. HUTH, *The Life and Writings of H. T. Buckle*, for an account of an attractive personality.

of statistics, first elaborated by the Belgian mathematician, Quetelet,*
'a branch of knowledge which, though still in its infancy, has ... thrown
more light on the study of human nature than all the sciences put
together'.[23] Statistics of crime and suicide, for example, show that
such actions are in part determined by environment, and reflect the
'great social law, that the moral actions of men are the product not
of their volition but of their antecedents'.[24]

With this background in mind, Buckle embarked upon an elaborate panorama of the roots of civilization, preliminary to his ample
project of a history of civilization in England. With a wealth of
footnotes, and a sweeping style, he marshals the far flung evidence
for the effect of environment upon the varying cultures of mankind.
Since 'wealth must accumulate before knowledge can begin', the
general aspect of nature, the quality of soil and climate, the basic
food supply, must determine the bias of a culture. Indian civilization, for example, is based on rice; hence the profound contrast between India and the West. A great population multiplying on a
cheap food supply implies exploitation, caste, callousness and waste.
The riverine lands of the Near East depended upon the date palm; in
Brazil, where the trade winds strike the Andes in a tropical latitude,
there is a 'bounty of nature ... so rank and luxuriant that nature
seems to riot in the very wantonness of power'. This environment
has been overwhelming. Here 'the forests are skirted by enormous
meadows, which reeking with heat and moisture, supply nourish-
ment to countless herds of wild cattle, that browse and fatten on
their herbage; while the adjoining plains, rich in another form of
life, are the chosen abode of the most ferocious animals ...' By all
this teeming life civilization has been smothered. 'The people,
ignorant and therefore brutal, practising no restraint, and recogniz-
ing no law, continue to live in their old and inveterate barbarism.'[25]

In Mexico and Peru, on the other hand, remarkable civilizations
have been built on maize and the banana. '... Both Mexicans and
Peruvians lived to a great extent on the produce of the banana; a
vegetable whose reproductive powers are so extraordinary that nothing but the precise and unimpeachable testimony of which we are
possessed could make them at all credible.'[26] Here, as in India,
cheap food has meant abundant labour, a one-sided civilization
dominated by a military aristocracy of wealth.

* Adolf Quetelet, 1796-1874, a native of Ghent; Professor of Mathematics at Brussels,
1820. Supervisor of Statistics for the Belgian Government, 1830. Convened the first
international congress of statisticians, Brussels, 1853.

All the early civilizations, Buckle points out, were in hot climates where nature is dangerous: 'indeed, generally, in Asia, Africa and America, the external world is more formidable than in Europe'. Hence the prevalence of fear in their religions. Consider, he says, the frightful Indian mythology, the cult of blood and pain, the acceptance of disease — an attitude which infected medieval Europe. It 'still lingers on among the vulgar;'[27] and traces of it may be found in the writings of the clergy, he remarks, airing a characteristic antipathy. In Greece, on the other hand, in a more manageable environment, mythology was homely. 'Jupiter was an amorous good natured king . . . Neptune was a sailor, Vulcan was a smith; Apollo was sometimes a fiddler, sometimes a poet, sometimes a keeper of oxen. As to Cupid, he was a wanton boy . . .' What a contrast to the cult of Siva and Kali, to the bestial monsters of Eastern religion! Here is a vivid example of the decisive effect of climate on mentality. 'The tendency of Asiatic civilization was to widen the distance between men and their deities; the tendency of Greek civilization was to diminish it.'

It follows that 'the history of the human race can only be understood by connecting it with history and the aspects of the natural universe'. Hence the unique achievement of Europe, with its favourable climate. Here man, not environment, has been dominant. Here is progress due to 'encroachment of the mind . . . upon the organic and the inorganic forces of nature'.[28] And this European achievement is only beginning. As John Stuart Mill wrote in his *Principles of Political Economy*, 'our knowledge of the properties and laws of physical objects show no sign of approaching its ultimate boundaries; it is advancing more rapidly and in a greater number of directions at once, than in any previous age or generation, and affording such frequent glimpses of unexplored fields beyond, as to justify their belief that our acquaintance with nature is still almost in its infancy'.[29]

Such already has been the achievement of the nineteenth century: it reflects, he states hopefully, the 'diminishing influence of physical laws and the increasing influence of moral laws'. It demonstrates that 'the laws of history are the laws of mind'. Conditioned as man's origins may be by environment, the interaction of mind and phenomena must produce, in favourable conditions, the rise of civilization and liberty.

On this basis, Buckle looked about him with a natural complacency. Although the majority of mankind may be content with 'slumbering on in a peaceful and decent mediocrity',[30] the intellectual climate of Europe has gradually improved. War and persecution are everywhere diminishing. 'That this barbarous pursuit is, in the progress of society, steadily declining, must be evident to even the most hasty reader of European history.' The recent Crimean conflict had been produced by the 'encroachment of the uncivilized Russians on the still more uncivilized Turks'. In the West the power and prestige of militarism is diminishing. While in Antiquity the best abilities were in the profession of arms, now only the fool of the family becomes a soldier or a clergyman, and the record of the Duke of Wellington has shown the ineptitude of the military at politics.[31] Today leadership has passed to the economists, and the greatest current influence is Adam Smith, whose *Wealth of Nations* 'looking at its ultimate results, is probably the most important book which has ever been written'.[32] The Bible, by implication, is dismissed.

Buckle proceeds to a panegyric upon the influence of the great economist. 'Such is the way in which great thinkers control the affairs of men, and by their discoveries regulate the march of nations.' Turning to the beneficent effects of modern inventions, in particular to 'the application of steam to the purposes of travelling', he insists that better communications will increase mutual tolerance and understanding. No longer will Englishmen believe that all Frenchmen subsist on frogs, or Frenchmen be convinced that all the English are victimized by spleen. Personal intercourse will resolve the matter. The old fears and hatreds of the past will fade before the liberating power of modern inventions, and the 'enormous evil of the monkish doctrine of original sin' will dissolve before the new technology. The keystone of peace will be the permanent alliance of England and France. 'Every new railroad that is laid down, and every fresh steamer that crosses the channel, are additional guarantees for the preservation of that long and unbroken peace which, during forty years, has knit together the fortunes of the two most civilized nations on earth.'[33] As the economic benefits of free trade increase the wealth of all classes, the importance of power politics, and, indeed, of government, will diminish. Echoing the sentiment of Saint-Simon, 'Plus des Alexandres, vive les Archimèdes!' Buckle insists that 'the gigantic crimes of Alexander or Napoleon become after a time, void of effect . . . but the discoveries of great men never leave us; they are immortal'. Opinion changes; knowledge remains, a cumulative legacy. Government is more 'quiescent' and the people more 'active'. The gates of the future stand wide for the progress of mankind.

Such is the flavour of Buckle's high spirited and influential book, which made him famous. It is the work of a comparatively young man: he died at forty-one. For all its occasional shallowness, it signifies a great broadening of the horizons of history. The vivid geographical sense, the eager Victorian exploration of exotic scenes and esoteric learning, the delight in a vivid style and in the startling impact of new ideas, the desire at once to edify and to shock, all display the vitality and self-confidence which are found only in rare and great phases of civilization. Beneath the prosperity and independence which Buckle reflects, there lurked, indeed, the massive social evils which Carlyle, Ruskin and Disraeli had denounced; but all aristocracies in history have exacted their price, and in that long perspective, the Victorian liberal middle class, which Buckle in its strength and weakness represents, need hardly be ashamed. For they created a whole range of culture and new knowledge of which their ungrateful posterity have been the beneficiaries. The naive confidence in the abolition of war, in the sovereign virtues of free-trade, in the benevolent possibilities of human nature, are a natural aspect of a sheltered civilian mentality, which had grown up in a country long free from invasion, world-powerful at sea and world-powerful in finance. This kind of sweeping self-confidence may appear today surprising and even vulgar, but the mentality it bred in England and North America later helped to sustain the conviction that defeat was impossible during the ordeals of the twentieth century. It is a reflection of successful government and humane purpose, and it is pervaded by a broad sense of the importance of environment characteristic of the new scientific knowledge.

I V

The career of W. E. H. Lecky was also singularly successful.*

* The Rt. Hon. William Edward Hartpole Lecky, 1838-1903, born in Dublin of Scots-Irish descent, son of a landowner and barrister. He was educated at Cheltenham (1852-55) and Trinity College, Dublin. His early *Leaders of Public Opinion in Ireland* 1861, met with little success, but his *History of the Rise and Influence of the Spirit of Rationalism in Europe*, 1865, won him immediate celebrity. There followed his *History of European Morals from Augustus to Charlemagne* (1869). In 1871 he married one of the ladies in waiting to Queen Sophia of the Netherlands. He then settled in London and began his *History of England [and Ireland] in the Eighteenth Century* (1878-90). In 1892 he was offered and declined the Regius Professorship of History at Oxford in succession to Freeman. In 1895 he became M.P. for Dublin University and in the following year published his *Democracy and Liberty*. His *Map of Life* appeared in 1903, followed by a volume of historical and political essays. Lecky was a man of equable temper, though hypersensitive to noise, being only

Like Buckle, he early inherited a fortune which enabled him to travel extensively and follow his bent. His early works were based on wide and curious learning, assimilated by 'diving into half the libraries of Europe'. Aimiably self-sufficient, he took enormous pains with his writing, and early perfected an admirable style. Apart from his fame as a narrative historian of the eighteenth century, his impact on mid-Victorian opinion was very great, both through his early investigation of the history of ideas, and his later comments on the political developments of his time. The *History of the Rise and Influence of the Spirit of Rationalism in Europe* (1865) is a landmark in the mellowing of liberalism. The narrative power and word painting of Macaulay had been bounded by the history of his own country. Now the learning of continental Europe was ransacked for a panoramic survey of the broad development of the tides of European thought. In some sense, Lecky, like Michelet and Thierry, was a romantic, but his romanticism was controlled by shrewd judgment. The curious by-ways of learning, old crazy dogmas of religious controversy, are juxtaposed with a serene conviction of progress in industrial and civilian life. There is an intense feeling for the past, a lively humour and pity, and a invincible faith in the achievements of the nineteenth century. Like Buckle, by whom he was early influenced, Lecky is fascinated by the effect of environment on ideas, convinced of the reality of progress. But he was aware also of the dangers that threatened the culture of which he was so representative.

able to write in conditions of absolute calm. He detested Cheltenham; but when his house of forty boys was broken up and he 'went into a house where there was only one other boy . . . he found it much more tolerable'. At Trinity College, Dublin, he displayed a meteoric talent for oratory, first developed in these congenial surroundings. But his main pleasure was travel. He writes as a young man from Italy − a country he preferred to all others − 'I have been a long time at Genoa, in a state of the most supreme felicity. I am hard at work on an enormous book [and] waiting with great impatience for a treatise on the devil by Psellus.' He had the highest conception of a writer's calling, and took elaborate pains with his style. 'Good writing', he says, 'is a very much harder thing than people who have never tried it imagine . . . Inspired by this passion, the writer abandons the lucrative paths of mediocrity to develop, amid the discouragement of his friends and the sneers of hostile critics, his peculiar talents, dedicating all his time and sacrificing all his pleasures to the attainment of his object, moulding and clarifying his sentences till he has made them flexible and melodious, capable of conveying the most delicate modulations of his thought − a faithful mirror of his mind.' He depicts the laborious hours essential for good craftsmanship. 'There are also innumerable little difficulties of style, arrangement and research, which no one but an author can know, and there falls upon one not infrequently an utter weariness, a despondency which is very painful. But by long patience something really comes out in the end.' See *A Memoir of the Rt. Hon. W. E. H. Lecky, M.P., O.M.*, by his wife. Longmans Green, 1910 − a book well worth consulting by anyone beginning a career as a writer, by academic Philistines, who look after the facts and leave the style to look after itself, and even by the public who enjoy the writer's art.

His *Rise of Rationalism* was followed up by the *History of European Morals from Augustus to Charlemagne* — a work of similar intention, now the more dated of the two. His most massive achievement was the eight volume *History of England in the Eighteenth Century*. His *Democracy and Liberty*, the work of his mature age, contains shrewd criticism of the radicals and socialists of his time, and accurately forecast many of the consequences of their political ideas. The first and the last of these books will here be briefly examined.

The two themes of the *Rise of Rationalism* are the decline of superstition before the influence of rational inquiry, and the supersession of the military and clerical outlook by the industrial spirit.* Lecky also greatly enriched current ideas on the mysterious causes of the transformation of the tone of thought. Why was it, he asked, that 'reasoning which in our age would have made no impression whatever, in the next age is received with enthusiastic applause'? In this context Lecky refers to Glanvil, the seventeenth-century scholar from whom Arnold took the legend of the Scholar Gipsy, and who first coined the phrase 'climates of opinion'.† Opening with a panorama of the witch persecution endemic in Europe from the Middle Ages to the eighteenth century, he inquires by what insensible gradations the revolution of ideas occurred which abolished this almost universal practice. With immense gusto and many picturesque examples, pointed by footnotes of curious learning, Lecky depicts the development of patristic and medieval superstition. The policy of the early Church towards magicians, the elaborate crimes of the Merovingian Queen Fredegunde, the opinions of the Byzantine philosopher Psellus on the nature of Demons, the excesses of the Flagellants and the sufferings of the Cabbalists, the widespread belief in lycanthropy and metempsychosis,‡ and the queer beliefs of the Cathari — all are swept into an easy narrative lit up by flashes of Victorian wit. 'Celibacy', for example, 'was universally regarded as the highest form of virtue, and in order to make it acceptable, theologians exhausted all the resources of their eloquence in describ-

---

* The first volume contains four chapters: on The Declining Sense of the Miraculous; on Magic and Witchcraft and the Miracles of the Church; on the Aesthetic, Scientific and Moral Developments of Rationalism; and on Persecution and its Antecedents. The second volume, in three chapters, continues the history of Persecution, and treats of the secularizing of Politics and the industrialization of Society.

† Later widely popularized by A. N. WHITEHEAD in his *Science and the Modern World*.

‡ 'It raged, however, especially where wolves abounded — among the Jura, in Norway, Russia, Ireland – in the Pyrenees and Greece. The Italian women usually became cats. Among the many mad notions of the Abyssinians, perhaps the maddest is their belief that blacksmiths and potters can change themselves into hyaenas, and ought, therefore, to be excluded from the sacrament.'

ing the iniquity of those whose charms rendered it so rare.' Apart from patristic, medieval and seventeenth-century sources, in particular the *Malleus Maleficarum*, Lecky cites many works of nineteenth-century scholarship — Maury, *Histoire de la Magie*; Michelet, *La Sorcière*; Plancey, *Dictionnaire Infernale*; Garinet; and Madden, *History of Phantoms*. Herder's *Philosophy of History* and works of Scandinavian lore were all drawn into the net. It is, indeed, still a rewarding occupation to follow up the tracks indicated in Lecky's well-placed footnotes — one which may be recommended as a valuable alternative to the study of the commentators on Marx's theory of surplus value, or the local government of Crewe.

Ranging over the aesthetic and moral developments of rationalism, Lecky traces the evolution of Christianity in terms of Christian art, from the lyrical frescoes of the catacombs to the severity of Byzantine mosaics, and explains the rise of the cult of Saints and images through the assimilation of barbarians incapable of abstract religion. Twelfth-century renaissance art is correlated with its habits of thought, and the environment of sixteenth-century Venice evoked in a fine romantic manner to explain the painting of Titian and Tintoretto. 'The thousand lights that glittered around the gilded domes of St. Mark, the palaces of matchless architecture resting on their own soft shadows in the wave, the long paths of murmuring water, where the Gondola sways to the lover's song, and where dark eyes lustrous with passion gleam from the overhanging balconies, the harmony of blending beauties, and the languid and voluptuous charm that pervades the whole, had all told deeply and fatally on the character of the people.' Romanticism in time is enriched by romanticism of place.

The absorption of religious by aesthetic feeling, he points out, culminates in the Renaissance: 'The age of the Cathedrals had passed. The age of the printing press had begun.'[34] Turning to the revolution in cosmology, Lecky once more relates the change in the climate of opinion to total environment. After a lucid and eloquent presentation of the notions entertained by Cosmas Indicopleustes on the nature of the universe, and an entertaining digression on the opinions of the Fathers about the Antipodes,* Lecky describes the 'besotted ignorance' of Science in medieval times, and dilates upon the revolution brought about in opinion by the 'discoveries of geology relating to the pre-adamite history of the globe'. They scout finally, he insists, the legend that death was the penalty of the Fall. 'Geology

---

* St. Boniface had some trouble with an Irish Saint in eighth-century Germany who asserted their existence.

has proved that countless ages before men trod this earth . . . death raged and revelled among its occupants . . . To deny this is now impossible: to admit it is to abandon one of the root-doctrines of the past . . .'[35] Yet this discarding of a fundamental doctrine of Christianity does not destroy the argument from design. 'Indeed it is, perhaps, not too much to say, that the more fully this conception of universal evolution is grasped, the more firmly a scientific doctrine of Providence will be established, and the stronger will be the presumption of a future progress.' Lecky, unlike Tennyson, was not appalled by the new scientific knowledge. Yet he displayed no merely Philistine complacency. He was well aware of the mystery of life and states it in terms which have not been superseded. 'Science can throw much light upon the laws that preside over the development of life; but what life is, and what its ultimate cause, we are utterly unable to say. An impenetrable mystery lies at the root of every living thing.'

Such is the broad, scholarly and imaginative treatment here deployed. On the waning of persecution and of ideological tyranny his book makes ironical reading. 'Among all the possible dangers that cloud the horizon, none appears more improbable than a coalition formed upon the principle of a common belief, and designed to extend the sphere of its influence.'[36] His belief in the sovereign virtue of the law of supply and demand, and in the Spencerian supersession of military societies by peaceful industrial states, were destined to prove no more accurate. But this confident, attractive and learned interpretation of the past furnished Victorian conservative optimists with a philosophy of history. It was Lecky, not Marx, who was representative of the general beliefs of his time. And this outlook, with its assurance and imaginative appeal, could attract minds too sensitive for the crude 'scientific' individualism of Herbert Spencer. Where Spencer spoke for the practical man with scientific inclinations, Lecky widened and enriched the range of nineteenth-century knowledge and spoke for a sophisticated upper-class culture which collectively, in its academic and bureaucratic influence, set the tone for dominant opinion.

The political outlook of this class, in its wisdom and its limitations, he also well expressed. His *Democracy and Liberty* is a thorough and comprehensive work,* comparable in its grasp of fact of Bryce's

---

* Published in two volumes, 1896, it opens with a comparison of eighteenth-century and Victorian democracy, and proceeds (chapter IV), to a discussion of Aristocracies and Upper Chambers. Chapter V deals with Nationalities, and chapter VI with

masterpiece on *American Democracy*. Written more than thirty years after his essay on *Rationalism*, Lecky's book was now to be reminiscent of de Tocqueville. The cardinal fact of the 'nineties was the 'displacement of power'.[37] The democracy de Tocqueville foresaw as inevitable had arrived. Like Mill and Spencer, Lecky was apprehensive of its tyranny. 'Equality is the idol of democracy', but since such levelling is unnatural, it can only be attained by constant interference with liberty, 'by a constant systematic, stringent repression of the natural development'. It is, therefore, bound to destroy the 'balance of opinions, interests and classes, on which constitutional liberty mainly depends'. It is even hostile to the authority of parliaments, 'which have hitherto proved the chief organ of political liberty'. It is likely to lead, in the long run, to despotism by plebiscite. 'To place the chief power in the most ignorant classes is to place it in the hands of those who naturally care least for political liberty, and who are likely to follow with an absolute devotion some strong leader.'[38] He regarded Trade Union power with suspicion, holding that it made for restrictive practices and technical conservatism, and he constantly warned his contemporaries of the dangers of centralized bureaucracy and of taxation employed as a means of social revolution. He pointed out that the first victims of socialism were likely to be 'the upper and middle classes who have chiefly valued constitutional liberty ... those classes it is the work of democracy to dethrone'. This clear appraisal of the realities of the situation was reinforced by his prophesy, amply fulfilled, of the uses of penal taxation '. . . which under a democracy is likely to take forms that are peculiarly hostile to liberty'. While his progressive contemporaries were gaily discarding traditional safeguards, Lecky remarks, 'I have already pointed out how this old fundamental principle of English freedom, that no one should be taxed except by his consent, is being gradually discarded.' As to the end of this process Lecky had no illusions.

With the decline of the upper bourgeoisie, and with them of the respect for the restraints on arbitrary power, he correctly foresaw the rise of modern demagogues — 'The instability of democratic politics . . . the spectacle of dishonest and predatory adventurers climbing by popular suffrage into positions of great power in the state.'[38] He went on to suggest possible safeguards by reform of the House of Lords and other revisions of parliamentary procedure. Lecky, in

Democracy and religious liberty. Vol. II examines democracy and moral laws (chapter VII) and contains a long and interesting survey of the development of socialism (chapter VIII). The concluding chapters discuss labour questions and women's suffrage.

fact, warned his own kind exactly of what was to be in store for them.

Similarly, he foresaw that mass democracy would tend to war. While wisely advocating that governments should be based on consent constitutionally elicited, Lecky also warned his contemporaries that the cult of national will can be extremely dangerous. Pushed to extremity, it becomes 'the readiest weapon in the hands both of a conqueror and of a revolutionist, and, by discrediting the force of all international treaties, deepening lines of division, and introducing elements of anarchy and rebellion into most great nations, it threatens the most valuable elements in our civilization'.[39]

Socialism, even of the Fabian kind, Lecky regarded as a reversion to a more primitive form of society — an 'archaism'. Taking his stand squarely on the ancient tradition of Locke, Bentham and the Mills, he regards property as the greatest safeguard to political freedom. The concentration of political and economic power in Government marks 'a revival of beliefs which had been supposed . . . long since finally exploded — the aspirations to customs belonging to early and rudimentary stages of society'.[40] State control of property is the essence of despotism, and today the 'most extreme power of property ever claimed by an oriental tyrant is attributed to a majority told by the head.'

Holding these views, his treatment of the history of socialism is hardly sympathetic. He did not, for example, find Karl Marx's mind congenial, and even went so far as to describe him as frigid, systematic, pedantic and arrogant. Nor did he sense the attractions of *Das Kapital*. 'It is not probable', he ventured to prophesy, 'that a work so long, so obscure, confused and tortuous in its meanings, or so unspeakably dreary in its style, has had many readers among the working class, or indeed in any class.' He even described it as 'highly pretentious'. Lecky also noted in Marx 'that curious Teutonic power of framing a picture of the world out of formulae and abstract reasonings, to the neglect of some of the most patent facts'. But he cited Burke on the power of myth. 'Burke has noticed that the weakest reasonings are sometimes the most dangerous, because they are united with the strongest passions.' Besides a rich contribution to the history of ideas and his massive achievement as an historian, Lecky had a shrewd eye for the situation in the late nineteenth century. It is often said that the Victorian ruling classes were strangely blind to the forces that were to undermine their world: that criticism cannot be brought against this brilliant historian.

CHAPTER III

THE LIFE OF INSTITUTIONS
MAINE: BAGEHOT: TYLOR

T HE historical bias of nineteenth-century thought was reinforced after the mid-century by better scientific method. A
picturesque sense of environment is everywhere apparent, along
with a new knowledge of the primitive background of civilization.
Political thought is related to ancient law and custom; to the behaviour of a wide range of savage peoples, now for the first time
being brought into the net of social anthropology. Here is no world-
historical vision of metaphysical 'laws', whereby the fate of mankind
is predicted according to the imagination of a prophetic philosopher,
but the findings of systematic historical and anthropological research.
Empirical and factual, if by modern standards oversimplified and
over ambitious, here is the mark of genuine science: a contrast to the
dogmatic system of Marx and Engels, with its originally romantic
origins.

The development was most typical in England, though it had
brilliant exponents in France: Renan, Taine and Tarde. Maine set
political problems in a new perspective by unearthing the roots of
Law and pointing out that constitutionalism was based on primitive
custom; he reinforced the historical evidence by facts from contemporary India. He explained that in the context of world history the
very idea of improvement by legislation was extremely rare, and
stressed the debt of Western society to the Roman concept of Natural
Law. He brought powerful criticism to bear on Austin's doctrine of
sovereignty, and vindicated a balanced constitution. Bagehot contributed a new sense of the actual working of government. He
examined how leadership arose in primitive societies, and pointed
out that mankind are led not by reason but by custom, myth and
the glamour of tradition. His analysis of the English Constitution is
famous, and he related the prevalent idea of progress to the slow
development of society. Like Maine, he stressed the rarity of advance
and the primitive elements still embedded in the social structure.
Bagehot's brilliant intuition was justified by the evidence collected
by Tylor, the greatest pioneer of British anthropology. Where Comte
and Spencer had endeavoured to subordinate sociology to a system,

Tylor, limiting his definition of progress to command over environment, made a more empirical approach. He revealed the undercurrent of barbarous customs and ideas beneath the tide of civilization, and set the evolution of Western culture against a world panorama of new anthropological knowledge.

All these shrewd writers, far from ignoring the primitive past, as had the elegant historians of the eighteenth century, show a certain satisfaction in revealing the lineaments of the primitive beneath the veneer of civilization. They all turn, as it were, a searchlight along the often horrid vista of the primitive past, lighting up some sinister objects in its glare. Unlike many of their continental contemporaries, they do not manifest despair at grim conclusions. They accept them and act upon them for the betterment of mankind. It was congenial to their minds to draw constructive conclusions from facts.

Much of Buckle's easy optimism, for example, was thus deflated, and a more realistic understanding achieved of the life of institutions. In the long historical background revealed, later nineteenth-century thought was to be set. Bagehot, in particular, anticipated many conclusions of the sociologists Durkheim and Graham Wallas.

II

The new historical method proved particularly valuable in the study of Law. Sir Henry Maine made a salutary criticism of political ideas, setting theories hitherto taken for granted in a new perspective.* His approach was followed up by Maitland and Pollock in the late nineteenth and early twentieth centuries: 'he did nothing less', writes the latter, 'than create the natural history of law'.†

By this approach he profoundly criticized both traditional doctrines of Natural Law, and the positivist aspects of Bentham and Austin.

* Sir Henry Maine, 1822-88, came of Scottish ancestry. Through the good offices of Dr. Sumner, Bishop of Chester and afterwards Archbishop of Canterbury, he obtained a nomination to Christ's Hospital in 1829. A scholar of Pembroke College, Cambridge, he became Tutor at Trinity Hall, 1845. He was Regius Professor of Civil Law, 1847-54, and Reader in Roman Law at the Inns of Court, 1854-62. In 1861 he published *Ancient Law*. 1862-69 Legal Member of Council for India; 1869-78 Professor of Jurisprudence at Oxford; 1871 *Village Communities in the East and West*; 1875 *The Early History of Institutions*. 1877 Master of Trinity Hall. 1883 *Dissertations on Early Law and Customs*; 1885 *Popular Government*. 1887 Professor of International Law, Cambridge. He died at Cannes in 1888. Maine was a brilliant scholar of frail physique: his lectures are distinguished by extraordinary range and grasp of essentials, and by an irony which renders them particularly telling.

† See his Introduction (p. xvi) to *Ancient Law. Its connection with the Early History of Society and its relation to Modern Ideas*. Murray (1906 edition).

It is most strikingly revealed in the first five chapters of *Ancient Law*, and in the last two chapters of *Early Institutions*.* In Maine's history of law there is a sense of broad horizons and far-reaching comparisons, alien from the atmosphere both of Blackstone and Bentham. In Vico alone is there a glimmering of such an historical and comparative approach, for Montesquieu had little sense of historical evolution, if his sense of environment had been vivid.

The nineteenth century in Western Europe is depicted as quite exceptional in the long, slow-moving, history of mankind. Maine contrasts modern Benthamite legislation with the 'dooms' whereby primitive societies asserted customary or habitual law. He makes particularly illuminating comparisons . . . 'The farther we penetrate into the primitive history of thought, the farther we find ourselves from a conception of law which at all resembles a compound of the elements which Bentham determined. It is certain that, in the infancy of mankind, no sort of legislature, nor even a distinct author of law, is contemplated or conceived of. Law has scarcely . . . the footing of custom; it is rather a habit.'[1] This background of custom, here so much stressed, is obviously of singular importance in political action. Austin realized its negative importance: Maine showed its constructive side. Hence the fundamental distinction, at the root of constitutionalism, between society and government — the traditional assumption, for example, that there is an ultimate appeal to a constitution which reflects a Law of Nature, and Burke's appeal to a tradition which expresses the total sense of a society, past, present and to come. Both are accorded an ancient and ramified pedigree. Moreover, Maine traced the rise of the kind of law, whereby custom became defined in a code, of which the rulers are not the source but the custodians, and revealed the deep roots of another vital aspect of political progress. His method, and that developed by his successors, cleared the ground for a new appreciation of the perennial problem of power. And he points out the contrast between Western societies, where some sort of legal code was 'nearly universally obtained early in the history of the Commonwealth', and the situation in the East, where the rise of religious oligarchies and the vast areas concerned retarded and distorted this development. 'We are not of course entitled to say that if the Twelve Tables had not been published the Romans would have been condemned to a

* *Lectures on the Early History of Institutions.* Seventh edition. Murray. London, 1914. The former covers Ancient Codes, Legal Fictions, the Law of Nature and Equity, the Modern History of the Law of Nature, and Primitive Society and Ancient Law; the latter, Sovereignty and Sovereignty and Empire.

civilization as feeble and perverted as that of the Hindoos, but thus much at least is certain, that *with* their code they were exempt from the very chance of so unhappy a destiny.'[2] Constitutionalism, he proved, was fundamental to the unusual success obtained by many Western societies in controlling power.

Through such broad comparisons Maine also stressed the rarity of progress in world history. 'It is only with the progressive societies that we are concerned, and nothing is more remarkable than their extreme fewness.' This fact was disconcerting for opinion in the 'sixties, and incompatible with the sanguine opinions of the French heirs of the eighteenth century, Saint-Simon and Comte. With Maine, we are in a more realistic and empirical world. 'In spite of overwhelming evidence,' he writes, 'it is most difficult for a citizen of Western Europe to bring thoroughly home to himself the truth that the civilization which surrounds him is a rare exception in the history of the world.'[3] In this wider context the confident proposals of Bentham appear startlingly unusual, if salutary. 'It is indisputable that much the greatest part of mankind has never shown a particle of desire that its civil institutions should be improved since the moment when external completeness was first given to them by their embodiment in some permanent record . . . There has been material civilization, but, instead of the civilization expanding the law, the law has limited the civilization . . . the stationary condition of the human race is the rule, the progressive the exception.'[4]

In making this routine of custom constructive the idea of Natural Law had played an important part. Maine thoroughly examined that ancient and pervasive idea. 'I shall attempt', he says, 'to discover the origin of these famous phrases, law of nations, law of nature, equity.'[5] He relates the Jus Gentium, originally 'an ignoble appendage' to the Roman 'jus civile', designed to deal with foreigners, to the Greek theory of the Natural Law. This Greek concept of a universal order behind phenomena had been defined by Stoic philosophers. The vague and world-wide concept of universal justice, reflecting a law of nature which brings harmony out of confusion, was related by the Romans to 'aequitas', technically over-riding privileges of class. All this was rooted in the past, but it now became dynamic. Its role in achieving political progress was decisive.

Maine thus brings a sweeping historical analysis to bear on two fundamental beliefs; on the rule of law, so deeply rooted in custom, and on successive interpretations of the Law of Nature.[6] The ideas he defined, now familiar, were the pioneering effort of his original mind. By cutting through ancient legal theory; by interpreting the development of thought in terms of history and environment, he was applying the most characteristic mid-nineteenth-century technique to the origins of both constitutional government and popular political ideas. His treatment of the origins of International Law was also salutary.[7,8]

While admitting the rarity of constitutional government, he unearthed the roots of the most effective institutions for the control of power. His sense of the importance of custom and tradition, and of the myths that expressed them, made him point out not only the rarity and the achievements of modern sovereignty, but also its limitations and its dangers.

In this context, he attacked Hobbes's total concept of sovereign power.[9] Far from being held in the grip of despotism, progressive societies have shown a gradual emancipation of the individual from patriarchal control, from tribal 'status' to independent 'contract'.[10] This criticism of Hobbes is elaborated and expanded in Maine's masterly treatment of sovereignty, in the twelfth and thirteenth lectures in *Early Institutions*. Austinian sovereignty derives, he points out, from Hobbes, who defined it 'with a keenness of intuition and lucidity of statement which have never been rivalled'.[11] Hobbes made the pioneer inquiry how sovereignty arose. Yet in the light of modern knowledge, Maine insists, the stark positivist assertions Austin derived from Hobbes need profound modification.

If the social facts are examined, this concept of sovereignty will appear to be an abstraction. 'It is arrived at by throwing aside all the characteristics and attributes of Government and Society except one.' Various forms of power are classified together, and the real roots of power, broad-based in the entire history and institutions of a community, are ignored. 'All that constitutes . . . the whole enormous aggregate of opinions, sentiments, beliefs, superstitions and prejudices, of ideas of all kinds, hereditary and acquired . . . is rejected by the analytical jurists.' This narrow conception of sovereignty can make for tyranny.

The insulated concept of law as simply the command of a superior, may be useful for legislative reform. It is also very dangerous. Although Austin wrote little more than forty years ago, 'he wrote before men's ideas were leavened to the present depth by experiment and observation'. Austin's law did not reflect the broader idea of natural order; rather, the kind of law created by the sovereign imposed in too wide a context. This belief, as Maine points out, was historically rare, since in primitive societies it is custom, and not the fiat of a ruler, which commands the most widespread and intimate obedience. Consider, for example, he says, the rule of Runjeet Singh, 'the Sikh despot of the Punjaub'. 'He could have commanded anything . . . Yet I doubt whether once in his life he issued a command which Austin would call a law.'[12] This sovereign 'took, as his revenue, a prodigious share of the produce of the soil. He harried villages which recalcitrated at his exactions, and he executed great numbers of men. But he never made a law. The rules which regulated the life of his subjects were derived from their immemorial usages, and these rules were administered by domestic tribunals, in families or village communities'. Moreover, the Sikh tyrant could not have changed these usages had he so desired. This kind of rule is typical of 'all Oriental communities in their native state, during their rare intervals of peace and order'. It is exercised by particular, often incalculable, commands. For law itself in the East is not the 'command of the sovereign, but the supposed command of the Deity'. This view of government is far more general in history, including the history of Europe, than the positivist outlook first defined by Hobbes as the result of an unusual scepticism, and developed by Bentham. Austin's attempt to include custom in the command of a superior by asserting that 'What the sovereign permits he commands', is irrelevant in this more primitive context, and not very convincing in any other. In the 'tax-taking Empires',[13] the modern idea of legislation was alien. The fiats of oriental despotism were 'a sudden and temporary interference with ancient multifarious usages left in general undisturbed'. The conception of a centralized, legislating state is ultimately derived from Rome, and peculiar to the West.

It follows that the attributes of sovereignty defined by Hobbes and Austin are peculiar to an important but statistically small part of humanity. And the kind of sovereign power exercised by Richelieu and admired by Hobbes was an innovation: it crushed the 'old multiform local activity of a feudal or quasi-feudal society'. 'We have heard of a village Hampden, but a village Hobbes is inconceivable.' The positivist outlook is the product of unusual circumstances, and 'no geniuses of an equally high order so completely divorced themselves from history as Hobbes and Bentham, or appear, to me at all events, so completely under the impression that the world has always been more or less as they saw it'. As for Hobbes's views that corporations are worms in the body politic, 'we now know that, if we are forced to use a physiological illustration, these groups must rather be compared to the primary cells out of which the whole human body has been built up'.[14] Here is a pointer to the pluralist outlook of Gierke and Maitland. As for the Benthamite idea of utility, of the greatest happiness of the greatest number considered on the basis of law and morals, 'which was grafted upon' the positivist theory of Hobbes, it depends on the unusual doctrine of the equality of mankind. 'I have myself heard an Indian Brahmin dispute it on the ground that ... a Brahmin was entitled to twenty times as much happiness as anyone else.'[15] Bentham, Maine argues, was not fool enough to believe that men are by nature equal. He made the hypothesis as a working rule of legislation, which on the scale on which modern legislation operates, demands the neglect of differences in the ruled.

Such is the powerful analysis to which Maine subjects some most influential political ideas. He placed the Hobbesian-Austinian concept of sovereignty in its historical setting and put it in a new light. He vindicated the sense of the organic nature of commonwealth which had always been invoked as the ultimate sanction for government. He brought the evidence of primitive societies to bear on the threat of the unbridled power of the nineteenth-century state, and by subjecting Austinian ideas to this criticism, reinforced, in the legal field, the more organic idea of society which was already being advanced by the later writings of J. S. Mill, and which was to develop further after him with T. H. Green.

The examples quoted by Maine in this context have been principally Indian or Classical. He was also widely learned in other and curious branches of the history of law. For example, his investigations into the extraordinary laws and customs of the tribal Irish assembled much remarkable data. The grotesque elaboration of the most ancient Irish code, the Book of Aicill, 'Composed of the dicta of two famous lawyers, Cormac and Cennfaeladh';* the precautions taken by the Brehons (who displayed, he believed, a Druid pedigree) to maintain their prestige in tribal society and secure 'their rights of feasting at the expense of other classes'; and the genial Irish assumption that 'chastity was the professional virtue of a special class', com-

---

* 'Four pages of the book of Aicill (a very large proportion in an ancient body of law) are concerned with injuries received from dogs in dog-fights ... in the case of the owners – in the case of the spectators – in the case of the "impartial interposer" – in the case of the "half interposer", i.e. the man who tries to separate the dogs with a bias in favour of one of them – in the case of an accidental looker on ... or of a youth under age.' 'The same law tract deals also with the curious subjects of injuries from a cat stealing in a kitchen, from women using their distaffs in a woman-battle, and from bees. . . .' Op. cit., p. 46.

bine to explain much that is socially attractive, and politically impossible, in the development of the island. Here he also found new evidence for the development of tribal ideas of kinship, starting from the original assumption that one's neighbour was either a relation, a slave, or an enemy, and proceeding to expand, by a fictitious assumption of ancestry, into the Septs and arch-tribes existing at the time of the English conquest. He describes the methods of reckoning wealth in cattle, so that the very word capital means reckoning by the 'head'; the effects of the predominance of cattle-thieving in Celtic communities as a major interest in life, and the extraordinary multiplication of 'Bishops' in the early Irish Church. Besides his great legal acumen, he thus also contributed to sociology.

This power of setting the Victorian situation in the light of world history is also finely expressed in his later work, *Popular Government.** While most contemporary writers accepted the 'democratic principle' as well nigh infallible, Maine pointed out that historically and geographically, modern democracy is unusual and precarious. 'Does the expectation', he asked, 'of the virtual permanence of government of the modern type rest upon historical evidence?' He concluded it did not.

Maine's survey of the geographical range of popular government is masterly, still to be read with profit. Seldom has a better survey of an actual situation been penned. It is as witty as it is accurate and able.† He points out that this form of government originated in England. But since the American constitution so derives, 'It now became possible for the continental Europeans to admire popular government without the somewhat bitter necessity of admiring the English . . .' Although, he writes, 'the British political model was followed by France, by Spain, by Portugal and by Holland and Belgium combined in the Kingdom of the Netherlands; and, after a long interval by Germany, Italy and Austria', its success has often been superficial. Since the Revolution, the French have had forty-four years of constitutional government, but thirty-seven of dictatorship. In Spain there have been forty-four military risings since 1812; in Germany the nominally constitutional government has been imposed within a monarchical frame. And while constitutionalism has won its most important success in the United States, it has

---

* *Popular Government, Four Essays*, 1885. It treats of The Prospects of Popular Government; The Nature of Democracy; The Age of Progress and The Constitution of the United States.

† It is significant that Maine records in the preface his debt to Lord Acton, a scholar of very different background who also took long views.

proved a singular farce in most of South America. Out of thirteen Presidents of Bolivia, thirteen had been assassinated or died in exile.

Outside the Anglo-Saxon areas, modern popular government has been most successful in the smaller states — Holland, Belgium and Scandinavia. Apart, therefore, from the huge areas of Eastern Europe, Asia and Africa where it is alien, popular government has always been fragile even in Europe. It is in truth exceptionally unstable. The impartial historian will 'note as a fact, to be considered in the most serious spirit, that since the century during which the Roman Emperors were at the mercy of the Praetorian soldiery, there has been no such insecurity of government as the world has seen since rulers became the delegates of the community'.[16]

With an insight justified by the events of the twentieth century, Maine emphasized the affinity between nationalism and democracy. Yet democracy and military efficiency are incompatible. 'No two organizations', he wrote, 'can be more opposed to one another than an army scientifically disciplined and equipped and a nation democratically governed'. Further, as weapons become more efficient, the power of military minorities is likely to increase. Nationalism, he believed, was 'full of the seeds of future civil convulsion'.[17] And popular government was imperilled by its tendency to violence.

Internally the dangers were also formidable. The extension of the suffrage was bound to increase the power of the 'Wire-Puller', and the organization and fervour of party. It is, indeed likely to become the basis of a conservative tyranny. Society will be 'drugged', apathetic, mediocre. Full popular government is even likely to prevent scientific enterprise, on which progress depends: 'the opposition between democracy and science . . . does not promise much for the longevity of popular government,' he concludes wrily.[18] There is hope perhaps in 'instructed' leadership, but the greatest leaders are enslaved by the stupidity of the masses, which leads towards a 'dead level of commonplace opinion'.[19] Alternatively, the cult of the expert is dangerous; 'society is to become the Church of a sort of political Calvinism, in which the elect are to be the men with exceptional brains'. Maine thinks this danger is not very great; popular democracy would not long put up with them.

Historically, the great ages of intellectual enterprise have been oligarchic. Athens, for example, was never a democracy in the modern sense. Moreover popular government may well be economically unsound. It assumes that 'the stock of good things in the world is unlimited'; it is more concerned with fair shares than with creating wealth. If these tendencies predominate, a complete democracy may well become 'a mutinous crew, feasting on the ship's provisions' but refusing to navigate the ship to port.[20] There will be lack of incentive, the danger of 'fiscal tyranny'. Maine refers with approbation to Herbert Spencer's *The Man versus the State*. He declares that either competition or slavery is necessary. Either have one or the other, or else '. . . pass through penury to starvation'.

This hard outlook, which modern events have sometimes substantiated, was reinforced by the strong sense, already apparent, of the debt which modern societies owe to past monarchies and empires. The entire modern state, Maine declares, is an 'inverted monarchy'. 'We ourselves live in the dust of Roman Imperialism, and far the largest part of modern law is nothing more than a sedimentary formation left by Roman legal reforms'.[21] The greatest legacy, and the best safeguard, to popular government is a balanced constitution. In that, he insists, lies the hope that modern democracy may control itself and survive. At present if the tendency towards mass democracy continued, 'we are drifting towards a type of government, associated with terrible events — a single Assembly . . . with full powers over the Constitution, which it may exercise at pleasure'.[22]

Maine has certainly thrown a cold douche over the sanguine assumptions of liberal democrats. His later Essays are still widely regarded as something to be deplored. Yet both his factual demonstration of the rarity of popular government and his sense of the dangers ahead proved him a reliable prophet. Like Lecky, he gave ample warning of the development of a situation which was to take liberal democrats by surprise. This power to dissociate himself from the predominant outlook of his age was due to a powerful geographical sense and an imaginative grasp of the development of civilization over long ages.

III

This sense of the precariousness of popular government, of a huge and static past, of the power of primitive ideas and the sparseness of progress, is also apparent in the realistic outlook of Walter Bagehot, the most brilliant of the English writers who applied the new historical ideas to political speculation. He was a versatile and forceful character.* His famous treatise on *The English Constitution*

---

* Walter Bagehot, 1826-77. Born at Langport, Somerset, where his father, a shipowner, was vice-chairman of Stuckey's Bank. Educated at Bristol and University College, London, he was called to the Bar in 1852. In 1858 he became editor of *The Economist*,

is the best known of his works,* but his *Physics and Politics,* or Thoughts on the Application of the Principle of Natural Selection and Inheritance to Political Society, is more important and more directly relevant to the present study.†

The theme of this remarkable book, so full of a new psychological insight, is the reality and method of gradual progress. Bagehot's conception of society is historical and organic; his affinities are with Burke and Maine rather than with Bentham. He observes, for example, that 'stupidity is essential to political freedom', and that the French were 'too clever to be free'. He regards the new sense of the past as most characteristic of his age, when 'everything is made an Antiquity'. He also believed, with Spencer, that acquired characteristics were heritable, and that the organic nature of society guaranteed the transmission and diffusion of previous achievement. Each civilization, he said, was not 'a line of detached dots, but a line of colour, surely enhancing shade by shade'. He compared the progress of mankind to an unfolding melody, 'making nicer music from finer chords', and maintained that the 'silent toil of the first generation became the transmitted aptitude of the next'.

Like Maine, by whom he was influenced, he traced the progress of early societies to the growth of the solidarity of Church and State. 'The King must be priest and prophet King; the two must be the same because they are the same,' and the 'object of such organization is to create what may be called the cake of custom'. Thus society emerged from its primitive incoherence. This is the 'hereditary drill' or 'mould of civilization . . . Rome and Sparta were drilling aristocracies and succeeded because they were such'.[23] 'The ages of monotony had their use, for they trained men for ages when they need not be monotonous.'[24] This sense of the deep irrational element in society contrasts with the facile rationalism of the Utilitarians, and

---

* *The English Constitution* contains nine chapters; they deal with the Cabinet, the Monarchy (two chapters); the House of Lords and the House of Commons; with Changes of Ministry; with Its supposed Checks and Balances; with The Pre-Requisites of Government and the Peculiar Form which they have inherited in England, and with Its History, and the Effects of that History.

† The 224 pages of *Physics and Politics* are divided into six chapters; 'The Preliminary Age', 'The Use of Conflict,' 'Nation Making' (twice investigated), 'The Age of Discussion', and 'Verifiable Progress Politically Considered'.

---

having married the daughter of the founder and proprietor. He wrote *The English Constitution* in 1867, *Physics and Politics* in 1872, and *Biographical Studies.* His collected works, in ten volumes, were edited, with a Life, by Mrs. R. Barrington (1915). Bagehot was a man of magnetic personality and striking appearance, with 'heavy black hair, flashing black eyes, a florid complexion, a lissom figure and a look of high animal spirits, but he had also something of good natured mockery in his glance'.

harks back, with a new scientific content, to the shrewd realism of Halifax the Trimmer. Bagehot's remark, for example, in *The English Constitution*, that 'the mass of the English people yield a deference rather to something else than to their rulers. They defer to what we may call the *theatrical show* of society ... Courts and aristocracies have the great quality which rules the multitude, though philosophers can see nothing in it — visibility.[25] This sentiment may be compared with Halifax's observation that 'monarchy is liked by the People for the Bells and Tinsel, the outward Pomp and Gilding and there must be milk for Babes, since the greater part of mankind are and ever will be included in that list'.[26] There is the same high spirited good humour, the same respect for oligarchical government, and a comparable pride in English institutions and political sense. Like Halifax, Bagehot is a man of the world, and this quality enhanced his political judgment. Unlike Halifax, he was able to employ the scientific approach of mid-nineteenth-century biology. A healthy society, in Bagehot's opinion, is still composed of a minority of elites and a great mass whose loyalty is determined by symbols. This situation reflects the healthy 'deference' of the common people for the spectacular side of society, which is actually ruled by inconspicuous persons of the middle class. It is precarious, since 'if you once permit the ignorant class to begin to rule, you may bid farewell to deference for ever ... A democracy will never, save after an awful catastrophe, return what has once been conceded to it, for to do so would be to admit an inferiority in itself, of which, except by some almost unbearable misfortune, it could never be convinced'.[27]

Bagehot, like de Tocqueville and Mill, regarded with apprehension the rule of the common man. His scepticism was rooted in a scientific outlook on society, as well as upon the outlook of his class. For he believed that imitation was a powerful and necessary force in maintaining social cohesion and traced with remarkable insight the causes of the evolution of national character. 'In the origin of states strong and eager individuals got hold of small knots of men and made for them a fashion which they were attached to and kept.' Hence the dislike felt by Plato and Aristotle for trade and for the influence of foreigners; 'the old oligarchy wanted to keep the type perfect'. Like the ages of monotony, 'the ages of isolation had their use, for they trained men for ages when they were not to be isolated'. Bagehot's sense of the need for gradual and natural adaptation is vivid and constant; it never penetrated the doctrinaire heads of contemporary revolutionaries, with their short cuts to the millennium. 'The development of the English Constitution', he writes, 'was of necessity slow, because a quick one would have destroyed the executive and killed the state, and because the most numerous classes, who changed very little, were not prepared for any catastrophic change in our institutions.'

The principle that representative institutions are not the mere instrument of the coercive power of a majority, but the means whereby government can find where the shoe pinches, is admirably brought out in Bagehot's remarks on English medieval parliaments, when he states that 'from thence the King learned, or had the means to learn, what the nation would endure, and what it would not endure'.[28]

The Tudor Parliament, he also rightly maintains, admirably served this purpose, and the very anomalies of its election made it the more representative — a 'feeler' he says, for government. For all legislation and improvements have to be tentative, gradual and wary. Bagehot's sense of the need for 'reformers' to carry the bulk of popular opinion with them reflects both the realism of Cromwell and the intuition of Burke. Compare the former's answer to the Leveller's 'We have to consider whether the spirit and temper of the nation are prepared to go along with it,' and the latter's 'the virtue, spirit, and essence of the House of Commons consists in its being the express image of the feelings of the nation'. Like Maine, he emphasizes that the very idea of progress and improvement is rare. 'The ancients had no conception of progress; they did not so much as reject the idea; they did not even entertain the idea.'[29] Yet even the most static and conservative societies must have made progress at some time. As he shrewdly remarks, they 'have, so to say screwed themselves into the uncomfortable corners of a complex life, which is odd and dreary, yet it is possible'. This observation, casually thrown off, is typical of Bagehot's insight, as again, when he remarks 'the progress of the military art is the most conspicuous, I was about to say the most *showy*, fact in human history'.[30]

Among the causes of that rare phenomenon, progress, Bagehot gives war an important place. Like most mid-nineteenth-century thinkers — Marx in particular — he believes that history proceeds by ascertainable 'laws'. 'Every one now admits that human history is guided by certain laws.' One of the laws, he maintains, is that war acts as a salutary instrument of natural selection. And although modern civilization is so elaborate, it does not make men unwarlike. 'Nowadays in all countries the great cities could pour out multitudes wanting nothing but practice to make good soldiers, abounding in bravery and vigour.' Here, acting on a singularly humane mind, is apparent the effect of the grim outlook of contemporary interpreters of science.[31]

It was the past that seemed depressing to this Victorian, not the future. The hard virtues of military aristocracies, it seemed, had broken the cake of custom which paralysed most cultures. They had imposed the salutary domination of progressive societies on 'arrested civilizations'. 'The hard impact of military virtues,' wrote Bagehot, 'beats meanness out of the world.' Marx's lust for class conflict reflects, in more vicious form, the same nineteenth-century assumption.

The harsh picture Bagehot gives of early societies reinforced this outlook. For the widening explorations of the mid-Victorian age, contact with the savages of Tierra del Fuego, of Australia, Borneo, the Burmese interior, and of Central Africa, had combined with the discoveries of the prehistorians to present a repulsive picture of human origins. This was made more convincing by their lack of psychological understanding of savages. On primitive peoples Bagehot parodied Addison's 'When wild in woods the noble savage ran' by his own lines 'When lone in woods the cringing savage crept.'

Continuing his survey of progress, Bagehot cites the habit of discussion in assemblies practised by the 'Aryan' race.* Further, the mixture of peoples, caused by trade and conquest and the practice of slavery, creates leisure. Without it, the patriarchs, for example, would not have had 'the steady calm which marks them'.[32] The effect of God-fearing armies is also salutary, and 'creeds and systems which conduce to a soft limp mind tend to perish'. The military contribution, of course, is limited; 'Military moral can

* The theory of an 'Aryan' linguistic group originating from Central Asia and derivative from Sanskrit, was based on the work of Sir Philip Jones in the late eighteenth century, and on Jacob Grimm's and Franz Bopp's philological speculations as revised by Schleicher, and popularized by Max Müller in his *Lectures on the Science of Language* in 1861. It was based on the hypothesis that Sanskrit was the root of the Indo-European language which included, in the West, the Greek, Latin and Teutonic speech. Neither Schleicher nor Müller regarded it as a term of racial affinity, and Müller had previously remarked 'that an ethnologist who spoke of an Aryan race was as bad as a philologist who spoke of a dolichocephalic dictionary'. (See PENNIMAN, op. cit., pp. 198-200.) It was believed that the original 'Aryan' speaking people lived in 'Ariana' in Central Asia, but their claims to linguistic paternity are disputed, since several European languages are older than Sanskrit. The legend of a blond Aryan 'race' is pure fantasy. It was subsequently argued, says Penniman, that the original Aryan tribe was a mixture of blondes and brunettes. These facts did not prevent the misinterpretation of the theory having great and terrible political consequences – an example of pernicious vulgarization, whereby the nineteenth and twentieth centuries created pseudo-scientific catchwords for which peoples were ready to die, in the same way as their ancestors were willing to perish for the popularized views of theologians.

direct the axe to cut down the tree, but it knows nothing of the quiet force by which the forest grows'.[33] Turning from the impact of war on the 'cake of custom', Bagehot examines with great insight the nature of leadership; he points out how men are led by 'catching' examples, rather than by argument, and attacks the deterministic view of history. Mind and character lead, not things. 'There is an odd idea that those who take what is called a "scientific view" of history need rate lightly the influence of individual character. It would be as unreasonable to say that those who take a scientific view of nature need think little of the sun.' His idea of evolution is creative, not passive. He cites homely examples from the rapidly changing tone in schools, following the influence of dominant boys, as showing the importance of personality in primitive societies.

His second essay on 'Nation Making' again shows how deeply the new discoveries of prehistory and anthropology had influenced his mind. He affirmed the reality of progress in face of the squalor of the primitive past, and of the limitations and fears of the minds of contemporary savages, 'so to say, tattooed over with monstrous images'. Here is a vivid contrast to the baseless fantasies of de Maistre, writing less than half a century before, who regarded primitive peoples as superior. Between de Maistre and Bagehot an intellectual revolution had supervened. He gives many examples of the incompetence and terror which afflict savages. 'They are playing a game — the game of life — with no knowledge of its rules'; they are 'like gamblers', and we well know how superstitious they are. Their religion centres on 'lucky beasts' and the enforcement of 'lucky rites'. There is little sense of property or family discipline. And the African chief who 'expressed his disgust at adhering to one wife by saying it was "like the monkeys",'[34] represented an enervated society. Such societies are always smashed by patriarchal peoples, who 'conquered the world in manhood because as children they were bred in homes where the tradition of passionate valour was steadied by the habit of implacable order'. The virtue of predatory conquerors swept superstition, self indulgence and incompetence into limbo.

In modern times progress has been peacefully achieved. In 'The Age of Discussion' Bagehot admirably suggests the origins of political and intellectual enterprise and liberty. It was in the small republics of Greece and Italy, he writes, 'that the chain of custom was first broken'. These states practised political discussion in their assemblies. Once this was habitual, all traditions were questioned and the desire for improvement came about. Normally men are paralysed

by custom, and only where there is political discussion can enterprise exist. In all customary societies bigotry is the ruling principle,
and 'one of the greatest pains to human nature is the pain of a new
idea'. 'It is, as common people say, "so upsetting".'[35] All centres
on the political structure, although much is due to the circumstances
of an age. For example, the England of Elizabeth I showed astonishing originality through combined intellectual, economic and geographical good fortune. 'The liberation of humanity', as Goethe used
to call it, was begun in another fortunate environment, in Greece.
A combination of political institutions and patriarchal tradition
allowed enterprise. The delicate plant of speculation managed to
survive, in spite of traditional hereditary despotism, or the new
tyranny of adventurers who dominated huge areas, having 'vaulted on
the backs' of the masses. Such liberties were extremely precarious
and were often smothered. There were many failed Romes, and free
cities only survived if originally distant from great centres of power.
Bagehot maintains that the intellectual freedom of the French
eighteenth-century 'despotism tempered by epigram' was kept
alive only through Dutch and English influence. He might have
added, like de Tocqueville, the astonishing effect of the tiny Puritan
communities of New England on the development of the entire North
American continent.

All this progress he traced ultimately to government by discussion.
Such a government is also 'the greatest hindrance to the inherited
mistake of human nature, to the desire to act promptly, which in a
simple age is so excellent but which in a later and complex time leads
to so much evil'.[36] This impulse reflects a wider problem. Reactions
suitable for a primitive environment are unsuited to modern life,
and the taming of political human nature is the great problem of our
time. Although Bagehot regards war and competition as necessary
to progress in the past, he assumes, like so many other thinkers of the
nineteenth century, that industrial civilization will bring easier
conditions. The mentality suited for civilized life, he admirably
defines as one of 'animated moderation'. It is, he believes, best
developed in England, where vigorous enterprise is often combined
with balanced judgment and the good sense to know where to stop.
Bagehot's ideal is oligarchic and bourgeois; that does not make it the
less suitable for an elaborate and interdependent society, or the less
salutary for the perennial problems of politics. Under all political
regimes, in foreseeable conditions, the problem of the control of
power is fundamentally similar, and Bagehot's solution of a wise and

flexible oligarchy, open to new ideas, is not to be despised. It is realistic in its good sense, its objectivity, its deliberate limitations.

These objectives are clearly defined in Bagehot's concluding chapter on 'Verifiable progress politically considered'. Here, for all his speculative brilliance, he takes up a thoroughly empirical position. Manning and Huxley, he says, would give hopelessly contradictory answers if the wider aspects of progress are considered. He therefore discards all ultimate speculation as unprofitable, and defines 'ascertainable progress' as a greater command of nature. This results in a 'confidence in the Universe', alien to the fear and superstition of primitive peoples. In energy and balance; in 'continuous well being' rather than 'wild excitement' and 'stupifying repletion'; in an organized pursuit of security and plenty. First things first, he says. Material progress is the basis of civilization.[37] It is of course precarious: lapses into 'atavism' are likely. There may easily be 'some strange recurrence to a primitive past', and societies may revert to the predominant monotony and conservatism normal in most places and times. Above all, there is danger that the excessive energy and restlessness inherited from the primitive past will shake the elaborate edifice of civilized life. None the less, he insists, command of environment and range of knowledge has vastly increased. This proven fact is mainly due to the salutary influence of political constitutionalism, which Bagehot had set against so wide and ancient a background.

I V

Tylor's masterpiece, *Primitive Culture, Researches into the Derivation of Mythology, Philosophy, Language, Art and Custom,** contains on its

* Sir Edward Burnett Tylor, 1832-1917. Started his career in a family business of brass-founders in the Midlands. He travelled for his health in North and South America and when in Cuba in 1856, met an archaeologist whom he accompanied to Mexico. His first book, *Anahuac, or Mexico and the Mexicans, Ancient and Modern*, a systematic study of a living culture, was published in 1861. In 1865 appeared his *Researches into the Early History of Mankind*, and in 1871, in the same year as DARWIN's *Descent of Man*, *Primitive Culture* (2 vols., 502 pp. and 471 pp. – 3rd edition revised 1891). It covers the Science of Culture, the Development of Culture, Survival in Culture, Emotional and Imitative Language, the Art of Counting, Mythology and Animism. The second volume deals with Animism, Rites and Ceremonies and a Conclusion. Tylor was the founder of systematic anthropology in England, opening up new fields of study, of which the religious aspect was to be further investigated by SIR JAMES FRAZER in *The Golden Bough*, and the social aspects by many scholars, of whom the best known to the public are now Malinowsky and Margaret Mead, and the most constructive is Evans-Pritchard. For a good short account of Tylor's significance see STANLEY CASSON, *The Discovery of Man*. London, 1939, pp. 238ff. 'It would indeed be difficult,' writes Casson, 'to estimate the enormous effect which Tylor's outlook had upon the development of anthropological thought.'

title page a quotation from de Brosses, 'Ce n'est pas dans les possibi-lités, c'est dans l'homme même qu'il faut étudier l'homme: il ne s'agit pas d'imaginer ce qu'il aurait pu ou dû faire, mais de regarder ce qu'il fait.' This concentration on facts, presented with studied and cool impartiality, sets the tone of a decisive book. It altered the perspective of political and religious ideas by setting them against the background of a primitive past and of the survival of savage thought in modern civilization: ... 'the English mind,' wrote this great pioneer investigator, 'not readily swayed by rhetoric, moves freely under the pressure of facts.'[38]

Only the contemporary German anthropologist Bastian* can be compared to Tylor in range, and he falls below him in exposition. For Tylor's temperate judgment is expressed in a dignified and trenchant style, enlivened by flashes of picturesque eloquence and humour. Throughout he insists on the practical implications of his science. 'The condition of culture among the various societies of mankind, in so far as it is capable of being investigated on general principles, is a subject apt for the study of laws of human thought and action.' Anthropology is highly relevant to the study of contem-porary society, where the uniform action of uniform causes may be traced, and 'various grades' mark 'the stages of development or evolution, each the outcome of previous history, and about to do its proper part in shaping the history of the future'. Like Buckle and Lecky, Tylor was convinced that human societies, like the rest of nature, obey ascertainable laws, which historians have been reluct-ant to investigate. 'To many educated minds there seems something presumptuous and repulsive in the view that the history of mankind is part and parcel of the history of nature ...' 'But let us take', he says, 'this admitted existence of natural cause and effect as our stand-ing ground, and travel ... as far as it will bear us. It is on the same basis that physical science pursues, with ever increasing success, its quest of laws of nature.'

This application of professional mid-nineteenth-century scientific method to the study of society is a landmark in the development of social thought. It at once puts traditional emotional responses and their mythology in a new light: it examines the pedigree of ideas, and brings comparative method to aid the sociologist. Here is a world of sober professional skill, very different from what Tylor calls 'the dashing invective of de Maistre', or from the isolated introspection of

* Adolph Bastian, 1826-1905, wrote a detailed account of exotic Civilizations – *Man in History* (1860), *The Peoples of Eastern Asia,* etc. See *Man,* vol. V, pp. 139-43.

Comte: something much more formidable and promising. It looks forward to the immense contributions of modern systematic sociology, and it retains a nineteenth-century clarity and eloquence of exposition. Irony and implication are here employed to point to devastating conclusions, and the vast field of human culture surveyed for the origin and the comparison of accepted prejudice. Tylor's aim is always practical. If early anthropology did not begin at home, its conclusions were consistently related to contemporary culture. 'Not merely as a matter of curious research, but as an important practical guide to the understanding of the present and the shaping of the future, the investigation into the origin and early development of civilization must be pushed on zealously.'[39] The result, though it led to over-ambitious claims to universal explanations, was to deepen knowledge of the entire basis of culture.

This research, he believed, would reveal certain limited but ascertainable laws of development. 'The tendency of modern inquiry is more and more towards the conclusions that if law is anywhere, it is everywhere . . . already it seems not too much to say that the vague outlines of a philosophy of primaeval history are beginning to come within our view.' Rudimentary as the 'science of culture' might be, certain uniformities of behaviour were apparent in primitive and savage societies all over the world. 'The ancient Swiss lake dweller may be set beside the medieval Aztec, and the Ojibwa of North America beside the Zulu of South Africa . . .' and 'if two independent visitors to different countries, say, a medieval Mohammedan in Tartary and a modern Englishman in Dahomy, or a Jesuit missionary in Brazil and a Wesleyan in the Fiji Islands, agree in describing some analogous art or rite or myth . . . it becomes difficult or impossible to set down such correspondence to accident or wilful fraud'.[40] Besides this evidence of broad similarity of development, there is also, Tylor believes, evidence for ascertainable progress in control of environment. As Gibbon remarked, 'The splendid days of Augustus and Trajan were eclipsed by a cloud of ignorance, and the barbarians subverted the laws and palaces of Rome. But the scythe, the invention or emblem of Saturn, still continued annually to mow the harvests of Italy . . . ' There is consequently, of course, no evidence of universal degeneration from a higher state, as de Maistre absurdly maintained, though there is evidence of broken down cultures, and the Irish were tying ploughs to their horses' tails in the seventeenth century. It had not occurred to them that harness might be more efficient. There was even a Malay tribe who deliberately 'gave up civilization'.

Yet, 'direct or devious,' the path of civilization 'lies forward.' Its objective is the 'general improvement of mankind by the higher organization of the individual and society, to the end of promoting at once man's goodness, power and happiness'. This gradual and chequered advance — 'civilization is a plant much more often propagated than developed' — is confirmed by the new evidence of prehistoric archaeology, 'a department of research only established on a scientific footing within the last few years', which has rendered previous speculations obsolete, and which holds the master key to the investigation of man's primeval condition.

This gradual, tentative, advance reflects the normal Darwinian principle of evolution. 'History within its proper field, and ethnography over a wider range, combine to show that the institutions that can best hold their own in the world gradually supersede the less fit ones, and that this incessant conflict determines the general resultant course of culture.'[11]

On this firm basis, Tylor boldly traces the similarity of primitive and savage ideas all over the world. He examines their contemporary survival in advanced civilizations 'which even now sets up in our midst primeval monuments of barbaric thought and life'. The intimate connection between modern cultures and primitive ideas, between Victorian England and a vast outer world, is proved by homely examples. What, he asks, are the origins of the familiar phrases — to sow wild oats, to raise the wind, to haul over the coals and to let the Devil take the hindmost? The first refers to the Scandinavian God Loki, the mischief-maker, who sows weeds among the crops; the second to the practices of wizards in Finland; the third to the ancient custom of ordeal, and the fourth to the belief that the devil claimed the last scholar of his class in the black arts for his fee.

The reader is also constantly confronted with outlandish origins in time and place.* Familiar proverbs and riddles prove to have extraordinary origins; the latter are characteristic of barbaric

* I, pp. 83-5. Even the familiar term 'Puss' evokes for Tylor the 'old Keltic name for the cat, Irish "Pus", Erse "Pusag", Gaelic "Puis".' 'Similar calls are known elsewhere in Europe . . . and there is some reason to think that the cat, which came to us from the East, brought with it one of its names, which is still current there, Tamil Pûsei . . .' Conversely, the name has spread out of Europe. 'Thus "boosi" is the recognized word for cat in the Tonga Islands . . . and not only is the European cat called a "puss-puss" in the Chinook jargon, but in the same curious dialect the word is applied to a native beast, the Cougar, now called "hyas puss-puss", i.e. great cat.' I, pp. 178-9.

societies all over the world — among Zulus, Anglo-Saxons and Poly-
nesians, among Mexicans and Scandinavians. The custom of drinking healths is related to sacrifice, even to the widespread barbaric
custom of walling up a victim in the foundations of a temple or a
fort.

Turning next, after a wealth of illustration, from such relics of
barbarism to the study of language, Tylor points out that it is a
clumsy instrument of expression. Evolved in primitive and savage
surroundings, it bears the marks of its origin. 'Compare', he says,
'the methods of language with the work it has to do.' Metaphor and
syntax 'the two great methods of naming thoughts and stating their
relation to one another . . . belong to the infancy of human expression'. The growth of language 'has far less to do with systematic
arrangement and scientific classification than with mere rough and
ready ingenuity and the great rule of thumb'. 'Let anyone,' he concludes, 'whose vocation it is to realize philosophical or scientific
conceptions and to express them in words, ask himself whether
ordinary language is an instrument planned for such purposes. Of
course it is not.' It has to be reinforced by gesture, and in general
the more gesture the lower the language. Language is, indeed, 'no
apt machine . . . but an old barbaric engine added to and altered,
patched and tinkered into some sort of capability.'[42] This treatment
of the limitations of language in a chapter of singular interest, foreshadowed a vital field of philosophical study. Here, as elsewhere,
Tylor indicated problems which have since loomed large.

Methods of calculation are equally primitive in origin. Those
incapable of mathematics will sympathize with the widespread
inability of savages to count. They will even applaud the action of
'question-worried' Tongans, who, exasperated beyond endurance
when asked to define numerals beyond their range, gave the per-
tinacious inquirers instead 'a little vocabulary of Tongan indecency'.[43]

Even more striking is the survival of animist myth in civilization.
Tylor intends to turn 'mythology to account as a means of tracing
the history of the laws of mind'; this is 'a branch of science scarcely
discovered till the present century'. The brisk eighteenth-century
rationalizations of the lexicographer Lemprière are irrelevant in this
study. It demands a more sympathetic approach. 'Starting with the
bold rough nature myths into which the savage moulds the lessons he
has learnt from his childlike contemplation of the universe, the
ethnographer can follow these rude fictions up into times when they
were shaped and incorporated into complex mythologic systems,

gracefully artistic in Greece, stiff and monstrous in Mexico, swelled into bombastic exaggeration in Buddhist Asia.'[44] Tylor passes in review a great accumulation of mythological lore, and asserts, with a wealth of curious illustration, the world-wide distribution of certain fundamental myths. The universal relation of mankind to animals is a notion by no means confined to the age of Darwin. 'To suppose', he remarks slyly, 'that theories of a relation between man and the lower mammalia are only a product of advanced science would be an extreme mistake.' Such legends were still common in Europe in the Middle Ages; for example, the well-known belief, so long and so widely held on the continent, that the English have tails. 'That zealous and somewhat foul-mouthed reformer, Bishop Bale writes, 'Johan Capgrave and Alexander of Esseby sayth, that for castynge of fyshe tayles at thys Augustyne, Dorsett Shyre menne hadde Tayles ever after. But Polydorus applieth it unto Kentish men at Stroud by Rochester for cutting of Thomas Becket's horse's tail. Thus hath England in all other land a perpetuall infamy of tayles by theyr wrytten legendes of lyes . . .'[45] This imputation was also made by the Sicilians against Richard I, with unpleasant consequences to themselves. It has now dwindled in our own country into 'a common-place of local slander' between Cornwall and Devon.

Needless to say, many stories of giants and monsters had been given wide circulation in the early middle ages through the writings of St. Isidore.* They often reflect folk memories of aboriginal peoples, bound up with weird legends of prehistoric burial mounds and haunted megalithic sites.

A more intimate primitive thought pervades civilization. Tylor investigates the development of the belief in an after life. Though the 'continuance theory' is part of the natural religion of primitive peoples, it is only in some higher civilizations that the rewards and penalties of heaven and hell have had vivid and decisive effects. They have been made 'to further goodness and to check wickedness according to the shifting rules by which men have divided right from wrong'.[46] With the advance of knowledge, it seems, such beliefs fade, so that they are 'alike absent from the beliefs of classes of men at the two extremes of culture'. The acceptance of this cool conclusion, without rhetoric or fuss, is characteristic of Tylor and the tradition he represents. It contrasts with the frantic blasphemies, self pity and self dramatization of a Schopenhauer or a Nietzsche. With calm good sense Tylor accepts this deprivation with

* For the contribution of this worthy to political thought see W.P.T., pp. 151-3.

a certain quiet integrity and regret. 'Yet he who believes that his thread of life will be severed once and for ever by the fatal shears, well knows that he wants a joy in life, which belongs to him who looks for a life to come.'

Along with these shifting beliefs in immortality, the custom of ancestor worship and propitiation of the dead is also world-wide — on the whole a beneficent influence. It shades into devil worship and also into the cult of Christian Saints. Among such local deities 'may be counted the diabolic soul of a certain wicked British officer, whom native worshippers in the Tinnevelly district still propitiate by offering at his grave the brandy and cheroots he loved in life'.[47] In Christian Europe, the habitation of the local God became the sanctuary of the local Saint, and a 'system of spiritual division of labour was in time worked out with wonderful minuteness in the vast array of professional saints'.

Throughout the ages the deep animal emotions of the people have thus been swayed by comparable ideas. They have been manipulated by a queer and often pathological minority — a situation since reflected in the vagaries of political fanatics. 'Thus, even in the lower culture, a class of sickly brooding enthusiasts begin to have that power over the minds of their lustier fellows, which they have kept in so remarkable a way through the course of history.'[48] Had Tylor's knowledge been more widely assimilated, the ascendancy of Marx, of Treitschke, or of Nietzsche might have been anticipated.

Behind this often pathological leadership, extends a dark vista of beliefs. The charms and amulets, the jujus and the fetishes, the sacred 'pillars', the stones stained with sacrificial blood, all reflect an animism which lurks close beneath the surface of civilized life. If in the West 'physics, chemistry and biology have seized whole provinces of ancient animism, the visionary temptations of the Hindu ascetic and the medieval saint are happening in our own day, though their place is rather in a medical handbook than in the record of miracles'. Individually an atavistic horror of darkness still haunts the civilized mind — 'in the dark ... evil spirits swarm'. 'Animals stare and startle when we see no cause', and 'the dogs could see Hela the [Scandinavian] death goddess move unseen by men'.[49] There are still few civilized men to whom the thought of ghost and doppelganger cannot bring a shiver down the spine.

Against this world-wide primitive background, latent even in the most advanced civilization, and conditioning the most modern thought, Tylor set the confident culture of his own Victorian age.

No one before had so intimately and systematically related nine-teenth-century civilization to its origins and to contemporary primitive peoples. Here is an investigation of human motives based on elaborate and systematic study, a marshalling of facts which profoundly illuminate the working of society. While this approach is now considered over-simplified and too linear, it is far more valuable than the intuitions dredged up by half-crazy philosophers from the depths of their sub-conscious minds, the projection of individual frustration and repression. Here, and not in the cloudy generalities of metaphysical assertion, is a valuable contribution of the new nineteenth-century professionalized knowledge. Tylor himself was profoundly concerned to establish the close connection between modern culture and its primitive origins. 'The thing that has been, will be', and the study of primitive motives and ideas throws light on motives now at work. The liberalism of the 'seventies was thus given ample warning of the powerful and irrational force which its shallow optimism ignored. Maine, Bagehot and Tylor all took a far more realistic view, and when Graham Wallas and Durkheim and Trotter later took up the theme, they were only following an approach already defined by the great pioneers of the mid-century.

Tylor's outlook, like that of most of his contemporaries, was consistently historical. The historian of society, he wrote, in the conclusion of his great book, 'must be called upon to show the hereditary standing of each opinion and practice'. This historical perspective modified the confidence with which he regards the advance of civilization. He is far more sober and realistic than Buckle or the early Lecky. 'It is our happiness to live', he writes, 'in one of those eventful periods of intellectual and moral history, when the oft-closed gates of discovery and reform stand open at their widest. How long these good days may last, we cannot tell.'[50] With vast anthropological knowledge behind him, Tylor could not share any naive hopes. 'It may be', he continues, 'that the increasing power and range of the scientific method, with its stringency of argument and constant check of fact, may start the world on a more steady and continuous course of progress than it has moved on heretofore. But if history is to repeat itself according to precedent, we must look forward to stiffer, duller ages of traditionalists and commentators, when the great thinkers of our time will be appealed to by men who slavishly accept their tenets, yet cannot or dare not follow their methods through better evidence to higher things.' This reversion to normal, to the statistically predominant 'cake of custom', is now apparent in the intellectually arrested orthodoxy of Stalinist Marxism. If this blight is not to spread, it will be through the maintenance of the standards which Tylor goes on to define. 'In either case, it is for those among us whose minds are set on the advancement of civilization, to make the most of present opportunities, that even when in future years progress is arrested, it may be arrested at the higher level.' To promote this progress the anthropologist must use his knowledge. 'To the promotion of what is sound . . . in modern culture ethnography has double help to give.' Far from fatalistically accepting the march of events, 'where barbaric hordes groped blindly, cultured men can often move onward with clear view'. And their function is to eradicate as well as to improve. 'It is a harsher, and at times even painful, office of ethnography to expose the remains of crude old culture which have passed into harmful superstitions, and to mark them out for destruction.' 'The science of culture', he concludes, 'is essentially a reformer's science.'[51]

So by a massive accumulation of fact, interpreted by a vivid imaginative sympathy, and described with great literary skill, Tylor had brought his contemporaries face to face with the intimate, bloody, and irrational background of all civilization. By implication his book purged contemporary superstition, and still leaves an impression of profound conviction. The outlook to which it leads is saddened but clear. It accepts the limitations of the human lot, and armed with new knowledge and the characteristic Victorian passion for truth, which Tylor shared with Darwin and Huxley, it faces the austere implications of modern science with a decent irony and sober confidence. For here, in increased knowledge, was also the prospect of amelioration and control. Tylor's influence was to dominate anthropology. It was carried on, modified, by the work of Durkheim; it made for an outlook empirical, cautious and sure. 'An inspection of the geographical distribution of art and knowledge among mankind,' he wrote, 'seems to give some grounds for the belief that the history of the lower races, as of the higher, is not the history of a course of degeneration, or even of equal oscillation to and fro, but a movement, which, in spite of frequent stops and relapses, has on the whole been forward; that there has been from age to age a growth of man's powers over nature which no degrading influences have been able permanently to check.' On this basis of ascertained fact, the advance of society could be systematically promoted, and he looked forward to the day when anthropology should develop 'from a derided byeway to truth, to a time when its help and decisions are sought by governments'. In spite of current catastrophes, and a less ambitious method than Tyler envisaged, that help is today being increasingly invoked.

v

The three writers here described have in common a sober and practical judgment, and the capacity to accept uncomfortable conclusions without excitement. Maine points out the rarity of progress, the dangers which attend the concentration of power necessary for improvement by legislation, and the limits of the range of constitutional government. Bagehot, with his vivid sense of the irrational element in civilization, and understanding of the routine and discipline which custom and isolation have imposed in the long and broad course of history, also set Victorian liberal optimism in a more realistic light. And he brilliantly described how illogically, in fact, English constitutional custom proceeds. Tylor, with his far ranging investigation of primitive habits and beliefs, also insists in the irrational and primitive aspect of society. While well aware of the grin of savagery behind the mask of culture, he sought to make anthropology constructive, an aid to government. In contrast to the hysterical reactions of philosophers, fascinated or horrified at the implications of Darwinism, they all display a cautious, empirical, respect for truth. All three, accepting the facts and carrying on J. S. Mill's conception of social studies already described, set about the business of gradually improving society in the light of new knowledge. This desire for improvement, and the sense of the importance of the whole life of institutions, was to be reinforced by the theoretical enrichment of the theory of Constitutional government made by T. H. Green. This contribution will now be examined.

CHAPTER IV

NEO-HEGELIAN HUMANISM
T. H. GREEN: F. H. BRADLEY

THE reaction against Utilitarian laissez-faire and individualism, already apparent in the later work of J. S. Mill, was given a creative, if rather esoteric and local content, by a group of academic writers whose political influence long predominated in British universities. The movement began in Balliol, an Oxford college whose liberal humanists combined high ideals with a formidable rigour of mind. Jowett, the famous Master of Balliol, created a tradition of academic brilliance, humane insight and worldly success. He was deeply influenced by Platonic and German philosophy. He was concerned, like so many of the thinkers examined in this study, to retain a Christian basis for morality while assimilating new knowledge. His influence was pervasive, vigorous and salutary. The tradition of Victorian Balliol made an impact on society probably unique in the history of a British academic institution.* It was predominantly directed to the expansion of humane values in legislation and high policy, and to immediate missionary enterprise through settlements in industrial cities. The most brilliant and level-headed exponent of the liberal aspect of its political theory was T. H. Green.† His

---

* Symbolized by the transformation of its architecture in the 'sixties, which still gives the college the aspect of a battleship.

† Thomas Hill Green, 1836-82, was born in the West Riding of Yorkshire, son of the Rev. Valentine Green, rector of Birkin, who came of a Leicestershire family of Puritan descent. Educated at Rugby, he early displayed strong moral feelings, a 'certain solid wilfulness' and an independent mind. 'He was a boy apart,' writes a contemporary. 'Even then, he seemed to us boys to have something of the character of Cromwell about him – his favourite hero . . . A sixth fellow . . . in whose presence no one in the house would have found it possible to use a bad word or tell a ribald story; a water drinker in those days, when he was probably the only one of four hundred to be so.' 'With a boy like this,' says his biographer, Nettleship, 'it is not surprising that few of his fellows were intimate.' In 1855 he entered Balliol, where he came under the influence of Jowett, whom he greatly admired. 'The more I see of him, the more I am convinced of his remarkable goodness and genius.' As a freshman he took, at first, a grim view of the University, 'the functionaries being wholly given to quiet dishonesty and the undergraduates to sensual idleness'. After his election to a Fellowship in 1860 and a Tutorship in 1866, he apparently mellowed, though he was not without a certain studied faroucheness sometimes found in academic circles. In 1864-65 he undertook an inspectorship of Schools in the Midlands, and with the election of Jowett to the Mastership of Balliol in 1870, he undertook the main administrative duties of the College. He arranged that exhibitions should be awarded to extra-mural students and started a hostel for them in St. Giles; and in 1867 he carried through the abolition of compulsory chapel in Balliol and the substitution of a roll call. In 1871 he married Charlotte Symonds, sister of John Addington Symonds. Apart from

Lectures on the Principles of Political Obligation, which were delivered in 1879-80 and published after his death in 1882, form the most valuable, closely reasoned, and practical case for Victorian Liberal humanism.* The book is exacting to the reader: it cuts to the root of fundamental problems and remains indispensable to the study of nineteenth-century politic thought. This approach was later developed by Edward Caird, who was Master of Balliol (1893-1907) in succession to Jowett, and by William Wallace, a Balliol man who succeeded Green. Arnold Toynbee, a Fellow of Balliol, founded Toynbee Hall in the east end of London. He died in 1882, at thirty-one. Bernard Bosanquet, a scholar of Balliol, became a Fellow of University College, and lectured for the London Ethical Society and for charity organizations. As Professor of Moral Philosophy in the University of St. Andrews (1903-8), he elaborated the metaphysical Hegelian element of this school of thought. F. H. Bradley, a Fellow of Merton College, Oxford, also had affinities with this group of Oxford Idealists, but he is far more conservative — a highly sophisticated and eloquent metaphysician, whose brilliant, rather feverish, eloquence advocates a negative attitude to politics, very different from the moral zeal apparent in the others. His view of the duty of political philosophers and his influence towards a cult of the state, will also be examined.

II

L. T. Hobhouse, a most effective critic of the later and more theoretical manifestations of Idealism, remarked of Green, 'his living interest was in practical life, and the strength of his grasp lay upon

* The book was edited by Nettleship after Green's death, and is prefaced by an extract from his lectures, *Prolegomena to Ethics*, 'on the different senses of freedom applied to Will and the Moral Progress of Man' (25 pp). It is then divided as follows: The Grounds of Political Obligation; Spinoza; Hobbes; Locke; Rousseau; Sovereignty and the General Will (Rousseau and Austin); Will, not Force the Basis of the State; Has the Citizen any Rights Against the State? Private Rights, the Right to Life and Liberty; The Rights of the State over the Individual in War; The Right of the State to promote Morality, etc. In all, 347 pages in the edition, with preface by Bosanquet, published in 1921.

his teaching, which was gaining great influence, Green was the first Fellow of a College to be elected a Town Councillor for Oxford City. In 1875 he opened a 'Coffee Tavern' in St. Clements as a counter-attraction to the three hundred odd public houses then extant in the town, and in 1876 he became President of an optimistic brotherhood, 'the Oxford Band of Hope Temperance Union'. In 1878 he was elected to the Whyte Chair of Moral Philosophy. He died suddenly from septicaemia in 1882. Of puritan and evangelical mind, and a philosopher and personality of quietly compelling power, Green possessed singular humour, force and humanity. His appearance as a young man was striking, 'Thick black hair, dark eyebrows, eyes of rich brown with a particularly steadfast look . . an air of solidity and quiet strength.'

the hard problems of social reform'.* And again, 'in his polished lectures Green never forgets that theoretical principles affect life'. Politics, in the view of all these writers, is a branch of ethics. The aim of the state is to promote the good life. Since they were sceptical of Thomism, which had always taken a similar view, they were forced to create for themselves a new philosophy as a basis for the moralization of power. The Scottish influence, later so important in their theory, made for a metaphysical approach, for they were not content with a pragmatic basis for humane action.† They drew upon a long tradition of political thought going back to Plato and Aristotle, and derived also from Spinoza, Rousseau and Kant. They were impressed by Hegel's dynamic and abstract philosophy; and influenced, like Mill, by the humanitarian ideals of Comte, though not by Comte's atheism. Hegel's more humane ideas were lifted from their original and sometimes sinister context, developed and modified.‡ The later, more academic, manifestations of Idealism, in particular Bosanquet's theory of the State, have been scarified by Hobhouse and Plamenatz, who have made formidable criticisms of the collectivist and metaphysical tendencies of this school.

Meanwhile, these reforming humanists accustomed the later Victorians to a new conception of the State. They were behind the reforms of the 'seventies and of later liberal administrations. Since the aim of the State was the good life, conditions must be created in which its attainment is possible by all — a very large order to be carried out by government and by the institutions it harmonized. Here, already, was a powerful influence making for the Welfare State. When, ten years later, the Fabian onslaught on capitalism developed, the ground, as Sidney Webb was to remark, was already prepared by Liberal legislation, the basis of Fabian achievement. The first foundations of the Socialist State were laid by Liberal humanists and its legislation enacted by statesmen trained, as was Asquith, in this Oxford way of thought.§

* L. J. HOBHOUSE, *The Metaphysical Theory of the State*. Allen & Unwin, 1918, p. 122.
† Green, who was thoroughly English, distrusted the wilder side of Hegel; the later Scottish idealists, on the other hand, accepted and elaborated it.
‡ See Lord Lindsay's opinion of Hegel, already quoted.
§ As Laski pointed out, the influence of Jowett and Green on Asquith was direct. Temperamentally a Whig, the Prime Minister was willing to support Lloyd George and Churchill.
'Why', asks Laski, 'did so matured a Whig take up this attitude? Asquith was a Balliol man, in an era when Benjamin Jowett, its Master, had set out to make the College a nursery of statesmanship. Jowett had already shown the direction of his interest in the important part he had played in helping to get Civil Service reform accepted. He was, too, engaged in his well-known translation of Plato. A task not, I think, unconnected

Today the work of T. H. Green seems less original than it did to contemporaries. It restates, in dynamic and philosophical form, a very old constitutional tradition, going back into the mists of Antiquity, for it is based on the time-honoured distinction between society and government. Since Burke had made his eloquent and conservative contribution to that theme, and Coleridge had rather vaguely elaborated it, a raw Utilitarian individualism had intervened, and Austin has taken and developed from Hobbes and Bentham the idea of strictly positive Law. Green was original in attempting to recreate a new inspiration for criticism of government, as well as a court of ultimate appeal. Emergent Will, the best sense of the whole society, provided a dynamic version of the old static framework of Natural Law familiar in medieval thought, the reflection of Divine revelation as defined, for example, by Hooker. As already emphasized, this idea of emergent will is apparent in various guises; in the thought of Spinoza, in the political writings of Rousseau, and in the *Weltbürgerlich* philosophy of Kant. Since Hume's criticism of Natural Reason, will, not analytic thought, had come to be regarded as the expression of creative freedom. Some queer versions of the most influential of these conceptions, Rousseau's General Will, had already played an immense part in the world. It was now skilfully reinterpreted. Though an obvious myth not susceptible to analysis — as such later riddled by Pareto and Sorel* — it symbolized a social fact — the changing, creative, development of society as a whole in which all the people were included. By asserting that 'Will not Force' was the basis of State, Green was giving his political ideas a dynamic neo-Hegelian aspect. 'Will', in this context, was hardly a happy term for so instinctive a process, but Rousseau's idiom is generally misleading. To modern minds, who take for granted the importance of the fabric of society, and the massive life which institutions spontaneously generate, this assertion of the social framework

* See the former's unsympathetic analysis of the idea, which he regards as a meaningless, if politically useful, 'sentiment'. See *The Mind and Society*, vol. III, Section 1608 (pp. 1048ff), 'Sentiment in Thinking'. For Sorel's opinion of Rousseau vide *infra*, p. 406. PLAMENATZ, in his *Consent, Freedom and Political Obligation*, London, 1938, also has some incisive criticisms.

with the return to the Greek ideal of the state, so essential a part of the new political philosophy. He gave the major tone to the College. And Asquith's tutor was T. H. Green, not only himself a man of noble heart and distinguished mind, but the thinker who – more than any other – symbolizes the turning away from the old individualism . . . the general atmosphere of Balliol and the special contacts he made there, accustomed Asquith early in life to the acceptance of doctrine to which, temperamentally, he would not have been naturally inclined.' See *Ideas and Beliefs of the Victorians*, Sylvan Press, 1949, p. 421.

as against the executive will not seem startling. At the time it seemed an innovation. The new fields which Green and his followers re-discovered through the study of Greek and German political thought were soon also to be charted and examined by English sociologists. Apart from the cardinal work of Durkheim in France, Graham Wallas and L. T. Hobhouse were later to enrich this neo-Hegelian awareness of the life of society. With the development of a more precarious situation in the twentieth century, the unconscious drives of society were to be regarded with greater distrust. But by the turn of the century, the objectives of both liberal and scientific humanists were destined to coincide. Both realized the importance of institutions for the development of personality, both desired to use them for the furtherance of the good life, both desired a demo-cratic society and the extension of humane values. They believed in the integrity, the importance and the goodness of free personality. The state, wrote Green, has a liberating function; it should 'hinder hindrances to the good life'. It should encourage and harmonize institutions which embodied a way of life directed to good ends, in which self was transcended in a wider freedom. Hobhouse, a spokes-man of the scientific humanists, writing in 1917 in darker mood, puts the matter more grimly. He desires to avert the misery of man-kind. He hopes to extend into public life, national and international, the morality of the 'simple relation of man to man', to humanize the State. His view is the antithesis of Herbert Spencer's brutal and influential gospel of ruthless competition.

T. H. Green's theory assumes the potential creative power and goodness of men, all of whom have something to contribute accord-ing to their talents and limitations, all of whom are included. This liberalism, whether idealist or scientific, repudiates St. Augustine's or de Maistre's belief in original sin which can only be redeemed by supernatural revelation, or Nietzsche's distinction between masses and elites, his contempt and detestation of ordinary mankind. It would seem, also, to have little in common with any modern cult of the social protectorate, however well intentioned, and it is at total enmity with Marxist-Stalinist doctrines of inevitable class war and monolithic dictatorship. It implies rather a liberation of creative power than the imposition of any social pattern upon it. It is a hope-ful creed; anthropocentric, yet attempting transcendence. It could be shared by agnostics as well as Anglicans of uncertain belief. If in Bradley it produced a vague metaphysical religion with a conservative bias, in Green it led to powerful movements of reform. It was defined by academic men in a sheltered society when the prospects of peace and progress seemed good. With their vivid intellectual life, unworldly standards of wealth and duty, and strong middle-class family loyalty, they continued to assert, in spite of the predominant materialism of their age, the place of humane ideals in society and their faith in the power of the classes and the people to assimilate them. Reinforcing denunciations by Carlyle, Ruskin and Matthew Arnold of the 'Barbarians' and the 'Philistines', they proved an extremely influential minority. They belonged to a milieu very different from the militarist world of Treitschke's Berlin period, of French Royalist nationalism, or of Kipling. Different, too, from the close bitter world of the revolutionary refugees, or the stark horizons of Schopenhauer and Nietzsche, atheists, who because they could not have everything, believed in nothing. These elevated, fundamentally religious, minds, with their neo-Greek, neo-Puritan, creed of self-rewarding morality, their careful charitable lives, their strong social conscience, were guarded by the fleets and guns of the greatest naval power in the world. They could afford their optimism. Yet their reforms were realized in legislation while their country was entering an armaments race that led to catastrophes which were to shake the foundations of the liberal world. So when the reforms which they advocated were coming to fruition, their initiative, like the Fabians', seemed dwarfed by the colossal realities of world conflict and economic dislocation, which threatened to make the Welfare State seem provincial and out of place — a fool's paradise in a sinking civilization.

But the size of events does not alter their moral quality, and in the still small voice of radical humanism there may yet be found, in principle, a remedy for the massive brutalities of a militant age. It was the expression of a high and powerful civilization which asserts creative personality, the achievements of the human spirit, against the impoverishment and subnormality of war. Such humanism, backed by adequate power and more effective sociology, realized in wider institutions, may yet have a decisive effect. It sums up, in important aspects, and in a new idiom, the best sense of that tradition of political thought which had come down from a pre-industrial past; which had been carried on by de Tocqueville and J. S. Mill, and which was to be further developed by Acton.

The foundations of this liberal outlook as defined by Green are worth further attention. The style of the *Principles* is singularly dry, but it is uncompromising, muscular, exact. Green's other writings, in particular his treatment of the English Revolution in the seventeenth century, often glow with a vivid and compelling eloquence, although, in the light of more recent evidence few historians would now defend his nonconformist cult of Cromwell.* Green's outlook is thoroughly humanistic. Since consciousness imperfectly reflects the self-realization of God, the liberation of personality is the highest end of man. This can only be achieved through relating personality to institutions which represent the accumulated highest common good in society. The Stoics, with their Law of Nature; St. Paul, redeemed through Christ; Kant, formulating the doctrine of the Good Will; Hegel and the dynamic self-realization of the Absolute, had all contributed to this liberation. Like St. Paul, who distinguishes between appetite and salvation, Green distinguishes between objects of temporary desire, which 'interfere with the seeker's possibilities or his progress towards perfection', and permanent objectives which draw out the highest qualities. Although Hegel 'thinks of the state in a way not familiar to Englishmen', he thinks of it 'in a way not unlike that in which Greek philosophers thought of the πόλις, as a society governed by laws and institutions and established customs which secure the common good of society — enable them to make the best of themselves'.[1] When related to such institutions, individuals find 'a content or object which has been . . . brought into being by that consciousness itself as working through generations of men, and interests are thus applied to the man of a more concrete kind'.

Society, Green believed, with the optimism of his generation, was improving; 'the number of individuals whom society awakes to interest in objects contributory to [their] perfection tends to increase'. Here is a similar view to that expressed by Spencer, Buckle and Lecky. Even the conservative Bagehot, it will be recalled, shared the assumption. J. S. Mill hoped for it: Marx and Engels believed that social salvation would be accelerated by understanding of the laws which governed society. Though in profound disagreement with Spencer's individualism or Marxist dialectic, Green shared this common belief in progress. It was a practical objective, succinctly

---

* 'It was this exhilaration of energy in the Lord's work, not the vulgar ambition of Kingship that shone in Cromwell's countenance', etc. *Works*, vol. III, p. 354.

defined in his last public utterance. 'We may hope and pray', he said, 'for a condition of English society in which all honest citizens will recognize themselves and be recognized by each other as gentlemen.'[2] Such sober, yet idealistic, levelling-up to middle class standards, would prove, he thought, the basis of higher consciousness for some, and for a general improvement of moral tone for all. This optimism seems strange in a world which contained the conditions depicted by Marx and Engels, with the better aspects of the old order so much pulverized by the impact of great industry. But Green, a countryman by upbringing, was not so deeply preoccupied as Marx with industrial 'laws'. He set much store, too, by personal contacts; had little apprehension, it seems, that the coming of mass democracy might mean levelling down.

In this context, the state — and other institutions within it — regain the moral purpose denied by the Utilitarians and become a means, direct or indirect, of the enrichment of men's lives. This ideal is both Platonic and Puritan; it demands a strict self-discipline, an unflagging will, and a concern with other people's business. Here, in modern guise, is the outlook which was thought to have inspired some of the better Puritan Independents, without Calvinist fatalism or sense of sin. The state, therefore, has it duty: it should promote the good life by legislation and put down abuses that interfere with it. Here is a very wide commission. In the light of this cautious philosophy, Green concentrates on the 'object served by law',[3] and sets out to consider what is of permanent value in the institutions of modern Europe. He is also led to reconsider the old idea of a law of nature, '*jus naturae* . . . with reference to the moral end, as serving which alone law and the obligations imposed by law have their value'.[4] Ignoring the large field of medieval speculation, he is drawn to analyse the political thought of Spinoza, Hobbes, Locke and Rousseau with singular acuteness. Significantly he quotes, in a footnote, the German jurist Ulrici on Natural Law, or *Recht*. '*Recht* is that which is really necessary to the maintenance of the material conditions essential to the existence and perfection of human personality.' Amid the working of actual institutions, it reflects what ought to be. This view he cites against the negative Utilitarian theory that law should merely enforce contracts and prevent interference with individual enterprise — a view which has 'gained undue favour on account of the real reforms to which it has led'.[5]

With this standard in mind, Green embarks on a trenchant and still valuable historical survey. In the works of Spinoza, that pioneer humanist, he naturally finds some support. Quoting from the *Tractatus Politicus*, he admits that Spinoza founds his state on a ferocious idea of the law of nature, whereby every creature in 'suo esse perseverare conuntur', striving always to intensify its own being and power. And the state's right, according to Spinoza, can be only the reflection of superior force. But since the state expresses Reason, and its 'finis' is 'pax vitaeque securitas', it creates moral values within its own field, 'Homines enim civiles non nascuntur sed fiunt', and 'potentia' becomes 'jus'. Men are not born citizens, but they become so.[6]

Hobbes, with his fiction of contract, Green finds less realistic and less rewarding. The degradation of government into a mere convenience naturally disgusts him, as it had shocked Hobbes's contemporaries. It is through this positivist and limited view of law, Green insists, that there has since grown up an 'inveterate irreverence of the individual towards the State', an impoverishing hostility to the powers that be.

That hostility has been further fostered by Locke's theory of contract, with its dependence on artificial natural right, which existed prior to society. Only Spinoza has the correct, organic conception. But Locke, rightly, limits the power of government, since there should always be a power of society held in reserve against the executive. This idea is salutary, if negative, based on a static assertion of individual natural rights, rather than on a creative sense of society as a whole. It was not until Rousseau, with his dynamic idea of the General Will constantly at work, that the organic nature of the state, familiar to Antiquity, is again adequately asserted — an 'auguster thing' than mere government — the modern θεῖος νοῦς. Yet often Rousseau is misleading. Green begins a long liberal tradition of explaining him. For Rousseau confused the legal term sovereignty with the General Will. 'Thus the question of what really needs to be enacted by the state in order to secure the conditions under which a good life is possible, is lost sight of in the quest for majorities'. 'As the will of the people, in any other sense than the measure of what the public will tolerate, is really unascertainable in the great nations of Europe, the way is prepared for the sophistries of modern political management, for manipulating electoral bodies ... and procuring plebiscites.'[7] Further, Rousseau used the misleading old fiction of contract when his conception of society was organic. In analysing the views of this paradoxical romantic, Green is particularly wise. He concludes that Rousseau's conception of the General Will, as distinct from the will of all, is immensely valuable — 'the permanently valuable thing in Rousseau'.[8] But it could only be realized in Swiss cantons, and would certainly be stifled in societies on a greater scale. 'There was no state in Europe at his time in which his doctrine would not have inspired rebellion, and even under existing representative systems the conditions are not fulfilled . . .' Rousseau, therefore, has been misinterpreted. His views are invoked to justify the tyranny of demagogues, when the only system under which his General Will might harmoniously operate, would be one of direct democracy, of 'federated self-governing communes, small enough to allow each member an active share in the legislation. . .' .[9]

This early and penetrating examination of Rousseau, the firm extraction of the gold from the dross, is highly characteristic of Green's exact mind. Proceeding to discuss sovereignty and the General Will, Green makes a singularly thorough and fair examination of a fundamental problem, and endeavours to meet the most formidable objections to his argument. He attacks Austin's conception of positive law as the mere command of a superior, borrowed, he declares, from Hobbes. He contrasts this barren concept with Rousseau's idea of the creative General Will, and cites Maine's *Early Institutions* for the importance in society of custom, opinion and consent. As before emphasized, he reiterates an ancient constitutional tradition, found in classical and medieval thought, that the commonwealth as a whole is above the ruler. But he frees it from the fiction of contract and artificial natural rights; he endows it with an anthropocentric, dynamic and mystical content. It contrasts with the revealed and transcendental sanctions of the old pagan or Christian Natural Law, of which human law, according to Cicero and St. Thomas, is a reflection. Green thus invokes the then novel historical analysis of law. Sovereignty, he insists, is no mere fiat of arbitrary power; it no longer even resides in 'a determinate person or persons, but in the impalpable congeries of the hopes and fears of a people, bound together by common interests and sympathy, which we call the general will'.* If despotic power sets itself against this tide of habit and will, it cannot long survive. Constitutionalism as Maine insists, is rooted in custom and ways of life.

Yet it is dangerous, following Rousseau, to call the general will 'sovereign'. Sovereignty is associated with immediate coercive power, and 'when we have pronounced the general will sovereign, we are pretty sure to identify the general will with a vote of the

* p. 98. Compare Burke. 'The great contexture of the mysterious whole.'

majority of citizens'. This misinterpretation of liberal theory is, of course, constantly made, and probably passes for democratic theory in most minds today. Green, on the other hand, who sets the liberation of personality for the good life as the supreme purpose of his society, places the ultimate sanction not in a majority, but in the best sense of the whole people. Not in what they are but in what they may become.* As Bagehot had observed it in primitive societies, the general sense of the community was heavily conservative: in the progressive context of his time, Green attempts to preserve its sanction, with a new, creative, drive.

He accepted, however, one grave limitation. It was natural at the time, and it was to prove the greatest weakness of liberal thought. So anxious was Green to maintain the homogeneity of the state, that he never looks far beyond it. 'It is easy to conceive,' he writes, 'a better system than that of the great states of modern Europe, with their national jealousies, rival armies, and hostile tariffs; but the condition of any better state of things would seem to be the recognition of some single constraining power, which would be even more remote from the active co-operation of the individual citizen than the sovereign power of the great states at present.'[10] The answer, as pointed out by Proudhon, who had a similar concern for civic vitality, might be a federation. This could better combine local self-government with the rule of law in the wider sphere of international relations. It may seem curious that Green, with his passionate moral sense, his cult of personality, should have accepted the degenerate international framework of his time — the hypertrophy of the successor states of that ancient universal Christendom originally inspired by the great cosmopolitan Church he detested. But in the sanguine, progressive, atmosphere of the age, the consequence of international anarchy was masked, and if Green was wrong, he erred for good reason. Yet, in this context, Proudhon was the wiser man.

Not that Green ignored the evil aspects of the nation state. In passages afterwards criticized by Bosanquet, an overestimated and far less realistic thinker, who went much further along the collectivist road, he admits that the poorer classes at present may seem to have

* Here, in Plamenatz's opinion, the idealist school is on dangerous ground. For 'laws, customs and social conventions are not the least of the causes that have developed and made permanent in men some of the most unpleasant qualities which civilization has brought to light. We are always agitating against them, inspired to do so by the wise men of our time'. Green might have retorted: 'You can so agitate because you live under a liberal democratic state, and it is through your agitation that your society remains creative.'

little interest in it.[11] He even admits its dubious pedigree. 'Is it not seriously misleading,' he asks, 'when the requirements of the State have so largely arisen out of force directed by selfish motives, when the motive to obedience to these requirements is determined by fear, to speak of it as having a common source with the morality of which it is admitted that the essence is to be disinterested and spontaneous?'[12] Yet, in spite of these objections, he finds, like Burke and Hegel, that man is born into society, with common memories, tradition and customs, language and literature: 'intelligent patriotism' should be possible, not only passive loyalty. 'The citizens of the Roman Empire were loyal subjects . . . but they were not intelligent patriots, and chiefly because they were not, the Empire fell.' The ties which enmesh the individual in society should be comparable to those which bind him to his family life.

To support this dynamic view of the state, Green invokes the authority of science. The 'recognition of ends immanent in Nature, or ideas realized within it, is the basis of a scientific explanation of life'. But where the drive of more primitive organisms is blind, and all are conditioned by environment, the evolution of human societies is given 'character' by consciousness. The emergence of this character is tentative and uneven. 'In the earth-hunger of conquering hordes, in the passion of military despots, in the pride or avarice . . . which moved such men as Louis XI and Henry VIII . . . what is there of reference to such good?' But the will of tyrants, he maintains, is often diverted through circumstances beyond their control, and some good came of the conquests of Napoleon. 'It is thus that the actions of men, whom in themselves we reckon bad, are overruled by good', so that 'in some measure [even Napoleon] represented the struggle of mankind towards perfection'.[13]

Given the capacity for moral development through the enrichment of the 'character' of the state, and since such development can only come about in an ordered and free society, Green very reluctantly concedes to arbitrary governments the name of state. Here, in nineteenth-century terms, is the old medieval distinction between 'princeps' and 'tyrannus'; between 'regal' and 'regal and political' government.* 'We only count Russia', he writes, 'a state by a sort of courtesy.' It was a far-ranging distinction. It led to conclusions later developed in Green's views on war. He had practically denied

---

* Defined, for example, in the first treatise on political theory in the English tongue – FORTESCUE's *Governaunce of England*. 'There bith ij kindes off kyngdomes, regal, where the King is absolute, and regal and political where the Kynge may not rule the people bi other lawes than such as thai assenten unto.' Chap. I, see *W.P.T.*, p. 227.

moral sanction to methods of government still prevalent over vast areas of the world.

To describe really moral government, the term 'state', he continues, is hardly suitable. 'If any other word, indeed, can be found to express the same thing by all means let it be used instead.' The traditional term commonwealth might serve. All derives from the end — or the idea of it — served by commonwealth. There is 'no right but thinking makes it so'. Where St. Thomas or Fortescue invoked transcendent Natural Law, Green regards the moral sanction as immanent and emergent through man. It is the middle way between the optimism of the old Stoic view of natural law and the Epicurean pessimism which regards nature as sub-human.* In contrast to Marx, Green asserts that the ideal is 'not dependent on anything material, but has its being solely in consciousness'. This view reflects his monistic philosophy, which regards the whole universe and experience as one, so that the creative moralization of society reflects a cosmic event. Perhaps, he writes, 'we should find ourselves compelled to regard social good as a communication to the human consciousness, developing itself in time from an eternally complete consciousness', which here has its seat in the mind of man. In spite of this metaphysical ambience, the creed is anthropocentric. There is, first, an understanding that morality is rooted in custom; second, that constitutionalism is custom developed and rationalized and made more humane; and, third, an attempt to make that constitutionalism dynamic, since it is the means to fullness of life. Here is an answer to the doctrine of revolutionary class war; the development of the human spirit through the moralization of existing power. How far that moralization went will later be examined, when Green's remarks on war and property come to be considered.

Discussing the rights of free citizens, ἴσοι καὶ ὅμοιοι, 'doing and being done by', Green insists that even men subject to arbitrary power have rights as members of the human race:[14] through their 'social relation' as opposed to their subjection to government. Stateless persons, too, have human rights. And again, if the state falls away from the moral standard it exists to promote, it may be resisted. It is the old argument of Hunton, Lawson and Locke, without its theological idiom.[15] On the other hand, if the state is

---

* See W.P.T., p. 81. 'There is also a third view which regards values as emergent, which holds that in man and his societies the cosmic process becomes conscious of itself, and makes its natural "law" as it goes along.'

morally progressing, resistance is not morally justified. Here is at once a right of resistance, and, a wide opportunity for the reformer. Green doubtless has temperance legislation in mind. The rights of the State against individuals are thus regulated by its conformity or non-conformity to a subjective and evangelical-liberal conception of moral law.[16] The fate of the temperamentally rebellious, the topers, artists, Bohemians, and other oddly adjusted persons, will not be much more enviable in Green's commonwealth than in Plato's, though they will doubtless be treated with more sweetness and light.

In spite of his Puritan zeal for reform, especially in the matter of temperance, Green is in general a realist. The good aimed at must command popular consent; be 'such as the public conscience is capable of apprehending'. This apprehension must develop by discussion and missionary enterprise. Reform comes not from the fiat of authority, but from the General Will.

Green's morality is not static, if it is sometimes provincial. The outlook, a cosmopolitan critic might suggest, of the well conducted rectory or dissenting chapel. But in Green's state all are treated as ends, not as means, and there is free enterprise within the law. The General Will might thus in time become more colourful, more sophisticated, far more widely tolerant. For it encourages enterprise and is open to persuasion.

Against this sober humanism, based on an intuitive perception of good, and backed by a rather vague metaphysic, the private rights of individuals are further examined. They are related to war, nationalism, crime and property. In this remarkable book, one of the finest works of nineteenth-century political thought, largely the foundation of the later liberal creed and still full of interest, the great problems of political conduct are never burked. The answers may seem inadequate, but all the problems are raised.

How, for example, can the right to a 'free life' be reconciled with war? An apparently impersonal catastrophe, which 'breaks out' like a plague, it is an intentional waste. It violates basic rights and the habit of mutual protection. Can it ever be justified? Only if the integrity of free states is menaced by aggression. All are involved in complicity with aggression — 'in that radical (but conquerable because moral) evil of mankind which renders such a means of maintaining political freedom necessary'.[17] This view may imply the prevention of war by free states through the extension of civilized methods of government. It had already been carried further by

Kant. In his *Project for Perpetual Peace* he had written, 'It is a duty to make actual a condition of public justice.'[18] War, in fact, as de Maistre believed, is a punishment for sin, but not, as de Maistre insists, 'an external infliction brought about by agencies to which man is not a party'.*

Green was aware of the dangers of popular nationalism. Most wars have been brought about by dynastic, commercial or nationalist ambition, and a 'diffused desire for excitement'. But there is 'no such thing as an inevitable conflict between states', though, he alleges, the machinations of the Catholic Church create it. Aggression arises from the 'imperfect realization of civil equality in morally primitive states'. As from the pernicious view that there is one morality for states and another for men, it is untenable. Here is total hostility to doctrines of raison d'état. Yet Green's constructive proposals seem disappointing — a key perhaps, to the weakness of liberal optimism, with its failure to grasp the hard realities of world power.[19]

In fact the proposed alternative seems unconvincing. Since, it is argued, public spirit 'may take, and is every day taking, directions which lead to no collisions between one nation and another', the causes of conflict are likely to disappear. 'Localized philanthropy' does not imply aggression. 'Those in whom it is strongest are every day expressing it in good works which benefit their fellow citizens without interfering with the men of other nations.' This parochial method of 'setting an example' in a world of *Realpolitik* has never been very successful. Meanwhile, 'till all the methods have been exhausted by which nature can be brought into the service of man', he remarks, and 'everyone's capacities have full scope for development, there is no need to resort to war for a field in which patriotism may display itself'. The views of Treitschke, in a sense Green's opposite number in German universities, were quite contrary to this opinion. It was, indeed, singularly unfortunate that the security which British world power at that time guaranteed, led most English political thinkers to accept international conditions which was to bring so much of the

* Kant had argued that 'the rights of men are holy, whatever the cost to the ruling power', and pointed out that the 'wickedness of human nature may be seen undisguised in the relationship between peoples'. All are involved in this crime. The only remedy is an expanding federation of civilized mankind, 'where fortune so disposes that a powerful and enlightened people can constitute themselves a republic . . . it becomes a centre of Federal Union for other States'. Meanwhile, until war is thus rendered impossible, all are in varying degrees guilty, aggressors and defenders, and victory celebrations ought to be followed by 'penance for the great sin persisted in by mankind, the sin of not accepting a legalized constitution in relation to other nations, but through pride in their independence to resort to the barbarous method of war'. Green is less constructive – or less hopeful.

liberal achievement to ruin. Nowhere is this curious blindness better illustrated than in the ideas of this able and high-minded writer.

The blame, he thought, was not upon the system, or the masses. It was upon the military tradition of the upper class. This was a 'legacy of feudalism'. When πολιτεία has superseded the more primitive δυναστεία, all this will vanish. Meanwhile, Green, with his high moral patriotism, supports the nation state: 'the military system of Europe is no necessary incident of the relations between independent states, but arises from the fact that the organization of state-life, even with those peoples who have been brought under its influence at all, is still so incomplete.' A view similar to Mazzini's.[20]

Free trade also, he believed, in the manner of his time, was bound to make for peace.[21] Restrictions will disappear as class interests are brought under control — a queer prophesy in view of the economic nationalism of the Welfare State.[22] Once governments are really representative, there is 'no reason why they should not arrive at a passionless impartiality in dealing with each other'.[23] When this ideal is attained, 'the dream of an international court, with authority resting on the consent of independent states, may come to be realized. Such a result may seem very remote, but it is important to bear in mind that there is nothing in the intrinsic stature of independent states incompatible with it'. Voltaire had remarked, with better judgment, 'Les animaux carnassiers se déchireront toujours. . . .'

On crime and punishment, the *Principles of Political Obligation* say little that is new. Punishment is public retribution for breaking rules which render the good life possible. It is only justified if the system serves that end. It should be proportionate to the rights violated, and it should deter. The death penalty, the ultimate defence of society, is not an act of vengeance. It is only justifiable if deterrent. Lesser penalties are similarly defensive and should lead through shame to reformation.

Meanwhile the State should promote the development of personality — its highest aim. In principle, the promotion of habits of true citizenship seem necessarily to be confined to the removal of obstacles'.[24] But the obstacles are numerous and difficult to define. 'Under this', writes Green, 'should be included much that most states have hitherto neglected.' Education is the business of the state; health and housing; abuse of landed property; 'the massing of population without regard to conditions of health' in mushroom industries; unemployment. These are great obstacles. They can be tackled by both public and private initiative 'without vitiating spontaneity'. Here is an opening for large and revolutionary policies, pointing to wide horizions. Yet there is no attack on men of property, other than bad landlords: the liberal principle of self development predominates. On the two fundamental questions, war and poverty, Green was a conservative. 'Considered as representing the conquest of nature by the effort of free and variously gifted individuals, property must be unequal and no less must it be so if considered as a means by which individuals fulfil social functions.'[25] He rejects, out of hand, the common ownership of the means of production — does not think in these terms at all. Following prevalent opinion, he assumes the beneficent operation of the free market.[26] Given the ever expanding possibilities of modern production, the increased wealth of one man does not naturally mean the diminished wealth of the other. Here is a total contrast with Marx's picture of the proletarian who sells his labour to the capitalist and expects 'a tanning'.[27] It follows that the accumulation of capital through generations promotes profits and so wages. And 'there is nothing in the nature of the case to keep the labourer in a condition of living from hand to mouth'. Nothing in the economic system prevents them becoming small capitalists themselves. Their 'combination in work' gives them the chance to invest their savings. The condition of the lowest classes is due not to liberal capitalism, but to the plight of the landless labourers, whose 'ancestors were serfs' and who formed the proletariat of the great cities. It is laid at the door of feudalism, of the aristocracy and the landlords, not of the business men. 'The capital gained by one is not taken from another, but one man cannot acquire more land without others having less. Landlords who turn estates into "forest", remove villages, build insanitary houses and forbid "the erection of dissenting chapels",' are, of course, anti-social, but it is unfair to 'lay on the free development of individual wealth the blame which is really due to the arbitrary and violent manner in which rights over land have been acquired and exercised'.[28] As with war, so with poverty, the blame is put on the old feudal and military pedigree of society, which the beneficent action of free trade is expected to redeem.

Such, in broad outline, is the range, and the limitation, of Green's political philosophy. It had extended the function of the state far beyond that admitted by the Utilitarians, and helped to restore Burke's organic view of society with a neo-Hegelian metaphysical background and reforming zeal. By developing Rousseau's concept of the General Will as the cumulative highest achievement and best sense of the whole society, with which personality is linked and so developed, Green had asserted a constructive humanism. If its limitations in foreign affairs and economics now seem severe, it enriched the theory of constitutional self-government. Green owed much to Plato and Aristotle. Like the Greek pioneers of political thought, he believes that 'morality is not ambulatory', and he subordinates politics to life.

IV

Where T. H. Green inspired liberal reformers to practical endeavour, F. H. Bradley, who was even more deeply influenced by Hegel, held that institutions are likely to be better than individuals and so not much susceptible to improvement. Political philosophers, in his view, should be spectators, not prophets. His influence was far less direct than Green's, and mainly due to his prestige as a philosopher. He was primarily a metaphysician; his works standard reading for generations of some of the best minds in England. He attempted, while steeped in Hegel's historicism, to vindicate a solid basis for morality. Hence his prestige. He believed that individuals are entirely enmeshed in society, which is in a state of continual evolution, and that their morality was bound to be that of their time. Hence a conservative acceptance, akin to Hegel's admiration for the historical *fait accompli*, of things as they are. 'If you can be as good as your world', he wrote, 'you are lucky.' Here is a contrast to the improving Utilitarians or to Green; still more to the revolutionaries. In his curious, self-conscious way, Bradley's Hegelian sense of the 'cake of custom' has affinities with the conservatism of Bagehot and Maine. He even anticipates Durkheim's sense of the texture of society and ideas. But, unlike these thinkers, he was unconstructive.

Bradley was younger than Green and long outlived him.* He made his best known contribution to political thought in a work

* F. H. Bradley, 1846-1924. Son of the Rev. C. Bradley and half-brother of the Rev. A. C. Bradley, who was Master of Marlborough and afterwards Dean of Westminster. He was educated at Cheltenham and Marlborough (1861-63), where he excelled in Rugby football. He was an 'ardent member of the school rifle corps', and is said to have 'made acquaintance, while still a schoolboy, with Kant's *Critique of Pure Reason*'. In 1865 this model Marlburian entered University College, Oxford, where he took up rowing. In 1870 he was elected a life Fellow of Merton College, the appointment, under the old statutes, being conditional on celibacy. Here he was early stricken with severe illness, but lived in College for more than half a century, save for regular visits to Paris in the summer. Bradley's principal publications were: *Ethical Studies*, 1876; *Principles of Logic*, 1883; *Appearance and Reality*, 1893. In 1914 he was awarded the Order of Merit.

published well before Green's posthumous *Lectures on the Principles of Political Obligation*. In *Ethical Studies*, which first appeared in 1876, and were reprinted with new comments in 1927, Bradley launched an elaborate, ironical and picturesque attack on the old Utilitarian individualism, and all its brisk programme of improvement.*

While Green wished to reform society and Bosanquet was to carry on this tradition, Bradley was Olympian and detached. An aesthete among philosophers, an artist in ideas, his style is, perhaps, more striking than his thought. He wielded formidable powers of phrase, of ridicule and sarcasm. His alembicated prose belongs to the period of Matthew Arnold and Walter Pater. Very consciously above the battle, he declared that it was not for political philosophers to change institutions, any more than it is for art-critics to paint. This detachment increased his influence, for such lofty pronouncements are frequently regarded with awe, and Bradley's flair for a brilliant phrase, and the studied cadence of his prose, placed him among the foremost writers of his time, whatever the view now fashionable of his use of philosophical terminology.†

These delicate cobweb speculations, heavily qualified in a separate concluding remark, came to eloquent and vivid expression in the well-known essay 'My Station and its Duties', which appears to contain the key to his political views.[29] As a conservative statement of neo-Hegelian belief, it deserves attention. Here is another attempt to found morality on speculative intuition rather than on revelation, and an escape from the bare limitations of Utilitarian ethics. Bradley constantly insists that a man is entirely dependent on his social setting. He glances at the behaviour of gregarious animals, and at the probable origins of mankind; at the institutions of early society, 'actual existing communities with the common type impressed on all their members, their organic structure . . .'[30] Then, narrowing the subject 'to keep to what is familiar', he takes 'an Englishman as he is now', and traces the infinite ramifications of the life of a child born

---

* After two short prefaces (1876 and 1927), the book is divided into seven essays. 'The Vulgar Notion of Responsibility in Connection with the Theories of Free Will and Necessity'; 'Why Should I be Moral? Pleasure for Pleasure's Sake'; 'Duty for Duty's Sake'; 'My Station and its Duties'; 'Ideal Morality'; 'Selfishness and Self-sacrifice'; 'Concluding Remarks'.

† For example, the famous passage from his *Principles of Logic*. 'It may come from a failure in my metaphysics, or from a weakness of the flesh which continues to bind me, but the notion that existence could be the same as understanding strikes as cold and ghost-like as the dreariest materialism. That the glory of the world in the end is appearance leaves the world more glorious, if we feel it is the show of some fuller splendour; but the sensuous curtain is a deception and a cheat if it hides some colourless movement of atoms, some spectral woof of impalpable abstractions, or unearthly ballet of bloodless categories.'

at a given time from parents of a given race and culture. The infant is a social being, the heir to a complex and ancient past; 'and if Mr. Darwin's conjecture as to the development of man from a social animal be received, we must say that man has never been anything but social, and society never was made by individual men'.[31] As the child develops, 'The "icy chains" of universal custom are hardening themselves round his cradled life, . . . he grows with his world.' And Bradley here quotes Hegel 'that in respect of morality the saying of the wisest men of antiquity is . . . that to be moral is to live in accordance with the moral tradition of one's country; and in respect of education, the one true answer is that which a Pythagorean gave to him who asked what was the best education for his son, if you make him a citizen of a people with good institutions'.[32]

To assert a merely private morality is futile. The Stoic universal humanity, whereby all men participate in a world-wide reason, or the Kantian cosmopolitan brotherhood of all mankind, are here dismissed. For Bradley is committed to a new, relative, standard of morality, determined by the individual's setting in space and time. Here, again, is the neo-Hellenic morality of the πόλις; but here also Hegelian relativism steals into ethical thought, together with the new Hegelian sense of the unfolding of morality in time.

Institutions may be relative, but they reflect a metaphysical background. They represent the 'outer side' of the moral world, 'and there must be a soul; or else the body goes to pieces; everyone knows that institutions without the spirit in them are dead'. Bradley even here forgets his careful standards of prose in some very queer Hegelian jargon. 'In the moral organism', he writes, 'this spirit is in the will of the organs, as the will of the whole which, in and by the organs, carries out the organism and makes it alive, and which also (and this is the point to which attention is requested) is, and must be felt or known, in each organ as his own inward and personal will.'[33] Here is the impact of the Hegelian absolute, realizing itself through social personality in time. Even popular judgment, he continues, 'as expressed in uneducated vulgar opinion', understands that man is a social animal. But this fact reflects a cosmic process. Hence the vitality of public spirit, without which a nation cannot be strong. And that spirit must express personal will. Public spirit, in Bradley's opinion, is 'being inwardly aware of oneself as willing the good will' — a phrase shocking to modern logicians — and 'moral institutions are carcasses without personal morality . . .'[34] Thus the 'will of the whole becomes self conscious in us and to be moral a man must will his station and its duties. So I will to particularize a moral system'. The calculating interest of the 'peevish' Utilitarians is transformed into something warm, personal and spontaneous. This view, Bradley believes, is based on intellectual analysis, but it is also a faith. 'It is like faith, however, in this, that not merely by thinking ourselves, but by willing ourselves as such, can we look on ourselves as organs in a good whole. . .'[35]

So we grow into the good self around us. So it is possible to be 'reconciled to the world and to life'. Evils will not discourage us, 'since they point to the strength of a life which can endure such parasites and flourish in spite of them'; while 'still at the push, the doctrinaire and the quacksalver go to the wall, and . . . even that too is as it ought to be'.[36] Here is, indeed, a remarkable tribute to the 'best self' of society — in this instance, the nation state. Not, perhaps, the robust and natural patriotism of Burke, rather the worked-up emotion of a cloistered philosopher. All the more curious is the following encouragement to think with the blood. In the moral 'organism' there is a real 'identity of might and right' — in a crisis 'instincts are better and stronger than so-called principles'. There follows a paean on the state, which reaches its climax in a quotation from Hegel. For in the fullest crisis of the state's activity, in war, a man 'sees . . . what are called "rights" laughed at, "freedom", the liberty to do what one pleases, trampled on, the claims of the individual trodden under foot, and theories burst like cobwebs. And he sees, as of old, the heart of a nation rise high and beat in the breast of each one of her citizens, till her safety and her honour are dearer to each than life . . . and death seems a little thing to those who go for her to their common and nameless grave'. 'It is no mere extravagance', he continues, 'when a poet talks of a nation's soul.'*

After this rapture, the philosopher sinks into a quieter mood. 'The truth of individualism', he says, 'is saved, because, unless we have intense life and self-consciousness in the members of the state, the whole state is ossified.'[37]

Having reconciled the individual and society, Bradley examines the variation of moral standards. 'Morality', he asserts, 'is "relative" but none the less real.'[38] Since all progress has come through evolution, 'the notion that full fledged moral ideas fall down from heaven',

---

* This is not the place to quote the full passage from Hegel cited by Bradley, but the reader will realize its character from the following sentences. 'The realm of morality is nothing but the absolute spiritual unity of the essence of individuals . . . the moral substance looked at abstractedly from the mere side of its universality, is the Law, and, as this, is only thought.'

is false, and a 'human being is nothing if he is not the son of his time'. A good cannibal, it would follow, is a better citizen of his age than a conscientious objector in a modern garrison state. But in civilized society, he believed, with Green, that 'There is an objective morality in the accomplished will of the past and present . . . worked out by the infinite pain, the sweat and blood of generations, and now given to me by free grace . . . as a sacred trust'. This morality is 'stronger and higher than any caprice . . . of my own'. The power of public opinion, convention and tradition is glorified, without much impulse for reform. Here, in contrast to Green's view, was a reinforcement of the *status quo*. Hegel could be what one made him. Bradley insists that the morality of each stage of history is the only one possible. It follows that philosophers cannot transcend the outlook of their time, and 'political philosophy has not to play tricks with the state, but to understand it'. Political theory should be cautious, tentative, academic.

Here, indeed, is a timid, even discouraging outlook. For who, he asks, would go to a learned theologian, as such, in a religious difficulty, or to a political philosopher in practical politics? Here is the antithesis to the view of Green — always practical, well aware of the needs of the ordinary people. It is also totally hostile to the views of Aristotle and Plato; to the main medieval tradition as expressed by St. Thomas or Dante; to the constructive humanism of Spinoza, with his clear-cut definition of the end of the state as peace, or to the practical advice of Locke and the political theorists of the business commonwealth, or even to the desperate remedies of Hobbes, let alone the reforming zeal of Rousseau, Saint-Simon, Proudhon, or Comte, or Marx's determination to make history. If this was the view of sophisticated conservatism — and Bradley's opinions were widely fashionable — it is not remarkable that the Liberals, the Fabians, and the Marxists seized the initiative. This self conscious humanism, the work of an academic virtuoso, represents the decadence of late Victorian neo-Hegelian philosophy. In a world where, even in technologically advanced countries, the masses lived in conditions which made their sharing of the good life of their age impossible, and when poverty prevailed over most of the planet, when the great national states maintained a precarious peace only by elaborate power politics, such were the views of this sceptical English philosopher, his contribution to the two great problems of the nineteenth century, the problem of mass poverty and total war.

It is typical of this decadence that Bradley believes that the solution of practical problems comes by intuition. Here, again, is the Hegelian thinking with the blood — and that intuition is expressed by the αἴθησις of the φρόνιμος, by the perception of the leader, 'who has identified his will with the moral spirit of the community'. This representative person, in whom the collective spirit is strong, will act instinctively and lead by example: he will be the embodiment of his society's highest tradition. 'The final arbiters are the φρόνιμοι, persons with a will to do right. . . .'

And woe betide the critical individual! If you can be as good as your world, you are lucky. The will to be better than the world is to be already 'on the threshold of immorality'. The belief that 'everything would be better upside-down' is only tolerable in youth. It may even be an instrument of progress; but for mature minds, appreciative of the world, the desire for change is 'self conceit'.[39] 'We should consider', he says gravely, 'what we are, and what the world is.' Those who flaunt their individuality end as 'common Philistines'; for the licentious young the 'enchanted bower' soon becomes a 'hideous phantasm'. With maturity, the 'despised and common reality has become the ideal'. It follows that 'there is nothing better than my station and its duties, nor anything higher or more truly beautiful. It holds its own . . . against the worship of the individual, whatever form that may take'.[40] On second thoughts, Bradley admits that in his eloquence he has perhaps exceeded. For example, the community where the fusion of 'ought' and 'is', is to be attained, may be in a 'confused and rotten condition' — as are most fallible communities. It may also dawn on a sharp observer that 'the world is not altogether as it should be', so that he tries to make it better. Further, since we now know more about the morality of other places and times, a man feels more detached from his own age. And perhaps the creative artist, an expatriate in time, may aim beyond immediate values at higher beauty and truth. Bradley, indeed, admits that there may be higher things. 'The finite realization of "my station", was truth indeed, and a happiness that called to us to stay, but was too narrow to satisfy wholely the spirit's hunger.' 'My station and its duties' here, seems, retrospectively, transcended in a world of liberal theology outside the scope of this study. It may well be that Bradley's outlook leads to the conviction that such morality can only be transcended by grace.

Immediately, Bradley had written, in terms well suited to his audience, an eloquent vindication of a rather academic conservatism, and encouraged political philosophers to remain spectators in their field. His attack was directed originally against the angular doctrines of Utilitarian self-interest and improvement. It extends to broader fields of endeavour. He laughs at lovers, intellectuals and reformers — 'At frantic theories and vehement passions; at the frenzied apotheosis of the yet unsatisfied passion it calls love'; at kindness to genius 'too clever to do anything in particular', at 'stargazing virgins with souls above their spheres', and at those whose 'wish to be something in the world takes the form of wishing to do something with it'. Having thus left the room swept and garnished for any wandering devils to occupy, glorified the ugly features of the nation state, and abdicated leadership for political thought, Bradley concludes that this rather spiteful conservatism outweighs the teaching of all the writers who have spoken for human charity, enterprise and improvement. He concludes with a quotation from the *Frogs* of Aristophanes. 'Cuckoo,' says Dionysos, 'let go the scales; Aeschylos' side goes down . . . !' 'Cuckoo, indeed', the realist might reply.

v

T. H. Green and Bradley, the one optimistically, the other with an odd, defeatist, conservatism, had thus acclimatized an Hegelian sense of the organic texture of society and ideas, very different from the mechanical Utilitarian view. With a more sociological approach, meanwhile, Maine, Bagehot and Tylor had also come to a realistic outlook. They sensed the rarity of progress and of constitutional government, the strength of the primitive in its modern setting, and the precariousness of nineteenth-century civilization. This high mid-nineteenth century culture was now being subjected to a powerful attack.

CHAPTER V

MARX AND ENGELS, I

I T has already been observed that in pre-industrial Europe the benefits of civilization had hitherto been confined to minorities. With increased command of environment through better techniques, a new problem became urgent. How to assimilate the masses, now increasingly urban, into a potentially far more prosperous world, and liberate the full power of modern industry? This problem no previous civilization had been called upon to solve. Its urgency had first been realized by Saint-Simon: it had been the main preoccupation of the revolutionary and Utopian writers hitherto examined.

On this threshold of achievement, promising and precarious, a vast future was looming up. With it liberal economists and philosophers were preoccupied. In general they believed these problems could be solved through laissez-faire. And in spite of innovating criticism, the basic social and international framework, inherited from the eighteenth century, remained conservative save for the initiative of the new industrialists. Yet, for all the confidence of Spencer and Buckle, the problem of adaptation was extremely serious. The only forces strong enough to deprive mankind of the benefits of harnessed science were national and class war. Before the challenge of a changing environment, politically reflected in the democratic revolution which de Tocqueville and J. S. Mill had regarded as inevitable, and economically expressed by the new great industry, all resources of political wisdom, all available poise and judgment were urgently required. But nineteenth-century prophets of nationalism and class conflict, often with the best intentions and under gross provocation, contributed to undermine the foundations of ordered society. If this expanding civilization was not to be wrecked by the forces unleashed by modern science and its hard won achievement dissipated, a cautious political realism was imperative. In the world of the Industrial Revolution, as more urgently in the world of jet aircraft and atomic bombs, '*Circumspecte agatis*' was the obvious motto, not '*Pecca fortiter*'. The latter course was consistently recommended by economic pirates, nationalists, revolutionaries and nihilists in the later nineteenth century. It is recommended by their heirs today, when the wages of sin are even more imminently lethal.

Herbert Spencer's doctrine of savage competition has already been examined; the development of unbridled nationalism will later be investigated. It is now necessary to study the idea of inevitable class war, which Malthus' and Spencer's gospel had encouraged.

The fundamental doctrines of a new 'scientific' socialism were formulated by Marx and Engels. In spite of the genius of the one and the industry of the other, they combined the frequent political ineptitude of the peoples they jointly represent. Both were economic historians of great insight, but as prophets of revolution, they proclaimed inevitable class war and dictatorship. Marx, indeed, in his later years, admitted that in England the revolution might conceivably come about without violence; and Engels, at the end of his life, admitted that the early prophecies of social disruption were premature. He then even believed that, under more modern conditions, coup d'état might be superseded by infiltration. These admissions were to be eagerly cited by Western social democrats — Bernstein and Jaurès, for example — as against the more intransigent Communist doctrinaires. They have been savagely repudiated by Marx's Eastern interpreters.

A broad survey of their writings shows that Marx and Engels were at heart revolutionary romantics, in the tradition of 1789. Being Germans and authoritarians, they also believed that their goal could be won only through state power. Following economic revolution and the abolition of class, this power, the expression of the transitory bourgeois phase of history, would then wither away and give place to a civilization at last worthy of the name. This supersession of the State is already familiar in collectivist doctrines both of the Right and Left, in Saint-Simon and in Owen. For all this Utopian objective, the basic Marxist doctrine was one of class war and ruthless dictatorship.

There is one subject on which all great political thinkers had been unanimous. It is the danger of the abuse of power. This obvious political wisdom was ignored by prophets dazzled by a Communist Apocalypse. Marx and Engels were both men of formidable ability. They jointly created a social philosophy of massive range and insight, which radically altered and even enriched economic thought. They invoked, in a characteristically mid-nineteenth-century idiom, the authority of science for their political beliefs. They were actuated by a burning sense of mission, not unmixed with a desire for domination, for Marx has been well described as a 'domineering social misfit'. They differed from the usual run of revolutionaries by insisting that preparations must be long and systematic; that timing must be determined by a deep analysis of economic and political forces without which such revolutionary movements are bound to fail. They would succeed, they were convinced, only when the masses were behind them. And their incitement to violence was justified by an elaborate, yet basically simple, myth. It was only posthumously that their influence began to be really formidable. The internal feuds of Communists and Socialists, and the more powerful influence of nationalism, long prevented their success.

With the Russian Revolution, the doctrine, as reinterpreted by Lenin and Stalin, was to win great power. In England it was never congenial. The cult of Marxism began only after the Russian Revolution gave it prestige. Just as in the 'seventies the neo-Hegelianism of T. H. Green reflects the influence of a German philosopher long outmoded in his own country, so the English Marxists of the nineteen-thirties received their ideas with a Russian flavour. Subsequent events have provoked a reaction against this enthusiasm, and caused a reassertion of a more native realism and compromise.

For Marx and Engels were prophets, not political realists. They created the most original myth of the nineteenth century, if nationalism proved more compelling. In spite of its parade of scientific sanctions, communism won world influence as an atheist religion. It succeeded where Comte failed. It was the first successful rationalization of the needs, the ignorance, and the anger of the poor. It was at once gospel, explanation and programme. It combined Jewish moral indignation and prophecy with German system. It made the first massive, if technically primitive, analysis of the problem of poverty from the stand-point of the people. In its passion for social justice, hatred of exploitation and zeal for the oppressed, it proved what its founders meant it to be, a most formidable weapon of political warfare. It was directed primarily against the brutal laissez-faire capitalism and competitive anarchy justified by Herbert Spencer and derived from the worst aspects of Utilitarianism. No one of humane mind familiar with the writings of Malthus, James Mill and Spencer, will question the need for the Marxist attack; no one with rudimentary political sense will imagine that the Marxist cult of inevitable violence is the way out. Marx and Engels were at once idealists and sharp observers of the political scene. Neither had ever shouldered political responsibility; neither, in the words of a seventeenth-century critic of Hobbes, 'had ever had a finger in mortar'. For all their theoretical genius, they were working in a political medium they did not fully understand. They never appreciated the meaning of Constitutionalism, and in attempting good ends by evil means they fell into an ancient Machiavellian error.

So much tendentious literature has been written about Marxism, and so thick a haze of emotion and menace envelops the inquirer, that educated minds are repelled by it and ignorant minds are stunned. It is the more important to keep a level head. To set the claims of these nineteenth-century prophets against an older political tradition, and cut down to the essentials of the doctrine by a study of the texts. How many 'fellow-travellers' have read the complete text even of the first volume of *Das Kapital*? How many have investigated the voluminous and obscure writings which lead up to the *Communist Manifesto*? And how many of Marx's critics, either, are closely familiar with these documents? Yet no one can be politically equipped without first hand knowledge of the doctrine at its source.

Marx and Engels's theory has been variously reinterpreted, each version denouncing the rest as deviationist. But the basic programme of modern Communism is still to be found in this nineteenth-century dogma, of which the fundamental strategy has not been abandoned. In a changed environment it retains this old fashioned, period, quality. Doctrines of inevitable class war which might merely damage society in the days of the Crimean War or the Paris Commune, spell cosmic ruin and disaster in the age of thermo-nuclear weapons of mass destruction. If Marx's nineteenth-century doctrines of inevitable conflict are true, civilization is doomed.

The problem is thus urgent. It is to refer the reader to the original texts that the present pages have been written. Since the Marx-Engels partnership is inextricable, the analysis will proceed jointly in two chapters. The first will be devoted to the development of the doctrine up to the Revolutionary years 1848-49: the second to its systematization and reinforcement, from the beginning of the exile in England until the death of Engels. And for the first inquiry it will be necessary to cast back to the political milieu of the 'forties in Germany and France.

II

Karl Marx and Friedrich Engels were both highly cultivated intellectuals. They combined and reinterpreted the mid-nineteenth-century currents of collectivist thought. Marx was brought up by an indulgent father in the liberal and 'gemütlich' atmosphere of Trier.* At Bonn he led the usual easy student life. He married

* Karl Heinrich Marx, born 1818, son of Herschel Marx, a Jewish lawyer (Justizrat), who changed his name from Levi in 1817, and turned Christian in 1824. Karl's mother Henrietta Pressburg, came of Hungarian Jewish stock settled in Holland. In 1835 he attended the University of Bonn, and in the following year moved to Berlin. In 1841 he joined the staff of the *Rheinischer Zeitung*, edited by Moses Hess, at Cologne, becoming editor in 1842. In 1843 he married Jenny, daughter of Freiherr Ludwig von Westphalen, with whose family he had long been intimate. On the suppression of his paper, Marx moved to Paris. In 1844 his collaboration with Engels began. In 1845 he was expelled from Paris at the request of the Prussian government and moved to Brussels. During this period they published *The Holy Family* and wrote the *German Ideology*, which remained unpublished until after Marx's death. In 1847 appeared *Misère de la Philosophie*, written against Proudhon. The *Communist Manifesto* was published early in 1848. At the outbreak of the Revolution in 1848 Marx returned to Paris and then to Cologne, where he renewed his journalism. Arrested but acquitted by a Cologne jury, he was forced to leave the Rhineland in July 1849 for his part in the German Revolution. Its failure was the turning point in his life. From Paris he crossed to England in August 1849. Here he wrote *The Class Struggle in France*, the *18th Brumaire of Louis Bonaparte* and numerous other pamphlets. He lectured to German working men in London, and contributed to the *New York Tribune* for ten years. In 1859 appeared his *Critique of Political Economy*. In 1864 the First International was founded, which he turned into a centralized direction for world revolution until its dissolution in 1872, following his quarrel with Bakunin. In 1867 appeared the first volume of *Das Kapital* and in 1871 *The Civil War in France*, vindicating the Commune. In 1881 his wife died. His own death occurred on March 14th, 1883.

Marx was of thick-set build and dark complexion and known to his family circle as the 'Moor'. A Bohemian intellectual, he lived in the utmost confusion, over-worked desperately and ruined his health in sedentary labour. He was a deeply cultivated man with an immense admiration for Shakespeare, on whose works his family were brought up. He planned to write a book on Balzac and enjoyed the writings of Fielding, besides having a vast knowledge of German, French and classical literature. He was an amiable family man, but quite unpractical in the affairs of life. 'As far as accounts were concerned, the classic theoretician of money could never quite make his own tally', says his biographer, Mehring. He would seek consolation in mathematics, which exercised a soothing effect on him. His handwriting was appalling (see MEHRING, p. 283, for an example) and saved him from employment as a railway clerk at the nadir of his fortunes in 1861. In spite of the venom and bitterness of his public life, he enjoyed simple pleasures. There were picnics to Hampstead Heath on Sundays, when the family was in funds, when Frau Marx would bring a hamper containing 'a mighty roast of veal', and the 'Moor' would amuse the children by riding a donkey. Marx suffered from a liver complaint, and his later years were dogged by ill health, following decades of sedentary study. He was so short-sighted that he 'was always doubtful, when returning home when he was standing in front of his own house'.

The best short introduction to Marxism is I. BERLIN's brilliant *Karl Marx, his Life and Environment*. Oxford University Press, 2nd edition, 1948, q.v. for a good short bibliography. The standard life is *Karl Marx, the Story of his Life* by FRANZ MEHRING (1919), translated by E. Fitzgerald. Allen & Unwin, 1936. It is an able, partizan but well written book. Mr. J. Strachey says that every politically conscious British worker will find new inspiration and determination in its pages. See also E. H. CARR, *Karl Marx, a Study in Fanaticism*. For the *Communist Manifesto* see the edition by H. J. LASKI (1948). The best translation of *Das Kapital*, vol. I, is by E. and C. Paul, 1928. The earlier translation was made in 1889 by J. Moore and E. Aveling and edited by Engels. Allen & Unwin, 1938. The only complete edition of all Marx's writings is published by the Marx-Engels Institute in

Jenny von Westphalen, said to have been the most beautiful girl in Trier. In spite of poverty and exile, it was a happy marriage. His talents could have ensured a brilliant career, but his 'hide was not thick enough', he once remarked, 'to let him turn his back on the sufferings of humanity'. For Marx was an idealist whose belief in progress was inherited from a rationalist background. His objective, whatever his achievement, was the liberation of mankind. In spite of penury and squalor, the Marx household was always bourgeois. When they had retrieved some of their possessions from the pawnbroker, Frau Marx, who had a Scottish grandmother, could write 'once again I was able to count my old Scottish napkins with delight'. Close contact with the proletariat was never congenial, and Marx's biographer, Mehring, when describing the worst straits to which in the 'sixties they were reduced, refers to the proposal that they should 'move . . . into one of those blocks of buildings which had been run up to meet the needs of the poorer classes', as a 'counsel of despair'.

Worried by his son's 'wild frolics' at Bonn, the elder Marx sent him to Berlin. 'Other universities', wrote Marx, 'are positively Bacchanalian compared to this workhouse.' Here he assimilated the Hegelian and neo-Hegelian dialectic of inevitable thesis and antithesis, of the movement of history, of the relativity of ideas and standards. These theories became 'idées fixes'. Later a critical synthesis of Hegel and Feuerbach was to develop from this foundation, reinforced by the theories of English Classical Economists.

Hegel's political philosophy has already been sketched: Feuerbach's ideas therefore now deserve attention. This writer (1804-72), was a militant atheist, whose *Way of Christianity* had appeared in 1841.* He regarded religion not merely as a delusion, but as a disease. The more advanced the religion, the worse its effects. Like Proudhon, he held that man impoverishes himself by transferring his

---

* *Das Wesen des Christentums*, trans. M. Evans. London, 1877. See in particular his *Preliminary Theses on the Reform of Philosophy*, 1843 . . . (Sämtliche Werke, edited W. Bolin and F. Hodl, 10 vols. Leipzig, 1903-11). See H. DE LUBAC, *The Drama of Atheist Humanism*. London, 1949 and J. S. SPERLE, *La Pensée Allemande de Luther à Nietzsche*.

Moscow, but there are translations of most of the important pamphlets in Lawrence & Wishart's Marxist Leninist Library. They have also issued a *Selected Correspondence* in two volumes. For details of family life and some revealing photographs, see *Karl Marx. Eine Sammlung von Erinnerungen und Aufsätzen*. Ring Verlag, Zurich. The immense Marxist literature includes, in English, LASKI, *Communism*. O.U.P.; A. D. LINDSAY, *Karl Marx's Capital*; G. D. H. COLE, *What Marx really Meant*; S. HOOKE, *From Hegel to Marx*. See also J. PLEKHANOV, *Fundamental Problems of Marxism*; LABRIOLA, *Essai sur la Conception Matérialiste de L'Histoire*; G. SOREL, *La Décomposition du Marxisme*. For more critical accounts, see SABINE, GRAY, op. cit. and K. POPPER, *The Open Society and its Enemies*, vol. II, a particularly valuable work. R. CAREW HUNT, *The Theory and Practice of Communism*, is the best short introduction to the development of Marxist theory by Lenin and Stalin.

greatest achievements to an Abstraction. 'The poor man', he wrote, 'possesses a rich God.' This monstrous Projection — the embodiment of human desires — is a 'Vampire' on civilization. As a Russian disciple remarked, 'In history the name of God is the terrible club with which men of manifold inspiration, the great geniuses, have struck down the liberty, dignity, reason and prosperity of man.' Like Comte, Feuerbach made a cult of humanity, and desired that individuals should achieve happiness. He was a materialist, impatient of metaphysical abstractions; and he wished, like the rest of them, to deduce a 'science of man' from the 'laws' of environment. All progress, he believed, was conditioned by material circumstances, and anthropology demonstrated that ideas are strictly conditioned by food supply. 'Do you wish to improve the people?' he wrote in his most notorious utterance, 'then instead of preaching against sin, give them better food . . . Man is what he eats.'

Apart from his materialism, Feuerbach was no militant revolutionary. He had much in common with Comte, and while he admitted the importance of what he termed the 'stomach work' of Marx and Engels, he never had their preoccupation with economics and class war. Marx therefore savagely attacked him for his intellectual detachment, but agreed with his materialist atheism. It was always to colour Marx's thought and all the subsequent doctrine.

When, with this intellectual background, Marx, at the age of twenty-four, took up his editorship at Cologne, he at once proved his power as a political journalist. Next, in Paris, then the centre of a ferment of revolutionary ideas, he was to become deeply versed in the literature of French socialism and intimately acquainted with Proudhon and the Russian anarchist Bakunin. Here, too, he made the life-long friendship with Engels which was decisive for them both. Engels was already familiar with the doctrines of Ricardo, and the social facts first collected by the English Poor Law reports on which so much of their work was to be based. The influence of the Swiss economist Sismondi was also decisive for them both in the study of economic history.

These three elements are constant — a revolutionary and optimistic rationalism; the Hegelian view of history, crossed with Feuerbach's materialism; and the economic idiom of Ricardo in theory, and Sismondi, in social analysis. Yet Marx and Engels, though cosmopolitan linguists, remained intensely German. Marx's mentality was always that of a revolutionary refugee, and their eyes were turned towards their own kind. Nearly all their books were written in German. Their heavy, rancorous, controversies with fellow revolutionaries became the personal vendettas of Herr Doktor Marx against Herr Doktor Bauer; of Herr Doktor Engels against Herr Doktor Dühring. This gross form of controversy has set the tone for subsequent Marxist polemics. As Professor Berlin remarks, it inaugurated a new epoch in political vituperation. In his concern with Germany, Marx seldom misses a chance to denounce the 'Philistinism' of his compatriots. The *Communist Manifesto* was written for German workers in London, and directed at an audience in Germany, where the authors over-estimated the chance of revolution.

The intellectual development of Marx and Engels was thus early determined. By 1848, at the ages of thirty and twenty-eight respectively, their ideas seem set. This development had been marked by savage controversy, as Marx assimilated, or flung aside, the elements of existing revolutionary theory.

Besides these main currents, there is much else in these obscure and voluminous writings. They are naturally coloured by the intellectual fashion of their time. In particular, there is the usual mid-nineteenth-century conviction of progress, if of progress through suffering. And the belief, already frequently observed, in immutable and ascertainable historical Laws. Comte and Spencer, Buckle, Bagehot and Lecky, all believed in them. Marx and Engels were in this respect in no way original. Their system was merely more elaborate, more concerned with economics, more massive and more angular. In his well-known oration over Marx's grave, Engels makes the specific claim: 'On the 14th of March, at a quarter to three in the afternoon, the greatest living thinker ceased to think ... just as Darwin discovered the laws of evolution in organic nature, so Marx discovered the law of evolution in human history.'[1] He further, Engels declared, 'discovered the special law of motion governing the present day Capitalist method of production and the bourgeois society this method of production has created'. And he discovered the 'law' of surplus value, a conception now technically discredited.

Engels depicted a prophet, scientist and seer. If, to more modern thought, it seems a quaint notion that the vast and complex panorama of history and society can be explained by a few simple laws, to the nineteenth century the belief was natural and familiar.[2]

The other, all pervading, idea was also expressed by Engels on the same occasion. Marx, he said, 'was before all else a revolutionary ... fighting was his element'. His 'mighty vision' was expressed for all mankind; his task was 'impregnating the proletariat with mighty thoughts'. His purpose was not merely to interpret, but to change the world. Marx, indeed, was a shrewd observer, and wrote best as a political journalist.* Yet all is profoundly dated. The reader entering this ideological world seems to contemplate some archaic Victorian steam engine. The massive and obsolete machinery revolves; amid acrid fumes of ancient processes, the reek of coal smoke and the glare of flame upon the fog, the machine slowly begins to move. Steadily it proceeds along its determined rails to its scheduled destination.

The campaign to which Marx and Engels dedicated their lives was thus inspired with massive purpose. It implied the definition of doctrine, the laborious education of the masses into class consciousness, the elaborate assessment of the ripeness of the time for revolution. Yet the total picture is painted in stark extremes. As T. E. Lawrence observed of the Semites, 'they a were people of primary colours, or rather of black and white, who saw the world always in contrast'.† This prophetic and vengeful Jewish strain, with its vision of apocalypse and judgment, makes Marxism another great successful Semitic religion. Through all the Hegelian and economic jargon, two master ideas emerge; the belief in a 'science' of dialectical materialism, and in the need for a strategy of revolution.

The personality and contribution of Engels did nothing to modify Marx's mind. He was the able chief of staff for Marx's campaign; an indefatigable collaborator; modest, efficient, moderately rich; never a competitor. Talented as he was, his loyalty increased Marx's arrogance.

The partnership dates from their early years. It lasted till death. Beneath his rancorous polemics, Engels was a humane and even a genial character.‡ To the liberal revolutionary from the Rhineland,

---

* Vide *infra*. *The Eighteenth Brumaire of Louis Bonaparte*, which can compare with Machiavelli.

† Quoted in *W.P.T.*, p. 109, in analysing the Semitic element in Christianity.

‡ Friedrich Engels was born in 1820 at Barmen near Düsseldorf in the Northern Rhineland. He entered business at Barmen and Bremen. During his military service (1841-42) he became interested in military history and later wrote authoritative articles on the campaigns of Napoleon III in Italy and on the Franco-Prussian War. In 1842-43 he joined the cotton-spinning firm of Ermann and Engels in Manchester. On his way to England he first met Marx at Cologne, and in 1844 began to collaborate with him in Paris. In 1845 he published his *Condition of the.Working Class in England in 1844*, and the *Communist Manifesto* was written with his assistance. He took part in the German Revolution of 1849 at Cologne and Baden, where he was involved in street fighting. After the suppression of the risings, he fled to Vevey and finally joined Marx in London, having made the round voyage from Genoa. These escapades disturbed his father ('my fanatical and despotic governor'), who offered him a post at Calcutta. But he rejoined the business in

early Victorian Manchester had been a decisive shock. To this fate, it appeared, the world was heading as the Industrial Revolution went its way. The young man wrote a powerful, documented, indictment. From 1844 his collaboration with Marx was continuous. The Marx-Engels canon is thus framed and permeated by Engel's contribution. His *The Condition of the Working Class in England in 1844*, appeared in 1845; his *Anti-Dühring* in 1878; the study of *The Family* after Marx's death. The whole campaign opened with his indictment of capitalism in the hungry 'forties, which Communists claim as 'the first great document of scientific socialist thought'. Already, they believe, this genius had discovered the total explanation of history and politics at the age of twenty-four.

This first document now demands attention as the first step in the development of Marxism up to 1848. The assimilation of Hegel and Feuerbach will then be traced, and finally the *Communist Manifesto* itself will be more closely analysed. The writings after 1848 will be the subject of a separate chapter.

Manchester in March 1850, though he continued his collaboration with Marx, whom he subsidized through his worst struggles. 'Five pound notes, ten pound notes, and later even hundred pound notes constantly went from Manchester to London.' In 1864 he became a partner in the firm, and married his deceased mistress's sister. In 1869 he sold out his interest in the business for a large capital sum which enabled him to move to London, devote himself to study and propaganda and to provide Marx with the then tolerable income of £350 a year. Marx thus existed during his English exile mainly on the proceeds of a competitive cotton business in Manchester. As an independent capitalist, Engels could now leave the routine of 'dastardly' commerce, and in 1878 he published his *Anti-Dühring*, the most important of his works. In 1884, the year after Marx's death, appeared his *Origin of the Family, Private Property and the State*, based in part on the work of the American anthropologist, Lewis Morgan. In 1888 he also published a book on Feuerbach, but his main task after Marx's death was the collation and editing of Marx's numerous manuscripts, in particular the volumes II-III of *Das Kapital*. He died in 1895 and his ashes were scattered on the sea from a rowing boat at Eastbourne, a ceremony in which Bernstein participated.

Engels was a Rhinelander with a great sense of fun and a distinguished presence – a more worldly character than Marx. A tall spruce figure of military bearing and a good linguist, he was devoted to his Irish mistress, Mary Burns, and enjoyed such amenities of bourgeois life as fox hunting and a well stocked cellar. He sometimes uses similes from the hunting field, though they have a Teutonic flavour; 'The stiff necked cart horse of bourgeois common sense naturally shies at the ditch which separates reality from appearance . . . if we want to hunt over the rough country of abstract thought we must not ride a cart horse' (MEHRING, op. cit., p. 128). He had 'a great relish for his beer, especially if it was Viennese'. He played the part of benevolent uncle to the Marx household – an offset to the pawnbroker. 'In spite of all cotton trade', wrote Frau Marx in 1850, 'you will still remain the old Fritz . . . and will not become estranged from the holy cause of freedom . . . the children chatter much about Uncle Angels.' But to the outer world, when engaged in controversy, the poisonous rancour of his polemics equalled that of his formidable friend. The standard biography of Engels is by G. Mayer (translated G. and H. Highet and edited R. H. S. Crossman). It contains some revealing photographs, Engels as a young man having a jolly spaniel-like appearance. In later life he became a bearded Victorian figure, though he retained a sleek and well-groomed air, in contrast to that of his more Bohemian collaborator.

The Condition of the Working Class in England in 1844 was first published in German and not translated into English until 1886.* Its form closely anticipates the descriptive passages of *Das Kapital*. In a preface to the English edition of 1892, Engels admits that 'youthful ardour' made him miscalculate the chances of immediate revolution, but claims that conditions outside England are still critical. If his method had been anticipated by Sismondi and his disciple Buret, Engels had charted a new field in an economically more advanced economy.

The book is permeated by a sense of crisis. England, Engels insists, is the classic land of the Industrial Revolution. What is happening here will later come about in all industrial countries, and this transformation reflects a 'history which has no counterpart in the annals of humanity'. The impact of machinery had created a weird, inhuman, society; it had transformed London and the Midland cities into something strange. In the great towns 'The name merry old England conveys no meaning', and the nation is riven into two classes, rich and poor. Tracing the impact of the new steam-driven cotton mills on the weaving industry, with its handicrafts and rural background, Engels turns to the development of the 'broad coal fields' of England, and depicts the vast shift of population into the new towns. What is to become of these millions?

The new urban life horrified the young Rhinelander. London, in particular, with the 'brutal indifference' of its crowds, presented everywhere 'hard egotism on the one hand, and nameless misery on the other . . . reciprocal plundering under the protection of the law'.[3] Before impersonal economic power, the huge working class are helpless. They are driven into the slums of St. Giles, Whitechapel and Bethnal Green; into the closes of Edinburgh and Glasgow, into the grimy tenements of Leeds and Liverpool. Of Manchester Engels speaks with accurate first-hand knowledge. 'In a word we must confess that in the working-men's dwellings . . . no cleanliness, no convenience, and consequently no comfortable family life is possible; that in such dwellings only a physically degenerate race, robbed of all humanity, degraded, reduced morally and physically to bestiality,

---

* Translated New York, 1886 with preface by Engels. Allen & Unwin, 1892, 276 pp., London edition. It contains eleven chapters: 'The Industrial Proletariat'; 'The Great Towns'; 'Competition'; 'Irish Immigration'; 'Results'; 'Single Branches of Industry'; 'Remaining Branches of Industry'; 'Labour Movements'; 'The Mining Proletariat'; 'The Agricultural Proletariat'; 'Attitude of the Bourgeoisie towards the Proletariat'.

could feel comfortable and at home.'* This new slum-proletariat
is as ill clad as it is ill housed. 'The damp air of England,' writes this
German observer, 'with its sudden changes of temperature, more
calculated than any other to give rise to colds, obliges almost the
whole middle-class to wear flannel next the skin ...' This mid-
nineteenth-century precaution is denied the workers. They wear
cheap cotton, which absorbs the wet. And the Irish immigrants go
bare-foot. Engels quotes from Carlyle on *Chartism*, and describes
in harrowing detail the working-class diet of adulterated food and
black tea. Such are the results of the battle of all against all. Caught
in the uncontrollable rhythm of boom and slump, weakly, angular,
lean, the work-people 'nearly all suffer from indigestion'.⁴ Addicts of
patent medicines, they are 'hollow-eyed ghosts'; a surplus population,
always on the verge of unemployment. They hang about the streets
of the hideous towns. They are victims of social murder. Only the
Irish, with their pigs and their drink, retain a crazy good cheer.
Engels quotes Dr. Alison on scrofula, rickets and malnutrition among
the Scottish poor: he quotes appalling statistics of child mortality
from Dr. Cowan of Glasgow, and from the Commission of Inquiry
into the employment of children in 1841-43. On housing, Dr.
Holland — 'very frank for an English bourgeois' -- writes '*Hundreds
of our immediate neighbours* are annually destroyed, for want of the
most evident precaution.'⁵ Something, Engels insists, like Owen,
must be done.

Education in these industrial hells is atrocious. Illiteracy is
preponderant, agravated by the 'confused orthography of the
English language'. Children were ignorant who Christ was.† 'He
was Adam,' they said, 'He was the Saviour's Lord's son; he was a
King of London long ago.' In these conditions the vast majority
detest their work — a deep cause of demoralization. No wonder
Dr. Alison refers to the 'disorderly habits and profligate enjoyments
of the lower orders'. Flat feet, curvature of the spine, anaemia —
'whole generations wretched' — such is the price of bourgeois prosperity, such the price of England's industrial wealth. Engels
quotes Power's report on Leeds, Tufnell's report on Manchester.
He had reason to. The legacy still exacts its delayed revenge.

These conditions, Engels argues, will bring about inevitable
revolution. As 'schools of war the Unions are unexcelled'. In the

---

* p. 63. To reinforce his argument Engels quotes ALISON, *Principles of Population*; P.
GASKELL, *The Manufacturing Population of England*, and the conservative NASSAU SENIOR,
Letters on the Factory Act, 1837.
† Children Employment Commission Report.

mines, in great industry and in agriculture, the movement has already begun. For the last he cites Gibbon Wakefield on *Swing Unmasked; or the Cause of Rural Incendiarism* (1831). The game laws have further increased discontent, and labourers are exasperated by missionary sermons. 'Why doan't they zend the parzon az droans every day in Zalisbury Cathedral for nobody but bare ztones?' asked one of them. Engels quotes statistics of the ruin of the Welsh peasantry. The parallel with the closing chapters of *Das Kapital* is striking. He concludes by a savage denunciation of the bourgeoisie, quoting Carlyle's *Past and Present*, and attacking Malthus and the economists. English nationality, he rashly states, is annihilated in the working men; they are therefore not so inhibited by phlegm as the middle class, and are 'as passionate as foreigners'. There is 'nothing to be done with the bourgeois . . . he is dead to all active movement; he is losing his position in the forefront of England's historical development. The worker is taking his place'. Hardly an accurate prophecy on the verge of the great mid-Victorian period of middle-class achievement, in thought, literature, politics and industry. There are the usual accusations of money-grubbing, coldness and hypocrisy.

Revolution was inevitable, 'the bloodiest ever waged'. And Communism will be the way out. Still young and idealistic, Engels here attempts to transcend the consequences of the class war. 'Communism stands, in principle, above the breach between bourgeoisie and proletariat.' It wishes, indeed, to 'bridge over this chasm, to do away with all class antagonisms'. It is a movement for all humanity, not for the workers alone. He hopes there will be enough 'intelligent comprehension' to avoid the extremity of bitterness; he hopes that Communism will conquer the brutal elements in revolution. Later he was often to sing a different tune.

Engels had written a powerful and lucid indictment. If his tactical assessment was at fault, too much coloured, as all their thought, by the bitterness of the 'forties, he had assembled massive documentary evidence for the consequences of laissez-faire, and provided Marx with new data,* though, inevitably, both saw England through foreign eyes.

Such was the first aspect of the developing doctrine; the collection of facts about the most highly industrialized state, and the deduction

---

* His tendency to concentrate on the distress of handloom-weavers, in particular, a class then inevitably on the decline, and upon the standard of living of Irish immigrants, makes his indictment hardly representative of the over-all picture.

that the crises the system provoked must end in revolution. One must now turn to the theoretical background created by Marx out of his Hegelian and economic studies, from which the concept of Dialectical Materialism emerged.

The pedigree of Dialectical Materialism is naturally complex. On the dialectical side it derives primarily from Hegel, with whose ideas the reader will already be too familiar. The concept of dialectic, of thesis and antithesis, proceeding, by a qualitative revolutionary leap, to synthesis, has already been examined. It is basic to Marx's thought. Of the young Engels, an admirer writes, 'he had mastered Hegelian dialectics until they became second nature'. Transferred, by a false analogy, to the sphere of politics, at once metaphysical and apparently scientific, they are invoked to assert the necessity of revolution. In modern terms, history is thus an event in space-time, at once reflecting and contributing to individual experience: all standards are changing and relative. On the materialist side, the pedigree goes back to the philosophers of antiquity, to Heraclitus, Democritus and Lucretius. It also derives from the crude behaviourism of Hobbes. But like his fellow Jew, Spinoza, Marx was not content with a sceptical philosophy. The good humoured conservative empiricism of Hume was also uncongenial to his mind, with its Jewish and German thirst for total explanation. He attempts, like Spinoza, to infuse a mystical content into a sceptical outlook. But where Spinoza, with his cult of life, of political liberty, defined a humane and tolerant pantheism, Marx brought to materialism the idea of historically determined conflict, and the old Jewish faith in apocalypse and judgment, expressed in the revolutionary idiom of 1789.

While this study will concentrate on two main documents of Marxism, the *Communist Manifesto* and the first volume of *Das Kapital*, it is worth examining the development of the Marx-Engels system during its earlier phase, of which these two decisive works are the immediate and the long-term expression. As is usual with most political thinkers, the basic ideas are early apparent, expressed in terms which have the advantage of not being too generally familiar. For Marxist studies are numbed by hackneyed quotations.

The philosophical ideas later succinctly expressed in the *Communist Manifesto* were worked out by Marx and Engels during the middle 'forties in Paris and Brussels. This process can be seen in the rancorous *Holy Family* — the polemic against Bruno Bauer, a Feuerbachian deviationist — and in the *German Ideology*, a large work which was written to 'settle acounts with our philosophic conscience' and only published in fragmentary form after Marx's death.* In the *Holy Family* the idea that economic interest determined the political success of ideas is already worked out. The French Revolution was a triumph for the bourgeoisie, a failure only for the masses. For the final, proletarian interest, the old catch-words of liberty and equality were not enough. A new ideology, reflecting a new society, was imperative.

As already noted, the emancipation of Marx from the orthodox Hegelian idealism of his student days left him dissatisfied with Feuerbach's socially unconstructive views. In the *Theses on Feuerbach*, a short and singularly revealing document of four pages, discovered among Marx's papers after his death, and written in 1843, this criticism is clearly expressed.[6] 'The chief defect of all materialism up to now (including Feuerbach's) is, that, the object, reality, what we apprehend through our senses, is understood only in the form of the *object* or *contemplation*, but not as *sensuous human activity*, as *practice*.' The active side of consciousness was still relegated to abstraction. For Marx this was intolerable. Feuerbach's views are also too individualistic. Only as part of society is man able to act upon it: '. . . the essence of man is no abstraction inherent in each separate individual. In its reality, it is the ensemble of the social relations'. Where the old materialism thinks in terms of a contract, dialectical materialism thinks in terms of 'social humanity'. Only in this creative way can its objective be achieved. 'The philosophers have only interpreted the world differently, the point is to change it.' By combining Feuerbach's materialism with Hegelian dialectic, Marx retains the Hegelian drive. And he had stood the dialectic 'the right way up'.

This feat had not been achieved without rancour. He sneers, while attacking him, at conventional Germans shocked by Feuerbach. For his own part, he is concerned with real men. Against the idealists, he stressed environment. 'Ideas are not determined by consciousness, but consciousness by life.' All is determined by the stage of development of the means of production. 'The class which has the means of material production at its disposal has control at the same time over the means of mental production.'[7]

Revolution is thus intellectually as well as socially inevitable. Marx, still a young man, was writing in the Paris of 1843. His hopes were set on the transformation of society, this time in terms of working-class supremacy. Engels thought it inevitable owing to economic

* 'We abandoned the manuscript to the stinging criticism of the mice.'

conditions: Marx supplied the philosophical justification. 'It must be achieved not only because the ruling class cannot be overthrown in any other way, but also because the class overthrowing it can only in a revolution succeed in ridding itself of all the muck of ages and become fitted to found society anew.'[8] The roughs of Paris were to cleanse the world, among other things, of German metaphysicians. It was a naive hope. In principle, it remained in Marx's mind until his death.* It is expressed in the concluding sentence of the attack on Proudhon, the *Misère de la Philosophie*, in which Marx and Engels formulated their economic creed in terms of a Ricardo turned to socialism and a Hegel turned economist.

So the second stage in the development of the Marx-Engels theory had been attained. The facts collected by Engels were interpreted by a theory which retained Hegel's belief in the dialectical movement of history and in Feuerbach's materialism, yet was purged of metaphysics and of academic detachment. The total explanation demanded by the fashion of the day and the bias of their minds was being formulated.

IV

In the *Communist Manifesto* all these elements were combined.† They were also heavily reinforced by economic arguments, drawn in part from English classical economists, with their belief in iron economic laws. This view of the decisive importance of economics gave rise to a wide and simplified survey of the course of history. Thus a third element was finally assimilated into the original synthesis and into the philosophy of dialectical materialism that inspired it.

Like many famous documents, the *Manifesto* was a *pièce d'occasion*.‡

* See his idealizing of the thugs of the Paris Commune in 1871, 'The cocottes had refound the scent of their protectors – the absconding men of family, religion and, above all, of property. In their stead, the real women of Paris showed again at the surface – heroic, noble and devoted, like the women of antiquity. Working, thinking, fighting, bleeding Paris – almost forgetful, in its incubation of a new society, of the cannibals at its gates – radiant in the enthusiasm of its historic initiative.' The tone of this passage, with its reference to Antiquity, is still, in the 'seventies, that of the old romantics of the original Revolution. *The Civil War in France*, with an Introduction by Friedrich Engels, p. 50. Lawrence & Wishart, 1933.

† See *The Communist Manifesto, Socialist landmark*. Edited H. J. Laski. Allen & Unwin, 1948, pp. 124-68, and *The Manifesto of the Communist Party*, edited F. Engels, 1888 edition. This contains five prefaces by Engels. Lawrence & Wishart, 1933.

‡ 'It is evident', writes Laski, 'from the whole content of the *Manifesto*, that when it was written Marx and Engels were convinced that the day of reckoning was close at hand, and this is why there was a certain note of apocalyptic urgency about their discussions. It is not less evident that they believed – of course mistakenly – that the birthplace of the social revolution they anticipated was certain to be Germany.' Op. cit., p. 33.

It was jointly composed in Brussels, in January 1848, for German members of the Communist League in London. The original German draft was early translated into French. It appeared in English in 1850, and was translated into Italian, Danish and Flemish. It was done into Russian in 1863, published in America in 1872 and in Spain in 1886.

The powerful, melodramatic document is world famous. And, indeed, it is a masterpiece of political propaganda. It gives the essentials of Marxism, in concentrated and popular form; it has been compared with the American Declaration of Independence and the Declaration of the Rights of Man. The comparison goes far to explain the debasement of politics in the twentieth century. The *Manifesto*, like the later nineteenth-century slogans of nationalism, breathes hatred and revenge: it is disfigured by vulgar abuse, and it ends with incitement to violence on a world scale. It compares ill with the old masterpieces of political thought. Its most important, and erroneous, assumption, as Professor Popper well remarks, is that 'politics are impotent'.* It attacked all concepts of the rule of Law and self-government developed in answer to the central and perennial problem of politics, the control of power.

By asserting that economic forces are more fundamental than political institutions, Marx and Engels, like most pioneers, overplayed their hand. In politically mature countries the adjustment of economic forces by consent has since proved practicable. In response to popular will, constitutionally expressed, it has already gone far to supersede the class-struggle so imminent in the 'forties of the nineteenth century. The mitigation of the trade cycle by government intervention in the light of Keynesian economic theory; the levelling of gross inequalities of fortune by Liberal and Fabian welfare legislation, the widespread diffusion of small property in spite of the concentration of managerial power, the guarantee by government of basic economic security, have since largely cleared the jungle of laissez-faire without the disruption of society. But in great Asiatic and African areas, where constitutionalism has no ancient roots, Marx's incitement to violence still proves its force. And his assertion of the inevitability of conflict still haunts the world.

The *Manifesto* is designed in four parts. After a short statement of the major theme, the first, 'Bourgeois and Proletarians', surveys the historical evolution of society; the second defines the relations of

---

* See the *Open Society and its Enemies*, vol. II, 'The High Tide of Prophecy', for an admirable and witty analysis, pp. 111ff.

Communists to the Proletariat and to the goal of the classless society; the third, on Socialist and Communist literature, scarifies most other revolutionary theories. The fourth is tactical. It defines 'The position of the Communists in Relation to the various existing opposition Parties.'

The opening passage shows the authors' flair for propaganda. 'A spectre', they say, 'is haunting Europe — the spectre of Communism.' And Communism is now a power. Like Calvin, in the preface to his epoch-making *Institutes*, Marx and Engels at once define their aim. In fact Communism was not at the time at all formidable. Nationalism was much more powerful on the Continent; in England the influence even of the Chartists had become negligible. In stating that a weak movement was irresistible, the authors of the *Manifesto* observed a cardinal rule of political warfare.

Following this powerful opening, as of some dark symphony of Sibelius, the whole panorama of recorded history is telescopically reviewed. As seen by Marx and Engels, it was a nightmare. They had assimilated the static fatalism of the classical political economists, crossed with the dynamics of Hegel. Their blistering hatred of established society spiced their doctrine with extraordinary venom.

The essence of this doctrine, stripped of the powerful rhetoric of the *Manifesto* itself, is succinctly and soberly defined by Engels in his Preface of 1888. 'That in every historical epoch, the prevailing mode of economic production and exchange, and the social organization necessarily following from it, form the basis upon which is built up, and from which alone can be explained the political and intellectual history of that epoch; that consequently the whole history of mankind (since the dissolution of primitive tribal society, holding land in common ownership) has been a history of class struggles ... in which, nowadays, a stage has been reached when the exploited and oppressed class — the proletariat — cannot attain its emancipation from the sway of the exploiting and ruling class — the bourgeoisie — without, at the same time, once and for all emancipating society at large from all exploitation, oppression, class distinctions and class struggles.'

Reiterating the claim made over Marx's grave in 1883, Engels concludes, 'This proposition, which in my opinion, is destined to do for history what Darwin's theory has done for biology, we, both of us, had been gradually approaching for some years before 1845.'

Such a view of history, wildly hopeful and deterministically sombre, is now dramatically elaborated. The surge of class conflict and economic exploitation has broken successive class dominations, and swept the whole planet into the net of a world market. The new world-interest had smashed the tottering fabric of feudal society. The bourgeoisie now captured political power. From the fierce medieval communes, through the urban republics of Italy and Germany, and the alliance of monarchy and third estate, the new class has attained, in the modern representative state, exclusive political sway. The executive of the modern state is but a committee for managing the common affairs of the whole bourgeoisie'.[9]

And all this has been brought about by the inevitable process of Dialectical Materialism. In obedience to this compulsion, 'the bourgeoisie, wherever it has got the upper hand, has put an end to all feudal, idyllic relations. It has pitilessly torn asunder the motley feudal ties that bound man to his "natural superiors", and has left no other nexus between man and man than naked self-interest and callous "cash payment"'. Where Spencer and Buckle and Maine were to see, in the progress from status to contract, the secret of civilization's advance, Marx and Engels regarded it as the destruction of fundamental liberties. The bourgeoisie, they continue, 'has drowned the most heavenly ecstacies of religious fervour, of chivalrous enthusiasm, of philistine sentimentalism, in the icy water of egotistical calculation . . . The bourgeoisie has stripped of its halo every occupation hitherto honoured and looked up to with reverent awe. It has converted the physician, the lawyer, the priest, the poet, the man of science, into its paid wage labourers. The bourgeoisie has torn away from the family its sentimental veil. . . .'*

Under the same compulsion, bourgeois achievements have been staggering. 'It has been the first to show what man's activities can bring about. It has accomplished wonders far surpassing Egyptian pyramids, Roman aqueducts, and Gothic cathedrals, it has conducted expeditions that put in the shade all former exoduses of nations and crusades.' It has dominated the world.

'The cheap prices of its commodities are the heavy artillery with which it batters down all Chinese walls, with which it forces the barbarians' intensely obstinate hatred of foreigners to capitulate.' It had conjured vast towns into existence, which dwarf the greatest cities of the past, and 'rescued a considerable part of the population from the idiocy of rural life'. Huge agglomerations, massive enterprise, unheard of power — in their admiration for the *kolossal*, the

---

* Ten out of eleven of the thudding clauses of this indictment begin with the words The bourgeoisie . . .', pp. 128-31 (Laski edition).

authors of the *Manifesto* pay their tribute to the class they thought themselves fated to destroy.

This huge cosmopolitan development creates a civilization in which national and provincial differences are obliterated. No more than the prophets of Free Trade, did Marx and Engels foresee the power of economic nationalism. The picture they paint is the cosmopolitan vision of the Free Trader in reverse. It is painted with all the brave colours of nineteenth-century materialism. The whole panoramic description of the march of history is inspired with a profound admiration for power.

As the disruption of feudal ties came about through the force of bourgeois production — 'they had to be burst asunder; they were burst asunder' — today the same fate is overtaking bourgeois civilization. It is 'like the sorcerer who is no longer able to control the powers of the nether world whom he has called up by his spells'. Hence the periodical alternation of boom and slump, which put 'the existence of the entire bourgeois society on its trial, each time more threateningly'. The 'epidemic of over production', inherent in capitalist economy, creates the paradox of famine amid plenty. 'Society suddenly finds itself put back into a state of momentary barbarism ... and Why? Because there is too much civilization, too much means of subsistence, too much industry, too much commerce.' As bourgeois society staggers to destruction, a new class inevitably comes to power — the modern proletariat. It is created and organized by the very process of capitalist expansion. In the shadows of the future the workers wait. In the new society they will at last release and distribute the pent up force of modern production.

The first blind reaction of this new proletariat was to smash the machines and wreck the factories. They next attacked the remnant of the old order, the aristocracy and land owners, as in the French Revolution. The real enemy only became apparent with the rise of great industry and great towns. Now, urban and organized, they unite. The railways have increased their solidarity. Their economic interest is now reflected in politics, for 'every class struggle is a political struggle'. They are finding external reinforcement as 'a small section of the ruling class cuts itself adrift, and joins the revolutionary class, the class that holds the future in its hands'. For these intellectuals have at last 'raised themselves' to the level of comprehending what is going on.

In the dramatic, Hegelian, and predestined unfolding of history, the new urban proletariat now takes the place of the bourgeoisie as a world historic class.* It is distinct from the peasants and the petit-bourgeois, who cling to a way of life destined to disappear. Distinct also from the *lumpen-proletariat*, 'the social scum', who are more likely to become the 'bribed tool of reactionary intrigue'. This skilled proletariat is organized, modern and desperate. They have no property; they are without true family ties, devoid even of patriotism. They are crushed down into a cosmopolitan degradation 'stripped . . . of every trace of national character'. The worker is totally disillusioned with a civilization by which he has been victimized. 'Law, morality, religion, are to him so many bourgeois prejudices.'

The new theory was extremely formidable. It was a myth which rationalized, and compensated, the vast perennial grievance of the poor. This massive proletariat, Marx declares, the final historical world-revolutionary class, is a portent unique in history. It is the first class not to be a minority. 'The proletarian movement is the self-conscious independent movement of the immense majority, in the interest of the immense majority.' Before this inescapable threat, bourgeois society can only go its fated way. Inevitably it at once exasperates and organizes; it goes on thrusting the proletariat deeper into poverty, until 'pauperism develops more rapidly than population and wealth'. Society begins to break down. The ruling class is plainly no longer fit to rule; 'society can no longer live under the bourgeoisie'. 'The development of modern industry, therefore, cuts from under its feet the very foundation on which the bourgeoisie produces and expropriates products. What the bourgeoisie . . . produces above all, is its own grave diggers. Its fall and the victory of the proletariat are equally inevitable.'

Such is the mechanical, massive argument, at once abstract yet apparently practical, which forms the core of the *Communist Manifesto*. It is a masterpiece of propaganda. It is simple, authoritative, dogmatic; it struck home directly to the masses for which it was designed. It offered certainty, hope, and revenge. Rousseau had written 'man is born free but he is everywhere in chains'; now to Rousseau's heady phrases was added a sustained, apparently scientific, argument. Where Rousseau worked with gun-powder, here was dynamite.

Against the background of this grim, clear-cut dogma, expressed with lurid historical imagination, Marx and Engels proceed, in the second part of the *Manifesto*, to define their aims. First the position

* Compare Hegel's conception of world-historic nations.

and purpose of the Communist party is described. They are 'the most advanced and resolute section of the working class parties of every country, that section which pushes forward all others ... clearly understanding the line of march'. This militant élite is to weld the proletariat into a class, to destroy bourgeois supremacy and to win political power for the masses. Communists will not abolish small personal property, but they will abolish private ownership of the social means of production. For capital is social power. It must be deprived of the means of expropriating other men. Such confiscation will not destroy liberty and culture, it will only destroy bourgeois liberty and culture, which for the vast majority of wage earners do not exist. Middle class notions of freedom and law have no absolute validity; they reflect a phase of economic evolution. Civilization is thus identified with the proletariat. Universal moral, intellectual and aesthetic standards, the work of men of genius from all classes and times, are repudiated.

In the political sphere Marx's abstract dogmatism becomes even more glaring. Whatever the economic condition of society, basic political problems are constant. They are psychological and practical. The pages of Aristotle, Thucydides or Machiavelli centre on perennial problems of moral behaviour, upon the perennial problems of power. Yet the Marxist destruction of standards was later to be applied even to the realm of science and technology. After repudiating traditional politics and morality, Marx attacks the family. The 'bourgeois family', they assert, 'will vanish as a matter of course'. Like morality, it is again the mere reflection of economic evolution. And here the *Manifesto* deviates from assertion into abuse. It speaks of 'bourgeois claptrap about the family and education'. Drawing up an indictment against a whole class, Marx and Engels declare that 'the bourgeois sees in his wife the mere instrument of production ... Not content with having the wives and daughters of their proletarians at their disposal, not to speak of common prostitutes, [they] take the greatest pleasure in seducing each others wives'. 'Bourgeois marriage,' they declare wildly, 'is really a system of wives in common.'*

Defending the Communist plan to abolish nationalism, Marx

* This passage comes curiously from the pen of Engels. But Mehring finds no difficulty in glossing over his peccadilloes. 'He was a highly respected member of the Manchester Stock Exchange, and prominent both in the business and the pleasures of the English bourgeoisie, its fox hunting, its Christmas parties, but the *intellectual leader and fighter* had a treasure in a little house far away on the other side of the town, a child of Ireland, and in her arms he recovered his spirits, when he had grown all too tired of the bourgeois pack in whose midst he was compelled to live.' Op. cit., p. 232.

and Engels assert that its decline is now already doing so. Already 'the working men have no country, we cannot take from them what they have not got'. In view of the history of nationalism in the next hundred years, the following passage appears hardly a gem of prophecy. 'The national differences and antagonisms between peoples are daily more and more vanishing . . . united action of the leading civilized countries at least is one of the first conditions for the emancipation of the proletariat.' Nationalism, they assert hopefully, is only the result of internal class conflict. Finally, as if to make their contribution to the enrichment of civilization quite clear, Marx and Engels, both intellectuals of the deepest dye, repudiate the principles on which intellectual vitality is based. Since, in their view, the dreary compulsion of class war has dominated all history, notions of religious liberty and intellectual freedom merely reflect 'the sway of free competition within the domain of knowledge'. Here, indeed, is the cloven hoof of Teutonic professorial dogma. In the new society, a more than Comtian orthodoxy will plainly rule the world.

Having defined their views on property, the family, nationalism and intellectual liberty, the authors of the *Manifesto* describe their immediate objective. It is to substitute the rule of one class for that of another, 'to win the battle of democracy'. Not, save as an occasional tactical manœuvre, by democratic means. Violent revolution is the immediate programme. 'The objective of the proletariat will be to wrest by degrees all capital from the bourgeoisie, to centralize all means of production in the state, i.e. the proletariat organized as the ruling class.' Having seized power, the Communists will abolish landed property, impose a heavy graduated income tax, destroy all rights of inheritance and confiscate the property of all 'emigrants and rebels'. They will nationalize all banks and transport, win control of all instruments of production, and embark on a great agricultural plan. All citizens will be obliged to work. 'Industrial armies' will be established, especially on the land; the distinction between town and country will be gradually abolished. There will be free education, geared to industry, in state schools.

This part of the *Manifesto* ends on a panegyric on the new society. Having advocated an economic, political and intellectual tyranny which puts the amateurish ideas in Hobbes's *Leviathan* in the shade, Marx and Engels deprive their state of all constitutional safeguards, discard the rule of Law as a bourgeois prejudice, and make the extraordinary and Fourieresque assumption that this Minotaur will of itself dissolve. 'When,' they write, 'in the course of development, class distinctions have disappeared and all production has been concentrated in the hands of a vast association of the whole nation, the public power will lose its political character.' For here is the Hegelian negation of the negation. Having abolished the old order, the proletariat will have 'swept away the conditions for the existence of class antagonisms and of classes generally, and will have there-by abolished its own supremacy as a class'. The old early-nine-teenth-century romantic Utopia has reappeared.

Even the anarchist Bakunin found this too much. 'We be-lieve,' he wrote, criticizing Marxist *étatisme*, 'power corrupts those who wield it as much as those who are forced to obey it ... Intellectuals, positivists, doctrinaires, all who put science before life, defend the idea of the state and its authority ... the difference be-tween such revolutionary dictatorship and the modern state is only one of external trappings. In substance, both are a tyranny of the minority over the majority — in the name of the many and the supreme wisdom of the few — and so they are equally reactionary, devising to secure political and economic privilege to the ruling minority and the enslavement of the masses, to destroy the present order, only to erect their own rigid dictatorship on its ruins.'[10]

Bakunin's opinion is that of a fellow revolutionary. It is reinforced by the great political thinkers of the past and by the long history of the dangers of arbitrary power. Yet, having depicted a Leviathan without precedent in history, having destroyed the customary safe-guards, rationalized as Law and rooted in primitive custom, which from time immemorial have diminished the abuse of power in politically mature societies, these eloquent theorists assumed, with a strange echo of Rousseau, that 'in place of the old bourgeois society with its classes and class antagonisms, we shall have an association in which the free development of each is the condition of the free development of all'.

Marx and Engels had set out their dogma and defined their objectives. They proceed, in varying degrees, to attack all other forms of revolutionary thought. With savage precision the ninepins are successively knocked down. Feudal socialism is a blind reaction — 'the Holy water with which the priest consecrates the heart-burn-ings of the aristocrat'. The middle class socialism of Sismondi has done good critical service, but it would cramp the development of modern means of production. It is both reactionary and utopian: it has ended in a 'miserable fit of the blues'. For German or 'True'

socialism Marx reserves his most withering contempt. It is an emasculated version of French ideas; 'beneath the French criticism of the
bourgeois state they write dethronement of the category of the
general'. It is the 'bombastic representative of the petit-bourgeois
Philistine'. Most of it is foul and enervating. As for the reformist
levelling 'mutualism' of Proudhon, it is a mere screen for capitalist
interests — 'the bourgeois is a bourgeois for the benefit of the working
class'. And the Utopian socialism of Saint-Simon, Fourier and Owen
is premature, out of touch with economic realities. They reject the
class war and end in fantasy. Shirking the contest, they become
increasingly ineffective and even hinder the class struggle. Owenites
oppose Chartists, and Fourierists the exponents of direct action.

So with the self-righteousness of Calvinist theologians, and an acri-
mony all their own, the authors of the *Manifesto* relegate all rivals to
limbo. They strike the domineering note of the dusty and endless
vistas of Marxist controversy. There is no compromise, no humanity; all is ferocious and solemn, in the worst German academic
tradition. They conclude with some tactical advice, which does little
credit to their political foresight. The revolution, they insist, is
destined to take place in Germany, 'because that country is on the
eve of a bourgeois revolution that is bound to be carried out under
more advanced conditions of European civilization and with a much
more developed proletariat than that of England was in the seventeenth, and of France in the eighteenth century, and because the
bourgeois revolution in Germany will be but the prelude to an
immediately following proletarian revolution'. Marx spent the rest
of his life expecting this upheaval. In spite of disappointments, he
was hopeful to the end. As Professor Berlin points out, 'he was all
his life a convinced and uncompromising believer in a violent
working-class revolution'.

On the eve of this supposed upheaval the *Manifesto* concludes,
as it began, on an apocalyptic note. There is the same touch of
melodrama, reminiscent of 1789. 'The communists disdain to conceal their views and aims. They openly declare that their ends can
only be achieved by the forceful overthrow of all existing social conditions. Let the ruling classes tremble at a communist revolution. The
proletarians have nothing to lose but their chains. They have a world
to win. Working men of all countries unite.'

Marx and Engels had thus gathered up and simplified their earlier
thought. They had defined the dogma of their revolution, its theory,
its objectives, and its plan. They had created one of the great politi-

cal myths of world history. That the *Manifesto* is based on assumptions divorced from reality, and upon a distorted view of the past; that its economics are unsound, and its prophecies erroneous, is irrelevant to its power. Marx and Engels, doctrinaire theorists, believed, like other nineteenth-century 'discoverers' of the laws of history, in the objective truth of their analysis. This, too, is irrelevant. They had set out, like Comte and Herbert Spencer, to create a science of politics and implement it. They had created a new, atheist, religion.

This religion, though likely to provide the force which, alone, in primitive societies, could cause revolution, was unlikely to contribute to human solidarity and world-order. Where at the core of Christianity, for example, beneath the dogmatic conflicts to which it has given rise, there is humanity, the Marxist mythology is full of hate. On its own admission, it cuts across the far more ancient tradition of collaboration, of human commonwealth, of constitutional self-government. Yet that tradition reflects an unbroken primitive solidarity, continuing through the conflicts and exploitations which history records. Even their fellow revolutionaries could not accept the new myth: hence Proudhon's and Kropotkin's detestation of Marx.

Political realists may remark that the social effect of all religious and metaphysical beliefs is the maintenance of elites, the preservation of leadership.[11] And it may be argued that since Christian dogma was then losing its authority, a myth based on atheism and evolution was necessary to control the masses in the nineteenth and twentieth centuries. By facing, as Comte and Proudhon and Schopenhauer faced, the apparently stark facts of mid-nineteenth-century knowledge, by giving the people a substitute for the transcendental religion in which they had ceased to believe, a Communist elite, it can be argued, have today secured their own preponderance in powerful states. And, with it, that maintenance of privilege and leadership which has always been the condition of civilization. Hence the usefulness of the Marxist myth in its twentieth-century interpretation, in particular in politically and economically primitive areas.

Such a view is less realistic than it looks. Undiluted in a planetary twentieth-century context, the Marxist myth can lead only to a world-wide conflict that would destroy the civilization Marx was determined to transform.

Varying interpretations have naturally been made of Marxism, according to the Western, central European or Eastern background of those concerned. The Webbs, in their liberal constitutional setting, took what they wanted from it, but discarded its revolutionary violence. Bernstein in Germany and Jaurès in France endeavoured to adapt it to a social democratic programme. But the original writings would seem to demonstrate that the most faithful political interpreters of Marx have been Lenin and Stalin, with their historic background of tyranny and disregard for life. Inevitable class war and dictatorship are basic to the original creed. On the merest pragmatic considerations, a less barbarous political theory is better suited to the twentieth century, in particular since nuclear weapons have made theories of inevitable violence incompatible with the continuance of ordered society.

CHAPTER VI

MARX AND ENGELS, II

THE development of Marxist theory up to the Revolutions of 1848-49 has been indicated; its philosophic, political, and economic origins briefly surveyed. The dogma was the work of young men, ardent revolutionaries, expectant of the overthrow of middle-class domination and existing society.

These expectations failed. The remainder of Marx's life was passed in exile. To this second period belong the pamphlets and articles in which Marx's ability as a political journalist and Engels's power of exposition are most strikingly displayed. The highly technical *A Contribution to the Critique of Political Economy*; the masterpiece, the three great volumes of *Das Kapital*, of which only the first appeared while Marx was alive, are reinforced by the systematic, often lucid, explanation of the doctrine written by Engels, with Marx's collaboration, in the *Anti-Dühring*.

There were numerous other writings: *The Class Struggle in France* (1871); Engels on Feuerbach; Engels on the *Origin of the Family*. In the scale of this study only the more outstanding documents can be examined. First, one of the most powerful of Marx's pamphlets, *The Eighteenth Brumaire of Louis Bonaparte*, will be taken to represent Marx's historical analysis. Next, an attempt will be made to elucidate the economic theory contained in the *Contribution*, to chart the broad argument of the first volume of *Das Kapital*, and describe the flavour and impact of this formidable work. Then the *Anti-Dühring*, probably the most succinct exposition of the total theory, will be examined. Finally, the Marx-Engels contribution to the political thought of the nineteenth century will be related to other traditions.

The Eighteenth Brumaire was written in defiant and rueful mood. Exiled and in penury, in the smoke and grime of mid-Victorian London — his overcoat in pawn — Marx set himself to explain this shocking sequel to the failure of the Revolution. And he seized the opportunity to wring lessons from the failure. The pamphlet is regarded by Marxists as an 'object lesson in political analysis', occasioned by the first crude manifestation of proto-Fascism.* Written

---

* It was first published, in German, in the United States in 1852. The translation by E. and C. Paul (Allen & Unwin, 1926) is in seven chapters (127 pp.) with a fervid introduction by the translators. 'In the hope of making the study of this classic easier' they have even 'furthermore, ventured to write a foreword'. There is a laudatory preface by Engels

within a few weeks of Louis Napoleon's *coup d'état*, the tract insists upon total class war. Fiasco, Marx points out, is bound to occur when proletarian revolutionaries are deceived by the specious promises of bourgeois reform and think in terms of the obsolete ideology of 1789. The book, Engels claims, has fathomed an inevitable sequence of events. 'Never', he writes, 'have we had an example of so fine a penetration into the meaning of living history.' Thucydides, Tacitus, Machiavelli, he implies, were amateurs. For Marx, with his eagle eye, had perceived the 'great law' of the class struggle. He 'could never be taken unawares by events'.

The rise of the false Napoleon was exactly what was to be expected. 'For my part,' wrote Marx, 'I prove that the class war in France created circumstances and relationships that enabled a grotesque mediocrity to strut about in a hero's garb.' Marx, his collaborator in turn indefatigably insists, 'was the first to discover the great law which governs the march of history . . the more or less clear expression of struggles between social classes . . . This Law bears the same relationship to history as the law of the conservation of energy bears towards the physical sciences'.

This typically mid-nineteenth-century conviction pervades the entire pamphlet. But within these limits Marx achieved a biting analysis. The revolution failed, he argues, through lack of realism. It was premature, naive. 'In consequence the coup-de-main of February 1848 was answered by the coup-de-tête of December 1851.' Once for all it must be understood that the idea of liberal revolution is superseded. 'The legacy of the dead generations weighs like an alp upon the brains of the living.' The Roman phrases of 1789 spoke of liberty, but the real victors were the bourgeoisie. In the English revolution of the seventeenth century, 'in like manner . . . Cromwell and the English people had borrowed the phraseology, the emotions, and the illusions of the Old Testament as trappings for their own bourgeois revolution. As soon as they had reached the goal, as soon as the bourgeois transformation of English society had been effected, Locke supplanted Habakkuk'.* The proletarian revolution must now have its own ideas; 'the revolutionaries of the nineteenth century

---

* p. 25. Here is the *fons et origo* of a misinterpretation of the English Civil Wars which has been going on ever since at Marxist hands. For a more understanding modern view, see W. SCHENK, *The Concern for Social Justice in the Puritan Revolution.* Longmans, 1948.

---

and the text is followed by a phonetic glossary. Achilles, it is pointed out, should be pronounced 'A-kil-eez', and 'in partibus', 'in-pahrti-buhss, usually anglicized like omnibus'. Equipped with this knowledge, the unlettered will be able to grasp Marx's political analysis.

must let the dead bury their dead'. Self-criticism is the watch-word. A cold assessment of the position shows that sanguine hopes of victory were premature, in view of the 'materials to hand, the cultural level of the masses, existent circumstances and conditions'. Of course the alliance of plutocracy with the peasants, lower middle class and slum proletariat, has found expression in dictatorship. What else, he asks, with a sardonic, knowing, diagnosis, backed by the panoramic sense of situation apparent in the *Manifesto*, could the fools expect? Liberal politicians have been equally idiotic. In consequence they have been dragged from their beds in the fog and thrust into the Black Maria. Now the gloves are off, the class war declared, naked force in control.

A 'state of siege' has created a 'night in which all cats are grey and in which all the ghouls return'. This shows what 'bourgeois principles' are worth. Of course all that matters is interest. The rest is illusion. One must also distinguish between what men do and what they say and even believe. For 'upon the different forms of property . . . there is built a superstructure of diversified and characteristic sentiments, illusions, habits of thought and outlooks on life in general'. These ideas merely reflect the economic interests, indeed, the compulsions, of those concerned. Hence the folly of social democrats who attempt reconciliation of classes, who think in terms of compromise. Such views are contemptible before the reality of class war; the inexorable, massive march of events. Marx writes with blistering contempt of 'the incurable disease of parliamentary imbecility', and describes how, in obedience to the compulsion of their interest, the 'industrial bourgeoisie servilely acclaim the coup d'état'.

The peasants, too, are naturally wrong.[1] 'They have signed a covenant with the underworld of history.' The bureaucracy is wrong — they are 'understrappers', a 'dreadful parasitic growth'. The journalists are all venal — witness the 'huckstering clamour with which the newspapers mouth their slogans'. As for the slum proletariat, it sells itself to plutocracy, and the lower middle classes are imprisoned in ideas which reflect their mean occupations. All the world is united against the class-concious industrial proletariat.

Yet the very isolation of the proletariat, the stark conflict, helps 'to mass the revolutionary forces of destruction for the onslaught'. When the time is ripe and their day comes, 'Europe will leap to her feet and exclaim "Old mole! Cans't work i' the earth so fast? A worthy pioneer!" '[2]

The *Eighteenth Brumaire* concludes with a paean of hatred against the bourgeoisie and bureaucrats. Former revolutions have merely cemented their venal alliance. As for the peasants, they are in debt to the urban plutocrats, so that 'the mass of the French are a nation of troglodytes'. In time they will turn against the middle class usurers — for the state is a vampire, the tool of the bourgeoisie. All these things are necessary, Marx concludes, that the class conflict may be fulfilled.

II

The doctrine of class conflict was now to be reinforced by more elaborate economic sanctions. The core of Marx's economic theory is most succinctly expressed in his tortuous and technical *A Contribution to the Critique of Political Economy*, first published in 1859,* the year that saw the appearance of Darwin's *Origin of Species*. It was designed as the first instalment of a complete treatise; the full and classic formulation of the class conflict through the materialist interpretation of philosophy, history and economics. This design was never completed, but the first volume of *Das Kapital* repeated the basic labour theory of value in what Marx considered a relatively popular form.

Marx claims the authority of systematic research. On this, during the 'fifties, he had been engaged. 'This account of my studies in political economy', he writes, 'is simply to prove that my views, whatever one may think of them . . . are the result of many years conscientious research.'† Trained originally as a philosopher and a lawyer, Marx had early found himself 'embarrassed' by ignorance of economics. As a journalist he had to deal with the economic affairs of the Moselle peasantry, and with current controversies over Protection or Free Trade. He had therefore turned to master the 'science' of political economy, in which, he had come to believe, 'the anatomy of civil society' is to be sought. This conviction, which already dominated the *Communist Manifesto* and the *Eighteenth Brumaire*, is here again elaborately expressed. 'The mode of production in material life determines the general character of the social, political and spiritual processes of life.'³ Hegelian fatalism and Feuerbach's crass materialism were again reinforced by the belief in

---

* Translation from the second German edition by N. I. Stone (based on that of K. Kautsky, 1877), New York, 1904. This edition contains the unfinished and unpublished introduction written in 1857.

† Preface, p. 15. For another view of this research see DURKHEIM, *infra*, p. 453.

economic laws inherited from the classical economists. 'It is not', Marx again insists, in a famous phrase, 'the consciousness of men that determines their existence, but, on the contrary, their social existence determines their consciousness.'

As the ground swell of economic development undermines the laws of property, suitable to an earlier stage, 'with the change of the economic foundation the entire immense superstructure is more or less rapidly transformed'.[4] Here, again, with its massive appeal to practical minds, is the belief that the economic stage of production is decisive, and that its development can 'be determined with the precision of a natural science'. The ideological superstructure falls into place. It is merely a legal, political, aesthetic, philosophical projection 'in which men become conscious of this conflict and fight it out'. The radical assumption of conflict was here further reinforced by Marx's version of economic 'science'. And assuming that 'ideology' is peripheral, he again attempts to cut the ground from beneath the feet of those who maintain permanent standards of morality. 'Just as our opinion of an individual is not based on what he thinks of himself, so can we not judge of such a period of transformation by its own consciousness.'[5] History is intelligible only to those who have grasped the economic laws which form its basic and necessary explanation. This historical development has passed through four great phases. The first Asiatic, the second ancient, the third feudal, the fourth bourgeois (*Bürgerlich*).* In this vast, systematic development, which proceeds with the automatism of a machine, change conveniently comes about only when the 'material conditions for its solution' exist. The fourth phase of 'Bürgerliche Produktion' is now beginning to break down, as the previous Feudal stage declined. This last 'social formation' constitutes, *therefore*,† the closing chapter of the prehistoric stage of human society.

Against this now familiar world-historical background, the Marxist labour theory of surplus value must be set. It is said that William Morris, in a moment of exasperation, remarked, 'I am asked if I believe in Marx's theory of surplus value. To speak quite frankly, I do not know what Marx's theory of value is, and I'm damned if I want to know.'[6] This robust ignorance is still widely shared. Many, indeed, will feel Morris's outlook admirable. Since the theory is fundamental to Marxism, an outline of it will here be given. To

---

* This notorious Hegelian term, for which there is no exact equivalent in English, has a slightly different and less hostile nuance in the original German to the sound and meaning of the French 'bourgeois', which has had to be impressed into English to translate it.

† Italics mine.

master its inmost complexity and the voluminous and ferocious controversies which it occasioned, one must study the full text of the *Contribution*. It is comparatively short, and from its economic errors some of the fundamental flaws in Marxist theory derive.*

The technical arguments whereby Marx justifies his theory are now generally regarded as obsolete. Like Rousseau's mysterious General Will, it is still a formidable myth. For it claimed to prove that labour alone creates social wealth. This wealth is subsequently cornered by the capitalist, who thus inevitably robs the worker of his due. Every commodity, Marx assumes, quoting, like many writers before him, one of Aristotle's more misleading utterances, has a two-fold aspect. It has use value and exchange value. One can use one's shoes, for example, said the philosopher, for two purposes. The proper use is to wear them. But it is sometimes necessary to use them for barter. Their value will then no longer be to protect one's feet, but whatever can be obtained by the exchange. Now what determines their exchange-value as opposed to use-value? It is the amount of 'socially necessary working time' they represent. Labour-power is the fundamental element in wealth. Marx quotes that eminent contemporary of John Aubrey, Sir William Petty, whom he regards as the father of English classical political economy. Petty, who had made a great fortune out of the survey of Cromwellian Ireland, declared that 'labour was the father and earth the mother of wealth'. He was also Adam Smith's precursor in formulating a theory of division of labour.† He was fundamentally right. With a wealth of industry and elaborate notes, Marx now traces the development of the classical theory of value from Petty through Locke, Bishop Berkeley, Benjamin Franklin and Ricardo. All maintain the ancient emphasis on the importance of labour; Locke had, indeed, defined property as what a man had 'mixed his labour with'. It follows that the exchange value represents 'crystallized' labour. By the abstraction 'socially necessary labour time', Marx attempts to

* For the controversy see P. M. SWEEZY's edition of *Karl Marx and the Close of his System*, by Eugen Böhm-Bawerk, and Böhm-Bawerk's *Criticism of Marx by R. Hilferding*, New York, 1949. Also B. CROCE, *Historical Materialism and the Economics of Karl Marx* (1913).

† Marx cites in particular his *Essay Concerning the Multiplication of Mankind* (1686) and his *Political Arithmetick* (1699). (See C. H. HALL, *The Economic Writings of Sir William Petty*. C.U.P., 1899.) While citing his ideas, Marx depicts Petty in savage terms as a grasping and unscrupulous bourgeois. By contrast, Aubrey, in a more humane manner, writes 'He can be an excellent Droll (if he has a mind to it) and will preach extempore incomparably, either in the Presbyterian way, Independent, Cappucian Friar or Jesuite. He is a proper handsome man . . . a person of great worth and learning, and has such a prodigious working witt that is both fitt for and an honour to, the highest preferment.'

evade the difficulty of equating the value of the man-hours of a navvy with that of an expert.*

Since for purposes of exchange, crystallized labour is equivalent, how does the profit come about? The answer, according to Marx, is that the capitalist buys labour-power — the only commodity he can actually convert into money at a profit. For one commodity alone can give this return. It is labour-power itself. If, for example, a product takes six hours working time to produce, it can be sold for its proper exchange value, ten pounds. If the employer can force the workman, without raising his pay, to work a further three hours, the whole of the resulting surplus will be his. 'Surplus value' is unpaid working time. Thus the capitalist piles up his profits, all of which are robbery.

This theory, presented as an economic law of capitalist society, was naturally to prove a powerful incitement to revolution. If the whole of bourgeois civilization was built, according to the laws of its own being, on the brutal exploitation of the labour-power of the people, the class conflict took on the appearance of a Holy War.

Modern economic thought has long abandoned the view that commodities exchange according to the working time stored up in them. Price is in fact determined by supply and demand; by the amount of capital invested, the scarcity of the raw material involved and many other factors. As Lindsay remarks, 'if Marx's theory of value be taken as an account of what determines the actual value of concrete things, it is obviously untrue'.[7] Böhm-Bawerk, more savagely, writes of 'an abortive dialectic, more arbitrary and untrue to the facts than has ever before been known in the history of our science'.[8] Marx, he maintains — like Hegel, a philosophic genius — had built up what was economically 'a house of cards'. Professor Cole, on the other hand, defends the theory, no longer as a theory of value, but as 'a theory of capitalist exploitation'.[9]

As a basis for the picture of capital as a bloodstained vampire painted by Marx and Engels, it became widely influential. In a society where capital is monopolized by the few, Marx declared, the workers are inevitably exploited. The only way out is to collectivize the means of production. The class conflict, by the nature of economic laws as well as dialectical, is inevitable. This is the moral of the labour theory of value, and it was worked out with a wealth of detail and illustration in *Das Kapital*.

* The standardized term 'horse power' performs a similar function.

The vast enterprise was designed in three volumes. The first, the only one published in Marx's lifetime, will here be examined. With the prefaces to various editions, included at the end of the Paul translation, it, alone, runs to over nine hundred pages.*

Marx's 'Bible of the Working Classes' is a massive, rancorous and obscure book. It is less unreadable than its structure and opening chapters would suggest. Compared, for example, with the wastes of medieval and seventeenth-century theological controversy, or early-nineteenth-century economics, the work is relatively human. Apart from the obsolete economic jargon, particularly apparent in the headings and sub-headings, and particularly daunting in Part I (on Commodities and Money), the massive mechanical argument is sustained and clear. It is indeed overweighted with evidence and footnotes, but luridly lit up by a savage indignation. This mass of material makes the book, in Popper's words, 'a truly imperishable document of human suffering'.[10] In this aspect *Das Kapital* has much in common with Engels's slighter work of 1845.

It is also diversified by much curious learning. With all his hatred for 'bourgeois' culture, Marx was a most formidable scholar. Quotations from Greek and Latin poets, from Dante, Shakespeare and Goethe, came naturally to his polyglot and retentive mind. Vast obscure economic arguments give place to lucid and detailed descriptions of the conditions of the industrial and agricultural poor. They were culled from Reports on factories, on diet, housing, and public health, though how far an estimate of the whole range of these documents would give the picture Marx painted, awaits their further systematic study. There are quotations from Homer, Diodorus Siculus, Horace, and Antipater of Thessalonica. Marx made great game of some fatuous eighteenth-century Anglican divines — for example, of the Reverend J. Townsend, the 'High Church parson',

---

* *Capital. A Critique of Political Economy*, I. The process of Capitalist production. Translated from the 4th German edition by E. and C. Paul (Allen & Unwin, 1928). It is divided into seven parts. They deal with Commodities and Money; with The Transformation of Money into Capital; The Production of Absolute Surplus Value; The Production of Relative Surplus Value; The Production of Absolute Surplus Value and of Relative Surplus Value; with The Accumulation of Capital. There are prefaces to the 1st (German) edition of 1867; to the second of 1873, to the third edition of 1883 (both by Engels) and to the English translation of 1886. The second volume, on *The Process of Circulation of Capital*, was edited by Engels in 1885; translated E. Untermann (Chicago 1909). 610 pp. The third, on *The Process of Capitalist Production as a Whole*, was also edited by Engels in 1894 and translated E. Untermann (Chicago, n.d.). 1032 pp. Both presented a difficult task to the editor, and by the end of the third volume Engels's eyesight was severely impaired.

who 'writing with characteristic brutality glorified poverty as the necessary condition of wealth'.[11] He had a particular detestation for Oxford, that 'hot-bed of Protestant orthodoxy'.* Mr. Gladstone was another of Marx's hobbies. His remarks on the struggle for existence and the 'intoxicating augmentation of wealth and power' in the 'sixties, Marx found particularly detestable. These attacks often merge into hatred which clouds Marx's judgment, as when he prophesied that the United States was destined to take a bloody revenge upon England for the wrongs of Irish peasantry.

The preface to the first German edition of *Das Kapital* (1867) insists on the all-pervading importance of economic 'laws'. 'The subject of study in the present work is the capitalist method of production, and the relations of production and exchange appropriate to that method.' Marx intends to study not the symptoms of the 'natural laws' of capitalist production, but 'these laws in themselves, the tendencies which work out with an iron necessity towards an inevitable goal'.[12] By analysing, as had Engels, conditions in England, the most advanced capitalist country, he presents the Germans, with whom he is primarily concerned, with a 'picture of their own future'. Paying tribute to the work of English social statisticians, he remarks that the Germans would be terrified if they had the equivalent information about their own society. It could be collected 'if it were possible to find in Germany men as competent and as free from bias and from respect of persons, as are the British factory inspectors'. After this tribute to bourgeois civil servants, Marx reiterates what he held to be his central discovery. 'When a society has discovered the natural laws which regulate its own movement' (and the final purpose of my book is to reveal the economic law of motion of modern society) it can neither overleap the natural phases of evolution, nor shuffle them out of the world by decrees. But this much, at least, it can do; it can shorten and lessen the birth pangs.'

The German workers can now understand the revolution in which they are bound to be involved. It is predictable, scientifically inevitable. It is an ugly picture, and Marx admits that he has not been tender to capitalists. But 'if I speak of individuals, it is only in so far as they are personifications of economic categories . . .' 'I should be the last', he writes, 'to hold the individual responsible for conditions whose creature he himself is.' This detachment is rare in the Marx-Engels literature.

---

* He would have been surprised to know that in the nineteen-thirties the home of lost causes was to become a hot-bed of middle-class Marxism.

Marx concludes on the 'scientific' note of the first preface. 'I am ready to welcome scientific criticism. As far as concerns the prejudices of what is termed public opinion, to which I have never made any concessions, I shall continue to guide myself by the axiom of the great Florentine — 'Sequi il tuo corso, e lascia dir le genti'.

In the preface to the second German edition (1873), Marx's hate and scorn for the Germans colours what is a more philosophical argument. He reiterates his dogma of the class struggle. It is economically determined with all the rigidity of Ricardian theory. Nowhere is Marx more obviously the continuator of classical economics. But his main concern is to define his attitude to Hegel. 'For Hegel the thought process . . . is the demiurge of the real; and for him the real is only the outward manifestation of the idea. In my view, on the other hand, the ideal is nothing other than the material when it has been transposed and translated inside the human head.'[13] Yet Hegel was a great philosopher — though by the 'forties the 'peevish and arrogant German professors' treated him as 'a "dead dog".' Though he 'mystified' the dialectic, 'he was the first to expound the general form of its movement. In Hegel's writings dialectic stands on its head. You must turn it right way up again if you want to discover the rational kernel that is hidden away within the wrappings of mystification'.

Having again defined his attitude to Hegel, Marx returns to economics and deploys his argument from the doctrine of surplus value, already elaborated in the *Contribution to a Critique of Political Economy*. 'Capital', he wrote, 'is dead labour', and like the vampire, can only keep itself alive by 'sucking the blood' of living labour; it has a 'were-wolf's hunger' for surplus value. Social power has become private power and gold the Holy Grail. Marx quotes Timon of Athens:

> . . . Gold can place thieves
> And give them title, knee and approbation
> With senators on the bench . . . .[14]

The modern capitalist is driven by an insatiable appetite to hoard. His prosperity is based on commercial wealth won from the world market which began in the sixteenth century. This power is insatiable and irresponsible. 'Nul terre sans seigneur', said the medieval maxim, but money has no master. Impelled by 'auri sacra fames', the capitalist buys more and more labour power, piling up the surplus value it creates. 'The one who came to the market as the owner of money leaves it striding forward as a capitalist; the one who came to the market as the owner of labour-power brings up the rear as a worker. One of them self confident, self satisfied, with a keen eye to business; the other, timid, reluctant, like a man who is bringing his own skin to market, and has nothing to expect but a tanning.'[15]

The history of the production of surplus value is plain and horrible. In principle, it is alike, whether the monopolist be 'an Athenian devotee of the Good and the Beautiful, an Etruscan theocrat, a Roman citizen, a Norman Baron, an American slave owner, a Wallachian boyar, a modern landlord, or a capitalist'. But with growing civilization, exploitation must increase. For slaves only limited production is possible. They are clumsy and slow; in Virginia so brutish that mules must be employed rather than horses. As this exploitation develops, and the vampire of Capitalism saps a country's energy, even bourgeois government must interfere. It must curb 'the lavishness worthy of Tamerlane which . . . capitalists display in the expenditure of human life'. Hence the English Factory Acts, the beginning of the organization of labour. And here is the opening of the Hegelian antithesis to the thesis of capitalism. Already in England, in addition to the atrocity of urban conditions, the rural sources of labour are running dry. 'Flesh agents', sent to the West of England (in 1860) to Dorset and Wiltshire to recruit labour for the cotton mills found large areas already depopulated. Such in industrially advanced countries is the inevitable outcome of the laws of capitalist production: such will be the fate of all countries where great industry develops. Yet as a producer of wealth capitalism is unrivalled. As the extractor of surplus value, and exploiter of labour power, capitalism in its energy and remorseless efficiency has 'outsoared all the earlier systems of production, those that were based on forced labour'. At what a price!

'The subdivision of labour', Marx quotes from the Scottish Turkophile publicist, David Urquhart, 'is the assassination of a people.'* As modern machinery has developed, it has increased rather than diminished toil, to the applause of laissez-faire economists. Aristotle's

---

* David Urquhart, 1805-77, with whose various causes Marx became involved, gave Marx considerable assistance. He had fought in the Greek War of Independence, been employed on secret service in Turkey, and travelled widely in the Levant. He was M.P. for Stafford (1847-52), and denounced the results of great industry and the national sovereign state. See, in particular, his *Familiar Words as Affecting the Character of England and the Fate of England* (1855), and *An Appeal to the Pope to restore the Law of Nations* (1868). Urquhart was also the first to popularize Turkish Baths in England, and 'superintended the erection of the bath in Jermyn Street'. See his *The Turkish Bath, with a View to its Introduction in the British Dominions* (1856).

views were more humane, when he remarked that if 'weavers' shuttles were to weave of themselves', there would be no need for slaves; and Antipater of Thessalonica wrote of water mills 'we taste again the joys of the primitive life, learning to feast on the products of Demeter without labour'. 'Lacking the gift of Christianity', writes Marx, they thought machines would increase leisure; 'it never occurred to them to advocate the enslavement of the masses in order to transform a few vulgar and half educated upstarts into "eminent cotton spinners", "extensive sausage makers" and "influential blacking dealers".'

The impact of machinery has been decisive, necessary and horrible.[16] Historians should attend to these technical developments. Their importance only prehistorians have so far understood. They would then have realized the overwhelming power of machinery, distorting and wrecking all traditional civilization. It 'lays the worker low, abolishes humane relations, stultifies the masses and depopulates the country side'. But the rise of 'machinofacture' and the rule of capital have made the class-war nakedly apparent.

For by this stage Capitalism begins to bring about its own negation. 'It ripens the contradictions and antagonisms of the capitalist form of production, thus simultaneously ripening the factors that tend to revolutionize the old society and the factors that tend to build the new one'.[17] Meanwhile the capitalist, obeying his horrible compulsion, yet creates the means of production for the future classless society. 'Fanatically bent upon the expansion of value, he relentlessly drives human beings to production for production's sake, thus bringing about a division of social productivity and the creation of those material conditions of production which can alone form the real basis of a higher type of society, whose fundamental principle is the full and free development of every individual.'[18] Through the murk of mid-Victorian industry, Marx discerns the distant goal. There is light at the end of the tunnel. The theme on which the book was to conclude here sounds first with increasing power.* Then Marx swings back to a savage anatomy of present evils.

Though the capitalist is caught in a 'social mechanism of which he is the driving wheel' (the simile is characteristic), Marx relentlessly attacks bourgeois greed and callousness. He quotes Luther on usurers, and scarifies the 'petty-fogging ideologists',[19] and 'sycophants', who are the 'lackeys of the bourgeoisie'. But, underneath,

---

* The argument is fully stated twice, pp. 544ff and pp. 846ff, rising, as it were, in two waves.

the people are beginning to move. The 'learned squabbles' about the division of the spoil were 'hushed' in face of the July revolution; shortly afterwards, the urban proletariat of Lyons sounded the tocsin of revolt, and English labourers began to fire ricks and barns.[20] In his apocalyptic mood, Marx still exaggerated the significance of these disturbances: it is revealing that he still took them seriously.

Bentham, Malthus, James Mill and McCulloch now come in for some withering broadsides. The former humane old gentleman, the greatest legal reformer of his time, who could write with such brisk lucidity, is described as the 'arch-Philistine ... insipid, pedantic, leather-tongued oracle of the commonplace bourgeois intelligence of the nineteenth century. Bentham is among philosophers what Martin Tupper is among poets: neither of them could have been made anywhere else than in England'.[21] And Malthus, of course, is entirely unoriginal — a just representative of his class, the parsons whom Marx so detested. The class 'who have taken the motto "Be fruitful and multiply" as their specific biblical mission, with such success that they generally contribute to the increase of population to a quite unbecoming degree'. After this passing insult to Mr. Quiverfull, Marx turns to the broader problem of surplus population. It is the inevitable consequence of Capitalist development which needs its 'reserve army of hands', its fluctuating horde of unemployed, as the 'mechanism of capitalist production continually adapts the number of workers to capitalism's need for self expression'.

Marx proceeds to depict a panorama of industrial and agricultural misery; to extend his analysis to colonial development, and to draw to his conclusion, the climax of the book. Reiterating Engels' early theme, he quotes terrible statistics of malnutrition.* 'It is not too much to say', wrote Dr. Hunter, 'that life in parts of London and Newcastle is infernal.' In the depression of 1866, millions were starving. He depicts the condition of the peasantry in harrowing detail. He cites examples of depopulated villages, of semi-starvation and disease. Near Blandford, Wimborne and Poole in Dorset, for example — on Lord Shaftesbury's estates, he maliciously observes — the condition of the labourers is appalling. In Wiltshire cottages are dilapidated, gross overcrowding habitual. The labourers' diet, according to Dr. Hunter, is so inadequate that convicts are better fed. The system of nomadic labour gangs, who hire themselves to farmers is pernicious: according to the economist Thorold Rogers,

---

* From Dr. Smith's report to the Privy Council on the diet of the poor.

'the peasant has again become a serf'. In South Wales the already alarming number of idiots has increased; in Ireland mass emigration has been the only remedy. 'While rents accumulate, the Irishman, driven out of his country by sheep and bullocks, reappears on the other side of the Atlantic as a Fenian; and confronting the old Queen of the Seas, arises, threateningly and ever more threateningly the Giant Young Republic,

> Acerba fata Romanos agunt
> Scelusque fraternae necis. *Horace. Epode VII.*'[22]

Marx quotes Sir John Fortescue's *De Laudibus Legum Angliae*, with its picture of the sturdy peasantry of England, and cites More's attack on exploiters of the land.[23] Bacon, in his *Reign of Henry VII*, still desires a balanced economy; 'the pinnacle of civilization' had not yet been reached, when capitalism and exploitation are taken for granted. But a 'new terrible impetus was given to the forceful expropriation of the masses of the people during the sixteenth century by the Reformation'. Here is the germ of a familiar point of view, then novel, towards the Tudor period. As to the ruin of the yeomen, even the bourgeois Macaulay — 'a systematic falsifier of history' — admits they were the best element in the countryside. 'They had contrasted favourably with the drunken country squires and the squire's servants, the country clergymen, who had to marry their master's cast off mistresses', Marx observes, with gratuitous spite. The rise of great estates at the expense of the peasantry is traced through the eighteenth and nineteenth centuries; in particular the recent depopulation of the Highlands for deer forests. Vagrancy laws and state interference in the landlord's interest are savagely denounced.

It is a powerful, one-sided, indictment, then written from a startlingly new angle. The work of this urban intellectual, who studied rural England from statistics, has coloured much of the recent presentation of English economic history.

After a broad and massive recapitulation of his version of English economic development, Marx turns to the field of Colonial exploitation, an aspect of his book which was later to make wide appeal in Africa and the Far East. He paints a sombre and harrowing picture of the 'looting' of the East Indies, and of the West African Slave Trade in 'the rosy dawn of modern capitalism'. Exploitation and Christianity, he says, went hand in hand.[24] He cites Dutch ruthlessness in Java. the plunder of India by the English in the eighteenth century, the extermination of the Redskins by New England farmers, the Opium wars.

This exploitation of the internal and external proletariat, he insists, was the inevitable result of laissez-faire capitalism, whose interest was 'the making of surplus value to be the sole end and aim of mankind'.[25] He turns to examine the rise of the system of public credit, national debt and joint stock companies, in the early eighteenth century, which made this expansion possible, and relates it to child labour and the slave trade. As the indictment rises to its climax, Marx lays about him with growing fury. 'The nations', he writes in his typical idiom, which has since been so widely imitated, 'bragged cynically of every infamy which should serve as a means for the accumulation of capital.' Burke, who had a far shrewder eye than Marx for the incalculable consequences of the manipulation of power, comes in, like Bentham, for a brutal cut. He was a 'sycophant who, in the pay of the English oligarchy played the romanticist against the French Revolution . . . to the very marrow he was a commonplace bourgeois'.[26] Considering Marx's rich vocabulary, the epithet seems inadequate for this imaginative and feckless genius. Marx could see him only as the apologist of a system rooted in iniquity. 'Capital', he concludes, 'comes into the world soiled with mire from top to toe and oozing blood from every pore.'

Such is the ogre Marx depicts, such the iniquity of its exponents. Yet he concludes by reiterating that its development has been inevitable — the price paid for modern industrial power. The old handicraft method of production could only 'perpetuate mediocrity'. In due time it created forces ripe for its overthrow, and had to be destroyed. 'Hence the transformation of the pigmy property of the many into the Titan property of the few.' With 'ruthless vandalism' and driven by 'infamous passions', capitalists have achieved the necessary social concentration of economic power. The Hegelian antithesis now comes into operation. In a well-known passage Marx defines the inevitable goal. As the 'immanent laws' of capitalist production become manifest, the greater capitalists destroy the less. With growing efficiency and wider exploitation of the world market, a few monstrous concentrations of wealth are achieved. 'While there is thus a progressive diminution of the number of the capitalist magnates . . . there occurs a corresponding increase in the mass of poverty, oppression, enslavement, degeneration and exploitation; but at the same time there is a steady intensification of the wrath of the working class — a class which grows ever more numerous, and is disciplined, unified and organized by the very mechanism of the capitalist means of production.' At length this mass of misery and hatred, organized, militant and class conscious, turns upon its oppressors. The new society is incompatible with the capitalist husk. 'This bursts asunder. The knell of capitalist private property sounds. The expropriators are expropriated.'[27]

So 'with the inexorability of the law of nature', capitalism 'begets its own negation'. The trump of judgment sounds; the Hegelian Dialectic is fulfilled. The chosen people, the proletariat, are redeemed. The vision, first so powerfully defined in the *Communist Manifesto*, had received, nineteen years later, its massive theoretical sanction. In spite of the long years of exile and frustration, Marx's fierce romanticism had remained undimmed.

A comparison with the *Manifesto* will show little really new in the first volume of *Das Kapital*. It is based on the original adaptation of Hegel and Feuerbach, on the concept of surplus value and on Ricardian and Malthusian economics, on the idea of scientific 'law'. Arguments deployed in earlier writings are remorselessly recapitulated and hammered home, backed by elaborate economic disquisitions whose obscurity seemed the more compelling. There is the same paradox as in the *Manifesto*; the vendetta against Capitalists, depicted at the same time as victims of compulsive economic laws. This is reflected in another contradiction. The reluctant admiration for the disinterested officials who compiled the reports which are the basis of the most powerful parts of the book, contrasts with Marx's detestation of the English middle class — for he remained, it has been well said, 'always a German who lived very consciously *in partibus infidelium*'. But a more overwhelming contradiction pervades the whole theme. This learned doctor, with his wide European culture and incisive power of quotation and analysis, this 'highbrow', this romantic, whose 'hide was not thick enough' for the ordinary assumptions of life, had brought the full power of his genius to build a theory which discarded the cultural wealth of civilization as a mere phase in an economically determined class war. In pursuit of a politically impracticable aim, which no realist would ever sanction, he gave the weight of his authority to a clawing down of elites. Marx always showed particular detestation of the 'Philistines'. As the event has amply proved, the world he contributed to create was to be fit only for Philistines to live in. Politics, this visionary might have known, are not so simple. In spite of economic forces, the realities of power are constant, and the attempt to attain good ends by evil means brings its own nemesis. The destruction of values by Marxist atheist materialism was a poor prelude to the liberation of mankind.

IV

Engels's most important work, to which Marx contributed, was entitled *Herr Eugen Dühring's Revolution in Science*, generally known as the *Anti-Dühring*.[28] It appeared in 1878. Here is a comprehensive summary of the whole doctrine, which emerges from a spate of rancorous and clumsy abuse. Dühring was a Prussian socialist of provincial origin, who dared to attempt an alternative doctrine.[29] He got what might be expected. This social-democratic deviationist and systematizer, the exponent of a 'noisy pseudo-science, drowning everything with its booming sublime nonsense', was typical, they said (and who knew better?) of German intellectual arrogance. He is treated to all the amenities of the Marxist vocabulary. He is puerile, superficial — he writes 'simple balderdash'. But through these clouds of abuse, which the reader soon gets to ignore, the clearest obtainable picture of the total doctrine can be discerned.

In the section on philosophy Engels reiterates his typically mid-nineteenth-century belief that all history is governed by laws which nature, too, reflects: '. . . amid the welter of innumerable changes taking place in nature, the same *dialectical laws of motion* are in operation as those which in history govern the apparent fortuitousness of events'. These laws were first discerned by Hegel in a mystical form: his great achievement was to create a philosophy of history 'in which for the first time — and this is its great merit — the whole natural historical and spiritual world was presented as a process'. Dialectical materialism owes much to this view. 'It sees history as the evolution of humanity, and our problem as the *discovery of the laws of motion* of this process.' Marx 'discovered' them. As in the funeral speech, Engels couples this achievement with the 'discovery' of the 'law' of 'surplus value'. By this it was 'shown that even if the capitalist buys the labour power . . . at its full value as a commodity on the market, he yet extracts more value from it than he paid for'. 'Those two great discoveries', he insists, 'the materialist conception of history and the revelation of the secret of capitalist production by means of surplus value, we owe to Marx. With these discoveries socialism became a science.'

The reliability of this dialectical 'science' is not enhanced by Engels' metaphysics. Negation follows negation. It is the law of life. It applies everywhere. 'If we take an ornamental plant which can be modified in cultivation, for example a dahlia or an orchid, if we treat the seed of the plant which grows from it as a gardener does, we get as the result of this negation of the negation not only more seeds, but qualitatively better seeds . . . each repeated negation of the negation increases this improvement.' With a reckless analogy, Engels insists that 'the whole of geology is a science of "negated negations". It is the same in mathematics. It is the same, too, in history.'[30] In consequence, the course of events is 'bound' to move from the primitive common ownership of land, into the negative phase of private property, back to a more advanced communism which will release the full force of modern production. From early equality mankind is fated to move through inequality to social justice. 'The oppressors are oppressed. It is the negation of the negation.' Thus the great law of nature is fulfilled, the 'law of motion', and 'each class of things . . . has its own appropriate form of being negated'.[31]

It is clear, in this context, that Herr Dühring had no monopoly of nonsense.

The economic section of the book is more valuable. Here Marx takes over the argument, though he, too, develops the theme of inevitable negation. He opens up a new prospect of the vast possibilities of science. 'Modern large-scale industry has called into being on the one hand a proletariat, on the other a bourgeoisie.' They control the means of production. But, with every boom and crash, they prove to be 'a class under whose leadership society is racing to ruin like a locomotive whose jammed safety-valve, the driver is too weak to open'. Again the simile is revealing.[32] It follows that 'if the whole of modern society is not to perish, a revolution of the mode of production and distribution must take place'. This revolution will abolish all distinctions of class. 'On this tangible, material fact', Marx continues, 'which is impressing itself in a more or less clear form, but with invincible necessity, on the minds of the exploited proletarians — it is on this fact, and not on the conception of justice and injustice held by any armchair philosopher, that modern socialism's confidence of victory is founded.'[33]

The incongruity between modern means of production and bourgeois society is the key to the failure of the French Revolution. Why has 'Reason [now] become nonsense and good deeds a scourge'?[34] Simply because the social order is no longer relevant to the economic facts: '. . . the new forces of production have already outgrown the bourgeois form of using them'. Hence the ideological conflict has a material basis. It has not arisen 'in men's heads, as for example the conflict between original sin and divine justice, but it exists in the facts — objectively, outside of us'. In consequence, modern socialism is 'nothing but the reflex in thought of this actual conflict'. The dialectic was, of course, materialist.

For the means of production are now social. Yet they are still treated as the property of individuals. There is a 'glaring incompatibility' between social production and capitalist individual appropriation. The mighty forces of modern industry are misapplied: they are making chaos instead of plenty. They are out of control, lunging about in the welter of capitalist competition — terrifying forces from a new world. For capitalism has long thrust out the old order. Production for a world market has swamped the old local systems, and men have 'lost control of their social relationships'. All the traditional decencies are disrupted. 'It is the Darwinian struggle for individual existence, transferred from Nature to Society with intensified fury.'[35] 'The standpoint of the animal in Nature', Engels continues, 'appears as the last word in human achievement.' The struggle is exacerbated by the rhythmic vagaries of the market, which cannot keep pace with the spate of uncontrolled production. 'The production and exchange of all civilized peoples and of their more or less barbarian dependent peoples, is dislocated practically once in every ten years.' Five times since 1825 has this come about — this 'crise pléthorique', when 'the mode of production rebels against the mode of exchange'.[36] Meanwhile, the fluctuating reserve army of unemployed are at the mercy of elements of primeval fury. For the forces that move capitalist society are blind. Like the forces of nature, they must be understood. With understanding we can transfer them 'from demoniac monsters into willing servants'.

It is indeed a powerful diagnosis. As already suggested, there were to be other remedies. The social democratic Welfare State, Keynesian economic policy, the interventionist 'social engineering' of the New Deal, were in fact to avoid the stark alternative of revolution, and prove more in harmony with the perennial long term difficulties of administration. But seldom have the contradictions of laissez-faire society been better depicted.

State intervention, for Marx and Engels, was to be absolute and yet final. 'The first act in which the state really comes forward as the representative of society as a whole' would be the taking over of the means of production in the name of society. It would be also 'its last independent act as a State. The interference of the State power in social relations becomes superfluous in one sphere after another, and then ceases of itself'. After the realist diagnosis, comes the Utopian sequel: 'The Government of persons', concludes Engels, in a famous passage, echoing Saint-Simon, 'is replaced by the administration of things . . . the state is not abolished, *it withers away*.' It was a hopeful paradox.

This revolution will come not by willing it, but when the time is ripe. Class war, itself, is the result of limited techniques, of incompetent production. There will be no need for an exploiting class when the full power of modern machinery is given its head. Today the new forces pulsate against the restricting framework of the old society. The revolutionary tension exists. 'Their political and economic bankruptcy is hardly still a secret to the bourgeoisie themselves.' The time is ripe at last to unleash the full power of modern technology.

And once the old integument is sloughed off, what a prospect! Not merely unheard of material well-being, but the unrestrained 'development and exercise of their physical and mental faculties — this possibility now exists for the first time — but it does exist'.[37] Engels had recalled the great economic fact of the Industrial and Technological Revolutions — the masses for the first time could participate in civilization. 'At this point', he continues, 'in a certain sense, man finally cuts himself off from the animal world.' He becomes at last fully human, the master of nature. 'It is humanity's leap from the realm of necessity' to 'freedom'. Man now makes himself.

To carry through this 'world emancipating act' is the historic mission of the modern proletariat. The task of scientific socialism is to be their guide. And in the new society mankind will no longer be stunted by division of labour. Engels even reverts to Fourieresque and Owenite ideas of decentralized self-government, of a fusion of town and country, of the destruction of the hideous megalopolitan aspect of the nineteenth century. The great towns will perish with the great state. Man will also slough off the cramping bonds of superstitition, for religion is 'nothing but the phantastic reflections in men's minds of these external forces which control their daily lives'. It will vanish when external forces have been brought to heel. By some magic, the Dialectic, too, which, in the Marxist argument, should go on heaving away into the future, is now

344

becalmed. The brave new masters of society will find before them all the kingdoms of the earth.

Disentangled from current polemics, here is a lucid and eloquent argument. The original text of the *Anti-Dühring* is disfigured by deviations in hot pursuit of the unfortunate philosopher who was the occasion of its composition. But from the welter of Teutonic recrimination, the main theme emerges strong and clear. There is no doubt that the diagnosis was valuable. The sense of the possibilities of the modern industry correct; the ideal, within its atheist assumptions, humane. Here is the original core of all the socialist doctrines, Utopian and Marxist — the supersession of the politico-legal state by the shifting of the economic basis of power and ideas. It is the more depressing that politically Engels does not here go beyond the revolutionary violence of 1848, though in another context he was more hopeful.*

The over-riding dialectic still made their vision of history necessarily violent; though tentatively they admit that perhaps, in England, the change might come without savage revolution, as in his earliest work Engels had desired to transcend it. The desire for destruction also reflects the horror which inspires both *Das Kapital* and the *Anti-Dühring* for the ruthless world of animal competition specifically defended and given biological sanction by Herbert Spencer. Like Nietzsche, after them, they were now in revolt against the version of Darwinism which was then gaining increasing hold on public opinion. The old romantic vision of the free classless society, in which the full force of modern technology could be released, derived from Saint-Simon and even from Fourier, had been given a new partly Hegelian, partly economic, sanction by the 'scientific laws' that Marx and Engels claimed to have discovered. Before these 'laws' the practical considerations which obtain in politics, and of which the administrators, de Tocqueville, for example, had been well aware, and which the shrewd mind of Lecky had succinctly expressed, seemed the banal entanglements of an obsolete world. The constant facts which have been observed from Aristotle's *Politics* to Mill's *Essay on Liberty*, the danger and ever-present probability of arbitrary power, were dwarfed to these abstract thinkers by their conviction that they understood the development of a process which was inevitable. Here is the profound misjudgment so characteristic of their time. They understood the interdependence of economics, politics and thought; they made a fruitful hypothesis

* See Bernstein's quotation, *infra*, pp. 434-5.

for the reinterpretation of history. But they pitched their claims too high; and, as Lionel Curtis writes, 'Marx had failed to foresee the reactions which his own methods were destined to yield.'[38]

These mistakes were natural, given the circumstances and personalities concerned. For the idea of historical inevitability is highly typical of the nineteenth century. It combines the historical outlook, the most original aspect of the time, with the idea of scientific law applied to human society. It presents a total, materialist, explanation.

These certainties have since faded. Modern historians, with far wider data at their disposal, are unable to discern the operation of such simple historical laws. Hegel's conception of history, for example, to which Marx and Engels owed so much, is described by a representative American critic simply as poetry. 'A study of the vagaries of Hegel', he writes, '(who was not an historian) and of those he influenced directly and indirectly, should serve to make the historian of the twentieth century a more sophisticated practitioner of his craft.'[39]

In the philosophical arena, the Hegelian Dialectic, essential to Marxism, has been utterly discredited. A representative Logical Positivist political philosopher can write: 'Hegel's statement of it is difficult to deal with because he systematically confuses statements about language with statements about matter of fact, and irretrievably muddles up logical with psychological and biological arguments . . . Hegel's supposed foundation of politics is completely useless. It is not false but it is vacuous.'[†] The same writer riddles the Marxist dogma also, as 'a historicism much more vicious . . . than that of Hegel himself'. After a trenchant analysis, he declares that 'both "materialism" and "dialectical" in any positive and definite sense are useless words', and concludes that 'Marxist foundations . . . are worthless'.[‡]

In another field, Professor Evans-Pritchard, a representative modern anthropologist, declares that the great Victorian pioneers of that subject were too ambitious; too much taken with a 'passion for origins' and for total explanation. Vital as were their contributions, the basis of modern research, study now concentrates rather on the working of existing customs and institutions, and on how, in varying

---

* In particular Marx's erroneous prophecy that small property would be absorbed in the concentration of a few great fortunes, blinded him to the political effect of this diffusion in promoting both Fascism and Social democracy.

† T. D. WELDON, *The Vocabulary of Politics* (Pelican, 1953), London, pp. 107-10.

‡ Op. cit., 127-37, q.v.

contexts, survival and social equilibrium are maintained. These things can be directly observed by anthropologists, while broad generalizations about the evolution of man, for which there is no evidence for scientific certainty, are now regarded as impossible. While there is evidence for progress, in the sense of a gradual, tentative increase of control of environment, and for a cumulative enrichment of knowledge, there now seem no simple 'laws' of development applicable to all the vast and varying pattern of world history.[40] The Marxist concept of an inevitable pre-determined process, an economic 'law of motion', as ascertainable as the laws of physics, is only one of the many crude and materialist nineteenth-century attempts to reduce history to a pattern of simple quasi-scientific laws. To the complex, shifting, ramified, evidence of modern research, and before the limitations accepted by modern historical, social, and philosophical, method, this dogmatism is simply irrelevant — like the philosophy of Comte, a nineteenth-century curiosity. It is not irrelevant in the political field. There it remains — an extremely dangerous intellectual anachronism. It remains, also, a commanding myth. As interpreted by its most powerful modern exponents, its fundamental political assumptions have never been modified, or its long term strategy of world-revolution abandoned.

CHAPTER VII

UNBRIDLED NATIONALISM: TREITSCHKE

In his study of nationality, Dr. Herz well observes, 'it has been remarked of certain theological controversies of the Byzantine Empire, which gave rise to grave commotions, that popular passions have often been roused to the highest pitch by disputes about subjects which were far beyond the understanding of the human mind'.* These Byzantine conflicts are paralleled in our own time. The mythology of class warfare, with its parade of pseudo-scientific dogmas, has been examined. We now turn to modern nationalism. Both the dogmas of class war and nationalist aggression led to conflict about theories which are imponderable.

The origins of modern nationalism in the romantic movement are already familiar. The ideas of Herder and Hegel, for example, have previously been examined, and some attention given to the humanitarian, if conspiratorial, nationalism of Mazzini. The cult of the national past in romantic and popular guise is writ large in the history, the music and the official art of the age.† The nationalism of the first half of the century, which found expression in admiration for Garibaldi and Kossuth, had its origins in the romantic attitudes of the French Revolution. This outlook, savagely criticized by Marx in the *Eighteenth Brumaire*, had in its time shaken Europe and swept over wide areas during the Napoleonic Wars. Outside the more liberal countries, it persisted in the Iberian peninsula, and outside Europe, for example, in the Spanish American Republics, where it achieved some of its most picturesque and sanguinary results. The romantic Bohemian nationalism of the early and mid-century, co-existing with the 'monde' of Balzac, was reflected by famous liberal historians. In England it was combined with a habit of travel. The book-shelves, heavy with the volumes of Scott and Chateau-

---

* F. Herz, *Nationality in History and Politics*. Kegan Paul, 1944, p. 1, q.v. a comprehensive and learned analysis.

† See the romantic versions of the history of the English Parliament which adorn the entrance of the House of Commons, and the nineteenth-century battle canvasses which compare so ill with the earlier paintings at Versailles. Innumerable examples could be cited from all over Europe. I forbear to particularize on the sculptural atrocities dedicated, then and now, to the cult of nationalism, which merges, in the twentieth century, in a more primitive cult of the dead, expressed in innumerable megalithic War Memorials. The archaeologist of the future need have no difficulty in discerning a basic preoccupation of our time.

briand, with the works of Michelet and Niebuhr, with memoirs of travel in Spain and Greece and the Levant, the romantic prints and the water colours of Italy, reflected a high academic culture, a vague enthusiasm for popular liberty, and a secure assumption of world power. This liberalism, which had supported Greeks against Turks, and Italians against Austrians, was a rarefied aspect of the movement. It profoundly influenced policy even into the days of Asquith and of Grey. It long obscured the dangerous realities of the international position. These remained fundamentally unchanged up to the second World War. As Curtis well wrote in 1938, 'the Great War revealed a stronger devotion in masses of men to their national states than was ever seen in the world before . . . But between these states and their governments there is no law . . . Whilst governments are able, as never before, to order affairs within their sovereignty in accordance with justice and right, between these national governments there is nothing but anarchy'.[1]

With the turn of the century and the impact of misplaced Darwinian ideas of struggle and natural selection, with the failure of the revolutions of 1848-49, the capture of German national feeling by Bismarck, and the growing participation of the masses in political life, began the grosser implications of this romantic cult. The failure of the mid-century Papacy to come to terms with liberal thought, and its concentration on Italian interests; the deepening of class hatred following the June Days in Paris, and the rise of Louis Napoleon, combined to create an atmosphere very different from the relative optimism of the earlier half of the century.* Following the Franco-Prussian War, the situation steadily deteriorated. The typical prophet of Nationalism was no longer Mazzini; it was Treitschke.

The present chapter will examine the most influential example of this sombre nineteenth-century nationalism. Together with Marxism, this outlook was increasingly to oust transcendental religion, both among the masses and among the proletarian leaders who emerged after the first World War.

The development of nationalism has naturally been very widely studied.† It was to reach its most militant phase in the twentieth

---

* For the effects of Papal policy see Sir Llewellyn Woodward's valuable *Three Studies in European Conservatism*. His study of Pius IX contains the best treatment of this important and neglected subject, and observes the Risorgimento from a far more realistic point of view than that of most English historians.

† See in particular *Nationalism*, Royal Institute of International Affairs; F. Herz, op. cit.; C. J. H. Hayes, *Essays in Nationalism*. New York, 1926, O.U.P., 1939, and *The Historical Evolution of Modern Nationalism*. New York, 1931; R. Johannet, *Le Principe des Nationalités*.

century. In Germany it attained its most unbridled violence, and the German historian, Treitschke, will therefore be taken as representative of its most extreme later-nineteenth-century expression.

This German movement was to be paralleled in France. Here the social-democratic ideas of Jaurès was attacked by military and clerical parties, who proclaimed a mystique of national regeneration. The class conflict in France was bound up with the expression of nationalist opinion. The climax of this propaganda was not reached until the twentieth century, with Maurice Barrès. His *Scènes et Doctrines du Nationalisme* attacked foreigners, parliamentary government, socialism, freemasonry and the Jews. Charles Maurras's *Romantisme et Révolution* was an onslaught on the whole democratic movement deriving from 1789. He also advocated a return to dictatorship. But this form of nationalism never had the deep roots which German nationalism possessed in the *Volk*. It was bound up with French politics and primarily a movement of intellectuals. The basic peasant provincial foundation of France had a more negative, if militant, patriotism.*

In Great Britain during the later years of the century there was less specific nationalist propaganda. British supremacy was taken for granted, and interest was more concentrated on business and home politics. But there was a reaction from the casual and often negative attitude which Government and public opinion had adopted towards the Empire in the mid-century. With the publication of Seeley's *The Expansion of England* in 1883, the romantic Imperialism of Disraeli was theoretically reinforced.† The conception of trusteeship, defined by Burke, was revived and encouraged by the higher standards of administrative competence which followed civil service reform. The British development of indirect rule, a policy also paralleled in French colonial administration, and the achievements and outlook of British Colonial government of the twentieth century, are outside the scope of this study. In general, continental opinion little realized how prevalent was British popular apathy

* See in particular E. SEILLIÈRE, *Le Péril Mystique dans l'Inspiration des Démocraties Contemporaines; Philosophie de l'Impérialisme.*

† It was Seeley who coined the phrase that England appeared to have 'conquered and peopled half the world in a fit of absence of mind'.

Paris, 1923; and SIR E. BARKER, *National Character and the Factors in its Formation.* London, 1927. LORD ACTON's Essay on Nationality (*History of Freedom and other Essays*, pp. 270-300) written in the 'sixties, is a document of prophetic insight. See as well E. H. CARR, *Nationalism and After.* Macmillan, 1945, and my *The Unity of European History*, chap. XII. Cape, 1948. For further documentation, see KOPPEL PENSON, *Bibliographical Introduction to Modern Nationalism.*

towards the Empire, and how intangible were the ties which bound the Dominions to the Home Country. In fact, the absence of concerted foreign policy gravely handicapped these enormous areas in playing their part in the maintenance of peace in Europe. The spectacle of so much wealth and territory, so loosely organized, proved a standing provocation to German colonial ambition. It is not, therefore, in France, where the extreme theory of nationalism remained the province of party politicians and intellectuals, or in Great Britain, where the Imperialism of Rhodes and Kipling was seldom representative, where common policies were often frustrated by the particularism of the Dominions, and energies fully occupied by the administration of India and of huge colonial territories, that later-nineteenth-century nationalism found most vivid and popular expression. It was not in countries already satiated, and even burdened, with colonial possessions, that these aspirations were most extreme. It was in Germany that the theory of unbridled nationalism found most powerful expression. It is therefore worth examining the ideas of the most representative exponent of German nationalism at this time. They are based on a view of human nature akin to de Maistre's, but where de Maistre thought to counter original sin by the authority of the Church, while regarding war as a spiritual compulsion, Treitschke asserted redemption through the nation state as well as war.

While, in liberal democratic England theoretical Imperialism was at a discount, and Green and his disciples were propounding their theory of the general will and making their academic contribution towards a peaceful theory of government, and while the Fabian socialists were soon to define the constitutional outline of the welfare state, a different atmosphere had long been apparent in Bismarck's Germany. Following the failure of 1848, German unity had at last come about through a series of gradual and calculated manœuvres. Predominant political thought in Germany was naturally influenced by this achievement; it was reflected with singular fidelity in the ideas of Treitschke.* As Lord Balfour remarked in his Olympian

* Heinrich von Treitschke, born at Dresden in 1834, son of a Saxon general, partly of Czech descent. Educated in strict classical learning and influenced by liberal ideas, he was involved in the liberal revolt in Dresden, 1848. In 1851 he attended Bonn University and came under the influence of the liberal Dahlmann, and at Leipzig he developed an interest in economic history under Roselar. He was also influenced by von Rochau's *Realpolitik*. Owing to deafness, he was prevented from following a military career. 1855, Privatdozent at Leipzig; 1856, published patriotic poems *Vaterländische Gedichte*; 1857, lectured on the Politics of Aristotle and Machiavelli: involved in Pan-German movement; 1861, *Die Freiheit*, an attack on J. S. MILL's *Liberty*; 1862, *Das Deutsche Ordensland*

and scathing introduction to the translation of the *Politik*, 'Political theories, from those of Aristotle downwards, have ever been related, either by harmony or contrast, to the political practice of their day, but of no thesis is this more glaringly true than of those expounded in these volumes.' They reflect, he points out, 'the mature thought of one who had seen the success of Bismarck'.

Yet Treitschke does more than express this predominant theme. He summed up and publicized many other strains in German thought. He goes back to Herder and Fichte, Hegel and Niebuhr and the lawyer Savigny. Treitschke is ultimately a muddled thinker, but he is representative; he 'thinks with the blood', with a vivid sense of history and a singular power of phrase.

His great reputation was made as an historian — he was the Macaulay of the Bismarckian Empire — and on the congenial subject of the Teutonic Knights of Prussia he could made a heady and often brilliant evocation of dramatic times. By 1862 he was already the propagandist of Prussian leadership. 'There is hardly even an outline sketch to convey to the mind of a south German boy an intuition of the most stupendous and fearful occurrence of the late Middle Ages — the northward and eastward rush of the German spirit and the formidable activities of our people as conqueror, teacher, discipliner of its neighbours.'[2] The sinister Order is held up for emulation to German youth, 'when the full harshness of our national spirit was displayed, when conquerors endowed with the triple pride of Christians, Knights and Germans, had to form front against the heathen'. The eagle ferocity of medieval Baltic Barons, fighting in

---

Preussen: Treitschke's Origins of Prussianism (The Teutonic Knights) translated G. and C. Paul, London, 1942. 1863, Professor of Political Science at Freiburg in Baden; *Federation and Centralization*; engaged in propaganda for Bismarck; 1866, Professor at Kiel; 1867, Professor at Heidelberg. After 1870, his thoughts turned to foreign policy and colonial expansion. 1871-84, member of the Reichstag; 1874, Professor at Berlin in succession to Ranke, who opposed the appointment. Editor of *Preussische Jahrbücher*. In Berlin he reached the summit of his widespread influence. His most widely read work, *Deutsche Geschichte im Neunzehnten Jahrhundert*, of which the first volume appeared in 1879, won him his greatest renown. (Translated G. and C. Paul. *History of Germany in the Nineteenth Century*.) He died in 1896. The *Politik*, which appeared after his death, is based on notes taken at lectures by his students. It sums up essays and lectures of the 'sixties and 'seventies and contains his essential ideas. It has been admirably translated, with an introduction by Lord Balfour, by Mrs. Blanche Dugdale and T. de Bille, 2 vols., Constable, 1916. It is divided into four books: the Nature of the State; The Social Foundation of the State; The Constitution of the State; and the Administration of the State. See also *Historische und Politische Aufsätze*, 1896. Leipzig, 4 vols. A. HAUSRATH, *Leben von Heinrich von Treitschke*, and H. W. C. DAVIS, *Political Thought of Heinrich Treitschke*, 1914. (In his anxiety to retain an open mind, during the outbreak of the first world war, Davis tends to over-emphasize the liberal elements in Treitschke.) ROHAN BUTLER's *Roots of National Socialism* does not suffer from this defect at all. See also G. P. GOOCH, *History and Historians in the Nineteenth Century*. London (1952 dition).

the cockpit of Eastern Europe against Poles, Balts, Letts and Lithu-
anians, was related to the quasi-philosophic 'Laws' of history which
the militant professor imagined he had discovered. For the heart of
Treitschke's doctrine is the glorification of war. States exist, he
believed, through 'ordeal by battle'. 'No state in the world may
renounce the "I" in its sovereignty.'[3] 'War', he insisted, 'is justified
because the great national personalities can suffer no compelling
force superior to themselves, and because history must always be in
constant flux.'[4] The state, he said, rather gratuitously, 'is no violet to
bloom unseen'. Since all history is a welter of competing sovereignties, and a healthy nation should display the punctilious sense of
honour reflected in the student custom of duelling, no state need
keep its treaties, since it cannot 'pledge its future to another'.[5] And
'No court of arbitration will ever succeed in banishing war from the
world.'[6] 'The grandeur of history', said Treitschke, 'lies in the perpetual conflict of nations.'[7] Like Hegel, he had a wild vision of
historical fate, with nations 'blossoming' and 'shrivelling', so that
even a balance of power is impossible; and as the European states
strive for world domination, the whole planet will be engulfed in
titanic conflicts. For the 'world beyond Europe is bulking larger
and larger upon Europe's horizon, and there is no doubt that the
European nations must go out to it and subdue it, directly or indirectly, to themselves'.[8] Along with this savage belligerence, goes a
paradoxical aspiration towards a comity of nations in an 'international mosaic', sometimes reminiscent of Mazzini. The 'Divine
light', . . . he said, 'is broken by countless facets among the separate
peoples'.[9] But where Mazzini asserted a 'sisterhood' of nations,
Treitschke asserts a desperate masculinity — 'the features of history',
he said, 'are virile'. Neurosis is writ large in the gospel of this
eloquent professor, whose deafness debarred him from a military
career. There is, indeed, much in common between Treitschke and
Nietzsche, though Treitschke was inferior in speculative power.
Both were physically handicapped, both were educated in Greek
thought by a strict classical discipline which encouraged a revolt
against German middle-class materialism. Both were frustrated
warriors. But where Nietzsche early freed himself from his Protestant upbringing and became a militant atheist, Treitschke retained
a confused Lutheran mysticism. He could address his audiences as
'We Christians'.

This worshipper of power began as a liberal. He retained to the
end some liberal conceptions of the state. He was never a totalitarian;

he criticized Hegel on that score, and he would have been horrified at the centralization of the Hitlerite state. He disliked bureaucracy and the German examination system; he favoured local self-govern-ment and justified the state as a means for moral development. He can write, for example, 'the state does not identify itself with physical power for its own sake; it is Power in order to protect and further the highest welfare of the human race'.[10] Unhappily, as Lord Russell observes of Hegel, he seems to think that everything important takes the form of war.[11] 'We have already seen that war is both justifiable and moral and that the ideal of perpetual peace is not only impossible but immoral as well.'[12]

His romantic conception of the state, so typical of the nineteenth century, derives directly from Herder. Herder, he wrote, 'first taught the German people to think historically . . .'[13] This out-look is also rooted in a bitter hostility both to the cosmopolitan world-order asserted in the old Thomist (he calls it Jesuit) version of Natural Law, and in an equal detestation of the commonsense materialism of the 'English Manchester School'. Further, Treitschke's romantic love of the German Folk, extending from the cult of old Fritz and Teutonic Knights to a sense of the solid virtues of the peasantry, was expressed in brutal disparagement of almost all other peoples. In particular, he detested the French and the Poles. He also despised the Belgians and the Dutch: he refers constantly to the vulgarity of the 'Yankees' and regards the Latin races as effeminate. But his strongest hatred is reserved for the English, of whom he dis-plays extreme jealousy. He alternately admires them for blowing Hindus from guns during the Mutiny, while colonizing vast terri-tories overseas, and despises them for their desire to avoid war and for their alleged greed, hypocrisy and shallowness, which contrasts with the profundity of the German character. His compatriots, he thinks, are too humble, 'always in danger of enervating their nationality through possessing too little rugged pride'.[14] A nation, he warned the Germans, cannot dispense with arrogance.

Incongruously enough, Treitschke's lectures were modelled upon the *Politics* of Aristotle — 'that greatest masterpiece' as he rightly remarked, 'of political theory'.* Most of the lectures begin by a reference to the Philosopher. Man, he insists, is a profoundly politi-cal animal. In reaction against the convention of social contract

---

* Introduction, p. xxxii. Hence, in part, the curious leniency which Davis displays towards this political philosopher in a criticism written in 1914, with its motto 'Fas est ab hoste doceri'.

current in the eighteenth century, and against the anaemic counting-house morality of English and Scots economists, Treitschke has something in common with Green. There is also a great deal of quasi-religious Hegelian assertion about the lofty necessity of nature, and peoples attaining to what they deserve. 'In the course of the world's history a Divine ordinance is perceptible', and one can observe 'the objectively revealed will of God as unfolded in the State'. For just as the citizen of Aristotle's πόλις, by his very nature and capacity for speech, is part of the organic life of the state, so in nineteenth-century Europe, where the nation has superseded the πόλις, 'it is the essence of creative genius to be national'. The state is primordial, rooted in tradition; 'who would respect the banners of the state if the power of memory had fled?'[15] Quoting Fichte, he declares, 'the individual man sees in his country the realization of his earthly immortality'. Legal fictions are not enough. States are the great collective personalities of history '. . . visibly girt about with armed might'.[16] To such an interpretation had Aristotle come.

The other formative influence was Machiavelli. He was the first political thinker, Treitschke affirmed, to understand that the state is power. Bodin next made the first realistic definition of sovereignty, and Gustavus Adolphus, that just soldier, declared, 'I recognize no power above me, but God and the conqueror's sword.' As Machiavelli held a cynical view of mankind, so Treitschke believed that 'nothing is truer than the Biblical doctrine of Original Sin, which is not to be uprooted by civilization to whatever point you may bring it'.[17] Will, not intelligence, is the moving force of events, and brute force and craft are the weapons of the statesman, so that the greatest political leaders display a ruthlessness beyond ordinary morality. Those architects of power, a Frederick the Great, or a Bismarck, represent the highest human achievement. 'The great political thinkers have their meed of fame, but the men of action are the real heroes of history.'[18] Such artists in violence and cunning have always understood, as Machiavelli pointed out, that 'the state is power'.[19] The riddle of history is solved by personalities who create the future. This will to power has affinities with the vulgarization of Nietzsche's ideas current in the early twentieth century. As Machiavelli remarked, 'For when the entire safety of our country is at stake, no consideration of what is just and unjust . . . must intervene', so Treitschke wrote 'When a nation's existence is at stake, there is no outside power whose impartiality can be trusted . . . the appeal to arms will be valid until the end of history, and therein lies the sacredness of war.'[20] Machiavelli was a 'mighty thinker, who co-operated with Martin Luther for the liberation of the state'.[21] He was 'the first to declare distinctly that the state is power' and those who will not face this fact had 'better leave politics alone'. But Machiavelli's 'downright terrifying frankness' is too limited. He neglected to create any moral justification of power. Indeed, this flatness of moral sense is wrong. Treitschke goes beyond him; accepting the Italian's discovery that the state is power, he provides it with a mad morality of its own. In obedience to this morality, the statesman must commit what to private individuals would be crime. 'The statesman has no right to warm his hands with smug self laudation at the smoking ruins of his fatherland, and comfort himself by saying, "I have never lied".'[22] His path is, inevitably, strewn with broken lives.* But this fact reflects the realities of politics, which emerge not from compromise or good will, but from the clash of interest and force. Only the historian, who 'moves in the world of real will', and scorns the 'braying laughter of the vulgar', or the 'gross calculations of Philistine materialists', knows what the true statesman is about.

It follows that Treitschke's state is neither the 'night watchman' of laissez-faire liberals nor the totalitarian society of Hegel. 'The state is no Academy of Arts, still less is it a Stock Exchange: it is Power.'[23] This authority is expressed through the army and the police. But the world of intellect and art is outside it: 'what does it matter what people think if they obey?' As for economics, since 'passion and stupidity' must be counted among the great powers of economic life, the economic process can never be beneficent if uncontrolled. It took Scottish philosophers to imagine the 'crazy contention that the brute in man would raise man above the brute'.[24] Naturally harmony can never come from the competing interests of society. It can come only from the state, '. . . from the power that stands above it armed with the strength to restrain its wild passions'. State power will not monopolize all activities: it will merely monopolize the essentials — military and legal and, to some extent, economic force. So it will adjust and protect the dynamic life of a people. Local affairs can be left subject to self government, 'which enlists the best elements in the community in the daily service of the state'.[25] For the government is not the whole of a people's life, '. . . its function is only to surround the whole, regulating and protecting it'.[26] Here Treitschke's early constitutional liberalism persists: it was reinforced by a vague

* It was said, for example, of Lloyd George that 'he went through life with as much consideration as a cactus hedge'.

religious ideal, which made him advocate freedom of the church from the state. 'The end of all friction between them', he said, 'would be a sign of the stagnation of one or the other.'[27] Yet the main function of the state, besides maintaining order and unity, is war. These internal liberties are not very significant and have been over-emphasized. The essential Treitschke is displayed when he remarks that although Clausewitz had revealed the necessity of war, in the effeminate hands of civilian politicians it has been forgotten. 'But God above will see to it that war will return again — a terrible medicine for mankind diseased.'

What kind of society did he envisage, when it was not engaged in war? What was it that this steely concentration of military and police power would protect? Treitschke's views were here thoroughly conservative and ordinary. He accepted the rigid class divisions of the Germany of his day, for his dynamic view of history was confined to the clash of nation states. The tendency of society, he believed, was inevitably aristocratic, and 'social life is built up on class organization'. Dreams of social equality and betterment are delusions. 'Millions must plough and forge and dig', he asserts, 'in order that a few thousands may write and paint and study. It sounds harsh, but it is true for all time, and whining and complaining can never alter it.'[28] 'The masses', he concludes, 'must ever remain the masses. There can be no culture without kitchen maids.'

This outlook set little store by the possibilities of applied science. He scorned the idea that progress meant progress in amenities. He also made a cult of the peasants, who think with the blood, and showed dislike of the 'jaded victims of over-culture'. The virtues of poverty were much admired by Treitschke. He criticized the 'arrogance of learning', and respected homely virtues. The modern Greeks, he complained, would never evict the Turk from Constantinople, since they cared more for intellectual speculation than military service. 'It would be a disaster if still more Germans wish to matriculate.' As for the stifling of talent under a conservative order, 'let us hear no more clap-trap about the disinherited'. 'Who disinherited them? What are they disinherited of?' The people did not create civilization. They should be left to their own tasks.

And among a sturdy peasantry will always be found an honourable warrior spirit. Treitschke detested the vulgarity of great commercial cities, and his admiration of aristocrats, soldiers and peasants was bound up with hatred for the Philistine middle class. As will later be apparent, he particularly detested the Jews. Lassalle for him was 'devilish', and Marx's ideas reflected a base materialism. Property is the legitimate extension of personality; the idea of 'social justice' is preposterous, since there can never be enough wealth to go round. Although the state can protect its citizens from the unfair competition of foreigners (though in general free trade is desirable), and control the 'unnatural and cosmopolitan' capital of the Rothschilds, it has no business to engage directly in production itself. It must be confined to its essential function — the guardian of ultimate power. Poverty is inevitable: it is well known that 'God gives no external reward to virtue in this present life'. In any case, 'the state does not exist for the purpose of producing money's worth'.[29]

As government has no business to do more than adjust the economic process, so it has 'little creative power over intellectual life, but is limited to protecting it and offering superficial assistance'.[30] The life of the spirit and of the mind must be the concern of church and home. Education must be free and vital, and based on a strict study of the classics: 'Greek has the most beautiful literature that the world has ever known.' The spirit of this classical humanism can only be caught from outstanding teachers, and the concern of universities is to find them. 'One of the finest characteristics of youth is its ready recognition of genius.' Treitschke bitterly attacks the pedantry of contemporary German education, and declares that the nation is crippling itself by specialization.* Cramming with shallow information is no substitute for the depth and insight of real learning. And education should be the discipline of an elite, free within its own bounds. Women will, of course, be excluded from it. Art must also be independent, though the state will offer opportunities for monumental sculpture. It certainly did in Bismarck's Germany. But states 'may not meddle', Treitschke declared, with the inner light of art.[31]

When we return to the world of politics, these humanist ideals — the relics of his classical and liberal upbringing, and the expression of his brilliant sense of the drama and atmosphere of history, for it was as an historian he had won fame — give place to the brassy vulgarity of late-Bismarckian Berlin. For a nation to realize its mission it must be *kolossal*. Small peoples are ridiculous.[32] The Swiss he regards with contempt, for big countries are 'better economically', and alone able to wage a great war. 'A splendid security springs

---

* 'What reason can there be for plaguing boys with a few chemical formulae? Did not Goethe tell us that the human mind assimilates nothing that does not appeal to it?' (I, p. 374). The bureaucrats did not take the hint.

from the mere largeness of the scale', and wide horizons liberate the mind. Goethe and Kant were great in spite of the *Kleinstäterei* from which they sprang, not because of it. Inferior races must simply be overwhelmed: and a people whose 'role in history is played out' will disappear, as 'the Redskins in America withered before the Basilisk eye of the Palefaces'.[33] Extirpation or absorption — such is their fate. As the international system becomes 'more aristocratic' with the rise of larger states, overseas territories become essential for a great people. The alternative is 'the appalling prospect' of England and Russia dividing the world between them. And it is 'hard to say whether the Russian knout or the English money bags would be the worst alternative'.[34] As it is, 'England has conquered half the world'.[35] It follows that the next German objective is clear; '. . . the outcome of our next successful war must be the acquisition of colonies by any possible means'.[36] It was a theme which went beyond Bismarck, a major motive of both world wars. No one, at least, can say that Germans of that day, or of Hitler's, failed to give warning of their intentions. Nor, we must admit, do they ever go to war without invoking moral sanctions. 'The cry for war in 1870', said Treitschke, 'was the voice of the German conscience making itself heard'.[37]

With this desire for expansion — a desire shared by other nations in the late nineteenth century — went a singular complacency. Not only were Europeans infinitely superior to the rest of the world — so that their mission is 'to dominate the whole world as one great aristocracy' — but Germans are by nature the master race of Europe. As previously observed, Treitschke has never a good word to say for other peoples. This provincialism, redeemed only by a romantic vision of old Greece, needs further attention, since it coloured all Treitschke's thought and infected generations of German youth. In general, of course, he assumes, the Northern peoples are always morally superior to Southerners. They have a 'manly earnestness of spirit' which contrasts with Mediterranean indolence. And when they do relax, for example when resting on walks in the woods, it will be observed that their posture is superior: for 'the Latin has no feeling for the beauty of the forest; when he takes his repose in it, he lies upon his stomach, while we rest upon our backs'.[38] And Germans, of course, are 'far too good-natured'. This is perhaps natural. Compare the surroundings of Heidelberg and, in particular, the Rhineland — where the people 'have wine in their bones' — with the foggy atmosphere of England. 'There are days in London when the fog is so thick that spleen is in the air.'* And how can one expect real culture, where, as in England, there is no scenery? Could one expect anything else from an island festering with snobbery and prudishness? Naturally Germans have greater sensibility than this Philistine people — for 'the soul is lost to poetry who does not feel the inspiration of Heidelberg or Bonn'. And how maddening the unfairness of fate which has allowed this myopic English race so vast a place in the sun! Again and again Treitschke recurs to the colonizing exploits of the English — 'We have still', he says, 'a great deal to learn from them.' Their colonial administration is 'magnificent'. We must master this strange paradox whereby these degenerate shopkeepers have captured half the world. 'There are 100,000,000 overseas English.' It is too much! 'We must, and will,' he cries, 'take our share in the domination of the world by the white races!'[39] Germans must realize the 'sacredness of our civilizing mission'.† These exhortations alternate with contempt. England is termed that 'Carthage' for not assisting Germany in face of French aggression in 1870. 'We seem to hear that reverend snuffle . . . oh hypocrisy! Oh cant, cant, cant!' If this pacifism goes on, the mistress of the seas will 'sell her war fleet to the highest bidder'.

As for the French, they are arrogant, temperamental and mean. They are 'born calculators'. They 'import the arithmetical spirit even into the kindly relations of family life'. They are selfish and sensual, dominated by women: 'in every century they have lived under petticoat government'.[40] But while the Frenchman, with his bourgeois comfort, limits the size of his family, the German view of life is entirely different, for 'we hold that a man should be a man'. This damning of the consequences is natural, for 'the German is a hero born, and believes that he can hack and hew his way through life'. Bolder, freer, larger families result.

Unfortunately this desire to replenish a master race is shared by inferior nations. The fecundity of the Poles, for example, is disgusting. 'These people require no further provision for matrimony than a supply of potatoes and Schnapps sufficient for two days.'[41] Slovaks and Vlaks, too, threaten to swamp superior German and Magyar stocks in Central Europe, and, as for the Irish, 'they breed like rabbits'. The Austrians come in for Treitschke's particular dislike, and

* I, p. 222. An interesting study might be written on the effect of the legend of the English climate on continental political thought.
† TREITSCHKE's *History of Germany in the Nineteenth Century* is full of bitter propaganda. It was Blücher, naturally, who won the battle of Waterloo. See H. W. C. DAVIS, op. cit., chap. x.

he tends to despise Scandinavians, who are merely 'sub-Germans'. As for the Dutch — look at their language! It is 'irresistibly comic', 'a sailor's dialect framed to express the lowest and most ordinary ideas'. Such coarseness shows that the modern Dutch are no longer German. They are, in any case, mere money-grubbers and physically degenerate. And the Italians are now become a mere nation of dilettanti, who find beauty 'only in the ankle of a ballerina or the throat of a prima donna'. When they are not admiring ballerinas, the Italians admire viragos. The only distinguished southern people were the ancient Greeks ('Greeks and Germans — perhaps the two noblest nations in the world's history!') and the sixteenth-century Spaniards, who sacrificed themselves for an idea. 'We cannot contemplate such stupendous political idealism without a kind of horror-stricken admiration.' So 'the gifted Spanish race drained its life blood for the political idea of the supremacy of the Church'.[42]

Such Quixotry would never distinguish Americans. Like all Anglo-Saxon people, they are materialists, and compared with cultured Germans, raw and vulgar: 'the peculiar thinness of intellectual atmosphere in young countries is repellent'. As for the coloured peoples, they are naturally servants and will always remain so, while 'mulatto' peoples combine the worst of both worlds — like mules. But the most despicable of all races are the Jews. In this insidious and subversive people the 'trading instinct is developed into the wildest passion'.[43] Curiously enough, they have an astonishing 'racial conceit'. With a deadly hatred of anything Christian, they are always, everywhere, 'an element of national decomposition'. Good German folk must beware of this evil thing: 'Whenever he finds his life sullied by the filth of Judaism, the German must turn from it.'[44]

These widespread animadversions and demands for war did not come from some crazy and venal journalist. They came from the Professor of History at the University of Berlin, the most popular historian of his day, the successor of Ranke. Into these lectures, says Davis, 'he wove the best of his political ideas'. It is easy to imagine how topical the references could be made; how this brilliant historical romantic could play upon his audience. For the ideas of Treitschke, as they must appear to anyone familiar with the course of German history, closely reflect the political and emotional development of the Germany of his day. First there is the assertion of state-power — the passionate desire to surround the nation with a framework of steel. Through blood and iron, German unity had been accomplished:

thus alone the ancient highly civilized states of the south had been welded into the structure of Bismarck's Reich. The union had been consecrated on the battlefield of Sedan and proclaimed at Versailles. Underneath was the age-old North German tradition of military enterprise in the east, symbolized by Treitschke's cult of the Teutonic Knights. 'Who can understand', he had written, 'the inmost nature of the Prussian people and the Prussian state, unless he has familiarized his mind with the pitiless racial conflicts whose vestiges . . . live on mysteriously in the habits of our people?'[45] Behind the reiteration of the need for order and internal cohesion, still lies the recurring night-mare of the Thirty Years War; the old dreams of medieval Teutonic Empire and its disruption. All this is coloured by a specious liberal-ism — for Treitschke is the child of the Romantic age. 'Everything new', he wrote, 'in the nineteenth century is the work of Liberalism.' His early nationalism had been liberal, with its desire for freedom of speech and religion, and for economic liberty. He had advocated the forms of constitutional government, a world of 'free men in a free state'. But all was steeped in nationalism, and in the romantic historian's delight in the spectacle of action. For in his historical insight, not in his wild political thought, lay the genius of this limited and forceful mind. No one who reads the brilliant evocation of the medieval *Drang nach Osten*, or the panoramic treatment of the German resistance to Napoleon, can deny Treitschke's literary power.

By European standards, this prophet, like Carlyle, was a provin-cial. He was also singularly blind to the most important fact of the nineteenth century — the vast pervasive influence of science. Unlike Nietzsche, he was not much influenced by the implications of the new doctrine of evolution. He scorned the role of technology in history.* He had no vision of the possibilities, for peace or war, of modern invention. Though he had a picturesque, and, indeed, obsessive, feel for geography, for the romance and mystery of the sea and the mountains, for the drama of history in its perennial setting, he held that events were determined by mysterious and providential laws. 'Who is so blind', he asked, 'that he cannot see in the march of events of these latest days the divine wisdom which constrains us Germans to become a nation?'[46] Material progress is uncertain and unimportant. The spiritual significance of events is vital. All is displayed by the unfolding of a Divine plan and 'the destinies of

---

* 'The discovery of the use of manure was the most ancient in agriculture and produced the greatest effect, for when the tribes attained that knowledge, they became stationary and their whole way of life was changed' (I, p. 57). This homely discovery, he implies, was far more important than the invention of any number of gadgets.

states are accomplished by processes of attraction and repulsion whose final consummation is hidden from mortal eyes'. While there may be truth in this assertion, since if history proceeds on Treitschke's principles, there may soon be no mortal eyes left to see it, the idea is strictly meaningless — a debased poetry, the projection of a mal-adjusted spirit. This need for emotional excitement may explain the haste and eagerness with which Treitschke proclaims his cult of war. For that cult is the core of his creed. Again and again, with an extraordinary insistence, he asserts the necessity of war. 'The arbitrament of force is the logical outcome of the nature of the State. The mere fact of the existence of many States involves the necessity of war.'[47] The dream of peace, said Frederick the Great, is 'a phantom'. Consider, he insists, not without reason, the facts of the current situation. While the liberal world has been talking about disarmament for decades — what are the facts? 'Armaments are everywhere becoming . . . more formidable.' We live, he shouts with exultation, in a warlike age. Clausewitz was right — war is 'the forceful continuation of policy'. As the century has developed, we have seen the moral majesty of war.

It was natural, perhaps, that Treitschke should accept the frame-work of European nation states into which he was born, but some deep neurosis must explain the glee with which he welcomes the clash of arms. Modern war, he insists, .must be swift and utterly ruthless. 'The bloodstained savagery of a quick war of annihilation is more humane.'[48] For war is 'the remedy for ailing peoples' and 'Aryan races are above all things conquerors'. What pathological desire for reassurance is behind these assertions? And what queer death-wish is behind the phrase 'the grandeur of war lies in the utter annihilation of puny man in the great conception of the state'?

Treitschke was, indeed, the prophet of a feverish age. Of the militarism of nineteenth-century Prussia, of the heel-clicking, metallic arrogance of the nineteenth-century Prussian officer-caste, of the efficiency of a mighty military tradition, with all its undertones of tension and guilt. And the obverse of all this self-assertion was total collapse. The despair of politics, the cynical opportunism. That, too, came down from the days of *Simplicissimus* and the Thirty Years War. For the Germans of Treitschke's day were the victims of their own historic fate, and their popular professor blared his war cry across the lecture halls of Berlin. So much achievement, in so evil a frame! Only the supersession of nineteenth-century nationalism can liberate that tortured and forceful spirit.

With Treitschke had come the climax of bourgeois militarized romanticism, of the cult of the nation state. He expressed the aspirations of crude nineteenth-century minds. His influence was to be surpassed by a philosopher with more penetrating insight. The mind of Nietzsche cut through all this backwash of the old romantic nineteenth century: it ranged forward into far more frightening territories, and faced the implications of Darwinian evolution, the atheism of Feuerbach and Schopenhauer, and the transformation of middle class culture. And where Treitschke was an old-fashioned Prussian nationalist, Nietszsche was to be something more outlandish — the cosmopolitan prophet of the annihilation of the liberal world.

CHAPTER VIII

THE CULT OF THE IRRATIONAL
SCHOPENHAUER: NIETZSCHE

WHILE Treitsçhke was proclaiming his unbridled nationalism, a yet more radical attack was being made against both
the Christian and the humanist position. The assault came
from within the humanist camp. It was directed as much against
the materialist aims of Marxist or Utopian revolutionaries as against
the conservatives or social democrats. Not since the Middle Ages
had so profound a denial of life been formulated. The major prophets were Schopenhauer and Nietzsche.

The origins go back a long way. Schopenhauer's negative pessimism had its roots in the eighteenth century and in the romantic age.
One must cast back in time to understand him. But his influence
was very gradual, and only came to fruition in the later decades of
the period under review. Nietzsche, on the other hand, is post-
Darwinian. He is in raging reaction against the conclusions of the
great mid-nineteenth-century scientists, against the belief in progress,
material amelioration and popular government. Where Schopenhauer imported a quasi-Eastern despair of politics, Nietzsche formulated a neo-Pagan cult of power. His belief in action for action's sake
was to be reinforced by the post-Marxian anarchist Sorel, whose
attack on liberal democratic ideas was to contribute directly to the
rise of Fascism. Both had affinities with the philosopher Bergson,
with his destructive, counter-revolutionary political influence.

II

The introspection displayed by Schopenhauer and Nietzsche was
already apparent in Herder and Hegel and the Romantic writers of
their day. As this romanticism developed, it had often achieved
benevolence and sensibility — in hatred of oppression, humanitarian
reform, the championship of small nationalities, the emancipation of
the slaves. But there was another side to the picture; the obsession
with self, the cult of farouche egotism, of utter despair.

It could, of course, prove politically demoralizing. When this
romanticism, and its disillusionment, was bound up with philosophy,
and when that philosophy was German, sad results might be

expected. Driven to its logical conclusion, the new outlook could lead not to the transcendental humanism of Hegel, that heady substitute for religion, but to a blistering atheism and a suicidal despair. Life, it could be argued by soured romantics, was intrinsically evil; love was a cheat; politics a game for fools. When such views were expressed with violent originality and startling eloquence by a philosopher of genius, his influence could be formidable. The romantic youth of late nineteenth-century Germany, in particular, always alert for a new pessimistic philosophy, were swayed by the writings of Schopenhauer like ripe wheat before the wind. The views of this philosopher lead to a despair of politics, to an exaltation of elites who claimed the right to practise a morality different from that of the people. Even to a horror of life and scorn of humanitarian motives which helped to darken the political scene in the later nineteenth century. Unlike other subsequent prophets of despair, Schopenhauer was an authentic philosopher; a profound and brilliant writer whose views command respect. It was the effect of these opinions on intellectuals obsessed by philosophical abstractions which was to be deplored.

A well-to-do eccentric of compelling personality and striking appearance, Schopenhauer had brought to the problems of his age the attack and confidence of the eighteenth century and a more than eighteenth-century subtlety of mind.* He had grown up under the

* Arthur Schopenhauer, born at Danzig, 1788, of aristocratic mercantile family. He was called Arthur, since the name, being similar in all languages, would be useful in business. His father was an extravagant, neurotic, *bon viveur*, who died through falling from an attic window into a canal after a nervous breakdown; his mother was highly intelligent but 'dépourvue de tout esprit d'ordre' and 'surprise d'avoir donné naissance à un pessimiste incurable'. In 1793 they migrated to Hamburg, and Schopenhauer studied at Göttingen and Dresden. Inheriting a comfortable fortune, he was able to devote himself to study, having no inclination for business. In 1819 was published his most important book, *The World as Will and Perception*, which at first had little success. After studying art in Italy, he attended the University of Berlin where he conceived a deep antipathy to Hegel and his academic following. He then settled in Frankfurt, and in 1836 published his *Will in Nature*. Three years later appeared his *Liberty and Will*, and in 1860, the year of his death, his *Parerga and Paralipomena*. He was a man of wide erudition and broad interests. Schopenhauer was able to pursue his original bent independently of academic employment, but he craved academic recognition: he detested the Jews for their 'vulgar optimism', while his hatred of professors was more intimate. In principle he disliked women (though he appears not always to have been impervious to them) and preferred the company of his dog, a white poodle named Atma. 'In old age he had a blue and limpid eye, thin lips with a touch of sarcasm, round which played a delicate smile. His vast forehead, set off by two tufts of white hair at the sides, revealed an aristocratic distinction, sparkling with wit and mischief.' He was a brilliant linguist, with the fine manners of an eighteenth-century aristocrat. He is said to have possessed the largest known head of his time, for it measured 5.5, while Kant's was 4.10, Talleyrand's 4.9 and Napoleon's a mere 4.5. His collected works are published in fifteen volumes, edited P. Deussen, Munich 1911-33. For a masterly account of his writings see T. Ribot, *La Philosophie de Schopenhauer*. Paris, 1874; M. Zwemmer, *Arthur Schopenhauer*. Leipzig, 1862; Foucher de Careil, *Hegel et Schopenhauer*. Paris, 1862; T. Ruyssen, *Schopenhauer*. Paris, 1911. *Die Welt als Wille und Vorstellung* is translated by R. B. Haldane and J. Kemp.

influence of Byron and the romantics, whom he frequently quotes. He was also one of the first Europeans to be well versed in Indian philosophy, with its political abnegations and desire for escape from the world of appearance. Following Kant, he accepted the limitations of mind before phenomena, anticipated modern views on the importance of the sub-conscious, attempted to fuse matter and spirit in emergent will, and regarded intelligence as a bye-product of the blind process of life. Here is a cult of Will, but it is not a Good Will. Kant, he believed, advocated a 'slave morality' as an escape from correct conclusions. The world is an enigma and philosophy strictly empirical, dictated by experience. A blind will to live sustains the world and in man the Life-Force first attains full consciousness. 'Man is the only creature that is astonished at his own existence.' He is the only 'metaphysical animal' — the intelligent monkey. Hence the popular need for religion, which is the poetry and philosophy of the people. The greatest spirits are beyond such compensations, and beyond the rules of ordinary morality. Like Spinoza, Schopenhauer regarded the world as a totality, but he does not find the world good. Man is the culmination of life, since a more intelligent being could not bear to live. There is, of course, no personal survival, but while individuals perish, the unknowing (*unbewusst*) Life Force drives inexorably on. Hence Schopenhauer's detestation of what he regarded as the vulgarity of optimistic demagogues. 'They have come', he wrote, 'through hatred of Christianity to pretend that the world is an end in itself, and that life . . . makes for happiness, that the howling colossal suffering . . . is due to governments, and that without them there would be Heaven on earth.'[1] 'Howling colossal suffering' — here is the key to Schopenhauer's deepest mind.* The Eastern remedy of self-transcendence was his answer. This may be achieved by contemplation, by 'Menschenliebe' — a detached pity. And also by asceticism which cheats life of its purpose. Though Schopenhauer disapproves of it, his followers found the idea of suicide attractive, at once an affirmation of annihilation and of will. Had not Byron written

> Count o'er the joys thine eyes have seen,
> Count o'er thy days from anguish fre :;
> And know, whatever thou hast been,
> 'Tis something better — not to be.[2]

---

* This sensibility appealed in particular to Thomas Hardy, who was influenced by Schopenhauer, the *Dynasts* owing a good deal to this philosophy.

The basic human instinct is sex. This fraud keeps the whole hideous process alive. The instinct is the heart of the will to live; the concentration of the whole being. 'That is why,' he wrote, 'I call the sex organs the seat of the Will.' Here is the undying core of Life; the root and connection of the whole species, impersonal, animal, profound. But Nature recks nothing of individuals, and love is the future generation clamouring for life. Sexual relations are brutally impersonal; for the pleasure of a few 'epileptic moments' the individual is permanently trapped. The looks of lovers are sinister; 'the meditation of the . . . species'. They are furtive traitors, plotting to perpetuate pain. The 'drunkenness of the species' attains its end, regardless of the artificialities of romantic love. Not since the brave times of Tertullian and St. Augustine had such eloquent denunciations of normal instinct been put about.

This adolescent and sensational despair naturally made Schopenhauer's works widely notorious, and greatly contributed to their influence. It won popularity among those reacting from the extremities of romantic love, as well as among those who desired to appear sophisticated — both always a considerable proportion of articulate youth. For here was a philosophical justification for Byronic disillusionment. Here, said Schopenhauer's admirers, is a true realism, facing the appalling facts of battle, pestilence, loneliness and despair. Here, the cheating sophistries of romantic sentimentalists and the coarse optimism of fatuous reformers are unmasked. It was easy for Dante to describe Hell: when it came to describing Paradise he had little material for his imagination. The world, said Schopenhauer, like Hobbes before him, is a chaos of blind conflicting Wills, and they reflect the laws of man's own being.

The political influence of such a philosophy was naturally deleterious. Since life was an evil enigma, an Eastern quietism, remote from politics, should be attained. To these forerunners of existentialism, irresponsibility was the beginning of wisdom. 'Im *esse* nicht im *operari* liegt die Freiheit' — 'In being not in doing Freedom lies.' Appeals to duty or to utility were alike meaningless; the best that could be hoped is for politics not to interfere with private life. This embittered outlook tended to a characteristic despair of politics. For this nineteenth-century prophet infected with his brilliant pessimism a wide circle of admirers. In particular, his distinction between the common herd, whom he called the 'clockworks of nature', and the fine-drawn minority of master minds — of pioneers, beyond conventional morality and religion, who sensed the tragedy of Time—foreshadowed the doctrines of Nietzsche. Morality can only be attained by exceptionally talented individuals; 'It is as foolish to believe that our systems of morals and ethics will produce virtuous characters and saints as to think that our aesthetics will create poets, musicians and painters.'[3] History, in such a view, is largely meaningless, a catalogue of suffering. This outlook was violently opposed to the main current of nineteenth-century opinion. Hegel, Saint-Simon, Comte, Marx, the post-Darwinian political philosophers, as well as the liberal democrats, the psychologists, historians and anthropologists, were deeply committed to the idea of Progress. Schopenhauer defied them all.

Meanwhile his political scepticism made an appeal to liberal romantics, disillusioned after their failures in 1848. Since unhappiness is inevitable, aesthetic contemplation, detachment, and a certain distant pity were the proper reaction of a civilized man. With this detached view, he could write as follows: 'the question of the sovereignty of the people comes down ultimately to this — if anyone has the right to govern the people against its Will? I do not see how this can reasonably be admitted. Therefore, absolutely, the people is sovereign; but it is a sovereign that is a perpetual "minor", which must always remain in tutelage, and cannot even exercise its rights without running the greatest dangers. For like all minors, it easily becomes the plaything of cunning rascals, who are, therefore, termed demagogues'.[4] It follows that an absolute hereditary monarchy is the best form of government. But in any case, the individual cannot expect to find fulfilment in anything so vulgar as the state. Hence, among other reasons, Schopenhauer's detestation of Hegel. A spectator in politics, he cared mainly for the preservation of property and order.

Such, in a brief sketch, were the doctrines of this original pessimist. Rich, healthy and talented, his extreme sensibility to suffering and his capacity to face the worst implications of advanced mid-nineteenth-century opinion, plunged him in stormy gloom. His sensitive pessimism can certainly make the robust confidence of a Herbert Spencer or a Buckle look Philistine. Though he won little influence among his contemporaries, his effect on later generations was lasting. Here was an appeal to the self pity of disillusioned romantics, to the desire for separation from the herd, to a bold treatment of sexual morality, startling at the time. Had he been insulated in the Latin obscurity of medieval or sixteenth-century theological controversy, his opinions would have had no more effect than those of most heretics. With access to the full publicity of the nineteenth century, his influence was highly subversive. But it was never negligible. Apart from his influence on Nietzsche, by his definition of the idea of creative will he anticipated Bergson, and by his understanding of the sub-conscious he anticipated Freud.

III

Seldom has there been a stranger fatality than the life and influence of Friedrich Nietzsche.* The brilliant ideas of this psychopathic

* Friedrich Nietzsche, 1844-1900, was born at Röcken in Saxony in the North German plain. His father, a Lutheran pastor, died in 1849, and he was brought up at Naumburg in a conventional atmosphere by his mother, grandmother, sister and two maiden aunts. His desire to shock his contemporaries may in part be traced to this upbringing. In 1858 he went to the famous and strictly disciplined school at Pforta, and proceeded in 1864 to Bonn, where he disliked the roisterous beer-swilling of his contemporaries. At Leipzig he formed friendships with Deussen, the interpreter of Indian philosophy, and with the philologist Rohde. He was also influenced by Schopenhauer's philosophy. In 1867 he fell off a horse when engaged on military service, and only took part in the war of 1870 as a hospital orderly. In 1869, at the early age of twenty-four, the brilliant Hellenist was appointed Professor of Classical Philology at Basel. Here he remained until his resignation in 1879. He formed friendships with Burckhardt, the historian of the Renaissance, whom he much revered, with Wagner ('I could not have stood my youth', he wrote, 'without Wagner's music'), and with Frau Cosima, for whom he had a romantic affection. In 1878 his bitter quarrel with Wagner – 'what I never forgave Wagner? That he became Reichsdeutsch' – marked a turning point in his life. He resigned his Professorship, partly through ill-health, in the next year, and faced loneliness and penury in shabby pensions in the Alps and Italy, 'living in drab attic rooms, often without fire in winter, near-sighted almost to blindness, sitting alone night after night unable to read or sleep' (MORGAN, op. cit., p. 9). In 1880 he wrote *Zarathustra*, his favourite work. It was so little recognized that he had difficulty in publishing the last part. In 1885 his sister, to whom he was intimately devoted, married Bernard Forster, an anti-Semite 'rabble-raiser', who subsequently committed suicide after founding a Teutonic colony in Paraguay. 'You have gone over to my antipodes' . . . he wrote. 'I will not conceal from you that I consider the engagement an insult.' In 1888 Nietzsche's euphoria reached its climax in the production of *The Twilight of the Idols* and the *Ecce Homo*, but in January 1889 he collapsed in the street at Turin, attempting to embrace a mare being flogged by the driver of a carozza. His friend Overbeck found him in his lodgings, ploughing the piano with his elbow and shrieking in frenzy. Shouting his poems in the train, he was removed to a clinic in Basel, and thence to an asylum in Jena. He spent his last three years at Weimar, half paralysed and sunk in a docile imbecility. The fame which Nietzsche craved came only after his madness. After 1889 his doctrines spread like wildfire. Full advantage of this change was taken by his sister, now Frau Forster-Nietzsche, a woman of limited intelligence and unbridled fanaticism. But she had a good business sense and lived to ingratiate herself with Hitler. She cornered all Nietzsche's manuscripts and suppressed and distorted without compunction. The notorious *Will to Power* was compiled from an unrepresentative selection of his notes. 'The tragedy was played out,' writes Dr. Kaufmann, 'and a satyr play followed, while the author of *Antichrist* was lingering in his mother's house, hopelessly mad, his sister, under the same roof, employed her considerable propagandist talents in the service of that Teutonic "Christianity" and "chauvinistic racism" which Nietzsche loathed as a "scabies of the heart" '. Nietzsche was a man of small physique, with a high voice and neurotic mannerisms. He was proud of his Polish blood, and wore a heavy military moustache. He was passionately addicted to the mountains, and conceived some of his most brilliant and extraordinary ideas in the Alps. He was also extremely sensitive to music. When, as a youth in Cologne, he was conducted by a porter

genius were addressed to a minority of hypersensitive and serious minds. He attempted, in good faith, to face the bleak situation of the later nineteenth century. He acclaimed, like Proudhon and Feuerbach, the decline of Christianity, and endeavoured to create a new morality, reinterpret the course of history and chart the development of the future. He was primarily an aesthete and a moralist, not a philosopher. He was endowed with extraordinary insight, original eloquence and a total lack of political sense. He exercised, on his own level, a most powerful influence on the writers of the early twentieth century, notably on Sorel, Bernard Shaw, Gide and Stefan George. He was a pioneer of psychology, before Freud, and he claimed to stand not at the end of an epoch, but at its beginning. Elusive, feverish, self-consciously irresponsible, this extraordinary prophet is a forerunner, like Schopenhauer, of Existentialism and of a modern revolt against politics.

On a different level, his influence was to be more immediately political. His neo-Hellenic doctrine of the Overman (*Übermensch*)* an intellectual's vision compounded of Socrates and Caesar and Goethe, was applied, with an ambience of Wagner, to the racial dogmas he particularly detested, and vulgarized by the German Philistines he frantically denounced.† Christ, Nietzsche believed, was the only Christian, and he died on the Cross. His own fate was to be crucified by the vulgarity of his belated followers — a fate he apparently anticipated. And if ever an intellectual deserved that nemesis it was Nietzsche. His vanity and madness are inextricable from his apocalyptic and brilliant intuitions.

This baleful prophet was much influenced by Dostoevsky. Yet he was in the main stream of German culture. The influence of

---

* What one looked up to, not so much one who ruled.

† Earl Russell remarks, with sardonic wit, 'Nietzsche's superman is very like Siegfried, except that he knows Greek. This may seem odd, but that is not my fault.' *History of Western Philosophy*, 1961, p. 728.

---

to a brothel instead of an hotel, he recovered his poise by rushing to a piano. He suffered from migraine and insomnia and his madness was accompanied by a paralytic stroke at forty-four.

The German edition of Nietzsche's writings in twenty volumes is published by the Musarion Verlag, Munich, 1920-29. The complete works are available in English, edited by Oscar Levy, New York (Macmillan). His principal books are: *The Birth of Tragedy*, 1872; *Untimely Meditations*, 1873-76; *Human, All too Human*, 1878-80; *The Dawn*, 1881; *The Gay Science*, 1882; *Thus Spoke Zarathustra*, 1883-85; *Beyond Good and Evil*, 1886; *Towards a Genealogy of Morals*, 1887; *The Case of Wagner*, 1888; *The Twilight of the Idols*, 1889. After his madness appeared the *Antichrist* (written in 1885); *The Will to Power*, 1901 and 1906, and *Ecce Homo*, 1908. See, in particular, WALTER A. KAUFMANN, *Nietzsche, Philosopher, Psychologist, Anti-Christ*. Princeton, 1950 for the best critical account. See also *What Nietzsche Means*, G. A. MORGAN, JNR. Harvard, 1943.

romantic Hellenism was cardinal, but that of Goethe appears to have been very great, and many of the startling titles which made Nietzsche's works so sensational were suggested by his poetry. Although, too, he was no systematizer, but rather ego-centric, he had, in common with Hegel, a wild and intense vision of world history and a violent Germanic determination to fathom life to the depths. 'All truths', he said, 'are bloody to me.' In the nineteenth century exploration of intuition Nietzsche got to the bitter dregs.

His influence may thus be traced on two levels. On the one hand, he challenged, and changed, the outlook of elites. He shook the complacencies of widely received opinion, and gave warning of the implications of atheist humanism in its most immoderate guise. As a moralist and a prophet, Nietzsche is extremely formidable. And he was astringent. He raised problems latent in the closing nineteenth century. They can be faced and overcome. They cannot be ignored.

On the popular level, on the other hand, the vulgarization of Nietzsche's ideas has been pervasive, gloomy and demoralizing. His rhetorical and melodramatic stress on egoism and cruelty, his contempt for ordinary human life and disregard of law, his glorification of struggle and ruthlessness, and his conviction that the society in which he lived was decadent, were to spread like a blight over the early twentieth century. In the *Trahison des Clercs* Nietzsche was probably an even greater sinner than Marx and Treitschke. He certainly reaches the climax of the movement begun by Rousseau whereby the moralist has become an outcast, appealing to all and sundry through the seductions of style and epigram, and casting bread upon the troubled waters of a widening public. But the contrast with Marx is striking, though both were the savage enemies of bourgeois society. Where Marx founded and promoted a great political movement and based his political philosophy and programme on dialectical materialism, Nietzsche conducted his dialectic with himself and regarded the material aspect of life with singular indifference. The means of production, whether publicly or privately owned, bored Nietzsche profoundly; the Marxist goal of material well being seemed to him as much of a pig-sty as the bourgeois equivalent. To his agonized sensibility, the fate of the mass of mankind was a matter of no concern. All that counted were the elite few. Yet Marxist doctrines of the dictatorship of the proletariat through a Communist vanguard, and Fascist doctrines of elites, were to prove a political caricature of the 'Übermensch'. For Marx and Nietzsche were united in a common indifference to the dangers of the abuse of power. Between them they were to contribute handsomely to the bedevilment of mankind.

Nietzsche, he emphasized, was a prophet of the future. He was determined to face the worst implications of contemporary disbelief. Like Feuerbach, he regarded Christianity as a terrible and poisonous delusion. But he foresaw, apparently with exultation, the frightful consequences when it got about among the masses that the old myth was finished.

Darwin's discoveries, he believed, must undermine all standards. If 'doctrines . . . of the lack of a . . . distinction between man and animal . . . are hurled into the people for another generation',[5] if once they realize the implications of modern knowledge, an age of barbarism will begin. 'There will be wars such as have never happened on earth.'[6] 'This apocalyptic sense of . . . things to come,' writes Dr. Kaufmann, 'hangs over Nietzsche's thinking like a thunder cloud.'[7] The brooding sense of doom may have reflected the creeping madness in Nietzsche's mind, but in appraising the century of Coventry and Berlin, Stalingrad, Hiroshima and Nagasaki, Nietzsche's insight was accurate.

Naturally such frightful chaos must come about, for God is dead. 'Do we not feel the breath of empty space? Has it not become colder? God is Dead. God remains dead. And we have killed Him.'[8] What universal madness when mankind discovers that they have lost God! Yet 'Above all,' the Epicureans had said, 'leave God out.' 'Écrasez l'infame,' had been Voltaire's motto, and he strove with all the resources of his wit to further the betterment of humanity. The tough agnostic T. H. Huxley had felt no need, in face of 'irreparable loss . . . to renounce [his] manhood, and, howling, grovel in bestiality'.[9] The anthropologist Tylor, we have seen, kept a balanced mind.

This capacity to take agnostic conclusions without self dramatization and despair was impossible for Nietzsche. He represented more violent peoples than Epicurus, Voltaire or Huxley. Hence the need for a categorical answer — are values possible in a Godless world? Hence Nietzsche's raging onslaught on compromise, hypocrisy, and on stoic or bland indifference to questions obviously beyond the human mind. Hence his *Blitzschlag* of accepted values, and the title of his *Götzendämmerung oder wie man mit dem Hammer philosofiert.* * These forays into the unknown had a hectic brilliance, and a lightening power of phrase. They are shot through with Nietzsche's *folie des grandeurs.* 'Revaluation of all values; that is my

* *The Twilight of the Gods or Why one Philosophizes with a Hammer.*

373

formula for an act of ultimate self examination of mankind which in me has become flesh and genius. My lot is that I must be the first *decent* human being, that I know myself to be in opposition against the mendaciousness of millennia.'[10] 'I am no man,' he said, 'I am dynamite.'

In pursuit of this desperate purpose Nietzsche hammered home his attack. It was backed by a queer doctrine of 'inevitable recurrence' — dredged up from who knows what oriental and classical source. Individual lives must be lived, he believed, over and over again, 'grinding in the horror of existence like a cosmic dentist's drill'.[11] In face of this horror — the death of God, the recurrence of Fate, the Christian blasphemy of life, and the worthlessness of the common man, now swarming in new and sinister power with the coming of democracy — there is one way out. The glorification of life by a cosmopolitan world elite. One day they will realize in themselves the powers, beyond good and evil, of a new Humanity. They, alone, can accept with joy the fate of eternal recurrence. And they will manipulate the masses to suit the changing patterns of their design for life. They will displace God.

The conception of the 'übermensch', the goal of this elite, is very much an intellectual's dream, the compensation of a solitary genius. It has of course little to do with politics. Where Hegel believed that the highest values were realized through the state, Nietzsche repudiated and attacked it, as tending to destroy superior individuals. The 'will to power', the driving instinct of all life, rose to its apex only in personality. It won its greatest triumphs in the solitary victories of self discipline and self torture. To would-be disciples, Nietzsche exclaimed, 'Be yourselves'.

The foundation of Nietzsche's affirmation of life was thus the cult of superior personality. He had been a brilliant Hellenist, and his first publication showed strange insights into the culture of the Greeks, since often confirmed. He believed that the climax of Greek culture had been the age of Aeschylus, when a hard acceptance of fate and mastery of experience was uncontaminated by Plato. On the other hand, he could sometimes admire Socrates.* Here, he believed, was the great example of a ruthless, undeviating, quest for truth, even to the destruction of one's own deepest convictions. He held Greek civilization to have been far greater than anything since

---

* His ambivalent attitude to this philosopher is a matter of disagreement, but in spite of the incoherence and paradox which are among Nietzsche's notable characteristics, it would seem that the Socratic influence was powerful.

achieved. Following Burckhardt, he was also fascinated by the Renaissance; with Leonardo, in particular. Like Marx he had the profoundest admiration for Shakespeare. Spinoza's sense of the totality, fatalism, and self-sufficiency of life also appealed to him; but like most nineteenth-century Germans, he was hypnotized by Goethe — the hard self-creator, the universal man. The Greeks had known how to organize chaos; Goethe was the supreme architect of his own life. This Germanic search for a principle of self mastery is typical and fundamental. Far from feeling that the evolution of humanity out of animal beginnings was a guarantee of progress, Nietzsche deeply resented the 'hairy garments of our ape genealogy'. He therefore maintains that the distance between Shakespeare and the common man is wider than that between the common man and the ape: 'for genius becomes no longer animal'. The existence of a few master minds alone redeems our bestial nature, though why it should need redemption in the context of Nietzsche's thought is not apparent.

These master minds are creative artists, never technicians. The technician is merely a 'super-chimpanzee'. Through these splendid beings only, the Life Force realizes its end. Schopenhauer was wrong when he believed that the cosmic drive is mindless: it is at least creative. The task of great men is not to thwart but to guide nature. The idea of such cosmic self realization is familiar in Spinoza,[12] as in Schopenhauer. Since the basic drive in life is the will to power, the 'Overman' will come to terms with it: strictly guiding and developing himself according to its own law — something different for the *Herdenmoral* of the mob. So in the 'Great Noon' is the future, the artist-tyrants of a world culture will attain the happiness of Gods: 'full of power and love, full of tears and full of laughter, a happiness. which like the sun at evening continually gives away and sheds its inexhaustible wealth into the sea; and, like it, feels richest only then, when even the poorest fisherman rows with golden oars'. These neo-Hellenes will lead the world according to true justice, which is the will of the strong. Beneath them will exist the mass of specialized ordinary humanity, performing their necessary routine. These 'Overmen', spiritual, grand and terrible, will be the descendants of fierce 'new barbarians' who, in the twentieth and twenty-first centuries, will smash the decadent culture of the herd and the antheap. These 'men of prey' are to be born masters; like the original Hellenes, they will 'throw themselves on old mellow cultures'. They will be free of the Christian sense of sin. And they will be a new kind of barbarian, 'who come from the height'. Women, for them, will be 'the relaxation of the warrior'. Their friendship, like the ideal described in Plato's *Symposium* — curiously enough, the young Nietzsche's favourite book — will be an emulative self mastery.[13] They will be warriors of knowledge, with a resilient tenacity: 'Typus höchster Wohlgeratenheit'. They will realize at last the potentialities of life.

Along with this wild and glittering vision, went a ferocious onslaught against Christianity. Official Christianity had been a miasma and a blight; the Evangel of Jesus was followed by the 'Dysangel' of Paul, that 'genius in hatred'. The glad tidings were quickly superseded by the 'very worst'. Nietzsche found the idea of redemption particularly unpleasant, a relic of 'gruesome paganism'. The founder of Christianity was a kind of Idiot, in the Dostoevskian sense, who practised an ethic of total non-resistence, touched by a certain 'bucolic sweetness'. And of course Jesus was a political criminal, since he 'attacked the priesthood, the core of Jewry'. So he died for his own fault, not for the faults of others. And Pauline Christianity is a morality of slaves. Its sense of sin is a blasphemy and a castration of life.* Particularly revolting is the Christian attitude to sex. In pagan times 'the sexual symbol was venerable ... Christianity has made something unclean out of sexuality: it threw filth upon the origin, upon the presuppositions of our life'. As for the Pauline attitude to marriage, it is atrocious. 'How can one put a book into the hands of children and women which contains that vile word "to avoid fornication, let every man have his own wife ... it is better to marry than to burn".'† Christianity is a kind of subJudaism. The Old Testament is like the music of Handel, but the New the gospel of the 'sick animal in man'. For the Christian wants to get rid of himself. He wants to hide from the hard and brilliant realities of life. Proudhon had held the same view.

As prophet of the future, Nietzsche accepted what he held to be the truth, the facts of atheism and power addiction. For the sublimation of the Schopenhauerian Life Force comes about only through the supreme effort of controlled personality. And sublimation, Nietzsche demands, not denial. The crime of the medieval Church

---

* Nietzsche called the rise of Christianity a 'Sklavensaufstand'; the German Reformation the 'Bauernaufstand des Geistes' – a spiritual peasants revolt.

† *Antichrist*, p. 56. Nietzsche's own view of marriage was ambivalent. Sometimes he depicts a partnership in self-perfection, but the following passage is probably more representative. 'This one went out like a hero in quest of truths, and eventually he conquered for himself a little dressed up lie. His marriage, he calls it.'

was to have hunted down the healthy barbarian — comparable to the famous 'blond Bestie' (the lion) — only 'to put him behind bars in monasteries'.* There is more hope even for Cesar Borgia, with his clean cult of power, than for the nincompoop Parsifal, maundering about the Holy Grail.† In the stern process of self mastery (*Selbstbeherrschung*) one must have something to overcome. Passion must be controlled, not emasculated.

Along with the attack on Christianity, goes the onslaught, common to so many writers here surveyed, on the Philistine bourgeoisie. Nietzsche loathed and detested what he termed Herd Morality.‡ He foresaw, with justifiable horror, the worst features of the century of the common man. Mass uniformity, hatred of elites, state worship; nationalism, routine overwork to pointless ends; the barbarity of specialists — all were anticipated and indicted.§ The smugness, snobbery, and myopia of the petit-bourgeois milieu from which Nietzsche derived has never had a more savage enemy. He particularly disliked the German academic world, which he termed 'a Bedlam of learned Philistines . . .' 'Scholarly oxen', he called them. And 'the ant-hill swarming of the mongrel populace' is only the background to history.

So, against the banal ʻobjective of fair shares and comfort, Nietzsche sets the hard cosmopolitan ideal of the Overman. He little anticipated how this fantasy would appeal to the petit-bourgeois he despised. Had he lived to see it, the vulgarization of his ideas would probably have been the most agonizing consequence of his career. For the ideal was lofty. The last thing he desired was to see the herd aping genius. He dreaded the cosmic boredom of a universal mediocrity, ending perhaps in mass-suicide following obsession with violence and crime. At all costs this prospect must be transcended. 'A little pure air' needs letting in to the foetid parlours of provincial-

---

* *Götzendämmerung*, VII, 2. The term first appears in *Towards a Genealogy of Morals*, I, 11. The blond beast, says Dr. Kaufmann, is not in fact a racial concept. Here Nietzsche 'specifically refers to Arabs, Japanese and Greeks, no less than ancient Teutonic tribes, when he first introduces this notorious term'. '. . . and the "blondness" presumably refers to the beast, the lion, rather than the kind of man' (op. cit., p. 196). The legend that it was derived from the sight of German regiments going into action in 1870 is now discredited.

† Compare Jowett's alleged inquiry, 'And what were they going to do with the Grail when they found it, Mr. Rossetti?'

‡ In the nineteenth century this hostility appears particularly widespread among men of original mind. But it is likely that in most ages the great flood of orthodox mediocre ideas presents a similar aspect to genius. Witness the attitude of the seventeenth century to the medieval scholastics. In barbaric times this criticism subsides; everyone is in the same boat, e.g. Bede and St. Isidore.

§ See G. E. MORGAN, op. cit., pp. 324-7, for a formidable summary.

ism. One of the worst aspects of Luther's teaching was a provincial state-worship. 'Is there any idea whatever,' he wrote, 'behind this bull-headed nationalism? What value could it have to stir up their petty self conceits now, when everything points to common interests?' This 'absurd condition of Europe' must be transcended by new elites. For Nietzsche, the Hellenist, the admirer of the Renaissance, the European man, regarded Frederick Stupor Mundi as the cosmopolitan precursor of a European mind. Far from being the dupe of racial theories, which later invoked his name, he remarked 'How much mendacity and morass is involved in raising racial questions in the medley of Europe today. Maxim: to have intercourse with nobody who has any share in the mendacious race-swindle.'* Further, 'When Napoleon wanted to bring Europe into an association of states (the only human being who was strong enough therefor) they botched everything with their "Wars of Liberation," and conjured up the misfortune of the insanity of nationalities with the consequence of race-fights in such long mixed countries as Europe.'[14] He foresaw such an increase in Russian power that Europe would be forced to unite against it. With this cosmopolitan outlook, he disliked the racial propaganda of the post-Bismarckian Imperialists and denied their claim to descent from primitive Germans. 'Between the old German tribes and us Germans there is scarcely a conceptual relation, not to speak of a blood relationship.' In attacking the exclusiveness of race, rather than the exclusiveness of superior personality, he wrote — in the idiom of his time — 'the Aryan impulse has corrupted all the world'. For the masters of the future will be a cosmopolitan aristocracy of talent, not of blood.

Nietzsche admired cross-bred people: he also believed in the old-fashioned Lamarckian theory of the inheritance of acquired characteristics. His lack of scientific knowledge and misunderstanding of Darwin, encouraged him to dogmatize on such subjects, and, indeed, like so many nineteenth-century political theorists, to transfer pseudo-scientific concepts to unsuitable settings. He held that an hereditary caste of rulers can be created and maintained. So, after the first brave days of neo-pagan barbarism, when the decadent remnant of bourgeois civilization will be smashed in wars which are the preliminary to world government, mankind, in spite of themselves, will be forced into 'great politics'. Then the superb predatory types will gradually give place to complete men. 'Epicurean Gods', a law unto themselves.

* Quoted by KAUFMANN, p. 266.

But mere political activity is never the highest function of man. Personality is the supreme achievement. Carlyle was wrong in regarding the political hero as the supreme type. The 'Overman' is a philosopher and an artist. Such personalities alone will be the heirs of the ages. They will realize in themselves all the long striving of Mind — for 'nothing has been bought more dearly than the little bit of human reason and sense of freedom which is now the basis of our pride'. As Beethoven transcends Haydn, so the new morality, with its denial of the Christian conflict between spirit and matter, and its new acceptance of the limitations of life, will be realized by these enigmatic and intellectual thugs.

It is mainly in this fantastic and highly intellectual context that Nietzsche glorifies war. In general, he means intellectual strife, though he is not averse to the 'purgation' of the society he detested by the coarser means he had prophesied. 'You say, it is the good cause that hallows even war? I say to you: it is the good war that hallows any cause.'[15] This notorious and sybiline paradox was open to any interpretation. Repudiating both Christian compassion and the materialist improvement of the Philistine herd, Nietzsche claimed to stand on heights whence the cold peaks of a queer and glittering future could already be discerned.

In contrast to this cosmopolitan vision — a curious compound of neo-Hellenism, a romantic feeling for the Renaissance and the usual cult of Goethe, coloured by Schopenhauer's pessimism, by Hegel's doctrine of self-mastery through transcendent contradiction, and by an original and sinister psychological insight expressed with brilliant powers of phrase — this desperate moralist invoked a strange view of history. It helped, from its different angle, to contribute to the Marxist propaganda that civilization was degenerate, in an age when the vitality and genius of Europe and America had never been more obvious. At the close of a century of unprecedented and staggering expansion in knowledge and technique, when the foundation of new sciences were laid and traditional learning vastly enriched, this baleful prophet could see nothing but decline. Such, it seems, are the consequences of thinking with the blood. There got about among intellectuals a pessimism which was contradicted by the facts of the total world picture. It was sedulously propagated by the charlatans of learning, of whom Spengler was later to be the most notorious and the most influential. It proliferated in the soil churned up by two world wars, and it flourished amid the ruins of the mid-twentieth-century cities. This aspect of Nietzsche's doctrine was perhaps the worst of the legacies of nineteenth-century introspection.

But how, it may be asked, did this outlook infect intelligent opinion outside Germany? It appealed because, like Comte before him, Nietzsche faced the worst. He attempted to supply a 'medical kit for the soul'. He is a writer whose chaotic and powerful intuitions made a widespread appeal. His merciless insight, which clearly owed much to Dostoevsky, explored the world of neo-paganism as no one had done before. He rejoiced in the disappearance of the old inhibitions and the old dogmas. Like Hobbes, in the seventeenth century, he horrified but shook his contemporaries. On the question with which he was primarily concerned, deep problems of existence which must remain mysterious, Nietzsche made his startling contribution. He was essentially a non-political, aesthetic, moralist. His vision was an artist's. It imagined a minority of superior beings, weaving the web of human thought, as Plato's philosopher-king might have designed his pattern of the state. Nietzsche's casual political ideas, in all their irresponsibility, are conditioned by this subjective, aesthetic outlook. It was not exclusively warlike. 'In Nietzsche's vision', writes Dr. Kaufmann, 'the globe becomes a Greek gymnasium where all nations vie with each other, each trying to overcome itself and then excell all others.' He was also a psychologist who proclaimed with ruthless reiteration that the master impulse of life was power. And all this insight was conditioned and distorted by a ghastly acuteness of sensibility, by the self-torture of a genius who screamed from the housetops the forebodings which might well have occurred to any nineteenth-century moralist. Above all, he seemed to speak for his time in his reaction to the doctrine of evolution, which for some natures, who cry for the moon, seems degrading. For Nietzsche, it has been said, reacted to Darwin as Kant reacted to Hume.

Meanwhile, the other Nietzsche, the publicist, the showman, provoked his reward. The hyper-sensitive mind which ended in madness had defined a subjective, anti-social, ideal of personality. He had been the redoubtable adversary of the Philistine and the mob. And the Philistines, with a supreme irony of fate, took Nietzsche to their hearts. His doctrine of a cosmopolitan elite was transformed into a nationalist myth of vulgar 'racial' superiority: his hypersensitive scholarship parodied by the imitation of minor intellectuals. But in the practical field he had made one contribution. Nietzsche's sense that the main social reality was power, and that mankind are moved not by reason, but by myth, anticipated many psychological views in the early twentieth century. Of this outlook the pioneers have been Schopenhauer and Bergson: their influence was to be enriched by the systematic and documented analysis of Freud. An understanding of the irrational was to characterize the sociologists Durkheim and Graham Wallas, whose ideas will form the concluding study of this survey.

The irresponsibility of the artist was naturally displayed by Nietzsche. With his brilliant, brooding, insight into the future, and flashing power of phrase, this extraordinary prophet was a subjective individualist, lacking the rudiments of political judgment. Blinded with his original and private vision, he contributed to a destruction of the standards which he proclaimed. His emancipated followers, translating moral exhortations into political terms, put about ideas destructive of elites, and helped to rock to their foundations the most massive institutions of the nineteenth century. For Nietzsche's genius had depicted with unprecedented brilliance the consequences of an atheist humanism devoid of charity or commonsense. Debased and perverted, his influence was to contribute to the ideology of Fascism. And on a more immediately political level the irrationalist attack was to be pressed home against liberal democracy by Sorel.

CHAPTER IX

CATHOLIC ATTITUDES: THE ENCYCLICALS OF LEO XIII: ACTON

Tᴴᴱ high bourgeois culture of the mid-century long remained apparently impervious to the Marxist, nationalist and nihilist attack. But the assault was insidious. Socialism was gradually beginning to sap the foundations of private property; unbridled nationalism had achieved a European catastrophe in the Franco-Prussian war; and Nietzsche's brilliant negations and neo-pagan prophecies were only the most striking utterances of a spreading disbelief.

These developments had long been foreseen by the ancient and cosmopolitan Catholic Church. Benthamite atheist improvement had always been incompatible with Christian ideas; Spencer's rank individualism had cut across the tradition of Christian commonwealth, and even the neo-Hegelian T. H. Green, with his Puritan background, had been hostile to Rome. The Papacy regarded even this humanism as heretical, though Acton's liberal Catholicism came to terms with it. As for Marxist dialectical materialism and class war, Treitschke's nationalist frenzy and Schopenhauer's and Nietzsche's atheism, they were regarded as the logical developments of the profoundest error of the Enlightenment and the nineteenth century — the cult of man.

Two representative Catholic attitudes to this secular challenge will here be examined. Following the failure of Pius IX's liberal experiments, the Papacy had turned its back on all compromise with the nineteenth century. It had reverted to the policy of Gregory XVI, by whom even the liberal Catholicism of Lamennais had been discouraged, and the climax of this reaction had been signalized in 1870 by the proclamation of Papal infallibility. With the accession of Leo XIII, a more constructive policy was adopted. Ultimately the Catholic position remained uncompromising, but the Church entered the arena of politics with a modernized version of Thomist political thought. The liberal Catholics, meanwhile, of whom Lord Acton will be taken as representative, went much further along the path of compromise. They took their stand on the dictates of conscience and the old conception of Christian commonwealth, stated in terms which liberals and even socialists could assimilate.

In opening the campaign of Catholic action, the supreme authority of the Catholic Church denounced both the radical and socialist movements. The denunciation was lucid, comprehensive and entire. It extended retrospectively to the Reformation, when the unity of Christendom had been disrupted. It represented an unbroken patristic and medieval tradition. For those who hold Catholic beliefs it was, and remains, unanswerable.

It is expressed with all the medieval eloquence and clarity traditional to Papal pronouncements. The most famous of these documents are the Encyclicals *Inscrutabili·Dei Consilio*, 1878; *Immortale Dei*, 1885, which deals with basic questions of political thought; and *Rerum Novarum*, 1891, which is concerned with economic problems and class war.* The position here uncompromisingly asserted is familiar to anyone conversant with medieval thought. All centres upon the revelation of Christ, the reality of a future life, and the all pervading providence of God. The entire anthropocentric philosophy of liberal and socialist humanism is regarded as a manifestation of old heresy, and the course of modern civilization since the disruption of Christendom in the fifteenth century as disastrous. The picture is clear and exact. Through an 'insatiable craving for things perishable', the modern world is 'rushing wildly upon the straight road to destruction'.[1]

Agnostics and atheists have ignored God and Revelation. Naturally they are heading for disaster. 'Exclude the idea of futurity and forthwith the very notion of what is good and right would perish; nay, the whole scheme of the universe would become a dark and unfathomable mystery.'[2] Modern thought has concentrated only on the world, inevitably a place of suffering and exile, for only 'when we have given up this present life, then shall we really begin to live'.[3] The conditions of life are the result of sin. They are in-

* They are translated in *The Pope and the People*, Select Letters and Addresses on Social Questions by Pope Leo XIII, Pope Pius X, Pope Benedict XV, and Pope Pius XI. (Catholic Truth Society, revised edition, 1929.) For a more comprehensive Italian collection, see *Le Encicliche Sociali dei Papi da Pio IX a Pio XII 1864-1946*. A cura di Igino Giordani. Studium (Editrice), Rome, 1942. For a short but lucid introduction to modern Catholic political thought see F. CAVALLERA, *Précis de la Doctrine Sociale Catholique*. Paris, 1937. For a fuller treatment see ABBÉ J. LECLERCQ, *Leçons du Droit Naturel*: (I) *Le Fondement du Droit et de la Société* and (II) *L'État et la Politique*. Louvain, 1934. The most important subsequent Papal Encyclicals are Pius X's *Singulari quadam* (on Christian Trade Unions), 1912; Pius XI's *Quadragesimo Anno* (on the fortieth anniversary of *Rerum Novarum*), 1931; *Mit brennender Sorge* (on the Hitlerite persecution of the Catholic Church), 1937; *Divini Redemptoris* (on atheist Communism), 1937; Pius XII, *Pace nel mondo e collaborazione delle classi*, 1943.

evitable. In face of the fatuous dream of liberalism, 'nothing is more useful than to look upon the world as it really is'.* Let them strive as they may, 'no strength and no artifice, will ever succeed in banishing from human life the troubles that beset it'. However the political and social organization may be manipulated, there must always be inequality. Hierarchy must therefore be accepted and harmonized; with dignity, compassion and love. The ancient medieval ideal of Commonwealth under God is once more invoked against the innovations of Liberals and Communists. 'You understand as a matter of course, Venerable Brothers, that We are alluding to that sect of men who, under the motley and all but barbarous terms of Socialists, Communists and Nihilists are spread abroad throughout the world ... [and] Strive to carry out the purpose, long resolved upon, of uprooting the foundations of civilized society at large.'⁴ Their movement derives from 'venomous teachings which, like pernicious seed scattered far and wide among the nations, have provided in course of time death-bearing fruit'. It began in the sixteenth century, when 'atrocious war' was 'declared against the Catholic Faith by the Reformers'. It has culminated in the 'rejection of all revelation' and the 'enthronement of unaided reason'. In consequence, 'by an act of impiety unknown even to the very Pagans, governments have been organized without God'.⁵

Against this appalling error, the Church maintains its unshaken beliefs. These are lucidly and comprehensively described, with the ordered argument of a great tradition which has been confronted with barbarism before. The Christian Commonwealth is based on the all pervading Laws of God: political action is judged in terms of morality, and the standards of private and public life are one. The whole of life falls into place in this clear-cut picture of divine and human order, and amid the raging of the heathen the Church maintains certainty and calm.

The Christian community described is based upon the family. Marriage is a sacrament, no mere civil contract; indissoluble, absolute.† The family circle is the 'starting point of every city and every State'.⁶ And the family is subject to paternal authority. This implies property, freely disposable, which is no mere human inven-

---

* It is significant that Schopenhauer and the Church agree in this view, from an opposite approach.

† 'Truly it is hardly possible to describe how great are the evils that flow from divorce', (p. 37). And it is undesirable for Catholics to marry outside their religion. 'Care also must be taken for Catholics that they do not easily enter into marriage with those who are not Catholics, for when minds do not agree as to the observance of religion, it is scarcely possible to hope for agreement in other things.' *Arcanum Divinae*, p. 43.

tion, but derived from nature, prior even to the state. Beyond the family is society, for man is a social animal, and authority, without which society is impossible, derives from God: 'There is no power but from God; and those that are, are ordained by God.' Every civilized community must have a ruler, and 'this authority no less than society itself, has its source in Nature, and has, consequently, God for its nature. Hence it follows that all public power must proceed from God'.[7] Here is the authentic voice of medieval Thomism.

This power is not confined to any one form of government. 'It may take this or that form, providing only that it be of a nature to insure the general welfare.' But it must be bound up with the Church, which alone represents true religion, 'for it is a public crime to act as though there was no God'. The state has no right to be neutral, and to treat the Catholic Church as one with other religions; the only true religion is the one 'established by Jesus Christ Himself; which He commanded to His Church to protect and propagate'. The old question of the temporal and spiritual power is here resolved. In a state permeated by Catholic influence, the Laws 'aim at securing the common good', spiritual and temporal; 'the ruling powers are invested with a sacredness more than human, and are withheld from deviating from the path of duty'. Laws are not, in such a society, framed by the changing caprice of the mob. In liberal doctrine, on the other hand, which bases all government simply on the people's will, when the 'authority of God is passed over in silence', the state 'becomes nothing but a mere multitude'.[8] Such unbridled freedom is merely a 'liberty of self ruin'. Freedom of press and publication is therefore denied. One of the most dangerous of these liberties is the licence 'of thinking, and of publishing, whatsoever one likes'. Since truth is unchangeable, false opinions ought to be suppressed. The 'State is acting against the Laws and dictates of Nature whenever it permits the licence of opinion and of action to lead minds away from Truth . . .'. Further, the Church ought to influence state education, and 'curb all movements of the mind which are opposed to reason', for 'a state from which religion is banished can never be well regulated'. Doctrines of freedom of conscience are pernicious: the Encyclical of Gregory XVI, *Mirari vos* (1832), is cited against the separation of Church and State, in particular against the view that each man's conscience is his own guide. Here is a logical and authoritarian position. It is diametrically opposed to the Protestant doctrine of the spiritual priesthood of all believers, which, in the official opinion of the Catholic Church, can lead only to confusion. It is implacably hostile to the subjective atheism of Nietzsche, or even to any form of liberal thought.

In the purely political field, on the other hand, the doctrine is not authoritarian. It is constantly emphasized that since all power comes from God, political authority can never derive from the head of the state, but rather from the whole Commonwealth, and that varying forms of government promote welfare in different contexts. Since the 'real perfection of all creatures is found in the prosecution and attainment of their respective ends',[9] the end of the state is liberty within the bounds of Natural Law.

If a law is 'enacted contrary to reason or to the eternal Law, obedience is unlawful, lest, while obeying man, we become disobedient to God'. Since the laws of the state are subject to this ultimate appeal, 'an effectual barrier' will be 'opposed to tyranny'. Here is familiar medieval doctrine, to which constitutional government owes much, and which was acclimatized into English political thought by Hooker. It is the ideal of Christian Commonwealth, traditional, hierarchical, and, in this case, subject to the all embracing spiritual authority of Rome. For there is only one authority capable of pronouncing on the nature of divine, eternal and human Law, so that ultimately society is subject not to individual conscience, or the embodied popular will, but to Papal authority. On such a commonwealth alone is true freedom. It is not this discipline which reflects tyranny, but the boundless claim of the liberal state that the 'collective reason of the whole community' is supreme. And as for the positivist doctrine that sovereignty depends only on force, it can lead only to chaos, since it is precarious. 'Justice therefore forbids the state to be Godless.'[10]

It follows that the 'excesses of the unbridled intellect, which unfailingly end in the oppression of the untutored multitude', should be controlled in the interests of true liberty, which includes the eternal salvation of souls. And since the majority of men are 'either absolutely unable, or able only with great difficulty, to escape illusions', restriction of free discussion on the fundamentals of religion will in fact make liberty more secure. For the Church well knows, writes the Pope, how to 'weigh the great burden of human weakness.' The majority of mankind cannot maintain right conduct, and it is the duty of the Church to tend her sheep. Civil power, religion, and education must all be ultimately subject to spiritual sanctions. The alternative is the worship of man; the abuse of power; the destruction of civilized life.

Within these limits, Pope Leo XIII departed from the negative position of the mid-nineteenth-century Papacy, which had renounced contact with modern ideas. He is careful to insist that democratic methods are lawful. 'It is not in itself wrong to prefer a democratic form of government, if only the Catholic doctrine be maintained as to the origin and exercise of power.'[11] Further, the well-known *Rerum Novarum* faced the economic crisis of the late nineteenth century. Catholic initiative was encouraged in the economic field. For the Pope stresses the 'momentous gravity' of the social transformation created by modern industry. This position again derives from medieval origins. The old idea of commonwealth has been disrupted, since the 'ancient working-men's guilds were abolished in the last century, and no protective legislation took their place'.[12] Usury and greed have so prevailed that 'a small number of rich men have been able to lay upon the teeming masses of the labouring poor a yoke little less than slavery itself'. Yet the socialist attack on property is no way out. By destroying the worker's right to save, and to dispose freely of his labour, they undermine liberty itself. Collectivism, with its concentration of political and economic resources, presents too great a power to the State.

The possession of property has always distinguished man from the beasts. God has indeed 'granted the earth to mankind in general', but, contradicting Communist doctrine, the Pope declares that the 'limits of private possession has been left to be fixed by man's own industry'. The 'laws of nature' justify the institution of private property. Reverting to the original argument that the basis of society is the family, the Encyclical again lays down that property is a primordial right. Since it belongs to individuals, it must 'likewise belong to a man . . . [as] head of a family'.[13] If the state interferes with an obligation older than itself, it will rightly be 'an object of detestation rather than desire'. Undue state interference is therefore mischievous; and 'quite certain to harass and worry all classes of citizens and subject them to odious and intolerable bondage'. The main Collectivist doctrine must therefore be rejected, since it is 'directly contrary to the natural right of mankind and would introduce confusion into the commonweal'.

To attempt, indeed, to transform and level society is to fight against the very conditions of human life. 'It must . . . be recognized that the condition of things inherent in human affairs must be borne with, for it is impossible to reduce society to one dead level.'[14] The socialists are 'striving against nature in vain'; hankering for impossible felicity.

It is the lot of humanity to suffer and endure. 'For the consequences of sin', writes the Pope, as de Maistre had written earlier in the century, 'are bitter and hard to bear, and they must accompany men as long as life lasts.'

It is a familiar position. It is rooted in the slow moving agricultural world of the Middle Ages; sceptical of the improving confidence of the Utilitarians, or of the possibilities of plenty and well-being depicted by Saint-Simon, Fourier and Comte. Incompatible, too, with the liberal belief in progress and with the materialism of Marx. It had been attacked by Godwin and Proudhon; it was to be denounced by Sorel. It is alien to the pedestrian optimism of the Fabian Welfare State. Like a rock, the Papacy thus stood out against the whole tide of ideas which reflected the new ambitions of modern science. Subsequent events have set this resistance in a different light to that in which it appeared at the close of the nineteenth century.

Since the Socialist ideal is a delusion, life must be organized within the traditional framework of Christian Commonwealth. That will at least mitigate the inevitable rigours of any economic system by kindliness and mutual respect. The Encyclical invokes the Ciceronian and medieval ideal of rendering each man his just due, and the rich are exhorted to share their plenty, endow charities and deal kindly with dependants. Here, within its conservative assumptions, is a moral conception of society. It is very different to the nightmare justified by the misguided Anglican clergy who accepted and propagated the ideas of Malthus. For it is critical of unrestrained Capitalism. Wealth is a handicap to salvation, and St. Thomas has written 'a man shall not consider his material possessions his own, but as common to all, so as to share them without hesitation when others are in need. Whence the Apostle saith "Command the rich of this world . . . to offer with no stint. . . ."'[15] Poverty is no disgrace; 'God Himself chose to seem and be considered the son of a carpenter.' Here is the traditional, pre-industrial, conception of commonwealth, in which class distinction is taken for granted, in which each class works harmoniously in its proper station, and men are respected, not for their riches, but for their conduct and personality. A similar view of society is expressed, with varying codes of behaviour, in other ancient world religions.

Within this setting, which the workers must accept, thrift should be encouraged. There is here little conception of a modern, expanding, economy. 'If a workman's wages be sufficient . . . he will find it easy, if he be a sensible man, to practise thrift; and he will not fail, by cutting down expenses, to put by some little savings and thus secure a modest source of income. Nature itself would urge him to this.'[16]

The state, in this view, should humanize the existing system, hold a just balance between classes, and regard the poor as its special care. Taxation should not be excessive, and the ancient guilds can legitimately be revived and adapted as Christian Trade Unions. 'History asserts what excellent results were brought about by the Artificer's Guilds of olden times.'[17] For it is the natural right of man to form associations. As for attempts at monopoly, Christian working men may resist them by forming associations of their own. Moreover, Catholic action to improve the condition of the masses is strongly encouraged, though the clergy should always bear in mind that they belong to a sphere above material things.

In *Rerum Novarum* the supreme authority of the Catholic Church had, indeed, entered forcefully into the political and economic field. Like the other Encyclicals, it had made a shrewd and lucid appeal to two fundamental forces. First to the family, which was the basis of all Christian society. Here the influence of the priest is necessarily strong and the influence of women considerable. The second was to the small worker's desire to save for independence, rather than be subject to megalopolitan bureaucracy.

The outlook and policy expressed in the Encyclicals is thus strategically clear, while tactically efficient. It is logical throughout, and it follows systematically from Catholic beliefs. From the belief in the universal providence of God and in the supreme importance of a future life; from the conviction of original sin, which sets limits to the improvement of terrestrial conditions, and from the assumption that man can never be self sufficient. It is also laid down, as in other world-religions, that the Faith is the supreme and only revelation of God. The Catholic Church, alone, is the divinely ordained repository of revelation, and the representative of God on earth. As here expressed, this claim is theocratic; it goes back far into Antiquity, to the priesthoods of Mesopotamia and Egypt, and to the Roman Empire. The twentieth-century expressions of this outlook are outside the scope of this study. Though more flexible in the economic sphere, they do not differ in principle from its nineteenth-century assertion. Between this outlook — for believers logical, exact, secure — and all forms of atheist improvement and revolution there can clearly be no compromise.

III

The liberal Catholic thought of Lord Acton must now also be considered.* While hardly representative of the official Catholic position, Acton influenced important circles in England. He enriched the liberal idea of commonwealth, defended by de Tocqueville and J. S. Mill, and developed by T. H. Green, with a more cosmopolitan outlook. This range made his influence salutary. His unusual heredity and polyglot learning made him an original, even a disconcerting figure. He was primarily a great historian, a man of the European world, with a far-sighted, complex political judgment. The approach natural to one of his background even appears odd and foreign in the relatively parochial Liberal tradition to which he is related. Above all, it has been well observed that Acton had a 'prophetic preoccupation with the very questions with which the twentieth century found itself preoccupied'.[18] He was a European Catholic Humanist, concerned with the moralization of power.

* John Emerich Edward Dalberg, 8th baronet, 1st Baron Acton, 1834-1902. Came of an old Shropshire family whose seat was at Aldenham, near Bridgnorth. His grandfather, Sir Ferdinand Acton, had been first minister to the King of Naples. His mother was the heiress of the great Rhineland family of Dalberg, his Dalberg grandfather having been a Napoleonic Peer of France, and his uncle Archbishop-Elector of Mainz. After the death of Acton's father, his mother married the Whig Lord Granville. He was educated at Oscott, Paris, Edinburgh and Munich, where he studied with Döllinger. Acton travelled in Europe, Russia and America, and from 1859 to 1865 sat in Parliament as a Liberal. In 1863 he married the daughter of Count Arco Valley: in 1869 Gladstone made him a Peer. He was connected with various Liberal Catholic Reviews, the *Rambler*, *Home and Foreign Review*, and the *Chronicle*, and actively opposed the promulgation of the Papal dogma of Infallibility at the Vatican Council of 1870. From 1895 to 1898 he was a Lord in Waiting to Queen Victoria. Owing to his religion, Acton was rejected by three Cambridge colleges. He therefore studied in Germany and became one of the greatest exponents of the German school of historical scholarship dominated by Ranke. He was a prophet of the new documentary age. G. M. Trevelyan writes of him, 'Dons of all subjects crowded to his oracular lectures, which were sometimes puzzling but always impressive. He had the brow of Plato, and the bearing of a sage who is also a man of the great world.' (*Autobiography*, quoted Fasnacht, p. 131.) In 1886 he founded the *English Historical Review*, and in 1895 became Regius Professor at Cambridge. He died at Tegernsee in Bavaria. Acton was an extremely formidable and systematic scholar. 'In mere dogged power of reading he rivalled the heroic Dutch and German students of the seventeenth century.' (*Proceedings of the British Academy*, pp. 277-88 q.v.). He ransacked the bookshops of Europe and accumulated a library of 60,000 volumes. He was cosmopolitan. 'He was hardly more an Englishman in respect of his love for liberty, order and good sense, than he was a Frenchman in the fine edge of his wit, a German in his learning, an Italian in his flexibility' (op. cit.). Numerous remarks of devastating insight are scattered through his lectures and correspondence. If Acton's impartiality, perfectionism, and a certain lack of constructive power, could have a desiccating effect, the range and depth of the standards he set marked a new epoch in British historical studies. Acton's principal works are: *Lectures in Modern History*, 1906; *Historical Essays and Studies*, 1907; *The History of Freedom and other Essays*, 1907; *Lectures on the French Revolution*, 1910; *Essays on Church and State*, edited and introduced by Douglas Woodruff, 1952. See also, GASQUET, *Lord Acton and his Circle*; H. PAUL, *Letters of Lord Acton to Mary Gladstone*, 1913; J. N. FIGGIS and R. V. LAWRENCE, *Selections from the Correspondence of the 1st Lord Acton*, 1917; ARCHBISHOP DAVID MATHEW's *Acton*, and G. E. EASNACHT's *Acton's Political Philosophy*, an Analysis, 1952.

'Liberty', he declared, 'is not the power of doing what we like but the right of being able to do what we ought.'[19] He consistently asserts, not the authority of Rome, but the authority of conscience. In this 'secret monitor', he believed, is 'the audible voice of God, that never misleads or fails'.[20] Conscience alone is strong enough to 'confine the sphere of power'; to counteract the 'passion for power over others which can never cease to threaten mankind'. And always this assertion of conscience is 'tardy, the conflict intense, and the balance uncertain'.

Looking out over the panorama of modern history, Acton believed that a rhythmic movement could be discerned. On the one hand the assertion of expanding power; on the other the resistance it provokes. A movement 'away from force and cruelty to consent and association, the persistent appeal to common, simple, and evident maxims'. In his well-known letter to the contributors to the *Cambridge Modern History*, he could write: 'By Universal History I understand that which is distinct from the combined history of all countries, which is not a rope of sand, but a continuous development, and is not a burden to the memory, but an illumination of the soul.'[21] There was a morality of politics, he declared in his Inaugural, 'deposited by the stream of history'. The contrast with ideas of Schopenhauer, Treitschke and Nietzsche could not be more profound.

In the light of these values Acton's views on political thought were clear. The political expression of conscience is constitutional commonwealth. In spite of his Catholic background, Acton, like T. H. Green, admired the idea of commonwealth asserted by the Puritan radicals of the seventeenth century. The pedigree of constitutionalism, with its medieval and seventeenth-century origins, had been developed by Locke and Burke in England; by Jefferson and Hamilton in the United States. In North America, where the idea had been most fully and wisely realized, there had, indeed, been two strains in the assertion of liberty — Puritan and Cavalier. 'There was local self-government and federation in Connecticut, and spiritual self government and toleration in Rhode Island; and from there the two institutions spread to the United States, and when the time came, the cavaliers of Virginia, who went out under James I, surpassed the fugitives of the *Mayflower*. They produced the Declaration of Independence, and bequeathed to America religious liberty and the political function of the Supreme Court.'[22] The Declaration was a tremendous, world-achievement. 'It was,' he wrote, 'the system of an international extra-territorial universal Whig, far transcending the English model by its simplicity and rigour. It surpassed in force all the speculation of Paris and Geneva, for it had undergone the test of experiment, and its triumph was the most memorable thing that had been seen by man.'[23] Its influence on the early stages of the French Revolution was decisive. 'The French were not mere reckless innovators, they were confiding followers . . .' Acton's respect for American political achievement is profound.

In the light of his central conviction that 'achieved liberty is the goal of advancing civilization', Acton drew upon a cosmopolitan learning. His writings are irreconcilable with modern doctrines of relativism and of the political irresponsibility of historians. Always there is a moral purpose in view, a sense of the practical and grave implications of political ideas. 'Morality', he said, quoting Sir Thomas Browne, 'is not ambulatory.'

He found many neglected contributors to the development of constitutional government. To James Harrington, for example, the author of *The Commonwealth of Oceana*,* he pays tribute; to William Penn; to the Jesuit Sarasa and to Bishop Butler. He admired Fénelon for his humane views on balanced government, toleration and educational freedom.† He cites the freethinker Fontenelle as contributing to the idea of progress, in which he believed, and the Abbé Sieyès whose scheme for a French Constitution in 1791 had foundered in the power politics of the time. All these writers, he pointed out, are against theories of arbitrary power; against Carlyle, for example, who holds 'that great and salutary things are done for mankind by power concentrated, not by power balanced and cancelled and diffused'. They have all combined to build a 'rampart of tried conviction and accumulated knowledge, a fair level of general morality, education, courage and self-restraint . . . the reign of opinion, security of weaker groups, liberty of conscience which effectively secured, secures the rest'.

In contrast to Marx and Engels, Acton believed in the dominant power of ideas. The movement of thought, he declared, was the cause rather than the consequence of change. He can quote Ruskin:

---

* HARRINGTON'S *Oceana* was published in 1656. He was an aristocratic agrarian republican, with a great concern for the control of power in a balanced constitution. See H. F. B. RUSSELL SMITH, *Harrington and his Oceana*. C.U.P., 1914.

† Fénelon, François de Salignac de la Motte, 1651-1715. A forerunner of liberal Catholicism, whose immediate influence was swamped by Bossuet on the one hand and Diderot and Voltaire on the other. Tutor to the Duke of Burgundy, 1685; Archbishop of Cambrai, 1694. He was rusticated to his See in 1697. His principal works are *Télémaque*, 1699; *Dialogues des Morts*, 1700; *Tables de Chaulnes*, 1711; *Lettre sur les occupations de l'Académie*, 1716. See *Œuvres Complètes*. Paris, 1848-52.

'The real history of mankind is that of the slow advance of resolved deed following laboriously just thought.'* In the long battle which conscience has fought against arbitrary power, the Greek attempt to moralize politics is outstanding. Acton particularly admired both Plato and Aristotle. 'The *Laws* of the one and the *Politics* of the other, are, if I may trust my own experience, the books from which we may learn most about the principles of politics. The penetration with which those great masters of thought analysed the institutions of Greece and exposed their vices, is not surpassed by anything in later literature.' Acton naturally detested the doctrines of Machiavelli, and the philosophical justification of Machiavellianism constructed by Hobbes. They are the political prophets of the modern world of sovereign state power — 'a narrow and disedifying section of history'. After Hobbes, he wrote, 'all liberty resided in the restoration of conscience'. It is remarkable how close are Acton's arguments to the vindication of Aristotle and the assertion of conscience and constitutionalism made by Hobbes's contemporaries.¹⁴ Acton had a similar detestation of arbitrary government. Speaking of the new state power of the Emperor Charles V, he writes, 'It was the supreme manifestation of the modern state according to the image which Machiavelli had set up, the State that suffers neither limit nor equality, and is bound by no duty to nations and to men, that thrives on destruction and sanctions whatever things constitute an increase of power.' Acton also invokes patristic and scholastic authority against unbridled power. Hence his citation of St. Thomas Aquinas, though he remarks that 'Aquinas devised Whiggism to prop religious absolutism.' 'But stick to this:' he wrote, 'that in that Society out of which modern European States have grown, the corporation was the first thing, the sovereign State the second.'¹⁵ Acton emphasized this medieval descent of the Whig tradition, through Hooker to Locke. It was to be enriched by the fine assertion of Burke: 'the principles of true politics are those of morality enlarged: and I now do not, nor will ever admit, any other'.

Since constitutional, balanced, government is the public expression of morality, Acton never accepted the prevalent nineteenth-century cult of popular will or positivist law. Its unrestrained exercise must destroy the personal liberty Rousseau claims to guarantee. Liberty is rather the result of precarious, elaborate, long-term contrivance: it is not the alleged freedom of the noble savage or of the mass plebis-

---

* See Notes to the Inaugural in *Lectures on Modern History*, pp. 319ff, for many valuable and original ideas.

cite. It can never be *étatist*. It has been most powerfully promoted by the disruption of the united front of Church and State: by the saying 'Render unto Caesar the things that are Caesar's and unto God the things that are God's.' Room was then left for the assertion of personal responsibility. In this context Acton admired Butler's *Analogy*, to which, he maintained, Kant was indebted. For Kant believed that 'Conscience proves God'.

Liberty of conscience naturally demands toleration. Hence Acton's deep admiration for Locke, who separated the sphere of government from that of religion. Civil liberties also imply freedom of opinion, freedom of the press; a wide scope for self-determination for all the varying groups within society. 'State absolutism', Acton declared, 'is the modern danger.' It was acute in the decadence of Antiquity. 'The political ideas of the Theodosian or Justinian Code are those of a Society ground to atoms by the wheel of revolution.' In healthy States there must be divided powers; toleration for minorities; the capacity for ordered change. Acton quotes Hamilton that 'there ought to be a principle in government capable of resisting the popular current'.[26] Hence the virtue of representative democracy developed in England and in the Federal institutions of the United States — a barrier to the abuse of power both by dictators and majorities. Acton shared de Tocqueville's and J. S. Mill's fear of the tyranny latent in the multitude. Tyranny, in whatever guise, is always the enemy of conscience and commonwealth. Acton's most famous aphorism was that 'Power tends to corrupt, and absolute power corrupts absolutely.'* He told his audience at Cambridge to 'suspect power more than vice'.

Hence Acton's profound distrust of nationalism, rare at the time. Then as now, of all the current threats of arbitrary power, the unbridled sovereignty of the national or supra-national state was the most dangerous. Few Liberal political philosophers faced this fact. Dr. G. M. Trevelyan remarks that when Acton declared that states based on racial unity might prove dangerous to freedom, he was puzzled. 'I did not see what he meant at the time, but I do now!'[27]

With his long Catholic perspective and European learning, Acton saw this nineteenth-century phenomenon in an unusual light. Hence his declaration that since the aim of healthy patriotism is freedom, 'the greatest adversary of the rights of nationality is the modern theory of nationality'.[28] It identifies national cultures with national

* It is contained in his letter to Dr. Creighton, 1887, in *Historical Essays and Studies*, p. 504.

sovereignty. The best states, he believed, combine various cultures within a flexible frame. The monolithic, racial state is the antithesis of this idea. Hence Acton's uncompromising declaration: 'If we take the establishment of liberty for the realization of moral duties to be the end of civil society . . . the theory of nationality . . . is a retrograde step in history.' For nationality, he wrote, 'does not aim either at liberty or prosperity, both of which it sacrifices to the imperative necessity of making the nation the mould and measure of the State. Its course will be marked with material as well as moral ruin.'[29]

Besides this attack on current nationalist slogans, Acton also faced the other dominant problem of his age. The economic question was far more real to him than to most Liberals. Besides his belief in the unfolding of a moral purpose in history and in gradual progress, he had a lively sense of the economic foundations of society. 'In 1873', writes Fasnacht, 'he tried hard to persuade Gladstone to read Marx's *Capital*, expressed surprise that Gladstone had not yet had time to read it, and indicated the book's importance as the *Koran* of the new Socialists.'[30] Whether his advice was taken is not known.

Seventeenth-century thinkers, he believed, had first extended the idea of commonwealth from politics to economics. Harrington, who had written that 'a commonwealth is nothing but a national conscience', had depicted with minute care the economic aspect of his ideal state. He was also the author of 'what Americans have called the greatest discovery since the printing press. For he has given the reason why the great rebellion failed . . . he says it failed because it failed to redistribute the property of the kingdom'. This concern with economic history gave Acton a greater understanding than most of his contemporaries of the mounting influence of Socialist ideas. In his firm insistence on viewing economic problems in moral terms, paralleled in the Papal Encyclicals already examined, Acton reflects one of the most ancient and venerable principles of Christianity. Efforts towards the gradual redistribution of wealth, within the accepted constitutional frame, may be necessary and morally justified. But they must not enthrone the arbitrary power of the majority. For to live and flourish, a society must be flexible and based on a widespread possession of property.

Acton viewed his age with an Olympian impartiality, ripened by close experience of European affairs. History, he remarks, 'promotes the faculty of resistance to contemporary surroundings'. Such studies transcend frontiers and 'compel us to share the existence of societies wider than our own, to be familiar with distant and exotic types . . .

to live in the company of heroes, and saints, and men of genius, that no single country could produce'.[31] In this long and world-wide perspective he emphasized three dominant facts. First, that the predominance of world power had passed to the Atlantic, Oceanic, states—to the American Federation which he regarded as the greatest political achievement in the world, and to the British Commonwealth. Secondly, that this centre of constitutional government which had realized, albeit imperfectly, the greatest measure of conscience and liberty, was confronted with the inheritors of a militarist, autocratic tradition. This had been most fully developed in Central and Eastern Europe in the eighteenth century, which had marked the apex of the dynastic great state. 'That,' he wrote, 'is the tremendous power, supported by millions of bayonets, which grew up in the days of which I have been speaking at Petersburg, and which was developed, by much abler minds, chiefly at Berlin; and it is the greatest danger that remains to be encountered by the Anglo-Saxon race.[32] Thirdly, he pointed out that the extension of modern technological civilization must inevitably be worldwide, transcending nationality and class. 'We have dethroned necessity,' he said, 'in the shape both of hunger and of fear, by extending the scene from Western Europe to the whole world, so that all shall contribute to the treasure of civilization, and by taking into partnership in the enjoyment of its rewards, those who are far off as well as those who are below.' If today this may seem too hopeful a sentiment, it reflects economic potentialities since further developed.

Its optimism was natural in a time of peace, when the liberal-democratic world seemed at the height of its political and economic prestige. Acton spoke, indeed, during a lull in the perennial conflict he discerned rising between the moralization of power and its abuse. With renewed pressure, he implied, the area of moralization would extend. For 'it is by the combined efforts of the weak, made under compulsion, to resist the reign of force and constant wrong, that, in the rapid change but slow progress of four hundred years, liberty has been preserved, and secured, and extended, and finally understood'.

In the complex, oracular, and far-sighted utterances of this liberal Catholic historian, are ideas extraordinarily relevant to the present day. Here, in a broad and highly sophisticated perspective, the fundamental questions are surveyed. Acton remarked of himself that he was both a sincere Catholic and a sincere Liberal; for he had 'renounced everything in Catholicism which was not compatible with liberty and everything in politics which was not compatible with Catholicism'. The mind of the pupil of Döllinger, the Liberal Catholic professor who left the Church, displays more affinity with the Protestant doctrine of the 'inner light' than with the high official doctrine of Rome, or even with the Encyclicals of Leo XIII. The belief in conscience is the heart of this outlook. For Christians, and, indeed, for Humanists, it seems constructive and wise.

What, in the light of modern psychology, has the twentieth century to say to it? That is a question which theologians and psychologists may well investigate. It is unlikely that psychological investigation of the roots of moral conduct will render Acton's political advice the less valuable.* His outlook remains one of the most powerful and elaborate expressions of the universal human instinct for mutual aid. It aims at the control of power for the biological benefit of the species, expressed in the idiom of the most adaptable, realist, and comprehensive ideas of the august European Catholic civilization of which he was himself so representative.

* In this context see, in particular, REV. VICTOR WHITE, O.P., *God and the Unconscious*, with a foreword by C. G. Jung, for a useful introduction to this important field.

CHAPTER X

GEORGES SOREL
MYTH AND ANARCHY

WHEN Pope Leo XIII restated Catholic political principles and Acton developed the idea of commonwealth as the expression of conscience, both were adapting traditional ideas to a new mass society. By the closing decades of the nineteenth century great urban industry and world-wide expansion had altered the scale of Western civilization and brought the mass of the people to the threshold of political and economic power. Only political ideas which took account of these facts remained relevant. Revolutionary theories, insignificant hitherto, now achieved greater influence. Ruling circles had either to come to terms with them or promote counter-revolution on a popular scale.

In the wealthier Western states, prospects of compromise were better than in the mid-century. In England liberal legislation had been influenced by T. H. Green and Bosanquet, Tory democracy had been devised by Disraeli, and growing prosperity had diminished discontent. The Fabian socialists began to extend the moralization of politics into the field of economics within the constitution, ultimately to absorb Liberalism into social democracy. In Germany, prosperity and nationalism distracted the masses from extremist programmes, and Bernstein revised Marx. In France, social democracy found expression in the writings and oratory of Jaurès. Though German social democrats were to be trampled under the heel of militarism, and the murder of Jaurès long crippled socialist leadership in France, the dominant trend of socialism in the West remained constitutional.

But this development had brutal enemies. Apart from the basic inadequacy of European institutions, still organized in competing sovereign states, the tide of class war and nihilism had been rising since the turn of the nineteenth century. Ideas taken from Marx and Nietzsche were to be combined by Sorel, a forerunner of Fascism. Before the main development of social democracy and its reinforcement by a new environmental and psychological sociology is examined, account must be taken of his ideas. Where the Fabians were to make their selection from Marxism, and Bernstein and Jaurès their revision of it, Georges Sorel gave a new twist to the Marxist revelation. He declared that the revisionists were traitors and blended the Marxist class war with a new Nietzschean Myth. He differs from Marx in being pessimistic, with a sombre view of life, akin sometimes to de Maistre's. Hence his contribution to Fascism. He preached anarchy because he held, with Bergson, that the tide of events is not susceptible to control; that the future could not, as Marxists held, be foreseen. History proceeds in a series of creative improvisations, each age being characterized by the Myth which reflects the interest of its dominant class. His thought derives from ideas which descend from Vico, Marxist determinism, Nietzsche and Bergson.* The scepticism of this misguided moralist made his attitude ambivalent. He wavers between the improvisations of the Right and the Left. His principal effect on the twentieth century was upon Italian Fascism. He made a destructive perversion of a new psychological approach to politics, here discoloured, like the thought of Nietzsche, by moral and religious disillusion.

To the irrationalism of Nietzsche and Bergson and the class hatred of Marx, he added anarchist ideas taken from Proudhon. While he was devoid of immediate political judgment, his criticisms are striking. He is a gadfly of political philosophy. His ideas, if often pernicious, are astringent to humbug. He understood that what counted in politics were myths for which men would die. Like Nietzsche, Sorel was primarily a moralist. Along with a Bergsonian cult of will, he believed in the assertion of human dignity by *Homo Faber*, by a proletarian elite. Like his forerunner, Proudhon, he was a Puritan, compensating himself for the spectacle of ordinary human nature. A man whose lost faith made him observe life with sceptical gloom, who brought strange gleams of insight to deep problems, and the vulgarization of whose ideas affected the gutter-elites of whom Mussolini and Goebbels are representative. But all his work shows strong individuality. Like Pareto, he was an engineer, and his thought reflects the technician's desire for results.†

---

* For Bergson's ideas see the admirable account in BERTRAND RUSSELL's *History of Western Philosophy*. London, 1946, p. 828. Here he quotes probably the most politically relevant passage of Bergson's works. 'All the living hold together and all yield to the same tremendous push. The animal takes its stand on the plant, man bestrides animality, and the whole of humanity in space and in time is an immense army, galloping beside and before and behind each other in an overwhelming charge, able to beat down every resistance and to clear every obstacle, perhaps even death.' This intoxicating philosophy, with its belief in intuition and 'becoming', was later to contribute to Fascist improvisation and to the cult of irresponsible Will, with its background from Schopenhauer and Nietzsche.

† Georges Sorel, 1847-1922, cousin of Albert Sorel, the historian, was born at Cherbourg. Educated at the École Polytechnique, 1865-67, he became an engineer, serving successfully in the Direction des Ponts et Chaussées until his early retirement in 1892. As a provincial engineer, he had solaced his mind by omnivorous reading, and in 1889 he

Sorel's numerous writings are contradictory and confused. 'A self taught man,' he writes, 'exhibiting to other people the notebooks which have served for my own instruction ... That is why the rules of the art of writing have never interested me very much.'[1] But certain ideas are dominant. First, the assumption, common to Marx and Nietzsche, that liberal democratic society is doomed, and what he terms 'bourgeois' thought 'decadent'. It is doomed, not for the abstract considerations described by Nietzsche, but because modern industry demands a civilization of self governing producers, free from the interference of the state. Traditional culture has hitherto been parasitic. Sorel is determined to make all things new. 'For twenty years', he writes, 'I worked to deliver myself from what I retained of my education.' Next, he declares, the decisive events of history are influenced not by the leadership which liberal historians describe, but by myths created by the people independently of the surface

published his first considerable work, the *Procès de Socrate*, in which he maintained that the authorities had been right to condemn the philosopher. In the same year Bergson profoundly influenced his outlook. After his retirement he took up with a circle of Marxist students, and contributed an article on Vico to their review, *Le Devenir Social* (1895-98). After the death of his wife, to whom he was devoted, and who came of working-class background, he retired in 1897 to live with one of her nephews at Boulogne-sur-Seine. There he lived for the rest of his life, 'dans une petite villa d'employé modeste ... nulle existence plus bourgeoise que celle de ce révolutionnaire'. Like Labriola in Italy and Bernstein in Germany, he was critical of the 'clericalism' of Marx's followers and attempted to renew the revolutionary class struggle by founding his 'New School of Syndicalism' (1899), following the publication of *L'Avenir Socialiste des Syndicats* in the preceding year. From 1900 he became the 'Socrates' of the circle which met in the bookshop of Charles Péguy and produced 'Les Cahiers de la Quinzaine'. In 1901 he published *La Ruine du Monde Antique*, and in 1904 his *Introduction à l'Économie Moderne*, in which he abandoned all compromise with reformist socialism, following his disgust with the behaviour of both sides over the Dreyfus case. In the next year appeared the remarkable *Système Historique de Renan* in which he developed his study of political myths. In 1908 there appeared his *Réflexions sur la Violence*, of which an Italian version had already been published in 1905 (*Lo Sciopero Generale e la Violenza*), and in the same year *Les Illusions du Progrès* and the *Décomposition du Marxisme*. In 1909 appeared *La Révolution Dreyfusienne*. Sorel's views had now moved more to the right, and he collaborated with Barrès and Maurras and the 'Action Française'. The first world war left him cynical towards both sides, but the Russian Revolution roused his enthusiasm. In 1918 appeared his *Matériaux pour une Théorie du Prolétariat*, which is concerned with immediate politics. His last work is entitled *De l'Utilité du Pragmatisme*, 1921. Sorel's production was remarkable and only the most important writings are here cited; but his style shows little consideration for the reader and he believed that reading ought to be difficult, to provoke thought. 'Chez Sorel,' remarks his biographer and critic, M. Perrin, 'la diversité des sources n'a d'égale que le désordre de l'exposition et l'obscurité du style.' He might have added, its vitriolic quality. The reader, says Berth, 'is like a traveller in a strangely various country, with a guide possessed of bizarre and malicious humour'. Sorel, 'ce terrible vieillard', had a striking appearance. With fresh complexion, white hair and violet eyes, he was a dapper figure of conventional habits and a brilliant conversationalist. His influence in England and America was negligible, and in France he had little importance during his lifetime outside his own circle. But he had great prestige in Italy, and influenced Pareto and Mussolini. The best short account of his ideas is by P. L. PERRIN, *Les Idées Sociales de Georges Sorel*. Alger, 1925. See also JOHANNET, *Itinéraires d'Intellectuels*; GUY-GRAND, *La Philosophie Syndicaliste*; E. BERTH, *Marchands, Intellectuels, et Politiciens*; J. R. BLOCH, *Carnaval est Mort*.

rationalizations of intellectuals. These two ideas lead to a double attack on 'intellectuals' as such, and to the repudiation of any reformist constitutional programme. The workers, he believes, must keep themselves uncontaminated from bourgeois leadership and exploitation. The whole intellectual capital of civilization, the range of professional knowledge, the achievements of the arts, are labelled 'bourgeois culture' and repudiated.

But the most sinister creation of the old order is the state. As against Bernstein and Jaurès, Sorel thinks it superlatively corrupt. Far from the means of the gradual transmission and broadening down of civilization, the state is something that must be smashed. Hence a detestation of the Fabians and of Jaurès. They would merely substitute one set of corrupt politicians for another. To take over the machinery of the bourgeois state is not enough; it must be destroyed. Hence the error even of the Marxist conception of proletarian dictatorship.

The only way out is Anarcho-Syndicalist class war. This conflict must be inspired by the supreme myth of the age, the General Strike. Paradoxically, the destructive myth was to herald an age of untrammelled production. The 'Syndicat', which has more in common with the Soviet than with the Trade Union, is the 'cell' whereby the proletarian masses will be inspired to wreck bourgeois society and repudiate its leadership. Even, perhaps, to galvanize decadent capitalism into its old vitality, so that the Marxist scriptures may be fulfilled and the proletariat inhérit a world in the full vigour of production. Out of the Syndicates will come not only a society of self-governing producers, but, Sorel's fourth master idea, a moral revolution. For Sorel, like Proudhon, was an idealist. He romanticized the elite technician — the pioneer of a cleaner world. Puritan in sexual morality, atheist in religious belief, here is another cult of man.

So the first two assumptions, the decadence of bourgeois culture and importance of myth, lead to total revolution and the discarding of the state. The Anarcho-Syndicalists must create their own future. It will be mysterious. Sorel, with his cult of will, cannot foretell the manifestations of the Life-Force, in themselves their own end. Influenced by Schopenhauer and Nietzsche, by Bergsonian Creative Evolution, he saw in the destruction of the state an immediate and all-embracing goal. Yet he regards himself not so much as a prophet, as an observer of the doings of the Life Force through the proletariat. 'Gesta Vitae', as it were, 'per Populos'.

So from Sorel's works these major ideas emerge. The decadence of bourgeois civilization; the importance of myth; the need to destroy the state by Syndicalist class war inspired by the General Strike, and economic and moral redemption by the released creativeness of proletarian producers.

This gospel of destruction, akin sometimes to the ideas of Nietzsche, was wildly unsuited to the elaborate and precarious structure of modern civilization. Sorel is in fact careless of the actual interests of the proletariat. For this engineer of roads and bridges, the bogus mythology of the General Strike was the supreme tactic. He appears, too, singularly blind to the appalling evils of modern war and to the urgent necessity for international order. Impatient of all existing institutions, he looked first to Lenin (who regarded him with contempt) as the founder of the 'Rome of the proletariat'; then to Mussolini, of all people. An obsession with French politics — in particular with the dreary Dreyfus case and with the part subsequently played by Jaurès — gives him scope for a poisonous irony.

As an observer of society and a critic of thought, Sorel is more interesting. In the first of his main contributions, the attack on bourgeois civilization and leadership, his criticisms are trenchant. No one has better put the case against all the values in which liberal democrats have believed. To understand the twentieth century one must take account of Sorel. Like Nietzsche's, his criticisms can be answered: they cannot be ignored.

In the wide range of his works the early *La Ruine du Monde Antique, Conception matérialiste de l'Histoire,* compares the alleged dissolution of democratic society with the collapse of Graeco-Roman Antiquity.* Sorel admired the hard pagan virtues, but he relates early Christianity to Sorelian socialism.[2] The intellectuals of Antiquity, Sorel believes, undermined the civic and imperial myths which were its strength.

Yet the decline of Antiquity was different from the break up of the eighteenth-century order. The former marked a dead end — 'véritable culbute idéologique' — one of the 'ricorsi' which Vico had seen in history. This social and economic decadence was only painfully restored by the barbarians, in spite of the handicap imposed on them by Christianity. The French Revolution, on the other hand, occurred in an expanding society. Far from marking a collapse, it

---

* The second edition, published by Rivière, Paris, 1925, runs to 323 pages. It describes the impact of Christian ideas on Antiquity, and deals with the 'monkish corruption of education' and with the effect of Christianity on economic life. Chapter VII is entitled 'The State as the Servant of the Church'; Sorel also treats of 'Intolerance and Fanaticism' (Formation des Milieux Superstitieux) and the financial methods of the Church.

was a great 'mutation of property'. It was due not to intellectual convictions but to a massive change in habits of life. Here the promise of a mass civilization of producers first appeared. Irrelevant liberal ideologists, who attempt, like the Christians, to impose their intolerance and misunderstanding on this vast social and economic change, must be brushed aside. They will interfere with production and rob it of its fruits. For these modern slaves to abstraction, these despicable secular clerics, are as incapable of directing great scale production as were the barbarians of using the broken-down institutions of the Graeco-Roman world.[3] The Christian 'economy of asceticism' was parasitic: useless to the kind of progress (command of environment) in which Sorel believed. 'It contains no element which assures the passage to superior forms.'[4] As for Christian literature, there was nothing original in that, either, except for the 'drama' of the religious life, which was confined to a few and 'unconstructive'. Christianity had merely taken over the pagan concept of the 'good life' for an idle minority and developed it in selfish and ascetic terms. 'In a society of idlers, of rich parasitic patricians, . . . what was there better than such wisdom?' 'Although, of course,' he adds characteristically, 'most will prefer debauchery.'[5] Christian education, also, had nothing to contribute. It merely took over a pernicious system of literary culture and conserved it. This 'parasitism of literary talent' still deeply infects civilization. Sorel idealized the cult of manual work. This destructive intellectual set little store by the more strenuous enterprises of the mind.

Socrates, regarded by John Stuart Mill as a hero of intellectual liberty, has for Sorel, says Perrin, but one title to fame: he was the precursor of Dr. Pangloss.* This attack already shows implacable hostility to the assumptions of liberal thought.

The onslaught is further worked out in the *Les Illusions du Progrès*, Sorel's most interesting work, where the influences of Marx and Bergson are equally apparent.† Here he again insists on the need to

---

* How right, Sorel implies, were the authorities to have the old bore put down.

† *Les Illusions du Progrès*. Paris, 1908. 390 pp. It is divided into five chapters: 'Ideologies of Progress', 'The Conquering Bourgeoisie', 'The Eighteenth-Century Outlook', 'The Audacity of the Third Estate' and 'Theories of Progress'. They are followed by appendices on 'Greatness and Decadence' and the 'March to Socialism'. Topics of the first chapter include: The Influence of Polite Society on Literature, Fontenelle and Pascal's Criticism: the influence of Descartes and Condorcet. The second chapter treats of the Theory of Contract and contains an onslaught on Locke, Rousseau and the Physiocrats. The third attacks Diderot, and the 'Mathematical Appraisal of Social Questions'. The fourth deals with Turgot, the Cult of the Noble Savage and with Charlevois. The fifth concentrates on the popularization of ideas by Madame de Staël, on de Tocqueville and on Proudhon. Both appendices are worth examination. In the first the alleged

penetrate to the roots of society. For its laws are mysterious. The obscurities of Marx more deeply reflect life and history than the artificial and shapely simplifications of liberal thought. The ideas or myths of an epoch are those of its dominant class, and since the most characteristic ideology of the middle class is the idea of progress, it should be carefully examined. For the historian must concentrate upon the outlook of the 'winners' in a given epoch.

Another typical bourgeois myth is the idea of the general Will. Inheriting the admiration of the old régime for strong government, social democrats have always demanded centralization. Hence the cult of popular Will, a new myth to justify the old state. Naturally, the idea is fantastic. With the social grades on such different levels of development, so that the leaders may be living intellectually several centuries before the majority, who trail in varying stages of political consciousness behind them, it is ridiculous even to imagine a general Will. Yet the myth has worked. Popular opinion is always subordinated in each epoch to the ideas of elites. Behind these ideas — 'which nobody has and in which every one is supposed to participate' — are concealed the fundamental causes of human action. Just as the historian reconsiders historical persons, so myths and slogans should be reassessed. 'It is in democratic times, especially, that one can say that mankind is governed by the magic power of great words rather than by ideas, by formulae rather than by reason, by dogmas of which no one knows the origin, rather than by doctrines founded on observation.'

There is no better example of such dogma than the myth of progress. It should be historically analysed, in terms of class. Following the Marxists, Sorel regards 'bourgeois' ideology as repellent. It owes much, he thinks, to the 'neo-fetishism' of Comte, though his Religion of Humanity was little regarded, and his hierarchy of 'bourgeois saints laïques' is ridiculous. Middle-class thinkers, indeed, have never escaped from the assumptions of the eighteenth century. To destroy this outlook is not only 'a question of conscience but of immediate practical interest'. French 'Enlightenment', which set the tone for all Europe, was profoundly artificial, conditioned by the mentality of class. The great French tradition of clarity and elegance was

degeneracy of Law is discussed, Revolutions, and 'Genius and Mediocrity in Democratic society'. In the second, there is an analysis of Marx's 'Hegelian Prejudices'; a description of the 'reduction of the workers to the role of insects', and an inquiry into the conditions under which Marx's predictions would be correct. It concludes with a vindication of 'Real Progress, or Technical Progress in Production'. A comparison between Bury's 'Idea of Progress' and Sorel's treatment of the same theme makes profitable reading.

regarded by this ruthless iconoclast as dangerous and misleading. Its very elegance masks the truth. Writers become good craftsmen, 'clever advocates', who establish an artificial orthodoxy. Here, he says, are to be found the origins of the doctrine of progress. It reflects the outlook of a class. 'In formulating his famous principle of methodical doubt', for example, Descartes was only 'applying to thought the habits of an aristocrat'.[6] Such writers have little respect for tradition, and while Pascal yearned for the constant presence of God, Descartes, intoxicated with the prospects of new knowledge was, in effect, content with His absence.

Naturally this bold scepticism was attractive to people of quality, to the *gens du monde*. It justified their desire 'to talk with assurance on subjects imperfectly understood', relying on native wit, and reckless of middle-class caution. When the practical middle class came to predominance, this aristocratic desire for clarity was reinforced by the demand for a total explanation, by a confidence in reason, which reaches its climax in Herbert Spencer. 'Hence', says Sorel, 'the insensate confidence in the decisions of enlightened people which has remained the ideological basis of the superstition of the modern state.'[7] Hence, also, the illusions of liberal rationalism, with its view of history as the education of the human race. In that originally eighteenth-century outlook, the mysterious, complex and irrational process of history is reduced, with deceptive lucidity, to an intelligible and elegant compass. Such simplification was natural to writers who catered for a beau monde 'which turned everything into conversation'. If French literature lacks the depth of a Shakespeare or a Goethe — *cherchez la femme*. Reason, tolerance, humanity — they are the values of the salon. Modern democrats have never escaped from this stuffy, artificial, inheritance.

'There is no reason', either, 'to think opinion made by the Press any better than that made in salons.'[8] All attempts to assimilate the masses into bourgeois culture should be resisted. 'An education which aims to make the people participate in middle-class culture is useless to the proletariat.' The Welfare State is brushed aside. In English terms, W.E.A. activities, extra-mural studies — all are pernicious. Sorel turns to a vitriolic attack on both secular and classical education in France — the latter, he says, has descended to 'the level of fetishes'. Intellectuals, indeed, show for their abstractions the respect of savages for their hieroglyphs. Could there be a worse or more cruel government than that of 'mandarins'? The pretended century of enlightenment was the supreme age of humbug, of the 'bric-à-brac of the *Encyclopedia*'. Even Saint-Simon is tarred with this brush. As for the religion of Comte, 'one might as well worship the Bibliothéque Nationale'. Like de Maistre, Sorel holds that the healthy gloom of medieval Catholicism, the sombre dignity of Calvin's beliefs, more nearly reflect the realities of life. They were perverted into fatuous and delusive hope through the shallow optimism of ideologists. This rationalist nonsense reflects the class bias of parasitic minds. Actually it is emotion, not reason, that dominates mankind. All political life is an improvisation before fate.

The French, of course, will always accept anything sufficiently theoretical. Rousseau's sophistries are a notable example. His own countrymen knew better. The *Contrat Social* was regarded in Geneva as a seditious libel and burnt. But Rousseau was a supreme popularizer; he condensed ideas, largely taken from Locke, into a 'masterpiece of style which is wonderfully obscure'. He thus proved himself a master of myth, and altered the development of history. The power of this myth was extraordinary. It did not matter in the least that Rousseau was unintelligible. 'Enlightened people dare not admit that they cannot understand arguments that are presented in very sophisticated language by an illustrious writer.' The idea of the General Will and the Marxist theory of Value — notable and perennial torments for students of political thought — both prove, says Sorel, 'how important obscurity can be in giving force to a doctrine'. Of course it is quite beside the point to try to understand either.[9] But when, later, Rousseau's book came into the hands of the small bourgeoisie, it became a programme of immediate action. 'Everyone found in it what he wished.'[10]

Of course the idea of government by all is a fiction; yet it is the last word of democratic political thought. But the theory of the bourgeois state merely reflects a class myth. It is outdated. The whole ideology must be superseded by the proletariat, by the Syndicats, a 'powerful means of moralization'.[11] The objective is not to capture the bourgeois machine, but to deprive it of life.

Further, he again emphasizes, the whole middle-class outlook is vitiated by the cult of concentrated state power. It was inherited from the ancien régime; it is now unchecked by the Church, and backed by the myth of the General Will. What future can it have but tyranny? The danger of the omnipotent state was ever in Sorel's, as in Proudhon's, mind. Eight years before, he had written, in a society in which state, church and property exist, 'there is some chance of finding chinks without being completely crushed'[12] . . . But what can one do when the state will be 'alone, absolute in temporal and spiritual affairs, and more absolute than the Pope, because it will be represented by the expert — the man of science'? Here is the danger even of Saint-Simonean planning: the opportunity for demagogues to capture power and stultify the Revolution. Of this 'political clerisy', the intellectuals, the parasites who sell ideas, Jaurès — that Sorelian bugbear — is the representative. He has the mentality of a successful cattle merchant.

Along with the attack on democratic politicians, here is another denunciation of middle-class culture. This omnivorous reader, this self-taught beneficiary of organized knowledge, again had to undermine the intellectual capital of civilized society. History, as interpreted by liberals in terms of the leadership of individuals of genius and elites of talent, is unreal. He denies the creativeness, the decisive influence, of individuals. So-called great men are only the 'carriers of symbols' which the creative and irrational imagination of the masses have made. This is a process intellectuals cannot understand. He quotes Anatole France —'c'est toujours à l'insu des lettrés que les foules ignorantes créent des dieux'. The moving power of history is the proletariat; the 'individualist and aristocratic doctrine of talents' is false.[13] Here Sorel's sceptical view of elites and masses reinforces his political programme.

In his most notorious, though not his most able, book he worked this programme out. In the *Reflections on Violence* anarcho-syndicalism is interpreted in terms of the synthetic myth of the General Strike.* Reiterating ideas previously formulated, it is primarily a call to misguided action. The introductory 'Letter to Halévy' contains some of Sorel's most striking phrases. 'But philosophy', he says, 'is perhaps, after all, only the recognition of the abysses which lie on each side of the footpath that the vulgar follow with the serenity of somnambulists —'† Profound understanding of life, he argues darkly, produces pessimism, for conventional philosophy and industrial civilization have created false hopes. The prosperous urban Greeks of Antiquity were shallow, regarding the world with a trader's mentality as 'an

* *Reflections on Violence*, translated by T. E. Hulme. Allen & Unwin, 1915, 297 pp. It is in the main a collection and expansion of articles which appeared in the Italian paper *Il Divenire Sociale*. It opens with a long letter to Daniel Halévy and is divided into seven chapters: 'Class War and Violence', 'Violence and the Decadence of the Middle Classes', 'Prejudices against Violence', 'The Proletarian Strike', 'The Political General Strike', 'The Ethics of Violence and the Ethics of the Producers'. Sorel had a remarkable flair for an arresting title, as the names of all his books witness. The startling title and chapter headings probably account for the book's notoriety above his other works.

† *Reflections* (Letter to D. Halévy), p. 6. Thus, it may be added, keeping philosophers alive.

immense shop full of excellent things'.[14] The concept of Natural Law is equally empty, a mere projection of the mind. He quotes Pascal: 'three degrees of latitude nearer the Pole reverse all jurisprudence, a meridian decides what is truth'.[15] It is impossible, he says, to reason about justice, a relative term. International arbitration, with its appeal to abstract right — that decrepit Rosinante — merely evokes a secularized mythology. There can be no justice in politics.

With the rise of Calvinism, the shallow and vulgar optimism of the Renaissance gave place to a juster estimate of life. But Protestantism soon became 'soft' and degenerated into 'mere lax Christianity'. Then 'the immense success of industrial civilization ... created the belief that, in the near future, happiness would be produced automatically for everybody'. All this reformist optimism is nonsense. The syndicalists will have a tougher outlook, both in theory and politics. With the destruction of bourgeois ideology, 'the partiamentary régime, so dear to intellectuals, will be finished with — it is the abomination of desolation'![16] The kind of social democracy which says 'do what you like, but don't kill the goose', [the bourgeois state] must give place to a militant, destructive creed. For in a crisis the fanatics, the extremists, win. The early Christians, as he had said in the *Illusions of Progress*, who really counted were the Tertullians — the men who refused compromise. Bruno, who was burnt for his '*convictions*', is more important than Galileo, who was merely 'certain — with that particular kind of *certitude* about the accepted theories of science which instruction ultimately produces'.[17] The idea of a dynamic myth, of a Holy Army, is the contribution to political theory which we draw from Bergson. He was concerned with the inner self, constantly creative in Duration, not Time. This creative consciousness, whereby we invent our world, must be applied to the eternal improvisations of politics. It must be expressed in a mythology accepted by the masses, not as description 'of things', but as means of action.[18] For action is what counts.

And myth is a redoubtable weapon. 'People who are living in this world of "myths" are secure from all refutation'. It was a queer gospel for the increasingly precarious, interdependent, world of the twentieth century. Sorel glories in this dark thinking with the blood. He repudiates a constructive programme. 'We on the contrary have invented nothing at all, and even assert that nothing can be invented.' He has merely asserted that 'a new culture might spring from the struggle of the revolutionary trade unions against the employers and the State'. He is original, he declares again, only in repudiating the leadership of intellectuals. He has no wish at all to direct the great surge of proletarian vitality; only to put the workers on guard against 'bourgeois' thought. 'The proletariat must be preserved from the experience of the Germans who conquered the Roman Empire: the latter were ashamed of being barbarians, and put themselves to school with the rhetoricians of the Latin decadence; they had no reason to congratulate themselves upon having wished to be civilized.'[19] 'I do not believe . . . that I am labouring in vain,' he continues, 'for in this way I help to ruin the prestige of middle-class culture, a prestige which up till now has been opposed to the complete development of the principle of the "class war".'[20] The heady vintage of Bergsonian intuition is mixed with the muddy brew of Marxist determinism.

From this theoretical background emerges the full myth of the General Strike. Sorel apparently believed that it was already 'established in the minds of the workers'.[21] The myth was to spread through the Syndicalist cells; the infecting of the syndicates by anarchism is one of the outstanding events of the early twentieth century.

The great surge of proletarian violence, even if unsuccessful, creates a revolutionary state of mind. In pursuit of his new proletarian culture, cut off from the past, he denounces all attempts to avoid class war. 'Social duty', he writes, 'no more exists than international duty.' Sorel pours vitriolic contempt on the 'cowardice' of the middle class, who 'continue to pursue the chimera of the social peace'.[22] The natural bellicosity of the French, which subdued most of the continent under Napoleon, must be turned inwards.

It is essential, he insists, to keep the bourgeois on the run. A watered-down Capitalism would merge into a dreary sub-bourgeois state. So the class war must be kept going; the capitalists driven to fight. Proletarian violence is 'the only means by which the European nations, at present stupefied by humanitarianism, can recover their former energy'. Sorel need not have worried on that score.

He recurs to the contrast between the creative French Revolution, coming in a time of prosperity, and the Christian revolution which took over a bankrupt and decadent world. He proceeds to a glorification of Napoleon, to quotations from de Tocqueville on the dangers of democratic centralization, and to the assertion that the General Strike is not illegal since it ranks as an operation of war. But he pays the English a fine compliment. They 'are distinguished', he says, 'by an extraordinary lack of understanding of the class war'.[23]

Sidney Webb he finds peculiarly contemptible. He 'enjoys a reputation for competence that is very much exaggerated: all that can be put to his credit is that he has waded through uninteresting blue books and has had the patience to compose an extremely indigestible compilation on the history of trade unionism; he has a mind of the narrowest description'. Sorel, as one might expect, underestimates that formidable political influence.

This miscalculation was due in part to his insularity. To his obsession with French political intrigue, to the constant harping on the Dreyfus case and its consequences, to the dreary feud with Jaurès which runs with a certain gross humour, a kind of bass accompaniment, throughout the books.* He labours the comparison between the corrupt demagogues of social democracy, blackmailing the rich, imposing their own will on the masses in the guise of constitutional government, and the clean Proudhonian enterprise of the Syndicalist elite.

To keep the myth alive there must be unremitting agitation. 'Consider', he says, 'the ethics of violence'. Consider how few were the Christian martyrs, yet what a resounding legend they made! One need not necessarily achieve violence on a scale so large as to wreck society: 'there is no danger of civilization succumbing under the consequences of the development of brutality'. The myth of the General Strike — the widespread revolutionary state of mind — may indeed, foster the class war 'by means of incidents which would appear to middle-class historians of small importance, as the execution of a few Christians seemed insignificant to established opinion in Rome'.[24] There is even a 'good chance' of a Syndicalist revolution succeeding without resort to the centralized terror of bourgeois intellectual fanatics.[25] Good clean violence in factory and shipyard, railroad and power station — that Sorel admires. When this violence is side-tracked into 'cunning', into bargaining, as in the English trade unions, then there is spiritual death. Blows, on the contrary, beget heroism. Here, already, is part of the mythology of Fascism.

He becomes more interesting when he leaves his programme of action. Discussing the 'Ethics of Producers', he resumes a fruitful theme. What, he asks, with Renan, will replace the old myths? ' "On what will those who come after us live?" '[26] This is the great problem. We need, he insists, a new morality of producers, broad-

* Sorel's political opponents are apaches, imbeciles, assassins, etc., in the best tradition of French political abuse. For some fine specimens, see his remarks on Viviani (pp. 20-1), and Vandervelde (p. 49).

based on the creative impulse of the people. He quotes, with approval, the notorious remarks of Nietzsche about the blond beast, and asserts that this kind of master type still exists in the United States. Had Nietzsche lived to see the gathering tide of American prosperity, 'he would have been struck by the singular analogies which exist between the Yankee . . . and the ancient Greek sailor, . . . sometimes a pirate'.[27] After this unexpected compliment to capitalists in their wild state, he turns to rend Aristotle and the Catholics, with their 'consumer mentality', their contemptible ideas of stability and order. But for the 'free producers of tomorrow, working in factories, there are no masters'. They must show an heroic, an Homeric, élan. The incredible victories of the revolution were due to French individualism, 'to intelligent bayonets'. 'The same spirit is found in the working-class groups . . . eager for the general strike', that 'manifestation of individualistic force in the revolted masses'.[28] Ingenious artisans, working like creative artists, are inspired by Syndicalist cells. They will develop their missionary, and spontaneous, idea.* What a prospect for all-out production! Here is no 'Welfare' State, ridden by conservative bureaucrats, exploited by a clerisy, infested with the corruption of politicians. Here is a new, a healthy society, driven by its proper myth, fulfilling its own phase of a Vicoesque 'course' of history. The Holy Army is restored. This time it is not Satan who is the enemy: it is the bourgeoisie.

These ideas are further elaborated in the later *Materials for a Theory of the Proletariat*, a collection of early essays which was Sorel's penultimate work.† Here, again, the intellectuals are attacked. Sorel denounces their superstititious respect for the expert, the parasitism of 'democrats' and 'Mandarins', the glorification of the 'pontiffs of science'. The world of dreary abstractions, of tedious and artificial classification, in which this clerisy has its being, he finds most suitable for the mentality of women, such 'research fitting the female mind'. But the shrewder bourgeois realize that once women are let in, the

---

* Actually Sorel's curiously Philistine mind had no understanding for the real artist. He remarks 'the habits of the modern artist, founded in imitation of those of a jovial aristocracy, are in no way *necessary*' (p. 287n). There is to be no question of the upright workers, however creative, following the manners and customs of the Quartier Latin.

† It is divided into four parts: 'The Socialist Future of the Syndicates', 'The Basis of a Critique of Society', 'A Proletarian Writer' and 'The Organizing of Democracy'. There is an Appendix mainly devoted to Proudhon. The second and third chapters of Part I are notable. 'On the Illusion of the Superiority of Intellectual Work', 'On the Self Government of the Working Class' and 'On Petit-Bourgeois Mentality' (I, 5). Part II (1) deals with metaphysical aspects of Marxism, (2-4) with the 'Psycho-erotic Law', and 'The Nomadic Characteristics of Americans'. See also the criticism of 'Medieval' Socialism and the 'Elaboration of the Catastrophic Concept of the General Strike'.

prestige and rewards of their calling will be diminished. Hence their anxiety to exclude them from such suitable occupations. As science progresses, the workers can actually do without the so-called experts, who will dwindle into an intellectual proletariat. Sorel remarks, foolishly enough, that in medicine 'the progress of science and the better organization of assistance has already diminished the numbers of doctors used'.[29] Further, the managerial class is superfluous. Executive capacity is not rare.' The workers can soon provide their own self-governing institutions. 'The socialization of the means of production will translate itself into a prodigious lockout of intellectuals.' Their natural and meretricious role as exploiting politicians will no longer have any scope. 'Mort aux intellectuels!' cries this renegade of the École Polytechnique. For the collective soul is profoundly mysterious, and the tides of history are determined not by the puny laws of man's mind but by the purpose, or Bergsonian lack of it, of creative Life.

The habits of this new proletarian age will be chaste. There is 'a psycho-erotic "law"' which demands the conservation of energy. Fourier's 'penchant for perverse debauchery' is quite out of order. Sorel, indeed, makes a cult of the family. But the proletarian family will extend to 'free unions'. As in so many French writers, the ideal of the 'femme forte' is glorified.* The proletarian woman is to be a 'compagnon sévère et intelligente'.

Within their self-governing factories, meanwhile, the workers will develop their creative tasks. The cult of the General Strike will pass into the cult of work. Like 'skilled vine dressers', absorbed in their art, they will feel like a gardener about his dahlias. Accustomed to exploits of sabotage, habituated to violence and destruction, the Syndicalist elites, Sorel assumes, will quickly revert to the routine and responsibility of modern industry. For here is 'an economic epic'. 'Rejuvenated by the feelings roused by proletarian violence', they will be inspired by Sorelian myth to an 'entirely epic state of mind'. Here is the answer to the supreme question of the age — by what shall we live? An ideology for the new civilization of the people. 'It is to violence,' Sorel concludes, 'that socialism owes the high ethical values by means of which it brings salvation to the modern world.'

And why, the reader may ask, is Sorel held to be important? He had, indeed, little influence in his own country in his own time. He was destructive, immediately irresponsible. His ideas were part of

---

* Vide *supra* for this perennial theme in Saint-Simon, Comte, even Proudhon.

the wave of irrationalism promoted by Bergson. But he is a writer, like de Maistre, who raises profound problems. He was in tune with two most formidable facts of his age. The growing political and economic power of the masses, and the new psychological interpretation of politics. He combines Marx's belief in the class war with a Nietzschean understanding of myth, and a new understanding of the subconscious mind. Above all, he brings a profound pessimism to bear on politics. His view of life was sombre, and his morality puritan. In history he saw no plan and little progress: in politics only improvisation: in ideas only myth. This dark revolutionary sceptic was to provide Fascism with a much needed political philosophy. He was to make a major contribution to the disasters of the twentieth century.

CHAPTER XI

SOCIAL DEMOCRACY: THE FABIANS:
WILLIAM MORRIS: BERNSTEIN: JAURÈS

WHILE Sorel contributed to destructive ideas, foreshadowing major tendencies of the mid-twentieth century, the main stream of social-democratic thought developed from liberal, Marxist and communitarian origins. And, reinforcing it, there arose a new, constructive, and powerful sociology.

The development of social democracy will be examined under four aspects. First, the political theory of the British Welfare State, expressed in the well-known *Fabian Essays* and in the writings of William Morris. Next, the German Bernstein's revision of Marxism will shortly be described. Finally, the speeches and writings of Jaurès, far the most eloquent and intellectually able of all the many exponents of early European social democracy, will be analysed.

It has been well remarked that the origins of British socialism were Methodist, not Marxist. The Fabians and Morris took only what they wanted from Marx, and it was not much. Continental preoccupation with theory was far greater. Bernstein goes to elaborate lengths to prove himself Marx's true interpreter. In France, Jaurès draws upon Fourier, and in particular, Proudhon. He brilliantly, if tortuously, maintains that Marx, at his best, was neither rigid nor materialist. Both were constitutional writers who desired a creative socialist society, with its roots both in the people and in the traditional civilization now to become their own. In a welter of recrimination, the claims of Bernstein and Jaurès were bitterly denied by the socialists of the Left. They accepted total, world-wide, class war and worked for revolutionary dictatorship. Their ideas were realized not in Western Europe but in Russia, where Western theories are often acted upon with startling completeness and where arbitrary government had long been normal. Since the present study deals with Western political ideas, the Russian version of Communism is outside its range.

But there is another aspect of political thought at the turn of the century which demands further attention — a revolutionary development. Where Darwin had opened up the vistas of evolution, the psychologists were now exploring the depths of the sub-conscious mind. The new psychology was systematic and scientific; not the intuitions of Nietzsche or Sorel, but the cautious and documented conclusions of methodical investigation. This environmental and psychological approach to the study of society was to be far more effective than the over-ambitious attempts of Comte and Spencer. It was to prove a powerful reinforcement to constitutional government. As Lasswell remarks, 'Without science, democracy is blind and weak. With science, democracy will not be blind and may be strong'.[1] Political motives and ideas were now to be examined, as it were, from within. Not in the light of revelation or eternal Law, but of psychological projection. Freud was later to express this outlook. 'The fateful question of the human species seems to me to be to what extent the cultural process developed in it will succeed in meeting the derangements of communal life caused by the human instincts of aggression and destruction.'[2] Here is a clear, dispassionate, outlook. Its influence was bound in time to be as important and pervasive as that of Darwin. In terms of social psychology and the study of myths, the political thought of the future is likely to proceed.

Following the analysis of British, German and French social democratic thought, two important pioneers of this sociology will therefore be examined. The first, Émile Durkheim, was to have great scientific influence. Graham Wallas was to popularize a new approach in England and America. Both these writers represent a reinforcement of civilized government by new knowledge. Nietzsche, Bergson and Sorel had stated with brilliant eloquence that mankind are led not by reason, but by myth. But they had demanded a politically irresponsible exploitation of that belief. Durkheim and Wallas, on the other hand, continuing the scientific approach of their nineteenth-century predecessors, were concerned to help government and promote welfare. Both represent the promise of a new constructive humanism. They stand only on the threshold of that development, which it would require another volume to describe. Durkheim, in particular, was the master of a new technique, which he applied to problems normally the subject of passion and propaganda.

II

Against this background the political theory of the British Welfare State now claims attention. The Fabians were constitutionalist administrators. Backed by Trade Union power, they were to inspire peaceful but profound social change. The other side of British social democracy was visionary, sentimental; revolutionary in an amateurish way. It demanded a fuller life for all. It reached back to seventeenth-century radicalism and to Owen. It was later to inspire sporadic guild socialist revolts against Fabian bureaucracy.

In both its aspects British social democracy was insular. It was also very powerful, with the mass of working class opinion increasingly behind it. It developed in an incongruous setting, against a panorama of growing armaments and nationalism, of vast, inescapable continental and Imperial responsibilities. It assumed an economy of peace and plenty. Both were denied it by the monstrous events of the first half of the twentieth century. The educated, peaceful, social democracy at which it aimed was therefore more immediately realized in smaller states — in Sweden and Switzerland, for example. Here, mainly through the accidents of geography, governments avoided the cataclysms which strained and impoverished the scene of the British social democratic experiment.

The appearance of *Fabian Essays* reflects a late Victorian background.* Opposite the title-page of the first edition there is a revealing cartoon. Clad only in a cap of liberty and a scarf, a figure is poised modestly on one knee. Grasping an enormous pen, it confronts a rather Beardsley devil, crouched in shocked and puzzled apprehension over a large globe. With the other hand, the figure displays a scroll that frames the picture and bears the title of the work. This ninetyish drawing, with its suggestion of bearded figures with loose ties and knickerbockers, bicycling through a garden suburb, evokes at once the placid atmosphere of the time.†

The Preface to the first edition is resolutely constitutional. It is written in a plain style, with a touch of Puritan complacency, and inspired by the will to improve. The writers, it says, 'are all Social Democrats, with a common conviction of the necessity of vesting the

---

* *Fabian Essays* by BERNARD SHAW, the RT. HON. THE LORD PASSFIELD, GRAHAM WALLAS, The LORD OLIVIER, WILLIAM CLARKE, ANNIE BESANT, HERBERT BLAND, with a foreword by the original editor. Jubilee Edition, London. Allen & Unwin, 1948. First Edition, 1889. Like the *Communist Manifesto*, it contains various prefaces: the original of 1889, one by Shaw in 1908, by Webb in 1920, and again by Shaw in 1948. The 'Basis of Socialism' is first defined; the economic by Shaw, the historical by Webb (Passfield), the industrial by Clarke, the moral by Olivier. The 'Organization of Society' is next examined; Property Under Socialism, by Wallas; Industry by Annie Besant; the Transition to Social Democracy by Shaw; the Outlook by Bland. The whole is rounded off by a Shavian postscript in the Jubilee Edition — a piece of characteristically able exhibitionism.

† It compares poorly with the well drawn title-page of another famous document, the *Leviathan* of THOMAS HOBBES — the measure, perhaps, of the spiritual contrast between the mid-seventeenth and late-nineteenth centuries.

organization of society and the material of production in a State identified with the whole people by a complete Democracy'.[3] The authors, in 1889, have only most modest and accurate pretentions. The *Essays*, they point out, are merely re-printed lectures; 'any Sunday paper which contains a lecture list will shew where some, if not all, of the seven lectures may be heard for nothing'. Here is a different opening from the melodramatic and ferocious phrases of the *Communist Manifesto*, or from the numinous rhetoric of world-historical philosophers. 'There are', the writers continue, firmly ignoring Marx, 'at present no authoritative teachers of Socialism ... The essayists make no claim', they say, 'to be more than communicative learners.' There is a final note of qualified self confidence. In 1908 Shaw wrote 'in the main, we have nothing to withdraw, nothing to regret, nothing to apologize for, and much to be proud of'. The texture of the first preface is sub-fusc.

It was also extremely formidable. Far more successful than the writings of most continental revolutionaries. Sixty years later Shaw could add, 'as I write a Fabian Socialist is Prime Minister of Britain'. Anyone who has read the preceding pages will have noticed that it is unusual for political theorists to become Cabinet Ministers. It was just this sobriety and provincialism, this constitutional limitation of purpose, which was to appeal to the predominant mass of the twentieth century British, with their curious docility, observed already by Bagehot. The programme seemed to offer at once betterment and safety first. Shaw, of course — so un-English — was disillusioned by the outcome. He complained later that the constitutionalism was a mistake. In his old age, he wanted — or pretended to want — to abolish the party system, break up the constitution and achieve something far more positive and dictatorial. But the rich famous writer was less realistic than the young reformer. Had revolution been the note of the Fabians, their staggering success would never have come about. Shaw himself says, 'the distinctive mark of the Fabian Society was its resolute constitutionalism ... When the greatest Socialist of that day, the poet and craftsman William Morris, told the workers that there was no hope for them save in revolution, we said that if that were true there was no hope at all for them'. This constitutional bias was reinforced by the brilliant journalism of the young Shaw, by the mole-like industry of Webb, by the cautious observation of Graham Wallas. It is typical of the whole movement, but unimportant, that by far the weakest aspect of the Essays is theoretical.

Besides their resolute constitutionalism, the Fabians had two other strong cards. They had accepted from de Tocqueville that complete mass democracy was inevitable. Here they had the advantage of their political opponents; of the limited realism of Lecky, for example, or of romantic Conservative doctrines. This sense of the irresistible tide of contemporary mass civilization, which owes much to Marx, is apparent in all their work. From Marx they derived their other card, the sense of the importance of the means of production and of the constriction of productive power under current forms of capitalism. But here is none of de Tocqueville's scepticism, of his fear of the state; and little of Marx's ferocity, though some of this theory is Marx and water. In contrast to Marx's hostility to bourgeois ideas, there is a constant appeal, as in J. S. Mill and Green, to traditional morality, to the cultured and the good. 'The gambling spirit', says Shaw, 'is the enemy.' We must make order, decency, social justice, *welfare*. Immediately they were much influenced by Henry George's then fashionable doctrine of the taxation of land values.* Rent, in particular, is unjust and inefficient. Private right must give way, they insist, to 'public weal'. The present system reflects the ambitions of 'that modern Plutarch, Mr. Samuel Smiles'. It creates riches; it does not create wealth. Luxuries are piling up, but 'in the things that are wanting for the welfare of the people we are abjectly poor'. All follows from the maladjustments of an uncontrolled economy, the perversion and waste of productive power. Hence 'a grotesquely hideous march of civilization from bad to worse'. Effective propaganda, if a strange judgment in view of the great improvement of English social conditions in the later nineteenth century. But revolutions, it is well known, are made not by the down-trodden but by the discontented.

By the present system, they argue, the masses are deprived of purchasing power, their potential contribution stifled. 'All attempts yet made', writes Shaw, 'to construct true societies . . . have failed: the nearest things to societies so far achieved have been civilizations, which have rotted into centres of vice and luxury, and eventually been swept away by uncivilized races. That our own civilization is already in an advanced stage of rottenness may be taken as statistically proved.'† This sweeping assertion, in the vein of Proudhon and Kropotkin, anticipating the blistering attacks of

* Henry George, born San Francisco, 1838, died New York, 1897. His most influential book was *Progress and Poverty*, 1879.

† p. 22. When in the Election of 1951 Mr. Attlee remarked, 'we have to clear up the mess of centuries', he was only following this view.

Sorel, must have made some appeal in the atmosphere of fin-de-siècle, then invading literary circles. The period also saw a singular and growing Philistinism among the English ruling class. The Fabians made their appeal against it, to those who wished to be in the van of culture — always an influential minority. The truly sophisticated, they said, were not the sceptics of a decadent society, but those who could apprehend the main tide of civilization's advance. Against the cynicism of the aesthetes and the indifference of the Philistines, they also invoked the name of science. This argument was most effectively deployed by Wells, whose influence over the younger generation was destined to be enormous, and is now too little appreciated.* Although he satirized the Fabians, he was dominated by this idea. With a wider vision, he was to be the greatest early-twentieth-century prophet of popularized scientific humanism and world order.

Shaw already strikes this note of confidence, 'The source of our social misery is no eternal well-spring of confusion and evil, but only an artificial system . . .' Man, he argues, with a similar optimism, is well able to set his house in order. Active benevolence can combat and vanquish the ancient inheritance of folly and exploitation. The two enemies, he argues, have been the fatuous optimism of laissez faire and the misinterpretation of science which has lately reinforced it. The old economic fatalism has been disastrously revived by mistaken notions of the evil of Nature. The apparent implications of Darwin's discoveries had been eagerly canvassed by the advocates of economic piracy. The black struggle depicted by Herbert Spencer had been exactly what these 'realists' had expected. Here was Nature, they had said, at it again. Socialism seemed the dream of sentimentalists. Actually, says Shaw, characteristically turning the tables on his adversaries, the Socialists have science on their side. 'Socialism now challenges individualism, scepticism, pessimism, worship of Nature personified as a devil — on their own ground of science.' For a truly scientific social order would sweep away the squalor and evil of the past, the 'idiotic waste of magnificent opportunities for noble and happy living'.⁴ It is exactly the belief of Wells; the confident assertion of emancipated middle class intellectuals, borne up by the continuing tide of late Victorian and Edwardian prosperity, full of hope in reason and humanity. Economics, Shaw concludes, once the Dismal, now the Hopeful Science, can point to

* See E.M. EARLE, 'H.G. Wells, "British Patriot in Search of a World State",' in *Nationalism and Internationalism*. Princeton, 1948, for a wise appreciation of his importance.

the emancipation of mankind. It is the mission of social democracy to use the power of the existing state to end the disorder, which postpones a creative and splendid future.

Sidney Webb strikes the same note, but without Shaw's flashy dialectical skill. He is pedestrian, indefatigable and self-confident. The gradual advent of Socialism is inevitable. It reflects a social evolution now for the first time intelligible. It is bound to develop in the 'social organism'.* This idea, apparent in so much mid-nineteenth-century thought, was accepted and developed by Webb, who writes with a quiet, remorseless, didactic complacency. And, the focus of the social organism is the sovereign nation state, though its general vitality should be assured by the development of municipal Socialism. For nowadays there is no need of violent revolution. 'No philosopher now looks for anything but the gradual evolution of the new order from the old, without breach of continuity or abrupt change of the entire social tissue . . .' Gimcrack pre-evolutionary Utopias — 'the impossible ideal of Humanity-intoxicated Frenchmen' — are now obsolete. Social evolution has changed all that. That is why both the great political parties in England have long been 'drifting before a nameless undercurrent', to them mysterious. For Socialism is merely the inevitable outcome of democracy — its economic sequel. And the rise of democracy has been the outstanding political event of the century. This fact shrewd observers have long apprehended. De Tocqueville, in 'a classic which everyone quotes and nobody reads', 'hammered this truth into the reluctant ears of the old world two generations ago'. In Webb's opinion this overwhelming tide, far from being destructive, was blindly but benevolently bearing the country to 'social salvation'. For Webb, like Green and Morris, had faith in the people, in their desire and capacity to assimilate the culture which he was anxious to diffuse. This steady social evolution is reflected in changing ideas, but it does not imply class conflict. Rather a solid development of a social conscience, of refinement of manners. 'It is', writes Webb, 'through the slow and gradual turning of the popular mind to new principles that social reorganization bit by bit comes.' The rhythm of the sentence is characteristic. This salutary development is apparent to all perceptive minds; to 'students of society who are abreast of their time'. Progress is taken for granted.

It will be 'constitutional and peaceful' — 'in this country at least', he

---

* For a striking and once fashionable interpretation of the idea, see BENJAMIN KIDD: notably in his *Social Evolution,* 1894 and *The Science of Power,* 1918.

adds with an insular touch. These changes will come about by consent; being prepared for in the minds of all, they will not cause dislocation. They will succeed, since they are not regarded as 'immoral' by the masses, for democracy is the control of the people by themselves. Socialism, after all, implies merely the economic application of democratic principles. Here, in the Fabian view, is the advance on the liberalism of Mill and Green. Mere political levelling will never achieve social justice: 'the people must gain control of the main instruments of wealth production'. How this control will be administered is not here discussed. Webb was to examine that later. He assumes that the owners of property will merely fight a delaying, rearguard action; that they will submit to their own gradual supersession. Curiously enough, following two world wars, and the extension of state power into spheres never before admitted, this prophecy was to be partially realized in England in little more than half a century. Prosaic, ordinary, devoid of any profound political philosophy, ignoring the abysmal and fundamental questions posed by Dostoevski, Nietzsche or Sorel, this persevering, level-headed, administrator had accurately assessed the desires of the majority of his countrymen. He spoke, it seems, too, for a new middle-class oligarchy of administrators, who were destined in the twentieth century to achieve an impersonal power. Just as John Locke, the spokesman of the Whig oligarchy, shelved the deepest problems of political philosophy by seeming firmly unaware of them, so this patient exponent of lower middle-class interest, now, in his different context, did the same.

A rather anaemic survey of the course of English history, of the consequences of the Industrial Revolution and the rise of democracy, reinforce the argument. The philosophic Radicals come in for severe criticism. Coleridge had done his best to drown their inhuman theories in German transcendental philosophy; Carlyle 'who knew how to compel men to listen to him', had denounced them with all his eloquence; now the scientific idea of the social organism will give raw individualists their *coup de grace*. For look, exclaims Webb, with enthusiasm, how far that organism has already developed! Already the social legislation of both parties has greatly diminished the freedom of the capitalist. Already, on every side, he is being registered, inspected and controlled and ultimately superseded by the community. And all this has been brought about under the pressure of events by 'practical men who are not socialists'. There follows an extraordinary panegyric of the state. Today it makes rueful reading.* He seems to gloat over the numerous inspectors already in circulation. Pages are devoted to the amenities of municipal socialism. Consider, he says, the gasometers, the dispensaries, the public reading rooms; observe, he writes with sober eagerness, the Municipal public conveniences. Already slaughter houses and Scotch herrings have come into the civic net. Think of the wash-rooms, the sewers, the drains, the neat cemeteries; remark the development of municipal tramways — 'the tramway mileage belonging to local authorities has increased fivefold since 1878'. These things, he implies, are in themselves satisfying. 'It need hardly be added, that the advantages to the public are immense.'

Nor are the needs of popular instruction neglected. Free libraries, museums and reading-rooms are now common. The masses can already inform themselves on history, philosophy and current affairs. They can discuss the questions of the day. In cities whose squalor Engels had denounced, the intellectual and aesthetic needs of the people are beginning to be met. Already 'Liverpool provides Science lectures'; Manchester 'builds and stocks' (the word is revealing) 'an Art Gallery'; Birmingham 'runs a school of design' and Bradford (always practical) 'supplies water below cost price'. The guarantee of all this progress is the creation of an encouraging municipal debt. 'This Municipal socialism has been rendered possible by the creation of a local debt', now over one hundred and eighty-one million pounds. And all over the great cities the rates are going up.

Webb concludes with a grave evocation of the authority of science. Darwin's conclusions do not reinforce individualism and laissez faire. Rather they demand the planned evolution of human society. 'Evolution', as Professor Huxley declares, 'is the substitution of conscious co-ordination among the units of each organism for blind anarchic competition.' In human societies, conscious adaptation is now possible. This idea is slowly sinking in. It is all part of an 'irre-sistible glide into collectivist Socialism'.[5] Unlike Proudhon, Webb had no fear of the tentacular state. Nor did the danger to liberty, always apparent to shrewd observers since Aristotle, from full democracy which combines political with economic power, seem

---

* Anyone who reads the full text will appreciate Max Beerbohm's caricature of 'Mr. Sidney Webb on his birthday'. The reformer is depicted kneeling on the boards of a bare room: with happy concentration, he is unpacking and arranging a box of small wooden figures. For each docile citizen there is an inspector. On the walls are two pictures, one a plain diagram of human nature, the other, labelled 'The State', the head and shoulders of a lovely girl. See SIR MAX BEERBOHM, A Survey, p. 49. Heinemann, 1921.

menacing. There might, he admitted, be political atavism — a just opinion in view of the history of social democracy on much of the continent in the next fifty years — but 'so long as democracy in political administrations continues, . . . socialism will be its obverse'.

The belief in the 'social organism' also leads to a glorification of the Community; 'its life transcends that of any of its members'. Webb admires the superior organization of the German state, which in his opinion, in 1870 showed its 'decisive superiority' to the French. All this cult of the social organism linked up with the neo-Hegelian movement already described, which was providing liberal democrats with a new and sophisticated philosophy.

Webb's appeal is more to popularized science. The alliance of socialism with centralized bureaucracy was the natural result of the Webbs' passion for order and genius for detail. This led them later to make their greatest contribution to the political success of the movement through a famous and massive treatment of administrative problems, outside the aspects of political theory here considered. But the basic mental attitude which inspired this achievement is nowhere better revealed than in this early *Essay*. With that before them, there was no need for reformers to expect any other outcome from Socialist capture of political power than the situation which has since developed. In its strength and in its weakness, the Fabian programme is here already plainly revealed. Its success was due to the alliance between these doctrinaire leaders with the surge of popular discontent and aspiration. 'Every increase in the political power of the proletariat will most surely', wrote Webb in conclusion, 'be used by them for their economic and social protection.' The word comes naturally from the most successful advocate of the modern *Protectorat Social*.

William Clarke and Graham Wallas also believed that socialism is the expression of an overwhelming, inevitable, process. 'There has been, and is proceeding,' writes the former, 'an economic evolution practically independent of individual desires and prejudices.' This optimistic fatalism looks back over the horrors of the early industrial age, and out at the menace of the great contemporary trusts and combines, with a cautious confidence. There are no illusions about the difficulties in the way — indeed, a tactical realism, one of the secrets of Fabian success. 'The human race', Clarke continues, reasonably enough, 'generally contrives to exhaust every device which stupidity can suggest' before the right line is taken. At first socialist legislation may even hamper production, but in the long run the old individualism is doomed.[6] Since the change is inevitable, it can be peaceful. The aim is a co-operative commonwealth. Socialists must educate the masses 'to take up the threads as they fall from the weak hands of a useless possessing class'. Like Webb, he assumes that the owners will admit their own supersession. 'By this means', he concludes, 'the class struggle, with its greed, hate and waste, will be ended.' Here, again, is a significant contrast to Marx. The ideal is sensible, limited and hygienic. 'Practical, peaceful life, the people's life', he says, quoting Walt Whitman.

Graham Wallas, too, is convinced that science is on their side. He cites 'the growing recognition, due in part to Darwin, of causation in the development of individuals and societies'. Nor has he much expectation of sudden improvement. It was to be Wallas's special task to analyse the actual working of society; he was far the most able sociologist among them, his contribution cautious and moderate.[7] He believed in the 'slow often unconscious progress of the time spirit', which he thought needed prodding. We must 'find out what must be', shape and accelerate tendencies already there. It is expedient, he insists, to dwell on the limitations of the Fabian programme. He refers to the 'tentative and limited social democracy I have sketched'. What a contrast to the queer visions of earlier revolutionaries!

This homespun caution exacts its price. It cannot be said that his essay is inspiring. Commonsense, he believes, will convert the masses to socialism. 'A man will soon see how poor a means of production of food is his own fire when compared with the public kitchen' — a banal appeal. And when 'the present anarchy is overpast', the public will desire intellectual improvement. 'Education, refinement, leisure, the very thought of which now maddens them, would be part of their daily life.'[8] For under socialism they will have security. Without security there can be no culture. Socialism will 'remove that constant apprehension of undeserved misfortune which is the peculiar result of Capitalist production'. The stress on security was to colour the theory and practice of subsequent socialist government. The idea is suburban, practical and sincere. Academic, serious, Philistine and provincial, these able administrators and careful statisticians were also expressing in a wider context a secular variation of a perennial English theme — levelling puritanism. Unlike the Levellers, they had this time a great tide of popular support beginning to build up behind them. When the time came, the ideology of the trade unions was provided by these admirable, systematic and hope-

ful men; Shaw, genius and mountebank, the dynamo of the original
movement, taking no part in the subsequent political triumphs.*

The programme and mentality revealed in the preceding pages
was characteristic of a prosperous and insular environment. There
are two outstanding assumptions behind the political theory of
Fabian socialism. First, that capital assets of the old system will
remain secure, and the socialists take over a going concern. The
England in which these writers were an obscure minority was then
at the peak of world power; it was immensely rich, the centre of a
great Empire, the financial focus of the world, supreme at sea. In
the plethoric imperialism of the 'nineties the Fabians were regarded
as harmless cranks. Though they expressed a revolt against the
cosmopolitan plutocracy then coming to dominate British society,†
they shared one assumption with their enemies; the continuance of
the prosperity on which the experiment was to be built. When the
Welfare State which they had so largely inspired came to be constructed, it was begun in a country half crippled by two world wars.

The second outstanding Fabian doctrine was a belief in centralized
government. Order, security, regimentation, were dear to their tidy
minds. The Fabians showed a curious lack of the suspicion of power
displayed by the radicals with whose moral purpose they had so much
in common. Faced with what they regarded as a monstrous problem
of social hygiene, they turned hopeful eyes towards the new bureaucracy, developing since Gladstone's legislation of the 'seventies. The
evils of over-organization, so apparent to the twentieth century,
when the threat of the modern Minotaur is so imminent,‡ were less
conspicuous in 1889, before the garrison and the Welfare State had
been developed and even combined.

Yet in accepting and exploiting the enormous power of modern
bureaucracy, the Fabians were in tune, as they believed themselves
to be, with the predominant drift of social power in their century.
What other weapon, they might have argued, looking back over the
last fifty years, would have moved the great inert mass of bewildered

* There are a great many fireworks in his 1948 Epilogue. He is now, he declares, only
interested in providing a basic income for all – (£4000 a year) – which will make 'every
family a breeding place for an aristocracy of talent'. For he thinks political salvation can
only come through a 'Democratic Aristocracy' as against 'underdog authority or government by the unfittest'. If meant seriously, this is a total repudiation of the faith in mass
democracy on which Fabianism rests. (See pp. 218ff.)

† The later campaigns of Belloc and Chesterton against the Edwardian plutocracy won
no popular following, since neither of these brilliant Catholic writers were insular or
representative.

‡ See J. J. CHEVALLIER, 'Le Minotaure des temps modernes . . . avec son corps énorme et sa toute
petite tête'. Les Grandes Œuvres Politiques de Machiavel à nos Jours. Paris, 1948, p. 399.

democracy, and struck to the root of the ignorance, ill-health, malnutrition and unemployment which were one of the legacies of the mid-Victorian Age?

The use of this weapon implied a dangerous concentration of state power. Lecky, Maine and Acton, all resolute constitutionalists, had foreseen that popular rule might become single chamber government and destroy the balance of the constitution. They were shrewd prophets. Grave danger of tyranny over minorities and destruction of elites has since developed. It has been increased by the exigencies of war, and of preparations for it. The concentration of bureaucratic political and economic power and a levelling of standards has been hitherto the price of the attack on the darker aspect of liberal civilization.

III

In the history of political thought the outlook of the artist is seldom represented. Great poets — Dante or Milton — have turned their minds to the major problems of government, but the artist in all ages tends to adapt himself to the patronage of his time. He is preoccupied more with problems of technique than with problems of state. In general, and enviably, he is a spectator; above or outside the battle, with his own loyalties. When in the nineteenth century, with the decline of religious belief, the role of the prophet was secularized, Carlyle had deeply influenced opinion and stirred the conscience of his time. He had been obsessed with the ugliness of the new industrial civilization. His influence had been reinforced by Ruskin, through whom the point of view of the artist struck home on society. The attack on the Philistines had its origin far back in the Victorian age, and in Pugin's and G. E. Street's cult of Medievalism.

Where Ruskin had denounced, William Morris, on whom he had exercised deep influence, was determined to act.* He came from a

* William Morris, 1834-96. Born at Walthamstow, Essex, son of William Morris and Emma Shelton, of Welsh and Worcestershire origins. His father was a well-to-do discount broker, and Morris was brought up at Woodford Hall, Essex. On coming of age he inherited £900 a year. In 1848 he was sent to Marlborough, and 'a childhood', writes his biographer, 'on the edge of Epping Forest was fitly followed by a boyhood on the edge of Savernake.' Marlborough then provided ample liberty. There were no organized games as in F. H. Bradley's time; no uniform, and no prefects. Morris spent formative years exploring the Wiltshire countryside. He developed his love for Church architecture: a revealing letter survives describing his first visit to Avebury. He remained at Marlborough until Dr. Wilkinson's Headmastership culminated in the organized rebellion of 1851. Among his contemporaries Morris left a reputation for amiable eccentricity and bouts of ungovernable temper. Proceeding to Exeter College, Oxford, where, he after-

comfortable background, and brought to vast and dreary social problems the breezy attack of the Victorian well-to-do. He was drawn in middle age to face the condition of society through the difficulties encountered by his original aim; to revive healthy standards of craftsmanship in architecture, stained glass, dyeing, tapestry, printing and furniture. The mechanized vulgarity of his day convinced him that industrial society must be radically transformed: it was 'so beastly ugly'. 'Apart from the desire to produce beautiful things,' he wrote, 'the leading passion of my life has been its hatred of modern civilization.' Detesting its 'eyeless vulgarity', he endeavoured to restore what he held to be medieval standards. He appealed from the commercial 'pigskins stuffed with money' to the broad submerged masses of England. Like Owen and Proudhon, this pre-Raphaelite medievalist believed in the people. His craftsmanship and his poetry were better understood by the class he denounced, from which he came, and whose privileges he did so much to undermine. Morris brought to the socialist movement an inspiration the Fabians could never compass. A humanist and a poet, reckless of political consequences, he preached a new way of life. But if he could return to contemporary England, he would probably attack with equal vehemence the more soulless aspects of the Welfare State.

In contrast to the Fabians, Morris detested all forms of centralized power. He is in the tradition of Fourier, Owen and Proudhon. With him, anarchist and communitarian influence was continued in the pedigree of British Socialism. Though his ideas may seem dwarfed

wards declared, there was 'no teaching and no discipline', Morris abandoned his intention of taking Holy Orders and struck up a life-friendship with Edward Burne-Jones. Both found the then unspoilt surroundings of Oxford congenial. 'Beyond the grey garden walls of St. John's and Wadham, all was unbroken country.' Morris's early, and much of his middle life, were devoted to poetry and craftsmanship. He formed one of the Pre-Raphaelite brotherhood that gathered round Rossetti, and in 1861 founded the firm of William Morris and Co. which produced furniture, wall papers and stained glass. He turned to politics in the 'eighties, joining the Democratic Federation in 1883. The Socialist League was founded in the following year; for the rest of his life he took a vehement interest in the Socialist movement, forcing himself into political activities naturally repugnant to him. In his prime Morris presented the appearance of a 'Baltic Sea-Captain'; he talked incessantly in a 'husky shout' and wore emancipated clothes. Like many eccentrics, 'it was only in conventional dress that he looked really peculiar'. The atmosphere of Morris's life can be sensed by a visit to Kelmscott Manor, where he intermittently lived and worked from 1871 to 1896. There is a collected edition of Morris's works in twenty-four volumes (London, 1912). His principal political works are: *Hopes and Fears for Art*, 1882; *Signs of Change*, 1888; *News from Nowhere*, 1891; *How I Became a Socialist*, 1894; *Architecture, Industry, and Wealth*, 1902. See the *William Morris* selection *On Art and Socialism* by HOLBROOK JACKSON. London, 1947. The best biography is J. W. MACKAIL's *The Life of William Morris*, 2 vols. (1899). See also A. VALLANCE, *William Morris, his Art, his Writings and Public Life*; A. CLUTTON BROCK, *William Morris*. London, 1914; J. B. GLASIER, *William Morris and the Early Days of the Socialist Movement*, 1921, and *The Social Philosophy of William Morris*, by ANNE A. VON HELMHOLTZ-PHELAN (Duke University Press, 1927).

by the brutal and world-wide problems of today, and if he under-estimated the dismal and massive compulsions of economic environ-ment, he loudly maintained the values which are the artist's particu-lar concern. 'We are all', remarks a character in *News from Nowhere*, his Utopian romance, 'bent on the same enterprise, making the most of our lives.' 'The society', he wrote later, 'which does not give a due opportunity to all its members to exercise their energies pleasur-ably has forgotten the end of life.'⁹ He could define socialism as follows: 'What I mean by socialism is a condition of society in which there should be neither rich nor poor, neither master nor master's man, neither idle nor overworked, neither brain-sick brain workers, nor heart-sick hand workers, in a word, in which all men would be living in equality of condition and would manage their affairs un-wastefully and with full consciousness that harm to one would mean harm to all — the realization at last of the meaning of the word Commonwealth.' In *The Dream of John Ball* the priest remarks, 'Forsooth, brothers, fellowship is heaven and lack of fellowship is hell. Fellowship is life.' Morris, says one of his admirers, 'appeals to love, not to hatred, to the making of life and happiness, not to the evoking of the powers of destruction and death'.* It was an ideal which he summed up in the slogan 'One for all and all for one'. This enthusiasm was expressed in the songs Morris wrote for the socialist movement. Sentimental, rumbustious, and sincere.

Come hither, lads, and harken, for a tale there is to tell,
Of the wonderful days a-coming when all shall be better than well.
And the tale shall be told of a country, a land in the midst of the sea
And folk shall call it England in the days that are going to be.

The ideal he depicts is peaceful, agrarian and domestic. What after all, he asks, is worth winning? Not power, military glory, Empire.

Nay, what, save the lovely city, and the little house on the hill?

He exhorts the workmen no longer to 'lie in the hell our hands have

---

* J. B. GLASIER, *Socialism in Song*. An appreciation of WILLIAM MORRIS's *Chants for Socialists*. Manchester, 1920. Glasier points out that Morris was a pioneer in this field. Edward Carpenter's 'England Arise' had never much taken on, and Jim Connel's 'Red Flag', the popular battle cry of the Movement, 'is a bold vibrant hymn with a fine international note; it suffers, however, from its rather penetential air.' 'Pilgrims of Hope' and 'Chants for Socialists', are available, he says, in a 'dainty little volume . .. beautifully printed and handy to the pocket'. The songs are entitled 'The Day is Coming', 'The Voice of Toil', 'No Master', etc. Orwell was perhaps indebted to them for his songs in *Animal Farm*.

won'. 'Shoulder to shoulder, e're the world grows older', they are to
create beauty and commonwealth.

> Or who are these, with eyes aflame,
> And hands to deal and do?

They are the workers of his imagination.

Morris also became a socialist since he believed that work should
be enjoyable. Life should be full, balanced, vigorous; and happiness,
toleration and courtesy, the natural expression of man. They would
be achieved through a simple life, devoid of luxury. In contrast to
Treitschke, he thought servants unnecessary. The classless society
would be simple and, indeed, austere. He was first converted to
socialism by reading J. S. Mill's arguments against it, which put the
other side with so much lucidity. He was then quite ignorant of
economic theory. 'When I joined the Democratic Federation I had
never so much as opened Adam Smith or heard of Ricardo and Karl
Marx.' Owen he had always admired. 'The honoured name of
Robert Owen', he wrote, represented 'the nobler hopes of our day,
just as More was of his.' Saint-Simon, Fourier and Proudhon had
maintained their gospel in a darkening world. He particularly
admired Fourier, 'since his doctrine of the necessity and possibility of
making labour attractive is one which socialism can by no means do
without'. Marx, he believed, had revealed to the workers that under
Capitalism they were inevitably exploited, and that their emancipation was equally inevitable. Morris had assimilated the Marxian
doctrine that the monopoly of capital disinherited the worker.* He
appealed also to the professional classes to turn from being the
hangers-on of plutocracy and to throw in their lot with the mass of the
people. All these influences were fused and subordinated in Morris's
passionate dislike of the moral and aesthetic consequences of great
industry. He describes 'the ghastly wastes of Lancashire and the ever-
growing squalor of London'. Was it 'all to end', he asked, 'in a
counting-house on top of a cinder heap?'

Hence the indictment of poverty, war and modern government.
'We sit starving', he writes, as Shaw wrote in *Fabian Essays*, 'amid our
gold — the Midas of the Ages.' Competitive capitalism did not even
release the full power of modern industry. It produced 'artificial
famine'. In consequence, degradation — lives 'too much beset with

---

* Of *Das Kapital* he wrote that he 'suffered agonies of confusion of the brain over
reading the pure economics of that great work . . . Anyhow, I read what I could . . .
JACKSON, op. cit., p. 276.

sordid anxiety for them to be able to think and feel with the more fortunate people . . .' The whole basis of society, with its contrast of rich and poor, was 'incurably vicious'. Hence, he believed, the weakness of modern art, with no roots in the people.

What business, indeed, have we with art, unless all can share it? Like Tolstoi, he represents 'the conscience-stricken gentry'. He can write of 'feasting within earshot of a patient on the rack'. Haunted by this conviction, he threw himself into all the squalid bickering of sparse audiences at street corners. He was, perhaps, driven to these uncongenial courses by an underlying sadness. Morris was an agnostic, much influenced by the study of the Icelandic Sagas in the original. He felt more at home in Reykjavik than in Rome. This saga-philosophy had its undercurrent of pessimism.*

He was also driven to revolution by the craftsman's exasperation with inefficient technique. Mass-poverty of the people, Morris believed, was due to the misuse of machinery. War, that other scourge of humanity, is imbecile waste. It is the consequence of the nation state. The political unit, he believed, should be no longer the nation but the commune. What, he demanded, was a nation? 'A body of people kept together for purposes of rivalry and war with similar bodies, and when competition shall have given place to combination, the function of the nation shall be gone.'[10]

This detestation of government was reflected in Morris's tactics as well as his strategy. He tends to waver between the token revolution depicted in *News from Nowhere*, and the hope that the socialist commonwealth can be achieved by consent. But he is predominantly a revolutionary, and his attacks on the ruling classes are often ferocious. He never believed that society could be saved by a system. 'The paraphernalia of official authority' is 'after all a burden, even when it is exercised by the delegation of the whole people and in accordance with their wishes.' He hoped that the transformation would come through the pressure of opinion, and by acknowledgment of the need for change; by 'the intelligence of civilization'. It might be that the monopolists would one day give up their privileges uncompelled, 'yield with a good grace'.[11] His main stress was on propaganda, permeation, not political manœuvre. He warned his followers, in his more realistic moments, to remember 'how hard other tyrannies have died'. He understood, also, the underdog envy which could rise from the 'intellectual slavery of the masses'. Even

---

* See A. CLUTTON BROCK, op. cit., p. 119, q.v. for an interesting treatment of this side of William Morris.

the dangers of an intellectual proletariat; of a class with factual knowledge and without leisure or tradition; of the cult of mean and tabloid information.

Hence his insistence on humane upbringing. His romantic vision of a quasi-medieval commonwealth went along with a sense of educational mission. 'I believe,' he wrote, 'that socialism is advancing and will advance more and more as education spreads.'[12] Here was a greater hope than in any political action. Morris was haunted by the waste of contemporary society. By the sense of 'Innumerable lives which are spent in toil, unrelieved by hope and uncheered by praise'. Work, he believed, should bring happiness. Only a technological incompetence no longer necessary could excuse the drudgery to which the vast mass of mankind are condemned. 'Nothing', he wrote, 'shall convince me that such a labour as this is good or necessary to civilization.'

Morris was admitted to be the most influential socialist of his day. The vision of this craftsman and poet hung before the eyes of Fabian administrators. Was it a mirage? At first glance, the attempt to revert to a quasi-medieval and largely pre-industrial society seems unpractical. Brought up in comfort and independence, Morris habitually ignored the precariousness of the hard-won civilization he condemned — the gruelling struggle out of which, in harder climates and vaster territories, the great majority of mankind have painfully achieved the rudiments of minority culture. Even the Victorian men of the world, Maine and Lecky, for example, with their wary realism, would seem to put this idealist out of court. The revolutionaries of the Continent, stained and hardened in their struggle with the police-state, would regard such tactics as amateurish and indefensible.

Yet Morris's influence, like Owen's, was decisive for British socialism. Fabian statistics could never command the enthusiasm Morris could arouse. He eloquently expressed the perennial communitarian distrust of government, and the artist's detestation of the ugliness of nineteenth-century industry. Above all, he insisted that politics and industry should be subordinated to life. 'For after all,' he wrote, 'what is the true end of all politics and all commerce if it is not to bring about a state of things in which all men may live a life at peace . . . ?'

Was his Utopia a tame and provincial dream? After his time the evils of centralized power and top-heavy industry, class hatred and nationalism, were destined to increase. If the conquest of poverty has been rendered technologically more practicable, the results of the misuse of science have become even more appalling. It may be that the diffusion of economic and political power, greater equality of possessions, and a habit of civilized conduct widely spread, are inexorably demanded by the conditions of modern life. It may seem an ordinary ideal. Such objectives were scorned and derided by Treitschke and Nietzsche and Sorel. Yet Morris was perhaps the realist.

Mutatis mutandis, an egalitarian and pacific society, within a wider world-order, may prove the only way of survival. And upon some such classless and provincial commonwealth, a more powerful, varied and cosmopolitan civilization might in time be built. For as St. Paul said, without charity men are but sounding brass, and as Aristotle insists, without the good life, power is meaningless.[13] If the course of events since Morris's time have dwarfed and obscured his vision, they have emphasized the cardinal importance of the values he untiringly vindicated.

The British social-democratic movement which followed the liberal political reforms of the nineteenth century, had thus begun its double attack on the citadels of great capitalism. On the one hand were the Fabians, with their steady administrative zeal, command of detail, and belief in the capture of political power within the constitution. They accepted bureaucracy and the centralized state. They believed in the social organism and in the inevitability of democratic progress. They forged the weapons which were in time to win massive political power. Their disciples were to attempt a gradual and peaceful strangulation of the old order. They were the heirs of the Utilitarian improvers, representative also of a new interest. They laid the bureaucratic, formidable and centralized foundation of the Welfare State.

On the other hand was William Morris. He represents the visionary sentiment which also inspired the socialist movement. The ideal of the simple life; of the early W.E.A.; of the garden suburb, of emancipated children and the hikers on the downs. As the Fabians derived from Utilitarian reform and the liberal humanism of T. H. Green and Bosanquet, so Morris carried on the influence of Owen. Both these strains are interwoven in the humane, agnostic and insular ideology of early British socialism. They still persist.* This outlook was at once a limitation and a strength. Outside in the world, vast and sinister manœuvres of armed power were being

* See *New Fabian Essays*, edited R. H. S. Crossman, 1952.

slowly conducted. The glamour of royalty and the prestige of arms remained predominant, the rivalry of Imperial interests. At the focus of the gathering thundercloud lay the centre of the enormous British Empire. Already it was beginning to show the first symptoms of economic decline, and still it was the greatest naval and financial power in the world. Weighted with these responsibilities, the rulers of this vast concern peered into the darkening future, while, within the confines of the island, Fabian administrators and poetic revolutionaries wove their miniature ideas. To the superficial observer their astonishing and rapid influence may seem surprising. After two world wars and unprecedented economic upheaval, a Socialist government was to be swept to power by the votes of a huge electorate. It was to preside over a social revolution which sent its repercussions across the entire Commonwealth. In a deeper historical perspective, this change was, perhaps, inevitable and even salutary. For the Socialists had faced the next stage in the great problem of the nineteenth and twentieth centuries, the peaceful adaptation of traditional ways of life to the mass society created by the industrial and technical revolutions. In the British tradition of compromise, and with a less insular bias, their Conservative rivals were to do the same. The constitutional and moral standards of Greene and Acton were carried on with twentieth-century politics.

I V

While the Fabians and William Morris were developing social democratic thought in England, Bernstein (1850-1932), in Germany, was beginning a fundamental revision of Marxism.* He had much in common with the Fabians, but he differed from them in a constant preoccupation with Marxist beliefs, and in a concern for theoretical consistency from which the English writers were exempt. This concern does not prevent his revision of Marxism from being deeply considered. But while the theorists of British social democracy presented a solid front, and with time and opportunity, were to

* Eduard Bernstein was born of Jewish parents, the son of a minor railway-employé in Berlin. He became a bank clerk, but in 1878 abandoned this employment for Social-Democratic journalism. He spent over twenty years in exile in Switzerland and England, and organized clandestine Social-Democratic congresses at Zurich. For his family background see *Eduard Bernstein von 1850-1872. Kindheit und Jugendjahre* (Berlin, 1926), and for his often entertaining impressions of England *My Years of Exile, Reminiscences of a Socialist.* Trans. B. Miall. London, 1921. His principal works are: *Die Voraussetzungen des Sozialismus und die Aufgaben der Sozialdemokratie,* 1899 (translated by Alexandre Cohen, as *Socialisme Théorique et Socialdémocratie Pratique.* Recherches Sociales. Stock. Paris, 1900). *Geschichte und Theorie des Sozialismus,* 1901; *Sozialismus und Demokratie in der grossen Englischen Revolution,* 1922.

provide leadership and win power, the theoretical virtuosity of their German counterparts gave rise to damaging internal feuds which handicapped German social democrats in politics. And where the constitutionalism of the Fabians was appropriate to their stable British surroundings, the constitutionalism of the Germans was later to prove vulnerable in a world of provincial separatists, militant Communism, Fascist Freikorps and untamed military power.

The *Voraussetzungen des Sozialismus*, Bernstein's most important book, contains a great deal of good sense in terms of Germany of 1899, though not of Hitlerite Germany. Its tone is rather apologetic. He is struggling, with some diffidence and with an eye to the opinion of his political colleagues, out of the original Marx -Engels orthodoxy. The *Communist Manifesto*, he declares, was strategically right. He merely points out that the tactical timing for revolution was unsound. It would not only be 'useless' but 'stupid' to deny that the mounting economic crises which were to wreck bourgeois society have not developed as predicted.[14] On the contrary, the prosperity of capitalist civilization has greatly increased. The middle class has changed; it has certainly not been destroyed. Further, liberalism has increasingly diffused political power. 'The more that the political institutions of modern states are democratized, the more the necessity ... of great political catastrophes disappears.'[15] Speculations about a political apocalypse are now irrelevant. The task is to take advantage of the situation; to prepare the working class for political responsibility, and take the next step into economic justice from the vantage point of political democracy. To achieve power one must have political rights; the immediate task is to extend them. 'In our time', he wrote, 'we achieve by the ballot box ... reforms which a century ago needed bloody revolution.' He demands, he insists, only realism from his fellow socialists. He intends only to 'combat the ... vestiges of Utopian thought in Socialist theory'.[16] With this end in view, he quotes the later Engels with effect. For in a preface, written in 1894, to his earlier *Class War in France*, Engels himself had admitted it was time to abandon the barricades. Power should be won gradually, by legal means. History, he had written, has proved us wrong in expecting one more crisis and then explosion.[17] The conditions as they were in 1848 had altered: the method of struggle had therefore changed. 'The common form of all the old revolutions,' Engels had continued, 'was that they were revolutions of minorities. Now majority revolutions by the capture of mass opinion are necessary.' Otherwise the superior technical power of the modern state will win. The struggle must then be long, slow and obstinate. The right to vote must, therefore, be exploited. From a 'means of duping the people' it must be transformed into an instrument of emancipation. The day of revolutions by small politically conscious minorities, at the head of politically unconscious masses, is over. Now the correct tactical move is to capture the bourgeois administration.* This will produce a 'steady, spontaneous and irresistible' change which will 'come about as quietly as a process of nature'. The irony of world history, Engels had pointed out, 'has turned everything upside down. We revolutionaries . . . are prospering much more by legal methods than by illegal ones . . . the parties of order, as they call themselves, will be destroyed by the legal state they have themselves created'. Engels had even compared the communists to the early Christians, who thirty years after the worst persecutions, had obtained official recognition through legal means and the pressure of opinion.

This tactical abandonment of the apocalypse, sanctioned by Engels, implied an empirical outlook alien to the dialectic certainty of orthodox Marxist thought. Bernstein, who had been much influenced by English ideas, was accused by his more rigid colleagues of wearing 'English spectacles'. Engels, it was alleged, was in his dotage when he wrote the compromising words.

But Bernstein went further. An attack on the Dialectic itself could now hardly be avoided. Marx, he maintained, had indeed created in the Dialectic a key to great historical discoveries; he had perceived historical forces as living things. But his very genius had drawn him into excessive dogma, into a kind of quasi-Calvinist determinism, now in need of correction before the development of events. It is necessary, he argued, to emancipate thought from the rigid *Kräfteparallelogramm* of the Dialectic. Marx and Engels, in fact, had left to their successors the task of restoring harmony between theory and practice. And we now see the materialist concept of history in a different light. The original theory can thus be perfected through criticism inspired by realism and respect. The Dialectic, if rigidly interpreted, now constitutes a 'perfidious element' in Marxist thought; an obstacle, no longer a key.[18] This basically Hegelian theory, in which the Prussian 'Polizeistaat' culminated, is inefficient under modern conditions.

---

* It is interesting to note that the same view was taken by Hitler. After the failure of the Munich *putsch*, he set himself to create a mass movement which was aimed at the constitutional capture of the machinery of the state. In Russia, on the other hand, where more primitive conditions prevailed, Lenin achieved power by the minority coup recommended by the more orthodox Marxist tactics.

The old theory, too, had always demanded the internal collapse of capitalist society as the prelude to revolution. The actual prosperity of the bourgeois world, the diffusion of capital, the mixing of classes, must therefore appear an obstacle. If, on the other hand, one regards the increase and diffusion of wealth and democracy as the great socialist chance to capture political power, the situation is encouraging. We must abandon the theory of 'necessary misery'. Bernstein quotes figures for the increase of the income groups £150-£1000 a year in England from 300,000 in 1851 to 990,000 in 1881.[19] Similar increases have occurred in France. If the orthodox theory of surplus value had been correct, this diffusion of smaller capitalist property could never have occurred. 'The capitalist magnates ought to have their bellies much fuller.' In Germany, also, the vast majority of enterprises are on a small scale. In France, Austria and Switzerland, the peasant agricultural interest still predominates. The vitality of small enterprise is incontestable. And the development of modern credit has increased popular purchasing power. Local depression may be still expected, but breakdown is inconceivable. And what of the rise of the salaried managerial class?

The modern wage-earners, he also insisted, are no longer a homogeneous mass. Peasant and industrial operatives cannot be equated, and the objective of peasants everywhere is land. Marx and Engels had before their eyes only the undifferentiated masses of the age of the Revolution.[20] Hence, in part, their belief in centralization and revolution for its own sake. Under the complex conditions of modern society, where revolution may lead to economic paralysis, the object should be quite different: to pass 'without violent convulsions from the actual social order to a superior one'.[21] Hence, he wrote, 'it seems to me also advisable to moderate declarations of war against liberalism. Socialism is its legitimate heir'.[22] In fact the conquest, not the destruction, of the bourgeois political system is the 'primordial and indispensable condition' for a realization of socialist aims. Feudal institutions, which are rigid, may have needed destruction by violence. Modern liberal institutions are quite different, capable of transformation and development. There is no need, he insists, to destroy them. Moreover, the fact must be accepted that the modern proletariat are not, as Marx and Engels had believed, without a country. They are now full national citizens, increasingly bound up with the interests of their state. The entire dissolution of nations is now unlikely: nor is it desirable. The British socialist, Hyndman, admits that naval supremacy is necessary to his country.

Similarly, Bernstein argues that Germany needs colonies, though they should be humanely administrated.[23] The old idea of cosmopolitan revolution is obsolete. Geographical and political realities must be faced.*

Following the anglicized ideas that Plekhanov, Kautsky and Rosa Luxemburg found so reprehensible, Bernstein quotes, in the original, the English proverb 'never swop horses whilst crossing a stream'. He also declares that the English have a useful word — 'cant'. It dates from the seventeenth century and signifies false rhetoric and pious jargon. Plekhanov has called him an 'enemy of scientific socialism'. Scientific socialism, indeed! If ever the word science has become pure 'cant' it has here.[24] Plekhanov had also said that Bernstein, with his weak intellect, had been imposed upon by the prosperity of English capitalism. Marx, with his redoubtable genius, had been impervious to it, though he lived so long in the island. Undaunted, Bernstein replied that one can be right even against Marx. 'The great scientific mind was at the same time the prisoner of a doctrine.' The task is how to rid communist thought of its Utopian Dialectic legacy. Nor should we entertain illusions about the proletariat. It is ridiculous to say that all virtue is confined to one class. Even now, the mass of the workers are not politically advanced enough for the exercise of power. Intelligent working men understand this. Only intellectuals, who have never lived with the people, idealize them — an old song which age has not made more attractive. We must now take the workers as they are. Plekhanov may call him a Philistine: he is merely a realist. English Trade Union leaders know better than intellectuals what they are about. They encourage the Temperance movement; they know how necessary it is. Only the gradual long-term working of social democracy will raise the political capacity of the people. How can we 'exact from a class of which the majority are badly lodged, ill educated and underpaid, the high degree of intelligence and morality, which would come from the establishment and duration of the socialist community?'[25]

Social democracy, he declared, with an elephantine joke, needs a Kant against cant. This task he has undertaken. Bernstein is determined, in all humility, to separate the wheat from the chaff. Reality must never be obscured by dogma. It is fatal to resist the tide of economic and political development. It is, actually, a profoundly un-Marxist thing to do. The strategy of revolution must, indeed, remain constant; its tactics and ideology must be flexible.

* See Professor F. A. HAYEK, *The Road to Serfdom*. London, 1944, in this context.

On the modern evidence, catastrophe and class war are not inevitable. The old slogans are superseded.

So Bernstein struggled out of the toils of Marxist dogma into an outlook not dissimilar to that of Fabian socialism. Unfortunately for his followers, it was a theory not then well suited to its German surroundings, to the harsh realities of Wilhelmine political and military power.

v

The social democratic writers hitherto examined have been able but uninspired, while the Utopian William Morris, with his sentimental and aesthetic revolt, is so characteristically English as to have exercised little influence outside the island. It was for the French to produce far the most forceful, eloquent and versatile exponent of social democracy at that time. The greatest orator in the old style in France, it has been claimed, since Bossuet; one of the most brilliant products of the École Normale Supérieure; a 'paysan cultivé' with his roots in Languedoc; an untiring politician and publicist, Jean Jaurès seems an incarnation of militant French humanism. He was the greatest socialist leader in Europe, and his assassination, at fifty-four, on the eve of the first world war, was a symbolic disaster.*

* August Marie Joseph Jean Jaurès was born at Castres in the upland province of Tarn in Languedoc in 1859. His father was a small cloth-dealer and farmer. He entered the Collège Sainte-Barbe at Paris and passed first into the École Normale Supérieure in 1878. He taught at Albi and Toulouse, where from 1885 to 1898 he was Maître de Conférences and later a Professor of Philosophy. In 1885 he was elected Deputy for Tarn, and at once made his mark in politics. Defeated in the election of 1889, he was re-elected in 1893 and joined the Socialist Party. He played a vigorous part in the Dreyfus controversy, in the launching of L'Humanité (1904), in internal debate with Guesde on Socialist policy, and in the formation of socialist unity in 1905. He provoked bitter hatred from the parties of the Right, in particular from Charles Maurras, collaborator of 1940-44. Following the incitements of proto-fascist journalism, Jaurès was assassinated in a café on July 31st, 1914.

Jaurès' academic career was outstanding and he was a compelling and popular personality. With his rural origins, he had a profound love of nature, of the 'humming life of his beloved Midi'. He was impervious to corruption and lived at Passy in a modest establishment. 'De façon générale,' wrote M. Levy, 'il est fort maladroit dans les milles détails de l'existence courante. Il n'a pas le moindre souci de l'élégance vestimentaire. Ses chapeaux sont légendaires. Et aussi ses manchettes. Mal attachées, elles s'échappent parfois de la chemise au cours de l'action oratoire. Un soir, l'une d'elles est recueillie par les membres des Jeunesses et mise en tombola pour une fête socialiste.' (Op. cit., p. ix, q.v.) His appearance was forcible and reassuring. 'Again', writes Rappoport, 'I see his plump face, eager and happy, like a kindly bearded ogre; his small eyes bright and smiling . . . I see him pacing up and down the platform walking with heavy steps like a bear.' His bold handwriting is characteristic. (See RAPPOPORT, p. viii.)

His principal works are: De Primis Socialismi Germanici Lineamentis, Toulouse, 1891; Les Preuves, 1898; Études Socialistes (Cahiers de la Quinzaine, Paris, 1901); Discours Parliamentaires, 1889-94. Paris, 1904; Contributions to L'Histoire Socialiste (undated), (12 vols.) second edition edited A. Mathiez, 1922-24; L'Armée Nouvelle, first edition (undated), second edition, Paris, 1915 (8 vols.). See Œuvres edited Max Bonnafous. Rieder, Paris,

'Solide, trapu, large d'épaules . . . un homme bien accroché au sol de France,' Jaurès attempted to be at once a patriot and an internationalist. He was a formidable personality. 'A veritable athlete of the platform,' writes his biographer Rappoport, 'he cried, he thundered, he stormed . . . he was at once passionate and exact. Clear and keen thought alternated with sumptuous metaphor.' Jaurès was a Hellenist, a connoisseur of literature, a gourmet and raconteur. If, on occasion, a conventional rhetoric disguises contradictory thought, all is informed by a broad human sympathy. This intellectual leadership, so characteristically French, was deployed in a milieu of shifting, unstable and rancorous politics. His opponents of the Right called him a traitor. 'M. Jaurès,' wrote l'Action Française, 'c'est l'Allemagne' — a public enemy. Out of this welter of political hatred, focused on the Dreyfus case, which was to colour French political life for decades, Jaurès's ideas emerge. Their rich humanity is worth study in the light of the sometimes anaemic tradition of British socialist thought. Here are ideas still well worth consideration by those concerned with neo-Fabian social democracy. Jaurès had none of Webb's Philistinism, nor the touch of crankery which limited Morris's appeal. His mind was broad-based on a more vigorous humanism, at once French and European.

His thought may be regarded under four headings. The revision of Marxism; the anticipation of the Fascist danger; the attempt to combine patriotism with international solidarity, and the assertion of a humanist socialism reflecting 'la dignité humaine'. Like Bernstein, he was deeply preoccupied with Marxist theory. But he discarded the more rigid dogmas with greater zest. He attempted, he declared, to vindicate Marx against his own rhetoric and the misinterpretation of his narrower followers. Marx, he maintained, never stood for pure materialism: consider how he detests the Utilitarians. He had described with new insight how broad economic forces permeate men's minds and condition the human spirit; they are 'forces sociales, des forces collectives, des forces historiques, dont la puissance dépasse celle des mobiles individuels et égoïstes'.[26] Yet, intimate and powerful as they may be, he argued — against Lafargue — far from dominating thought, they are in turn dominated by it. 'La

1931-39 (9 vols.). The best selection is by L. Lévy, with an introduction, Anthologie de Jean Jaurès, Penguin Editions, London, 1947.

See also: CHARLES RAPPOPORT, Jean Jaurès: l'homme, le penseur, le socialiste. Paris, 1915; L. Lévy-Bruhl, Quelques Pages sur Jean Jaurès. Paris, 1916; MARGARET PEASE, Jean Jaurès, Socialist and Humanitarian. London, 1916; J. HAMPDEN JACKSON, Jean Jaurès, his Life and Work. London, 1943.

complication presque infinie de la vie humaine ne se laisse pas réduire brutalement, mécaniquement à une formule économique.' Mind is conditioned by the past, but we need not oppose material and ideal. They are combined in an indissoluble evolution. It was fatuous, he declared, to substitute 'a series of abstract and artificial revolutions' for the more profoundly revolutionary development defined with so much insight by Marx as an economic historian.

This humanity and sense of economic history always coloured Jaurès's thought. He therefore stressed continuity. Though a socialist, he did not depreciate the history of France. 'My friends,' he told a working-class audience, 'we are the true heirs of our ancestral hearths.' The modern world, he pointed out, was the first great civilization with a knowledge of its distant past. Like Michelet, by whom he was deeply influenced, he sensed the great sweep of French history in all its rich variety of national and provincial life. 'Je trouve médiocres', he said, 'les hommes qui ne savent pas reconnaître dans le présent la force accumulée des grandeurs du passé et le gage des grandeurs de l'avenir.' Here was no Sorelian or extreme Marxist repudiation of the past, rather an enrichment of a great tradition. He therefore never depicts the state as the mere executive committee of the bourgeoisie. He regarded the constitution as a rampart against clerical and military reaction. It is socialism, he insists, that will give the full content to the Declaration of the Rights of Man. Like Bernstein, he thought it right for socialists to participate in bourgeois governments. It was impossible, he said, to decide that burning question by 'the blind invocation of the formula of Class War'. 'C'est le devoir du prolétariat socialiste de marcher avec les fractions bourgeoises qui ne veulent pas revenir en arrière.' Like Bernstein, he believed that it is no concern of socialists to push the bourgeois world into deeper degradation. 'Nous n'avons pas voulu de cette flétrissure de honte sur l'aurore du prolétariat.'* To maintain that the people has no part in the State, 'condemned to be nothing until it becomes everything', is to turn back the great march of events and to destroy all that the proletariat has won. Such abstract fanaticism of thought is fatal; it alienates poten-

* For this controversy see, in particular, *Les deux Méthodes. Conférence par Jean Jaurès et Jules Guesde.* Lille, 1900. Guesde, like Sorel, insisted that 'l'embourgeoisement' would be fatal to the revolution. See in particular p. 9 and pp. 32-3 (Éditions du Parti Socialiste. Paris, 1931). The contrast between Jaurès and Guesde was symbolic. The one, a Southern Frenchman, a typical radical bourgeois of the Left centre; the other, the austere, pedantic prophet of Marxism, coming from the dour mining area of North-Eastern France.

tial followers. All the great revolutions of history have been made by infiltration.

With his strong sense of continuity, Jaurès foresaw, with remarkable insight the threat to social democracy of movements destined to contribute to Fascism and Nihilism. France, he believed, was menaced by 'le retour offensive de toutes les forces du passé, par le retour offensive de la barbarie féodale'. The proletariat should combine with all elements of bourgeois society hostile to reaction and destruction for its own sake. For such destruction was idiotic. He warned the youth of France not to be seduced by the already fashionable cult of the irrational. In particular, against his fellow *normalien* and contemporary, Bergson. 'Distrust those', he said, 'who ... in the name of philosophy, of instinct or intuition, preach the abdication of intelligence.'[27] This objectivity was encouraged by Durkheim, by whom Jaurès was influenced.

Though he detested militarism, Jaurès was a patriot. Though a pacifist, he composed *L'Armée Nouvelle*, a large work on the regeneration of the French forces. And here, perhaps, is the greatest weakness of his thought. On the one hand he had the reputation of an internationalist with pacifist convictions, and worked to that end: he denounced an international system which drifted into war of its own momentum. Even in democratic countries, he remarks, 'War can be unchained without the consent of the people, without their knowledge.' He warned his public that 'system-ridden and infatuated men can create the irreparable'; that 'War and peace are still unaffected by the law of democracy.' In one mood, he could incite the peoples to 'break these governments of delirium, rapine and murder'. If, he declared in July 1914, at Brussels on the eve of his death, 'appeal is made to secret treaties with Russia, we shall appeal to public Treaties with Humanity'. He could advocate France's repudiation of her alliances, an attempt to mediate between Great Britain and Germany. In the circumstances, a dangerous and foolish position.*

In another mood, he was very different. It was impossible, he said, to accept the mutilation of Alsace and Lorraine. He could write of 'l'haleine épaisse du César tudesque'. He desired social regeneration through a reconstituted, defensive, army. And his sympathies were always in the Western camp. He understood, as have few Frenchmen, the strength of the British Commonwealth. It was

---

* For an able treatment of the Socialist attitude to war see MILORAD M. DRACHKOVITCH, *Les Socialismes Français et Allemand et le Problème de la guerre 1870-1914. Droz. Geneva,* 1953.

regarded, he said, by its components as 'a protection, not a prison'. And although the United States might seem the embodiment of ruthless capitalism, it also embodied the Puritan passion for justice and liberty.

With these contradictions, his contribution to international problems did not go much beyond Mazzini's. He shared the weakness of most contemporary liberal and social-democratic international thought. 'Mais ce qui est certain', he could write in *l'Armée Nouvelle*, 'c'est que la volonté irréductible de l'Internationale est qu'aucune patrie n'ait à souffrir dans son autonomie . . . C'est dans l'Internationale que l'indépendance des nations a sa plus haute garantie.'[28] Like Mazzini, he sought a regenerated patriotism within sovereign states. 'La grande force collective, la grande passion collective des peuples organisés, au lieu de se déchaîner en violence d'orgueil et de convoitise, sera soumise à la loi supérieure de l'ordre humain, réglée et pénétrée jusqu'en son fond par l'idée du travail, de la justice et de la paix.'

Jaurès tends to swamp the facts of power and conflict in a cataract of eloquent humanism. Yet his broad vitality was alien to national or class hate. His socialism was an affirmation of life. He can cite the example of General Hoche, who when a political prisoner, consoled himself by reading Rabelais. Jaurès was an optimist, with a redoubtable confidence in the future. 'Pas d'idéal ascétique', he wrote, 'la justice ne sera pas achetée au prix des joies de la vie.' A remark worth pondering by socialist bureaucrats.[29] He praised Saint-Simon and Fourier because they advocated a world of plenty and expansion. 'Le fouriérisme et le saint-simonisme ne sont pas la négation . . . de la vie moderne, mais au contraire son élargissement passioné.' Fourier, in particular, understood that disorder and injustice might be remedied not by paralysing production, but by vastly increasing it. Proudhon, as well, had made a realistic contribution. He had understood the power of the small proprietor better than Marx. Following Proudhon, Jaurès repudiates the tentacular state. 'Le Socialisme', he declared, 'n'est pas l'Étatisme.' 'Whether the *patron* calls himself the State or Schneider, there is always the same dependence and the same penury: and if socialism were to become merely the extension of actual state ownership . . . it would be nothing but a gigantic fraud.' The existing State may of course be politically exploited, but it must also be transformed. In its present form it is 'the servant of a brutal machine which pounds and crushes the workers as a steam press crushes grapes, which exudes riches for the fortunate and leaves only a sterile residue for the poor'. True socialism will not merely take over from a crumbling state its hierarchy of servile bureaucrats and 'son patronat d'État dur au salarié et compliqué d'aridité fiscale, pour bâtir avec ces deux pierres usées la maison fraternelle'.[30] The socialist State will not be simply the greatest of capitalists, exploiting the people. It will be the permanent guardian of individual liberty. It must create the highest freedom, and in 'organized collectivism the full force of individual initiative will expand'.[31] It was on personality, the cult of Human Rights, on the 'high dignity of the Spirit of Man', that the socialist society must be built. The great achievement of the fathers of socialism had been 'to interrupt the old song of human misery', to canalize into constructive channels the spiritual force long wasted in superstition. Marxist determinism applied, he insisted, only to what Marx had termed the pre-historic phase of history. Now it was the task of his interpreters to thrust out from the reign of the unconscious into an historic age. Then at last the fullness of life will be expressed. Already, he declared, the economic system which has enslaved humanity is beginning to be transformed. 'C'est comme le premier frisson qui dans la forêt humaine n'emmène que quelques feuilles, mais qui annonce les grands souffles prochains et les vastes ébranlements.' Though upon the waves of economic determinism 'the poor fisherman's barque may rise to discern the first rays of dawn', the moralization of history will be an achievement of the spirit. In the well-known preface to the *Histoire-Socialiste*, he writes, the inspiration of the work derives at once from Marx, from Michelet, and from Plutarch. Thus the interpenetration of classes will be secured, the class war transcended, the cataclysm avoided and France and small property secured. From Marx will come the understanding of the great forces of economic change, from Michelet spiritual insight, from Plutarch the affirmation of will.*

It was a sanguine and vigorous exposition of socialist humanism. Was such a gospel doomed before the reaction of Left and Right? It was long to be out of fashion among intellectuals in France. The cult of violence for its own sake, of despair of politics and individualist 'disengagement', was to bring in its returns during the second world war. Today Jaurès is often dismissed as a mere orator in the old nineteenth-century style, a man altogether too eloquent, too visionary. In the existentialist cafés such 'engagement' is regarded as naive.

* See *Histoire Socialiste, 1789-1900. Sous la direction de Jean Jaurès* (12 vols.) first edition (undated), vol. I, p. 8. The frontispiece of peasants, mattock, fork and scythe on shoulder, advancing with their wives and children into a rich countryside lit by a rising sun, makes a significant comparison with the more bookish Fabian design.

Modern conditions make the engagement of intellectuals a necessity. Today the *Trahison des Clercs* is going out of fashion. The fact remains Bernstein had miscalculated the milieu of social democracy in Germany. Had Jaurès miscalculated it in France? That has been the great question of French politics ever since the Dreyfus case. Or did Jaurès, as one may hope, express through all the instability and bitterness of French politics, the realist spirit of the France of which he was so vigorous an embodiment, and so prove himself the greatest exponent of early-twentieth-century social democracy in Europe?

CHAPTER XII

MODERN SOCIOLOGISTS: DURKHEIM ON ENVIRONMENT: GRAHAM WALLAS AND SOCIAL PSYCHOLOGY

B Y the close of the nineteenth century the political theory of social democracy had been defined. It was increasingly to influence the West. With trans-Atlantic backing, it was to take deeper root in Europe and beyond, and to provide, over great Asiatic and African territories, a modern version of constitutional self-government, a constructive alternative to Communist revolution.

This new version of constitutional commonwealth was to find massive reinforcement in modern scientific sociology. The latest achievement of professional knowledge, the underlying motif of the whole period, it had now become extremely important. The relatively crude attempts of Comte were no longer representative, if the original inspiration is Saint-Simonian.

The two major and pervasive discoveries which profoundly affected the study of society, Darwin's creation of a new and spreading sense of environment in space and time, and the individual and social implications of the new psychology, were to have wide sociological effects. The sociologists had long been developing important ideas foreshadowed by Montesquieu, Saint-Simon, Comte and the mid-century anthropologists, of whom Tylor has been taken as an example. In France an analytical approach, with an emphasis on environment and institutions, had come to dominate historical speculation in the writings of Taine.* It was to reach its fuller expression in Émile Durkheim, a writer to whom modern anthropologists and students of society are deeply indebted.

In England, on a more political level, a rather similar, less massive, technique was explored by Graham Wallas, whose contribution to Fabian ideas has already been noticed, and who brought a new psychological observation to bear on the workings of society. L. T. Hobhouse, the critic of Idealism, also made some contribution in

---

* A fine modern example of this tradition are the works of SEIGNOBOS, whose *A History of the French People* (Trans., London, 1933) and *The Rise of European Civilization*. Cape, 1939, are monuments of dry objectivity, in which political events are strictly subordinated to the history of society. There is still room for such a treatment of English history.

this field in his *Morals in Evolution.** Durkheim and Wallas may be taken as more representative. They can here only be briefly considered. The reader will find it rewarding to investigate this original and fruitful study, which leads into all the elaborate techniques of contemporary sociology. In the light of this systematic research, now carried on most fully in America, the Marxist claim to have devised a science of politics will not bear examination, though Marxist emphasis on environment has given the new method support. The combination of humanism and science, which these writers represent, is clearly of great value in strengthening the theory of civilized government and in adapting constitutionalism to the modern world.

II

The writings of Durkheim are extensive and technical.† Here only his most important work, *Les Règles de la Méthode Sociologique* and his *Le Socialisme* will be briefly examined. Together with his *De la Division du Travail Social*, they marked a new approach to the environmental study of civilized as well as of primitive societies. Here the social fabric, invoked by Green and his followers, as the expression of will and the basis of sovereignty, is objectively analysed. Such a departure was of great importance to political theory, and should be closely related to the older tradition. Old problems are freshly illuminated — the basis of authority, the relation of the individual and the state, of society to government; the conflicting theories of positive and customary law.

Following Durkheim, sociologists have since tended to abandon mid-nineteenth-century attempts at total explanation. The reckless historicism of Comte, for example, and the more fruitful, but still over-sanguine, attempts of Maine, Bagehot and Tylor are now superseded. A new technique has been applied to the study of the actual

* There were also the pioneers of crowd psychology, notably LE BON, *The Crowd, a study of the Popular Mind*, 1895; SIGHÈLE, *La Foule Criminelle*, and TROTTER, *Instincts of the Herd in Peace and War*, 1915.
† Émile Durkheim, 1858-1917. Born at Épinal, he studied in France and Germany, and became Professor at Bordeaux. His principal works are *De la Division du Travail Social*, 1893; *Les Règles de la Méthode Sociologique*, 1895; *Le Suicide*, 1897; *Le Socialisme, sa Définition, ses Débuts*, 1897; *Les Formes Élémentaires de la vie Religieuse*, 1912; *Éducation et Sociologie*, 1922. There is a translation of *Les Règles de la Méthode Sociologique* by S. A. Solavey and J. H. Mueller, with an introduction by G. E. G. Catlin. Chicago, 1938. See also C. Bouglé's preface to DURKHEIM's *Sociologie et Philosophie*, 1924, and G. DAVY, *Émile Durkheim, Contemporary Social Theories*. For the most notable application of Durkheim's method to primitive peoples, see, in particular, LÉVY-BRUHL, *Les Fonctions Mentales dans les Sociétés Inférieures* and E. E. EVANS-PRITCHARD, *Social Anthropology*. For a modern edition of *Les Règles de la Méthode Sociologique*, see tenth edition. Presses Universitaires de France, 1947.

structure of contemporary institutions and ways of life. Discarding the nineteenth-century passion for origins and the glamour of abstract speculation — whereby, in Tylor's own words, theories of the law of nature, social contact and the like 'enjoy a universal preference over sober research' — contemporary scholars examine the social patterns which make best for equilibrium and survival in a given setting.[1] In this context the clinical approach of Durkheim is particularly valuable. 'Le devoir de l'homme d'État', he writes, 'n'est plus de pousser violemment les sociétés vers un idéal qui lui paraît séduisant, mais son rôle est celui du médecin; il prévient l'éclosion des maladies par une bonne hygiène et, quand elles sont déclarées, il cherche à les guérir.'[2] This remark is worth pondering by political enthusiasts of all creeds. Not that Durkheim displays the rather supercilious defeatism of Bradley: on the contrary, he believes that social myths — themselves an organic part of the social fabric — are the medium in which the human spirit naturally develops.

Here is a vitally important idea. It is the basis for a new creative outlook — a reinforcement, without metaphysical assertions, of the social will of Green; a contribution at once to the understanding and the control of power. Aristotle had attempted, in a limited context, both the moralization of power and the analysis of society; Spinoza had held it to be the concern of political philosophers not to laugh at men or weep over them, but to understand them, and Green had developed from Rousseau the idea of a creative general will. Here, from a rather unexpected quarter, is an outlook salutary for contemporary problems, at once modern and rooted in the oldest tradition of political thought.*

Durkheim was no inhuman analyst of fated phenomena. As the doctor, to whom he refers, understands the importance of the patient's psychological state, and desires to collaborate with and conserve the patient's natural instincts and vitality, Durkheim aims at preserving civilization, as at preserving life. We have here no mere sceptical utilitarianism; rather, as with Spinoza, a conception of society as justified by the values it can realize.

Realism and exactness are also Durkheim's aims. 'Notre principal objectif, en effet, est d'étendre à la conduite humaine le rationalisme scientifique, en faisant voir, que, considérée dans le passé, elle est réductible à des rapports de cause et effet, qu'une opération non moins rationnelle peut transformer ensuite en règles d'action pour l'avenir.'[3]

* The pluralistic legal implications of this political theory were to be examined and developed by Duguit in France, by Lindsay and Laski in England.

'What we call our positivism', he insists, 'is simply the consequence of this rational method . . . that is to say, it ought not to be confounded with the metaphysical positivism of Comte and Mr. Spencer.' And he appeals, as Green and his disciples never did, to the scientists. He demands from the reader a 'state of mind similar to that of chemists and physiologists when exploring new ground . . .' The sociologists have been too confident. 'Not only do they think themselves obliged to dogmatize on all problems at once', but they believe they hold the key to problems of extreme complexity. Yet social realities must be treated as facts — even if they are not material. There is a sociology of knowledge. States of mind are as relevant as material environment, even if conditioned by it, and in our analysis of society 'the idea we have of it — that, too, is a fact'* — as Sorel realized.

How does society, in this aspect, think for and of itself? Such a medium exists, reflecting and modifying the minds of all those born into it in space and time. Burke's 'great contexture of the mysterious whole'; Green's 'impalpable congeries of the hopes and fears of a people . . . which we call the general will', both express a living reality. It must be taken account of. 'Notre principe fondamental: [c'est] la réalité objective des faits sociaux.' All consciousness is determined, as Hegel and Bradley pointed out, by its social setting. Just as the sensible world 'weighs on and colours' all our minds, so the social milieu determines 'our religion, our morality and our techniques'. Within the fabric of a given society, there is, indeed, a whole scale of personal feelings (gamme des nuances individuelles), but sooner or later, limits are imposed by the all-pervading medium in which individuals exist. This fact, this limitation, must be understood and accepted before any effective adjustment of society can be made. Durkheim sets about his analysis with constructive purpose — not as a defeatist spectator. Here is an enrichment of Hegel's idea of a spontaneous, creative society, so attractive to Green and Morris, and without the metaphysical dogma and nationalism which disfigured Hegel's thought or the class hate of Sorel.

There are, says Durkheim, two overwhelming social facts. First, the queer, changing, life of society, which seems to have its own mysterious laws; secondly, that equally fluid medium, our ideas about it. We contemplate our societies, in fact, like an observer looking at a film through defective lenses, or an addict of imperfect

* Here is opened up the whole field of the sociology of knowledge, of which, in the 'thirties, Karl Mannheim was to be the most influential exponent. See his *Ideology and Utopia*. London, 1936; *Man and Society*. London, 1940, etc. These books, though outside the range of the present study, are of particular value and contain massive bibliographies.

television. Static general rules and revelations, final for all men in all places and times, lose their validity. True 'Natural law' — the law which makes for survival — will emerge, he implies, in a different ideological form in different societies.

Durkheim regards the views of earlier sociologists in this light. They were too ambitious. They had no technique. Now, at Bordeaux, he says, we have been able to get down to the facts. What are they? First, the institutions and mentality of a given society. These are embodied in law, public opinion, language and dress. These conventions are very powerful. 'Not only are these ways of conduct or thought outside the individual, but they are endowed with an imperative and coercive power, whereby they impose them-selves on him, whether he likes it or not.'[4] They form a way of life. And all are borne along by mysterious currents determined by material and mental environment, a changing context, *sui generis*. Here is a Marxian sense of environment, without Marx's dialectical materialism, and with a great emphasis on the power of thought. In this broad tide a general will can emerge. 'Chacun est entraîné par tous.' It is thus that civilizations are built, and it is thus, alas, also, 'que des individus, parfaitement inoffensifs pour la plupart, peuvent, réunis en foule, se laisser entraîner à des actes d'atrocité'. The substructure of politics, law, economics — all society — is pervaded by this psychic ambience. As in biology, structure and life are interdependent. It follows that a 'social fact' may be defined as 'any mode of action, fixed or not, liable to bring to bear exterior compulsion on individuals.[5] Society and ideas form a single texture'.

Conventional political thought and sociology have treated abstract concepts as a law unto themselves. But ideas, as much as institutions, are evolved in the struggle for existence. They have no independent vitality, and are only real as social facts. Thus the state, family, and the rest, seem, to abstract academic theorists, the reflection of all-powerful ideas; 'that is why so many thinkers have only seen social arrangements as more or less arbitrary and artificial'. We are thus tempted to believe in abstractions. Such sociology remains unreal. The great nineteenth-century concepts — evolution, progress and the like, are ideas, not facts. 'What alone can be observed are particular societies, which grow, develop and die . . .' Actual societies are a continuous process, and each phase is not the lineal descendant of the one preceding it. On the contrary, 'the sequence of societies cannot be expressed by a geometrical line; it is much more like a tree with branches spreading in different directions'. Comte merely dogmatized — 'il constate'. Specious and oversimplified, like all abstract philosophies of history, his theory cannot do justice to the infinitely complex and ramified phenomena he pretends to explain. He presents an objective for sociology which is an illusion. The same, of course, applies to Marx. In the present state of knowledge, we are in the position of medieval doctors. We use such terms as 'state', 'sovereignty', 'democracy', and so on, as if they were scientific. Actually, they 'only awake confused notions in us, mixtures of instincts and impressions, vague prejudices and passions'. The sociologist must escape from these vulgar '*idola*'. Like Descartes, he must put aside all preconceptions. Rather such universal phenomena as kinship, custom, or domestic ways of life ought to be investigated. 'Never take as the object of research anything but a group of happenings previously defined by certain exterior characteristics common to them all, and include in the same research all that responds to that definition.'⁶ Such a study cuts clean across the abstractions of much nineteenth-century political thought.

This procedure, familiar in the treatment of primitive peoples, is applied by Durkheim to civilized societies. In the light of this method, the mysteries about the General Will, what Rousseau really meant, and similar conundrums, take on a new aspect. We are approaching a more real appreciation of actual human affairs. And there is no rigid standard. The morality of savages may be a perfectly natural and, indeed, satisfactory response to their environment. It must be judged, not in relation to our own customs, but in relation to its own setting, for morality is what public opinion in a given time and place approves. But this does not imply that one morality is as good as another. There are always two kinds of morality; one making for survival, the other for death. The normal and the pathological. Societies are like individuals. They may be in good or in bad health. Thus a technologically advanced society may thwart healthy impulse and 'darken the heart', while a technically primitive people may be happier, since they are psychologically better adjusted.* Here, at last, Durkheim's clinical approach gives a firm standard of judgment. Health means happiness, right adjustment to environment. How far short of this standard are the monstrous garrison states of the mid-twentieth century, and the bogus, abstract, pseudo-scientific ideas of class and race conflict which they reflect! 'The happy develop-

* F. H. Bradley held a similar view, but made nothing constructive of it. Margaret Mead's account of the anthropology of primitive peoples in relation to modern western societies has followed up this theme; see her *Coming of Age in Samoa*. New York, 1928; *Male and Female*. London, 1951, etc.

ment of vital forces results', says Durkheim quietly, 'from adaptation to milieu.'[7] It follows, today, that the annihilation and impoverishment of millions, and the destruction of techniques, must result from clinging to abstract ideas of nineteenth-century nationalism and class conflict in the age of the hydrogen bomb. Misery and ruin are the natural penalities of political illusions which do not reflect environment.

It does not, of course, follow that adaptation should be uniform. Savage physique, for example is unsuitable for a townsman. Whatever. is most widespread and advantageous in a given context is healthy and normal. A laissez-faire economy may be suitable in Europe, for certain historical and social conditions: whether it is normal now depends on whether circumstances have changed. Adaptation is the test. We must avoid 'chasing chimaeras', and work to adjust our societies to the changing facts of their day. Crude nineteenth-century theories, which explain all history and lay down 'laws' of inevitable development, are out of date. Nationalism and Marxism, in particular, by implication, are discredited. With this end in view, one must study all the varying richness of society — cutting across traditional categories. We are not concerned, either, with 'humanity' in general, or with England or France in particular. We are concerned with the 'degree of social differentiation', with the changing and various structures of many peoples all over the world.

Yet, while avoiding doctrines of linear progress or 'inevitable' conflict, the sociologist must also take history into account. He must trace the rise of complex societies from the primitive horde, the transition from clans to tribes and villages, and place the peoples studied in the ramified tree of human development. One can distinguish societies by the simplest tests. By the continuance or absorption of tribal elements; by the rise and failure of urban organization; by the place of the family in relation to the whole economy. We must look for the social fabric — no mere sum of individuals. We must explain society by society.[8]

So examined, human organizations do not appear intentional. They are not the mechanical and rationalized structures envisaged by Hobbes and the Utilitarians. As Burke understood, they are organic, changing, mysterious and alive. Compare the independent attitude of individuals to each other and their subordination to the total, and often unconscious, adaptation imposed by society as a whole; by language, customs, tradition and law. The old rationalist and contractual fallacy is dismissed: the 'determining cause of social facts must be sought among antecedent social phenomena, not in the consciousness of individuals alone'.

The development of the social medium is spontaneous. Division of labour, for example, occurred through the need of mankind to adapt themselves to a changing situation, not by deliberate contrivance.[9] The Hobbesian antithesis between competing individuals and external constraint — the artificial, mechanical, creations of will — now appears a paradox. Spencer's theory that social harmony reflects increasing individualism is equally false. Objective analysis shows a very different picture — the richness of a vast social medium which spontaneously reinforces and canalizes the habits and the instincts of man. Such a view alone is practical — 'elle sort des entrailles mêmes de la réalité'.[10] The picture is therefore world-wide. Naturally we cannot unravel the complex variety of such primordial institutions — marriage for example — 'except by following its integral development across all social species'. Our sociology must be universal and comparative; no longer merely descriptive, and no longer enslaved to abstract ideas. 'La sociologie', he concludes, 'n'a pas à prendre de parti entre les grandes hypothèses que devisent les métaphysiciens.' It simply examines nature and causes, and the results of a given social pattern. It makes no 'a priori' assumptions: it merely asks how and why?

Society, thus understood, he insists, will not be classified by political labels. We are not primarily interested in these things. We are concerned rather to understand the whole vast phenomenon — 'what it needs, how it works'. The conclusions of such objective and far-flung study are unlikely to coincide with any political panaceas. The sociologist sees the problem in other terms. This approach is particularly well illustrated in Durkheim's analysis of socialism. In view of the prevalence of socialist doctrines, he felt bound to examine them. In 1895-96 he lectured on the subject, but soon turned, with some relief, to more strictly scientific studies. 'Durkheim', writes Mauss, 'était profondément opposé à toute guerre de classes ou de nations.'* As a scientific sociologist, he regarded such doctrines with profound distrust. His comparatively short analysis is one of the most valuable of his works; a model of impartiality and good sense. A close friend of Jaurès, his sympathies were with the Left, but he was unusual among his contemporaries in regarding even

---

* *Le Socialisme, sa Définition, ses Débuts, la Doctrine Saint-Simonienne.* Edited M. Mauss. Alcan, Paris, 1928. Many of the ideas in the book were appropriated, without acknowledgement, by Sorel.

the Dreyfus case with scientific detachment. This objectivity colours his whole view.

Thus equipped, he dealt the Marxist claim to have discovered 'a science in politics' a scientific blow. The data, he coolly pointed out, on which it was based, were totally inadequate. We know far too little, he insisted, of the complex variety of institutions, in all their world-wide range in space and time, to hazard so dogmatic and complete an explanation. All that Marxism can claim is 'une certaine tournure scientifique', and any speculation about the future is necessarily uncertain. 'The bases of methodical induction concerning the future, above all of an induction of such extent, are not available . . . that is why, strictly speaking, there can be no such thing as scientific socialism.'[11] Marx's reckless nineteenth-century methods shocked this careful investigator. 'In the *Kapital*', he writes, 'the whole theory of value is established in a few lines'. The so-called 'research' behind it is undertaken to establish a doctrine already defined. The facts were made to support the argument.

As a sociologist, on the other hand, Durkheim was quick to recognize the power of Marxism as myth. 'Le socialisme n'est pas une science, une sociologie en miniature, c'est un cri de douleur et, parfois, de colère, poussé par les hommes qui sentent le plus vivement notre malaise collectif.'[12] It is a formidable movement, but its claim to objectivity cannot be taken seriously. 'What would one say to a doctor who took the answers or the desires of his patient for scientific observations?' The recurrence of the medical comparison is significant.

Counter-revolutionary theories are equally unscientific. All are projections of different needs and circumstances. In themselves, for the social scientist, they are only of 'mediocre' interest; as phenomena for investigation they are of great importance. And how interesting the symptoms are! First we must inquire their duration. Are they endemic in society, co-eval with its origins? If so, they cannot be eradicated: fundamental readjustments must be made. Or is socialism something new, something ephemeral? What rearrangements may then be necessary? We are not interested in further dialectical debate; we are concerned to find out origins, nature and needs. We must do for socialism what we have already attempted in analysing the family, marriage, the incidence of suicide or crime.

At what level must the analysis begin? Is socialism an attack on property or upon the state? Is it primarily an economic or a political

myth? Durkheim concludes that its fundamental concern is economic. This applies to all varieties of socialism. Saint-Simon is therefore its most typical early exponent. Here is the characteristic
subordination of politics to economics. He concludes that all kinds
of socialism display a common 'aspiration towards the rearrangement
of the social body to effect a displacement of the industrial apparatus
in the whole organism; to take it out of the shadows in which it
functions automatically, to submit it to the light and to social
control'. Both 'socialism from above and below' are thus a common
symptom of the need for this social readjustment. It is naturally
reflected in a new outlook, for that is to be expected in a society as
much as in an individual. 'Imaginez que, dans l'organisme indivi-
duel, une de nos fonctions végétatives, située jusque-là en dehors de
la conscience, vienne à y être reliée par des voies de communication
directes, c'est le fond même de notre vie psychique qui serait profondément changé par cet afflux de sensations nouvelles.' The
modern approach to politics has naturally been profoundly altered
by socialist thought. But it does not follow that all previous ideas
are invalidated. The doctrines of class war and total revolution, he
implies, can never claim scientific authority.

Such an impartial attitude was naturally exasperating to political
enthusiasts. Durkheim admits that his solutions are at first unlikely
to have a wide appeal. But the sociologist must persevere. 'The role
of the Sociologist...is to emancipate us from all parties.'[13] He will not
offer new doctrines; he will create a new atmosphere. In time, this
atmosphere will infect even politicians. Authoritative, impartial,
the fruit of systematic research into human thought and institutions
in all their rich cosmopolitan variety across the world, sociology can
afford to follow its own path. 'Only methodical experiment will
snatch their secret' from the social facts. The fetishes of political
life, symbolical of old lusts, are at once necessary and provisional.
The sociologist must take account of them, but he will not rely on
them, or believe in them. His science, like all advanced knowledge,
is esoteric. But this detachment, this impartiality and remoteness,
will ultimately, Durkheim hopes, enhance its prestige. And as the
method spreads more and more, and educated minorities develop;
as the strains and complexities and failures brought about by political
illusions more obviously demand adjustment; as scientific invention
comes increasingly to dominate men's lives, they will be led by this
new comparative method into a final deflation of slogans in the dry
light of objective knowledge.

This scientific approach does not, with Durkheim, imply a sceptical materialism.* He ascribes great importance to ideas; to collective beliefs and the psychological states they reflect. They are the vital bonds of society, with a life of their own. Their relation to material environment is as close as a 'chemical synthesis'. The collective myths of society are immensely important. They are the medium in which human values are realized. Durkheim is no mere worshipper of a materialist social organism; 'La société n'est pas un système d'organes et de fonctions ... elle est le foyer d'une vie morale.' In this setting the forces of life come to self-consciousness and nature surpasses herself. The purpose of sociology is to understand and adjust; to ensure survival through adaptation, and to promote the development of the human spirit in the medium in which alone it can become articulate. Here, as with Spinoza, the originator of this kind of approach, an immediately utilitarian purpose leads to creative morality and richer achievement. With Durkheim the mysterious tides of society, sensed by Rousseau and more fully interpreted by Green as a basis of political morality, and brilliantly sketched by Bagehot, and eloquently described by Bradley, now began to be systematically and scientifically examined. The conclusions reflect the application of new techniques. They imply the abandonment of the old abstract assumptions, deriving from the eighteenth century and the Utilitarians, of the consistent reasonableness of man. They regard transcendent ideas of Natural Law and Revelation as part of the natural and changing idioms of human thought. Natural in a given stage of time and place, they are bound to alter. Sociology is concerned not with abstract and final truth, but with the health and sickness of society; with the contribution political and social ideas and customs make to survival. This pragmatic method, when applied to political thought, creates distrust of ideologies and creeds. It regards all such manifestations of the human spirit from a world-view, knowing that behaviour which is admired in one setting has been thought criminal in another. It is intolerant only of ideas which make for destruction and impoverishment of life.

It thus gives empirical and impartial methods a new and broader inspiration, drawn from familiarity with the vast range of manners and customs over the whole world. It is an appropriate outlook for a time when world communications grow swiftly closer every year. It crudely foreshadows, perhaps, the outlook of a world civilization. Here we are concerned not only with the political aspect of society,

* See C. BOUGLÉ's admirable preface, 1924, to the *Sociologie et Philosophie.*

but with the whole rich organic and cosmopolitan content of social life. It is the true sequel to the transformation of environmental studies wrought by Darwin in the nineteenth century.

In this modern view the political philosopher is no longer a prophet or an exponent of revelation. Such an outlook is old-fashioned, deriving from the days of witch-doctors and priest-kings. He is now an expert in the way societies work; on the well being of the social order; on the proper method of adjustment to a changing world. He is a leader, not a defeatist spectator, now engaged by a humane and absorbing purpose — the enhancement of life. He is concerned to promote health and maximum vitality, and to secure the adaptation to environment of which, in all the animal world, health and happiness are the natural manifestations.

III

Durkheim's outlook was to be paralleled by another great expansion of knowledge; the revelation of the depths of the sub-conscious mind by modern psychology. Of this development Graham Wallas is a representative pioneer.

The work of Graham Wallas, like that of Durkheim, marks the growing influence of a sociological view of politics. Though he seldom follows up his conclusions, and is preoccupied with questions of current affairs and local government, the novelty of his outlook is significant. His approach is unpretentious and parochial. He writes with the 'clever young mechanic' in mind; the 'young school mistress in her bed sitting room a few streets off . . . (ought she to spend herself in a reckless campaign for the suffrage?) He desires, in the early socialist manner, 'A good life for an unprivileged population'. But towards this objective he makes a new approach. Like Durkheim, he reflects the intellectual revolution brought about by the Darwinian view of the importance of environment, and, more than Durkheim, he is a pioneer of the application of psychology to politics, a forerunner of a great expansion of sociological study in England and, on a greater scale, in America.

Like Sorel, Wallas attacked the rationalist assumptions still fashionable. Bagehot had criticized this outlook with eloquence and precision, and Tylor had marshalled wide evidence of primitive motives in civilized society. But a vague belief in the rationality of popular political judgment was still reflected in political thought. In his preface to the 1920 edition, Wallas ruefully declares that these liberal beliefs had been profoundly shaken by the first world war, which had underlined his own conclusions.* A second world war, and the partial realization of the political levelling that Wallas desired, have again emphasized their importance.

Educated in the tradition of classical humanism, Wallas is concerned with the 'good life'. Not that his conception of it is very Greek.† He desires, indeed, to interpret it in terms of the Welfare State. Since human beings are wayward and irrational, this sober objective can only be reached by taking account of their limitations. Hence the title of his opening chapter, 'Impulse and Instinct in Politics'. His aim is 'not only to deepen and widen our knowledge of political institutions, but open an unworked mine of political invention'. Like Bergson, Sorel, William James and Durkheim, Wallas, in his context, is representative.

The impulse and instinct which still predominate in civilized societies, he argues, are the 'result not of any contrivance by the actor, but of the survival in the past of the fittest of many varying tendencies to act'. Take, for example, the impulse to own property. This is not abstract, uniform and unvarying, as Utilitarian economists wrongly supposed; and not necessarily limited to the family, defined by them as 'those persons' for whom 'in Western Europe for whose support a man is legally responsible'.[14] He suggests that a thorough investigation of such impulses in politics is desirable: it would include fighting instinct, impulses of curiosity and competition. Like Hobbes, but with far richer knowledge at his disposal, he wants to base efficient government on scientific psychology. He observes that in general the force and depth of impulses relates not to their importance in civilized life, but to 'the point at which they appeared in an evolutionary past'.[15] The greatest problem of politics is to adapt those primordial desires to modern environment. Like Durkheim, Wallas takes a biological view. Consider for example the question of solitude and gregariousness. Our ancestors for generations were adjusted to co-operative but small societies. Hence the maladjustment and tension of megalopolitan man. It is far more important to resolve this maladjustment than to vapour about abstractions. But the 'habitual intellectualism of the writers of political Utopias' prevents them observing what is obvious and urgent. At present, in

---

* Vide *Human Nature in Politics*. First published London, 1908. (1920 edition.)
† See his suburban attitude to sport. 'Many of the sons and daughters of the owners of railways and coal mines . . . were "fed up" with motoring or bridge, or even with the hunting and fishing which meant a frank resumption of palaeolithic life without the spur of palaeolithic hunger.' Preface, p. xix.

the pursuit of political panaceas, the basic sociological objectives are ignored. While politicians mouth obsolete slogans, untold frustration and misery is going on.

These matters should be taken into urgent account. They are bound up with another study still in its infancy, the psychology of the crowd. Wallas refers to Tarde and le Bon, though he rather smugly observes that 'the exaggerations . . . one seems to notice when reading French psychologists on this point, may be due to their having been made among a Latin and not a Northern race'.[16] Turning to the acute question of colour prejudice, he remarks that this seems due rather to secondary motives than to inevitable instinct, since white children easily take to coloured attendants, and persons of different colours fall in love. There is not here the same deep instinctive aversion as that found between the camel and the horse.

This biological approach to problems which are a focus of political passion is salutary. It reflects a view of man as an animal imperfectly adapted to recent changes of environment. It is also apparent in Wallas's concept of 'political entities', roughly the equivalent of Durkheim's 'social facts'. Political philosophers have intellectualized behaviour, which is the consequence of instinct and impulse. Following Bagehot, Wallas points out that political opinions result 'not from reasoning tested by experience, but from unconscious or half-conscious inference fixed by habit'. Sociology must learn to forecast and manipulate these irrational responses, as science, by creating hypotheses, has gone far to master nature.

But the political philosopher can never apply exact laws to his material. 'Again and again in the history of political thought men have believed themselves to have found this standard.' Plato's ideal City, Hobbes's theorem of politics, Locke's Natural Rights, Rousseau's Social Contract, Bentham's Felicific Calculus, all are inadequate. Wallas might have added that typical nineteenth-century dogma, Dialectical Materialism. In the light of modern psychology all such explanations are unreal. We must set about a more humble and ultimately more rewarding task; we must collect the facts on which a more tentative and truly scientific hypothesis can be constructed. 'In . . . collecting the material for a political science, we must adopt the method of the biologist, who tries to discover how many common qualities can be observed and measured in a group of related beings, rather than that of the physicist, who constructs, or used to construct, a science out of a single quality common to the whole material world.'[17]

These sociological facts should be arranged under three heads: descriptive, quantitative, environmental. Political thought should be related to them. At present, political science can only be compared to medicine when Galen and Hippocrates were the sole basis of study. Even Bryce still adopts the old rationalist fallacy. He begins by depicting an ideal 'intelligent, disinterested, democracy'. A society, he at once admits, which does not exist. 'No doctor would now begin a medical treatise' with the remark, 'the ideal man requires no food, and is impervious to the action of bacteria, but this ideal is for removed from the actualities of any known population.'[18] Practical politicians, therefore, tend to despise 'abstract political philosophy' in which man is depicted as without impulse and passion. What, asks Wallas pertinently, does abstract 'political philosophy' mean? No medical writer would speak of an 'abstract anatomical science in which men have no livers'. Political thought is thus discredited because concerned with obsolete ideas. No longer 'exactly believed in', they still 'exercise a kind of shadowy authority . . .' It is significant that Wallas, like Durkheim, makes a medical comparison. Only, he insists, if we take man and society as they are, can we construct a political science which can be taken seriously. Difficult though this project must be in view of the 'infinite complexity of the actual world', the day of *a priori* abstractions is on the wane.[19]

Quantitative methods are needed, based on statistics and thorough investigation. Armed with deeper psychology and wider knowledge, and following tentative empirical methods, political science may at last become objective. Will it simply result in the cynical manipulation of the masses and reinforce 'those methods of exploiting human nature which have hitherto been the trade secret of the elderly and disillusioned?' Or will it result in despair? Suppose, for example, the bees became 'conscious of their own nature, and of the waste of life and toil which goes on in the best-ordered hive'. They might merely conclude 'that no greatly improved organization is possible for creatures hampered by such limited powers of observation and inference, and enslaved by such furious passions. They might be forced to recognize that as long as they were bees, their life must remain bewildered and violent and short'.[20] It may even prove that control can be established only by selective breeding; perhaps 'by altering the human type itself'.

Such measures are at present unnecessary and impracticable. But we have already made a most important advance. Darwinian science and modern psychology have transformed our outlook. No previous change of perspective is comparable — 'the new history of man and his surroundings, stretching back through . . . unthought of ages, the substitution of an illimitable vista of ever-changing worlds for the imagined perfection of the ordered heavens, and above all, the intrusion of science into the most intimate regions of ourselves'.[21] This new self-consciousness must inevitably permeate political thought. 'Those who have eaten of the tree of knowledge cannot forget.' Like Durkheim, Wallas believes that a destruction of slogans is bound to come. Or rather, Wallas hints, perhaps a deliberate transformation of slogans, a manipulation of new Myths.

The conception of Science is one of them — the Myth, perhaps, of the twentieth century. Originating among a few specialists, it has now spread over the entire world. 'In every class-room and laboratory in Europe and America the conscious idea of Science forms the minds and wills of thousands.' Moreover, he points out, it had penetrated 'as the political conception of Liberty or of Natural Right never penetrated, to non-European races'.[22] Here is a constructive, contemporary idea, a focus perhaps for a new world-wide Humanism.

Reverting to his original theme, the adaptation of representative government to modern conditions and alien peoples, Wallas insists that we must not merely adapt but invent. He suggests expedients whereby government by consent may be acclimatized in areas where it is not native. Where it is already established, he hopes that greater social equality, and, above all, education, will greatly increase the 'margin of safety in democracy'. Like engineers building a bridge, we must calculate the strain the materials will stand. As an example of successful social engineering, he cites the substitution of competitive examination for patronage in the recruitment of civil servants.

Turning to international affairs, he criticizes both the sentimental nationalism of Mazzini and Bismarck's 'realpolitik'. The former had declared that the nation was 'the intermediate term between humanity and the individual', and believed that 'a pact of humanity' would be signed between 'free and equal peoples'; the latter, that the facts of geography, dictated by Providence, were bound to create great competing sovereign powers. Actually, Wallas insists, peoples are not so distributed. In 'Macedonia . . . bands of Bulgarian and Greek patriots, both educated in the pure tradition of Mazzinism, are attempting to exterminate the rival populations in order to establish their own claim to represent the purposes of God as indicated by the position of the Balkan mountains'.[23] Further, the colonial expan-

sions of the great powers make nationalist dogma even more dangerous. He foresaw the frightful consequences of the collision of rival
Imperialisms. Unless nationalism could be curbed, he expected
'centuries of warfare and steady regression'. 'In the waste of blood
and treasure and loyalty, of modern civilization, two Empires', he
predicted, 'England and Germany, or America and China may
remain.' 'Both', he continues, 'will possess an armament which
represents the whole "surplus value" beyond mere subsistence,
created by its inhabitants. Both will contain white and yellow and
brown and black men hating each other across a wavering line on the
map of the world.'[24] Finally, after a total Armageddon, only one
world Empire will survive. Then, at last, mankind, though hardly,
one would think, in a position to do so, 'diminished to half their
number, will be compelled to consider . . . the organized exploitation
of the globe from the point of view of mere humanitarianism'. World
conquest will be the price of world peace.

In face of this prospect, brought nearer by subsequent events,
Wallas again appeals to science. Since Darwin's discoveries, the
human race appears no longer as either 'a chaos of individuals' or
a 'mosaic of homogeneous nations'. It can be understood as one
great biological group, the product of a common evolution. Unhappily, 'political Darwinism' encouraged ruthless competition. The
struggle for life had been transferred to a struggle for Empire and
endowed with scientific prestige. Such ideas are a travesty of the
facts. They must be counteracted not only by reason but by a new
Myth. 'If this habit of mind is to be destroyed, it must be opposed
not merely by a new argument, but by a conception of man's relation
to the universe which creates emotional force as well as intellectual
conviction.' Here is a wider, but similar, appeal to Green's.

That ideal must be world-wide Scientific Humanism. 'An idea',
he writes, 'of the whole existence of our species is at last a possible
background to our individual experience.' Already mass communications transcend the old boundaries of the world. 'The sharp new
evidence of the camera brings every year nearer to us its surface of
ice and rock and plain, and the wondering eyes of alien peoples.'
Today these considerations are more obvious and intensified. Wallas
had pointed out, at a time when nationalism was an almost universal
obsession, the ultimate need for world government under the conditions created by modern science.

The same overriding sense of the adaptation of institutions and
mentality to changed environment pervades Wallas's other pioneer

work, *The Great Society*.* 'The main task of civilization', he declares, 'is to produce a new environment where stimulation of our existing dispositions shall tend towards the good life.' As in the previous volume, the influence of Aristotle is paramount. 'The master task of civilized mankind', is to examine the contemporary conditions of the 'good life'. We must face the difficulty by adapting primordial impulses to the 'Great Society', created by modern industry, something unprecedented in the world. Not only unprecedented, but extremely precarious: 'why should we expect an organization to endure which has been founded in a moment of time by human beings whose bodies and minds are the result of age long selection under far different conditions?'

In face of this dangerous situation, and with a similar desire for efficient government in mind, Wallas follows the method of Hobbes, 'the father of modern social psychology'.[25] He attempts a broad exploratory survey. He criticizes Bentham, who ignored animal psychology; 'the word instinct does not occur in the enormous index of his collected works'.[26] But he repudiates the cult of impulse in Bergson and Sorel.[27] Such a cult is far too dangerous in the precarious conditions of the Great Society. Wallas's homespun good sense here contrasts with the politically irresponsible brilliance of these two architects of ruin. Where Bentham's psychology was inadequate, so also was Hobbes's ascription of all political behaviour to fear. So, too, was Comte's oversimplified belief in the Law of Love. Bagehot, who was afraid of the consequences of the extension of the franchise, over-emphasized the stupidity of the people, while Tarde and William James set too much store by imitation. There is also much more evidence, which Kropotkin has collected, for the power of mutual aid. The behaviour of crowds results more from defective institutions than from innate bestiality. Custom, solidarity, in primitive societies, is the basis of survival. And custom is the foundation of law. In an admirable passage, Wallas quotes from the Njal Saga on the practical benefits achieved by the transition out of violence through custom to law. 'For with Law', says Njal, 'shall our land be built up and settled, and with lawlessness wasted and spoiled.'[28] The rule of law, constitutional government, is the sophistication of custom, itself the reflection of a universal impulse to primitive mutual aid, sublimated in Acton's conscience and commonwealth.

* *The Great Society, a Psychological Analysis.* London, 1914. It is divided into two parts, one a psychological exploratory review, the other on how to organize the great society in terms of Thought, Will and Happiness.

Constitutional methods of government reflect this instinct. Properly handled, the prevalent impulses of mankind are not anti-social. They only become destructive when baulked by wrong institutions, which social psychology can adjust or remove. The aim which Wallas depicts is similar to Lasswell's recently defined 'commonwealth of mutual deference'.* Here the causes of destructiveness would be understood and removed. Wallas rejects the then fashionable concept of a 'social organism', for which he declares there is no evidence, but he explores methods of reorganizing Thought, Will and Happiness.† He ranges widely over current English problems; the improvement of the efficiency of the Cabinet, House of Commons and Civil Service. He is particularly anxious to humanize the workings of bureaucracy and he examines methods of mass communication then available. He believes that a compromise between individualist enterprise, collective control and syndicalist independence may yet be achieved. The society at which he aims is classless; rather similar, it seems, to that towards which Scandinavia, Switzerland and New Zealand have since developed. It would reflect what he terms in his classical idiom, 'the Mean', or 'Middle Way'.

In conclusion he has his misgivings. He declares that an element of 'the Extreme' must be allowed for, if social democratic commonwealth is to be redeemed from mediocrity. In Wallas's mind, thoughout, there is conflict between the wide horizons of the Aristotelian outlook and the preoccupations and ideals of the industrial and suburban society in which he was enmeshed. Though his vision was broad, it was vague and it was insular. These limitations, familiar in the exponents of the Welfare State, detract little from the importance of Wallas's statement of constructive principles of social engineering and popularization of scientific sociology.

I V

Durkheim and Wallas thus represent the beginning of a movement of profound significance. The first stressed the importance of environment and of social organization, based, not upon abstract political theory, but upon permanent and world-wide human needs. The second stressed the importance of the subconscious mind and of the primitive inheritance which mankind bring with them out of

* See H. D. LASSWELL, *The Analysis of Political Behaviour*, in particular his chapters 'The Developing Science of Democracy' and 'Psychology Looks at Morals and Politics'. London, 1947.
† *The Great Society*, XI-XIII.

the enormous prehistoric past. From this men have emerged in the process of biological selection, and it has left its ineffaceable mark. Both take a scientific view of political problems, beyond political slogans. This social science has much the same relation to politics as medicine to biology. It is concerned to promote survival, to enhance life, to harmonize and to adjust. If the ultimate mysteries which religion and metaphysics had hoped to penetrate remain opaque, society at least, like other aspects of life, may in time be susceptible to control. This sociology is designed to remove institutional and personal causes of maladjustment and conflict. From the exploratory analysis of Durkheim and the fruitful generalizations of Wallas, a whole vast modern sociology was destined to develop. This new, cosmopolitan, and impartial outlook may well achieve the fundamental and urgent task of adapting political theory and practice to a revolutionized environment in the light of new social and psychological knowledge. Here modern political thought is likely to reach constructive conclusions. It may reinforce constitutional government by a systematic and deeper knowledge of the social medium in which all government must work. It can destroy the pretensions of dogmatic and abstract theory and destructive myth, and it is in this genuinely scientific perspective, suited to the modern world, that the nineteenth-century political ideas examined in this study must today be regarded. It can enrich the principles of commonwealth stated by Green and Acton, with skills of wider scope than Green could envisage, and of a scientific efficiency outside the range of Acton's traditional view.

RETROSPECT: A NEW HUMANISM

At the opening of this study it was observed that all nineteenth-century political thought was conditioned by the Industrial and Technical revolutions. Hitherto the environment of mankind had been predominantly rural, the wealth of civilization commercial, not industrial, and the tempo of thought determined by a slow and predictable routine. By the end of the period the picture had been transformed. To-day, still hardly adapted to the tempo of the nineteenth century, mankind is confronted, in a world setting, with a situation so extraordinary that there is widespread effort to ignore it.

As already remarked, it is of personal concern to all who read these pages that the political misuse of science should be arrested and political thought swiftly directed to that end. It is therefore topical to inquire how far, during the nineteenth century, political theorists improved political behaviour, how far they worsened it? Did they help to adapt conduct to environment? That is the primary concern. For political behaviour is still largely determined by nineteenth-century ideas. By the main stream of liberal and social-democratic ideas, by the national, class-conscious and nihilist attack upon it, and by the new environmental and psychological approach since developed. It is also worth recapitulating what was original in nineteenth-century speculation, how far it enriched the inheritance of previous ages. And it is urgent to relate these conclusions to our own time.

II

The objectives formulated by civilized minorities in pre-industrial times have been described in a previous volume. It may be recalled that a 'good life', with its concept of vital, many-sided ἀρετή, formed the Greek political ideal. In varying forms, together with the idea of universal Law, reflecting a cosmic order, it coloured the political thought of pagan Antiquity, in which the hard and splendid humanism of the Graeco-Roman world state was celebrated. With the influence of Christianity, a more emotional and compassionate ideal had been defined; the Humanist ideal of the good life was replaced by that of the Christian warrior or the saint. Political thought was assimilated to a theological world-outlook, and expressed in exact terms of Thomist morality. Power came to be regarded as part of a geometrically clear-cut scheme of Divine, Natural and Temporal Law, and political actions judged in terms of merit or of sin. With the disruption of the medieval synthesis, the revival of Humanism, the formulation of Baconian and Cartesian method, and the development of medieval Christendom into sovereign states, the conception of political power becomes more utilitarian and the ideal of conduct more limited and practical. But the Humanist and Christian heritage still affected the political ideas of the eighteenth century. Though the Encyclopedists were anti-clerical sceptics, their ideal was reasonable and humane. By the close of the eighteenth century, there remained a coherent and reputable doctrine. Though restricted to a minority, it defined and in part realized political principles Western civilization still imperfectly embodies. These principles, only partially effective even in constitutional states, have already been described and previously summed up in terms of rational objectivity, law, compassion and liberty. They are the basis of a Christian and Humanist Commonwealth.* On this inheritance were brought to bear the new ideas of the nineteenth century.

Against this background, the two original contributions of the Romantic Age may be recalled. First, the cult of Will, of intuition, of history expressed in national terms: secondly, the idea of 'improvement' based on an increasing body of professional knowledge. The first had been early expressed by Herder and more elaborately by Hegel. It had origins in Rousseau and in Burke; it was to reach its most influential cosmopolitan expression in Mazzini, and its most sophisticated national expression in T. H. Green. By giving the new democratic state a dynamic philosophy, this outlook strengthened constitutional government and promoted the objectives defined by de Tocqueville and J. S. Mill. In terms of conscience Acton assimilated it. It affected the political theory of the Welfare State.

The idea of creative will was compounded of many elements. Its inspiration was Humanist and Hellenic, as well as northern and romantic. It was primarily concerned with the enrichment of personality, and bound up with a vast enthusiasm for the expansion of knowledge and the enrichment of culture. It was the expression of a wealthy and powerful society. Here, it seemed, continuing prosperity would promote reasonableness and compassion. This cult of good-will could appear a substitute for transcendental religion, though it derived also from the Protestant cult of conscience and the 'inner

* Vide *W.P.T.*, Conclusion, and the Introduction to the present study.

light'. It had abandoned the clear-cut Thomist political thought. In the last resort, in spite of its metaphysical ambience, it was anthropocentric. It may therefore be regarded as a break with the ancient tradition of Catholic Christianity, with its doctrine of original sin, total cosmic explanation and carefully devised discipline. In spite of Mazzini's cosmopolitan ideas, it weakened European solidarity. As Leo XIII declared, this decline had been going on since the Reformation. It was not only a sin of omission. Romantic thought encouraged an aggressive nationalism. Hegel depicted not merely a national state, where individuals found freedom, but a dialectical struggle between world historic peoples. Combined with the cult of world historical men, it was to create singular havoc, and 'turned upside down' in terms of Marxist class war, to prove even more disastrous. Not the Liberals, but the Utopian visionaries, Saint-Simon, Comte and Proudhon, understood the external implications of the nation state. Liberalism was flawed with the fatal defect. It never achieved in the international field what it achieved nationally. Wilsonian Liberals of the nineteen-twenties were still living on the capital of Mazzinian ideals. Acton, alone, had a constructive view.

The second, even more far-reaching, nineteenth-century contribution had been 'improvement'. The theme sounds steadily throughout the period with increasing power. The clear-cut, over-simplified, Utilitarian outlook was mellowed and reinforced by environmental and historical studies. All institutions became no longer sacrosanct, but malleable. Utilitarian improvement is ancestral to modern pragmatic sociology.

In spite of the defects of liberalism in the international field, the idea of Christian and Humanist commonwealth had thus been doubly enriched. Liberal Romantics and laissez-faire Utilitarians replaced eighteenth-century order, Catholic or Rationalist, by a dynamic way of life, where personality, national aspirations and economic enterprise had free play. Both assumed the reality of progress — as Sorel pointed out, the most characteristic idea of middle-class society.

This outlook had horrified conservative minds. De Maistre had denounced it; Coleridge had turned away from it; Carlyle fulminated against it. But the revolutionary technocrats attacked it in a new way. They desired to create a new orthodoxy, not a new freedom. Across the broad and rushing cataract of early nineteenth-century liberalism and 'improvement', with its cult of political and economic liberty, the old and new exponents of totalitarian order gazed at one another. On the one side, the uncompromising Catholic Church: on the other, the would-be creators of a dogmatic Humanist religion. It was not for nothing that Comte's disciple Harrison described his beliefs as 'Human Catholicism'. Here a new influence entered nineteenth-century thought; the first amateurish design of a project later attempted by Marxist Communism in the U.S.S.R.

All this Western development must be set against the continuing predominance of military régimes in central and Eastern Europe, and the old contrast between the social and economic development of East and West. Against the background, also, of the continuing influence of the Catholic Church, particularly in Mediterranean Europe, and its refusal, until the later years of the century, of any compromise. Yet, in spite of conservative hostility and revolutionary attack, Liberalism remained by far the most powerful current of Western political thought in the nineteenth century, expressing a predominant class interest. On balance, there can be little doubt, it improved political behaviour. It was a sound response to nineteenth-century conditions. In spite of the brutalities of laissez-faire economic theory, it was to modify such crude assumptions. It showed healthy flexibility; it was to broaden into social democracy and tame revolution, with its nemesis — arbitrary power. Within a national framework, intellectual liberty had wide play, and Western liberal civilization was a culture of outstanding brilliance. Like our own, the time was one of unexampled expansion in knowledge. In view of recent political catastrophes, this fact is often forgotten. All this achievement was based on the political liberties won in the early nineteenth century and developed simultaneously in vast territories overseas.

III

The second half of the period saw the rise of a new major theme. The foundation of liberalism was private property, the mainspring of individual enterprise. Green still asserted the inviolability of private capital. Now this assumption began to be heavily assailed. There had been various constructive criticisms and outright attacks on laissez-faire capitalism in the early nineteenth century. The technocrats, Saint-Simon and Comte, desired even greater power for bankers and administrators, and the enlargement of production by centralized planning. To the left of them had been Owen, with his paternal socialism, intensive education, and small co-operatives.

Finally came the anarchists, the theoretical Godwin and the more constructive Proudhon. They desired to undermine the state and release a society of self-governing producers. These movements had all been politically ineffective. But by the 'fifties, a new force gradually became important. Marx and Engels were creating a far more formidable basis of attack. This time on property itself. It was complete with an elaborate philosophy of revolution and a clear tactical programme. Here the characteristic mid-nineteenth-century appeal to science developed into an explanation of all history in terms of dialectical materialism, and into a claim that now, for the first time, the 'laws' of historical evolution had been properly understood. In the 'sixties the authority won by Darwin in biology was claimed by Marx in social science.

Along with this typically nineteenth-century dogma, went militant atheism and a revolutionary appeal to class war. Where Saint-Simon, Comte and Owen, in varying ways, desired collaboration in a commonwealth and the protection of private property, and where Proudhon hoped for the disappearance of poverty and class distinction in the self-governing group, superseding a centralized and megalopolitan society, Marx and Engels were determined to seize and exploit the power of the bourgeois state. They represented the whole of history as the record of exploitation and class conflict, and brought into political thought a fanaticism unparalleled since the religious wars of the seventeenth century.

The parting of the ways between Marx and Proudhon was decisive for mid-nineteenth-century socialism. It was the natural sequel to the darkening of the moral scene that mid-century science was held to demand. Where the humanism of Saint-Simon, Owen or Mazzini had been benevolent and optimistic, with its religion of progress and association, the humanism of Marx was poisoned by political hatred and materialism, invoked as the driving force of history and revolution. This ferocity had been occasioned in part by the ruthless economic theory of Malthus and Ricardo, with its sacrifice of personality to economic 'laws', and in reaction to the savage competition Herbert Spencer had endowed with a quasi-scientific biological sanction and which pervaded most mid-nineteenth-century sociology. Malthusian economics and Spencerian individualism provoked and deserved the Marxist attack. Further, although Marx was asserting humane values against the cruelties of laissez-faire and pseudo-Darwinian competition, the German origins of Marxism were evident in a characteristic worship of the state, incompatible with its 'withering away'. And the violent principles inherited from 1789 encouraged incessant conflict. For all the enrichment of economic studies by Marxian analysis, it is not surprising that the Marxist programme only succeeded in a politically primitive society.

By the later decades of the nineteenth century the new major theme, the attack on laissez-faire society, had developed and divided. On the one hand the heirs of Saint-Simonian technocracy desired a managerial society as advocated by Comte. On the other, reformers of the anarchist stamp of Owen and Proudhon envisaged various forms of economic commonwealth, often superseding the state. The 'scientific' Marxists, meanwhile, having declared that the key to revolution was the seizure of the means of production by the elite class-conscious proletariat, were ready to use the bourgeois state for this end, in accordance with an Hegelian philosophy of history which demonstrated that this outcome was inevitable.

This double development of revolutionary thought coincided with the spread of the Industrial and Technical Revolutions into areas hitherto immune. The industrial masses were becoming more critical of bourgeois plutocracy and privilege, and demanding a greater share in political power. The question, as de Tocqueville, with his usual insight, had observed, was not whether mass democracy would achieve power, but how it was to achieve it. How far were the new revolutionary movements compatible with predominant constitutionalism, with its theory of a general will? And how far could they blend with the new professional knowledge, already concentrating on social problems, — the over ambitious, but realistic approach, for example, of Maine and Bagehot? Marxist economic analysis, if not Marxist dialectic, had much in common with the new study of the life of institutions, with its strong sense of environment and realist acceptance of fact. In the economic field, indeed, the traditional outlook was often shallow in comparison with the deeper Marxist insight. Marx's plan to release the full power of industry and bring a new well-being to the masses was not unlike the objectives of liberal capitalism. But politically the Marxists were barbarians, with their revolutionary violence and dictatorship, bringing, as Bernstein was to point out, inevitably disastrous consequences to the Marxist ideal itself.

Apart from the threat against property, another onslaught was being made on the liberal democratic world. Nationalism had always been bound up with the cult of popular will, and liberalism conditioned by it. Now, just as the Utopian socialism which followed the revolution had become embittered, and turned from the benevolent ideals of Owen and Fourier to the class warfare of Marx, so the romantic ideals of Herder and Mazzini had begun to lapse into the ferocious nationalism of which Treitschke has been taken as the most typical exponent. Here, again, the decline of religious belief played its part. Popularized doctrines of the survival of the 'fittest'; grim pictures of a prehistoric past of savage aggression, and a growing familiarity with primitive cultures where callousness was habitual, made political thought more sombre. Comte might combine atheism with a religion of Humanity, and Proudhon combine it with a cult of 'la dignité humaine': after the biologists had depicted a world of brutish struggle, and the physicists a world of blind mechanism, both benevolence and dignity seemed precarious. The Hegelian idea that history proceeds in terms of vast national conflicts had begun to capture the minds not only of intellectuals, but of whole peoples, reinforced by the misguided belief that such conflict was salutary. The ideal of a Christian Europe had been fading since the sixteenth century. Now cosmopolitan Enlightenment was being swallowed up in the surge of popular self-assertion. De Maistre's warning seemed justified that without the authority of the cosmopolitan Church, destructive individualism and perverted science would wreck society. With the prestige of science colouring the determinist and abstract ideas to which de Tocqueville had thought democracies particularly susceptible, savage myths of race superiority and inevitable conflict augmented an originally romantic nationalism.

These ideas were increasingly influential. They were reinforced by the political structure of Europe. As liberal constitutional ideas were embodied in massive institutions and so proved lasting, nationalism was also embedded in the texture of society. National sovereignty remained unquestioned by influential opinion. Save by a few anarchists and Utopians, it was accepted. Even the liberal T. H. Green took it for granted. Federal institutions, the natural corollary of liberalism, were to develop mainly in small areas, in Switzerland, for example, or in great extra-European territories overseas. In Europe, generally, attempts to create international institutions were negligible, while the popular acceptance of the nation state was reflected and ensured by all the glamour of ceremonial and tradition.

There were thus two perils which the liberal democratic ship had to face. The sudden tides of revolutionary upheaval that growing plutocracy encouraged, and the recurrent and spreading whirlpools of nationalist conflict. But there was another danger which was more intimate. The threat of mutiny on board the ship itself.

I V

Through the chequered course of nineteenth-century political thought, one objective had been constant. The desire to liberate personality and improve circumstance through control of environment by organized knowledge. Both liberals and revolutionaries had concurred in a belief in Man and in Progress. Even de Maistre and Carlyle had not totally despaired of politics. Saint-Simon and Comte had planned prosperous and efficient communities; Hegel had envisaged a state where, whatever its external relations, liberty would be self-fulfilled. Mazzini and Proudhon had seen in the regenerated nation state and the federation of producers the fulfilment of the moral and physical nature of man. Now, agnostics and atheists, often deprived of pagan consolations, produced radically destructive ideas. Soured Romantics and failed Christians struck attitudes of despair. In many aspects, the fin de siècle combined most of the disadvantages of Christianity and Paganism.

Schopenhauer had been one of the first to propagate this outlook. With his intellectual roots in the age of Byron, he posthumously exercised his greatest influence in the age of Darwin. His radical pessimism was unusual in a modern European philosopher, though it had many parallels in the East and affinities with the medieval Manichees. Here is a horror of life, similar to that felt by de Maistre, but without the consolations of Redemption. Here, also, is political quietism, an early contribution to the *Trahison des Clercs*. This influence was to be reinforced by popular misconceptions of Darwinian theory, depicting progress as the result of foredoomed and savage competition between individuals, states and empires. Here was a neo-Paganism far more ferocious than the old classical religion of family and civic gods — politically destructive. The official cults of Antiquity had been directed to order, prosperity and peace. Here, in a highly sophisticated culture, had emerged the lineaments of the beast. It had its fitting sequel in the disasters in the twentieth century. For these atrocities were not only the result of political maladjustment: they were the logical outcome of fundamental elements in nineteenth-century culture.

This pessimism and belief in violence was paralleled by a cult of irresponsibility. Since, in this view, there can be no objective appraisal of any situation, for all men are children of their age and unable to get beyond it, and all experience is 'existential', strictly confined by personality and environment, self expression can best be achieved through blind action for action's sake. Nietzsche's brilliant insight into the limitations of reason and his heady gospel of intuition, won, on a higher level, the kind of celebrity afterwards achieved by Spengler. For he expressed the mood of his time; the logical result of atheist subjectivity, the nemesis of the romantic cult of the individual. This nihilism was sometimes more destructive than Marx's attack on the liberal constitutional state. The original Marxist theory had been created by men steeped in European learning; strategically anxious to extend the benefits of traditional culture, if ruthless and misguided political tacticians. Following the Bergsonian doctrine of action for its own sake, and the deliberate manipulation of Myth, Sorel's anarcho-syndicalist ideas, too, foreshadowed Fascist violence. As Liberal democracy moved towards a constitutionalist attack on the citadels of Capitalism, towards the Welfare State and the New Deal, it was confronted not only with the threat of class war and nationalism, but with a cult of political irresponsibility and sheer destruction. Outside the esoteric doctrines of medieval heresy, this had no parallel since the barbarian irruptions of Dark Ages.

From a mid-twentieth century view, this mutiny and misgiving among the crew of the Western ship appears the natural, but not the permanent, sequel to the development of certain aspects of nineteenth-century thought. In particular of its atheism. It also reflected a political and economic situation which was institutionally unsound, and the long-term reaction of a dying romanticism and a misconceived science. Schopenhauer, oppressed by 'howling colossal suffering'; Nietzsche, with his revolt against Darwinism; Sorel with his hatred of bourgeois society and culture, his admiration for a destructive *Homo Faber*, were all soured romantics. They could not face the sobering, but not disastrous, conclusions of new scientific knowledge and old political experience. And there were disreputable prophets, not here examined. The racial ideas of Gobineau and of Houston Stewart Chamberlain, the quasi-astrological predictions of a Spengler, the nihilism of a whole world of self-pitying minor intellectuals rotten with introspection.

Such was the dangerous situation towards the close of the nineteenth century. For all its superficial power and prosperity, liberal constitutionalism, with its belief in intellectual and political assimilation, faced a searching challenge. Not only from a revolt of the masses, expressed in terms of militant class war and nationalist hysteria, but from a fundamental despair of politics among intellectuals, no longer engaged by religious belief or humanitarian conviction. If the contribution of the early nineteenth century to political behaviour had, on the whole, been salutary, this aspect of its later contribution was disastrous.

How far was this reaction permanent? How far representative of the most powerful tendencies of nineteenth-century thought? On closer inspection, it would seem that this virus of a European minority may well have been working itself out, the final decadence of the romantic age on its Byronic and destructive side.

v

On the problems thus created, a fresh analysis was now brought to bear. Following the rise of Darwin's influence, it marked another great advance of modern social science. The Darwinian discoveries had transformed environmental studies and placed all political and social problems in a new perspective. They had related political and social thought to a vast background of prehistoric time and to the whole field of biology. This biological and historical view was already apparent in Comte and Spencer. With the assimilation of Darwinism a more realistic approach developed. The study of the life of institutions, as undertaken by Maine and Bagehot, was broadened by the anthropological studies of Tylor, which were related to civilized society. The over-ambitious and linear historical approach of these pioneers was to be adapted to the new facts accumulated, by the more empirical, cautious, mind of Durkheim.

This environmental outlook, far more truly scientific than the dogmatic and romantic myths of Marxist political theory, was now reinforced in the late nineteenth century, by the development of psychology. For the first time the importance of subconscious impulse was understood, and its social implications examined. Darwinian understanding of the huge animal past which, as Graham Wallas emphasized, still so largely determines conduct, was enriched by a new knowledge of individual and social psychology. There developed not only a deeper social psychology, but a sociology of knowledge. At first, modern psychology seemed to accentuate pessimism. With greater maturity, the new outlook made for a more dispassionate and constructive view. And a new social psychology was in time to prove the most original and practical contribution of later-nineteenth-century thought, one more aspect of the expansion of professional knowledge already emphasized. For these psychological discoveries marked the greatest intellectual revolution since the time of Darwin. The charting of the subconscious mind was to be the most original and important intellectual achievement of the early twentieth century. It had its origins in the closing decades of the nineteenth. It went along not only with Bergsonian and Nietzschean cults of blind action, but with salutary movements in philosophy, a clearing of the decks, the development of pragmatism and of logical analysis. Among the psychologists, the work of Wundt and William James, in particular, had widespread influence before the more clinical and documented investigations of Freud. Ideas began to be looked at, as it were, from the inside. Ideologies existed, not as absolutes but as projections.

This revelation of a whole new field of knowledge seemed disconcerting. Rational calculation, it appeared, the heart of liberal doctrine, were no longer reliable. Even the more civilized societies were apparently dominated by atavistic instinct and sub-conscious impulse. In politics, it seemed, Bergson, Nietzsche and Sorel were right: a good myth was more powerful than a good education. Romantic pessimism and nihilist despair appeared to be provided with a new charter of personal and political irresponsibility.

This divorce of environmental and psychological understanding from political principle and constructive sociology was never necessary. It proceeded from an old-fashioned nineteenth-century reaction to the new techniques. In fact, as Durkheim and Wallas pointed out, here was a new promise of control. It was likely not to undermine, but reinforce constructive environmental studies, and the new psychological knowledge as to contribute to the foundations of a New Humanism. The emergence of this modern Humanism was the most original aspect of the later nineteenth century. It is worth relating to the urgent problems of our time, since it may well reinforce the political tradition of objectivity, law, compassion and liberty which Acton had summed up, and which had won its way to considerable influence before the advent of modern industrial society.

This outlook now seems likely to command the support of a growing body of opinion. All are now inevitably 'engaged' in politics, in view of the threat to the very life of civilization implied by destructive and obsolete ideas. Ideas which have been abstract and dogmatic, and are now giving way to an empirical view.

For the reign of myth has proved more and more disastrous. The combined effects of national and class conflict, economic and spiritual bankruptcy following world war, the atrocious suffering, the impoverishment of life, may at least, the humanist can argue, have acclimatized men not to expect too much. If, it is claimed, this belief should win acceptance, a more adult outlook, akin to the realism of Greek philosophers and dramatists in the dawn of civilization, may be expected. It could be reinforced with the knowledge which the long effort of European genius has after many centuries accumulated and deserved. Once the exaggerated hopes of dogma and metaphysics had faded, it could be argued, and the claims of romantic individualism had been modified, might not a new constructive Humanism emerge?

Whatever one's view of it, such a development may perhaps be expected. In the light of Darwinian principles, some such adaptation may contribute to survival. Like the new psychology, this new pragmatism seems to express a side of nineteenth-century political thought which has persisted most steadily and powerfully throughout the course of this survey – the continuing expansion of professional knowledge. While the romantic movement ramified and altered, and while revolutionaries of various kinds were attempting to change the world, the process of technical expansion, mental and material, was inexorably passing all previous bounds. In the field of invention, this revolution had plunged ahead with terrifying speed, dragging political and economic institutions after it. But sociology, psychology and positivist philosophy were also bringing their increasing returns. Slowly creating new and subtler techniques of adjustment and control: limiting the objectives, increasing the power. In this New Humanist view, the situation may seem comparatively hopeful, if precarious.

It is certainly that. Nationalist frenzy, class war and nihilism have brought civilization to a pretty pass. They have undermined the constructive political tradition inherited from the eighteenth century and beyond. But the domination of aristocrats, clergy and liberal elites, it can now be recognized, had always been precarious. Following the gradual disruption of the old slow-moving society by the industrial revolution, and with the full development of industrial democracy, elites were naturally liable to be absorbed.

Others are likely to emerge. In contrast to their predecessors, modern creative minorities may command wider influence through new mass communications and statistical techniques. If, in the view of these modern minorities, reality seems no longer accessible to dogma or metaphysics, life must go on. At least, modern Humanists maintain, society is better under control. Not in the crude Comtian sense, but in terms of far more subtle and extensive knowledge. If the questions dogmatists and romantics had put the Universe remain unanswered, the questions put by scientific method have brought in increasing returns. They may well, the humanist can argue, reinforce constitutional methods of government with unprecedented knowledge. Bacon had said, 'Natura non vincitur nisi parendo'. Perhaps the pendulum has swung too far. First to the side of optimism, to the dream of abstract and romantic perfection; afterwards to the side of sadism and despair. It may now be coming to rest in a more practical and biologically sounder view. The only view, it could be argued, compatible with the changed conditions of environment created by twentieth-century science.

If this outlook is justified, has the sobering process occurred in time? Can the destruction of lethal slogans be achieved before the primordial passions behind the great nationalist and revolutionary myths, inherited from the Romantic age, wreak hideous destruction through misused science? Or are such violent myths, based on atavistic sub-conscious impulse, always the natural political expression of mankind?

VI

If the Humanist outlook be accepted, there is some encouragement in a survey of the past. When, from even a pragmatic view, one looks back across the history of political thought, it is possible to discern powerful constructive ideas making for enrichment of life. Ideas complete and satisfactory in their own time; healthy in their own setting, which have all symbolized human solidarity and mutual aid. The ideological projections of this primordial instinct have been varied but incessant. They would appear, in the West, to be reflected in the idea of commonwealth. If not, it would never have survived so effectually, or dominated such huge areas of the world. A theological or abstract idiom for this impulse to mutual aid may appear alien to modern Humanists, as may the ideas of remote contemporary peoples. As Bradley pointed out, we are all inescapably conditioned by our own time. But, although the idiom of thought is constantly changing, the basic human preoccupations are constant. The fundamental concern has always been vitality and survival. By this standard the modern sociologist, following Durkheim, judges all societies in Space and Time. By this standard, the value of the changing patterns of political thought according to environment can be assessed. The fading of the old idea of dogmatic and final truth, of metaphysical total explanation, does not therefore, in this Humanist view, lead to nihilist despair. The New Humanism certainly has its own standards. Far more sophisticated, yet rooted in the outlook of primitive societies, with their concern for survival and cult of life. Judged by them, the course of European political thought becomes chequered but still coherent. Certain political ideas, and certain institutions, are inspired by a morality which is the expression of the basic instinct for mutual aid. In widely changing idioms and contexts, they have promoted life. Others have brought ruin. Laboriously, with many setbacks, by trial and error, in sparse favourable conditions, political ideas and procedures have been elaborated tending to advancement of life. In the Humanist outlook, the new psychology and pragmatism enables them to be viewed with understanding, detachment and respect.

In this perspective, perhaps, the evolution of political thought may now be regarded. In the great river valleys where civilization began, primitive tribal solidarity developed the cult of priest and priest-King, of the divine ruler, the Shepherd of the People. Here was little speculation, but administrative routine which enabled the material basis of civilized life to be secured. Then, in the Greek cities, political thought first became articulate. Here the ideal of the 'good life' was projected, the subtlest nuances of political behaviour analysed. No political philosophy has ever surpassed this achievement, as no drama has surpassed the works of Aeschylus and Sophocles. For the Baconian concept of knowledge as power is but Aristotle's objectivity methodized. The vocabulary of political speculation was here created, and Humanist standards set. It is no matter that Plato thought in terms of abstract Ideas which in our own time seem poetry; for the deepest expressions of human experience come from poets. Nor is it important that Aristotle thought in terms of a tiny πόλις and of a society economically insignificant. The great Greek achievement was to attempt the moralization of power and to create an ideology for this purpose. In this task, Plato pointed to one solution; Aristotle to another. Both are agreed that politics should be subordinated to life. And when this Humanism was expanded in Stoic concepts of universal natural Law, the idea of an ordered cosmos, of which Law was the reflection, gave classic Humanism a broader, politically constructive, content. These abstractions were never without root. They were the projection, in ideal terms, of the interest of the primitive community against the usurpation of individual power; against chaos and death. Thus, already, the danger of tyranny by government, a vampire on its own people, began to be diminished. The principle of commonwealth, with its roots, as Kropotkin pointed out, in the mutual aid of primitive societies, was here, in idealist and abstract terms, affirmed. We may discern in the Hellenic attempt at the subordination of politics to the good life, and the Greco-Roman concept of Natural Law and world government, the projection, on a civic and supernational scale, of a basic adaptation.

This idea was constantly abused. It became the sanction for vast bureaucratic tyranny and despotic law. There remained the belief that government was ultimately responsible to something beyond itself, and the idea of world order. This view was vastly enriched by Christian influence, with the new value set upon individuals, all candidates for salvation. Here, again, seen in Humanist psychological terms, a vast projection was accomplished. The great hierarchy of God and the Cosmic order; the pattern of salvation, of Heaven and Hell. Politically it gave new sanctions against the tyrant; against war and destruction and the breaking-up of laws. It tamed the barbarians. And they also brought their own rudimentary and primeval customs of self government. The ideal of commonwealth survived, enriched by Christian compassion and hope and barbarian vitality. It made a total picture of experience, appropriate for that age, and went on making it. The Encyclicals of Leo XIII have still the same idiom as the *Summa* of St. Thomas Aquinas. Here, looking back over the centuries, from a modern psychological view, Humanism can again discern political theories making for enrichment of life. Here, spontaneously expressed, at the suitable time and place and in its own idiom, is a pattern of ideas which promotes solidarity and commonwealth. The attempt, expressed in the Classical and Christian terms, at the subordination of irresponsible power to human needs.

These Greco-Roman and Medieval Christian political ideas were assailed by enemies with which we are familiar. Arbitrary power, barbarian rapine and destruction. From without and within, they rocked civilization. Yet all through this evil, this denial of life, civilization had held men's loyalty through their minds. Such is the power of the beliefs created by the human spirit, and such is their function in the struggle for survival. Both Hellenic and Greco-Roman Humanism and Catholic Christianity predominately expressed a fundamental solidarity.

If, on the humanist assumptions, the course of more recent history is also examined in the light of modern psychology, similar evidence may come to light. In the sixteenth and seventeenth centuries, along with the Protestant challenge to the Catholic Church, and the disruption of Christendom into dynastic and ultimately national centres of power, the old projections of human solidarity were transformed and asserted in a new context. In particular, the predominantly Protestant ideal of conscience, of inner light, reinforced the sense of political responsibility. As in the earliest days of Christianity, power was again criticized by conscience. And if the idea of a Christian Commonwealth became limited to a more national setting, the characteristic new seventeenth-century secular Myth was again universal. It was a development of the Renaissance ideal of the complete, competent man, full of versatility and 'virtu', dominating his world. It was also reinforced by a new, unprecedentedly powerful technical method, original to the West. This idea of Mechanism, was to transform the circumstances of mankind and dominate the planet. In its turn, it was projected; into belief in a mechanical, intelligible, system of cosmic laws. That, in turn, enhanced life. But it was a dangerous hypothesis; unlike the myth of Hellenic and Christian Natural Law. And it was a more aggressive, dynamic, ideal. It thrust out into the world, speculative and practical; it broke down old organic societies. It uprooted; it destroyed; it built. The dream of Mechanism, like the dream of Classical Humanism and Christianity, had brought in its returns. Such is the picture, presented in modern humanist terms.

The idioms, times and places, of these developments, here briefly touched upon, have been sketched in a preceding volume. How, in the nineteenth century, following the industrial and technical revolutions, the perennial theme has worked out, has been broadly indicated in these pages. For with the romantic movement and the new sense of history, the Cartesian tradition was criticized and enriched. On the one hand, constitutional commonwealth had been inspired and democratized by the romantic concept of Will. It had further been reinforced by the steady development of professional and scientific knowledge. Against this development, the usual forces of cruelty, hatred and destruction had launched their attack. It came this time from the new barbarians bred by the industrial revolution, and from the intellectual barbarism bred by misconceived science. It came, too, as the logical consequence of the disruption of the old unity of Classical and Christian civilization into sovereign states, and from the competition of world-wide Empires. But the nineteenth-century conflict was to grow more desperate than the conflicts of previous ages. It was now global. And with every increase of the power of destruction, more was at stake.

To this crisis modern Humanism can perhaps bring a new outlook to promote constructive politics. Darwinian science and Freudian psychology, as well as events, have shown the precariousness of civilization. They have also dissolved many illusions. Not merely romantic illusions, but those of misplaced mechanism and atheist pseudo-scientific explanation. The generalizations of Hegel and Marx are still a potent myth. They are no longer regarded by objective modern sociologists as scientifically true. And they are desperately dangerous in a modern context.

For we are today, all of us, Christians and Humanists, Marxists and the Common Man, down to essentials. What, in the present environment, makes for survival? What for death? The answer is plain. The modern expression of the primeval instinct for collaboration that has always made for survival. Rationality, the power to appraise surroundings and combine to turn them to account. Respect for law, rooted in common custom, since only law prevents tyranny and creates commonwealth. Compassion, the impulse to mutual aid. Liberty, the power of genius and initiative. To realize more fully these ancient principles in political terms is to adapt our institutions to the supreme fact of our time, the cosmically destructive power of science misused. Which of the ideas described in this volume promote these principles, the reader must decide. They imply the transcending of ideological, national, and class conflict in a common will for life. This course is plainly indicated by the present world situation. Before the tremendous power of modern weapons of mass destruction, it demands the creation, by such steps as are immediately practicable, of a supra-national commonwealth, implementing a rule of World Law. Its objectives the guidance of policy by compassion, according to biologically sound patterns of mutual aid rather than conflict, and the maintenance of the creative minorities on which all knowledge and civilization depend. Such can be a universal project for survival.

This outlook is not intolerant. It applies only one test to political ideas. Does a given ideology enhance life? For those for whom Classical Humanism or Christianity are final truth, it has no enmity. Rather it invites their collaboration. It is hostile only to cults of death. It has, therefore, numerous enemies in the modern world. But in its breadth lies strength. And it is broadened by the knowledge won by the two great discoveries of the nineteenth and early twentieth centuries. They were made by Darwin and Freud: the antiquity of man in the vast context of animal evolution, and the power of the subconscious mind. All political thought is thus seen in terms of environment and psychology. Political truth becomes varied in its idiom, but recognizable by one test — the enhancement of the quality of life. In this pragmatic view, political myths have their relative truth, if there is no rigid standard in the endless change of evolution. For as men and societies proceed through space and time, they carry with them, thrusting into the unknown, an ambience of ideas, similar in its purpose to the physical atmosphere which so thinly envelopes the planet. This ambience of Myth changes with the centuries and with its geographical setting. If it promotes life it is political truth: if death, it is error.

This contemporary Humanism may well express a vastly enriched version of the ideas described in the introduction to the preceding volume. They have inspired primitive societies all over the planet — survival, well being, plenty, life. It possesses unheard of power in modern organized knowledge. It can reinforce the empirically tested power of constitutional government to promote civilization by the organized common sense of science applied to politics.

It also faces unprecedented danger—a danger which derives from the misuse of scientific power by men enslaved to obsolete nineteenth-century metaphysical myths of inevitable national and class conflict. But it can draw on resources which are also of unparalleled scope. It is world-wide, transcending all frontiers. Its exponents are world citizens. For the New Humanism makes its appeal to the entire planet. If it cannot yet penetrate the barriers now created by the Kremlin, it can affect vast and powerful communities about the world. It may yet come to appeal across all frontiers. Already, within the tentative framework of the United Nations and its agencies, European, Atlantic and Pacific Commonwealths are coming into being. Where the background of early nineteenth-century society, as depicted in the introduction of this volume, was European, still predominantly agricultural, predictable and slow, the background to modern political thought has become swiftly moving and world-wide. Modern Humanism can survey the ideological kaleidoscope of the past, not only of Europe but of the world, with new understanding. It is concerned with the whole planet; with all the rich diversity of culture and language of the earth. Today, its background is predominantly Atlantic. Here it has its roots. Here, it may be, there can yet develop the spirit of a World Society, of which the technical expressions are the jet aircraft, supersonic speed and instantaneous radio and television. Over this society there looms a hideous threat: the mushroom cloud which follows the flash of the nuclear bomb. But before it lies, also, the promise of the ordered cities, the far-flung territories, of a World Commonwealth of all Mankind and of the enrichment of life they may express.

NOTES

Book One, Chapter I

[1] Neff, op. cit., pp. 46-7.
[2] Butler, op. cit., p. 25.
[3] p. 25n.
[4] Quoted by Butler, op. cit., 26
[5] Quoted by Butler, op. cit., p. 28.
[6] A. D. Lindsay, op. cit., p. 55.
[7] *History of Western Philosophy*, p. 765.
[8] *Philosophy of Right*, paragraph 260, as quoted by Lindsay, p. 61.
[9] Para. 343.
[10] Para. 345.
[11] Para. 331.
[12] Para. 347.
[13] *The Myth of the State*, p. 267. Yale University Press, 1945.
[14] Para. 348.
[15] Para. 351.
[16] *The Philosophy of History*, p. 9.
[17] p. 10.
[18] p. 14.
[19] p. 30.
[20] p. 31.
[21] p. 34.
[22] p. 39.
[23] p. 50.
[24] p. 52.
[25] p. 54.
[26] p. 67.
[27] p. 74.
[28] ibidem.
[29] p. 86.
[30] p. 96.
[31] pp. 98-9.
[32] p. 103.
[33] p. 107.
[34] p. 345.
[35] p. 407.
[36] p. 414.
[37] p. 441.
[38] p. 456.
[39] p. 457.

Book One, Chapter II

[1] Annual Biography and Obituary, 1833, p. 363, quoted in *D.N.B.*
[2] J. B. Bury, *The Idea of Progress*, p. 171.
[3] *Outlines of Historical Jurisprudence*, I, 129.

NOTES

[4] *Fragment*, p. 5. Harrison edition.
[5] p. 13.
[6] p. 12.
[7] p. 22.
[8] p. 25.
[9] p. 30.
[10] p. 50.
[11] p. 80.
[12] *Principles*, p. 123.
[13] p. 124.
[15] p. 144n.
[14] p. 163n.
[16] p. 177.
[17] p. 196.
[19] pp. 227-8.
[19] pp. 281-8.
[20] p. 420.
[21] p. 406.
[22] p. 428n.
[23] *Province of Jurisprudence*, p. 289. 1832 edition.
[24] p. 288.
[25] p. 35.
[26] p. 5.
[27] p. 200.
[28] p. 20.
[29] See MANNING, op. cit.
[30] *Province*, p. 288.
[31] p. 57.
[32] p. 58.
[33] p. 279n.

BOOK ONE, CHAPTER III

[1] *Soirées de St. Pétersbourg*, vol. I, pp. 72-3.
[2] Quoted by FAGUET, op. cit., p. 8.
[3] *Du Pape*, p. 10.
[4] p. 257.
[5] p. 135.
[6] p. 258.
[7] p. 380.
[8] *Soirées*, vol. I, pp. 30, 31.
[9] Romans, vii, 19 and 24.
[10] See *W.P.T.*, p. 388 ff.
[11] *Soirées*, vol. I, p. 91.
[12] p. 101ff.
[13] p. 105.
[14] Vol. II, p. 14.
[15] Vol. II, p. 13.
[16] See *W.P.T.*, p. 177.

[17] op. cit., p. 153.
[18] *Chartism, Miscellaneous Essays*, vol. III, Ashburton Edition, p. 290.
[19] *Sartor Resartus*, World's Classics, p. 189.
[20] *Sartor*, p. 138.
[21] *Past and Present*, World's Classics, p. 69.
[22] *Past and Present*, World's Classics, p. 68.
[23] *The Myth of the State*, p. 198.
[24] *Sartor*, p. 151.
[25] *Chartism*, p. 321.
[26] ibidem, p. 276.
[27] Vide *supra*, p. 310.
[28] *Chartism*, p. 326.
[29] *Past and Present*, p. 264.
[30] *Chartism*, p. 269.
[31] *Shooting Niagara*, p. 591.
[32] p. 589.
[33] *French Revolution*, vol. I, p. 56, World's Classics.
[34] *Niagara*, p. 591.
[35] *Sartor*, p. 165.
[36] *Chartism*, p. 290.
[37] *Past and Present*, p. 20.
[38] *Sartor*, p. 168.
[39] p. 282.
[40] Vide Professor BASIL WILLEY, *Nineteenth-Century Studies*, p. 130.

BOOK ONE, CHAPTER IV

[1] Vol. I, *Œuvres Choisies*, pp. 6-60.
[2] p. 27.
[3] p. 55.
[4] See *W.P.T.*, p. 404ff.
[5] Quoted Markham, p. 20.
[6] *Œuvres Complètes*, vol. 40, pp. 236-44.
[7] Quoted Markham, pp. 72-3 from *Organizateur*, *O.C.*, vol. 20, pp. 17-26.
[8] *Essai Sur l'Europe*. First, uncensored, edition. October 1814, 112 pp. *Œuvres*, vol. I, p. 158ff.
[9] p. 167.
[10] pp. 172-3.
[11] Vide *W.P.T.*, p. 262ff.
[12] *Essai*, p. 197, *O.C.*, vol. 23.
[13] p. 148.
[14] p. 186.
[15] *Procés*, p. 33.
[16] p. 155.

BOOK ONE, CHAPTER V

[1] pp. 1-317. 1875 translation.
[2] *Nineteenth-Century Studies*, pp. 187-203.

[3] *System*, vol. I, p. 274.
[4] H. GOUHIER, *La Jeunesse d'Auguste Comte*, vol. I, p. 71.
[5] op. cit.
[6] L. POWYS, *Glory of Life*.
[7] Compare Saint-Simon, *supra*, p. 103.
[8] *Plan, System*, vol. IV, p. 535.
[9] MILL, op. cit., p. 123.
[10] *General View (System)*, vol. I, p. 317.
[11] *General View (System)*, vol. I, p. 36.
[12] *Plan, System*, vol. IV, p. 529.
[13] p. 530.
[14] Compare Plato's *Statesmen* and *Laws*, quoted *W.P.T.*, pp. 53ff.
[15] *System*, vol. IV, p. 133.
[16] *General View (System)*, vol. I, p. 103.
[17] ibidem, vol. I, p. 168.
[18] *General View (System)*, vol. I, p. 63.
[19] ibidem, p. 311.
[20] ibidem, vol. I, p. 266.
[21] *System*, vol. IV, p. 111.
[22] *System*, vol. I, p. 213.
[23] *Physics and Politics*, p. 58.
[24] *System*, vol. IV, p. 129.
[25] BASIL WILLEY, op. cit., p. 202.
[26] GOUHIER, op. cit., vol. I, p. 6.

BOOK ONE, CHAPTER VI

[1] *Spirit of the Age*, p. 18, 1904 edition, quoted in Priestley, op. cit.
[2] I, p. 99.
[3] II, p. 535.
[4] I, p. 110.
[5] I, p. 5.
[6] I, p. 12.
[7] II, p. 114.
[8] See *W.P.T.*, p. 341.
[9] II, p. 133.
[10] II, p. 207.
[11] II, p. 211.
[12] II, p. 512.
[13] I, p. 44.
[14] II, p. 510.
[15] *Œuvres*, vol. I, p. 263.
[16] I, p. 203.
[17] I, p. 166.
[18] See in particular IV, p. 175ff.
[19] IV, p. 546.
[20] V, p. 7ff.
[21] IV, p. 13.
[22] COLE, op. cit., p. 95.

[23] *A New View*, p. 20.
[24] *An Address*, p. 154, 1819.
[25] p. 155.
[26] p. 53.
[27] p. 40.
[28] p. 6.
[29] *An Address*, p. 106.
[30] p. 150.
[31] *Report*, p. 253.
[32] p. 247.
[33] p. 254.
[34] p. 257.
[35] p. 268.
[36] p. 275.
[37] p. 277.
[38] p. 288.
[39] p. 294.
[40] p. 297.

Book One, Chapter VII

[1] Vide *supra*, pp. 398ff.
[2] *Propriété*, p. 132.
[3] *Justice*, p. 308.
[4] I, p. 424.
[5] I, p. 431.
[6] I, p. 429.
[7] II, p. 60.
[8] II, p. 123, q.v. for some curious opinions.
[9] II, p. 288, see pp. 257-93, for political catechism.
[10] III, p. 152ff.
[11] IV, p. 71.
[12] *La Guerre*, p. 426.
[13] p. 427.
[14] p. 507.
[15] Vide *supra*, p. 395.
[16] *Nouvelles Observations sur l'Unité Italienne*, p. 81, cited by Amoudruz, op. cit., p. 106.
[17] ibidem, p. 110.
[18] N. Bourgeois, op. cit., p. 47.
[19] *De la Capacité*, p. 51.
[20] p. 61.
[21] p. 70.
[22] p. 87.
[23] p. 90.
[24] p. 91.
[25] p. 96.
[26] p. 101.

NOTES

Book One, Chapter VIII

[1] V, p. 273.
[2] V, p. 274.
[3] V, p. 275.
[4] V, p. 278.
[5] V, p. 326.
[6] I, p. 238.
[7] *The Duties of Man*, IV, twelve chapters, pp. 204-366.
[8] IV, p. 223.
[9] IV, p. 240.
[10] *On the Encyclical of Pius IX*, V, p. 340.
[11] 2 V, 278.
[12] V, 277.
[13] VI, p. 98-214, 1847.
[14] VI, p. 156.
[15] VI, p. 259.

Book One, Chapter IX

[1] *Democracy*, I, Introduction, p. 6 (Bradley edition.)
[2] Vide *W.P.T.*, p. 163ff.
[3] *Democracy*, p. 66.
[4] p. 74.
[5] p. 93.
[6] p. 94.
[7] p. 183.
[8] p. 184.
[9] p. 185.
[10] Chap. xix, p. 284, Commager edition.
[11] ibidem., p. 286.
[12] Chap. xx, p. 300.
[13] Chap. xxvii, p. 417.
[14] Chap. xxx, p. 457.
[15] Vol. II, p. 331 (Bradley edition)
[16] Vol. II, p. 334.
[17] *System*, pp. 476-7.
[18] p. 531ff.
[19] p. 552.
[20] p. 557.
[21] p. 564.
[22] *Essay*, p. 8 (McCallum edition).
[23] p. 37.
[24] p. 41.
[25] p. 82.
[26] *Subjection*, 188 pp. (3rd edition, 1870).
[27] p. 36.
[28] p. 48.
[29] p. 57ff.
[30] p. 65.

[31] p. 82.
[32] p. 96.
[33] p. 105.
[34] p. 138.
[35] p. 147.

BOOK TWO, CHAPTER I

[1] *On Representative Government*, p. 305 (1861 edition).
[2] T. K. PENNIMAN, *A Hundred Years of Anthropology*, p. 94, q.v.
[3] E. L. WOODWARD, *The Age of Reform*, p. 493.
[4] ibidem, p. 501.
[5] op. cit., p. 292.

BOOK TWO, CHAPTER II

[1] *Autobiography*, vol. II, p. 460.
[2] *Social Statics*, p. 14 (1868 edition).
[3] p. 44.
[4] p. 229.
[5] *The Man Versus the State*, p. 358.
[6] Quoted from *Social Statics*, ed. 1851, pp. 322-5, 380-1, in *The Man Versus the State*, p. 357.
[7] *Social Statics*, p. 316.
[8] *The Man Versus the State*, p. 289.
[9] p. 293.
[10] p. 297.
[11] p. 322.
[12] p. 369.
[13] p. 399.
[14] p. 403.
[15] p. 408.
[16] *Principles of Sociology*, II, pp. 200-1.
[17] II, p. 206.
[18] *Autobiography*, vol. II, p. 469.
[19] ibidem, pp. 470-1.
[20] *History*, vol. I, p. 4.
[21] I, p. 5.
[22] I, p. 21.
[23] I, p. 31.
[24] I, p. 29.
[25] I, pp. 94-6.
[26] I, pp. 100-1.
[27] I, p. 110.
[28] I, p. 139.
[29] J. S. MILL, op. cit., vol. II, pp. 246-7.
[30] I, p. 162.
[31] I, p. 173.

[32] p. 194.
[33] I, p. 203.
[34] *Rationalism*, I, p. 259.
[35] I, p. 279.
[36] II, p. 109.
[37] *Democracy*, I, p. 212ff.
[38] I, p. 215.
[39] I, p. 398.
[40] II, p. 185.

BOOK TWO, CHAPTER III

[1] *Ancient Law*, p. 7.
[2] p. 18.
[3] p. 27.
[4] pp. 27-8.
[5] Vide pp. 50-8, *passim*.
[6] p. 99.
[7] p. 103.
[8] pp. 106-7.
[9] p. 124.
[10] p. 174.
[11] *Early Institutions*, p. 355.
[12] p. 380.
[13] p. 384.
[14] p. 396.
[15] p. 399.
[16] *Popular Government*, p. 21.
[17] p. 27.
[18] p. 37.
[19] p. 38.
[20] p. 46.
[21] p. 65.
[22] p. 126.
[23] *Physics and Politics*, p. 28.
[24] p. 30.
[25] *The English Constitution*, p. 236. (World's Classics Edition, Oxford, 1928).
[26] Vide *W.P.T.*, p. 370.
[27] *The English Constitution*, p. 240.
[28] *English Constitution*, p. 245.
[29] *Physics and Politics*, p. 41.
[30] ibidem, p. 44.
[31] But see J. U. NEF, *War and Human Progress*. Chicago, 1951.
[32] *Physics and Politics*, p. 73.
[33] p. 79.
[34] p. 124.
[35] p. 163.
[36] p. 193.

[37] See *W.P.T.*, chap. 1.
[38] *Primitive Culture*, Preface to 2nd edition, 1873.
[39] I, p. 24.
[40] I, pp. 6-9.
[41] I, p. 69.
[42] I, pp. 238-9.
[43] I, p. 241.
[44] I, p. 275.
[45] I, p. 384.
[46] II, p. 106.
[47] II, p. 112.
[48] II, p. 132.
[49] II, p. 196.
[50] II, p. 452ff.
[51] II, p. 453.

BOOK TWO, CHAPTER IV

[1] p. 6.
[2] NETTLESHIP, op. cit., p. 80.
[3] p. 29.
[4] p. 35.
[5] p. 39.
[6] For a fuller treatment of this theme of Spinoza's creative Humanism see *W.P.T.*, p. 377.
[7] p. 83.
[8] p. 90.
[9] p. 92.
[10] p. 127.
[11] See BOSANQUET, *The Philosophical Theory of the State*, pp. 269-70ff, 1899 (1923 edition).
[12] p. 128.
[13] p. 135.
[14] p. 145.
[15] See my *Hobbes and His Critics*, p. 98ff.
[16] p. 149.
[17] p. 165.
[18] op. cit. Grotius Society Publications, No. 7.
[19] p. 174.
[20] p. 177.
[21] Compare, for example, Buckle and Lecky.
[22] See F. A. HAYEK, *The Road to Serfdom*.
[23] p. 179.
[24] p. 209.
[25] p. 221.
[26] p. 221.
[27] Vide *supra*, p. 335.
[28] p. 228.
[29] *Ethical Studies*, pp. 160-206.

[30] p. 165.
[31] p. 170.
[32] p. 173, from HEGEL, *Philosophische Abhandlungen*, Werke, vol. I, pp. 399-400 (1832).
[33] p. 177.
[34] pp. 177-8.
[35] p. 182.
[36] p. 184.
[37] p. 187.
[38] p. 190.
[39] p. 199.
[40] p. 201.

BOOK TWO, CHAPTER V

[1] F. ENGELS, *The 14th March, 1883*, Marx-Engels-Lenin Institute, Moscow-London, 1933.
[2] See Durkheim on Marx, *infra*, p. 453.
[3] *Condition*, p. 24.
[4] p. 105.
[5] p. 107.
[6] Reprinted in the *German Ideology*, I-III, p. 197ff. (Marx and Lenin Library.)
[7] *German Ideology*, I, p. 39.
[8] p. 19.
[9] *Manifesto*, p. 128.
[10] Quoted by I. BERLIN, op. cit., p. 219.
[11] See *W.P.T.*, chap. 1.

BOOK TWO, CHAPTER VI

[1] *Brumaire*, p. 73.
[2] p. 72.
[3] *Critique*, p. 11.
[4] p. 12.
[5] p. 12.
[6] J. B. GLASIER, *William Morris*, p. 32.
[7] Introduction to B. CROCE, op. cit.
[8] SWEEZY, op. cit., p. 115.
[9] G. D. H. COLE, *What Marx Really Meant*. London, 1934, p. 207.
[10] POPPER, op. cit., vol. II, p. 312, q.v. for much wise comment.
[11] *Capital*, p. 715.
[12] p. 863.
[13] p. 873.
[14] p. 113 (Act IV, Scene 3).
[15] p. 165.
[16] p. 435.
[17] p. 544.
[18] p. 651.

[19] p. 670.

[20] pp. 655-6.

[21] p. 671.

[22] p. 789.

[23] p. 796, vide *W.P.T.*, p. 264.

[24] p. 833.

[25] p. 836.

[26] p. 843n.

[27] p. 846.

[28] *Anti-Dühring*. Second edition, 1885. Modern Edition in Marxist-Leninist Library. Allen & Unwin, 1934.

[29] For a brief account of him see R. d'O. BUTLER, op. cit., pp. 176-85.

[30] *Anti-Dühring*, p. 154.

[31] p. 158.

[32] p. 176.

[33] p. 177.

[34] p. 294.

[35] p. 301.

[36] p. 304.

[37] p. 311.

[38] CURTIS, *Civitas Dei. The Commonwealth of God* (Macmillan, 1938), p. 819ff, q.v.

[39] C. W. COLE, 'The Heavy Hand of Hegel', in *Nationalism and Internationalism*. Essays inscribed to Carlton J. H. Hayes, edited Edward Mead Earle, C.U.P., New York, 1950, p. 78.

[40] See E. E. EVANS-PRITCHARD, *Social Anthropology*. London, 1950, pp. 41ff.

BOOK TWO, CHAPTER VII

[1] CURTIS, op. cit., p. 818.

[2] *Origins of Prussianism*, op. cit., p. 18.

[3] *Politics*, II, p. 596.

[4] *Politics*, II, pp. 597-8.

[5] *Politics*, I, p. 28.

[6] *Politics*, II, p. 598.

[7] *Politics*, I, p. 21.

[8] *Politics*, II, p. 586.

[9] I, p. 19.

[10] II, p. 588.

[11] Vide *supra*, p. 39.

[12] II, p. 599.

[13] *Politics*, Introduction, p. xxxiii.

[14] I, pp. 19-20.

[15] I, p. 14.

[16] I, pp. 17-18.

[17] Introduction, p. xl.

[18] I, p. 25.

[19] I, p. 19.

[20] I, p. 29.
[21] I, p. 83.
[22] I, p. 104.
[23] II, p. 391.
[24] I, p. 46.
[25] I, p. 52.
[26] I, p. 53.
[27] I, p. 333.
[28] I, p. 42.
[29] I, p. 389.
[30] I, p 362
[31] I, p. 387.
[32] I, p. 35.
[33] I, p. 132.
[34] I, p. 34.
[35] I, p. 117.
[36] I, p. 119.
[37] I, p. 141.
[38] I, p. 206.
[39] I, p. 231.
[40] I, p. 244.
[41] I, p. 226.
[42] I, p. 50.
[43] I, p. 298.
[44] I, p. 302.
[45] Quoted in *Origins of Prussianism*, p. 19.
[46] *Deutsche Kämpfe*, I, p. 307. Quoted by Davis.
[47] *Politics*, II, p. 599.
[48] *Origins*, pp. 55-6.

BOOK TWO, CHAPTER VIII

[1] *Parerga*, vol. II, para. 126.
[2] Quoted by RIBOT, op. cit., p. 143.
[3] Quoted by RIBOT, p. 119 from *Die Welt*, vol. I, para. 53.
[4] *Parerga*, vol. II, para. 126.
[5] *Untimely Meditations*, 11. 9.
[6] *Ecce Homo*, iv, 1.
[7] KAUFMANN, p. 75.
[8] *Joyful Wisdom*, 125.
[9] See his letter to Kingsley on the death of Huxley's son. *Life and Letters*, vol. I, p. 318.
[10] *Ecce Homo*, vol. IV, p. 1.
[11] MORGAN, op. cit., p. 357.
[12] See *W.P.T.*, p. 377ff.
[13] KAUFMANN, p. 320, from *Joyful Wisdom*, 14.
[14] p. 277, from *Jenseit*, xvi, 368.
[15] p. 338.

NOTES

BOOK TWO, CHAPTER IX

[1] *The Pope and the People, Inscrutabili*, pp. 1-3.
[2] p. 144, *Rerum Novarum*.
[3] ibidem.
[4] p. 12, *Quod Apostolici Muneris* (1878).
[5] p. 14.
[6] p. 17.
[7] p. 47, *Immortale Dei*. See *W.P.T.*, pp. 208, 210 on St. Thomas, and p. 356ff on Hooker.
[8] See *W.P.T.*, p. 436, on Burke.
[9] See *W.P.T.*, p. 234, on Dante's 'Beatitudo vitae, quae in operatione propriae virtutis consistit.'
[10] *The Pope and the People*, p. 83.
[11] p. 93.
[12] p. 134.
[13] p. 139.
[14] p. 141.
[15] p. 145.
[16] p. 158.
[17] p. 160.
[18] See Douglas Woodruff's Introduction to *Essays on Church and State by Lord Acton*. London, 1952.
[19] op. cit., p. 423.
[20] *Lectures on Modern History*, p. 31.
[21] p. 317.
[22] p. 199.
[23] *Lectures on the French Revolution*, p. 20.
[24] See my *Hobbes and his Critics*.
[25] GASQUET, *Lord Acton and his Circle*, p. 232.
[26] *Historical Essays*, p. 130.
[27] *Autobiography*, quoted by FASNACHT, op. cit., p. 131.
[28] *The History of Freedom and other Essays*, p. 297. Compare Proudhon, *supra*, p. 163.
[29] p. 299.
[30] FASNACHT, p. 117.
[31] *Lectures on Modern History*, p. 5.
[32] p. 289.

BOOK TWO, CHAPTER X

[1] *Reflections on Violence*, translated by T. E. Hulme. Allen & Unwin, 1915 (Letter to Halèvy), p. 3.
[2] *La Ruine*, p. 311.
[3] p. 320.
[4] p. 105.
[5] p. 67.
[6] *Illusions*, p. 45.
[7] p. 50.
[8] p. 59.

[9] p. 107.
[10] ibidem.
[11] p. 332.
[12] *La Ruine*, p. 319.
[13] p. 235.
[14] *Reflections* (Letter), p. 12.
[15] p. 17 (Fragment 294, Braunschweig Edition quoted).
[16] p. 19.
[17] p. 26.
[18] p. 32.
[19] p. 38.
[20] p. 39.
[21] p. 35.
[22] *Reflections*, p. 71.
[23] p. 132.
[24] p. 213.
[25] *La Ruine*, p. 315.
[26] p. 269.
[27] p. 272.
[28] pp. 284-5.
[29] *Matériaux*, p. 91.

BOOK TWO, CHAPTER XI

[1] H. D. LASSWELL, *The Analysis of Political Behaviour*. London, 1948, p. 12.
[2] S. FREUD, *Civilization and Its Discontents*, p. 143. London, 1930.
[3] *Fabian Essays*, pp. xxxix-xl.
[4] p. 27.
[5] p. 56.
[6] p. 94.
[7] See pp. 456ff for a fuller account of him.
[8] p. 139.
[9] *The Socialist Ideal*, HOLBROOK JACKSON, op. cit., p. 322.
[10] p. 314, *True and False Society*.
[11] p. 297, *The Hopes of Civilization*.
[12] Letter to Manchester Examiners, March 1883.
[13] See *W.P.T.*, p. 15.
[14] *Socialisme Théorique*, Preface to German edition.
[15] ibidem., p. xxxviii.
[16] p. xliv.
[17] *Les Luttes des Classes en France*, 1848-50 (Modern Edition. Paris, 1948).
[18] *Socialisme Théorique*, p. 46.
[19] p. 46.
[20] p. 152.
[21] p. 217.
[22] p. 218.
[23] p. 256.
[24] p. 280.

[25] p. 303.

[26] JEAN JAURÈS et PAUL LAFARGUE, *Idéalisme et Matérialisme dans la Conception de l'Histoire.* Arras, 1894. (Edition Idées et Combats), Paris, 1945, p. 8 q:v., *passim.*

[27] *Anthologie de Jean Jaurès,* op. cit., p. 195.

[28] *Anthologie,* p. 25.

[29] *Anthologie,* p. 123 (from *Études Socialistes,* pp. 354-59, q.v.).

[30] p. 147.

[31] pp. 149-50 (see *Études,* vol. I, pp. 288-91).

BOOK TWO, CHAPTER XII

[1] Quoted by EVANS-PRITCHARD, op. cit.

[2] *Règles de la Méthode Sociologique,* p. 75.

[3] p. ix.

[4] p. 4.

[5] p. 14.

[6] p. 35.

[7] p. 50.

[8] p. 103.

[9] p. 93.

[10] p. 121.

[11] *Le Socialisme,* p. 5.

[12] p. 6.

[13] *Méthode,* p. 141.

[14] *Human Nature in Politics,* p. 38.

[15] p. 40.

[16] p. 55.

[17] p. 121-2.

[18] p. 127.

[19] p. 138.

[20] p. 179.

[21] p. 181.

[22] p. 186.

[23] p. 278.

[24] p. 284.

[25] *The Great Society,* p. 84.

[26] p. 37.

[27] p. 116.

[28] *Njal Saga,* p. 123, quoted p. 171.

BIBLIOGRAPHY

The following are the principal texts on which this study is based.
For books on particular authors and general subjects the reader is recommended to consult the notes.

A. The Political Thought of the Romantic Age

HERDER, J. G., *Sämtliche Werke* (Berlin, 1877-1913).

HEGEL, G. W. F., *Hegel's Philosophy of Right*. Trans. T. M. Knox, Oxford, 1942. *The Philosophy of History*. Trans. J. Sibree (1857), Revised edition, New York, 1944. *Werke*, Berlin, 1832-40.

BENTHAM, J., *Collected Works*, ed. J. Bowring, 11 vols., Edinburgh, 1843-49. *A Fragment of Government*, and *An Introduction to the Principles of Morals and Legislation*, ed. W. Harrison, Oxford, 1948.

AUSTIN, J., *The Province of Jurisprudence Determined*, London, 1832. *Lectures on Jurisprudence*, ed. R. Campbell, 2 vols., London, 1869.

MAISTRE, J. DE, *du Pape*, Paris, n.d. *Soirées de St. Pétersbourg*, Brussels, 2 vols., 1838. *Œuvres Complètes*, Lyons, 14 vols., 1884-47.

COLERIDGE, S. T., *Complete Works*, 7 vols., London, 1884.

CARLYLE, T., *Collected Works*, Ashburton edition, 17 vols., London, 1885-88.

SAINT-SIMON, C. H. DE R., COMTE DE, *Œuvres Complètes de Saint-Simon et d'Enfantin*, Paris, 47 vols., 1865-76 (vols. 15, 18-23, 37-40). *Œuvres Choisis de Saint-Simon*, ed. Lemonnier, 3 vols., Brussels, 1859, q.v. for *Introduction aux Travaux Scientifiques du Dix-neuvième siècle*. *Textes Choisis*, ed. C. C. A. Bouglé, Paris, 1925. *Selected Writings*, ed. and trans. with an introduction by F. M. H. Markham, Oxford, 1952.

COMTE, A., *Cours de Philosophie Positive*, 6 vols., Paris, 1864. *System of Positive Polity*, trans. H. J. Bridges, 4 vols., London, 1875-77. *The Positive Philosophy of Auguste Comte*, ed., translated and condensed by Harriet Martineau, 2 vols., London, 1853.

GODWIN, W., *Enquiry concerning Political Justice and its Influence on Morals and Happiness*, ed. F. E. L. Priestley, 3 vols., Toronto, 1946.

FOURIER, F. C. M., *Œuvres Complètes*, 6 vols., Paris, 1846-48.

OWEN, R., *A New View of Society and Other Writings* (selection), Everyman edition, ed. G. D. H. Cole.

PROUDHON, P. J., *Œuvres Complètes*, ed. C. C. A. Bouglé et H. Moyset, Paris, 1923-. *Selection* (ed. Bouglé), Paris, 1930.

MAZZINI, G., *The Life and Writings of Giuseppe Mazzini*, 6 vols., London, 1890-91.

TOCQUEVILLE, A. DE, *Democracy in America*, the Henry Reeve text as revised by F. Bowen, ed. Phillips Bradley, 2 vols., New York, 1945. *Democracy in America* (abridged), trans., H. Reeve, ed. H. S. Commager, World's Classics, Oxford, 1946. *L'Ancien Régime*, ed. G. W. Headlam, Oxford, 1904. *Œuvres Choisis*, ed. R. Elvin, London, 1946.

MILL, J. S., *A System of Logic*, London, 1843. *On Liberty*, and *Considerations on Representative Government*, ed. R. B. McCallum, Oxford, 1946. *On Subjection of Women*, London, 1869

BIBLIOGRAPHY

B. *The Political Thought of the Age of Darwin*

SPENCER, H., *Social Statics*, London, 1851. *A System of Synthetic Philosophy*, London, 1862-82. *Descriptive Sociology*, London, 1873. *The Man Versus the State*, London, 1884. *Autobiography*, ed. D. Duncan, 2 vols., London, 1904.

BUCKLE, H. T., *The History of Civilization in England*, 2 vols., 1857, 1861.

LECKY, RT. HON. W. E. H., *History of the Rise and Influence of the Spirit of Rationalism in Europe*, 2 vols., London, 1865 (1910 ed.). *History of European Morals from Augustus to Charlemagne*, London, 1869. *Democracy and Liberty*, 2 vols., London, 1896.

MAINE, SIR H., *Ancient Law, its connection with the Early History of Society and its relation to Modern Ideas*, ed. Sir F. Pollock, 1906, London, 1861. *Lectures on the Early History of Institutions*. London, 1874 (1914 ed.). *Popular Government, Four Essays*, London, 1885.

BAGEHOT, W., *The English Constitution* (1867), World's Classics, Oxford, 1928. *Physics and Politics*, London, 1872.

TYLOR, SIR E. B., *Primitive Culture*, 2 vols. (1871), revised ed., 1891.

GREEN, T. H., *Lectures on the Principles of Political Obligation*, ed. B. Bosanquet (1921 ed.). *Works*, ed., with Memoir, by R. L. Nettleship, 3 vols., 1885-88.

BRADLEY, F. H., *Ethical Studies* (second edition), Oxford, 1927

MARX, K., *The Holy Family; The German Ideology; The Poverty of Philosophy; The Manifesto of the Communist Party* (ed. F. Engels, 1888); *The Eighteenth Brumaire of Louis Bonaparte; The Civil War in France.* (Lawrence and Wishart's Marxist-Leninist Library.) *The Communist Manifesto*, ed. H. J. Laski, London, 1948. *A Contribution to the Critique of Political Economy*, trans. M. C. Stone, New York, 1904. *Capital, a Critique of Political Economy* (vol. I), trans. E. and C. Paul, London, 1928. *Capital: The Process of Circulation of Capital* (vol. II), and *The Process of Capitalist Production as a Whole* (vol. III), are translated by E. Untermann, Chicago, 1909; and n.d. Vol. IV on *Theories of Surplus Value*. (Untranslated.)

ENGELS, F. (see Marx), *The Condition of the Working Classes in England in 1844* (translation), New York, 1886. *Herr Eugen Dühring's Revolution in Science* (1878). (See Marxist-Leninist Library.)

TREITSCHKE, H. VON, *The Politics of*, trans. by Blanche Dugdale and T. de Bille, with introduction by Lord Balfour, 2 vols., London, 1916. *Die Politik*, Leipzig, 1899-1900. *Historische und Politische Aufsätze*, 4 vols., Leipzig, 1896.

SCHOPENHAUER, A., *Sämtliche Werke*, ed. P. Deussen, Munich, 1911-33.

NIETZSCHE, F. W., *Complete Works*, ed. O. Levy, Edinburgh, 1909-11.

LEÒ XIII, *The Pope and the People*, Select Letters and Addresses on Social Questions by Pope Leo XIII, Pope Pius X, Pope Benedict XV, and Pope Pius XI (Catholic Truth Society, revised ed., 1929). *Le Encicliche Sociali dei Papi da Pio IX a Pio XII*, ed. I. Giordani, Rome, 1942.

ACTON, SIR J. E. E. B., 1st Lord, *Lectures in Modern History*, London, 1906. *Historical Essays and Studies*, London, 1907. *The History of Freedom and Other Essays*, London, 1907. *Lectures on the French Revolution*, London, 1910. *Essays on Church and State*, ed. D. Woodruff, 1952.

BIBLIOGRAPHY

SOREL, G., *La Ruine du Monde Antique*, Paris, 1901. *Reflections on Violence*, trans. T. E. Hulme, London, 1916. *Les Illusions du Progrès*, Paris, 1908. *Matériaux d'une Théorie du Prolétariat*, Paris, 1919.

Fabian Essays (1889), ed. SHAW, BERNARD, 1948, London.

MORRIS, W., *The Collected Works of*, 24 vols., 1910-15. Stories in Prose and Verse, Shorter Poems, Lectures and Essays, ed. G. D. H. Cole. On Art and Socialism (selection), Holbrook Jackson, London, 1947.

JAURÈS, J., *Œuvres de*, ed. M. Bonnefous, Paris, 1931-39. *Anthologie de*, ed. L. Lévy, London, 1947.

DURKHEIM, E., *De la Division du Travail Sociale*, Paris, 1893. *Règles de la Méthode Sociologique*, Paris, 1895. *Le Socialisme, sa Définition, ses Débuts*, Paris, 1897. *Les Formes Élémentaires de la vie Religieuse*, Paris, 1922. *Sociologie et Philosophie*, ed. with introduction by C. C. A. Bouglé, Paris, 1924.

WALLAS, G., *Human Nature in Politics*, London, 1908. *The Great Society*, a Psychological Analysis, London, 1914.

INDEX

INDEX

Bentham, Jeremy (*Cont.*)
ideas of, 57-66; on Blackstone, 58-62; on utility, 63ff and persecution, 65; salutary influence of, 66; contrasted with counter-revolutionaries, 75-6; not appreciated by Carlyle, 96, 101; criticized by Mazzini, 177; J. S. Mill and, 196; limitations of, 198; and Spencer, 225; and Lecky, 247; compared with Maine, 250; attacked by Marx, 337; Wallas on, 458.

Bergson, Henri, and Schopenhauer, 365, 370, 381; and Sorel, 399n, 408, 409; Jaurès on, 441, 457, 475.

Berlin, I., 78n, 302n; on political vituperation, 305; on Marx as revolutionary, 322.

Bernstein, E., 222, 299; loyal act of, 307n, 324, 398, 401, 414; revises Marxism, 433-8; life, 433n; on Social Democracy, 434; and tactics of revolution, 435; terms Dialectic perfidious, 435; on diffusion of property, 436; on working class, 437; Jaurès and, 440, 470.

Bestor, A. E., on Communitarians, 134n.

Bismarck, 135; and Treitschke, 351ff, 362; Wallas on, 460.

Blackstone, Sir W., 52; *Commentaries* of, 59-60; life of, 59-60n; Bentham on, 61-2, 72; cited by de Maistre, 81; Maine and, 250.

Blücher, Treitschke on, 36on.

Bodin, J., 29; and Hegel, 42; Treitschke on, 355.

Böhm-Bawerk, E., 33on; on Marx, 331.

Bolingbroke, Lord, 28.

Bolivar, 53n, 170.

Bolivia, Presidents of, their fate, 256.

Bonald, L. de, 77.

Boniface, St., of Crediton, and Antipodes, 244n.

Bopp, F., philologist, 261.

Bosanquet, B., 28, 275, 284; and Bradley, 292, 432.

Bossuet, Bp., 28, 438.

Boucher de Perthes, discoveries of, 219.

Bracton, H., 29.

Bradley, F. H., 28, 40n, 73, 275; political philosophy of, 291-7; life, 291n; and Hegel, 291ff; and Bagehot, 291; prose of, 292, 292n; his moral relativism, 293; on the state, 294-5; an academic virtuoso, 295; pessimism of, 296-7; and Durkheim, 447, 448.

Bright, John, 134.

Brosses, C. de, and Comte, 119; quoted by Tylor, 265.

Browne, Sir Thomas, quoted by Acton, 392.

Bruno, G., 408.

Bryce, Lord, 459.

Buckland, Dean, on the flood, 218.

Buckland, W. W., 67n; on Austin, 68-9.

Buckle, H. T., 222, 228; historical outlook of, 237-41; life, 237n; influenced by Comte, 237; compared with Marx, 237; on Quetelet, 238; geographical sense of, 238-9; on progress, 239-40; representative, 241; and Lecky, 242; compared with Tylor, 270; contrasted with Schopenhauer, 269.

Burckhardt, J., and Nietzsche, 37on, 375.

Burns, Mary, Engels's mistress, 307, 319n.

Bury, Prof. J. B., on Encyclopedists, 56; and Comte, 118n.

Butler, Bp., and Hutcheson, 55; Acton on, 392, 394.

Butler, R. d'O., on German nationalism, 30; and Herder, 32.

Burke, Edmund, and Fichte, 30; and Herder, 32, 38; Austin on, 72; Disraeli and, 77; and de Maistre, 81; and Coleridge, 90-1; on political duty, 92;, 104; and Godwin, 136, 169, 199, 229; Maine and, 250; related to Green, 277, 290; compared with Bradley, 294; termed sycophant by Marx, 339; on Empire, 350; Acton on, 391; and Durkheim, 448, 466.

Byron, 78; and Comte, 120; and Mazzini, 171; quoted, 176; influences Schopenhauer, 367; quoted, 367, 472.

Byzantines, theological conflicts among, 348.

Caird, E., 117n; on Comte, 119, 122, 275.

Calvin, John, 82; and Carlyle, 95, 100, 221, 256; compared to Marx, 315; admired by Sorel, 406, 408.

Cambridge, University, and Paley, 51; and Lord Acton, 390-1.

Capgrave, J., anecdote by, 269.

Carlyle, Thomas, 28-9, 77-8; on Utilitarians, 94; political thought of, 94-100; and Calvin, 95; compared with Nietzsche, 96; denounces Malthus, 97; and Rousseau, 97; no Imperialist, 99; on aristocracy of talent, 99-100; and Darwin, 218, 227; and Engels, 309, and Treitschke, 362; Acton on, 392; Webb on, 421, 426, 467.

Cassirer, E., on Hegel, 40; on Carlyle, 96, 99.

Catholic Church, and Liberalism, 76-7; de Maistre on, 8off; Saint-Simon on, 112; and Positivism, 126; and Proudhon, 164; Mazzini, on, 173; and Green, 288; modern political theory of, 383, 389; and Acton, 390-7; and Sorel, 403ff, 471, 479, 480.

Cats, La Bruyère on, 87; injuries from Irish, 254n; Eastern origins and nomenclature of, 267n.

Chamberlain, H. S., 473.

INDEX

Charlemagne, 48, 102; Comte on, 131, 179.

Charles V, Emperor, 48; Acton on, 393.

Chateaubriand, F. R. de, 29-30, 212, 349.

Chesterton, G. K., 425n.

Chevallier, J. J., on *'Minotaur'*, 425.

Chinese, 14, 21; 'prosaic Empire' of, 47, 129; pageantry among, 221; education, 231; customs of, 235, 461.

Christian Martyrs, disproportionate influence of, 410.

Cicero, 84, 132.

Clarendon, Edward, 1st Earl of, 58.

Clausewitz, 347, 363.

Cobbett, W., 135, 152.

Codrington Library, 60n.

Cole, Prof. G. D. H., 144n; on theory of value, 331.

Coleridge, S. T., 28, 74, 77; political ideas of, 90-4; debt to Burke, 91; and Kant, 91; on Commonwealth, 92; against Utilitarians, 92; on Constitutionalism, 93, 97, 104; and Owen, 137, 277; Webb on, 421, 467.

Comte, Auguste, 29, 101; and Saint-Simon, 103, 106, 114; political thought of, 117-33; chequered life of, 117n; debt to Saint-Simon, 118; as sociologist, 119; on Positivism, 120; J. S. Mill on, 121; technocrat, 121, 122; on education, 127; and European union, 128-9; Positivist Calendar of, 129-30; his significance, 132-3; and Proudhon, 156; and J. S. Mill, 195, 198-9, 201, 212-15, 221-2, 227; compared with Maine, 251; and Green, 276, 295; Feuerbach and, 304; Marx and, 305, 347, 369; and Nietzsche, 380; and Leo XIII, 380; Sorel on, 404, 445; and Durkheim, 446-8; insight of, 467.

Condorcet, A. N. de, and Saint-Simon, 113, 119; his influence on Mazzini, 169, 177.

Congreve, R., and Positivist Religion, 130n.

Cosmas Indicopleustes, 244.

Cowles-Pritchard, strange hypothesis of, 219

Cowper, William, on Westminster School, 54.

Crewe, local government in, 244.

Crimean War, Buckle on, 240.

Cromwell, Oliver, callousness of, 64, 96; cult of, 274n, 280; misinterpreted by Marx, 326.

Cudworth, Rev. R., admired by de Maistre, 86; Coleridge and, 94.

Curtis, Lionel, quoted on Marx, 346; on International Anarchy, 349.

D'ALEMBERT, and Saint-Simon, 102.

Dante, 118, 130; quoted by Mazzini, 174, 295, 332; and by Marx, 334, 426.

Darfur, queer custom in, 235.

Darwin, 27, 88, 212; profound influences of, 215-22; his humane outlook, 217; misinterpreted, 218; Spencer on, 229-30; and Tylor, 272; and Marx, 305, 328, 364; Nietzsche on, 373, 378, 380, 414; and Freud, 415; Durkheim and, 446; Wallas related to, 461, 472, 474-5, 482.

Davis, H. W. C., on Treitschke, 352n, 360n, 361.

Declaration of Independence, favourably compared with *Communist Manifesto*, 314.

Descartes, Saint-Simon on, 104, 108, 132; Sorel on, 405.

Diderot, D., 56.

Diodorus Siculus, on Gauls, 139n, 332.

Diogenes, and Alexander, 45n.

Disraeli, B., and Coleridge, 90; on Anglican Church, 92; calls J. S. Mill a governess, 196; Imperialism of, 350, 398.

Dog-fights, Irish Law on, 254n.

Döllinger, 390n, 397.

Douglas, Norman, 168.

Douglas, Prof. D. C., 31n.

Dorset, a tale of, 269; Marx on rural distress in, 335.

Dostoevsky, on fear of freedom, 76; and Nietzsche, 380; uncongenial to Fabians, 421.

Dreyfus case, and Sorel, 402, 410; and Jaurès, 344.

Duguit, 68, 447n.

Dühring, E., 305, 307 (*see* Engels).

Dunbar, James, cautious optimism of, 56.

Durkheim, E., 222; and Bagehot, 249; and Tylor, 271, 272, 328n, 381, 415; and Jaurès, 441, 445; sociology of, 446-56; related to Green and Comte, 446; Bradley and, 447; compares statesman's task to doctor's mandate, 447; on sociology of knowledge, 448; and life of institutions, 448-9; on sociology beginning at home, 450-1; and comprehending the world, 452; criticizes Marx, 453; on Socialism, 454; Spinoza and, 455; importance of, 445-6, 475, 478.

ELAGABALUS, Proudhon on, 161.

Elizabeth I, 198; political finesse of, 206; Bagehot and, 263.

Encyclicals, Papal, 383-9 (*see* Catholic Church).

Enfantin, Saint-Simonian enthusiast, 114; sensational trial of, 115; criticized by Proudhon, 160n.

Engels, F., influenced by Fourier, 140, 212, 222, 236; doctrines of, 299-347; compares Marx to Darwin, 305; life and genial character of, 306-7n; on English working class, 302-10; and Dialectical

INDEX

Grimm, J., philologist, 261 .

Grotius, H., 29; wiser than Hegel, 44n, 66.

Guesde, J., his controversy with Jaurès, 44n.

Guizot, F., 135.

HALIFAX, LORD, shrewder than Hegel, 43n., 58.

Hamann, J. G. and Romantic movement, 31.

Hamilton, A., 391.

Hampden, J., contrasted with Hobbes, 253.

Handel, G. F., 376.

Hardy, Thomas, and Hegel, 42; on J. S. Mill, 195, 206; influenced by Schopenhauer, 367.

Harrington, J., Acton on, 392, 395.

Haydn, J., 381.

Hayek, F. A., and economic nationalism, 195n.

Hazlitt, W., on Godwin, 136.

Hegel, G. W. F., 27, 28, 30; political thought of, 36-50, and Marx, 36; life of, 36-7n; and Aristotle, 37; on creative will, 40; defines the Absolute, 41; Dialectic of, 42; a callous thinker, 42; on Nation State, 42-3; on *Geist*, 45; and Heroes, 45; on negroes, 47; on Frederick the Great, 49; on God, 49; Austin and, 69, 73, 75; nationalism of, 76, 102; and Comte, 119, 132, 169, 172, 180; limitations of, 191, 199, 212; and Green, 280; and Bradley, 291; jargon of, 293-4, 297; and Marx, 303ff, and Dialectical Materialism, 311, 313, 331; Marx on, 334; an American view of, 346; and Treitschke, 353; and Schopenhauer, 366, 369, 372; contrasted with Nietzsche, 374; Durkheim and, 448; and Nihilism, 472.

Helvétius, C. A. and Bentham, 55, 56, 176.

Herder, J. G., 27, 28, 30; political thought of, 31-4; influenced by Kant and Hamann, 31; life of, 31n; defines folk nation, 32, 33; and Mazzini, 33, 35-7; contrasted with Bentham, 75; his influence on Carlyle, 96, 169; J. S. Mill and, 199; Treitschke and, 352, 354, 466, 471.

Herz, Dr., on ideology and nationalism, 358.

Highlanders, rational dress of, 149.

Hitler, 44, 171, 221.

Hobbes, Thomas, 29, 51, 52; Hutcheson on, 54-5; and Utilitarians, 59, 67n; related to Austin, 71; and de Maistre, 79, 86, 159; attacked by Proudhon, 160; J. S. Mill on, 198, 221; and Spencer, 228, 233; Maine on, 252-3; and Hampden, 253; Green on, 282-3; Bradley and, 295; and Dialectical

Materialism, 311; outdone by Marx, 320; Schopenhauer and, 368; compared with Nietzsche, 380; Acton on, 393; his *Leviathan*, 416n; and Durkheim, 451-2; and Wallas, 458, 462.

Hobhouse, L. T., on T. H. Green, 275-6, 445.

Hodgskin, T., and Spencer, 226, 227.

Hog-Reeves, Anglo-Saxon, 186.

Holdsworth, Sir W., on Coleridge, 91.

Holy Grail, 334; and Nietzsche, 377; Jowett on, 377n.

Homer, 118, 332.

Hooker, R., 94; and Leo XIII, 386.

Horace, 332; quoted by Marx, 338.

Humbolt, W. von, quoted by J. S. Mill, 202.

Hume, 27, 29, 33, 51, 82; Coleridge impervious to, 91n, 133, 277, 311.

Hunton, P., related to Green, 286.

Hutcheson, Francis, and Bentham, 54-5.

Huxley, T. H., on Comte's ignorance of science, 119n, 215; on Darwin, 216n; confutes Bp. Wilberforce, 220; Bagehot on, 263; and Tylor, 272; and Nietzsche, 373; on evolution, 422.

INDIAN PHILOSOPHY, its influence on Schopenhauer, 367.

Irish, Saint and St. Boniface, 244n; pugnacity among the, 228; laws of the, 254-5; chastity among, 254; septs, 255; cattle thieving of, 255; bishops, 255; immigrants, 309; Engels on, 310; Treitschke on, 360.

Isidore of Seville, St., 377n.

JAMES, WILLIAM, 457, 462, 475.

Jaurès, Jean, 140, 299; and Marx, 324, 398, 401; and Dreyfus case, 402; bugbear of Sorel, 407; political thought of, 438-44; life and character, 438n; Humanist outlook of, 439; repudiates class war, 440; an internationalist, 441; and a patriot, 442; on Social Democracy, 442; and Human Rights, 443.

Jefferson, 33; Acton on, 391.

KANT, 27, 28, 29; compared with Herder, 32, 35; world citizenship of, 41; and Coleridge, 91, 102, 214; and Green, 276; on war, 288, 359; criticized by Schopenhauer, 367, 380; Acton on, 394, 437.

Kaufmann, W. A. on Neitzsche, 370n; quoted, 373; on blonde beast, 377n, 378n, 380.

Kautsky, and Bernstein, 437.

Ker, W. P., on Scandinavian Sagas, 90.

Keynes, J. M., 235; and Marx, 314.

Kidd, B., 420n.

INDEX

Engels, 304, 305; on Dialectical Materialism, 311, 312; on Hegel, 312, and *Communist Manifesto*, 313-24; Bakunin on, 321; on Louis Napoleon, 325-6; on surplus value, 319-31; on capital, 332-40; on Anglican clergy, 332; quotes Shakespeare, 334; David Urquhart and, 335; on expropriation, 340, 369; Nietzsche and, 372; and Leo XIII, 388; and Sorel, 399; Fabians and, 414, 417-18, 424; Morris on, 429; Bernstein on, 433, 438; and Jaurès, 439ff; criticism by Durkheim, 449, 453, 469.

Maurras, C., 349, 438n.

Mauss, M., on Durkheim, 452.

Mazzini, G., 20; and Herder, 33, 50, 100; his debt to Saint-Simon, 104, 116, political thought of, 168-79; life, 168n; on Pan-European ideal, 169-70; business ventures of, 170n; on guerrillas, 170n; imprisoned, 171; on nationalism and progress, 172; and the people, 173-5; and Communism, 177; on Marx, 177n, 180, 211; and Green, 289, 349; contrasted with Treitschke, 353; and Jaurès, 442; Wallas on, 460, 466.

Mehring, F., on Engels, 307, 319n.

Melbourne, Lord, on Austin, 68.

Metternich, 77, 99.

Michelet, J., 77, 169; and Lecky, 242, 349; and Jaurès, 443.

Mill, James, 53n, 67n, 194n.

Mill, J. S., 22, 28, 97; and Comte, 117, 119, 122n; and Godwin, 137, 189; political thought of, 194-208; life 194-5n; on elites, 196; sociology of, 199; and Milton, 200; on Comte, 201, 202; on liberty, 203-4; and emancipation of women, 205-7, 213; on international anarchy, 214, 215, 224, on progress, 239; Lecky and, 246-7; and Maine, 254, 273; contrasted with Marx, 345; Acton and, 390, 394, 418, 466.

Milton, 83, 92, 200, 202.

Monkeys, Saint-Simon on, 106n; Huxley on ancestral, 220; and Darwin, 221; disparaged, 262; man compared to, 367, 373; resented by Nietzsche, 375.

Montesquieu, C. de S., 57; quoted by Saint-Simon, 111, and Comte, 119, 199; Maine and, 250; and Durkheim, 445.

Montgolfier, J., canonized by Comte, 127.

Moore, G. E., 235.

More, Sir Thos., compared with Saint-Simon on power politics, 110; related to J. S. Mill, 200, 202.

Morris, William, and Owen, 135; and Fourier, 140, 222, 329; Shaw on, 417; political ideas of, 426-33; life, 426-7n; and Ruskin, 426; aesthetic revolt of, 427; defines Socialism, 428; songs by, 428-9; and Marx, 429; and industrial revolution, 431-2.

Mussolini, B., and Hegel, 44, 399; and Sorel, 402.

NAPOLEON, 19, 34; as world-historic man, 45n; a terrible example, 77; ignores Saint-Simon, 108; on women, 128; execrated by Comte, 131n; insight of, 174; Buckle on, 240; Green on, 285, 362; admired by Nietzsche, 378; praised by Sorel, 409.

Napoleon, III, Proudhon on, 164; attacked by Marx, 326ff.

Natural Law, 27; and Hegel, 39ff; and Bentham, 59; in atomic age, 73n; and Darwinism, 221; Maine on, 251; Green on, 277; *et passim*, 281; Leo XIII on, 385ff; and modern psychology, 479-801.

Neanderthal Man, 219.

Neff, Prof. E., on Herder, 30-2.

Neolithic Revolution, 21; farmers, 46.

New Deal, 473.

New England, de Tocqueville on, 186, 263.

New Humanism, 476ff.

Newton, I., Saint-Simon on, 104; council of, 107.

New York, 73, 175.

Niebuhr, B. G., 349.

Nietzsche, F., and soured Romantics, 78, 212, 222; unfavourably compared with Tylor, 269, 270; and Green, 278, 364-5; doctrines of, 370-81; life of 370n; atheism of, 373-4; on Superman, 374-5; on Christian attitude to sex, 376; on blond beast, 377; on Nationalism, 378; on war, 379; political irresponsibility of, 380; and Hobbes, 380; and Darwin, 380; and Sorel, 399, 401, 411, 413; and Fabians, 421, 432; Nihilism of, 473.

Njal, Saga, on law, quoted by Wallas, 462.

Novalis (F. L. von Hardenberg), 197.

OCCIDENTAL COMMITTEE, Comte on, 128; College, 129.

Original Sin, d'Holbach on, 56; St. Augustine on, 76; de Maistre on, 80ff; repudiated by Proudhon, 154; and Darwin, 216; Treitschke on, 355.

Ossian, 30.

Owen, W., 101; and Godwin, 138; ideas of 143-51; life, 144n; at New Lanark, 144; on education, 145; on mass purchasing power, 148; and agriculture, 149; and co-operatives, 150; attacked by Marx, 322; influence on Engels, 344; and Fabians, 416; influence on Morris, 468, 490.

Owl, Minerva's, 39.

Oxford Movement, limitations of, 220.

509

INDEX

Oxford University, laziness at, 54; idealism in, 274ff; a lost cause in, 333.

Ovid, on original sin, 86.

PAINE, TOM, 135-6.

Paley, Rev. W., 51, 56; on the Creator, 70; Godwin and, 136.

Palmerston, Lord, 99.

Papacy, 18; de Maistre on, 79, 83; Mazzini's criticisms of, 175; political theory of, 382-9; (*see* Catholic Church).

Parcours de Plaisirs, 142n.

Pareto, W., 79, 168; on Rousseau, 277n; Sorel and, 399.

Pascal, B., 405; on relativity of truth, 408.

Pater, W., and Bradley, 292.

Paul, Saint, and de Maistre, 76, 280; Nietzsche on, 376.

Paviland, Red Lady of, 218.

Peacock, T. L., on 'steam intellect', 76, 77; on Malthus, 94n.

Peel, Sir R., influenced by Utilitarians, 51.

Penn, William, 392.

Penniman, T. K., on real significance of Darwin, 217, 219; and Neanderthalers, 219n; on 'Aryan' race, 261n.

Percy's Reliques, 30.

Perugino, 168.

Peru, tyranny in, 232; happy situation of, 238.

Psellus, 242-3.

Peter the Great, and Russian recalcitrance, 87; J. S. Mill on, 198.

Petronius, 168.

Petty, Sir W., Marx and Aubrey on, 330n.

Phalanstères, 140-2, 148.

Pindar, 207.

Pius, IX, 382.

Plamenatz, J., 195n; on T. H. Green, 276; critical of Rousseau, 277n; and of Green, 284n.

Plato, 86; laws of, 123, 126; and Comte, 131, attacked by Proudhon, 161, 168; Jowett and, 274; influences Green, 276, 287; Bradley and, 295, 374, 380; Acton on, 393, 458.

Plekhanov, on Bernstein, 437.

Plutarch, 418; Jaurès on, 443.

Pollock, Sir F., on Bentham, 62; on Maine, 249.

Polydore Vergil, tale of, 269.

Popper, K., on power, 314; on *Das Kapital*, 332.

Powys, Llewellyn, on scientific humanism, 121.

Priestley, Dr., optimism of, 56.

Proudhon, P. J., 29, 102, 118; and Owen, 135; and Fourier, 142, 151; political ideas of, 152, 167; life, 152-3n; peasant origins of, 152-4; anti-clerical, 154; on women, 155; and economics, 155;

Federalism of, 155-6; on property, 156; Bakunin and, 158n; on Marx, 159; on morals of antiquity, 161; on War, 162; and nationalism, 162-3; and Europe, 164; on working-class leadership, 166; Mazzini on, 177, 180, 215; and Green, 284, 295, 304; attacked by Marx, 313, 322, 323, 388; Sorel and, 399, 401, 406; and Fabians, 418; influences Morris, 427-9; and Jaurès, 442, 467, 471.

Pufendorf, 66.

Puritans, admired by Green, 281.

QUAKERS, 134.

Quetelet, A., statistician, 238n.

RANKE, L. von, and Treitschke, 352n, 361.

Reade, Winwood, popularity of, 222.

Renan, E., 248; and Sorel, 410.

Rhodes, Cecil, and public opinion, 351.

Ricardo, D., and Marx, 304, 313, 330, 334, 429, 469.

Richelieu, Cardinal, 17; and French Academy, 107; Maine on, 253.

Richter, J. P., 36.

Rodrigues, Eugène, Saint-Simonian, 104.

Rodrigues, Olinde, 114.

Rockefeller Plaza, 23.

Roman Empire, economic problems of, 16, 21; depravity in, 161, 176; Maine on, 250-1; dust of, 257, 258; and Catholic church, 389; Sorel on, 402-3; and barbarians, 409.

Rome, 17, 41; panegyric on, 82-3; capture of, 88n; siege of 168n; Mazzini's cult of, 174, 178; republican, 186; competitors with, 263, 391.

Rossetti, D. G., and Jowett, 377n.

Rousseau, J-J, 19, 27, 29; and Herder, 33; on European order, 34n; 37; and Hegel 39; criticized by de Maistre, 82; denounced by Carlyle, 97; 101; his affinities with Proudhon, 153, 172, 276, 277; explained by Green, 280-3; 295; Marx and, 318; Nietzsche and, 372; Acton on, 393; Sorel on, 400; and Durkheim, 447, 450, 458, 466.

Runjeet Singh, despot of the Punjab, Maine on, 253.

Ruskin, John, and Carlyle, 90-1, 218, 227; and Green, 279; quoted by Acton, 393; his influence on Morris, 426.

Russell, Earl, on Hegel, 39; on Utilitarians, 51, 192n, 354; on Superman, 371n; on Bergson, 399.

Russians, 83; Saint-Simon on, 107; de Tocqueville on future of, 189; Green on, 285-6; and Treitschke, 359; Nietzsche on, 378. (*See* U.S.S.R.)

Treitschke, H. von, 20; and Hegel, 44n, 50, 76; contrasted with Mazzini, 171, 214, 222; and Tylor, 270, 349, 350; political thought of, 352-64; life, 351-2n; as historian, 352; on sovereignty, 353; on the State, 354; and Machiavelli, 355; on power, 356; on the masses, 357; anti-Semetic, 357; on education, 358; on master-race, 359; on Mediterranean peoples, 361; on Americans, 361; on Prussia, 362-3; on inevitability of war, 363; representative, 364; Nietzsche and, 365.

Turenne, H. de, on big battalions, 84.

Turgot, A. R., 119, 403.

Turks, improvidence of, 107; Saint-Simon on, 108, 191; beliefs of, 228; Buckle on, 240, 357.

Tylor, Sir Edward, critical of de Maistre, 79n, 222; compared to Bagehot, 248-9; 265-72; career of, 264n; and Bastian, 265; on de Maistre, 265; on social anthropology, 266; on progress, 267; on survivial of primitive ideas, 267, 297, 373, 445; and Wallas, 456, 474.

Tyrrel, Sir Walter, motives of, 65.

Ulrici, H., on *Recht*, 281.

Urquhart, David, and Marx, 335n.

Ussher's Chronology, 217.

U.S.S.R., 14, 22. (*See* Russia.)

United Nations, 17, 482.

United States, 20; world power of, 23, 135; de Tocqueville on, 184ff; Marx on, 333; migration to, 213; Treitschke on, 361; Acton on 394, 411, 482.

Utilitarianism, 27, 34; Lord Russell on, 51; descent of, 51; Bentham and, 52-66; Austin and 66-74; J. S. Mill re-interprets, 202ff; and Green, 274, 281, 290; attacked by Bradley, 291, 297, 300; and Durkheim 451, 467.

Vaux, Clothilde de, and Comte 107n; poem by, 128n.

Verdi, Giuseppe, 170.

Vico, 33; and de Maistre, 86; and Comte, 119, 168; admired by J. S. Mill, 199; compared with Maine, 250; and Sorel, 399; 400n, 402.

Vienna, Congress of, Saint-Simon on, 110; defended by Proudhon, 163.

Vinogradoff, and Blackstone, 58.

Visigoths, 48n, 163.

Voltaire, 28, 29, 33; and Coleridge 91n; and Mazzini, 171; on nation state, 289; Nietzsche and, 373.

Wagner, Richard, 76; and Nietzsche, 370n, 371.

Wakefield, Gibbon, cited by Engels on rural incendiarism, 310.

Wallace, A. R., and origin of species, 216n.

Wallas, Graham, 222; Bagehot and, 249; Tylor and, 271, 381, 415, 416n, 417, 423; on science and society, 424; and Durkheim, 445; pioneer sociologist, 456-64; on irrationality of mankind, 457; and political entities, 458; on rationalistic fallacy, 459; on science as myth, 460; and nationalism, 461; on scientific humanism, 461; and Hobbes, 462; and Bagehot, 462; related to Lasswell, 463, 464, 475.

Walpole, Horace, and Herder, 32, 57.

Washington, George, 33.

Watt, J., canonized by Comte, 127.

Webb, S., and Welfare State, 51; Owen and, 150; Green and, 276; related to Marx, 324; scorned by Sorel, 410; and Fabian Essays, 416n, 417ff; on progress, 420; on municipal Socialism, 422; and science, 423.

Weldon, T. D., on Hegel and Marx, 346.

Welfare State, 21, 51; Saint-Simon and, 105; debt to Owen, 149, 150, 279, 343, 388, 405, 411; political theory of, 414-26; and Wallas, 463.

Wells, H. G., 230; wide influence of, 419.

Westminster School, 53n; Bentham on, 54.

White, Rev. Victor, 397n.

Whitehead, A. N., 243n.

Whitman, Walt, quoted by Fabians, 424.

Wilberforce, Bp., 215; confuted by Huxley, 220.

Willey, Prof. Basil, on Coleridge, 90-1, 99; on importance of Comte, 120.

Wilson, President, and Mazzini, 179.

Wiltshire, Marx on rural poverty in, 335.

Wizards, in Finland, 267.

Woodward, Sir L., 77n; on limitations of the Oxford Movement, 220.

Wordsworth, W., 90n, 92.

Wundt, Wilhelm, 475.

Young, Edward, and Hamann, 31n.

Yxkull, Baron d', Hegelian enthusiast, 38n.

Zulus, Tylor on, 266, 267, 268.

511